CFA Institute®
CFA Program

AF886043

FIXED INCOME AND DERIVATIVES

CFA® Program Curriculum
2020 • LEVEL I • VOLUME 5

WILEY

ISBN 978-1-946442-80-2 (paper)
ISBN 978-1-950157-04-4 (ebk)

SKYC303317B-E776-47D5-A9A6-A9FD2EEA6310_091620

Please visit our website at
www.WileyGlobalFinance.com.

WILEY

CONTENTS

How to Use the CFA Program Curriculum

Congratulations on your decision to enter the Chartered Financial Analyst (CFA®) Program. This exciting and rewarding program of study reflects your desire to become a serious investment professional. You are embarking on a program noted for its high ethical standards and the breadth of knowledge, skills, and abilities (competencies) it develops. Your commitment to the CFA Program should be educationally and professionally rewarding.

The credential you seek is respected around the world as a mark of accomplishment and dedication. Each level of the program represents a distinct achievement in professional development. Successful completion of the program is rewarded with membership in a prestigious global community of investment professionals. CFA charterholders are dedicated to life-long learning and maintaining currency with the ever-changing dynamics of a challenging profession. The CFA Program represents the first step toward a career-long commitment to professional education.

The CFA examination measures your mastery of the core knowledge, skills, and abilities required to succeed as an investment professional. These core competencies are the basis for the Candidate Body of Knowledge (CBOK™). The CBOK consists of four components:

- A broad outline that lists the major topic areas covered in the CFA Program (https://www.cfainstitute.org/programs/cfa/curriculum/cbok);
- Topic area weights that indicate the relative exam weightings of the top-level topic areas (https://www.cfainstitute.org/programs/cfa/curriculum/overview);
- Learning outcome statements (LOS) that advise candidates about the specific knowledge, skills, and abilities they should acquire from readings covering a topic area (LOS are provided in candidate study sessions and at the beginning of each reading); and
- The CFA Program curriculum that candidates receive upon examination registration.

Therefore, the key to your success on the CFA examinations is studying and understanding the CBOK. The following sections provide background on the CBOK, the organization of the curriculum, features of the curriculum, and tips for designing an effective personal study program.

BACKGROUND ON THE CBOK

The CFA Program is grounded in the practice of the investment profession. Beginning with the Global Body of Investment Knowledge (GBIK), CFA Institute performs a continuous practice analysis with investment professionals around the world to determine the competencies that are relevant to the profession. Regional expert panels and targeted surveys are conducted annually to verify and reinforce the continuous feedback about the GBIK. The practice analysis process ultimately defines the CBOK. The

CBOK reflects the competencies that are generally accepted and applied by investment professionals. These competencies are used in practice in a generalist context and are expected to be demonstrated by a recently qualified CFA charterholder.

The CFA Institute staff, in conjunction with the Education Advisory Committee and Curriculum Level Advisors, who consist of practicing CFA charterholders, designs the CFA Program curriculum in order to deliver the CBOK to candidates. The examinations, also written by CFA charterholders, are designed to allow you to demonstrate your mastery of the CBOK as set forth in the CFA Program curriculum. As you structure your personal study program, you should emphasize mastery of the CBOK and the practical application of that knowledge. For more information on the practice analysis, CBOK, and development of the CFA Program curriculum, please visit www.cfainstitute.org.

ORGANIZATION OF THE CURRICULUM

The Level I CFA Program curriculum is organized into 10 topic areas. Each topic area begins with a brief statement of the material and the depth of knowledge expected. It is then divided into one or more study sessions. These study sessions—19 sessions in the Level I curriculum—should form the basic structure of your reading and preparation. Each study session includes a statement of its structure and objective and is further divided into assigned readings. An outline illustrating the organization of these 19 study sessions can be found at the front of each volume of the curriculum.

The readings are commissioned by CFA Institute and written by content experts, including investment professionals and university professors. Each reading includes LOS and the core material to be studied, often a combination of text, exhibits, and in-text examples and questions. A reading typically ends with practice problems followed by solutions to these problems to help you understand and master the material. The LOS indicate what you should be able to accomplish after studying the material. The LOS, the core material, and the practice problems are dependent on each other, with the core material and the practice problems providing context for understanding the scope of the LOS and enabling you to apply a principle or concept in a variety of scenarios.

The entire readings, including the practice problems at the end of the readings, are the basis for all examination questions and are selected or developed specifically to teach the knowledge, skills, and abilities reflected in the CBOK.

You should use the LOS to guide and focus your study because each examination question is based on one or more LOS and the core material and practice problems associated with the LOS. As a candidate, you are responsible for the entirety of the required material in a study session.

We encourage you to review the information about the LOS on our website (www.cfainstitute.org/programs/cfa/curriculum/study-sessions), including the descriptions of LOS "command words" on the candidate resources page at www.cfainstitute.org.

FEATURES OF THE CURRICULUM

OPTIONAL SEGMENT

Required vs. Optional Segments You should read all of an assigned reading. In some cases, though, we have reprinted an entire publication and marked certain parts of the reading as "optional." The CFA examination is based only on the required segments, and the optional segments are included only when it is determined that they might help you to better understand the required segments (by seeing the required material in its full context). When an optional segment begins, you will see an icon and a dashed vertical bar in the outside margin that will continue until the optional segment ends, accompanied by another icon. *Unless the material is specifically marked as optional, you should assume it is required.* You should rely on the required segments and the reading-specific LOS in preparing for the examination.

END OPTIONAL SEGMENT

Practice Problems/Solutions *All practice problems at the end of the readings as well as their solutions are part of the curriculum and are required material for the examination.* In addition to the in-text examples and questions, these practice problems should help demonstrate practical applications and reinforce your understanding of the concepts presented. Some of these practice problems are adapted from past CFA examinations and/or may serve as a basis for examination questions.

Glossary For your convenience, each volume includes a comprehensive glossary. Throughout the curriculum, a **bolded** word in a reading denotes a term defined in the glossary.

Note that the digital curriculum that is included in your examination registration fee is searchable for key words, including glossary terms.

LOS Self-Check We have inserted checkboxes next to each LOS that you can use to track your progress in mastering the concepts in each reading.

Source Material The CFA Institute curriculum cites textbooks, journal articles, and other publications that provide additional context or information about topics covered in the readings. As a candidate, you are not responsible for familiarity with the original source materials cited in the curriculum.

Note that some readings may contain a web address or URL. The referenced sites were live at the time the reading was written or updated but may have been deactivated since then.

Some readings in the curriculum cite articles published in the *Financial Analysts Journal*®, which is the flagship publication of CFA Institute. Since its launch in 1945, the *Financial Analysts Journal* has established itself as the leading practitioner-oriented journal in the investment management community. Over the years, it has advanced the knowledge and understanding of the practice of investment management through the publication of peer-reviewed practitioner-relevant research from leading academics and practitioners. It has also featured thought-provoking opinion pieces that advance the common level of discourse within the investment management profession. Some of the most influential research in the area of investment management has appeared in the pages of the *Financial Analysts Journal*, and several Nobel laureates have contributed articles.

Candidates are not responsible for familiarity with *Financial Analysts Journal* articles that are cited in the curriculum. But, as your time and studies allow, we strongly encourage you to begin supplementing your understanding of key investment management issues by reading this practice-oriented publication. Candidates have full online access to the *Financial Analysts Journal* and associated resources. All you need is to log in on www.cfapubs.org using your candidate credentials.

Errata The curriculum development process is rigorous and includes multiple rounds of reviews by content experts. Despite our efforts to produce a curriculum that is free of errors, there are times when we must make corrections. Curriculum errata are periodically updated and posted on the candidate resources page at www.cfainstitute.org.

DESIGNING YOUR PERSONAL STUDY PROGRAM

Create a Schedule An orderly, systematic approach to examination preparation is critical. You should dedicate a consistent block of time every week to reading and studying. Complete all assigned readings and the associated problems and solutions in each study session. Review the LOS both before and after you study each reading to ensure that you have mastered the applicable content and can demonstrate the knowledge, skills, and abilities described by the LOS and the assigned reading. Use the LOS self-check to track your progress and highlight areas of weakness for later review.

Successful candidates report an average of more than 300 hours preparing for each examination. Your preparation time will vary based on your prior education and experience, and you will probably spend more time on some study sessions than on others. As the Level I curriculum includes 19 study sessions, a good plan is to devote 15–20 hours per week for 19 weeks to studying the material and use the final four to six weeks before the examination to review what you have learned and practice with practice questions and mock examinations. This recommendation, however, may underestimate the hours needed for appropriate examination preparation depending on your individual circumstances, relevant experience, and academic background. You will undoubtedly adjust your study time to conform to your own strengths and weaknesses and to your educational and professional background.

You should allow ample time for both in-depth study of all topic areas and additional concentration on those topic areas for which you feel the least prepared.

As part of the supplemental study tools that are included in your examination registration fee, you have access to a study planner to help you plan your study time. The study planner calculates your study progress and pace based on the time remaining until examination. For more information on the study planner and other supplemental study tools, please visit www.cfainstitute.org.

As you prepare for your examination, we will e-mail you important examination updates, testing policies, and study tips. Be sure to read these carefully.

CFA Institute Practice Questions Your examination registration fee includes digital access to hundreds of practice questions that are additional to the practice problems at the end of the readings. These practice questions are intended to help you assess your mastery of individual topic areas as you progress through your studies. After each practice question, you will be able to receive immediate feedback noting the correct responses and indicating the relevant assigned reading so you can identify areas of weakness for further study. For more information on the practice questions, please visit www.cfainstitute.org.

CFA Institute Mock Examinations Your examination registration fee also includes digital access to three-hour mock examinations that simulate the morning and afternoon sessions of the actual CFA examination. These mock examinations are intended to be taken after you complete your study of the full curriculum and take practice questions so you can test your understanding of the curriculum and your readiness for the examination. You will receive feedback at the end of the mock examination, noting the correct responses and indicating the relevant assigned readings so you can assess areas of weakness for further study during your review period. We recommend that you take mock examinations during the final stages of your preparation for the actual CFA examination. For more information on the mock examinations, please visit www.cfainstitute.org.

Preparatory Providers After you enroll in the CFA Program, you may receive numerous solicitations for preparatory courses and review materials. When considering a preparatory course, make sure the provider belongs to the CFA Institute Approved Prep Provider Program. Approved Prep Providers have committed to follow CFA Institute guidelines and high standards in their offerings and communications with candidates. For more information on the Approved Prep Providers, please visit www.cfainstitute.org/programs/cfa/exam/prep-providers.

Remember, however, that there are no shortcuts to success on the CFA examinations; reading and studying the CFA curriculum *is* the key to success on the examination. The CFA examinations reference only the CFA Institute assigned curriculum—no preparatory course or review course materials are consulted or referenced.

SUMMARY

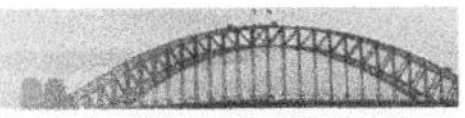

Every question on the CFA examination is based on the content contained in the required readings and on one or more LOS. Frequently, an examination question is based on a specific example highlighted within a reading or on a specific practice problem and its solution. To make effective use of the CFA Program curriculum, please remember these key points:

1. All pages of the curriculum are required reading for the examination except for occasional sections marked as optional. You may read optional pages as background, but you will not be tested on them.
2. All questions, problems, and their solutions—found at the end of readings—are part of the curriculum and are required study material for the examination.
3. You should make appropriate use of the practice questions and mock examinations as well as other supplemental study tools and candidate resources available at www.cfainstitute.org.
4. Create a schedule and commit sufficient study time to cover the 19 study sessions, using the study planner. You should also plan to review the materials and take practice questions and mock examinations.
5. Some of the concepts in the study sessions may be superseded by updated rulings and/or pronouncements issued after a reading was published. Candidates are expected to be familiar with the overall analytical framework contained in the assigned readings. Candidates are not responsible for changes that occur after the material was written.

FEEDBACK

At CFA Institute, we are committed to delivering a comprehensive and rigorous curriculum for the development of competent, ethically grounded investment professionals. We rely on candidate and investment professional comments and feedback as we work to improve the curriculum, supplemental study tools, and candidate resources.

Please send any comments or feedback to info@cfainstitute.org. You can be assured that we will review your suggestions carefully. Ongoing improvements in the curriculum will help you prepare for success on the upcoming examinations and for a lifetime of learning as a serious investment professional.

Fixed Income

STUDY SESSIONS

Study Session 14	Fixed Income (1)
Study Session 15	Fixed Income (2)

TOPIC LEVEL LEARNING OUTCOME

The candidate should be able to describe fixed-income securities and their markets, yield measures, risk factors, and valuation measures and drivers. The candidate should also be able to calculate yields and values of fixed-income securities.

Fixed-income securities continue to represent the largest capital market segment in the financial ecosystem and the primary means in which institutions, governments, and other issuers raise capital globally. Institutions and individuals use fixed-income investments in a wide range of applications including asset liability management, income generation, and principal preservation. Since the global financial crisis of 2008, evaluating risk—in particular, credit risk—for fixed-income securities has become an increasingly important aspect for this asset class.

FIXED INCOME

STUDY SESSION 14

Fixed Income (1)

This study session introduces the unique attributes that define fixed-income securities, then follows with an overview of global debt markets. Primary issuers, sectors, and bond types are explained. Key concepts for the calculation and interpretation of bond prices, yields, and spreads and coverage of interest rate risk and key related risk measures are presented. Securitization—the creation of fixed-income securities backed by certain (typically less liquid) assets—including the various types, characteristics, and risks of these investments end the session.

READING ASSIGNMENTS

Reading 42	Fixed-Income Securities: Defining Elements by Moorad Choudhry, PhD, FRM, FCSI, and Stephen E. Wilcox, PhD, CFA
Reading 43	Fixed-Income Markets: Issuance, Trading, and Funding by Moorad Choudhry, PhD, FRM, FCSI, Steven V. Mann, PhD, and Lavone F. Whitmer, CFA
Reading 44	Introduction to Fixed-Income Valuation by James F. Adams, PhD, CFA, and Donald J. Smith, PhD
Reading 45	Introduction to Asset-Backed Securities by Frank J. Fabozzi, PhD, CPA, CFA

READING

42

Fixed-Income Securities: Defining Elements

by Moorad Choudhry, PhD, FRM, FCSI, and Stephen E. Wilcox, PhD, CFA

Moorad Choudhry, PhD, FRM, FCSI, is at Cambridge & Counties Bank (United Kingdom). Stephen E. Wilcox, PhD, CFA, is at Minnesota State University, Mankato (USA).

LEARNING OUTCOMES

Mastery	The candidate should be able to:
☐	a. describe basic features of a fixed-income security;
☐	b. describe content of a bond indenture;
☐	c. compare affirmative and negative covenants and identify examples of each;
☐	d. describe how legal, regulatory, and tax considerations affect the issuance and trading of fixed-income securities;
☐	e. describe how cash flows of fixed-income securities are structured;
☐	f. describe contingency provisions affecting the timing and/or nature of cash flows of fixed-income securities and identify whether such provisions benefit the borrower or the lender.

INTRODUCTION

1

Judged by total market value, fixed-income securities constitute the most prevalent means of raising capital globally. A fixed-income security is an instrument that allows governments, companies, and other types of issuers to borrow money from investors. Any borrowing of money is debt. The promised payments on fixed-income securities are, in general, contractual (legal) obligations of the issuer to the investor. For companies, fixed-income securities contrast to common shares in not having ownership rights. Payments of interest and repayment of principal (amount borrowed) are a prior claim on the company's earnings and assets compared with the claim of common shareholders. Thus, a company's fixed-income securities have, in theory, lower risk than that company's common shares.

In portfolio management, fixed-income securities fulfill several important roles. They are a prime means by which investors—individual and institutional—can prepare to fund, with some degree of safety, known future obligations such as tuition payments or pension obligations. The correlations of fixed-income securities with common shares vary; but, adding fixed-income securities to portfolios including common shares is usually an effective way of obtaining diversification benefits.

Among the questions this reading addresses are the following:

- What set of features defines a fixed-income security, and how do these features determine the scheduled cash flows?
- What are the legal, regulatory, and tax considerations associated with a fixed-income security, and why are these considerations important for investors?
- What are the common structures regarding the payment of interest and repayment of principal?
- What types of provisions may affect the disposal or redemption of fixed-income securities?

Embarking on the study of fixed-income securities, please note that the terms "fixed-income securities," "debt securities," and "bonds" are often used interchangeably by experts and non-experts alike. We will also follow this convention, and where any nuance of meaning is intended, it will be made clear.[1]

The remainder of this reading is organized as follows. Section 2 describes, in broad terms, what an investor needs to know when investing in fixed-income securities. Section 3 covers both the nature of the contract between the issuer and the bondholders as well as the legal, regulatory, and tax framework within which this contract exists. Section 4 presents the principal and interest payment structures that characterize fixed-income securities. Section 5 discusses the contingency provisions that affect the timing and/or nature of a bond's cash flows. The final section provides a conclusion and summary of the reading.

2 OVERVIEW OF A FIXED-INCOME SECURITY

A **bond** is a contractual agreement between the issuer and the bondholders. There are three important elements that an investor needs to know about when investing in a bond:

- The bond's features, including the issuer, maturity, par value, coupon rate and frequency, and currency denomination. These features determine the bond's scheduled cash flows and, therefore, are key determinants of the investor's expected and actual return.
- The legal, regulatory, and tax considerations that apply to the contractual agreement between the issuer and the bondholders.
- The contingency provisions that may affect the bond's scheduled cash flows. These contingency provisions are options; they give the issuer or the bondholders certain rights affecting the bond's disposal or redemption.

1 Note that the term "fixed income" is not to be understood literally: Some fixed-income securities have interest payments that change over time. Some experts include preference shares as a type of fixed-income security, but none view them as a type of bond. Finally, in some contexts, bonds refer to the longer-maturity form of debt securities in contrast to money market securities.

This section describes a bond's basic features and introduces yield measures. The legal, regulatory, and tax considerations and contingency provisions are discussed in Sections 3 and 5, respectively.

2.1 Basic Features of a Bond

All bonds, whether they are "traditional" bonds or asset-backed securities, are characterized by the same basic features. **Asset-backed securities** (ABS) are created from a process called securitization, which involves moving assets from the owner of the assets into a special legal entity. This special legal entity then uses the securitized assets as guarantees to back (secure) a bond issue, leading to the creation of ABS. Assets that are typically used to create ABS include residential and commercial mortgage loans (mortgages), automobile (auto) loans, student loans, bank loans, and credit card debt, among others. Many elements discussed in this reading apply to both traditional bonds and ABS. Considerations specific to ABS are discussed in the introduction to asset-backed securities reading.

2.1.1 *Issuer*

Many entities issue bonds: private individuals, such as the musician David Bowie; national governments, such as Singapore or Italy; and companies, such as BP, General Electric, or Tata Group.

Bond issuers are classified into categories based on the similarities of these issuers and their characteristics. Major types of issuers include the following:

- Supranational organizations, such as the World Bank or the European Investment Bank;
- Sovereign (national) governments, such as the United States or Japan;
- Non-sovereign (local) governments, such as the state of Minnesota in the United States, the region of Catalonia in Spain, or the city of Edmonton in Canada;
- Quasi-government entities (i.e., agencies that are owned or sponsored by governments), such as postal services in many countries—for example, Correios in Brazil, La Poste in France, or Pos in Indonesia;
- Companies (i.e., corporate issuers). A distinction is often made between financial issuers (e.g., banks and insurance companies) and non-financial issuers; and
- Special legal entities that securitize assets to create ABS that are then sold to investors.

Market participants often classify fixed-income markets by the type of issuer, which leads to the identification of three bond market sectors: the government and government-related sector (i.e., the first four types of issuers listed above), the corporate sector (the fifth type listed above), and the structured finance sector (the last type listed above).

Bondholders are exposed to credit risk—that is, the risk of loss resulting from the issuer failing to make full and timely payments of interest and/or repayments of principal. Credit risk is inherent to all debt investments. Bond markets are sometimes classified into sectors based on the issuer's creditworthiness as judged by credit rating agencies. One major distinction is between investment-grade and non-investment-grade bonds, also called high-yield or speculative bonds.[2] Although a variety of considerations

2 The three largest credit rating agencies are Moody's Investors Service, Standard & Poor's, and Fitch Ratings. Bonds rated Baa3 or higher by Moody's and BBB– or higher by Standard & Poor's and Fitch are considered investment grade.

enter into distinguishing the two sectors, the promised payments of investment-grade bonds are perceived as less risky than those of non-investment-grade bonds because of profitability and liquidity considerations. Some regulated financial intermediaries, such as banks and life insurance companies, may face explicit or implicit limitations of holdings of non-investment-grade bonds. The investment policy statements of some investors may also include constraints or limits on such holdings. From the issuer's perspective, an investment-grade credit rating generally allows easier access to bond markets and at lower interest rates than does a non-investment-grade credit rating.[3]

2.1.2 *Maturity*

The maturity date of a bond refers to the date when the issuer is obligated to redeem the bond by paying the outstanding principal amount. The **tenor** is the time remaining until the bond's maturity date. The tenor is an important consideration in the analysis of a bond. It indicates the period over which the bondholder can expect to receive the interest payments and the length of time until the principal is repaid in full.

Maturities typically range from overnight to 30 years or longer. Fixed-income securities with maturities at issuance (original maturity) of one year or less are known as **money market securities**. Issuers of money market securities include governments and companies. Commercial paper and certificates of deposit are examples of money market securities. Fixed-income securities with original maturities that are longer than one year are called **capital market securities**. Although very rare, **perpetual bonds**, such as the consols issued by the sovereign government in the United Kingdom, have no stated maturity date.

2.1.3 *Par Value*

The **principal amount**, **principal value**, or simply **principal** of a bond is the amount that the issuer agrees to repay the bondholders on the maturity date. This amount is also referred to as the par value, or simply par, face value, nominal value, redemption value, or maturity value. Bonds can have any par value.

In practice, bond prices are quoted as a percentage of their par value. For example, assume that a bond's par value is $1,000. A quote of 95 means that the bond price is $950 (95% × $1,000). When the bond is priced at 100% of par, the bond is said to be trading at par. If the bond's price is below 100% of par, such as in the previous example, the bond is trading at a discount. Alternatively, if the bond's price is above 100% of par, the bond is trading at a premium.

2.1.4 *Coupon Rate and Frequency*

The coupon rate or nominal rate of a bond is the interest rate that the issuer agrees to pay each year until the maturity date. The annual amount of interest payments made is called the coupon. A bond's coupon is determined by multiplying its coupon rate by its par value. For example, a bond with a coupon rate of 6% and a par value of $1,000 will pay annual interest of $60 (6% × $1,000).

Coupon payments may be made annually, such as those for German government bonds or Bunds. Many bonds, such as government and corporate bonds issued in the United States or government gilts issued in the United Kingdom, pay interest semi-annually. Some bonds make quarterly or monthly interest payments. The acronyms QUIBS (quarterly interest bonds) and QUIDS (quarterly income debt securities) are used by Morgan Stanley and Goldman Sachs, respectively, for bonds that make quarterly interest payments. Many **mortgage-backed securities** (MBS), which are ABS backed by residential or commercial mortgages, pay interest monthly to match

---

3 Several other distinctions among credit ratings are made. They are discussed in depth in the reading on fundamentals of credit analysis.

the cash flows of the mortgages backing these MBS. If a bond has a coupon rate of 6% and a par value of $1,000, the periodic interest payments will be $60 if coupon payments are made annually, $30 if they are made semi-annually, $15 if they are made quarterly, and $5 if they are made monthly.

A **plain vanilla bond** or **conventional bond** pays a fixed rate of interest. In this case, the coupon payment does not change during the bond's life. However, there are bonds that pay a floating rate of interest; such bonds are called **floating-rate notes** (FRNs) or **floaters**. The coupon rate of a FRN includes two components: a reference rate plus a spread. The spread, also called margin, is typically constant and expressed in basis points (bps). A **basis point** is equal to 0.01%; put another way, there are 100 basis points in 1%. The spread is set when the bond is issued based on the issuer's creditworthiness at issuance: The higher the issuer's credit quality, the lower the spread. The reference rate, however, resets periodically. Thus, as the reference rate changes, the coupon rate and coupon payment change accordingly.

A widely used reference rate for FRNs has long been the **London interbank offered rate (Libor)**. Libor is a collective name for a set of rates covering different currencies for different maturities ranging from overnight to one year. Other reference rates include the Euro interbank offered rate (Euribor), the Hong Kong interbank offered rate (Hibor), or the Singapore interbank offered rate (Sibor) for issues denominated in euros, Hong Kong dollars, and Singapore dollars, respectively. Euribor, Hibor, and Sibor are, like Libor, sets of rates for different maturities up to one year. The process of phasing out Libor and the move to new references rates are discussed in CFA Level I Reading: "Fixed-Income Markets: Issuance, Trading, and Funding"

For example, assume that the coupon rate of a FRN that makes semi-annual interest payments in June and December is expressed as the six-month Libor + 150 bps. Suppose that in December 20X0, the six-month Libor is 3.25%. The interest rate that will apply to the payment due in June 20X1 will be 4.75% (3.25% + 1.50%). Now suppose that in June 20X1, the six-month Libor has decreased to 3.15%. The interest rate that will apply to the payment due in December 20X1 will decrease to 4.65% (3.15% + 1.50%). More details about FRNs are provided in Section 4.2.1.

All bonds, whether they pay a fixed or floating rate of interest, make periodic coupon payments except for **zero-coupon bonds**. Such bonds do not pay interest, hence their name. Instead, they are issued at a discount to par value and redeemed at par; they are sometimes referred to as **pure discount bonds**. The interest earned on a zero-coupon bond is implied and equal to the difference between the par value and the purchase price. For example, if the par value is $1,000 and the purchase price is $950, the implied interest is $50.

2.1.5 *Currency Denomination*

Bonds can be issued in any currency, although a large number of bond issues are made in either euros or US dollars. The currency of issue may affect a bond's attractiveness. If the currency is not liquid or freely traded, or if the currency is very volatile relative to major currencies, investments in that currency will not appeal to many investors. For this reason, borrowers in developing countries often elect to issue bonds in a currency other than their local currency, such as in euros or US dollars, because doing so makes it easier to place the bond with international investors. Issuers may also choose to issue in a foreign currency if they are expecting cash flows in the foreign currency because the interest payments and principal repayments can act as a natural hedge, reducing currency risk. If a bond is aimed solely at a country's domestic investors, it is more likely that the borrower will issue in the local currency.

Dual-currency bonds make coupon payments in one currency and pay the par value at maturity in another currency. For example, assume that a Japanese company needs to finance a long-term project in the United States that will take several years to become profitable. The Japanese company could issue a yen/US dollar dual-currency bond. The coupon payments in yens can be made from the cash flows generated in Japan, and the principal can be repaid in US dollars using the cash flows generated in the United States once the project becomes profitable.

Currency option bonds can be viewed as a combination of a single-currency bond plus a foreign currency option. They give bondholders the right to choose the currency in which they want to receive interest payments and principal repayments. Bondholders can select one of two currencies for each payment.

Exhibit 1 brings all the basic features of a bond together and illustrates how these features determine the cash flow pattern for a plain vanilla bond. The bond is a five-year Japanese government bond (JGB) with a coupon rate of 0.4% and a par value of ¥10,000. Interest payments are made semi-annually. The bond is priced at par when it is issued and is redeemed at par.

Exhibit 1 Cash Flows for a Plain Vanilla Bond

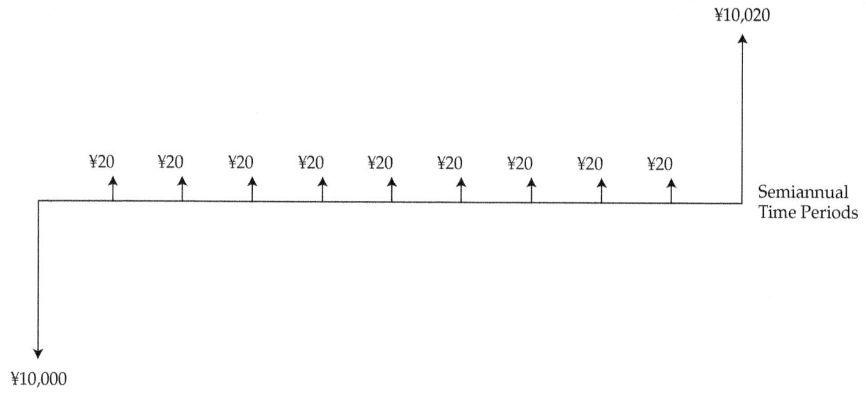

The downward-pointing arrow in Exhibit 1 represents the cash flow paid by the bond investor (received by the issuer) on the day of the bond issue—that is, ¥10,000. The upward-pointing arrows are the cash flows received by the bondholder (paid by the issuer) during the bond's life. As interest is paid semi-annually, the coupon payment is ¥20 [(0.004 × ¥10,000) ÷ 2] every six months for five years—that is, 10 coupon payments of ¥20. The last payment is equal to ¥10,020 because it includes both the last coupon payment and the payment of the par value.

EXAMPLE 1

1 An example of sovereign bond is a bond issued by:
   A the World Bank.
   B the city of New York.
   C the federal German government.

2 The risk of loss resulting from the issuer failing to make full and timely payment of interest is called:
   A credit risk.
   B systemic risk.
   C interest rate risk.

3 A money market security *most likely* matures in:
   A one year or less.

B between one and 10 years.

C over 10 years.

4 If the bond's price is higher than its par value, the bond is trading at:

A par.

B a discount.

C a premium.

5 A bond has a par value of £100 and a coupon rate of 5%. Coupon payments are made semi-annually. The periodic interest payment is:

A £2.50, paid twice a year.

B £5.00, paid once a year.

C £5.00, paid twice a year.

6 The coupon rate of a floating-rate note that makes payments in June and December is expressed as six-month Libor + 25 bps. Assuming that the six-month Libor is 3.00% at the end of June 20XX and 3.50% at the end of December 20XX, the interest rate that applies to the payment due in December 20XX is:

A 3.25%.

B 3.50%.

C 3.75%.

7 The type of bond that allows bondholders to choose the currency in which they receive each interest payment and principal repayment is a:

A pure discount bond.

B dual-currency bond.

C currency option bond.

Solution to 1:

C is correct. A sovereign bond is a bond issued by a national government, such as the federal German government. A is incorrect because a bond issued by the World Bank is a supranational bond. B is incorrect because a bond issued by a local government, such as the city of New York, is a non-sovereign bond.

Solution to 2:

A is correct. Credit risk is the risk of loss resulting from the issuer failing to make full and timely payments of interest and/or repayments of principal. B is incorrect because systemic risk is the risk of failure of the financial system. C is incorrect because interest rate risk is the risk that a change in market interest rate affects a bond's value. Systemic risk and interest rate risk are defined in Sections 5.3 and 4.2.1, respectively.

Solution to 3:

A is correct. The primary difference between a money market security and a capital market security is the maturity at issuance. Money market securities mature in one year or less, whereas capital market securities mature in more than one year.

Solution to 4:

C is correct. If a bond's price is higher than its par value, the bond is trading at a premium. A is incorrect because a bond is trading at par if its price is equal to its par value. B is incorrect because a bond is trading at a discount if its price is lower than its par value.

Solution to 5:

A is correct. The annual coupon payment is 5% × £100 = £5.00. The coupon payments are made semi-annually, so £2.50 paid twice a year.

Solution to 6:

A is correct. The interest rate that applies to the payment due in December 20XX is the six-month Libor at the end of June 20XX plus 25 bps. Thus, it is 3.25% (3.00% + 0.25%).

Solution to 7:

C is correct. A currency option bond gives bondholders the right to choose the currency in which they want to receive each interest payment and principal repayment. A is incorrect because a pure discount bond is issued at a discount to par value and redeemed at par. B is incorrect because a dual-currency bond makes coupon payments in one currency and pays the par value at maturity in another currency.

2.2 Yield Measures

There are several yield measures commonly used by market participants. The **current yield** or **running yield** is equal to the bond's annual coupon divided by the bond's price, expressed as a percentage. For example, if a bond has a coupon rate of 6%, a par value of $1,000, and a price of $1,010, the current yield is 5.94% ($60 ÷ $1,010). The current yield is a measure of income that is analogous to the dividend yield for a common share.

The most commonly referenced yield measure is known as the **yield to maturity**, also called the **yield to redemption** or **redemption yield**. The yield to maturity is the internal rate of return on a bond's expected cash flows—that is, the discount rate that equates the present value of the bond's expected cash flows until maturity with the bond's price. The yield to maturity can be considered an estimate of the bond's expected return; it reflects the annual return that an investor will earn on a bond if this investor purchases the bond today and holds it until maturity. There is an inverse relationship between the bond's price and its yield to maturity, all else being equal. That is, the higher the bond's yield to maturity, the lower its price. Alternatively, the higher the bond's price, the lower its yield to maturity. Thus, investors anticipating a lower interest rate environment (in which investors demand a lower yield-to-maturity on the bond) hope to earn a positive return from price appreciation. The reading on understanding risk and return of fixed-income securities covers these fundamentals and more.

3 LEGAL, REGULATORY, AND TAX CONSIDERATIONS

As a **bond** is a contractual agreement between the issuer and the bondholders, it is subject to legal considerations. Investors in fixed-income securities must also be aware of the regulatory and tax considerations associated with the bonds in which they invest or want to invest.

3.1 Bond Indenture

The **trust deed** is the legal contract that describes the form of the bond, the obligations of the issuer, and the rights of the bondholders. Market participants frequently call this legal contract the bond **indenture**, particularly in the United States and Canada. The indenture is written in the name of the issuer and references the features of the bond issue, such as the principal value for each bond, the interest rate or coupon rate to be paid, the dates when the interest payments will be made, the maturity date when the bonds will be repaid, and whether the bond issue comes with any contingency provisions. The indenture also includes information regarding the funding sources for the interest payments and principal repayments, and it specifies any collaterals, credit enhancements, or covenants. **Collaterals** are assets or financial guarantees underlying the debt obligation above and beyond the issuer's promise to pay. **Credit enhancements** are provisions that may be used to reduce the credit risk of the bond issue. **Covenants** are clauses that specify the rights of the bondholders and any actions that the issuer is obligated to perform or prohibited from performing.

Because it would be impractical for the issuer to enter into a direct agreement with each of many bondholders, the indenture is usually held by a trustee. The trustee is typically a financial institution with trust powers, such as the trust department of a bank or a trust company. It is appointed by the issuer, but it acts in a fiduciary capacity with the bondholders. The trustee's role is to monitor that the issuer complies with the obligations specified in the indenture and to take action on behalf of the bondholders when necessary. The trustee's duties tend to be administrative and usually include maintaining required documentation and records; holding beneficial title to, safeguarding, and appraising collateral (if any); invoicing the issuer for interest payments and principal repayments; and holding funds until they are paid, although the actual mechanics of cash flow movements from the issuers to the trustee are typically handled by the principal paying agent. In the event of default, the discretionary powers of the trustee increase considerably. The trustee is responsible for calling meetings of bondholders to discuss the actions to take. The trustee can also bring legal action against the issuer on behalf of the bondholders.

For a plain vanilla bond, the indenture is often a standard template that is updated for the specific terms and conditions of a particular bond issue. For exotic bonds, the document is tailored and can often be several hundred pages.

When assessing the risk–reward profile of a bond issue, investors should be informed by the content of the indenture. They should pay special attention to their rights in the event of default. In addition to identifying the basic bond features described earlier, investors should carefully review the following areas:

- the legal identity of the bond issuer and its legal form;
- the source of repayment proceeds;
- the asset or collateral backing (if any);
- the credit enhancements (if any); and
- the covenants (if any).

We consider each of these areas in the following sections.

3.1.1 *Legal Identity of the Bond Issuer and its Legal Form*

The legal obligation to make the contractual payments is assigned to the bond issuer. The issuer is identified in the indenture by its legal name. For a sovereign bond, the legal issuer is usually the office responsible for managing the national budget, such as HM Treasury (Her Majesty's Treasury) in the United Kingdom. The legal issuer may be different from the body that administers the bond issue process. Using the UK example, the legal obligation to repay gilts lies with HM Treasury, but the bonds are issued by the UK Debt Management Office, an executive agency of HM Treasury.

For corporate bonds, the issuer is usually the corporate legal entity—for example, Wal-Mart Stores Inc., Samsung Electronics Co. Ltd., or Volkswagen AG. However, bonds are sometimes issued by a subsidiary of a parent legal entity. In this case, investors should look at the credit quality of the subsidiary, unless the indenture specifies that the bond liabilities are guaranteed by the parent. When they are rated, subsidiaries typically carry a credit rating that is lower than their parent, but this is not always the case.

Bonds are sometimes issued by a holding company, which is the parent legal entity for a group of companies, rather than by one of the operating companies in the group. This issue is important for investors to consider because a holding company may be rated differently from its operating companies and investors may lack recourse to assets held by those companies. If the bonds are issued by a holding company that has fewer (or no) assets to call on should it default, investors face a higher level of credit risk than if the bonds were issued by one of the operating companies in the group.

For ABS, the legal obligation to repay the bondholders often lies with the special legal entity that was created by the financial institution in charge of the securitization process. The financial institution is known as the sponsor or originator. The special legal entity is most frequently referred to as a special purpose entity (SPE) in the United States and a special purpose vehicle (SPV) in Europe, and it is also sometimes called a special purpose company (SPC). The legal form for the special legal entity may be a limited partnership, a limited liability company, or a trust. Typically, special legal entities are thinly capitalized, have no independent management or employees, and have no purpose other than the transactions for which they were created.

Through the securitization process, the sponsor transfers the assets to the special legal entity to carry out some specific transaction or series of transactions. One of the key reasons for forming a special legal entity is *bankruptcy remoteness*. The transfer of assets by the sponsor is considered a legal sale; once the assets have been securitized, the sponsor no longer has ownership rights. Any party making claims following the bankruptcy of the sponsor would be unable to recover the assets or their proceeds. As a result, the special legal entity's ability to pay interest and repay the principal should remain intact even if the sponsor were to fail—hence the reason why the special legal entity is also called a bankruptcy-remote vehicle.

3.1.2 *Source of Repayment Proceeds*

The indenture usually describes how the issuer intends to service the debt (make interest payments) and repay the principal. Generally, the source of repayment for bonds issued by supranational organizations is either the repayment of previous loans made by the organization or the paid-in capital from its members. National governments may also act as guarantors for certain bond issues. If additional sources of repayment are needed, the supranational organization can typically call on its members to provide funds.

Sovereign bonds are backed by the "full faith and credit" of the national government and thus by that government's ability to raise tax revenues and print money. Sovereign bonds denominated in local currency are generally considered the safest of all investments because governments have the power to raise taxes to make interest payments and principal repayments. Thus, it is highly probable that interest and principal will be paid fully and on time. As a consequence, the yields on sovereign bonds are typically lower than those for otherwise similar bonds from other local issuers.

There are three major sources for repayment of non-sovereign government debt issues, and bonds are usually classified according to these sources. The first source is through the general taxing authority of the issuer. The second source is from the cash flows of the project the bond issue is financing. The third source is from special taxes or fees established specifically for the purpose of funding interest payments and principal repayments.

The source of payment for corporate bonds is the issuer's ability to generate cash flows, primarily through its operations. These cash flows depend on the issuer's financial strength and integrity. Because corporate bonds carry a higher level of credit risk than otherwise similar sovereign and non-sovereign government bonds, they typically offer a higher yield.

In contrast to corporate bonds, the source of payment for ABS does not depend on the claims-paying ability of an operating entity but on the cash flows generated by one or more underlying financial assets, such as mortgages or auto loans. Thus, investors in ABS must pay special attention to the quality of the assets backing the ABS.

3.1.3 *Asset or Collateral Backing*

Collateral backing is a way to alleviate credit risk. Investors should review where they rank compared with other creditors in the event of default and analyze the quality of the collateral backing the bond issue.

3.1.3.1 Seniority Ranking **Secured bonds** are backed by assets or financial guarantees pledged to ensure debt repayment in the case of default. In contrast, unsecured bonds have no collateral; bondholders have only a general claim on the issuer's assets and cash flows. Thus, unsecured bonds are paid after secured bonds in the event of default. By lowering credit risk, collateral backing increases the bond issue's credit quality and decreases its yield.

A bond's collateral backing might not specify an identifiable asset but instead may be described as the "general plant and infrastructure" of the issuer. In such cases, investors rely on seniority ranking—that is, the systematic way in which lenders are repaid in case of bankruptcy or liquidation. What matters to investors is where they rank compared with other creditors rather than whether there is an asset of sufficient quality and value in place to cover their claims. Senior debt is debt that has a priority claim over subordinated debt or junior debt. Financial institutions issue a large volume of both senior unsecured and subordinated bonds globally; it is not uncommon to see large as well as smaller banks issue such bonds. For example, banks as diverse as Royal Bank of Scotland in the United Kingdom and Prime Bank in Bangladesh issue senior unsecured bonds to institutional investors.

Debentures are a type of bond that can be secured or unsecured. In many jurisdictions, debentures are unsecured bonds, with no collateral backing assigned to the bondholders. In contrast, bonds known as "debentures" in the United Kingdom and in other Commonwealth countries, such as India, are usually backed by an asset or pool of assets assigned as collateral support for the bond obligations and segregated from the claims of other creditors. Thus, it is important for investors to review the indenture to determine whether a debenture is secured or unsecured. If the debenture is secured, debenture holders rank above unsecured creditors of the company; they have a specific asset or pool of assets that the trustee can call on to realize the debt in the event of default.

3.1.3.2 Types of Collateral Backing There is a wide range of bonds that are secured by some form of collateral. Some companies issue collateral trust bonds and equipment trust certificates. **Collateral trust bonds** are secured by securities such as common shares, other bonds, or other financial assets. These securities are pledged by the issuer and typically held by the trustee. **Equipment trust certificates** are bonds secured by specific types of equipment or physical assets, such as aircraft, railroad cars, shipping containers, or oil rigs. They are most commonly issued to take advantage of the tax benefits of leasing. For example, suppose an airline finances the purchase of new aircraft with equipment trust certificates. The legal title to the aircraft is held by the trustee, which issues equipment trust certificates to investors in the amount of the aircraft purchase price. The trustee leases the aircraft to the airline and collects lease payments from the airline to pay the interest on the certificates. When the certificates mature, the trustee sells the aircraft to the airline, uses the proceeds to retire the principal, and cancels the lease.

One of the most common forms of collateral for ABS is mortgaged property. MBS are debt obligations that represent claims to the cash flows from pools of mortgage loans, most commonly on residential property. Mortgage loans are purchased from banks, mortgage companies, and other originators and then assembled into pools by a governmental, quasi-governmental, or private entity.

Financial institutions, particularly in Europe, issue covered bonds. A **covered bond** is a debt obligation backed by a segregated pool of assets called a "cover pool". Covered bonds are similar to ABS but offer bondholders additional protection if the financial institution defaults. A financial institution that sponsors ABS transfers the assets backing the bonds to a special legal entity. If the financial institution defaults, investors who hold bonds in the financial institution have no recourse against the special legal entity and its pool of assets because the special legal entity is a bankruptcy-remote vehicle; the only recourse they have is against the financial institution itself. In contrast, in the case of covered bonds, the pool of assets remains on the financial institution's balance sheet. In the event of default, bondholders have recourse against both the financial institution and the cover pool. Thus, the cover pool serves as collateral. If the assets that are included in the cover pool become non-performing (i.e., the assets are not generating the promised cash flows), the issuer must replace them with performing assets. Therefore, covered bonds usually carry lower credit risks and offer lower yields than otherwise similar ABS.

3.1.4 *Credit Enhancements*

Credit enhancements refer to a variety of provisions that can be used to reduce the credit risk of a bond issue. Thus, they increase the issue's credit quality and decrease the bond's yield. Credit enhancements are very often used when creating ABS.

There are two primary types of credit enhancements: internal and external. Internal credit enhancement relies on structural features regarding the bond issue. External credit enhancement refers to financial guarantees received from a third party, often called a financial guarantor. We describe each type in the following sections.

3.1.4.1 Internal Credit Enhancement The most common forms of internal credit enhancement are subordination, overcollateralization, and reserve accounts.

Subordination, also known as **credit tranching**, is the most popular internal credit enhancement technique. It relies on creating more than one bond class or tranche and ordering the claim priorities for ownership or interest in an asset between the tranches. The cash flows generated by the assets are allocated with different priority to tranches of different seniority. The ordering of the claim priorities is called a senior/subordinated structure, where the tranches of highest seniority are called senior followed by subordinated or junior tranches. The subordinated tranches function as credit protection for the more senior tranches, in the sense that the most senior tranche has the first claim on available cash flows. This type of protection is also commonly referred to as a waterfall structure because in the event of default, the proceeds from liquidating assets will first be used to repay the most senior creditors. Thus, if the issuer defaults, losses are allocated from the bottom up—that is, from the most junior to the most senior tranche. The most senior tranche is typically unaffected unless losses exceed the amount of the subordinated tranches, which is why the most senior tranche is usually rated Aaa/AAA.

Overcollateralization refers to the process of posting more collateral than is needed to obtain or secure financing. It represents a form of internal credit enhancement because the additional collateral can be used to absorb losses. For example, if at issuance the principal amount of a bond issue is \$100 million and the value of the collateral is \$110 million, the amount of overcollateralization is \$10 million. Over time, the amount of overcollateralization changes. This can happen because of amortization, prepayments, or defaults (in the case of MBS). A major problem associated with overcollateralization is the valuation of the collateral. For example, one of the most significant contributors to the 2007–2009 credit crisis was a valuation problem with the residential housing assets backing MBS. Many properties were originally valued higher than the worth of the issued securities. But as property prices fell and homeowners started to default on their mortgages, the credit quality of many MBS declined sharply. The result was a rapid rise in yields and panic among investors in these securities.

Reserve accounts or **reserve funds** are another form of internal credit enhancement and come in two types: a cash reserve fund and an excess spread account. A cash reserve fund is a deposit of cash that can be used to absorb losses. An excess spread account involves the allocation into an account of any amounts left over after paying out the interest to bondholders. The excess spread, sometimes called excess interest cash flow, is the difference between the cash flow received from the assets used to secure the bond issue and the interest paid to bondholders. The excess spread can be retained and deposited into a reserve account that serves as a first line of protection against losses. In a process called "turboing," the excess spread can be used to retire the principal, with the most senior tranche having the first claim on these funds.

3.1.4.2 External Credit Enhancement The most common forms of external credit enhancement are bank guarantees and surety bonds, letters of credit, and cash collateral accounts.

Bank guarantees and **surety bonds** are very similar in nature because they both reimburse bondholders for any losses incurred if the issuer defaults. However, there is usually a maximum amount that is guaranteed, called the penal sum. The major difference between a bank guarantee and a surety bond is that the former is issued by a bank, whereas the latter is issued by a rated and regulated insurance company. Insurance companies that specialize in providing financial guarantees are typically called monoline insurance companies or monoline insurers. Monoline insurers played an important role in securitization until the 2007–2009 credit crisis. But financial guarantees from monoline insurers have become a less common form of credit enhancement since the credit crisis as a consequence of the financial difficulties and credit rating downgrades that most monoline insurers experienced.

A **letter of credit** from a financial institution is another form of external credit enhancement for a bond issue. The financial institution provides the issuer with a credit line to reimburse any cash flow shortfalls from the assets backing the issue. Letters of credit have also become a less common form of credit enhancement since the credit crisis as a result of the credit rating downgrades of several financial institutions that were providers of letters of credit.

Bank guarantees, surety bonds, and letters of credit expose the investor to third-party (or counterparty) risk—that is, the possibility that a guarantor cannot meet its obligations. A **cash collateral account** mitigates this concern because the issuer immediately borrows the credit-enhancement amount and then invests that amount, usually in highly rated short-term commercial paper. Because a cash collateral account is an actual deposit of cash rather than a pledge of cash, a downgrade of the cash collateral account provider will not necessarily result in a downgrade of the bond issue backed by that provider.

3.1.5 *Covenants*

Bond covenants are legally enforceable rules that borrowers and lenders agree on at the time of a new bond issue. An indenture will frequently include affirmative (or positive) and negative covenants. Affirmative covenants enumerate what issuers are required to do, whereas negative covenants specify what issuers are prohibited from doing.

Affirmative covenants are typically administrative in nature. For example, frequently used affirmative covenants include what the issuer will do with the proceeds from the bond issue and the promise of making the contractual payments. The issuer may also promise to comply with all laws and regulations, maintain its current lines of business, insure and maintain its assets, and pay taxes as they come due. These types of covenants typically do not impose additional costs to the issuer and do not materially constrain the issuer's discretion regarding how to operate its business.

In contrast, negative covenants are frequently costly and do materially constrain the issuer's potential business decisions. The purpose of negative covenants is to protect bondholders from such problems as the dilution of their claims, asset withdrawals or substitutions, and suboptimal investments by the issuer. Examples of negative covenants include the following:

- *Restrictions on debt* regulate the issue of additional debt. Maximum acceptable debt usage ratios (sometimes called leverage ratios or gearing ratios) and minimum acceptable interest coverage ratios are frequently specified, permitting new debt to be issued only when justified by the issuer's financial condition.
- *Negative pledges* prevent the issuance of debt that would be senior to or rank in priority ahead of the existing bondholders' debt.
- *Restrictions on prior claims* protect unsecured bondholders by preventing the issuer from using assets that are not collateralized (called unencumbered assets) to become collateralized.
- *Restrictions on distributions to shareholders* restrict dividends and other payments to shareholders such as share buy-backs (repurchases). The restriction typically operates by reference to the borrower's profitability; that is, the covenant sets a base date, usually at or near the time of the issue, and permits dividends and share buy-backs only to the extent of a set percentage of earnings or cumulative earnings after that date.
- *Restrictions on asset disposals* set a limit on the amount of assets that can be disposed by the issuer during the bond's life. The limit on cumulative disposals is typically set as a percentage of a company's gross assets. The usual intent is to protect bondholder claims by preventing a break-up of the company.
- *Restrictions on investments* constrain risky investments by blocking speculative investments. The issuer is essentially forced to devote its capital to its going-concern business. A companion covenant may require the issuer to stay in its present line of business.
- *Restrictions on mergers and acquisitions* prevent these actions unless the company is the surviving company or unless the acquirer delivers a supplemental indenture to the trustee expressly assuming the old bonds and terms of the old indenture. These requirements effectively prevent a company from avoiding its obligations to bondholders by selling out to another company.

These are only a few examples of negative covenants. The common characteristic of all negative covenants is ensuring that the issuer will not take any actions that would significantly reduce its ability to make interest payments and repay the principal. Bondholders, however, rarely wish to be too specific about how an issuer should run its business because doing so would imply a degree of control that bondholders legally want to avoid. In addition, very restrictive covenants may not be in the bondholders' best interest if they force the issuer to default when default is avoidable. For example, strict restrictions on debt may prevent the issuer from raising new funds that are necessary to meet its contractual obligations; strict restrictions on asset disposals may prohibit the issuer from selling assets or business units and obtaining the necessary liquidity to make interest payments or principal repayments; and strict restrictions on mergers and acquisitions may prevent the issuer from being taken over by a stronger company that would be able to honor the issuer's contractual obligations.

EXAMPLE 2

1 The term *most likely* used to refer to the legal contract under which a bond is issued is:

A indenture.

B debenture.

C letter of credit.

2 The individual or entity that *most likely* assumes the role of trustee for a bond issue is:

A a financial institution appointed by the issuer.

B the treasurer or chief financial officer of the issuer.

C a financial institution appointed by a regulatory authority.

3 The individual or entity *most likely* responsible for the timely payment of interest and repayment of principal to bondholders is the:

A trustee.

B primary or lead bank of the issuer.

C treasurer or chief financial officer of the issuer.

4 The major advantage of issuing bonds through a special legal entity is:

A bankruptcy remoteness.

B beneficial tax treatments.

C greater liquidity and lower issuing costs.

5 The category of bond *most likely* repaid from the repayment of previous loans made by the issuer is:

A sovereign bonds.

B supranational bonds.

C non-sovereign bonds.

6 The type of collateral used to secure collateral trust bonds is *most likely*:

A securities.

B mortgages.

C physical assets.

7 The external credit enhancement that has the *least* amount of third-party risk is a:

A surety bond.

B letter of credit.

C cash collateral account.

8 An example of an affirmative covenant is the requirement:

A that dividends will not exceed 60% of earnings.

B to insure and perform periodic maintenance on financed assets.

C that the debt-to-equity ratio will not exceed 0.4 and times interest earned will not fall below 8.0.

9 An example of a covenant that protects bondholders against the dilution of their claims is a restriction on:

A debt.

B investments.

C mergers and acquisitions.

Solution to 1:

A is correct. The contract between a bond issuer and the bondholders is very often called an indenture or deed trust. The indenture documents the terms of the issue, including the principal amount, the coupon rate, and the payments schedule. It also provides information about the funding sources for the contractual payments and specifies whether there are any collateral, credit enhancement, or covenants. B is incorrect because a debenture is a type of bond. C is incorrect because a letter of credit is an external credit enhancement.

Solution to 2:

A is correct. The issuer chooses a financial institution with trust powers, such as the trust department of a bank or a trust company, to act as a trustee for the bond issue.

Solution to 3:

A is correct. Although the issuer is ultimately the source of the contractual payments, it is the trustee that ensures timely payments. Doing so is accomplished by invoicing the issuer for interest payments and principal repayments and holding the funds until they are paid.

Solution to 4:

A is correct. A special legal entity is a bankruptcy-remote vehicle. Bankruptcy remoteness is achieved by transferring the assets from the sponsor to the special legal entity. Once this transfer is completed, the sponsor no longer has ownership rights. If the sponsor defaults, no claims can be made to recover the assets that were transferred or the proceeds from the transfer to the special legal entity.

Solution to 5:

B is correct. The source of payment for bonds issued by supranational organizations is either the repayment of previous loans made by the organization or the paid-in capital of its member states. A is incorrect because national governments rely on their taxing authority and money creation to repay their debt. C is incorrect because non-sovereign bonds are typically repaid from the issuer's taxing authority or the cash flows of the project being financed.

Solution to 6:

A is correct. Collateral trust bonds are secured by securities, such as common shares, other bonds, or other financial assets. B is incorrect because MBS are secured by mortgages. C is incorrect because equipment trust certificates are backed by physical assets such as aircraft, railroad cars, shipping containers, or oil rigs.

Solution to 7:

C is correct. The third-party (or counterparty) risk for a surety bond and a letter of credit arises from both being future promises to pay. In contrast, a cash collateral account allows the issuer to immediately borrow the credit-enhancement amount and then invest it.

Solution to 8:

B is correct. Affirmative covenants indicate what the issuer "must do" and are administrative in nature. A covenant requiring the issuer to insure and perform periodic maintenance on financed assets is an example of affirmative covenant. A and C are incorrect because they are negative covenants; they indicate what the issuer cannot do.

Solution to 9:

A is correct. A restriction on debt typically takes the form of a maximum acceptable debt usage ratio or a minimum acceptable interest coverage ratio. Thus, it limits the issuer's ability to issue new debt that would dilute the bondholders' claims. B and C are incorrect because they are covenants that restrict the issuer's business activities by preventing the company from making investments or being taken over, respectively.

3.2 Legal and Regulatory Considerations

Fixed-income securities are subject to different legal and regulatory requirements depending on where they are issued and traded, as well as who holds them. Unfortunately, there are no unified legal and regulatory requirements that apply globally.

An important consideration for investors is where the bonds are issued and traded because it affects the laws and regulation that apply. The *global bond* markets consist of national bond markets and the Eurobond market. A *national bond* market includes all the bonds that are issued and traded in a specific country and denominated in the currency of that country. Bonds issued by entities that are incorporated in that country are called *domestic bonds*, whereas bonds issued by entities that are incorporated in another country are called *foreign bonds*. If Ford Motor Company issues bonds denominated in US dollars in the United States, these bonds will be classified as domestic. If Volkswagen Group or Toyota Motor Corporation (or their German or Japanese subsidiaries) issue bonds denominated in US dollars in the United States, these bonds will be classified as foreign. Foreign bonds very often receive nicknames. For example, foreign bonds are called "kangaroo bonds" in Australia, "maple bonds" in Canada, "panda bonds" in China, "Samurai bonds" in Japan, "kimchi bonds" in South Korea, "matrioshka bonds" in Russia, "matador bonds" in Spain, "bulldog bonds" in the United Kingdom, and "Yankee bonds" in the United States. National regulators may make distinctions both between and among resident and non-resident issuers, and they may have different requirements regarding the issuance process, the level of disclosures, or the restrictions imposed on the bond issuer and/or the investors who can purchase the bonds.

Governments and companies have issued foreign bonds in London since the 19th century, and foreign bond issues expanded in such countries as the United States, Japan, and Switzerland during the 1980s. But the 1960s saw the emergence of another bond market: the Eurobond market. The Eurobond market was created primarily to bypass the legal, regulatory, and tax constraints imposed on bond issuers and investors, particularly in the United States. Bonds issued and traded on the Eurobond market are called **Eurobonds**, and they are named after the currency in which they are denominated. For example, Eurodollar and Euroyen bonds are denominated in US dollars and Japanese yens, respectively. Bonds that are denominated in euros are called euro-denominated Eurobonds.

Eurobonds are typically less regulated than domestic and foreign bonds because they are issued outside the jurisdiction of any single country. They are usually unsecured bonds and can be denominated in any currency, including the issuer's domestic currency.[4] They are underwritten by an international syndicate—that is, a group of financial institutions from different jurisdictions. In the past, Eurobonds typically were **bearer bonds**, meaning that the trustee did not keep records of who owned the bonds; only the clearing system knew who the bond owners were. Nowadays, Eurobonds as well as domestic and foreign bonds are **registered bonds** for which ownership is recorded by either name or serial number.

A reference is sometimes made to global bonds. A global bond is issued simultaneously in the Eurobond market and in at least one domestic bond market. Issuing bonds in several markets at the same time ensures that there is sufficient demand for large bond issues, and that the bonds can be purchased by all investors, no matter where these investors are located. For example, the World Bank is a regular issuer of global bonds. Many market participants refer to foreign bonds, Eurobonds, and global bonds as international bonds as opposed to domestic bonds.

The differences among domestic bonds, foreign bonds, Eurobonds, and global bonds matter to investors because these bonds are subject to different legal, regulatory, and as described in Section 3.3, tax requirements. They are also characterized by differences in the frequency of interest payments and the way the interest payment is calculated, which affect the bond's cash flows and thus its price. Note, however, that the currency in which a bond is denominated has a stronger effect on its price than where the bond is issued or traded. This is because market interest rates have a strong influence on a bond's price, and the market interest rates that affect a bond are those associated with the currency in which the bond is denominated.

As the emergence and growth of the Eurobond market illustrates, legal and regulatory considerations affect the dynamics of the global fixed-income markets. Exhibit 2 compares the amounts of total and international debt outstanding for the 15 countries that were the largest debt issuers at the end of December 2017. The reported amounts are based on the residence of the issuer.

Exhibit 2 Total and International Debt Securities by Residence of Issuer at the End of December 2017

Issuers	Total Debt Securities (US$ billions)	International Debt Securities (US$ billions)
United States	39,336	2,430
Japan	12,666	395
China	11,757	193
United Kingdom	6,024	3,183
France	4,597	1,531
Germany	3,712	1,292
Italy	3,298	853
Canada	2,428	914

4 Eurobonds denominated in US dollars cannot be sold to US investors at the time of issue because they are not registered with the US Securities and Exchange Commission (SEC). Most Eurobonds are sold to investors in Europe, the Middle East, and Asia Pacific.

Exhibit 2 (Continued)

Issuers	Total Debt Securities (US$ billions)	International Debt Securities (US$ billions)
Netherlands	2,181	2,106
Australia	2,149	610
Spain	2,015	546
Luxembourg	984	788
Ireland	863	846
Denmark	819	132
Sweden	803	506

Source: Based on data from the Bank of International Settlements, Table C1, available at www.bis.org/statistics/secstats.htm, (accessed 25 June 2018).

EXAMPLE 3

1 An example of a domestic bond is a bond issued by:
   - A LG Group from South Korea, denominated in British pounds, and sold in the United Kingdom.
   - B the UK Debt Management Office, denominated in British pounds, and sold in the United Kingdom.
   - C Wal-Mart from the United States, denominated in US dollars, and sold in various countries in North America, Europe, the Middle East, and Asia Pacific.

2 A bond issued by Sony in Japan, denominated in US dollars but not registered with the SEC, and sold to an institutional investor in the Middle East, is *most likely* an example of a:
   - A Eurobond.
   - B global bond.
   - C foreign bond.

Solution to 1:

B is correct. A domestic bond is issued by a local issuer, denominated in local currency, and sold in the domestic market. Gilts are British pound–denominated bonds issued by the UK Debt Management Office in the United Kingdom. Thus, they are UK domestic bonds. A is incorrect because a bond issued by LG Group from South Korea, denominated in British pounds, and sold in the United Kingdom, is an example of a foreign bond (bulldog bond). C is incorrect because a bond issued by Wal-Mart from the United States, denominated in US dollars, and sold in various countries in North America, Europe, the Middle East, and Asia Pacific is most likely an example of a global bond, particularly if it is also sold in the Eurobond market.

Solution to 2:

A is correct. A Eurobond is a bond that is issued internationally, outside the jurisdiction of any single country. Thus, a bond issued by Sony from Japan, denominated in US dollars but not registered with the SEC, is an example of a

Eurobond. B is incorrect because global bonds are bonds that are issued simultaneously in the Eurobond market and in at least one domestic bond market. C is incorrect because if Sony's bond issue were a foreign bond (Yankee bond), it would be registered with the SEC.

3.3 Tax Considerations

Generally speaking, the income portion of a bond investment is taxed at the ordinary income tax rate, which is typically the same tax rate that an individual would pay on wage or salary income. Tax-exempt securities are the exception to this rule. For example, interest income received by holders of local government bonds called municipal bonds in the United States is often exempt from federal income tax and from the income tax of the state in which the bonds are issued. The tax status of bond income may also depend on where the bond is issued and traded. For example, some domestic bonds pay their interest net of income tax. Other bonds, including some Eurobonds, make gross interest payments.

In addition to earnings from interest, a bond investment may also generate a capital gain or loss. If a bond is sold before its maturity date, the price is likely to have changed compared with the purchase price. This change will generate a capital gain if the bond price has increased or a capital loss if the bond price has decreased. From the stand point of taxes, a capital gain or loss is usually treated differently from taxable income. In addition, in some countries, there is a different tax rate for long-term and short-term capital gains. For example, capital gains that are recognized more than 12 months after the original purchase date may be taxed at a long-term capital gains tax rate, whereas capital gains that are recognized within 12 months of purchasing the investment may be taxed as a short-term capital gain. Very often, the tax rate for long-term capital gains is lower than the tax rate for short-term capital gains, and the tax rate for short-term capital gains is equal to the ordinary income tax rate, although there are exceptions. Not all countries, however, implement a capital gains tax. Furthermore, differences in national and local legislation often result in a very diverse set of aggregate country capital gains tax rates.

For bonds issued at a discount, an additional tax consideration is related to the tax status of the original issue discount. The original issue discount is the difference between the par value and the original issue price. In some countries, such as the United States, a prorated portion of the discount must be included in interest income every tax year. This is not the case in other countries, such as Japan. Exhibit 3 illustrates the potential importance of this tax consideration.

Exhibit 3

Original Issue Discount Tax Provision

Assume a hypothetical country, Zinland, where the local currency is the zini (Z). The market interest rate in Zinland is 10%, and both interest income and capital gains are taxed. Companies A and B issue 20-year bonds with a par value of Z1,000. Company A issues a coupon bond with an annual coupon rate of 10%. Investors buy Company A's bonds for Z1,000. Every year, they receive and pay tax on their Z100 annual interest payments. When Company A's bonds mature, bondholders receive the par value of Z1,000. Company B issues a zero-coupon bond at a discount. Investors buy Company B's bonds for Z148.64. They do not receive any cash flows until Company B pays the par value of Z1,000 when the bonds mature.

Exhibit 3 (Continued)

Company A's bonds and Company B's bonds are economically identical in the sense that they have the same maturity (20 years) and the same yield to maturity (10%). Company A's bonds make periodic payments, however, whereas Company B's bonds defer payment until maturity. Investors in Company A's bonds must include the annual interest payments in taxable income. When they receive their original Z1,000 investment back at maturity, they face no capital gain or loss. Without an original issue discount tax provision, investors in Company B's bonds do not have any taxable income until the bonds mature. When they receive the par value at maturity, they face a capital gain on the original issue discount—that is, on Z851.36 (Z1,000 – Z148.64). The purpose of an original issue discount tax provision is to tax investors in Company B's bonds the same way as investors in Company A's bonds. Thus, a prorated portion of the Z851.36 original issue discount is included in taxable income every tax year until maturity. This allows investors in Company B's bonds to increase their cost basis in the bonds so that at maturity, they face no capital gain or loss.

Some jurisdictions also have tax provisions for bonds bought at a premium. They may allow investors to deduct a prorated portion of the amount paid in excess of the bond's par value from their taxable income every tax year until maturity. For example, if an investor pays $1,005 for a bond that has a par value of $1,000 and matures five years later, she can deduct $1 from her taxable income every tax year for five years. But the deduction may not be required; the investor may have the choice either to deduct a prorated portion of the premium each year or to deduct nothing and declare a capital loss when the bond is redeemed at maturity.

EXAMPLE 4

1 The coupon payment is *most likely* to be taxed as:
   - A ordinary income.
   - B short-term capital gain.
   - C long-term capital gain.

2 Assume that a company issues bonds in the hypothetical country of Zinland, where the local currency is the zini (Z). There is an original issue discount tax provision in Zinland's tax code. The company issues a 10-year zero-coupon bond with a par value of Z1,000 and sells it for Z800. An investor who buys the zero-coupon bond at issuance and holds it until maturity *most likely*:
   - A has to include Z20 in his taxable income every tax year for 10 years and has to declare a capital gain of Z200 at maturity.
   - B has to include Z20 in his taxable income every tax year for 10 years and does not have to declare a capital gain at maturity.
   - C does not have to include anything in his taxable income every tax year for 10 years but has to declare a capital gain of Z200 at maturity.

Solution to 1:

A is correct. Interest income is typically taxed at the ordinary income tax rate, which may be the same tax rate that individuals pay on wage and salary income.

Solution to 2:

B is correct. The original issue discount tax provision requires the investor to include a prorated portion of the original issue discount in his taxable income every tax year until maturity. The original issue discount is the difference between the par value and the original issue price—that is, Z1,000 – Z800 = Z200. The bond's maturity is 10 years. Thus, the prorated portion that must be included each year is Z200 ÷ 10 = Z20. The original issue discount tax provision allows the investor to increase his cost basis in the bond so that when the bond matures, the investor faces no capital gain or loss.

4 STRUCTURE OF A BOND'S CASH FLOWS

The most common payment structure by far is that of a plain vanilla bond, as depicted in Exhibit 1. These bonds make periodic, fixed coupon payments and a lump-sum payment of principal at maturity. But there are other structures regarding both the principal repayment and the interest payments. This section discusses the major schedules observed in the global fixed-income markets. Schedules for principal repayments and interest payments are typically similar for a particular type of bond, such as 30-year US Treasury bonds. However, payment schedules vary considerably between types of bonds, such as government bonds versus corporate bonds.

4.1 Principal Repayment Structures

How the amount borrowed is repaid is an important consideration for investors because it affects the level of credit risk they face from holding the bonds. Any provision that periodically retires some of the principal amount outstanding is a way to reduce credit risk.

4.1.1 *Bullet, Fully Amortized, and Partially Amortized Bonds*

The payment structure of a plain vanilla bond has been used for nearly every government bond ever issued as well as for the majority of corporate bonds. Such a bond is also known as a **bullet bond** because the entire payment of principal occurs at maturity.

In contrast, an **amortizing bond** has a payment schedule that calls for periodic payments of interest and repayments of principal. A bond that is fully amortized is characterized by a fixed periodic payment schedule that reduces the bond's outstanding principal amount to zero by the maturity date. A partially amortized bond also makes fixed periodic payments until maturity, but only a portion of the principal is repaid by the maturity date. Thus, a **balloon payment** is required at maturity to retire the bond's outstanding principal amount.

Exhibit 4 illustrates the differences in the payment schedules for a bullet bond, a fully amortized bond, and a partially amortized bond. For the three bonds, the principal amount is $1,000, the maturity is five years, the coupon rate is 6%, and interest payments are made annually. The market interest rate used to discount the bonds' expected cash flows until maturity is assumed to be constant at 6%. The bonds are issued and redeemed at par. For the partially amortized bond, the balloon payment is $200 at maturity.[5]

5 The examples in this reading were created in Microsoft Excel. Numbers may differ from the results obtained using a calculator because of rounding.

Exhibit 4 Example of Payment Schedules for Bullet, Fully Amortized, and Partially Amortized Bonds

Bullet Bond

Year	Investor Cash Flows	Interest Payment	Principal Repayment	Outstanding Principal at the End of the Year
0	–$1,000.00			$1,000.00
1	60.00	$60.00	$0.00	1,000.00
2	60.00	60.00	0.00	1,000.00
3	60.00	60.00	0.00	1,000.00
4	60.00	60.00	0.00	1,000.00
5	1,060.00	60.00	1,000.00	0.00

Fully Amortized Bond

Year	Investor Cash Flows	Interest Payment	Principal Repayment	Outstanding Principal at the End of the Year
0	–$1,000.00			
1	237.40	$60.00	$177.40	$822.60
2	237.40	49.36	188.04	634.56
3	237.40	38.07	199.32	435.24
4	237.40	26.11	211.28	223.96
5	237.40	13.44	223.96	0.00

Partially Amortized Bond

Year	Investor Cash Flows	Interest Payment	Principal Repayment	Outstanding Principal at the End of the Year
0	–$1,000.00			
1	201.92	$60.00	$141.92	$858.08
2	201.92	51.48	150.43	707.65
3	201.92	42.46	159.46	548.19
4	201.92	32.89	169.03	379.17
5	401.92	22.75	379.17	0.00

Investors pay $1,000 now to purchase any of the three bonds. For the bullet bond, they receive the coupon payment of $60 (6% × $1,000) every year for five years. The last payment is $1,060 because it includes both the last coupon payment and the principal amount.

For the fully amortized bond, the annual payment, which includes both the coupon payment and the principal repayment, is constant. Thus, this annual payment can be viewed as an annuity. This annuity lasts for five years; its present value, discounted at the market interest rate of 6%, is equal to the bond price of $1,000. Therefore, the annual payment is $237.40. The first year, the interest part of the payment is $60 (6% × $1,000), which implies that the principal repayment part is $177.40 ($237.40 – $60). This repayment leaves an outstanding principal amount, which becomes the basis for the calculation of the interest the following year, of $822.60 ($1,000 – $177.40). The second year, the interest part of the payment is $49.36 (6% × $822.60), the principal repayment part is $188.04 ($237.40 – $49.36), and the outstanding principal amount is \$634.56 (\$822.60 – \$188.04). The fifth year, the outstanding principal amount is fully repaid. Note that the annual payment is constant but, over time, the interest payment decreases while the principal repayment increases.

The partially amortized bond can be viewed as the combination of two elements: a five-year annuity plus the balloon payment at maturity. The sum of the present values of these two elements is equal to the bond price of \$1,000. As for the fully amortized bond, the discount rate is the market interest rate of 6%, making the constant amount for the annuity \$201.92. This amount represents the annual payment for the first four years. For Years 1 through 4, the split between interest and principal is done the same way as for the fully amortized bond. The interest part of the payment is equal to 6% multiplied by the outstanding principal at the end of the previous year; the principal repayment part is equal to \$201.92 minus the interest part of the payment for the year; and the outstanding principal amount at the end of the year is equal to the outstanding principal amount at the end of the previous year minus the principal repayment for the year. In Year 5, investors receive \$401.92; this amount is calculated either as the sum of the interest payment (\$22.75) and the outstanding principal amount (\$379.17) or as the constant amount of the annuity (\$201.92) plus the balloon payment (\$200). As for the fully amortized bond, the interest payment decreases and the principal repayment increases over time. Because the principal amount is not fully amortized, interest payments are higher for the partially amortized bond than for the fully amortized bond, except the first year when they are equal.

Exhibit 4 does not address the complexity of the repayment structure for some bonds, such as many ABS. For example, MBS face prepayment risk, which is the possible early repayment of mortgage principal. Borrowers usually have the right to prepay mortgages, which typically occurs when a current homeowner purchases a new home or when homeowners refinance their mortgages because market interest rates have fallen.

EXAMPLE 5

1 The structure that requires the largest repayment of principal at maturity is that of a:

A bullet bond.

B fully amortized bond.

C partially amortized bond.

2 A plain vanilla bond has a maturity of 10 years, a par value of £100, and a coupon rate of 9%. Interest payments are made annually. The market interest rate is assumed to be constant at 9%. The bond is issued and redeemed at par. The principal repayment the first year is *closest* to:

A £0.00.

B £6.58.

C £10.00.

3 Relative to a fully amortized bond, the coupon payments of an otherwise similar partially amortized bond are:

A lower or equal.

B equal.

C higher or equal.

Solution to 1:

A is correct. The entire repayment of principal occurs at maturity for a bullet (or plain vanilla) bond, whereas it occurs over time for fully and partially amortized bonds. Thus, the largest repayment of principal at maturity is that of a bullet bond.

Solution to 2:

A is correct. A plain vanilla (or bullet) bond does not make any principal repayment until the maturity date. B is incorrect because £6.58 would be the principal repayment for a fully amortized bond.

Solution to 3:

C is correct. Except at maturity, the principal repayments are lower for a partially amortized bond than for an otherwise similar fully amortized bond. Consequently, the principal amounts outstanding and, therefore, the amounts of interest payments are higher for a partially amortized bond than for a fully amortized bond, all else equal. The only exception is the first interest payment, which is the same for both repayment structures. This is because no principal repayment has been made by the time the first coupon is paid.

4.1.2 *Sinking Fund Arrangements*

A **sinking fund arrangement** is another approach that can be used to achieve the same goal of periodically retiring the bond's principal outstanding. The term sinking fund refers to an issuer's plans to set aside funds over time to retire the bond. Originally, a sinking fund was a specified cash reserve that was segregated from the rest of the issuer's business for the purpose of repaying the principal. More generally today, a sinking fund arrangement specifies the portion of the bond's principal outstanding, perhaps 5%, that must be repaid each year throughout the bond's life or after a specified date. This repayment occurs whether or not an actual segregated cash reserve has been created.

Typically, the issuer will forward repayment proceeds to the bond's trustee. The trustee will then either redeem bonds to this value or select by lottery the serial numbers of bonds to be paid off. The bonds for repayment may be listed in business newspapers, such as the *Wall Street Journal* or the *Financial Times*.

As well as the standard version described above, another type of sinking fund arrangement operates by redeeming a steadily increasing amount of the bond's notional principal (total amount) each year. Any remaining principal is then redeemed at maturity. It is common to find utility and energy companies in the United States, the United Kingdom, and the Commonwealth countries that issue bonds with sinking fund arrangements that incorporate such a provision.

Another common variation is for the bond issue to include a call provision, which gives the issuer the option to repurchase the bonds before maturity—callable bonds are discussed in Section 5.1. The issuer can usually repurchase the bonds at the market price, at par, or at a specified sinking fund price, whichever is the lowest. To allocate the burden of the call provision fairly among bondholders, the bonds to be retired are selected at random based on serial number. Usually, the issuer can repurchase only a small portion of the bond issue. Some indentures, however, allow issuers to use a doubling option to repurchase double the required number of bonds.

The benefit of a sinking fund arrangement is that it ensures that a formal plan is in place for retiring the debt. For an investor, a sinking fund arrangement reduces the risk the issuer will default when the principal is due, thereby reducing the credit risk of the bond issue. But investors experience potential disadvantages with sinking fund arrangements. First, investors face reinvestment risk, the risk associated with having to reinvest cash flows at an interest rate that may be lower than the current yield to maturity. If the serial number of an investor's bonds is selected, the bonds will be repaid and the investor will have to reinvest the proceeds. If market interest rates have fallen since the investor purchased the bonds, he or she probably will not be able to purchase a bond offering the same return. Another potential disadvantage for investors occurs if the issuer has the option to repurchase bonds at below market prices. For example, an issuer could exercise a call option to buy back bonds at par on bonds priced above par. In this case, investors would suffer a loss.

Exhibit 5 illustrates an example of a sinking fund arrangement.

Exhibit 5

Example of a Sinking Fund Arrangement

The notional principal of the bond issue is £200 million. The sinking fund arrangement calls for 5% of the outstanding principal amount to be retired in Years 10 through 19, with the outstanding balance paid off at maturity in 20 years.

Year	Outstanding Principal at the Beginning of the Year (£ millions)	Sinking Fund Payment (£ millions)	Outstanding Principal at the End of the Year (£ millions)	Final Principal Repayment (£ millions)
0			200.00	
1 to 9	200.00	0.00	200.00	
10	200.00	10.00	190.00	
11	190.00	9.50	180.50	
12	180.50	9.03	171.48	
13	171.48	8.57	162.90	
14	162.90	8.15	154.76	
15	154.76	7.74	147.02	
16	147.02	7.35	139.67	
17	139.67	6.98	132.68	
18	132.68	6.63	126.05	
19	126.05	6.30	119.75	
20	119.75			119.75

There is no repayment of the principal during the first nine years. Starting the 10th year, the sinking fund arrangement calls for 5% of the outstanding principal amount to be retired each year. In Year 10, £10 million (5% × £200 million) are paid off, which leaves an outstanding principal balance of £190 million. In Year 11, the principal amount repaid is £9.50 million (5% × £190 million). The final repayment of the remaining balance (£119.75 million) is a balloon payment at maturity.

4.2 Coupon Payment Structures

A coupon is the interest payment that the bond issuer makes to the bondholder. A conventional bond pays a fixed periodic coupon over a specified time to maturity. Most frequently, the coupon is paid semi-annually for sovereign and corporate bonds; this is the case in the United States, the United Kingdom, and Commonwealth countries such as Bangladesh, India, and New Zealand. Eurobonds usually pay an annual coupon, although some Eurobonds make quarterly coupon payments. The norm for bonds issued in the eurozone is for an annual coupon, although there are exceptions.

Fixed-rate coupons are not the only coupon payment structure, however. A wide range of coupon types is offered in the global fixed-income markets. This variety exists to meet the differing needs of both issuers and investors.

4.2.1 *Floating-Rate Notes*

Floating-rate notes do not have a fixed coupon; instead, their coupon rate is linked to an external reference rate, such as Euribor. Thus, a FRN's interest rate will fluctuate periodically during the bond's life, following the changes in the reference rate. Therefore, the FRN's cash flows are not known with certainty. Large issuers of FRNs include government-sponsored enterprises (GSEs), such as the Federal Home Loan Banks (FHLB), the Federal National Mortgage Association ("Fannie Mae"), and the Federal Home Loan Mortgage Corporation ("Freddie Mac") in the United States, as well as banks and financial institutions in Europe and Asia Pacific. It is rare for national governments to issue FRNs because investors in sovereign bonds generally prefer fixed-coupon bonds.

Almost all FRNs have quarterly coupons, although counter examples do exist. FRNs usually pay a fixed spread over the specified reference rate. A typical coupon rate may be the three-month US dollar Libor + 20 bps (i.e., Libor + 0.20%) for a US dollar-denominated bond or the three-month Euribor + 20 bps for a euro-denominated FRN.

Contrary to plain vanilla, fixed-rate securities that decline in value in a rising interest rate environment, FRNs are less affected when interest rates increase because their coupon rates vary with market interest rates and are reset at regular, short-term intervals. Thus, FRNs have little interest rate risk—that is, the risk that a change in market interest rate affects a bond's value. FRNs are frequently favored by investors who expect that interest rates will rise. That said, investors still face credit risk when investing in FRNs. If an issuer's credit risk does not change from one coupon reset date to the next, the FRN's price generally will stay close to the par value. However, if there is a change in the issuer's credit quality that affects the perceived credit risk associated with the bond, the price of the FRN will deviate from its par value. A higher level of credit risk will lead to a lower price.

Additional features observed in FRNs may include a floor or a cap. A floor (floored FRN) prevents the coupon from falling below a specified minimum rate. This feature benefits the bondholders, who are guaranteed that the interest rate will not fall below the specified rate during a time of falling interest rates. In contrast, a cap (capped FRN) prevents the coupon from rising above a specified maximum rate. This feature benefits the issuer, because it sets a limit to the interest rate paid on the debt during a time of rising interest rates. It is also possible to have a collared FRN, which includes both a cap and a floor.

An inverse or reverse FRN, or simply an inverse floater, is a bond whose coupon rate has an inverse relationship to the reference rate. The basic structure is the same as an ordinary FRN except for the direction in which the coupon rate is adjusted. When interest rates fall, the coupon rate on an ordinary FRN decreases; in contrast, the coupon rate on a reverse FRN increases. Thus, inverse FRNs are typically favored by investors who expect interest rates to decline.

4.2.2 *Step-Up Coupon Bonds*

The coupon of a **step-up coupon bond**, which may be fixed or floating, increases by specified margins at specified dates. An example of a bond with a step-up coupon is a ten-year callable bond issued by the Federal Home Loan Bank on 3 August 2016. The initial coupon rate was 1.25% and steps up to 1.50% on 3 August 2018, to 2.00%

on 3 August 2020, to 2.50% on 3 August 2022, to 3.00% on 3 August 2023, to 4.00% on 3 August 2024, and finally to 6.00% on 3 August 2025 for the final year. The bond was first callable at par on 3 August 2018, at the time of the first step up.

Bonds with step-up coupons offer bondholders some protection against rising interest rates, and they may be an important feature for callable bonds. When interest rates increase, there is a higher likelihood that the issuer will not call the bonds, particularly if the bonds have a fixed rate of interest. The step-up coupon allows bondholders to receive a higher coupon, in line with the higher market interest rates. Alternatively, when interest rates decrease or remain stable, the step-up feature acts as an incentive for the issuer to call the bond before the coupon rate increases and the interest expense rises.

Redeeming the bond when the coupon increases is not automatic, however; the issuer may choose to keep the bond despite its increasing cost. This may happen if refinancing the bond is necessary and alternatives are less advantageous for this issuer. For example, a financial crisis may make it difficult for the issuer to refinance. Alternatively, the issuer's credit quality may have deteriorated, which would lead to a higher yield, potentially making the coupon rate on the new bond more expensive than that on the existing bond despite the stepped-up coupon. Although the issuer does not have to call the bond, there is an implicit expectation from investors that it will do so if the market price for the bond is above the call price. Failure to do so may be viewed negatively by market participants and reduce investors' appetite for that issuer's bonds in the future.

4.2.3 *Credit-Linked Coupon Bonds*

A **credit-linked coupon bond** has a coupon that changes when the bond's credit rating changes. An example of a bond with a credit-linked coupon is one of British Telecom's bonds maturing in 2020. It has a coupon rate of 9%, but the coupon will increase by 50 bps for every credit rating downgrade below the bond's credit rating at the time of issuance and will decrease by 50 bps for every credit rating upgrade above the bond's credit rating at the time of issuance.

Bonds with credit-linked coupons are attractive to investors who are concerned about the future creditworthiness of the issuer. They may also provide some general protection against a poor economy because credit ratings tend to decline the most during recessions. A potential problem associated with these bonds is that increases in the coupon payments resulting from a downgrade may ultimately result in further deteriorations of the credit rating or even contribute to the issuer's default.

4.2.4 *Payment-in-Kind Coupon Bonds*

A payment-in-kind (PIK) coupon bond typically allows the issuer to pay interest in the form of additional amounts of the bond issue rather than as a cash payment. Such bonds are favored by issuers who are concerned that the issuer may face potential cash flow problems in the future. They are used, for example, in financing companies that have a high debt burden, such as companies going through a leveraged buyout (a form of acquisition in which the financing consists primarily of debt). Because investors are aware of the additional credit risk associated with these bonds, they usually demand a higher yield for holding bonds with PIK coupons.

Other forms of PIK arrangements can also be found, such as paying the bondholders with common shares worth the amount of coupon due. With a PIK "toggle" note, the borrower has the option, for each interest period, to pay interest in cash, to make the interest payment in kind, or some mix of the two. Cash payments or payments in kind are frequently at the discretion of the borrower, but whether the payment is made in cash or in kind can be determined by an earnings or cash flow trigger identified in the indenture.

4.2.5 *Deferred Coupon Bonds*

A **deferred coupon bond**, sometimes called a **split coupon bond**, pays no coupons for its first few years but then pays a higher coupon than it otherwise normally would for the remainder of its life. Issuers of deferred coupon bonds are usually seeking ways to conserve cash in the years immediately following the bond issue, which may indicate poorer credit quality. Deferred coupon bonds are also common in project financing when the assets being developed do not generate any income during the development phase. A deferred coupon bond allows the issuer to delay interest payments until the project is completed and the cash flows generated by the assets being financed can be used to service the debt.

One of the main advantages of investing in a deferred coupon bond is that these bonds are typically priced at significant discounts to par. Investors may also find the deferred coupon structure to be very helpful in managing taxes. If taxes due on the interest income can be delayed, investors may be able to minimize taxes. This tax advantage, however, depends on the jurisdiction concerned and how its tax rules apply to deferred coupon payments.

A zero-coupon bond can be thought of as an extreme form of deferred coupon bond. These securities pay no interest to the investor and thus are issued at a deep discount to par value. At maturity, the bondholder receives the par value of the bond as payment. Effectively, a zero-coupon bond defers all interest payments until maturity.

4.2.6 *Index-Linked Bonds*

An **index-linked bond** has its coupon payments and/or principal repayment linked to a specified index. In theory, a bond can be indexed to any published variable, including an index reflecting prices, earnings, economic output, commodities, or foreign currencies. **Inflation-linked bonds** are an example of index-linked bonds. They offer investors protection against inflation by linking a bond's coupon payments and/or the principal repayment to an index of consumer prices such as the UK Retail Price Index (RPI) or the US Consumer Price Index (CPI). The advantage of using the RPI or CPI is that these indexes are well-known, transparent, and published regularly.

Governments are large issuers of inflation-linked bonds, also called **linkers**. The United Kingdom was one of the first developed countries to issue inflation-linked bonds in 1981, offering gilts linked to the UK RPI, its main measure of the rate of inflation. In 1997, the US Treasury introduced Treasury Inflation-Protected securities (TIPS) linked to the US consumer price index (CPI). Inflation-linked bonds are now more frequently being offered by corporate issuers, including both financial and non-financial companies.

A bond's stated coupon rate represents the nominal interest rate received by the bondholders. But inflation reduces the actual value of the interest received. The interest rate that bondholders actually receive, net of inflation, is the real interest rate; it is approximately equal to the nominal interest rate minus the rate of inflation. By increasing the coupon payments and/or the principal repayment in line with increases in the price index, inflation-linked bonds reduce inflation risk. An example of an inflation-linked bond is the 1% US TIPS that matures on 15 February 2048. The coupon rate remains fixed at 1% but the principal is adjusted every six months for changes in the CPI.

Exhibit 6 shows some of the national governments that have issued large amounts of inflation-linked bonds. It displays the amount of the linkers and the percentage of the total debt for each country. Sovereign issuers can be grouped into three categories. The first category includes countries such as Brazil and Colombia who have issued inflation-linked bonds because they were experiencing extremely high rates of inflation when borrowing. Thus, offering inflation-linked bonds was their only available alternative to raise funds. The second category includes the United Kingdom and

Australia. These countries have issued inflation-linked bonds in an effort to not only add credibility to the government's commitment to disinflationary policies but also to capitalize on the demand from investors still concerned about inflation risk. The third category, which includes the United States, Canada, and Germany, consists of national governments that are most concerned about the social welfare benefits associated with inflation-linked securities. Theoretically, inflation-linked bonds provide investors the benefit of a long-term asset with a fixed real return that is free from inflation risk.

Exhibit 6 Government Inflation-Linked Debt in Billions of USD as of Q4 2017 and the Percentage of Total Debt

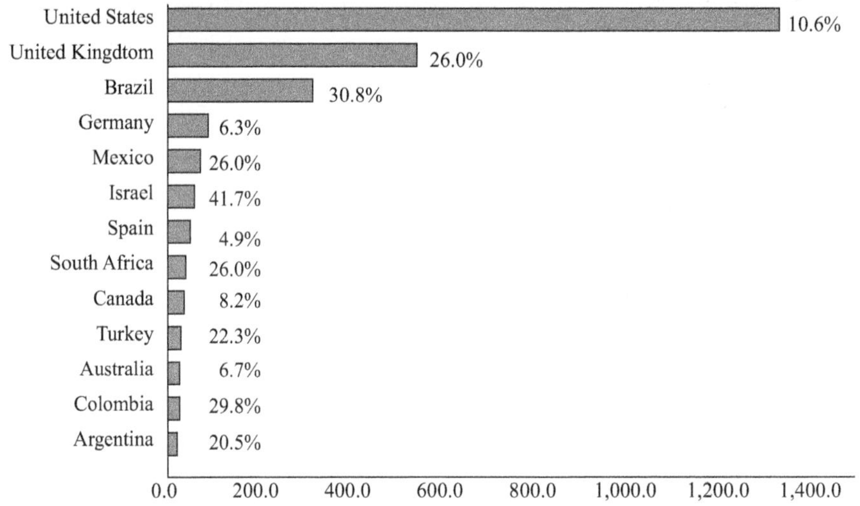

Source: Based on data from the Bank of International Settlements, Table C2, available at www.bis.org/statistics/secstats.htm, (accessed 28 June 2018).

Different methods have been used for linking the cash flows of an index-linked bond to a specified index; the link can be made via the interest payments, the principal repayment, or both. The following examples describe how the link between the cash flows and the index is established, using inflation-linked bonds as an illustration.

- *Zero-coupon-indexed bonds* pay no coupon, so the inflation adjustment is made via the principal repayment only: The principal amount to be repaid at maturity increases in line with increases in the price index during the bond's life. This type of bond has been issued in Sweden.
- *Interest-indexed bonds* pay a fixed nominal principal amount at maturity but an index-linked coupon during the bond's life. Thus, the inflation adjustment applies to the interest payments only. This is essentially a floating-rate note in which reference rate is the inflation rate instead of a market rate such as Euribor. These have been issued by insurance companies and major commercial banks but not typically by governments.

- *Capital-indexed bonds* pay a fixed coupon rate, but it is applied to a principal amount that increases in line with increases in the index during the bond's life. Thus, both the interest payments and the principal repayment are adjusted for inflation. Such bonds have been issued by governments in Australia, Canada, New Zealand, the United Kingdom, and the United States.
- *Indexed-annuity bonds* are fully amortized bonds, in contrast to interest-indexed and capital-indexed bonds that are non-amortizing coupon bonds. The annuity payment, which includes both payment of interest and repayment of the principal, increases in line with inflation during the bond's life. Indexed-annuity bonds linked to a price index have been issued by local governments in Australia, but not by the national government.

Exhibit 7 illustrates the different methods used for inflation-linked bonds.

Exhibit 7

Examples of Inflation-Linked Bonds

Assume a hypothetical country, Lemuria, where the currency is the lemming (L). The country issued 20-year bonds linked to the domestic Consumer Price Index (CPI). The bonds have a par value of L1,000. Lemuria's economy has been free of inflation until the most recent six months, when the CPI increased by 5%.

Suppose that the bonds are zero-coupon-indexed bonds. There will never be any coupon payments. Following the 5% increase in the CPI, the principal amount to be repaid increases to L1,050 [L1,000 × (1 + 0.05)] and will continue increasing in line with inflation until maturity.

Now, suppose that the bonds are coupon bonds that make semi-annual interest payments based on an annual coupon rate of 4%. If the bonds are interest-indexed bonds, the principal amount at maturity will remain L1,000 regardless of the CPI level during the bond's life and at maturity. The coupon payments, however, will be adjusted for inflation. Prior to the increase in inflation, the semi-annual coupon payment was L20 [(0.04 × L1,000) ÷ 2]. Following the 5% increase in the CPI, the semi-annual coupon payment increases to L21 [L20 × (1 + 0.05)]. Future coupon payments will also be adjusted for inflation.

If the bonds are capital-indexed bonds, the annual coupon rate remains 4%, but the principal amount is adjusted for inflation and the coupon payment is based on the inflation-adjusted principal amount. Following the 5% increase in the CPI, the inflation-adjusted principal amount increases to L1,050 [L1,000 × (1 + 0.05)], and the new semi-annual coupon payment is L21 [(0.04 × L1,050) ÷ 2]. The principal amount will continue increasing in line with increases in the CPI until maturity, and so will the coupon payments.

If the bonds are indexed-annuity bonds, they are fully amortized. Prior to the increase in inflation, the semi-annual payment was L36.56—the annuity payment based on a principal amount of L1,000 paid back in 40 semi-annual payments with an annual discount rate of 4%. Following the 5% increase in the CPI, the annuity payment increases to L38.38 [L36.56 × (1 + 0.05)]. Future annuity payments will also be adjusted for inflation in a similar manner.

EXAMPLE 6

1 Floating-rate notes *most likely* pay:

A annual coupons.

B quarterly coupons.

C semi-annual coupons.

2 A zero-coupon bond can *best* be considered a:

A step-up bond.

B credit-linked bond.

C deferred coupon bond.

3 The bonds that do **not** offer protection to the investor against increases in market interest rates are:

A step-up bonds.

B floating rate notes.

C inverse floating rate notes.

4 The US Treasury offers Treasury Inflation-Protected Securities (TIPS). The principal of TIPS increases with inflation and decreases with deflation based on changes in the US Consumer Price Index. When TIPS mature, an investor is paid the original principal or inflation-adjusted principal, whichever is greater. TIPS pay interest twice a year based on a fixed real coupon rate that is applied to the inflation-adjusted principal. TIPS are *most likely*:

A capital-indexed bonds.

B interest-indexed bonds.

C indexed-annuity bonds.

5 Assume a hypothetical country, Lemuria, where the national government has issued 20-year capital-indexed bonds linked to the domestic Consumer Price Index (CPI). Lemuria's economy has been free of inflation until the most recent six months, when the CPI increased. Following the increase in inflation:

A the principal amount remains unchanged but the coupon rate increases.

B the coupon rate remains unchanged, but the principal amount increases.

C the coupon payment remains unchanged, but the principal amount increases.

Solution to 1:

B is correct. Most FRNs pay interest quarterly and are tied to a three-month reference rate such as Libor.

Solution to 2:

C is correct. Because interest is effectively deferred until maturity, a zero-coupon bond can be thought of as a deferred coupon bond. A and B are incorrect because both step-up bonds and credit-linked bonds pay regular coupons. For a step-up bond, the coupon increases by specified margins at specified dates. For a credit-linked bond, the coupon changes when the bond's credit rating changes.

Solution to 3:

C is correct. The coupon rate on an inverse FRN has an inverse relationship to the reference rate. Thus, an inverse FRN does not offer protection to the investor when market interest rates increase but when they decrease. A and B are incorrect because step-up bonds and FRNs both offer protection against increases in market interest rates.

Solution to 4:

A is correct. TIPS have a fixed coupon rate, and the principal is adjusted based on changes in the CPI. Thus, TIPS are an example of capital-indexed bonds. B is incorrect because with an interest-index bond, it is the principal repayment at maturity that is fixed and the coupon that is linked to an index. C is incorrect because indexed-annuity bonds are fully amortized bonds, not bullet bonds. The annuity payment (interest payment and principal repayment) is adjusted based on changes in an index.

Solution to 5:

B is correct. Following an increase in inflation, the coupon rate of a capital-indexed bond remains unchanged, but the principal amount is adjusted upward for inflation. Thus, the coupon payment, which is equal to the fixed coupon rate multiplied by the inflation-adjusted principal amount, increases.

BONDS WITH CONTINGENCY PROVISIONS

5

A contingency refers to some future event or circumstance that is possible but not certain. A **contingency provision** is a clause in a legal document that allows for some action if the event or circumstance does occur. For bonds, the term **embedded option** refers to various contingency provisions found in the indenture. These contingency provisions provide the issuer or the bondholders the right, but not the obligation, to take some action. These rights are called "options." These options are not independent of the bond and cannot be traded separately—hence the term "embedded." Some common types of bonds with embedded options include callable bonds, putable bonds, and convertible bonds. The options embedded in these bonds grant either the issuer or the bondholders certain rights affecting the disposal or redemption of the bond.

5.1 Callable Bonds

The most widely used embedded option is the call provision. A **callable bond** gives the issuer the right to redeem all or part of the bond before the specified maturity date. The primary reason why issuers choose to issue callable bonds rather than non-callable bonds is to protect themselves against a decline in interest rates. This decline can come either from market interest rates falling or from the issuer's credit quality improving. If market interest rates fall or credit quality improves, the issuer of a callable bond has the right to replace an old, expensive bond issue with a new, cheaper bond issue. In other words, the issuer can benefit from a decline in interest rates by being able to refinance its debt at a lower interest rate. For example, assume that the market interest rate was 6% at the time of issuance and that a company issued a bond with a coupon rate of 7%—the market interest rate plus a spread of 100 bps. Now assume that the market interest rate has fallen to 4% and that the company's creditworthiness has not changed; it can still issue at the market interest rate plus 100 bps. If the original bond is callable, the company can redeem it and replace it with a new bond paying 5% annually. If the original bond is non-callable, the company must carry on paying 7% annually and cannot benefit from the decline in market interest rates.

As illustrated in this example, callable bonds are advantageous to the issuer of the security. Put another way, the call option has value to the *issuer*. Callable bonds present investors with a higher level of reinvestment risk than non-callable bonds; that is, if the bonds are called, bondholders have to reinvest funds in a lower interest rate environment. For this reason, callable bonds have to offer a higher yield and sell at a lower price than otherwise similar non-callable bonds. The higher yield and lower price compensate the bondholders for the value of the call option to the issuer.

Callable bonds have a long tradition and are commonly issued by corporate issuers. Although first issued in the US market, they are now frequently issued in every major bond market and in a variety of forms.

The details about the call provision are specified in the indenture. These details include the call price, which represents the price paid to bondholders when the bond is called. The call premium is the amount over par paid by the issuer if the bond is called. There may be restrictions on when the bond can be called, or the bond may have different call prices depending on when it is called. The call schedule specifies the dates and prices at which a bond may be called. Some callable bonds are issued with a *call protection period*, also called lockout period, cushion, or deferment period. The call protection period prohibits the issuer from calling a bond early in its life and is often added as an incentive for investors to buy the bond. The earliest time that a bond might be called is known as the call date.

Make-whole calls first appeared in the US corporate bond market in the mid-1990s and have become more commonplace ever since. A typical make-whole call requires the issuer to make a lump-sum payment to the bondholders based on the present value of the future coupon payments and principal repayment not paid because of the bond being redeemed early. The discount rate used is usually some pre-determined spread over the yield to maturity of an appropriate sovereign bond. The typical result is a redemption value that is significantly greater than the bond's current market price. A make-whole call provision is less detrimental to bondholders than a regular call provision because it allows them to be compensated if the issuer calls the bond. Issuers, however, rarely invoke this provision because redeeming a bond that includes a make-whole provision before the maturity date is costly. Issuers tend to include a make-whole provision as a "sweetener" to make the bond issue more attractive to potential buyers and allow them to pay a lower coupon rate.

Available exercise styles on callable bonds include the following:

- *American-style* call, sometimes referred to as continuously callable, for which the issuer has the right to call a bond at any time starting on the first call date.
- *European-style* call, for which the issuer has the right to call a bond only once on the call date.
- *Bermuda-style* call, for which the issuer has the right to call bonds on specified dates following the call protection period. These dates frequently correspond to coupon payment dates.

EXAMPLE 7

Assume a hypothetical 30-year bond is issued on 15 August 2019 at a price of 98.195 (as a percentage of par). Each bond has a par value of $1,000. The bond is callable in whole or in part every 15 August from 2029 at the option of the issuer. The call prices are shown below.

Year	Call Price	Year	Call Price
2029	103.870	2035	101.548
2030	103.485	2036	101.161
2031	103.000	2037	100.774
2032	102.709	2038	100.387
2033	102.322	2039 and thereafter	100.000
2034	101.955		

1 The call protection period is:
   - **A** 10 years.
   - **B** 11 years.
   - **C** 20 years.

2 The call premium (per $1,000 in par value) in 2033 is *closest* to:
   - **A** $2.32.
   - **B** $23.22.
   - **C** $45.14.

3 The call provision is *most likely*:
   - **A** a Bermuda call.
   - **B** a European call.
   - **C** an American call.

Solution to 1:

A is correct. The bonds were issued in 2019 and are first callable in 2029. The call protection period is 2029 – 2019 = 10 years.

Solution to 2:

B is correct. The call prices are stated as a percentage of par. The call price in 2033 is $1,023.22 (102.322% × $1,000). The call premium is the amount paid above par by the issuer. The call premium in 2033 is $23.22 ($1,023.22 – $1,000).

Solution to 3:

A is correct. The bond is callable every 15 August from 2029—that is, on specified dates following the call protection period. Thus, the embedded option is a Bermuda call.

5.2 Putable Bonds

A put provision gives the bondholders the right to sell the bond back to the issuer at a pre-determined price on specified dates. **Putable bonds** are beneficial for the bondholder by guaranteeing a pre-specified selling price at the redemption dates. If interest rates rise after the issue date, thus depressing the bond's price, the bondholders can put the bond back to the issuer and get cash. This cash can be reinvested in bonds that offer higher yields, in line with the higher market interest rates.

Because a put provision has value to the *bondholders,* the price of a putable bond will be higher than the price of an otherwise similar bond issued without the put provision. Similarly, the yield on a bond with a put provision will be lower than the yield on an otherwise similar non-putable bond. The lower yield compensates the issuer for the value of the put option to the investor.

The indenture lists the redemption dates and the prices applicable to the sale of the bond back to the issuer. The selling price is usually the par value of the bond. Depending on the terms set out in the indenture, putable bonds may allow buyers to force a sellback only once or multiple times during the bond's life. Putable bonds that incorporate a single sellback opportunity include a European-style put and are often referred to as one-time put bonds. Putable bonds that allow multiple sellback opportunities include a Bermuda-style put and are known as multiple put bonds. Multiple put bonds offer more flexibility for investors, so they are generally more expensive than one-time put bonds.[6]

Typically, putable bonds incorporate one- to five-year put provisions. Their increasing popularity has often been motivated by investors wanting to protect themselves against major declines in bond prices. One benefit of this rising popularity has been an improvement in liquidity in some markets, because the put protection attracts more conservative classes of investors. The global financial crisis that started in 2008 showed that these securities can often exacerbate liquidity problems, however, because they provide a first claim on the issuer's assets. The put provision gives bondholders the opportunity to convert their claim into cash before other creditors.

5.3 Convertible Bonds

A **convertible bond** is a hybrid security with both debt and equity features. It gives the bondholder the right to exchange the bond for a specified number of common shares in the issuing company. Thus, a convertible bond can be viewed as the combination of a straight bond (option-free bond) plus an embedded equity call option. Convertible bonds can also include additional provisions, the most common being a call provision.

From the investor's perspective, a convertible bond offers several advantages relative to a non-convertible bond. First, it gives the bondholder the ability to convert into equity in case of share price appreciation, and thus participate in the equity upside. At the same time, the bondholder receives downside protection; if the share price does not appreciate, the convertible bond offers the comfort of regular coupon payments and the promise of principal repayment at maturity. Even if the share price and thus the value of the equity call option decline, the price of a convertible bond cannot fall below the price of the straight bond. Consequently, the value of the straight bond acts as a floor for the price of the convertible bond.

Because the conversion provision is valuable to *bondholders*, the price of a convertible bond is higher than the price of an otherwise similar bond without the conversion provision. Similarly, the yield on a convertible bond is lower than the yield on an otherwise similar non-convertible bond. However, most convertible bonds offer investors a yield advantage; the coupon rate on the convertible bond is typically higher than the dividend yield on the underlying common share.

From the issuer's perspective, convertible bonds offer two main advantages. The first is reduced interest expense. Issuers are usually able to offer below-market coupon rates because of investors' attraction to the conversion feature. The second advantage is the elimination of debt if the conversion option is exercised. But the conversion option is dilutive to existing shareholders.

Key terms regarding the conversion provision include the following:

- The **conversion price** is the price per share at which the convertible bond can be converted into shares.

6 Although American-style putable bonds could be issued in theory, they are not observed in practice. The likely reason for the absence of continuously putable bonds is that issuers would not like to be surprised with having to raise cash to redeem the bonds at indeterminate times.

- The **conversion ratio** is the number of common shares that each bond can be converted into. The indenture sometimes does not stipulate the conversion ratio but only mentions the conversion price. The conversion ratio is equal to the par value divided by the conversion price. For example, if the par value is 1,000€ and the conversion price is 20€, the conversion ratio is 1,000€ ÷ 20€ = 50:1, or 50 common shares per bond.
- The **conversion value**, sometimes called the parity value, is the current share price multiplied by the conversion ratio. For example, if the current share price is 33€ and the conversion ratio is 30:1, the conversion value is 33€ × 30 = 990€.
- The **conversion premium** is the difference between the convertible bond's price and its conversion value. For example, if the convertible bond's price is 1,020€ and the conversion value is 990€, the conversion premium is 1,020€ – 990€ = 30€.
- **Conversion parity** occurs if the conversion value is equal to the convertible bond's price. Using the previous two examples, if the current share price is 34€ instead of 33€, then both the convertible bond's price and the conversion value are equal to 1,020€ (i.e., a conversion premium equal to 0). This condition is referred to as parity. If the common share is selling for less than 34€, the condition is below parity. In contrast, if the common share is selling for more than 34€, the condition is above parity.

Generally, convertible bonds have maturities of five to 10 years. First-time or younger issuers are usually able to issue convertible bonds of up to three years in maturity only. Although it is common for convertible bonds to reach conversion parity before maturity, bondholders rarely exercise the conversion option before that time. Early conversion would eliminate the yield advantage of continuing to hold the convertible bond; investors would typically receive in dividends less than they would receive in coupon payments. For this reason, it is common to find convertible bonds that are also callable by the issuer on a set of specified dates. If the convertible bond includes a call provision and the conversion value is above the current share price, the issuer may force the bondholders to convert their bonds into common shares before maturity. For this reason, callable convertible bonds have to offer a higher yield and sell at a lower price than otherwise similar non-callable convertible bonds. Some indentures specify that the bonds can be called only if the share price exceeds a specified price, giving investors more predictability about the share price at which the issuer may force conversion.

Although somewhat similar in purpose to a conversion option, a **warrant** is actually not an embedded option but rather an "attached" option. A warrant entitles the holder to buy the underlying stock of the issuing company at a fixed exercise price until the expiration date. Warrants are considered yield enhancements; they are frequently attached to bond issues as a "sweetener." Warrants are actively traded in some financial markets, such as the Deutsche Börse and the Hong Kong Stock Exchange.

Several European banks have been issuing a type of convertible bond called contingent convertible bonds. **Contingent convertible bonds**, nicknamed "CoCos," are bonds with contingent write-down provisions. Two main features distinguish bonds with contingent write-down provisions from the traditional convertible bonds just described. A traditional convertible bond is convertible at the option of the bondholder, and conversion occurs on the upside—that is, if the issuer's share price increases. In contrast, bonds with contingent write-down provisions are convertible on the downside. In the case of CoCos, conversion is automatic if a specified event occurs—for example, if the bank's core Tier 1 capital ratio (a measure of the bank's proportion of core equity capital available to absorb losses) falls below the minimum requirement set by the regulators. Thus, if the bank experiences losses that reduce its equity capital below the minimum requirement, CoCos are a way to reduce the bank's likelihood of default and, therefore, systemic risk—that is, the risk of failure of the financial system. When the bank's core Tier 1 capital falls below the minimum requirement, the CoCos immediately convert into equity, automatically recapitalizing the bank, lightening the debt burden, and reducing the risk of default. Because the conversion is not at the option of the bondholders but automatic, CoCos force bondholders to take losses. For this reason, CoCos must offer a higher yield than otherwise similar bonds.

EXAMPLE 8

1 Which of the following is **not** an example of an embedded option?

A Warrant

B Call provision

C Conversion provision

2 The type of bonds with an embedded option that would *most likely* sell at a lower price than an otherwise similar bond without the embedded option is a:

A putable bond.

B callable bond.

C convertible bond.

3 The additional risk inherent to a callable bond is *best* described as:

A credit risk.

B interest rate risk.

C reinvestment risk.

4 The put provision of a putable bond:

A limits the risk to the issuer.

B limits the risk to the bondholder.

C does not materially affect the risk of either the issuer or the bondholder.

5 Assume that a convertible bond issued in South Korea has a par value of ₩1,000,000 and is currently priced at ₩1,100,000. The underlying share price is ₩40,000 and the conversion ratio is 25:1. The conversion condition for this bond is:

A parity.

B above parity.

C below parity.

Solution to 1:

A is correct. A warrant is a separate, tradable security that entitles the holder to buy the underlying common share of the issuing company. B and C are incorrect because the call provision and the conversion provision are embedded options.

Solution to 2:

B is correct. The call provision is an option that benefits the issuer. Because of this, callable bonds sell at lower prices and higher yields relative to otherwise similar non-callable bonds. A and C are incorrect because the put provision and the conversion provision are options that benefit the investor. Thus, putable bonds and convertible bonds sell at higher prices and lower yields relative to otherwise similar bonds that lack those provisions.

Solution to 3:

C is correct. Reinvestment risk refers to the effect that lower interest rates have on available rates of return when reinvesting the cash flows received from an earlier investment. Because bonds are typically called following a decline in market interest rates, reinvestment risk is particularly relevant for the holder of a callable bond. A is incorrect because credit risk refers to the risk of loss resulting from the issuer failing to make full and timely payments of interest and/or repayments of principal. B is incorrect because interest rate risk is the risk that a change in market interest rate affects a bond's value.

Solution to 4:

B is correct. A putable bond limits the risk to the bondholder by guaranteeing a pre-specified selling price at the redemption dates.

Solution to 5:

C is correct. The conversion value of the bond is ₩40,000 × 25 = ₩1,000,000. The price of the convertible bond is ₩1,100,000. Thus, the conversion value of the bond is less than the bond's price, and this condition is referred to as below parity.

SUMMARY

This reading provides an introduction to the salient features of fixed-income securities while noting how these features vary among different types of securities. Important points include the following:

- The three important elements that an investor needs to know when investing in a fixed-income security are: (1) the bond's features, which determine its scheduled cash flows and thus the bondholder's expected and actual return; (2) the legal, regulatory, and tax considerations that apply to the contractual agreement between the issuer and the bondholders; and (3) the contingency provisions that may affect the bond's scheduled cash flows.
- The basic features of a bond include the issuer, maturity, par value (or principal), coupon rate and frequency, and currency denomination.
- Issuers of bonds include supranational organizations, sovereign governments, non-sovereign governments, quasi-government entities, and corporate issuers.
- Bondholders are exposed to credit risk and may use bond credit ratings to assess the credit quality of a bond.
- A bond's principal is the amount the issuer agrees to pay the bondholder when the bond matures.
- The coupon rate is the interest rate that the issuer agrees to pay to the bondholder each year. The coupon rate can be a fixed rate or a floating rate. Bonds may offer annual, semi-annual, quarterly, or monthly coupon payments depending on the type of bond and where the bond is issued.
- Bonds can be issued in any currency. Bonds such as dual-currency bonds and currency option bonds are connected to two currencies.

- The yield to maturity is the discount rate that equates the present value of the bond's future cash flows until maturity to its price. Yield to maturity can be considered an estimate of the market's expectation for the bond's return.
- A plain vanilla bond has a known cash flow pattern. It has a fixed maturity date and pays a fixed rate of interest over the bond's life.
- The bond indenture or trust deed is the legal contract that describes the form of the bond, the issuer's obligations, and the investor's rights. The indenture is usually held by a financial institution called a trustee, which performs various duties specified in the indenture.
- The issuer is identified in the indenture by its legal name and is obligated to make timely payments of interest and repayment of principal.
- For asset-backed securities, the legal obligation to repay bondholders often lies with a separate legal entity—that is, a bankruptcy-remote vehicle that uses the assets as guarantees to back a bond issue.
- How the issuer intends to service the debt and repay the principal should be described in the indenture. The source of repayment proceeds varies depending on the type of bond.
- Collateral backing is a way to alleviate credit risk. Secured bonds are backed by assets or financial guarantees pledged to ensure debt payment. Examples of collateral-backed bonds include collateral trust bonds, equipment trust certificates, mortgage-backed securities, and covered bonds.
- Credit enhancement can be internal or external. Examples of internal credit enhancement include subordination, overcollateralization, and reserve accounts. A bank guarantee, a surety bond, a letter of credit, and a cash collateral account are examples of external credit enhancement.
- Bond covenants are legally enforceable rules that borrowers and lenders agree on at the time of a new bond issue. Affirmative covenants enumerate what issuers are required to do, whereas negative covenants enumerate what issuers are prohibited from doing.
- An important consideration for investors is where the bonds are issued and traded, because it affects the laws, regulation, and tax status that apply. Bonds issued in a particular country in local currency are domestic bonds if they are issued by entities incorporated in the country and foreign bonds if they are issued by entities incorporated in another country. Eurobonds are issued internationally, outside the jurisdiction of any single country and are subject to a lower level of listing, disclosure, and regulatory requirements than domestic or foreign bonds. Global bonds are issued in the Eurobond market and at least one domestic market at the same time.
- Although some bonds may offer special tax advantages, as a general rule, interest is taxed at the ordinary income tax rate. Some countries also implement a capital gains tax. There may be specific tax provisions for bonds issued at a discount or bought at a premium.
- An amortizing bond is a bond whose payment schedule requires periodic payment of interest and repayment of principal. This differs from a bullet bond, whose entire payment of principal occurs at maturity. The amortizing bond's outstanding principal amount is reduced to zero by the maturity date for a fully amortized bond, but a balloon payment is required at maturity to retire the bond's outstanding principal amount for a partially amortized bond.
- Sinking fund agreements provide another approach to the periodic retirement of principal, in which an amount of the bond's principal outstanding amount is usually repaid each year throughout the bond's life or after a specified date.

- A floating-rate note, or floater, is a bond whose coupon is set based on some reference rate plus a spread. FRNs can be floored, capped, or collared. An inverse FRN is a bond whose coupon has an inverse relationship to the reference rate.
- Other coupon payment structures include bonds with step-up coupons, which pay coupons that increase by specified amounts on specified dates; bonds with credit-linked coupons, which change when the issuer's credit rating changes; bonds with payment-in-kind coupons that allow the issuer to pay coupons with additional amounts of the bond issue rather than in cash; and bonds with deferred coupons, which pay no coupons in the early years following the issue but higher coupons thereafter.
- The payment structures for index-linked bonds vary considerably among countries. A common index-linked bond is an inflation-linked bond, or linker, whose coupon payments and/or principal repayments are linked to a price index. Index-linked payment structures include zero-coupon-indexed bonds, interest-indexed bonds, capital-indexed bonds, and indexed-annuity bonds.
- Common types of bonds with embedded options include callable bonds, putable bonds, and convertible bonds. These options are "embedded" in the sense that there are provisions provided in the indenture that grant either the issuer or the bondholder certain rights affecting the disposal or redemption of the bond. They are not separately traded securities.
- Callable bonds give the issuer the right to buy bonds back prior to maturity, thereby raising the reinvestment risk for the bondholder. For this reason, callable bonds have to offer a higher yield and sell at a lower price than otherwise similar non-callable bonds to compensate the bondholders for the value of the call option to the issuer.
- Putable bonds give the bondholder the right to sell bonds back to the issuer prior to maturity. Putable bonds offer a lower yield and sell at a higher price than otherwise similar non-putable bonds to compensate the issuer for the value of the put option to the bondholders.
- A convertible bond gives the bondholder the right to convert the bond into common shares of the issuing company. Because this option favors the bondholder, convertible bonds offer a lower yield and sell at a higher price than otherwise similar non-convertible bonds.

PRACTICE PROBLEMS

1 A 10-year bond was issued four years ago. The bond is denominated in US dollars, offers a coupon rate of 10% with interest paid semi-annually, and is currently priced at 102% of par. The bond's:

A tenor is six years.

B nominal rate is 5%.

C redemption value is 102% of the par value.

2 A sovereign bond has a maturity of 15 years. The bond is *best* described as a:

A perpetual bond.

B pure discount bond.

C capital market security.

3 A company has issued a floating-rate note with a coupon rate equal to the three-month Libor + 65 basis points. Interest payments are made quarterly on 31 March, 30 June, 30 September, and 31 December. On 31 March and 30 June, the three-month Libor is 1.55% and 1.35%, respectively. The coupon rate for the interest payment made on 30 June is:

A 2.00%.

B 2.10%.

C 2.20%.

4 The legal contract that describes the form of the bond, the obligations of the issuer, and the rights of the bondholders can be *best* described as a bond's:

A covenant.

B indenture.

C debenture.

5 Which of the following is a type of external credit enhancement?

A Covenants

B A surety bond

C Overcollaterization

6 An affirmative covenant is *most likely* to stipulate:

A limits on the issuer's leverage ratio.

B how the proceeds of the bond issue will be used.

C the maximum percentage of the issuer's gross assets that can be sold.

7 Which of the following *best* describes a negative bond covenant? The issuer is:

A required to pay taxes as they come due.

B prohibited from investing in risky projects.

C required to maintain its current lines of business.

8 A South African company issues bonds denominated in pound sterling that are sold to investors in the United Kingdom. These bonds can be *best* described as:

A Eurobonds.

B global bonds.

C foreign bonds.

9 Relative to domestic and foreign bonds, Eurobonds are *most likely* to be:

A bearer bonds.

B registered bonds.

C subject to greater regulation.

10 An investor in a country with an original issue discount tax provision purchases a 20-year zero-coupon bond at a deep discount to par value. The investor plans to hold the bond until the maturity date. The investor will *most likely* report:

A a capital gain at maturity.

B a tax deduction in the year the bond is purchased.

C taxable income from the bond every year until maturity.

11 A bond that is characterized by a fixed periodic payment schedule that reduces the bond's outstanding principal amount to zero by the maturity date is *best* described as a:

A bullet bond.

B plain vanilla bond.

C fully amortized bond.

12 If interest rates are expected to increase, the coupon payment structure *most likely* to benefit the issuer is a:

A step-up coupon.

B inflation-linked coupon.

C cap in a floating-rate note.

13 Investors who believe that interest rates will rise *most likely* prefer to invest in:

A inverse floaters.

B fixed-rate bonds.

C floating-rate notes.

14 A 10-year, capital-indexed bond linked to the Consumer Price Index (CPI) is issued with a coupon rate of 6% and a par value of 1,000. The bond pays interest semi-annually. During the first six months after the bond's issuance, the CPI increases by 2%. On the first coupon payment date, the bond's:

A coupon rate increases to 8%.

B coupon payment is equal to 40.

C principal amount increases to 1,020.

15 The provision that provides bondholders the right to sell the bond back to the issuer at a predetermined price prior to the bond's maturity date is referred to as:

A a put provision.

B a make-whole call provision.

C an original issue discount provision.

16 Which of the following provisions is a benefit to the issuer?

A Put provision

B Call provision

C Conversion provision

17 Relative to an otherwise similar option-free bond, a:

A putable bond will trade at a higher price.

B callable bond will trade at a higher price.

C convertible bond will trade at a lower price.

18 Which type of bond *most likely* earns interest on an implied basis?

A Floater

B Conventional bond

C Pure discount bond

19 Clauses that specify the rights of the bondholders and any actions that the issuer is obligated to perform or is prohibited from performing are:

A covenants.

B collaterals.

C credit enhancements.

20 Which of the following type of debt obligation *most likely* protects bondholders when the assets serving as collateral are non-performing?

A Covered bonds

B Collateral trust bonds

C Mortgage-backed securities

21 Which of the following *best* describes a negative bond covenant? The requirement to:

A insure and maintain assets.

B comply with all laws and regulations.

C maintain a minimum interest coverage ratio.

22 Contrary to positive bond covenant, negative covenants are *most likely*:

A costlier.

B legally enforceable.

C enacted at time of issue.

23 A five-year bond has the following cash flows:

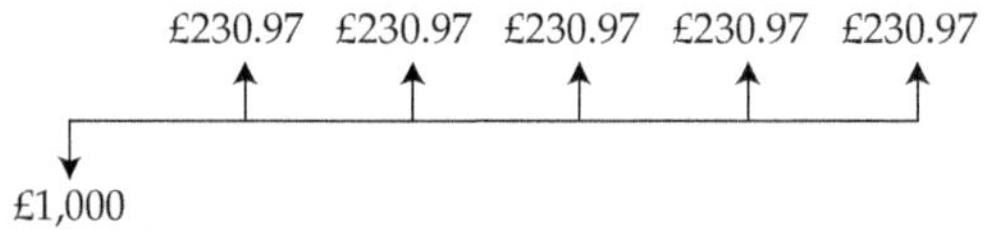

The bond can *best* be described as a:

A bullet bond.

B fully amortized bond.

C partially amortized bond.

24 Investors seeking some general protection against a poor economy are *most likely* to select a:

A deferred coupon bond.

B credit-linked coupon bond.

C payment-in-kind coupon bond.

25 The benefit to the issuer of a deferred coupon bond is *most likely* related to:

A tax management.

B cash flow management.

C original issue discount price.

26 Which of the following bond types provides the *most* benefit to a bondholder when bond prices are declining?

A Callable

B Plain vanilla

C Multiple put

27 Which type of call bond option offers the *greatest* flexibility as to when the issuer can exercise the option?

A A Bermuda call

B A European call

C An American call

28 Which of the following *best* describes a convertible bond's conversion premium?

A Bond price minus conversion value

B Par value divided by conversion price

C Current share price multiplied by conversion ratio

SOLUTIONS

1 A is correct. The tenor of the bond is the time remaining until the bond's maturity date. Although the bond had a maturity of 10 years at issuance (original maturity), it was issued four years ago. Thus, there are six years remaining until the maturity date.

   B is incorrect because the nominal rate is the coupon rate, i.e., the interest rate that the issuer agrees to pay each year until the maturity date. Although interest is paid semi-annually, the nominal rate is 10%, not 5%. C is incorrect because it is the bond's price, not its redemption value (also called principal amount, principal value, par value, face value, nominal value, or maturity value), that is equal to 102% of the par value.

2 C is correct. A capital market security has an original maturity longer than one year.

   A is incorrect because a perpetual bond does not have a stated maturity date. Thus, the sovereign bond, which has a maturity of 15 years, cannot be a perpetual bond. B is incorrect because a pure discount bond is a bond issued at a discount to par value and redeemed at par. Some sovereign bonds (e.g., Treasury bills) are pure discount bonds, but others are not.

3 C is correct. The coupon rate that applies to the interest payment due on 30 June is based on the three-month Libor rate prevailing on 31 March. Thus, the coupon rate is 1.55% + 0.65% = 2.20%.

4 B is correct. The indenture, also referred to as trust deed, is the legal contract that describes the form of the bond, the obligations of the issuer, and the rights of the bondholders.

   A is incorrect because covenants are only one element of a bond's indenture. Covenants are clauses that specify the rights of the bondholders and any actions that the issuer is obligated to perform or prohibited from performing. C is incorrect because a debenture is a type of bond.

5 B is correct. A surety bond is an external credit enhancement, i.e., a guarantee received from a third party. If the issuer defaults, the guarantor who provided the surety bond will reimburse investors for any losses, usually up to a maximum amount called the penal sum.

   A is incorrect because covenants are legally enforceable rules that borrowers and lenders agree upon when the bond is issued. C is incorrect because overcollateralization is an internal, not external, credit enhancement. Collateral is a guarantee underlying the debt above and beyond the issuer's promise to pay, and overcollateralization refers to the process of posting more collateral than is needed to obtain or secure financing. Collateral, such as assets or securities pledged to ensure debt payments, is not provided by a third party. Thus, overcollateralization is not an external credit enhancement.

6 B is correct. Affirmative (or positive) covenants enumerate what issuers are required to do and are typically administrative in nature. A common affirmative covenant describes what the issuer intends to do with the proceeds from the bond issue.

   A and C are incorrect because imposing a limit on the issuer's leverage ratio or on the percentage of the issuer's gross assets that can be sold are negative covenants. Negative covenants prevent the issuer from taking actions that could reduce its ability to make interest payments and repay the principal.

7 B is correct. Prohibiting the issuer from investing in risky projects restricts the issuer's potential business decisions. These restrictions are referred to as negative bond covenants.

A and C are incorrect because paying taxes as they come due and maintaining the current lines of business are positive covenants.

8 C is correct. Bonds sold in a country and denominated in that country's currency by an entity from another country are referred to as foreign bonds.

A is incorrect because Eurobonds are bonds issued outside the jurisdiction of any single country. B is incorrect because global bonds are bonds issued in the Eurobond market and at least one domestic country simultaneously.

9 A is correct. Eurobonds are typically issued as bearer bonds, i.e., bonds for which the trustee does not keep records of ownership. In contrast, domestic and foreign bonds are typically registered bonds for which ownership is recorded by either name or serial number.

B is incorrect because Eurobonds are typically issued as bearer bonds, not registered bonds. C is incorrect because Eurobonds are typically subject to lower, not greater, regulation than domestic and foreign bonds.

10 C is correct. The original issue discount tax provision requires the investor to include a prorated portion of the original issue discount in his taxable income every tax year until maturity. The original issue discount is equal to the difference between the bond's par value and its original issue price.

A is incorrect because the original issue discount tax provision allows the investor to increase his cost basis in the bond so that when the bond matures, he faces no capital gain or loss. B is incorrect because the original issue discount tax provision does not require any tax deduction in the year the bond is purchased or afterwards.

11 C is correct. A fully amortized bond calls for equal cash payments by the bond's issuer prior to maturity. Each fixed payment includes both an interest payment component and a principal repayment component such that the bond's outstanding principal amount is reduced to zero by the maturity date.

A and B are incorrect because a bullet bond or plain vanilla bond only make interest payments prior to maturity. The entire principal repayment occurs at maturity.

12 C is correct. A cap in a floating-rate note (capped FRN) prevents the coupon rate from increasing above a specified maximum rate. This feature benefits the issuer in a rising interest rate environment because it sets a limit to the interest rate paid on the debt.

A is incorrect because a bond with a step-up coupon is one in which the coupon, which may be fixed or floating, increases by specified margins at specified dates. This feature benefits the bondholders, not the issuer, in a rising interest rate environment because it allows bondholders to receive a higher coupon in line with the higher market interest rates. B is incorrect because inflation-linked bonds have their coupon payments and/or principal repayment linked to an index of consumer prices. If interest rates increase as a result of inflation, this feature is a benefit for the bondholders, not the issuer.

13 C is correct. In contrast to fixed-rate bonds that decline in value in a rising interest rate environment, floating-rate notes (FRNs) are less affected when interest rates increase because their coupon rates vary with market interest rates and are reset at regular, short-term intervals. Consequently, FRNs are favored by investors who believe that interest rates will rise.

A is incorrect because an inverse floater is a bond whose coupon rate has an inverse relationship to the reference rate, so when interest rates rise, the coupon rate on an inverse floater decreases. Thus, inverse floaters are favored by investors who believe that interest rates will decline, not rise. B is incorrect because fixed rate-bonds decline in value in a rising interest rate environment. Consequently, investors who expect interest rates to rise will likely avoid investing in fixed-rate bonds.

14 C is correct. Capital-indexed bonds pay a fixed coupon rate that is applied to a principal amount that increases in line with increases in the index during the bond's life. If the consumer price index increases by 2%, the coupon rate remains unchanged at 6%, but the principal amount increases by 2% and the coupon payment is based on the inflation-adjusted principal amount. On the first coupon payment date, the inflation-adjusted principal amount is 1,000 × (1 + 0.02) = 1,020 and the semi-annual coupon payment is equal to (0.06 × 1,020) ÷ 2 = 30.60.

15 A is correct. A put provision provides bondholders the right to sell the bond back to the issuer at a predetermined price prior to the bond's maturity date.

B is incorrect because a make-whole call provision is a form of call provision; i.e., a provision that provides the issuer the right to redeem all or part of the bond before its maturity date. A make-whole call provision requires the issuer to make a lump sum payment to the bondholders based on the present value of the future coupon payments and principal repayments not paid because of the bond being redeemed early by the issuer. C is incorrect because an original issue discount provision is a tax provision relating to bonds issued at a discount to par value. The original issue discount tax provision typically requires the bondholders to include a prorated portion of the original issue discount (i.e., the difference between the par value and the original issue price) in their taxable income every tax year until the bond's maturity date.

16 B is correct. A call provision (callable bond) gives the issuer the right to redeem all or part of the bond before the specified maturity date. If market interest rates decline or the issuer's credit quality improves, the issuer of a callable bond can redeem it and replace it by a cheaper bond. Thus, the call provision is beneficial to the issuer.

A is incorrect because a put provision (putable bond) is beneficial to the bondholders. If interest rates rise, thus lowering the bond's price, the bondholders have the right to sell the bond back to the issuer at a predetermined price on specified dates. C is incorrect because a conversion provision (convertible bond) is beneficial to the bondholders. If the issuing company's share price increases, the bondholders have the right to exchange the bond for a specified number of common shares in the issuing company.

17 A is correct. A put feature is beneficial to the bondholders. Thus, the price of a putable bond will typically be higher than the price of an otherwise similar non-putable bond.

B is incorrect because a call feature is beneficial to the issuer. Thus, the price of a callable bond will typically be lower, not higher, than the price of an otherwise similar non-callable bond. C is incorrect because a conversion feature is beneficial to the bondholders. Thus, the price of a convertible bond will typically be higher, not lower, than the price of an otherwise similar non-convertible bond.

18 C is correct. A zero-coupon, or pure discount, bond pays no interest; instead, it is issued at a discount to par value and redeemed at par. As a result, the interest earned is implied and equal to the difference between the par value and the purchase price.

19 A is correct. Covenants specify the rights of the bondholders and any actions that the issuer is obligated to perform or is prohibited from performing.

20 A is correct. A covered bond is a debt obligation backed by a segregated pool of assets called a "cover pool." When the assets that are included in the cover pool become non-performing (i.e., the assets are not generating the promised cash flows), the issuer must replace them with performing assets.

21 C is correct. Negative covenants enumerate what issuers are prohibited from doing. Restrictions on debt, including maintaining a minimum interest coverage ratio or a maximum debt usage ratio, are typical examples of negative covenants.

22 A is correct. Affirmative covenants typically do not impose additional costs to the issuer, while negative covenants are frequently costly. B is incorrect because all bond covenants are legally enforceable rules, so there is no difference in this regard between positive and negative bond covenants. C is incorrect because borrowers and lenders agree on all bond covenants at the time of a new bond issue, so there is no difference in this regard between positive and negative bond covenants.

23 B is correct. A bond that is fully amortized is characterized by a fixed periodic payment schedule that reduces the bond's outstanding principal amount to zero by the maturity date. The stream of £230.97 payments reflects the cash flows of a fully amortized bond with a coupon rate of 5% and annual interest payments.

24 B is correct. A credit-linked coupon bond has a coupon that changes when the bond's credit rating changes. Because credit ratings tend to decline the most during recessions, credit-linked coupon bonds may thus provide some general protection against a poor economy by offering increased coupon payments when credit ratings decline.

25 B is correct. Deferred coupon bonds pay no coupon for their first few years but then pay higher coupons than they otherwise normally would for the remainder of their life. Deferred coupon bonds are common in project financing when the assets being developed may not generate any income during the development phase, thus not providing cash flows to make interest payments. A deferred coupon bond allows the issuer to delay interest payments until the project is completed and the cash flows generated by the assets can be used to service the debt.

26 C is correct. A putable bond is beneficial for the bondholder by guaranteeing a prespecified selling price at the redemption date, thus offering protection when interest rates rise and bond prices decline. Relative to a one-time put bond that incorporates a single sellback opportunity, a multiple put bond offers more frequent sellback opportunities, thus providing the most benefit to bondholders.

27 C is correct. An American call option gives the issuer the right to call the bond at any time starting on the first call date.

28 A is correct. The conversion premium is the difference between the convertible bond's price and its conversion value.

READING

43

Fixed-Income Markets: Issuance, Trading, and Funding

by Moorad Choudhry, PhD, FRM, FCSI, Steven V. Mann, PhD, and Lavone F. Whitmer, CFA

Moorad Choudhry, PhD, FRM, FCSI, is at Cambridge & Counties Bank (United Kingdom). Steven V. Mann, PhD, is at the University of South Carolina (USA). Lavone F. Whitmer, CFA, is at Federal Home Loan Bank of Indianapolis (USA).

LEARNING OUTCOMES

Mastery	*The candidate should be able to:*
☐	a. describe classifications of global fixed-income markets;
☐	b. describe the use of interbank offered rates as reference rates in floating-rate debt;
☐	c. describe mechanisms available for issuing bonds in primary markets;
☐	d. describe secondary markets for bonds;
☐	e. describe securities issued by sovereign governments;
☐	f. describe securities issued by non-sovereign governments, quasi-government entities, and supranational agencies;
☐	g. describe types of debt issued by corporations;
☐	h. describe structured financial instruments;
☐	i. describe short-term funding alternatives available to banks;
☐	j. describe repurchase agreements (repos) and the risks associated with them.

INTRODUCTION

1

Global fixed-income markets represent the largest subset of financial markets in terms of number of issuances and market capitalization. These markets bring borrowers and lenders together to allocate capital globally to its most efficient uses. Fixed-income markets include not only publicly traded securities, such as commercial paper, notes, and bonds, but also non-publicly traded loans. The Institute of International Finance reports that the size of the global debt market surpassed USD 247 trillion in the first quarter of 2018.[1]

Understanding how fixed-income markets are structured and how they operate is important for debt issuers and investors. Debt issuers have financing needs that must be met. For example, a government may need to finance an infrastructure project, a new hospital, or a new school. A company may require funds to expand its business. Financial institutions also have funding needs, and they are among the largest issuers of fixed-income securities. Fixed income is an important asset class for both individual and institutional investors. Thus, investors need to understand the characteristics of fixed-income securities including how these securities are issued and traded.

Among the questions this reading addresses are the following:

- What are the key bond market sectors?
- How are bonds sold in primary markets and traded in secondary markets?
- What types of bonds are issued by governments, government-related entities, financial companies, and non-financial companies?
- What additional sources of funds are available to banks?

The remainder of this reading is organized as follows. Section 2 presents an overview of global fixed-income markets and how these markets are classified, including some descriptive statistics on the size of the different bond market sectors. Section 2 also identifies the major issuers of and investors in fixed-income securities and presents fixed-income indexes. Section 3 discusses how fixed-income securities are issued in primary markets, and how these securities are then traded in secondary markets. Sections 4 to 7 examine different bond market sectors. Section 8 discusses additional short-term funding alternatives available to banks, including repurchase agreements. Section 9 concludes and summarizes the reading.

2 OVERVIEW OF GLOBAL FIXED-INCOME MARKETS

Although there is no standard classification of fixed-income markets, many investors and market participants use criteria to structure fixed-income markets and identify bond market sectors. This section starts by describing the most widely used ways of classifying fixed-income markets.

2.1 Classification of Fixed-Income Markets

Common criteria used to classify fixed-income markets include the type of issuer; the bonds' credit quality, maturity, currency denomination, and type of coupon; and where the bonds are issued and traded.

2.1.1 *Classification by Type of Issuer*

One way of classifying fixed-income markets is by type of issuer, which leads to the identification of four bond market sectors: households, non-financial corporates, government, and financial institutions. Exhibit 1 presents data on global debt markets at the end of the first quarter of 2018 by these sectors. Each sector is broken down into mature markets (US, Euro area, Japan, and UK) and emerging markets. While

1 Institute of International Finance Global Debt Monitor, July 9, 2018.

the sectors are of roughly comparable sizes overall, in emerging markets the debt of non-financial corporates is proportionately higher and the financial sector lower than in the mature markets.

Exhibit 1 Global Debt by Sector at End of Q1 2018 in USD

USD trillion (% of Total)	Households	Non-Financial Corporates	Government	Financial Sector	Total
Mature Markets	34.7	42.0	51.3	50.3	178.3
	(19.5%)	(23.6%)	(28.8%)	(28.2%)	(100.0%)
Emerging Markets	11.9	31.5	15.2	10.4	68.9
	(17.3%)	(45.7%)	(22.1%)	(15.1%)	(100.0%)
Global Debt	46.5	73.5	66.5	60.6	247.2
	(18.8%)	(29.7%)	(26.9%)	(24.5%)	(100.0%)

Source: Institute of International Finance Global Debt Monitor, July 9, 2018

Exhibit 2 displays global debt by sector as a percentage of GDP for various mature and emerging market countries at the end of the first quarter of 2018. In general, debt in proportion to GDP is higher in developed countries. However, debt takes different forms in different countries.

Exhibit 2 Global Debt by Sector as Percentage of GDP

% of GDP	Households	Non-Financial Corporates	Government	Financial Sector	Total
United States	76.4	72.3	101.0	80.0	329.7
Japan	54.7	98.8	223.8	149.2	526.5
United Kingdom	86.3	84.2	104.8	180.9	456.2
China	49.2	162.9	47.8	39.4	299.3
South Korea	95.6	99.2	37.9	82.6	315.3
Brazil	24.9	44.3	83.9	33.8	186.9
Mexico	16.5	27.4	35.4	16.8	96.1
Israel	42.3	69.7	60.3	9.6	181.9
Nigeria	3.9	13.6	24.3	3.0	44.8

Source: Institute of International Finance Global Debt Monitor, July 9, 2018.

2.1.2 *Classification by Credit Quality*

Investors who hold bonds are exposed to credit risk, which is the risk of loss resulting from the issuer failing to make full and timely payments of interest and/or principal. Bond markets can be classified based on the issuer's creditworthiness as judged by credit rating agencies. Ratings of Baa3 or above by Moody's Investors Service or BBB– or above by Standard & Poor's (S&P) and Fitch Ratings are considered investment grade. In contrast, ratings below these levels are referred to as non-investment grade, high yield, speculative, or "junk." An important point to understand is that credit ratings are an assessment of the issuer's creditworthiness at a certain point in time; they are not a recommendation to buy or sell the issuer's securities. In addition, credit ratings are not static; they will change if a credit rating agency perceives that the probability of default for an issuer has changed.

One of the reasons why the distinction between investment-grade and high-yield bond markets matters is because institutional investors may be prohibited from investing in, or restricted in their exposure to, lower-quality or lower-rated securities. Prohibition or restriction in high-yield bond holdings generally arise because of a more restrictive risk–reward profile that forms part of the investor's investment objectives and constraints. For example, regulated banks and life insurance companies are usually limited to investing in very highly rated securities. In contrast, the sovereign wealth funds of both Qatar and Kuwait have no formal restrictions on what type of assets they can hold or on the percentage split between bond market sectors. Globally, investment-grade bond markets tend to be more liquid than high-yield bond markets.

2.1.3 *Classification by Maturity*

Fixed-income securities can also be classified by the original maturity of the bonds when they are issued. Securities that are issued with a maturity at issuance (original maturity) ranging from overnight to one year are money market securities. Some of these securities are issued by sovereign governments, such as Treasury bills. The corporate sector also issues fixed-income securities with short maturities. Examples include commercial paper and negotiable certificates of deposit. In contrast, capital market securities are securities that are issued with an original maturity longer than one year.

2.1.4 *Classification by Currency Denomination*

One of the critical ways to distinguish among fixed-income securities is by currency denomination. The currency denomination of the bond's cash flows influences which interest rates affect a bond's price. For example, if a bond is denominated in yen, its price will be primarily driven by the credit quality of the issuer and by Japanese interest rates.

Exhibit 3 presents data on debt as a percentage of GDP for several emerging market countries for local currency (LC) and foreign currency (FC) issuances at the end of the first quarter of 2018. Government debt is almost entirely in the domestic currency whereas corporate and bank debt differs considerably by country.

Exhibit 3 Debt by Local and Foreign Currency for several Emerging Markets

	Non-Financial Corporates		Government		Financial Sector	
% of GDP	LC	FC	LC	FC	LC	FC
Brazil	28.3	16.0	81.1	2.8	25.9	7.8
India	37.7	8.9	66.6	1.7	1.1	3.9
Mexico	7.2	20.2	29.8	5.6	13.8	3.0
Turkey	28.7	36.8	17.0	11.2	4.5	21.6

Source: Institute of International Finance Global Debt Monitor, July 9, 2018

2.1.5 *Classification by Type of Coupon*

Another way of classifying fixed-income markets is by type of coupon. Some bonds pay a fixed rate of interest; others, called floating-rate bonds, floating-rate notes (FRNs) or floaters, pay a rate of interest that adjusts to market interest rates at regular, short-term intervals (e.g., quarterly).

2.1.5.1 Demand and Supply of Fixed-Rate vs. Floating-Rate Debt Balance sheet risk management considerations explain much of the demand and supply of floating-rate debt. For instance, the funding of banks—that is, the money banks raise to make loans to companies and individuals—is often short term and issued at rates that change or reset frequently. When there is a mismatch between the interest paid on the liabilities (money the bank borrowed) and the interest received on the assets (money the bank lent or invested), banks are exposed to interest rate risk—that is, the risk associated with a change in interest rate. In an effort to limit the volatility of their net worth resulting from interest rate risk, banks that issue floating-rate debt often prefer to make floating-rate loans and invest in floating-rate bonds or in other adjustable-rate assets. In addition to institutions with short-term funding needs, demand for floating-rate bonds comes from investors who believe that interest rates will rise. In that case, investors will benefit from holding floating-rate investments compared with fixed-rate ones.

On the supply side, issuance of floating-rate debt comes from institutions needing to finance short-term loans, such as consumer finance companies. Corporate borrowers also view floating-rate bonds as an alternative to using bank liquidity facilities (e.g., lines of credit), particularly when they are a lower cost option, and as an alternative to borrowing long-term at fixed rates when they expect interest rates will fall.

2.1.5.2 Reference Rates The coupon rate of a floating rate bond is typically expressed as a reference rate plus a spread or margin. The spread is usually set when the bond is issued and remains constant until maturity. It is primarily a function of the issuer's credit risk at issuance: the lower the issuer's credit quality (the higher its credit risk), the higher the spread. The reference rate, however, resets periodically. Therefore, the coupon rate adjusts to the level of market interest rates each time the reference rate is reset. The choice of the reference rate is critical because the reference rate is the primary driver of a bond's coupon rate. Thus, the issuer's cost of financing and the investor's return from investing in the bonds depend on the reference rate.

Different reference rates are used depending on where the bonds are issued and their currency denomination. The **London interbank offered rate (Libor)** has long been the reference rate for many floating-rate bonds, in particular those issued in the US domestic and Eurobond markets. For example, a typical coupon rate for a floater denominated in British sterling that pays coupons semi-annually would be the sterling six-month Libor plus a spread. The coupon rate that is paid at the end of a six-month period is set based on the sterling six-month Libor at the beginning of the period, and it remains constant throughout the six months. Every six months, the coupon rate is reset in line with the sterling six-month Libor prevailing on the reset date. For floating-rate bonds denominated in US dollars, the reference rate usually has been the US dollar Libor—the US dollar three-month Libor if the coupons are paid quarterly or the US dollar 12-month Libor if the coupons are paid annually.

As illustrated in these examples, "Libor" is a collective name for multiple rates. Libor reflects the rate at which a panel of banks believe they could borrow unsecured funds from other banks in the London interbank money market for different currencies and different borrowing periods ranging from overnight to one year—the **interbank money market**, or **interbank market**, is the market of loans and deposits between banks for maturities up to one year. The sidebar describes how Libor is being phased out and likely will be replaced by new money market reference rates by the end of 2021.

The Phaseout of Libor[2]

Starting in 1986, daily Libor quotations for various currencies and maturities were set by the British Bankers' Association (BBA). Every business day, a select group of banks would submit to the BBA the rates at which they believed they could borrow from other banks in the London interbank market. Over time, the coverage grew to include 10 currencies and 15 borrowing periods. The submitted rates would be ranked from highest to lowest, and the upper and lower four submissions would be discarded. The arithmetic mean of the remaining rates became the Libor setting for a particular combination of currency and maturity. The 150 Libor quotations would then be communicated to market participants for use as reference rates in many different types of debt, including floating-rate bonds.

Problems with Libor first arose during the global financial crisis of 2007-2009 when the perceived default and liquidity risks of major international banks rose significantly. Some banks were allegedly submitting lowered rates to influence the market perception of their credit quality. In addition, some banks were allegedly altering their submitted rates to improve the valuation of their derivatives positions in contracts tied to Libor. In 2014, UK regulatory authorities transferred the administration of Libor from BBA to ICE (International Currency Exchange). Under ICE, the size for Libor quotations was reduced to 5 currencies and 7 maturities.

By 2017 it became apparent that the lack of activity in interbank borrowing and lending meant that Libor submissions were based more on judgment of market conditions than actual trades. Therefore, the decision was made that the panel of banks would no longer be required to submit quotations after 2021. In anticipation of the eventual demise of Libor, market participants and regulators have been working to develop new alternative money market reference rates. In the United States, it appears that the new rate will be SOFR (secured overnight financing rate). SOFR, which has begun to be reported daily by the US Federal Reserve, is based on actual transactions in the sale-repurchase agreement ("repo") market. (Repos are described in section 8.3 of this reading). In July 2018, Fannie Mae, a major institution in the US secondary mortgage market, issued USD 6 billion in floating-rate notes at SOFR plus a small spread.

Although there have been Libor quotations for currencies such as the euro and the yen, alternative interbank offered rates have been used for floating-rate debt issued in these currencies, such as the Euro interbank offered rate (Euribor) and the Tokyo interbank offered rate (Tibor), respectively. Similar sets of interbank offered rates exist in other markets, for instance, the Singapore interbank offered rate (Sibor), the Hong Kong interbank offered rate (Hibor), the Mumbai interbank offered rate (Mibor), and the Korea interbank offered rate (Koribor) for floating-rate debt issued in Singapore dollar, Hong Kong dollar, Indian rupee, and the Korean won, respectively. All these different interbank offered rates are sets of rates for borrowing periods of various maturities of up to one year. The processes to determine them are similar, except that the sets of banks and organizations fixing the daily rates are different. As Libor is eventually phased out, new reference rates in these currencies will emerge.

The use of these money market reference rates extends beyond setting coupon rates for floating-rate debt. These rates are also used as reference rates for other debt instruments including mortgages, derivatives such as interest rate and currency swaps, and many other financial contracts and products. As of 2018, it is estimated that nearly USD 350 trillion in financial instruments are tied to Libor. A major task going forward will be to renegotiate the terms on these contracts as Libor no longer is relevant.

---

2 This sidebar is based on "Libor: Its Astonishing Ride and How to Plan for Its End," by Liang Wu, a Numerix white paper, February 2018.

2.1.6 *Classification by Geography*

A distinction is very often made between the domestic bond, foreign bond, and Eurobond markets. Bonds issued in a specific country, denominated in the currency of that country, and sold in that country are classified as domestic bonds if they are issued by an issuer domiciled in that country and foreign bonds if they are issued by an issuer domiciled in another country. Domestic and foreign bonds are subject to the legal, regulatory, and tax requirements that apply in that particular country. In contrast, a Eurobond is issued internationally, outside the jurisdiction of the country in whose currency the bond is denominated. The Eurobond market has traditionally been characterized by less reporting, regulatory and tax constraints than domestic and foreign bond markets. These fewer constraints explain why approximately 80% of entities that issue bonds outside their country of origin choose to do so in the Eurobond market rather than in a foreign bond market. In addition, Eurobonds are attractive for issuers because it gives them the ability to reach out to more investors globally. Access to a wider pool of investors often allows issuers to raise more capital and usually at a lower cost.

Investors make a distinction between countries with established capital markets (developed markets) and countries where the capital markets are in earlier stages of development (emerging markets). For emerging bond markets, a further distinction is made between bonds issued in local currency and bonds issued in a foreign currency, such as the euro or the US dollar.

Emerging bond markets are much smaller than developed bond markets. But as demand from local and international investors has increased, issuance and trading of emerging market bonds have risen in volume and value. International investors' interest in emerging market bonds has been triggered by a desire to diversify risk across several jurisdictions in the belief that investment returns across markets are not closely correlated. In addition, emerging market bonds usually offer higher yields (return) than developed market bonds because of the higher perceived risk. Emerging countries typically lag developed countries in the areas of political stability, property rights, and contract enforcement, which often leads to a higher credit risk and higher yields. Many emerging countries, however, are less indebted than their developed counterparts and benefit from higher growth prospects, which appeals to many investors.

2.1.7 *Other Classifications of Fixed-Income Markets*

There are various other ways of classifying fixed-income markets. Market participants may classify fixed-income markets based on some specific characteristics associated with the fixed-income securities. Specific market sectors that are of interest to some investors are inflation-linked bonds and, in some jurisdictions, tax-exempt bonds. Issuance of either type of bond tends to be limited to certain types of issuers. Inflation-linked bonds or linkers are typically issued by governments, government-related entities, and corporate issuers that have an investment-grade rating. They offer investors protection against inflation by linking the coupon payment and/or the principal repayment to an index of consumer prices.

Tax-exempt bonds can only be issued in those jurisdictions that recognize such tax exemption. In the United States for example, there is an income tax exemption for some of the bonds issued by governments or by some non-profit organizations. In particular, local governments can issue **municipal bonds** (or **munis**) that are tax exempt (they can also issue taxable municipal bonds, although tax-exempt munis are more frequently issued than taxable munis). Tax-exempt bonds also exist in other jurisdictions. For example, the National Highways Authority of India (NHAI) issues tax-exempt bonds. In countries that implement a capital gains tax, there may be tax exemptions for some types of bonds. In the United Kingdom for example, government gilts are not subject to capital gains tax.

EXAMPLE 1

Classification of Fixed-Income Markets

1 Which of the following is *most likely* an issuer of bonds?

A Hedge fund

B Pension fund

C Local government

2 A bond issued by a city would *most likely* be classified as a:

A supranational bond.

B quasi-government bond.

C non-sovereign government bond.

3 A fixed-income security issued with a maturity at issuance of nine months is *most likely* classified as a:

A capital market security.

B money market security.

C securitized debt instrument.

4 The price of a bond issued in the United States by a British company and denominated in US dollars is *most likely* to:

A change as US interest rates change.

B change as British interest rates change.

C be unaffected by changes in US and British interest rates.

5 Interbank offered rates are *best* described as the rates at which a panel of banks can:

A issue short-term debt.

B borrow unsecured funds from other major banks.

C borrow from other major banks against some form of collateral.

6 A company issues floating-rate bonds. The coupon rate is expressed as the three-month Libor plus a spread. The coupon payments are *most likely* to increase as:

A Libor increases.

B the spread increases.

C the company's credit quality decreases.

Solution to 1:

C is correct. Major issuers of bonds include sovereign (national) governments, non-sovereign (local) governments, quasi-government agencies, supranational organizations, and financial and non-financial companies. A and B are incorrect because hedge funds and pension funds are typically investors in, not issuers of, bonds.

Solution to 2:

C is correct. Non-sovereign (local) government bond issuers include provinces, regions, states, and cities. A is incorrect because supranational bonds are issued by international organizations. B is incorrect because quasi-government bonds are issued by agencies that are either owned or sponsored by governments.

Solution to 3:

B is correct. Money market securities are issued with a maturity at issuance (original maturity) ranging from overnight to one year. A is incorrect because capital market securities are issued with an original maturity longer than one year. C is incorrect because securitization, which leads to the creation of securitized debt instruments, does not relate to a bond's maturity but to the process that transforms private transactions between borrowers and lenders into securities traded in public markets.

Solution to 4:

A is correct. The currency denomination of a bond's cash flows influences which country's interest rates affect a bond's price. The price of a bond issued by a British company and denominated in US dollars will be affected by US interest rates.

Solution to 5:

B is correct. Interbank offered rates represent a set of interest rates at which major banks believe they could borrow unsecured funds from other major banks in the interbank money market for different currencies and different borrowing periods ranging from overnight to one year.

Solution to 6:

A is correct. The coupon payments of a floating-rate bond that is tied to the three-month Libor will reset every three months, based on changes in Libor. Thus, as Libor increases, so will the coupon payments. B is incorrect because the spread on a floating-rate bond is typically constant; it is set when the bond is issued and does not change afterward. C is incorrect because the issuer's credit quality affects the spread and thus the coupon rate that serves as the basis for the calculation of the coupon payments, but only when the spread is set—that is, at issuance.

2.2 Fixed-Income Indexes

A fixed-income index is a multi-purpose tool used by investors and investment managers to describe a given bond market or sector, as well as to evaluate the performance of investments and investment managers. Most fixed-income indexes are constructed as portfolios of securities that reflect a particular bond market or sector. The index construction—that is, the security selection and the index weighting—varies among indexes.[3] Index weighting may be based on price or value (market capitalization).

There are literally dozens of fixed-income indexes globally, capturing different aspects of the fixed-income markets discussed earlier. One of the most popular set of indexes is the Bloomberg Barclays Global Aggregate Bond Index, which represents a broad-based measure of the global investment-grade fixed-rate bond market. It has an index history beginning on 1 January 1990 and contains three important components: the US Aggregate Bond Index (formerly Lehman Aggregate Bond Index), the Pan-European Aggregate Bond Index, and the Asian-Pacific Aggregate Bond Index. These indexes reflect the investment-grade sectors of the US, European, and Asian-Pacific bond markets, respectively.

With respect to emerging markets, one of the most widely followed indexes is the J.P. Morgan Emerging Market Bond Index (EMBI) Global, which includes US dollar-denominated Brady bonds (bonds issued primarily by Latin American countries in

3 Fixed-income indexes are discussed in greater details in the CFA Reading on "Security Market Indexes".

the late 1980s under a debt restructuring plan aimed at converting bank loans into tradable securities), Eurobonds and loans issued by sovereign and quasi-sovereign entities in several emerging markets.

Another popular set of indexes is the FTSE Global Bond Index Series, which has been set up to provide coverage of different classes of securities related to the government and corporate bond markets. It includes indexes of global government bonds, euro-denominated government bonds from emerging markets, sterling- and euro-denominated investment-grade corporate bonds, and covered bonds from Germany and other European Union issuers. Covered bonds are debt obligations issued by banks and backed (secured) by a segregated pool of assets.

Many other fixed-income indexes are available to investors and investment managers to measure and report performance.

2.3 Investors in Fixed-Income Securities

The overview of fixed-income markets has so far focused on the supply side. Before discussing bond issuers in greater detail, it is important to consider the demand side because demand for a particular type of bond or issuer may affect supply. After all, market prices are the result of the interaction between demand and supply; neither one can be considered in isolation. For example, an increase in demand for inflation-linked bonds as a result of investors' desire to protect the value of their portfolios against inflation risk may lead governments to issue a greater quantity of this type of bond. By issuing relatively more inflation-linked bonds for which there is demand, a government not only manages to sell its bond issue and get the funds required, but it may also benefit from a lower cost of financing.

There are different types of investors in fixed-income securities. Major categories of bond investors include central banks, institutional investors, and retail investors. The first two typically invest directly in fixed-income securities. In contrast, retail investors often invest indirectly through fixed-income mutual funds or exchange-traded funds (ETFs).

Central banks use open market operations to implement monetary policy. **Open market operations** refer to the purchase or sale of bonds, usually sovereign bonds issued by the national government. By purchasing (selling) domestic bonds, central banks increase (decrease) the monetary base in the economy. Central banks may also purchase and sell bonds denominated in foreign currencies as part of their efforts to manage the relative value of the domestic currency and their country's foreign reserves.

Institutional investors, including pension funds, hedge funds, charitable foundations and endowments, insurance companies, and banks, represent the largest groups of investors in fixed-income securities. Another major group of investors is sovereign wealth funds, which are state-owned investment funds that tend to have very long investment horizons and aim to preserve or create wealth for future generations.

Finally, retail investors often invest heavily in fixed-income securities because of the attractiveness of relatively stable prices and steady income production.

Fixed-income markets are dominated by institutional investors in part because of the high informational barriers to entry and high minimum transaction sizes. Fixed-income securities are far more diverse than equity securities because of the variety of types of issuers and securities. In addition, unlike common shares that are primarily issued and traded in organized markets, the issuance and trading of bonds very often occurs in **over-the-counter (OTC) markets**. Thus, fixed-income securities are more difficult to access than equity securities. For these reasons, institutional investors tend to invest directly in bonds, whereas most retail investors prefer to use investment vehicles, such as mutual funds and ETFs.

EXAMPLE 2

Investors in Fixed-Income Securities

1 Open market operations describe the process used by central banks to buy and sell bonds to:
   - A implement fiscal policy.
   - B control the monetary base.
   - C issue and repay government debt.

2 Retail investors *most often*:
   - A do not invest in fixed-income securities.
   - B invest directly in fixed-income securities.
   - C invest indirectly in fixed-income securities through mutual funds or exchange-traded funds.

Solution to 1:

B is correct. Open market operations refer to the purchase or sale of bonds, usually sovereign bonds issued by the national government, as a means of implementing monetary policy. By purchasing (selling) bonds, central banks increase (decrease) the monetary base in the economy, thus controlling the money supply. A is incorrect because open market operations help facilitate monetary policy, not fiscal policy (which is the taxing and spending by the national government). C is incorrect because although Treasury departments and some central banks may facilitate the issuance and repayment of government debt, open market operations specifically refer to the implementation of monetary policy.

Solution to 2:

C is correct. Retail investors often invest in fixed-income securities because of the attractiveness of relatively stable prices and steady income production. However, because most retail investors lack the expertise to value fixed-income securities and are not large enough investors to buy and sell them directly, they usually invest in fixed income indirectly through mutual funds and exchange-traded funds.

PRIMARY AND SECONDARY BOND MARKETS

3

Primary bond markets are markets in which issuers initially sell bonds to investors to raise capital. In contrast, **secondary bond markets** are markets in which existing bonds are subsequently traded among investors. As with all financial markets, primary and secondary bond markets are regulated within the framework of the overall financial system. An established independent regulatory authority is usually responsible for overseeing both the structure of the markets and the credentials of market participants.

3.1 Primary Bond Markets

Issuances in primary bond markets are frequent. Different bond issuing mechanisms are used depending on the type of issuer and the type of bond issued. A bond issue can be sold via a **public offering** (or **public offer**), in which any member of the public may buy the bonds, or via a **private placement**, in which only a selected investor, or group of investors, may buy the bonds.

3.1.1 *Public Offerings*

Investment banks play a critical role in bond issuance by assisting the issuer in accessing the primary market and by providing an array of financial services. The most common bond issuing mechanisms are underwritten offerings, best effort offerings, and auctions. In an **underwritten offering**, also called a **firm commitment offering**, the investment bank guarantees the sale of the bond issue at an offering price that is negotiated with the issuer. Thus, the investment bank, called the **underwriter**, takes the risk associated with selling the bonds. In contrast, in a **best effort offering**, the investment bank only serves as a broker. It only tries to sell the bond issue at the negotiated offering price if it is able to for a commission. Thus, the investment bank has less risk and correspondingly less incentive to sell the bonds in a best effort offering than in an underwritten offering. An **auction** is a bond issuing mechanism that involves bidding.

3.1.1.1 Underwritten Offerings Underwritten offerings are typical bond issuing mechanisms for corporate bonds, some local government bonds (such as municipal bonds in the United States), and some asset-backed securities (such as mortgage-backed securities). The underwriting process typically includes six phases.

The underwriting process starts with the determination of the funding needs. Often with the help of an adviser or advisers, the issuer must determine how much money must be raised, the type of bond offering, and whether the bond issue should be underwritten.

Once the issuer has decided that the bond issue should be underwritten, it must select the underwriter, which is typically an investment bank. The underwriter of a bond issue takes the risk of buying the newly issued bonds from the issuer, and then resells them to investors or to dealers who then sell them to investors. The difference between the purchase price of the new bond issue and the reselling price to investors is the underwriter's revenue. A relatively small-size bond issue may be underwritten by a single investment bank. It is more common for larger bond issues, however, to be underwritten by a group, or syndicate, of investment banks. In this case, the bond issue is referred to as a **syndicated offering**. There is a lead underwriter that invites other investment banks to join the syndicate and that coordinates the effort. The syndicate is collectively responsible for determining the pricing of the bond issue and for placing (selling) the bonds with investors.

The third phase of an underwritten offering is to structure the transaction. Before the bond issue is announced, the issuer and the lead underwriter discuss the terms of the bond issue, such as the bond's notional principal (total amount), the coupon rate, and the expected offering price. The underwriter or the syndicate typically organizes the necessary regulatory filings and prepares the offering circular or prospectus that provides information about the terms of the bond issue. The issuer must also choose a trustee, which is typically a trust company or the trust department of a bank, to oversee the master bond agreement. The bond offering is formally launched the day the transaction is announced, usually in the form of a press release. The announcement specifies the new bond issue's terms and conditions, including the bond's features, such as the maturity date, the currency denomination, and the expected coupon range, as well as the expected offering price. The issuer also releases the offering circular or prospectus. The final terms may differ from these terms because of changes in market conditions between the announcement day and the pricing day.

The success of the bond issue depends on the underwriter or syndicate's discernment in assessing market conditions and in pricing the bond issue accordingly. The pricing of the bond issue is, therefore, an important phase of an underwritten offering. Ideally, the bond issue should be priced so that the amount of bonds available is equal to the demand for the bonds by investors. If the offering price is set too high, the offering will be undersubscribed—that is, there will be insufficient demand for the bond issue. As a consequence, the underwriter or syndicate will fail to sell the entire bond issue. Alternatively, if the offering price is set too low, the offering will be oversubscribed. Underwriters may aim at a small oversubscription because it reduces the risk of being unable to sell the entire bond issue. But a large oversubscription indicates that the offering terms were probably unfavorable to the issuer in that the issuer might have raised the desired amount of capital at a lower coupon rate.

Between the announcement of a bond issue and the end of the subscription period, the underwriter or syndicate must gauge what the demand for the bond issue is and at what price the bond should be offered to ensure that the entire bond issue is placed without running the risk of a large oversubscription. There are different ways for underwriters to do so. The bond issue is usually marketed to potential investors. This may be by an indirect approach, such as an advertisement in a newspaper, a commonly used approach for bond issued by household names, or through direct marketing and road shows, aimed at institutional investors such as pension funds and insurance companies. The underwriter or syndicate may also approach large institutional investors and discuss with them the kind of bond issues they are willing to buy. These buyers are known as the "anchor." For some, but not all, bond issues, the grey market is another way for underwriters to gauge investor's interest. The **grey market**, also called "when issued" market, is a forward market for bonds about to be issued. Trading in the grey market helps underwriters determine what the final offering price should be.

The pricing day is the last day when investors can commit to buy the bond issue, and it is also the day when the final terms of the bond issue are agreed on. The following day, called the "offering day," the underwriting agreement that includes the bond issue's final terms is signed. The underwriting process then enters the issuing phase. The underwriter or the syndicate purchases the entire bond issue from the issuer, delivers the proceeds, and starts reselling the bonds through its sales network.

The underwriting process comes to an end about 14 days later, on the closing day, when the bonds are delivered to investors. Investors no longer receive a paper settlement; instead, the bond itself is represented by a global note that is typically held by the paying agent.

3.1.1.2 Shelf Registration A **shelf registration** allows certain authorized issuers to offer additional bonds to the general public without having to prepare a new and separate offering circular for each bond issue. Rather, the issuer prepares a single, all-encompassing offering circular that describes a range of future bond issuances, all under the same document. This master prospectus may be in place for years before it is replaced or updated, and it may be used to cover multiple bond issuances.

Under a shelf registration, each individual offering is prefaced with a short issue announcement document. This document must confirm that there has been no change to material elements of the issuer's business, or otherwise describe any changes to the issuer's financial condition since the master prospectus was filed. Because shelf issuances are subject to a lower level of scrutiny compared with standard public offerings, they are only an option for well-established issuers that have convinced the regulatory authorities of their financial strength. Additionally, certain jurisdictions may only allow shelf registrations to be purchased by "qualified" institutional investors—that is, institutional investors that meet a set of criteria set forth by the regulators.

3.1.1.3 Auctions An auction is a method that involves bidding. It is helpful in providing price discovery (i.e., it facilitates supply and demand in determining prices) and in allocating securities. In many countries, most sovereign bonds are sold to the public via a public auction. For example, in 2017, the United States conducted 277 public auctions and issued approximately $8.5 trillion of new securities such as Treasury bills, notes, bonds, and Treasury Inflation-Protected Securities (TIPS). The public auction process used in the United States is a **single-price auction** through which all the winning bidders pay the same price and receive the same coupon rate for the bonds. In contrast, the public auction process used in Canada and Germany is a **multiple-price auction** process, which generates multiple prices and yields for the same bond issue.

The US sovereign bond market is one of the largest and most liquid bond markets globally, so we will illustrate the US single-price auction process. This process includes three phases: announcement, bidding, and issuance. First, the US Treasury announces the auction and provides information about the bond issue, such as the amount of securities being offered, the auction date, the issue date, the maturity date, bidding close times, and other pertinent information.

After the auction announcement is made, dealers, institutional investors, and individual investors may enter competitive or non-competitive bids. With competitive bids, a bidder specifies the rate (yield) that is considered acceptable; if the rate determined at auction is lower than the rate specified in the competitive bid, the investor will not be offered any securities. In contrast, with non-competitive bids, a bidder agrees to accept the rate determined at auction; non-competitive bidders always receive their securities. At the close of the auction, the US Treasury accepts all non-competitive bids and competitive bids in ascending order of their rates (lowest to highest) until the amount of bids is equal to the amount the issuer requires. All bidders receive the same rate, based on the highest accepted bid. This single-price auction process encourages aggressive bidding and potentially results in a lower cost of funds (i.e., lower coupon rate) for the U.S Treasury because all the winning bidders pay the same price.

On the issue day, the US Treasury delivers the securities to the winning bidders and collects the proceeds from investors. After the auction process is complete, the securities are traded in secondary markets like other securities.

Exhibit 4 shows the results of a US Treasury public auction.

Exhibit 4 Results of a US Treasury Public Auction on 23 July 2018

TREASURY NEWS

Department of the Treasury • Bureau of the Fiscal Service

For Immediate Release
July 23, 2018

CONTACT: Treasury Auctions
202-504-3550

TREASURY AUCTION RESULTS

Term and Type of Security	182-Day Bill
CUSIP Number	912796QU6
High Rate [1]	2.140%
Allotted at High	29.02%
Price	98.918111
Investment Rate [2]	2.193%
Median Rate [3]	2.110%
Low Rate [4]	2.085%
Issue Date	July 26, 2018
Maturity Date	January 24, 2019

	Tendered	Accepted
Competitive	$128,928,869,200	$43,206,629,200
Noncompetitive	$793,540,100	$793,540,100
FIMA (Noncompetitive)	$1,000,000,000	$1,000,000,000
Subtotal [5]	**$130,722,409,300**	**$45,000,169,300 [6]**
SOMA	$0	$0
Total	**$130,722,409,300**	**$45,000,169,300**

	Tendered	Accepted
Primary Dealer [7]	$98,935,000,000	$20,122,560,000
Direct Bidder [8]	$6,105,000,000	$5,205,000,000
Indirect Bidder [9]	$23,888,869,200	$17,879,069,200
Total Competitive	**$128,928,869,200**	**$43,206,629,200**

[1] All tenders at lower rates were accepted in full.
[2] Equivalent coupon-issue yield.
[3] 50% of the amount of accepted competitive tenders was tendered at or below that rate.
[4] 5% of the amount of accepted competitive tenders was tendered at or below that rate.
[5] Bid-to-Cover Ratio: $130,722,409,300/$45,000,169,300 = 2.90
[6] Awards to TreasuryDirect = $384,924,100.
[7] Primary dealers as submitters bidding for their own house accounts.
[8] Non-Primary dealer submitters bidding for their own house accounts.
[9] Customers placing competitive bids through a direct submitter, including Foreign and International Monetary Authorities placing bids through the Federal Reserve Bank of New York.

Source: Based on information from www.treasurydirect.gov.

The rate determined at auction was 2.140%. T-bills are pure discount bonds; they are issued at a discount to par value and redeemed at par. Investors paid 98.918111% of par—that is, $9,891.81 per $10,000 in par value. The US Treasury received bids for $130.7 billion, but only raised $45.0 billion. All the non-competitive bids ($793.5 million) were accepted, but only a third ($43.2 of the $128.9 billion) of competitive bids was accepted. Note that half the competitive bids were submitted with a rate lower than 2.110% (the median rate). All successful bidders, however, received the rate of 2.140%, which is the essential feature of a single-price auction.

Exhibit 4 also identifies the types of bidders. Most US Treasury securities are bought at auction by primary dealers. **Primary dealers** are financial institutions that are authorized to deal in new issues of US Treasury securities. They have established business relationships with the Federal Reserve Bank of New York (New York Fed), which implements US monetary policy. Primary dealers serve primarily as trading counterparties of the New York Fed and are required to participate meaningfully in open market operations and in all auctions of US Treasury securities. They also provide the New York Fed with market information. Institutional investors and central banks are the largest investors in US Treasury securities; only a very small amount of these bonds is purchased directly by individual investors.

3.1.2 *Private Placements*

A private placement is typically a non-underwritten, unregistered offering of bonds that are sold only to an investor or a small group of investors. Typical investors in privately placed bonds are large institutional investors. A private placement can be accomplished directly between the issuer and the investor(s) or through an investment bank. Because privately placed bonds are unregistered and may be restricted securities that can only be purchased by some types of investors, there is usually no active secondary market to trade them. However, trading may be possible under certain conditions. For example, restricted securities issued under Rule 144A in the United Sates cannot be sold to the public, but they can be traded among qualified institutional investors. Even if trading is possible, privately placed bonds typically exhibit lower liquidity than publicly issued bonds. Insurance companies and pension funds are major buyers of privately placed bonds because they do not need every security in their portfolio to be liquid and they often value the additional yield offered by these bonds.

Private placements sometimes represent a step in the company's financing evolution between **syndicated loans** (loans from a group of lenders to a single borrower further discussed in Section 6.1) and public offerings. Privately placed bonds are often issued in small aggregate amounts, at times by unknown issuers. Many investors may not be willing to undertake the credit analysis that is required for a new name, in particular if the offering amount is small. Unlike in a public offering in which the bonds are often sold to investors on a take-it-or-leave-it basis, investors in a private placement can influence the structure of the bond issue, including such considerations as asset and collateral backing, credit enhancements, and covenants. It is common for privately placed bonds to have more customized and restrictive covenants than publicly issued ones. In addition to being able to negotiate the terms of the bonds and align them with their needs, investors in private placements are rewarded by getting the bonds, which is not always the case in public offerings in which investors cannot know for sure when the issue will become available and how many securities they will be allocated.

Private placements are also offered by regular bond issuers, in particular for smaller amounts of capital raised in major currencies, such as US dollars, euros, or sterling. Private placements are usually more flexible than public offerings and allow regular issuers to tailor the bond issue to their own needs.

3.2 Secondary Bond Markets

Secondary markets, also called the "aftermarket," are where existing securities are traded among investors. Securities can be traded directly from investor to investor, or through a broker or dealer to facilitate the transaction. The major participants in secondary bond markets globally are large institutional investors and central banks. The presence of retail investors in secondary bonds markets is limited, unlike in secondary equity markets.

The key to understanding how secondary bond markets are structured and function is to understand liquidity. Liquidity refers to the ability to trade (buy or sell) securities quickly and easily at prices close to their fair market value. Liquidity involves much more than "how quickly one can turn a bond into cash." This statement implicitly assumes a long position, but some market participants need to buy quickly when covering a short position. The other aspect of liquidity that is often ignored is that speed of trading alone does not constitute a liquid market. One can always buy something quickly by offering a very high price or sell something quickly by accepting a very low price. In a liquid market, trading takes place quickly at prices close to the security's fair market value.

There are two main ways for secondary markets to be structured: as an organized exchange or as an over-the-counter market. An **organized exchange** provides a place where buyers and sellers can meet to arrange their trades. Although buy or sell orders may come from anywhere, the transaction must take place at the exchange according to the rules imposed by the exchange. In contrast, with OTC markets, buy and sell orders initiated from various locations are matched through a communications network. Thus, OTC markets need electronic trading platforms over which users submit buy and sell orders. Bloomberg Fixed Income Electronic Trading platform is an example of such a platform through which dealers stand ready to trade in multiple bond markets globally. Although there is some trading of government bonds and very active corporate bonds on many stock exchanges around the world, the vast majority of bonds are traded in OTC markets.

The liquidity demands of fixed-income investors have evolved since the early 1990s. The type of investors who would buy and hold a bond to maturity that once dominated the fixed-income markets has been supplanted by institutional investors who trade actively. The dynamics of global fixed-income markets reflect this change in the relative demand for liquidity.

We will illustrate how secondary markets work by using the example of Eurobonds. The most important Eurobond trading center by volume is in London, although a large number of market participants are also based in Brussels, Frankfurt, Zurich, and Singapore. Liquidity is supplied by Eurobond market makers, of which approximately 35 are registered with the International Capital Market Association (ICMA). ICMA is an association of banks and other financial institutions that provides a regulatory framework for international bond markets and that is behind much of the established uniform practices that are observed by all market participants in the Eurobond market.

The level of commitment to the different sectors of the market varies among market makers. The **bid–offer spread** or **bid–ask spread**, which reflects the prices at which dealers will buy from a customer (bid) and sell to a customer (offer or ask), is very often used as an indicator of liquidity. It can be as low as 5 bps for very liquid bond issues, such as issues of the World Bank, to no price quoted for illiquid issues. A reasonable spread is of the order of 10–12 bps, whereas an illiquid spread may be in excess of 50 bps. When there is no bid or offer price, the issue is completely illiquid for trading purposes.

Settlement is the process that occurs after the trade is made. The bonds are passed to the buyer and payment is received by the seller. Secondary market settlement for government and quasi-government bonds typically takes place either on a cash basis or on a $T + 1$ basis. With cash settlement, trading and settlement occur on the same day. With $T + 1$ settlement, settlement takes place the day after the trade date. In contrast, corporate bonds usually settle on a $T + 2$ or $T + 3$ basis, although settlement can extend to $T + 7$ in some jurisdictions. Trades clear within either or both of the two main clearing systems, Euroclear and Clearstream. Settlement occurs by means of a simultaneous exchange of bonds for cash on the books of the clearing system. An electronic bridge connecting Euroclear and Clearstream allows transfer of bonds from one system to the other, so it is not necessary to have accounts at both systems. Both systems operate on a paperless, computerized book-entry basis, although a bond issue is still represented by a physical document, the global note mentioned earlier. All participants in either system will have their own internal account set up, and they may also act as agent for buyers or sellers who do not possess an account.

EXAMPLE 3

Bond Markets

1 Which of the following *best* describes a primary market for bonds? A market:

  A in which bonds are issued for the first time to raise capital.

  B that has a specific location where the trading of bonds takes place.

  C in which existing bonds are traded among individuals and institutions.

2 US Treasury bonds are typically sold to the public via a(n):

  A auction.

  B primary dealer.

  C secondary bond market.

3 In a single-price bond auction, an investor who places a competitive bid and specifies a rate that is above the rate determined at auction will *most likely*:

  A not receive any bonds.

  B receive the bonds at the rate determined at auction.

  C receive the bonds at the rate specified in the investor's competitive bid.

4 A bond purchased in a secondary market is *most likely* purchased from:

  A the bond's issuer.

  B the bond's lead underwriter.

  C another investor in the bond.

5 Corporate bonds will *most likely* settle:

  A on the trade date.

  B on the trade date plus one day.

  C by the trade date plus three days.

Solution to 1:

A is correct. Primary bond markets are markets in which bonds are issued for the first time to raise capital. B is incorrect because having a specific location where the trading of bonds takes place is not a requirement for a primary bond market. C is incorrect because a market in which existing bonds are traded among individuals and institutions is the definition of a secondary, not primary, market.

Solution to 2:

A is correct. US Treasury bonds are typically sold to the public via an auction. B is incorrect because primary dealers are often bidders in the auction; they are financial institutions that are active in trading US Treasury bonds. C is incorrect because any bond issue coming directly to the market is considered to be in the primary, not the secondary, market.

Solution to 3:

A is correct. In a single-price bond auction, a bidder that enters a competitive bid specifies the rate (yield) that is considered acceptable. If the rate specified in the competitive bid is above the rate (yield) determined at auction, the investor will not be offered any securities.

Solution to 4:

C is correct. Secondary bond markets are where bonds are traded among investors. A and B are incorrect because a bond purchased from the bond's issuer or from the bond's lead underwriter would happen in the primary, not secondary, market.

Solution to 5:

C is correct. Corporate bonds typically settle on a $T + 2$ or $T + 3$ basis—that is, two or three days after the trade date—although settlement can extend to $T + 7$ in some jurisdictions. A and B are incorrect because it is government and quasi-government bonds, not corporate bonds, that typically settle either on a cash basis or on a $T + 1$ basis.

SOVEREIGN BONDS

4

National governments issue bonds primarily for fiscal reasons—to fund spending when tax revenues are insufficient to cover expenditures. To meet their spending goals, national governments issue bonds in various types and amounts. This section discusses bonds issued by national governments, often referred to as **sovereign bonds** or **sovereigns**.

4.1 Characteristics of Sovereign Bonds

Sovereign bonds denominated in local currency have different names in different countries. For example, they are named US Treasuries in the United States, Japanese government bonds (JGBs) in Japan, gilts in the United Kingdom, Bunds in Germany, and obligations assimilables du Trésor (OATs) in France. Some investors or market participants may refer to sovereign bonds as Treasury securities or Treasuries for short, on the principle that the national Treasury department is often in charge of managing a national government's funding needs.

Names may also vary depending on the original maturity of the sovereign bond. For example, US government bonds are named Treasury bills (T-bills) when the original maturity is one year or shorter, Treasury notes (T-notes) when the original maturity is longer than one year and up to 10 years, and Treasury bonds (T-bonds) when the original maturity is longer than 10 years; in Spain, the sovereigns issued by Tesoro Público are named letras del Tesoro, bonos del Estado, and obligaciones del Estado depending on the sovereign's original maturity, one year or shorter, longer than one year and up to five years, or longer than five years, respectively. Although very rare, some bonds, such as the consols in the United Kingdom, have no stated maturity date.

The majority of the trading in secondary markets is of sovereign securities that were most recently issued. These securities are called **on-the-run**. The latest sovereign bond issue for a given maturity is also referred to as a **benchmark issue** because it serves as a benchmark against which to compare bonds that have the same features (i.e., maturity, coupon type and frequency, and currency denomination) but that are issued by another type of issuer (e.g., non-sovereign, corporate). As a general rule, as sovereign securities age, they trade less frequently.

One salient difference between money market securities, such as T-bills, and capital market securities, such as T-notes and T-bonds, is the interest provision. T-bills are pure discount bonds; they are issued at a discount to par value and redeemed at par. The difference between the par value and the issue price is the interest paid on the borrowing. In contrast, capital market securities are typically coupon (or coupon-bearing) bonds; these securities make regular coupon payments and repay the par value at maturity. Bunds pay coupons annually, whereas US Treasuries, JGBs, gilts, and OATs make semi-annual coupon payments.

4.2 Credit Quality of Sovereign Bonds

Sovereign bonds are usually unsecured obligations of the sovereign issuer—that is, they are not backed by collateral but by the taxing authority of the national government. When a national government runs a budget surplus, excess tax revenues over expenditures are the primary source of funds for making interest payments and repaying the principal. In contrast, when a country runs a budget deficit, the source of the funds used for the payment of interest and repayment of principal comes either from tax revenues and/or by "rolling over" (refinancing) existing debt into new debt.

Highly rated sovereign bonds denominated in local currency are virtually free of credit risk. Credit rating agencies assign ratings to sovereign bonds, and these ratings are called "sovereign ratings." The highest rating (i.e., highest credit quality and lowest credit risk) is AAA by S&P and Fitch and Aaa by Moody's. In 2018, only a handful of sovereign issuers were rated at this (theoretically) risk-free level by these three credit rating agencies, including Germany, Singapore, Canada, Sweden, Norway, Denmark, Luxembourg, Australia, Switzerland, the Netherlands, and the United Kingdom. Notably, S&P downgraded the US from AAA to AA+ in 2011.

Credit rating agencies make a distinction between bonds issued in the sovereign's local currency and bonds issued in a foreign currency. In theory, a government can make interest payments and repay the principal by generating cash flows from its unlimited power (in the short run at least) to tax its citizens. A national government also has the ability to print its own currency, whereas it is restricted in being able to pay in a foreign currency only what it earns in exports or can exchange in financial markets. Thus, it is common to observe a higher credit rating for sovereign bonds issued in local currency than for those issued in a foreign currency. But there are limits to a government's ability to reduce the debt burden. As the sovereign debt crisis that followed the global financial crisis has shown, taxing citizens can only go so far in paying down debt before the taxation becomes an economic burden. Additionally, printing money only serves to weaken a country's currency relative to other currencies over time.

The national government of a country that has a strong domestic savings base has the luxury of being able to issue bonds in its local currency and sell them to domestic investors. If the local currency is liquid and freely traded, the sovereign issuer may also attract foreign investors who may want to hold that sovereign issuer's bonds and have exposure to that country's local currency. A national government may also issue debt in a foreign currency when there is demand for the sovereign issuer's bonds, but not necessarily in the sovereign's local currency. For example, demand from overseas investors has caused national governments such as Switzerland and Sweden to issue sovereign bonds in US dollars and euros. Emerging market countries may also have to issue in major currencies because international investors may be willing to accept the credit risk but not the foreign exchange (currency) risk associated with emerging market bonds. When a sovereign issuer raises debt in a foreign currency, it usually swaps the proceeds into its local currency.

4.3 Types of Sovereign Bonds

National governments issue different types of bonds, some of them paying a fixed rate of interest and others paying a floating rate, including inflation-linked bonds.

4.3.1 *Fixed-Rate Bonds*

Fixed-rate bonds (i.e., bonds that pay a fixed rate of interest) are by far the most common type of sovereign bond. National governments routinely issue two types of fixed-rate bonds: zero-coupon bonds (or pure discount bonds) and coupon bonds. A zero-coupon bond does not pay interest. Instead, it is issued at a discount to par value and redeemed at par at maturity. Coupon bonds are issued with a stated rate of interest and make interest payments periodically, such as semi-annually or annually. They have a terminal cash flow equal to the final interest payment plus the par value. As mentioned earlier, most sovereign bonds with an original maturity of one year or less are zero-coupon bonds, whereas bonds with an original maturity longer than one year are typically issued as coupon bonds.

4.3.2 *Floating-Rate Bonds*

The price of a bond changes in the opposite direction from the change in interest rates, a relationship that is fully explained in the reading on understanding the risk and return of fixed-income securities. Thus, investors who hold fixed-rate bonds are exposed to interest rate risk: As interest rates increase, bond prices decrease, which lowers the value of their portfolio. In response to public demand for less interest rate risk, some national governments around the world issue bonds with a floating rate of interest that resets periodically based on changes in the level of a reference rate such as Libor. Although interest rate risk still exists on floating-rate bonds, it is far less pronounced than that on fixed-rate bonds.

Examples of countries where the national government issues floating-rate bonds include Germany, Spain, and Belgium in developed markets and Brazil, Turkey, Mexico, Indonesia, and Poland in emerging markets. The largest sovereign issuer, the United States, began issuing floating-rate bonds in January 2014. Two other large sovereign issuers, Japan and the United Kingdom, have never issued bonds whose coupon rate is tied to a reference rate.

4.3.3 *Inflation-Linked Bonds*

Fixed-income investors are exposed to inflation risk. The cash flows of fixed-rate bonds are fixed by contract. If a particular country experiences an inflationary episode, the purchasing power of the fixed cash flows is eroded over time. Thus, to respond to the demand for less inflation risk, many national governments issue inflation-linked bonds, or linkers, whose cash flows are adjusted for inflation. First issuers of inflation-linked bonds were the governments of Argentina, Brazil, and Israel. The United States introduced inflation-linked securities in January 1997, calling them Treasury Inflation-Protected Securities (TIPS). Other countries where the national government has issued inflation-linked bonds include the United Kingdom, Sweden, Australia, and Canada in developed markets and Brazil, South Africa, and Chile in emerging markets.

As explained in the reading on fixed-income securities, the index to which the coupon payments and/or principal repayments are linked is typically an index of consumer prices. Inflation-linked bonds can be structured a variety of ways: The inflation adjustment can be made via the coupon payments, the principal repayment, or both. In the United States, the index used is the Consumer Price Index for All Urban Consumers (CPI-U). In the United Kingdom, it is the Retail Price Index (RPI) (All Items). In France, there are two inflation-linked bonds with two different indexes: the French consumer price index (CPI) (excluding tobacco) and the Eurozone's Harmonized Index of Consumer Prices (HICP) (excluding tobacco). Although linking the cash flow payments to a consumer price index reduces inflation risk, it does not necessarily eliminate the effect of inflation completely because the consumer price index may be an imperfect proxy for inflation.

EXAMPLE 4

Sovereign Bonds

1 Sovereign debt with a maturity at issuance shorter than one year are *most likely*:

A floating-rate instruments.

B zero-coupon instruments.

C coupon-bearing instruments.

2 Floating-rate bonds are issued by national governments as the *best* way to reduce:

A credit risk.

B inflation risk.

C interest rate risk.

3 Sovereign bonds whose coupon payments and/or principal repayments are adjusted by a consumer price index are *most likely* known as:

A linkers.

B floaters.

C consols.

Solution to 1:

B is correct. Most debt issued by national governments with a maturity at issuance (original maturity) shorter than one year takes the form of zero-coupon instruments. A and C are incorrect because floating-rate and coupon-bearing instruments are typically types of sovereign debt with maturities longer than one year.

Solution to 2:

C is correct. The coupon rates of floating-rate bonds are reset periodically based on changes in the level of a reference rate such as Libor, which reduces interest rate risk. A is incorrect because credit risk, although low for sovereign bonds, cannot be reduced by linking the coupon rate to a reference rate. B is incorrect because although inflation risk is lower for floating-rate bonds than for fixed-rate bonds, floating-rate bonds are not as good as inflation-linked bonds to reduce inflation risk.

Solution to 3:

A is correct because sovereign bonds whose coupon payments and/or principal repayment are adjusted by a consumer price index are known as inflation-linked bonds or linkers. B is incorrect because floaters describe floating-rate bonds that have a coupon rate tied to a reference rate such as Libor. C is incorrect because consols are sovereign bonds with no stated maturity date issued by the UK government.

NON-SOVEREIGN GOVERNMENT, QUASI-GOVERNMENT, AND SUPRANATIONAL BONDS 5

This section covers the bonds issued by local governments and by government-related entities.

5.1 Non-Sovereign Bonds

Levels of government below the national level such as provinces, regions, states, and cities issue bonds called **non-sovereign government bonds** or **non-sovereign bonds**. These bonds are typically issued to finance public projects, such as schools, motorways, hospitals, bridges, and airports. The sources for paying interest and repaying the principal include the taxing authority of the local government, the cash flows of the project the bond issue is financing, or special taxes and fees established specifically for making interest payments and principal repayments. Non-sovereign bonds are typically not guaranteed by the national government.

As mentioned in Section 2.1.7, bonds issued by state and local governments in the United States are known as municipal bonds, and they often offer income tax exemptions. In the United Kingdom, non-sovereign bonds are known as local authority bonds. Other non-sovereign bonds include those issued by state authorities such as the 16 *Lander* in Germany.

Credit ratings for non-sovereign bonds vary widely because of the differences in credit and collateral quality. Because default rates of non-sovereign bonds are historically low, they very often receive high credit ratings. However, non-sovereign bonds usually trade at a higher yield and lower price than sovereign bonds with similar characteristics. The additional yield depends on the credit quality, the liquidity of the bond issue, and the implicit or explicit level of guarantee or funding commitment from the national government. The additional yield is the lowest for non-sovereign bonds that have high credit quality, are liquid, and are guaranteed by the national government.

5.2 Quasi-Government Bonds

National governments establish organizations that perform various functions for them. These organizations often have both public and private sector characteristics, but they are not actual governmental entities. They are referred to as quasi-government entities, although they take different names in different countries. These quasi-government entities often issue bonds to fund specific financing needs. These bonds are known as **quasi-government bonds** or **agency bonds**.

Examples of quasi-government entities include government-sponsored enterprises (GSEs) in the United States, such as the Federal National Mortgage Association ("Fannie Mae"), the Federal Home Loan Mortgage Corporation ("Freddie Mac"), and the Federal Home Loan Bank (FHLB). Other examples of quasi-government entities that issue bonds include Hydro Quebec in Canada or the Japan Bank for International Cooperation (JBIC). In the case of JBIC's bonds, timely payments of interest and repayment of principal are guaranteed by the Japanese government. Most quasi-government bonds, however, do not offer an explicit guarantee by the national government, although investors often perceive an implicit guarantee.

Because a quasi-government entity typically does not have direct taxing authority, bonds are repaid from the cash flows generated by the entity or from the project the bond issue is financing. Quasi-government bonds may be backed by collateral, but this is not always the case. Quasi-government bonds are usually rated very high by the credit rating agencies because historical default rates are extremely low. Bonds that are guaranteed by the national government receive the highest ratings and trade at a lower yield and higher price than otherwise similar bonds that are not backed by the sovereign government's guarantee.

5.3 Supranational Bonds

A form of often highly rated bonds is issued by supranational agencies, also referred to as multilateral agencies. The most well-known supranational agencies are the International Bank for Reconstruction and Development (the World Bank), the International Monetary Fund (IMF), the European Investment Bank (EIB), the Asian Development Bank (ADB), and the African Development Bank (AFDB). Bonds issued by supranational agencies are called **supranational bonds**.

Supranational bonds are typically plain vanilla bonds, although floating-rate bonds and callable bonds are sometimes issued. Highly rated supranational agencies, such as the World Bank, frequently issue large-size bond issues that are often used as benchmarks issues when there is no liquid sovereign bond available.

EXAMPLE 5

Non-Sovereign Government, Quasi-Government, and Supranational Bonds

1 Relative to sovereign bonds, non-sovereign bonds with similar characteristics *most likely* trade at a yield that is:
   A lower.
   B the same.
   C higher.

2 Bonds issued by a governmental agency are *most likely*:
   A repaid from the cash flows generated by the agency.
   B guaranteed by the national government that sponsored the agency.
   C backed by the taxing power of the national government that sponsored the agency.

Solution to 1:

C is correct. Non-sovereign bonds usually trade at a higher yield and lower price than sovereign bonds with similar characteristics. The higher yield is because of the higher credit risk associated with non-sovereign issuers relative to sovereign issuers, although default rates of local governments are historically low and their credit quality is usually high. The higher yield may also be a consequence of non-sovereign bonds being less liquid than sovereign bonds with similar characteristics.

Solution to 2:

A is correct. Most bonds issued by a governmental agency are repaid from the cash flows generated by the agency or from the project the bond issue is financing. B and C are incorrect because although some bonds issued by governmental agencies are guaranteed by the national government or are backed by the taxing power of the national government that sponsored the agency, bonds are most likely repaid first from the cash flows generated by the agency.

CORPORATE DEBT

6

Companies differ from governments and government-related entities in that their primary goal is profit; they must be profitable to stay in existence. Thus, profitability is an important consideration when companies make decisions, including financing decisions. Companies routinely raise debt as part of their overall capital structure, both to fund short-term spending needs (e.g., working capital) as well as long-term capital investments. We have so far focused on publicly issued debt, but loans from banks and other financial institutions are a significant part of the debt raised by companies. For example, it is estimated that European companies meet 75% of their borrowing needs from banks and only 25% from financial markets. In Japan, these percentages are 80% and 20%, respectively. However, in the US debt capital is much more significant: 80% is from financial markets and just 20% from bank lending.[4]

6.1 Bank Loans and Syndicated Loans

A **bilateral loan** is a loan from a single lender to a single borrower. Companies routinely use bilateral loans from their banks, and these bank loans are governed by the bank loan documents. Bank loans are the primary source of debt financing for small and medium-size companies as well as for large companies in countries where bond markets are either under-developed or where most bond issuances are from government, government-related entities, and financial institutions. Access to bank loans depends not only on the characteristics and financial health of the company, but also on market conditions and bank capital availability.

A syndicated loan is a loan from a group of lenders, called the "syndicate," to a single borrower. A syndicated loan is a hybrid between relational lending and publicly traded debt. Syndicated loans are primarily originated by banks, and the loans are extended to companies but also to governments and government-related entities. The coordinator, or lead bank, originates the loan, forms the syndicate, and processes the payments. In addition to banks, a variety of lenders participate in the syndicate, such as pension funds, insurance companies, and hedge funds. Syndicated loans are a way for these institutional investors to participate in corporate lending while diversifying the credit risk among a group of lenders.

In recent years, a secondary market in syndicated loans has developed. These loans are often packaged and securitized, and the securities created are then sold in secondary markets to investors.

Most bilateral and syndicated loans are floating-rate loans, and the interest rate is based on a reference rate plus a spread. The reference rate may be Libor, a sovereign rate (e.g., the T-bill rate), or the prime lending rate, also called the "prime rate." The prime rate formerly reflected the interest rate at which banks lent to their most

4 SIFMA 2018 Outlook

creditworthy customers, but it now tends to be driven by the overnight rate at which banks lend to each other. Bank loans can be customized to the borrower's needs. They can have different maturities, as well as different interest payment and principal repayment structures. The frequency of interest payments varies among bank loans. Some loans are bullet loans, in which the entire payment of principal occurs at maturity, and others are amortizing loans, in which the principal is repaid over time.

For highly rated companies, both bilateral and syndicated loans can be more expensive than bonds issued in financial markets. Thus, companies often turn to money and capital markets to raise funds, which allows them to diversify their sources of financing.

6.2 Commercial Paper

Commercial paper is a short-term, unsecured promissory note issued in the public market or via a private placement that represents a debt obligation of the issuer. Commercial paper was first issued in the United States more than a century ago. It later appeared in the United Kingdom, in other European countries, and then in the rest of the world.

6.2.1 *Characteristics of Commercial Paper*

Commercial paper is a valuable source of flexible, readily available, and relatively low-cost short-term financing. It is a source of funding for working capital and seasonal demands for cash. It is also a source of **bridge financing**—that is, interim financing that provides funds until permanent financing can be arranged. Suppose a company wants to build a new distribution center in southeast China and wants to finance this investment with an issuance of long-term bonds. The market conditions for issuing long-term bonds may currently be volatile, which would translate into a higher cost of borrowing. Rather than issuing long-term bonds immediately, the company may opt to raise funds with commercial paper and wait for a more favorable environment in which to sell long-term bonds.

The largest issuers of commercial paper are financial institutions, but some non-financial companies are also regular issuers of commercial paper. Although the focus of this section is on corporate borrowers, sovereign governments and supranational agencies routinely issue commercial paper as well.

The maturity of commercial paper can range from overnight to one year, but a typical issue matures in less than three months.

6.2.2 *Credit Quality of Commercial Paper*

Traditionally, only the largest, most stable companies issued commercial paper. Although only the strongest, highest-rated companies issue low-cost commercial paper, issuers from across the risk spectrum can issue commercial paper with higher yields than higher-rated companies. Thus, investors in commercial paper are exposed to various levels of credit risk depending on the issuer's creditworthiness. Many investors perform their own credit analysis, but most investors also assess a commercial paper's credit quality by using the ratings provided by credit rating agencies. Exhibit 5 presents the range of commercial paper ratings from the main credit rating agencies. Commercial paper rated adequate or above (shaded area of Exhibit 5 is called "prime paper," and it is typically considered investment grade by investors.

Exhibit 5 Commercial Paper Ratings

Credit Quality	Moody's	S&P	Fitch
Superior	P1	A1+/A1	F1+/F1
Satisfactory	P2	A2	F2
Adequate	P3	A3	F3
Speculative	NP	B/C	F4
Defaulted	NP	D	F5

In most cases, maturing commercial paper is paid with the proceeds of new issuances of commercial paper, a practice referred to as "rolling over the paper." This practice creates a risk that the issuer will be unable to issue new paper at maturity, referred to as rollover risk. As a safeguard against rollover risk, credit rating agencies often require that commercial paper issuers secure **backup lines of credit** from banks. The purpose of the backup lines of credit is to ensure that the issuer will have access to sufficient liquidity to repay maturing commercial paper if rolling over the paper is not a viable option. Therefore, backup lines of credit are sometimes called "liquidity enhancement" or "backup liquidity lines." Issuers of commercial paper may be unable to roll over the paper because of either market-wide or company-specific events. For example, financial markets could be in the midst of a financial crisis that would make it difficult to roll over the paper. A company could also experience some sort of financial distress such that it could only issue new commercial paper at significantly higher rates. In this case, the company could draw on its credit lines instead of rolling over its paper. Most commercial paper issuers maintain 100% backing, although some large, high credit quality issues carry less than 100% backing. Backup lines of credit typically contain a "material adverse change" provision that allows the bank to cancel the backup line of credit if the financial condition of the issuer deteriorates substantially.

Historically, defaults on commercial paper have been relatively rare, primarily because commercial paper has a short maturity. Each time existing paper matures, investors have another opportunity to assess the issuer's financial position, and they can refuse to buy the new paper if they estimate that the issuer's credit risk is too high. Thus, the commercial paper markets adapt more quickly to a change in an issuer's credit quality than do the markets for longer-term securities. This flexibility reduces the exposure of the commercial paper market to defaults. In addition, corporate managers realize that defaulting on commercial paper would likely prevent any future issuance of this valuable financing alternative.

The combination of short-dated maturity, relatively low credit risk, and a large number of issuers makes commercial paper attractive to a diverse range of investors, including: money market mutual funds, bank liquidity desks, corporate treasury departments, and other institutional investors that have liquidity constraints. Most commercial paper investors hold their position to maturity. The result is little secondary market trading except for the largest issues. Investors who wish to sell commercial paper prior to maturity can either sell the paper back to the dealer, to another investor, or in some cases, directly back to the issuer.

The yield on commercial paper is typically higher than that on short-term sovereign bonds of the same maturity for two main reasons. First, commercial paper is exposed to credit risk unlike most highly rated sovereign bonds. Second, commercial paper markets are generally less liquid than short-term sovereign bond markets. Thus, investors require higher yields to compensate for the lower liquidity. In the United States, the yield on commercial paper also tends to be higher than that on short-term municipal bonds for tax reasons. Income generated by investments in commercial paper is usually subject to income taxes, whereas income from many municipal bonds is tax exempt. Thus, to attract taxable investors, bonds that are subject to income taxes must offer higher yields than those that are tax exempt.

6.2.3 *US Commercial Paper vs. Eurocommercial Paper*

The US commercial paper (USCP) market is the largest commercial paper market in the world, although there are other active commercial paper markets in other countries. Commercial paper issued in the international market is known as Eurocommercial paper (ECP). Although ECP is a similar instrument to USCP, there are some differences between the two. These differences are shown in Exhibit 6.

Exhibit 6 USCP vs. ECP

Feature	US Commercial Paper	Eurocommercial Paper
Currency	US dollar	Any currency
Maturity	Overnight to 270 days[a]	Overnight to 364 days
Interest	Discount basis	Interest-bearing or discount basis
Settlement	T + 0 (trade date)	T + 2 (trade date plus two days)
Negotiable	Can be sold to another party	Can be sold to another party

[a] In the United States, securities with an original maturity greater than 270 days must be registered with the Securities and Exchange Commission (SEC). To avoid the time and expense associated with a SEC registration, issuers of US commercial paper rarely offer maturities longer than 270 days.

A difference between USCP and ECP is related to the interest provision. USCP is typically issued on a discount basis—that is, USCP is issued at a discount to par value and pays full par value at maturity. The difference between the par value and the issue price is the interest paid on the borrowing. In contrast, ECP may be issued at, and trade on, an interest-bearing or yield basis or a discount basis. The distinction between the discount and the interest-bearing basis is illustrated in Exhibit 7. Some aspects of the calculation, such as the day count convention, are discussed in the introduction to fixed-income valuation reading.

Exhibit 7

Interest Calculation: Discount vs. Interest-Bearing Basis

A US bank and a German industrial company both issue \$50 million of 180-day, 5% commercial paper. The US bank issues its commercial paper domestically, and the German industrial company issues Eurocommercial paper.

US bank:

Issues \$50,000,000 180-day USCP.

Interest is \$1,250,000 [\$50,000,000 × 0.05 × (180/360)].

Interest on USCP is on a discount basis. Proceeds received are \$48,750,000 [\$50,000,000 – \$1,250,000].

At maturity, the bank repays the par value of \$50,000,000.

Exhibit 7 (Continued)

German industrial company:

Issues $50,000,000 180-day ECP.

Interest is $1,250,000 [$50,000,000 × 0.05 × (180/360)].

Interest on ECP is on an interest-bearing basis. Proceeds received are the par value of $50,000,000.

At maturity, the company repays $51,250,000 [$50,000,000 + $1,250,000].

The amount of interest is the same for both companies. In the case of USCP, investors receive the interest by getting a discount on the par value when the commercial paper is issued. In the case of ECP, investors receive the interest by getting an additional payment (or add-on) to the par value when the commercial paper is repaid. However, note that the investors' return is not the same. Investors earn 2.56% on their 180-day investment in USCP ($1,250,000 ÷ $48,750,000) versus 2.50% on their 180-day investment in ECP ($1,250,000 ÷ $50,000,000).

Typical transaction sizes in ECP are also much smaller than in USCP, and it is difficult to place longer-term ECP with investors. The ECP market also exhibits less liquidity than the USCP market.

6.3 Corporate Notes and Bonds

Companies are active participants in global capital markets and regularly issue corporate notes and bonds. These securities can be placed directly with specific investors via private placements or sold in public securities markets. This section discusses various characteristics of corporate notes and bonds.

6.3.1 *Maturities*

There is no universally accepted taxonomy as to what constitutes short-, medium-, and long-term maturities. For our purposes, short term refers to original maturities of five years or less; intermediate term to original maturities longer than five years and up to 12 years; and long term to original maturities longer than 12 years. Those securities with maturities between 1 and 12 years are often considered notes, whereas securities with maturities greater than 12 years are considered bonds. It is not uncommon, however, to refer to bonds for all securities, irrespective of their original maturity.

In practice, most corporate bonds range in term to maturity between 1 and 30 years. In Europe, however, there are also bond issues with maturities of 40 and 50 years. In addition, companies and sovereigns have issued 100-year bonds; these are called "century bonds." For example, in 2017 Austria issued EUR 3.5 billion in bonds that will mature in 2117.

The first century bond was issued by the Walt Disney Company in 1993 as part of its **medium-term note** program. Medium-term note (MTN) is a misnomer. As the Disney example illustrates, MTNs can have very long maturities. From the perspective of the issuer, the initial purpose of MTNs was to fill the funding gap between commercial paper and long-term bonds. It is for this reason that they are referred to as "medium term." The MTN market can be broken into three segments: short-term securities that carry floating or fixed rates, medium- to long-term securities that primarily bear a fixed rate of interest, and structured notes. MTNs have the unique characteristic of being securities that are offered continuously to investors by an agent of the issuer. This feature gives the borrower maximum flexibility for issuing securities on a continuous basis. Financial institutions are the primary issuers of MTNs, in particular short-term ones. Life insurance companies, pension funds, and banks are among the largest buyers of MTNs because they can customize the bond issue to their needs and stipulate the amount and characteristics of the securities they want to purchase. These investors are often willing to accept less liquidity than they would get with a comparable publicly issued bond because the yield is slightly higher. The cost savings in registration and underwriting often makes MTNs a lower cost option for the issuer.

6.3.2 *Coupon Payment Structures*

Corporate notes and bonds have a range of coupon payment structures. Financial and non-financial companies issue conventional coupon bonds that pay a fixed periodic coupon during the bond's life. They also issue bonds for which the periodic coupon payments adjust to changes in market conditions and/or changes to the issuer's credit quality. Such bonds typically offer investors the opportunity to reduce their exposure to a particular type of risk. For example, FRNs, whose coupon payments adjust to changes in the level of market interest rates, are a way to limit interest rate risk; some of the inflation-linked bonds whose coupon payments adjust to changes in the level of a consumer price index offer a protection against inflation risk; credit-linked coupon bonds, whose coupon payments adjust to changes in the issuer's credit quality, are a way to reduce credit risk. Whether the periodic coupon is fixed or not, coupon payments can be made quarterly, semi-annually, or annually depending on the type of bond and where the bonds are issued and traded.

Other coupon payment structures exist. Zero-coupon bonds pay no coupon. Deferred coupon bonds pay no coupon initially, but then offer a higher coupon. Payment-in-kind (PIK) coupon bonds make periodic coupon payments, but not necessarily in cash; the issuer may pay interest in the form of securities, such as bonds or common shares. These types of coupon payment structures give issuers more flexibility regarding the servicing of their debt.

6.3.3 *Principal Repayment Structures*

Corporate note or bond issues have either a serial or a term maturity structure. With a **serial maturity structure**, the maturity dates are spread out during the bond's life; a stated number of bonds mature and are paid off each year before final maturity. With a **term maturity structure**, the bond's notional principal is paid off in a lump sum at maturity. Because there is no regular repayment of the principal outstanding throughout the bond's life, a term maturity structure carries more credit risk than a serial maturity structure.

A sinking fund arrangement is a way to reduce credit risk by making the issuer set aside funds over time to retire the bond issue. For example, a corporate bond issue may require a specified percentage of the bond's outstanding principal amount to be retired each year. The issuer may satisfy this requirement in one of two ways. The most common approach is for the issuer to make a random call for the specified percentage of bonds that must be retired and to pay the bondholders whose bonds are called the sinking fund price, which is typically par. Alternatively, the issuer can deliver bonds to the trustee with a total amount equal to the amount that must be retired. To do so, the issuer may purchase the bonds in the open market. The sinking fund arrangement on a term maturity structure accomplishes the same goal as the serial maturity structure—that is, both result in a portion of the bond issue being paid off each year. With a serial maturity structure, however, the bondholders know which bonds will mature and will thus be paid off each year. In contrast, the bonds retired annually with a sinking fund arrangement are designated by a random drawing.

6.3.4 *Asset or Collateral Backing*

Unlike most highly rated sovereign bonds, all corporate debt is exposed to varying degrees of credit risk. Thus, corporate debt is structured with this risk in mind. An important consideration for investors is seniority ranking—that is, the systematic way in which lenders are repaid if the issuer defaults. In the case of secured debt, there is some form of collateral pledged to ensure payment of the debt. In contrast, in the case of unsecured debt, claims are settled by the general assets of the company in accordance with the priority of payments that applies either legally or contractually and as described in the bond indenture. Within each category of debt (secured and unsecured), there are finer gradations of rankings, which are discussed in the reading on credit analysis.

There is a wide range of bonds that are secured by some form of collateral. Companies that need to finance equipment or physical assets may issue equipment trust certificates. Corporate issuers also sell collateral trust bonds that are secured by securities, such as common shares, bonds, or other financial assets. Banks, particularly in Europe, may issue covered bonds, which are a type of debt obligation that is secured by a segregated pool of assets. Asset-backed securities are also secured forms of debt.

Companies can and do default on their debt. Debt secured by collateral may still experience losses, but investors in secured debt usually fare better than in unsecured debt in bankruptcy proceedings. Investors who face a higher level of credit risk typically require a higher yield than investors exposed to very little credit risk.

6.3.5 *Contingency Provisions*

Contingency provisions are clauses in the indenture that provide the issuer or the bondholders rights that affect the disposal or redemption of the bond. The three commonly used contingency provisions are call, put, and conversion provisions.

Callable bonds give issuers the ability to retire debt prior to maturity. The most compelling reason for them to do so is to take advantage of lower borrowing rates. By calling the bonds before their maturity date, the issuer can substitute a new, lower cost bond issue for an older, higher cost one. In addition, companies may also retire debt to eliminate restrictive covenants or to alter their capital structure to improve flexibility. Because the call provision is a valuable option for the issuer, investors demand compensation ex ante (before investing in the bond). Thus, other things equal, investors require a higher yield (and thus pay a lower price) for a callable bond than for an otherwise similar non-callable bond.

Companies also issue putable bonds, which give the bondholders the right to sell the bond back to the issuer at a predetermined price on specified dates before maturity. Most putable bonds pay a fixed rate of interest, although some bonds may have step-up coupons that increase by specified margins at specified dates. Because the put provision is a valuable option for the bondholders, putable bonds offer a lower yield (and thus have a higher price) than otherwise similar non-putable bonds. The main corporate issuers of putable bonds are investment-grade companies. Putable bonds may offer them a cheaper way of raising capital, especially if the company estimates that the benefit of a lower coupon outweighs the risk associated with the put provision.

A convertible bond is a hybrid security that lies on a continuum between debt and equity. It consists of a long position in an option-free bond and a conversion option that gives the bondholder the right to convert the bond into a specified number of shares of the issuer's common shares. From the point of view of the issuer, convertible bonds make it possible to raise funds that may not be possible without the incentive associated with the conversion option. The more common issuers of convertibles bonds are newer companies that have not established a presence in debt capital markets but who are able to present a more attractive package to institutional investors by including an equity upside potential. Established issuers of bonds may also prefer to issue convertible bonds because they are usually sold at a lower coupon rate than otherwise similar non-convertible bonds because of investors' attraction to the conversion provision. However, there is a potential equity dilution effect if the bonds are converted. From the investor's point of view, convertible bonds represent a means of accessing the equity upside potential of the issuer but at a lower risk–reward profile because there is the floor of the coupon payments in the meantime.

6.3.6 *Issuance, Trading, and Settlement*

In the era before electronic settlement, there were some differences in the processes of issuing and settling corporate bonds depending on where the securities were registered. This is no longer the case; the processes of issuing and settling bonds are now essentially the same globally. New corporate bond issues are usually sold to investors by investment banks acting as underwriters in the case of underwritten offerings or brokers in the case of best effort offerings. They are then settled via the local settlement system. These local systems typically possess a "bridge" to the two Eurobond systems, Euroclear and Clearstream. As for Eurobonds from the corporate sector, they are all issued, traded, and settled in the same way, irrespective of the issuer and its local jurisdiction.

Most bond prices are quoted in basis points. The vast majority of corporate bonds are traded in OTC markets through dealers who "make a market" in bonds and sell from their inventory. Dealers do not typically charge a commission or a transaction fee. Instead, they earn a profit from the bid–offer spread.

For corporate bonds, settlement differences exist primarily between new bond issues and the secondary trading of bonds. The issuing phase for an underwritten offering usually takes several days. Thus, settlement takes longer for new bond issued than for the secondary trading of bonds, for which settlement is typically on a $T + 2$ or $T + 3$ basis.

EXAMPLE 6

Corporate Debt

1 A loan made by a group of banks to a private company is *most likely*:
   - A a bilateral loan.
   - B a syndicated loan.
   - C a securitized loan.

2 Which of the following statements relating to commercial paper is *most accurate*? Companies issue commercial paper:
   - A only for funding working capital.
   - B only as an interim source of financing.
   - C both for funding working capital and as an interim source of funding.

3 Maturities of Eurocommercial paper range from:
   - A overnight to three months.
   - B overnight to one year.
   - C three months to one year.

4 A bond issue that has a stated number of bonds that mature and are paid off each year before final maturity *most likely* has a:
   - A term maturity.

B serial maturity.

C sinking fund arrangement.

Solution to 1:

B is correct. A loan from a group of lenders to a single borrower is a syndicated loan. A is incorrect because a bilateral loan is a loan from a single lender to a single borrower. C is incorrect because securitization involves moving assets, such as loans, from the owner of the assets into a special legal entity.

Solution to 2:

C is correct. Companies use commercial paper as a source of funding working capital and seasonal demand for cash, as well as an interim source of financing until permanent financing can be arranged.

Solution to 3:

B is correct. Eurocommercial paper ranges in maturity from overnight to 364 days.

Solution to 4:

B is correct. With a serial maturity structure, a stated number of bonds mature and are paid off each year before final maturity. A is incorrect because a bond issue with a term maturity structure is paid off in one lump sum at maturity. C is incorrect because a sinking fund arrangement, like a serial maturity structure, results in a portion of the bond issue being paid off every year. However, with a serial maturity structure, the bonds are paid off because the maturity dates are spread out during the life of the bond and the bonds that are retired are maturing; the bondholders know in advance which bonds will be retired. In contrast, the bonds retired annually with a sinking fund arrangement are designated by a random drawing.

STRUCTURED FINANCIAL INSTRUMENTS

7

Structured financial instruments represent a broad sector of financial instruments. This sector includes asset-backed securities (ABS) and collateralized debt obligations (CDOs). CDOs are securities backed by a diversified pool of one or more debt obligations, and like ABS, they are discussed in the reading on asset-backed securities. A common attribute of all these financial instruments is that they repackage and redistribute risks.

Our focus in this section is on structured financial instruments apart from ABS and CDOs. These instruments typically have customized structures that often combine a bond and at least one derivative. Some of these instruments are called structured products. The use of derivatives gives the holder of the structured financial instrument exposure to one or more underlying assets, such as equities, bonds, and commodities. The redemption value and often the coupons of structured financial instruments are linked via a formula to the performance of the underlying asset(s). Thus, the bond's payment features are replaced with non-traditional payoffs that are derived not from the issuer's cash flows but from the performance of the underlying asset(s). While there is no universally accepted taxonomy used to categorize structured financial instruments, we will present four broad categories of instruments in this reading: capital protected, yield enhancement, participation, and leveraged instruments.

7.1 Capital Protected Instruments

Suppose an investor has $100,000 to invest. The investor buys zero-coupon bonds issued by a sovereign issuer that will pay off $100,000 one year from now. Also suppose the cost of buying the zero-coupon bonds is $99,000. The investor can use the $1,000 left over from the purchase of the zero-coupon bond to buy a call option on some underlying asset that expires one year from now. Buying a call option gives the investor the right to buy the underlying asset in one year at a pre-determined price. The investor will receive $100,000 when the zero-coupon bond matures and may also gain from the upside potential of the call option, if any. This combination of the zero-coupon bond and the call option can be prepackaged as a structured financial instrument called a **guarantee certificate**. The zero-coupon bond provides the investor capital protection; at maturity, the investor will receive 100% of the capital invested even if the call option expires worthless. The call option provides upside potential if the price of the underlying asset rises and a limited downside if the price of the underlying asset falls. The downside is limited to the price, often called the premium, paid for the call option. In our example, the maximum loss the investor faces is $1,000, which is the price paid for the call option.

Capital protected instruments offer different levels of capital protection. A guarantee certificate offers full capital protection. Other structured financial instruments may offer only partial capital protection. Note that the capital protection is only as good as the issuer of the instrument. Should the issuer of guarantee certificates go bankrupt, investors may lose their entire capital.

7.2 Yield Enhancement Instruments

Yield enhancement refers to increasing risk exposure in the hope of realizing a higher expected return. A **credit-linked note (CLN)** is an example of a yield enhancement instrument. Specifically, it is a type of bond that pays regular coupons but whose redemption value depends on the occurrence of a well-defined credit event, such as a rating downgrade or the default of an underlying asset, called the reference asset. If the specified credit event does not occur, the investor receives the par value of the CLN at maturity. But if the specified credit event occurs, the investor receives the par value of the CLN minus the nominal value of the reference asset to which the CLN is linked.

A CLN allows the issuer to transfer the effect of a credit event to investors. Thus, the issuer is the protection buyer and the investor is the protection seller. Investors are willing to buy CLNs because these securities offer higher coupons than otherwise similar bonds. In addition, CLNs are usually issued at a discount. Thus, if the specified credit event does not occur, investors will realize a significant capital gain on the purchase of the CLN.

7.3 Participation Instruments

As the name suggests, a participation instrument is one that allows investors to participate in the return of an underlying asset. Floating-rate bonds can be viewed as a type of participation instrument. As discussed earlier, floaters differ from fixed-rate bonds in that their coupon rate adjusts periodically according to a pre-specified formula. The coupon formula is usually expressed as a reference rate adjusted for a spread. A floater has almost zero interest rate risk because changes in the cash flows limit the effect of changes in interest rates on the floater's price. Thus, floaters give investors the opportunity to participate in movements of interest rates. For example, the Italian government issued in June 2005 floaters set to mature in June 2020. The coupon payments are delivered annually and determined by the formula of 85% of the 10-year constant maturity swap rate, a widely-used type of interest rate. Thus, investors who hold these floaters participate partially in movements of the 10-year constant maturity swap rate.

Most participation instruments are designed to give investors indirect exposure to a specific index or asset price. For example, investors who are precluded from investing in equity directly may get indirect equity exposure by investing in participation instruments that are linked via a formula to the performance of equity indexes. Many structured products sold to individuals are participation instruments linked to an equity index. In contrast to capital protected instruments that offer equity exposure, these participation instruments usually do not offer capital protection.

7.4 Leveraged Instruments

Leveraged instruments are structured financial instruments created to magnify returns and offer the possibility of high payoffs from small investments. An **inverse floater** is an example of a leveraged instrument. As the name suggests, an inverse floater is the opposite of a traditional floater. The cash flows are adjusted periodically and move in the opposite direction of changes in the reference rate. So, when the reference rate decreases, the coupon payment of an inverse floater increases.

A general formula for an inverse floater's coupon rate is:

$$\text{Inverse floater coupon rate} = C - (L \times R)$$

where C is the maximum coupon rate reached if the reference rate is equal to zero, L is the coupon leverage, and R is the reference rate on the reset date. Note that the coupon leverage indicates the multiple that the coupon rate will change in response to a 100 basis points (bps) change in the reference rate. For example, if the coupon leverage is three, the inverse floater's coupon rate will decrease by 300 bps when the reference rate increases by 100 bps.

Inverse floaters with a coupon leverage greater than zero but lower than one are called deleveraged inverse floaters. Inverse floaters with a coupon leverage greater than one are called leveraged inverse floaters. For example, the Barclays Bank PLC issued a 15-year bond in January 2010 having quarterly payments. The coupon rate was fixed at 7.50% for the first three years and then in January 2013 transformed into a leveraged inverse floater paying 7.50% *minus* the euro 3-month Libor. In this case, the coupon leverage is one. Thus, for a 100 bps increase in the euro 3-month Libor, the coupon rate of the leveraged inverse floater will decrease by 100 bps. Inverse floaters often have a floor that specifies a minimum coupon rate; for example, a floor may be set at zero to avoid the possibility of a negative interest rate. This inverse floater does not have a maximum coupon rate. At the July 2018 reset, euro 3-month Libor was minus 0.32%, so the coupon rate for the following quarter was 7.82%.

EXAMPLE 7

Structured Financial Instruments

1 If an investor holds a credit-linked note and the credit event does not occur, the investor receives:

A all promised cash flows as scheduled.

B all coupon payments as scheduled but not the par value at maturity.

C all coupon payments as scheduled and the par value minus the nominal value of the reference asset to which the credit-linked note is linked at maturity.

2 A structured financial instrument whose coupon rate is determined by the formula 5% – (0.5 × Libor) is *most likely*:

A a leveraged inverse floater.

B a participation instrument.

C a deleveraged inverse floater.

Solution to 1:

A is correct. If the credit event does not occur, the issuer must make all promised cash flows as scheduled—that is, the regular coupon payments and the par value at maturity.

Solution to 2:

C is correct. A structured financial instrument whose coupon rate moves in the opposite direction of the reference rate is called an inverse floater. Because the coupon leverage (0.5) is greater than zero but lower than one, the structured financial instrument is a deleveraged inverse floater. In this example, if the reference rate increases by 100 bps, the coupon rate decreases by 50 bps. A is incorrect because the coupon leverage would have to be higher than one for the structured financial instrument to be a leveraged inverse floater. B is incorrect because a participation instrument is designed to give investors indirect exposure to a particular underlying asset.

8 SHORT-TERM FUNDING ALTERNATIVES AVAILABLE TO BANKS

Funding refers to the amount of money or resources necessary to finance some specific project or enterprise. Accordingly, funding markets are markets in which debt issuers borrow to meet their financial needs. Companies have a range of funding alternatives, including bank loans, commercial paper, notes, and bonds. Financial institutions such as banks have larger financing needs than non-financial companies because of the nature of their operations. This section discusses the additional funding alternatives that are available to them. The majority of these funding alternatives have short maturities.

Banks, such as deposit-taking (or depositary) institutions, typically have access to funds obtained from the retail market—that is, deposit accounts from their customers. However, it is quite common for banks to originate more loans than they have retail deposits. Thus, whenever the amount of retail deposits is insufficient to meet their financial needs, banks also need to raise funds from the wholesale market. Wholesale funds include central bank funds, interbank deposits, and certificates of deposit. In addition to filling the gaps between loans and deposits, banks raise wholesale funds to minimize their funding cost. At the margin, wholesale funds may be less expensive (in terms of interest expense) than deposit funding. Finally, financial institutions may raise wholesale funds as a balance sheet risk management tool to reduce interest rate risk, as discussed in Section 2.1.5.1.

8.1 Retail Deposits

One of the primary sources of funding for deposit-taking banks is their retail deposit base, which includes funds from both individual and commercial depositors. There are several types of retail deposit accounts. Demand deposits, also known as checking accounts, are available to customers "on demand." Depositors have immediate access to the funds in their deposit accounts and use the funds as a form of payment for transactions. Because the funds are available immediately, deposit accounts typically pay no interest. In contrast, savings accounts pay interest and allow depositors to accumulate wealth in a very liquid form, but they do not offer the same transactional convenience as demand deposits. Money market accounts were originally designed to compete with money market mutual funds. They offer money market rates of return and depositors can access funds at short or no notice. Thus, money market accounts are, for depositors, an intermediate between demand deposit and savings accounts.

8.2 Short-Term Wholesale Funds

Wholesale funds available for banks include reserve funds, interbank funds, and certificates of deposit.

8.2.1 *Reserve Funds*

Many countries require deposit-taking banks to place a reserve balance with the national central bank. The reserve funds help to ensure sufficient liquidity should depositors require withdrawal of funds. When a bank cannot obtain short-term funding, most countries allow that bank to borrow from the central bank. In aggregate, the reserve funds act as a liquidity buffer providing comfort to depositors and investors that the central bank can act as lender of last resort.

Treatment of interest on reserve funds varies among countries, from a low interest payment, to no interest payment, to charges for keeping reserve funds. Additionally, there is an opportunity cost to the banks for holding reserves with the central bank in that these funds cannot be invested with higher interest or loaned out to consumers or commercial enterprises. Some banks have an excess over the minimum required funds to be held in reserve. At the same time, other banks run short of required reserves. This imbalance is solved through the **central bank funds market**, which allows banks that have a surplus of funds to loan money to banks that need funds for maturities of up to one year. These funds are known as central bank funds and are called "overnight funds" when the maturity is one day and "term funds" when the maturity ranges from two days to one year. The interest rates at which central bank funds are bought (i.e., borrowed) and sold (i.e., lent) are short-term interest rates determined by the markets but influenced by the central bank's open market operations. These rates are termed the **central bank funds rates**.

In the United States, the central bank is the Federal Reserve (Fed). The central bank funds and funds rate are called Fed funds and Fed funds rates, respectively. Other short-term interest rates, such as the yields on Treasury bills, are highly correlated with the Fed funds rate. The most widely followed rate is known as the Fed funds effective rate, which is the volume-weighted average of rates for Fed fund trades arranged throughout the day by the major New York City brokers. Fed funds are traded between banks and other financial institutions globally and may be transacted directly or through money market brokers.

8.2.2 *Interbank Funds*

The interbank market is the market of loans and deposits between banks. The term to maturity of an interbank loan or deposit ranges from overnight to one year. The rate on an interbank loan or deposit can be quoted relative to a reference rate, such as an interbank offered rate or as a fixed interest rate. An interbank deposit is unsecured, so banks placing deposits with another bank need to have an interbank line of credit in place for that institution. Usually, a large bank will make a two-way price, indicating the rate at which it will lend funds and the rate at which it will borrow funds for a specific maturity, on demand. Interest on the deposit is payable at maturity. Much interbank dealing takes place on the Reuters electronic dealing system, so that the transaction is done without either party speaking to the other.

Because the market is unsecured, it is essentially based on confidence in the banking system. At times of stress, such as in the aftermath of the Lehman Brothers' bankruptcy in 2008, the market is prone to "dry up" as banks withdraw from funding other banks.

8.2.3 *Large-Denomination Negotiable Certificates of Deposit*

A **certificate of deposit** (CD) is an instrument that represents a specified amount of funds on deposit for a specified maturity and interest rate. CDs are an important source of funds for financial institutions. A CD may take one of two forms: non-negotiable or negotiable. If the CD is non-negotiable, the deposit plus the interest are paid to the initial depositor at maturity. A withdrawal penalty is imposed if the depositor withdraws funds prior to the maturity date.

Alternatively, a negotiable CD allows any depositor (initial or subsequent) to sell the CD in the open market prior to the maturity date. Negotiable CDs were introduced in the United States in the early 1960s when various types of deposits were constrained by interest rate ceilings. At the time, bank deposits were not an attractive investment because investors earned a below-market interest rate unless they were prepared to commit their capital for an extended period of time. The introduction of negotiable CDs enabled bank customers to buy a three-month or longer negotiable instrument yielding a market interest rate and to recover their investment by selling it in the market. This innovation helped banks increase the amount of funds raised in the money markets. It also fostered competition among deposit-taking institutions.

There are two types of negotiable CDs: large-denomination CDs and small-denomination CDs. Thresholds between small- and large-denomination CDs vary among countries. For example, in the United States, large-denomination CDs are usually issued in denominations of $1 million or more. Small-denomination CDs are a retail-oriented product, and they are of secondary importance as a funding alternative. Large-denomination CDs, in contrast, are an important source of wholesale funds and are typically traded among institutional investors.

Like other money market securities, CDs are available in domestic bond markets as well as in the Eurobond market. Most CDs have maturities shorter than one year and pay interest at maturity. CDs with longer maturities are called "term CDs."

Yields on CDs are driven primarily by the credit risk of the issuing bank and to a lesser extent by the term to maturity. The spread attributable to credit risk will vary with economic conditions and confidence in the banking system in general and in the issuing bank in particular. As with all debt instruments, spreads widen during times of financial turmoil as a result of an increase in risk aversion.

8.3 Repurchase and Reverse Repurchase Agreements

Repurchase agreements are another important source of funding not only for banks but also for other market participants. A **repurchase agreement** or **repo** is the sale of a security with a simultaneous agreement by the seller to buy the same security back from the purchaser at an agreed-on price and future date.[5] In practical terms, a repurchase agreement can be viewed as a collateralized loan in which the security sold and subsequently repurchased represents the collateral posted. One party is borrowing money and providing collateral for the loan at an interest rate that is typically lower than on an otherwise similar bank loan. The other party is lending money while accepting a security as collateral for the loan.

5 Repurchase agreements can be structured such that the transaction is terminable on demand.

Repurchase agreements are a common source of money market funding for dealer firms in many countries. An active market in repurchase agreements underpins every liquid bond market. Financial and non-financial companies participate actively in the market as both sellers and buyers of collateral depending on their circumstances. Central banks are also active users of repurchase agreements in their daily open market operations; they either lend to the market to increase the supply of funds or withdraw surplus funds from the market.

8.3.1 *Structure of Repurchase and Reverse Repurchase Agreements*

Suppose a government securities dealer purchases a 2.25% UK gilt that matures in three years. The dealer wants to fund the position overnight through the end of the next business day. The dealer could finance the transaction with its own funds, which is what other market participants, such as insurance companies or pension funds, may do in similar circumstances. But a securities dealer typically uses leverage (debt) to fund the position. Rather than borrowing from a bank, the dealer uses a repurchase agreement to obtain financing by using the gilt as collateral for the loan.

A repurchase agreement may be constructed as follows: The dealer sells the 2.25% UK gilt that matures in three years to a counterparty for cash today. At the same time, the dealer makes a promise to buy the same gilt the next business day for an agreed-on price. The price at which the dealer repurchases the gilt is known as the **repurchase price**. The date when the gilt is repurchased, the next business day in this example, is called the **repurchase date**. When the term of a repurchase agreement is one day, it is called an "overnight repo." When the agreement is for more than one day, it is called a "term repo." An agreement lasting until the final maturity date is known as a "repo to maturity."

As in any borrowing or lending transaction, the interest rate of the loan must be negotiated in the agreement. The interest rate on a repurchase agreement is called the **repo rate**. Several factors affect the repo rate:

- The *risk* associated with the collateral. Repo rates are typically lower for highly rated collaterals, such as highly rated sovereign bonds. They increase with the level of credit risk associated with the collateral underlying the transaction.
- The *term* of the repurchase agreement. Repo rates generally increase with maturity because long-term rates are typically higher than short-term rates in normal circumstances.
- The *delivery requirement* for the collateral. Repo rates are usually lower when delivery to the lender is required.
- The *supply and demand conditions* of the collateral. The more in demand a specific piece of collateral is, the lower the repo rate against it because the borrower has a security that lenders of cash want for specific reasons, perhaps because the underlying issue is in great demand. The demand for such collateral means that it considered to be "on special." Collateral that is not special is known as "general collateral." The party that has a need for collateral that is on special is typically required to lend funds at a below-market repo rate to obtain the collateral.
- The *interest rates of alternative financing* in the money market.

The interest on a repurchase agreement is paid on the repurchase date—that is, at the termination of the agreement. Note that any coupon paid by the security during the repurchase agreement belongs to the seller of the security (i.e., the borrower of cash).

When a repurchase agreement is viewed through the lens of the cash lending counterparty, the transaction is referred to as a **reverse repurchase agreement** or **reverse repo**. In the above example, the counterparty agrees to buy the 2.25% UK gilt that matures in three years and promises to sell it back the next business day at the agreed-on price. The counterparty is making a collateralized loan to the dealer. Reverse repurchase agreements are very often used to borrow securities to cover short positions.

The question of whether a particular transaction is labeled a repurchase agreement or a reverse repurchase agreement depends on one's point of view. Standard practice is to view the transaction from the dealer's perspective. If the dealer is borrowing cash from a counterparty and providing securities as collateral, the transaction is termed a repurchase agreement. If the dealer is borrowing securities and lending cash to the counterparty, the transaction is termed a reverse repurchase agreement.

8.3.2 *Credit Risk Associated with Repurchase Agreements*

Each market participant in a repurchase agreement is exposed to the risk that the counterparty defaults, regardless of the collateral exchanged. Credit risk is present even if the collateral is a highly rated sovereign bond. Suppose that a dealer (i.e., the borrower of cash) defaults and is not in a position to repurchase the collateral on the specified repurchase date. The lender of funds takes possession of the collateral and retains any income owed to the borrower. The risk is that the price of the collateral has fallen following the inception of the repurchase agreement, causing the market value of the collateral to be lower than the unpaid repurchase price. Conversely, suppose the investor (i.e., the lender of cash) defaults and is unable to deliver the collateral on the repurchase date. The risk is that the price of the collateral has risen since the inception of the repurchase agreement, resulting in the dealer now holding an amount of cash lower than the market value of the collateral. In this case, the investor is liable for any excess of the price paid by the dealer for replacement of the securities over the repurchase price.

Although both parties to a repurchase agreement are subject to credit risk, the agreement is structured as if the lender of funds is the most vulnerable party. Specifically, the amount lent is lower than the collateral's market value. The difference between the market value of the security used as collateral and the value of the loan is known as the **repo margin**, although the term **haircut** is more commonly used, particularly in the United States. The repo margin allows for some worsening in market value, and thus provides the cash lender a margin of safety if the collateral's market value declines. Repo margins vary by transaction and are negotiated bilaterally between the counterparties. The level of margin is a function of the following factors:

- The *length* of the repurchase agreement. The longer the repurchase agreement, the higher the repo margin.
- The *quality* of the collateral. The higher the quality of the collateral, the lower the repo margin.
- The *credit quality* of the counterparty. The higher the creditworthiness of the counterparty, the lower the repo margin.
- The *supply and demand conditions* of the collateral. Repo margins are lower if the collateral is in short supply or if there is a high demand for it.

EXAMPLE 8

Short-Term Funding Alternatives Available to Banks

1 Which of the following are **not** considered wholesale funds?

A Interbank funds

B Central bank funds

C Repurchase agreements

2 A large-denomination negotiable certificate of deposit *most likely*:

A is traded in the open market.

B is purchased by retail investors.

C has a penalty for early withdrawal of funds.

3 From the dealer's viewpoint, a repurchase agreement is *best* described as a type of:

A collateralized short-term lending.

B collateralized short-term borrowing.

C uncollateralized short-term borrowing.

4 The interest on a repurchase agreement is known as the:

A repo rate.

B repo yield.

C repo margin.

5 The level of repo margin is higher:

A the higher the quality of the collateral.

B the higher the credit quality of the counterparty.

C the longer the length of the repurchase agreement.

Solution to 1:

C is correct. Wholesale funds refer to the funds that financial institutions lend to and borrow from each other. They include central bank funds, interbank funds, and certificates of deposit. Although repurchase agreements are an important source of funding for banks, they are not considered wholesale funds.

Solution to 2:

A is correct. Large-denomination negotiable certificates of deposit (CDs) can be traded in the open market. B is incorrect because it is small-denomination, not large-denomination, negotiable CDs that are primarily purchased by retail investors. C is incorrect because it is non-negotiable, not negotiable, CDs that have a penalty for early withdrawal of funds.

Solution to 3:

B is correct. In a repurchase agreement, a security is sold with a simultaneous agreement by the seller to buy the same security back from the purchaser later at a higher price. Thus, a repurchase agreement is similar to a collateralized short-term borrowing in which the security sold and subsequently repurchased represents the collateral posted. A is incorrect because collateralized short-term lending is a description of a reverse repurchase agreement. C is incorrect because a repurchase agreement involves collateral. Thus, it is a collateralized, not uncollateralized, short-term borrowing.

Solution to 4:

A is correct. The repo rate is the interest rate on a repurchase agreement. B is incorrect because the interest on a repurchase agreement is known as the repo rate, not repo yield. C is incorrect because the repo margin refers to the difference between the market value of the security used as collateral and the value of the loan.

Solution to 5:

C is correct. The longer the length of the repurchase agreement, the higher the repo margin (haircut). A is incorrect because the higher the quality of the collateral, the lower the repo margin. B is incorrect because the higher the credit quality of the counterparty, the lower the repo margin.

SUMMARY

Debt financing is an important source of funds for households, governments, government-related entities, financial institutions, and non-financial companies. Well-functioning fixed-income markets help ensure that capital is allocated efficiently to its highest and best use globally. Important points include the following:

- The most widely used ways of classifying fixed-income markets include the type of issuer; the bonds' credit quality, maturity, currency denomination, and type of coupon; and where the bonds are issued and traded.
- Based on the type of issuer, the four major bond market sectors are the household, non-financial corporate, government, and financial institution sectors.
- Investors make a distinction between investment-grade and high-yield bond markets based on the issuer's credit quality.
- Money markets are where securities with original maturities ranging from overnight to one year are issued and traded, whereas capital markets are where securities with original maturities longer than one year are issued and traded.
- The majority of bonds are denominated in either euros or US dollars.
- Investors make a distinction between bonds that pay a fixed rate versus a floating rate of interest. The coupon rate of floating-rate bonds is often expressed as a reference rate plus a spread. Interbank offered rates, such as Libor, historically have been the most commonly used reference rates for floating-rate debt and other financial instruments but are being phased out to be replaced by alternative reference rates.
- Based on where the bonds are issued and traded, a distinction is made between domestic and international bond markets. The latter includes the Eurobond market, which falls outside the jurisdiction of any single country and is characterized by less reporting, regulatory and tax constraints. Investors also make a distinction between developed and emerging bond markets.
- Fixed-income indexes are used by investors and investment managers to describe bond markets or sectors and to evaluate performance of investments and investment managers.
- The largest investors in bonds include central banks; institutional investors, such as pension funds, hedge funds, charitable foundations and endowments, insurance companies, mutual funds and ETFs, and banks; and retail investors, typically by means of indirect investments.
- Primary markets are markets in which issuers first sell bonds to investors to raise capital. Secondary markets are markets in which existing bonds are subsequently traded among investors.

- There are two mechanisms for issuing a bond in primary markets: a public offering, in which any member of the public may buy the bonds, or a private placement, in which only an investor or small group of investors may buy the bonds either directly from the issuer or through an investment bank.
- Public bond issuing mechanisms include underwritten offerings, best effort offerings, shelf registrations, and auctions.
- When an investment bank underwrites a bond issue, it buys the entire issue and takes the risk of reselling it to investors or dealers. In contrast, in a best-efforts offering, the investment bank serves only as a broker and sells the bond issue only if it is able to do so. Underwritten and best effort offerings are frequently used in the issuance of corporate bonds.
- The underwriting process typically includes six phases: the determination of the funding needs, the selection of the underwriter, the structuring and announcement of the bond offering, pricing, issuance, and closing.
- A shelf registration is a method for issuing securities in which the issuer files a single document with regulators that describes and allows for a range of future issuances.
- An auction is a public offering method that involves bidding, and that is helpful in providing price discovery and in allocating securities. It is frequently used in the issuance of sovereign bonds.
- Most bonds are traded in over-the-counter (OTC) markets, and institutional investors are the major buyers and sellers of bonds in secondary markets.
- Sovereign bonds are issued by national governments primarily for fiscal reasons. They take different names and forms depending on where they are issued, their maturities, and their coupon types. Most sovereign bonds are fixed-rate bonds, although some national governments also issue floating-rate bonds and inflation-linked bonds.
- Local governments, quasi-government entities, and supranational agencies issue bonds, which are named non-sovereign, quasi-government, and supranational bonds, respectively.
- Companies raise debt in the form of bilateral loans, syndicated loans, commercial paper, notes, and bonds.
- Commercial paper is a short-term unsecured security that is used by companies as a source of short-term and bridge financing. Investors in commercial paper are exposed to credit risk, although defaults are rare. Many issuers roll over their commercial paper on a regular basis.
- Corporate bonds and notes take different forms depending on the maturities, coupon payment, and principal repayment structures. Important considerations also include collateral backing and contingency provisions.
- Medium-term notes are securities that are offered continuously to investors by an agent of the issuer. They can have short-term or long-term maturities.
- The structured finance sector includes asset-backed securities, collateralized debt obligations, and other structured financial instruments. All of these seemingly disparate financial instruments share the common attribute of repackaging risks.
- Many structured financial instruments are customized instruments that often combine a bond and at least one derivative. The redemption and often the coupons of these structured financial instruments are linked via a formula to the performance of the underlying asset(s). Thus, the bond's payment features are replaced with non-traditional payoffs that are derived not from the issuer's cash

flows but from the performance of the underlying asset(s). Capital protected, yield enhancement, participation and leveraged instruments are typical examples of structured financial instruments.

- Financial institutions have access to additional sources of funds, such as retail deposits, central bank funds, interbank funds, large-denomination negotiable certificates of deposit, and repurchase agreements.
- A repurchase agreement is similar to a collateralized loan. It involves the sale of a security (the collateral) with a simultaneous agreement by the seller (the borrower) to buy the same security back from the purchaser (the lender) at an agreed-on price in the future. Repurchase agreements are a common source of funding for dealer firms and are also used to borrow securities to implement short positions.

PRACTICE PROBLEMS

1 In most countries, the bond market sector with the smallest amount of bonds outstanding is *most likely* the:

A government sector.

B financial corporate sector.

C non-financial corporate sector.

2 The distinction between investment grade debt and non-investment grade debt is *best* described by differences in:

A tax status.

B credit quality.

C maturity dates.

3 A bond issued internationally, outside the jurisdiction of the country in whose currency the bond is denominated, is *best* described as a:

A Eurobond.

B foreign bond.

C municipal bond.

4 When classified by type of issuer, asset-backed securities are part of the:

A corporate sector.

B structured finance sector.

C government and government-related sector.

5 Compared with developed markets bonds, emerging markets bonds *most likely*:

A offer lower yields.

B exhibit higher risk.

C benefit from lower growth prospects.

6 With respect to floating-rate bonds, a reference rate such as the London interbank offered rate (Libor) is *most likely* used to determine the bond's:

A spread.

B coupon rate.

C frequency of coupon payments.

7 The variability of the coupon rate on a Libor-based floating-rate bond is *most likely* due to:

A periodic resets of the reference rate.

B market-based reassessments of the issuer's creditworthiness.

C changing estimates by the Libor administrator of borrowing capacity.

8 Which of the following statements is *most accurate*? An interbank offered rate:

A is a single reference rate.

B applies to borrowing periods of up to 10 years.

C is used as a reference rate for interest rate swaps.

9 An investment bank that underwrites a bond issue *most likely*:

A buys and resells the newly issued bonds to investors or dealers.

B acts as a broker and receives a commission for selling the bonds to investors.

C incurs less risk associated with selling the bonds than in a best efforts offering.

10 In major developed bond markets, newly issued sovereign bonds are *most* often sold to the public via a(n):

A auction.

B private placement.

C best efforts offering.

11 Which of the following describes privately placed bonds?

A They are non-underwritten and unregistered.

B They usually have active secondary markets.

C They are less customized than publicly offered bonds.

12 A mechanism by which an issuer may be able to offer additional bonds to the general public without preparing a new and separate offering circular *best* describes:

A the grey market.

B a shelf registration.

C a private placement.

13 Which of the following statements related to secondary bond markets is *most accurate*?

A Newly issued corporate bonds are issued in secondary bond markets.

B Secondary bond markets are where bonds are traded between investors.

C The major participants in secondary bond markets globally are retail investors.

14 A bond market in which a communications network matches buy and sell orders initiated from various locations is *best* described as an:

A organized exchange.

B open market operation.

C over-the-counter market.

15 A liquid secondary bond market allows an investor to sell a bond at:

A the desired price.

B a price at least equal to the purchase price.

C a price close to the bond's fair market value.

16 Corporate bond secondary market trading *most often* occurs:

A on a book-entry basis.

B on organized exchanges.

C prior to settlement at $T + 1$.

17 Sovereign bonds are *best* described as:

A bonds issued by local governments.

B secured obligations of a national government.

C bonds backed by the taxing authority of a national government.

18 Which factor is associated with a more favorable quality sovereign bond credit rating?

A Issued in local currency, only

B Strong domestic savings base, only

C Issued in local currency of country with strong domestic savings base

19 Which type of sovereign bond has the lowest interest rate risk for an investor?

A Floaters

B Coupon bonds

C Discount bonds

20 Agency bonds are issued by:

A local governments.

B national governments.

C quasi-government entities.

21 The type of bond issued by a multilateral agency such as the International Monetary Fund (IMF) is *best* described as a:

A sovereign bond.

B supranational bond.

C quasi-government bond.

22 A bond issued by a local government authority, typically without an explicit funding commitment from the national government, is *most likely* classified as a:

A sovereign bond.

B quasi-government bond

C non-sovereign government bond.

23 Which of the following statements relating to commercial paper is *most accurate*?

A There is no secondary market for trading commercial paper.

B Only the strongest, highly rated companies issue commercial paper.

C Commercial paper is a source of interim financing for long-term projects.

24 Eurocommerical paper is *most likely*:

A negotiable.

B denominated in euro.

C issued on a discount basis.

25 For the issuer, a sinking fund arrangement is *most similar* to a:

A term maturity structure.

B serial maturity structure.

C bondholder put provision.

26 When issuing debt, a company may use a sinking fund arrangement as a means of reducing:

A credit risk.

B inflation risk.

C interest rate risk.

27 Which of the following is a source of wholesale funds for banks?

A Demand deposits

B Money market accounts

C Negotiable certificates of deposit

28 A characteristic of negotiable certificates of deposit is:

A they are mostly available in small denominations.

B they can be sold in the open market prior to maturity.

C a penalty is imposed if the depositor withdraws funds prior to maturity.

29 A repurchase agreement is *most* comparable to a(n):

A interbank deposit.

B collateralized loan.

C negotiable certificate of deposit.

30 The repo margin is:

A negotiated between counterparties.

B established independently of market-related conditions.

C structured on an agreement assuming equal credit risks to all counterparties.

31 The repo margin on a repurchase agreement is *most likely* to be lower when:

A the underlying collateral is in short supply.

B the maturity of the repurchase agreement is long.

C the credit risk associated with the underlying collateral is high.

SOLUTIONS

1 C is correct. In most countries, the largest issuers of bonds are the national and local governments as well as financial institutions. Thus, the bond market sector with the smallest amount of bonds outstanding is the non-financial corporate sector.

2 B is correct. The distinction between investment grade and non-investment grade debt relates to differences in credit quality, not tax status or maturity dates. Debt markets are classified based on the issuer's creditworthiness as judged by the credit ratings agencies. Ratings of Baa3 or above by Moody's Investors Service or BBB– or above by Standard & Poor's and Fitch Ratings are considered investment grade, whereas ratings below these levels are referred to as non-investment grade (also called high yield, speculative, or junk).

3 A is correct. Eurobonds are issued internationally, outside the jurisdiction of any single country. B is incorrect because foreign bonds are considered international bonds, but they are issued in a specific country, in the currency of that country, by an issuer domiciled in another country. C is incorrect because municipal bonds are US domestic bonds issued by a state or local government.

4 B is correct. Asset-backed securities (ABS) are securitized debt instruments created by securitization, a process that involves transferring ownership of assets from the original owners to a special legal entity. The special legal entity then issues securities backed by the transferred assets. The assets' cash flows are used to pay interest and repay the principal owed to the holders of the securities. Assets that are typically used to create securitized debt instruments include loans (such as mortgage loans) and receivables (such as credit card receivables). The structured finance sector includes such securitized debt instruments (also called asset-backed securities).

5 B is correct. Many emerging countries lag developed countries in the areas of political stability, property rights, and contract enforcement. Consequently, emerging market bonds usually exhibit higher risk than developed markets bonds. A is incorrect because emerging markets bonds typically offer higher (not lower) yields than developed markets bonds to compensate investors for the higher risk. C is incorrect because emerging markets bonds usually benefit from higher (not lower) growth prospects than developed markets bonds.

6 B is correct. The coupon rate of a floating-rate bond is expressed as a reference rate plus a spread. Different reference rates are used depending on where the bond is issued and its currency denomination, but one of the most widely used set of reference rates is Libor. A and C are incorrect because a bond's spread and frequency of coupon payments are typically set when the bond is issued and do not change during the bond's life.

7 A is correct. Changes in the coupon rate of interest on a floating-rate bond that uses a Libor reference rate are due to changes in the reference rate (for example, 90-day Libor), which resets periodically. "Therefore, the coupon rate adjusts to the level of market interest rates (plus the spread) each time the reference rate is reset."

8 C is correct. Interbank offered rates are used as reference rates not only for floating-rate bonds, but also for other debt instruments including mortgages, derivatives such as interest rate and currency swaps, and many other financial contracts and products. A and B are incorrect because an interbank offered rate such as Libor or Euribor is a set of reference rates (not a single reference rate) for different borrowing periods of up to one year (not 10 years).

9 A is correct. In an underwritten offering (also called firm commitment offering), the investment bank (called the underwriter) guarantees the sale of the bond issue at an offering price that is negotiated with the issuer. Thus, the underwriter takes the risk of buying the newly issued bonds from the issuer, and then reselling them to investors or to dealers who then sell them to investors. B and C are incorrect because the bond issuing mechanism where an investment bank acts as a broker and receives a commission for selling the bonds to investors, and incurs less risk associated with selling the bonds, is a best efforts offering (not an underwritten offering).

10 A is correct. In major developed bond markets, newly issued sovereign bonds are sold to the public via an auction. B and C are incorrect because sovereign bonds are rarely issued via private placements or best effort offerings.

11 A is correct. Private placements are typically non-underwritten, unregistered bond offerings that are sold only to a single investor or a small group of investors.

12 B is correct. A shelf registration allows certain authorized issuers to offer additional bonds to the general public without having to prepare a new and separate offering circular. The issuer can offer multiple bond issuances under the same master prospectus, and only has to prepare a short document when additional bonds are issued. A is incorrect because the grey market is a forward market for bonds about to be issued. C is incorrect because a private placement is a non-underwritten, unregistered offering of bonds that are not sold to the general public but directly to an investor or a small group of investors.

13 B is correct. Secondary bond markets are where bonds are traded between investors. A is incorrect because newly issued bonds (whether from corporate issuers or other types of issuers) are issued in primary (not secondary) bond markets. C is incorrect because the major participants in secondary bond markets globally are large institutional investors and central banks (not retail investors).

14 C is correct. In over-the-counter (OTC) markets, buy and sell orders are initiated from various locations and then matched through a communications network. Most bonds are traded in OTC markets. A is incorrect because on organized exchanges, buy and sell orders may come from anywhere, but the transactions must take place at the exchange according to the rules imposed by the exchange. B is incorrect because open market operations refer to central bank activities in secondary bond markets. Central banks buy and sell bonds, usually sovereign bonds issued by the national government, as a means to implement monetary policy.

15 C is correct. Liquidity in secondary bond markets refers to the ability to buy or sell bonds quickly at prices close to their fair market value. A and B are incorrect because a liquid secondary bond market does not guarantee that a bond will sell at the price sought by the investor, or that the investor will not face a loss on his or her investment.

16 A is correct. The vast majority of corporate bonds are traded in over-the-counter (OTC) markets that use electronic trading platforms through which users submit buy and sell orders. Settlement of trades in the OTC markets occurs by means of a simultaneous exchange of bonds for cash on the books of the clearing system "on a paperless, computerized book-entry basis."

17 C is correct. Sovereign bonds are usually unsecured obligations of the national government issuing the bonds; they are not backed by collateral, but by the taxing authority of the national government. A is incorrect because bonds issued by local governments are non-sovereign (not sovereign) bonds. B is incorrect because sovereign bonds are typically unsecured (not secured) obligations of a national government.

18 C is correct. Bonds issued in the sovereign's currency and a strong domestic savings base are both favorable sovereign rating factors. It is common to observe a higher credit rating for sovereign bonds issued in local currency because of the sovereign's ability to tax its citizens and print its own currency. Although there are practical limits to the sovereign's taxing and currency-printing capacities, each tends to support a sovereign's ability to repay debt. A strong domestic savings base is advantageous because it supports the sovereign's ability to issue debt in local currency to domestic investors.

19 A is correct. Floaters are bonds with a floating rate of interest that resets periodically based on changes in the level of a reference rate, such as Libor. Because changes in the reference rate reflect changes in market interest rates, price changes of floaters are far less pronounced than those of fixed-rate bonds, such as coupon bonds and discount bonds. Thus, investors holding floaters are less exposed to interest rate risk than investors holding fixed-rate discount or coupon bonds.

20 C is correct. Agency bonds are issued by quasi-government entities. These entities are agencies and organizations usually established by national governments to perform various functions for them. A and B are incorrect because local and national governments issue non-sovereign and sovereign bonds, respectively.

21 B is correct. The IMF is a multilateral agency that issues supranational bonds. A and C are incorrect because sovereign bonds and quasi-government bonds are issued by national governments and by entities that perform various functions for national governments, respectively.

22 C is correct. Bonds issued by levels of government below the national level—such as provinces, regions, states, cities, and local government authorities—are classified as non-sovereign government bonds. These bonds are typically not guaranteed by the national government.

23 C is correct. Companies use commercial paper not only as a source of funding working capital and seasonal demand for cash, but also as a source of interim financing for long-term projects until permanent financing can be arranged. A is incorrect because there is a secondary market for trading commercial paper, although trading is limited except for the largest issues. B is incorrect because commercial paper is issued by companies across the risk spectrum, although only the strongest, highly rated companies issue *low-cost* commercial paper.

24 A is correct. Commercial paper, whether US commercial paper or Eurocommercial paper, is negotiable—that is, investors can buy and sell commercial paper on secondary markets. B is incorrect because Eurocommercial paper can be denominated in any currency. C is incorrect because Eurocommercial paper may be issued on an interest-bearing (or yield) basis or a discount basis.

25 B is correct. With a serial maturity structure, a stated number of bonds mature and are paid off on a pre-determined schedule before final maturity. With a sinking fund arrangement, the issuer is required to set aside funds over time to retire the bond issue. Both result in a pre-determined portion of the issue being paid off according to a pre-determined schedule.

26 A is correct. A sinking fund arrangement is a way to reduce credit risk by making the issuer set aside funds over time to retire the bond issue. B and C are incorrect because a sinking fund arrangement has no effect on inflation risk or interest rate risk.

27 C is correct. Wholesale funds available for banks include central bank funds, interbank funds, and negotiable certificates of deposit. A and B are incorrect because demand deposits (also known as checking accounts) and money market accounts are retail deposits (not wholesale funds).

28 B is correct. A negotiable certificate of deposit (CD) allows any depositor (initial or subsequent) to sell the CD in the open market prior to maturity. A is incorrect because negotiable CDs are mostly available in large (not small) denominations. Large-denomination negotiable CDs are an important source of wholesale funds for banks, whereas small-denomination CDs are not. C is incorrect because a penalty is imposed if the depositor withdraws funds prior to maturity for non-negotiable (instead of negotiable) CDs.

29 B is correct. A repurchase agreement (repo) can be viewed as a collateralized loan where the security sold and subsequently repurchased represents the collateral posted. A and C are incorrect because interbank deposits and negotiable certificates of deposit are unsecured deposits—that is, there is no collateral backing the deposit.

30 A is correct. Repo margins vary by transaction and are negotiated bilaterally between the counterparties.

31 A is correct. The repo margin (the difference between the market value of the underlying collateral and the value of the loan) is a function of the supply and demand conditions of the collateral. The repo margin is typically lower if the underlying collateral is in short supply or if there is a high demand for it. B and C are incorrect because the repo margin is usually higher (not lower) when the maturity of the repurchase agreement is long and when the credit risk associated with the underlying collateral is high.

READING

44

Introduction to Fixed-Income Valuation

by James F. Adams, PhD, CFA, and Donald J. Smith, PhD

James F. Adams, PhD, CFA, is at J.P. Morgan (USA). Donald J. Smith, PhD, is at Boston University Questrom School of Business (USA).

LEARNING OUTCOMES

Mastery	*The candidate should be able to:*
☐	a. calculate a bond's price given a market discount rate;
☐	b. identify the relationships among a bond's price, coupon rate, maturity, and market discount rate (yield-to-maturity);
☐	c. define spot rates and calculate the price of a bond using spot rates;
☐	d. describe and calculate the flat price, accrued interest, and the full price of a bond;
☐	e. describe matrix pricing;
☐	f. calculate annual yield on a bond for varying compounding periods in a year;
☐	g. calculate and interpret yield measures for fixed-rate bonds and floating-rate notes;
☐	h. calculate and interpret yield measures for money market instruments;
☐	i. define and compare the spot curve, yield curve on coupon bonds, par curve, and forward curve;
☐	j. define forward rates and calculate spot rates from forward rates, forward rates from spot rates, and the price of a bond using forward rates;
☐	k. compare, calculate, and interpret yield spread measures.

INTRODUCTION

1

Globally, the fixed-income market is a key source of financing for businesses and governments. In fact, the total market value outstanding of corporate and government bonds is significantly larger than that of equity securities. Similarly, the fixed-income market, which is also called the debt market or bond market, represents a significant investing opportunity for institutions as well as individuals. Pension funds, mutual funds, insurance companies, and sovereign wealth funds, among others, are major fixed-income investors. Retirees who desire a relatively stable income stream often hold fixed-income securities. Clearly, understanding how to value fixed-income securities is important to investors, issuers, and financial analysts. This reading focuses on the valuation of traditional (option-free) fixed-rate bonds, although other debt securities, such as floating-rate notes and money market instruments, are also covered.

Section 2 describes and illustrates basic bond valuation, which includes pricing a bond using a market discount rate for each of the future cash flows and pricing a bond using a series of spot rates. Valuation using spot rates allows for each future cash flow to be discounted at a rate associated with its timing. This valuation methodology for future cash flows has applications well beyond the fixed-income market. Relationships among a bond's price, coupon rate, maturity, and market discount rate (yield-to-maturity) are also described and illustrated.

Section 3 describes how bond prices and yields are quoted and calculated in practice. When bonds are actively traded, investors can observe the price and calculate various yield measures. However, these yield measures differ by the type of bond. In practice, different measures are used for fixed-rate bonds, floating-rate notes, and money market instruments. When a bond is not actively traded, matrix pricing is often used to estimate the value based on comparable securities.

Section 4 addresses the maturity or term structure of interest rates. This discussion involves an analysis of yield curves, which illustrates the relationship between yields-to-maturity and times-to-maturity on bonds with otherwise similar characteristics. Various types of yield curves are described.

Section 5 focuses on yield spreads over benchmark interest rates. When investors want relatively higher yields, they have to be prepared to bear more risk. Yield spreads are measures of how much additional yield over the benchmark security (usually a government bond) investors expect for bearing additional risk. A summary of key points and practice problems conclude the reading.

2 BOND PRICES AND THE TIME VALUE OF MONEY

Bond pricing is an application of discounted cash flow analysis. The complexity of the pricing depends on the particular bond's features and rate (or rates) used to do the discounting. This section starts with using a single discount factor for all future cash flows and concludes with the most general approach to bond valuation. The general approach to bond valuation is to use a series of spot rates that correspond to the timing of the future cash flows.

2.1 Bond Pricing with a Market Discount Rate

On a traditional (option-free) fixed-rate bond, the promised future cash flows are a series of coupon interest payments and repayment of the full principal at maturity. The coupon payments are on regularly scheduled dates, for example, an annual payment bond might pay interest on 15 June of each year for five years. The final coupon typically is paid together with the full principal on the maturity date. The price of the bond at issuance is the present value of the promised cash flows. The **market discount rate** is used in the time-value-of-money calculation to obtain the present value. The market discount rate is the rate of return required by investors given the risk of the investment in the bond. It is also called the **required yield**, or the **required rate of return**.

For example, suppose the coupon rate on a bond is 4% and the payment is made once a year. If the time-to-maturity is five years and the market discount rate is 6%, the price of the bond is 91.575 per 100 of **par value**. The par value is the amount of principal on the bond.

$$\frac{4}{(1.06)^1} + \frac{4}{(1.06)^2} + \frac{4}{(1.06)^3} + \frac{4}{(1.06)^4} + \frac{104}{(1.06)^5} =$$

$$3.774 + 3.560 + 3.358 + 3.168 + 77.715 = 91.575$$

The final cash flow of 104 is the redemption of principal (100) plus the coupon payment for that date (4). The price of the bond is the sum of the present values of the five cash flows. The price per 100 of par value may be interpreted as the percentage of par value. If the par value is USD100,000, the coupon payments are USD4,000 each year and the price of the bond is USD91,575. Its price is 91.575% of par value. This bond is described as trading at a **discount** because the price is below par value.

Suppose that another five-year bond has a coupon rate of 8% paid annually. If the market discount rate is again 6%, the price of the bond is 108.425.

$$\frac{8}{(1.06)^1} + \frac{8}{(1.06)^2} + \frac{8}{(1.06)^3} + \frac{8}{(1.06)^4} + \frac{108}{(1.06)^5} =$$

$$7.547 + 7.120 + 6.717 + 6.337 + 80.704 = 108.425$$

This bond is trading at a **premium** because its price is above par value.

If another five-year bond pays a 6% annual coupon and the market discount rate still is 6%, the bond would trade at par value.

$$\frac{6}{(1.06)^1} + \frac{6}{(1.06)^2} + \frac{6}{(1.06)^3} + \frac{6}{(1.06)^4} + \frac{106}{(1.06)^5} =$$

$$5.660 + 5.340 + 5.038 + 4.753 + 79.209 = 100.000$$

The coupon rate indicates the amount the issuer promises to pay the bondholders each year in interest. The market discount rate reflects the amount investors need to receive in interest each year in order to pay full par value for the bond. Therefore, assuming that these three bonds have the same risk, which is consistent with them having the same market discount rate, the 4% bond offers a "deficient" coupon rate. The amount of the discount below par value is the present value of the deficiency, which is 2% of par value each year. The present value of the deficiency, discounted using the market discount rate, is –8.425.

$$\frac{-2}{(1.06)^1} + \frac{-2}{(1.06)^2} + \frac{-2}{(1.06)^3} + \frac{-2}{(1.06)^4} + \frac{-2}{(1.06)^5} = -8.425$$

The price of the 4% coupon bond is 91.575 (= 100 – 8.425). In the same manner, the 8% bond offers an "excessive" coupon rate given the risk because investors require only 6%. The amount of the premium is the present value of the excess cash flows, which is +8.425. The price of the 8% bond is 108.425 (= 100 + 8.425).

These examples demonstrate that the price of a fixed-rate bond, relative to par value, depends on the relationship of the coupon rate to the market discount rate. Here is a summary of the relationships:

- When the coupon rate is less than the market discount rate, the bond is priced at a discount below par value.
- When the coupon rate is greater than the market discount rate, the bond is priced at a premium above par value.
- When the coupon rate is equal to the market discount rate, the bond is priced at par value.

At this point, it is assumed that the bond is priced on a coupon payment date. If the bond is between coupon payment dates, the price paid will include accrued interest, which is interest that has been earned but not yet paid. Accrued interest is discussed in detail in Section 3.1.

Equation 1 is a general formula for calculating a bond price given the market discount rate:

$$PV = \frac{PMT}{(1+r)^1} + \frac{PMT}{(1+r)^2} + \cdots + \frac{PMT + FV}{(1+r)^N} \quad (1)$$

where

PV = present value, or the price of the bond
PMT = coupon payment per period
FV = future value paid at maturity, or the par value of the bond
r = market discount rate, or required rate of return per period
N = number of evenly spaced periods to maturity

The examples so far have been for an annual payment bond, which is the convention for most European bonds. Asian and North American bonds generally make semiannual payments, and the stated rate is the annual coupon rate. Suppose the coupon rate on a bond is stated to be 8% and the payments are made twice a year (semiannually) on 15 June and 15 December. For each 100 in par value (FV = 100), the coupon payment per period is 4 (PMT = 4). If there are three years to maturity, there are six evenly spaced semiannual periods (N = 6). If the market discount rate is 3% per semiannual period (r = 0.03), the price of the bond is 105.417 per 100 of par value.

$$\frac{4}{(1.03)^1} + \frac{4}{(1.03)^2} + \frac{4}{(1.03)^3} + \frac{4}{(1.03)^4} + \frac{4}{(1.03)^5} + \frac{104}{(1.03)^6} = 105.417$$

If the actual par value of the bond investment is in Singapore dollars—for instance, SGD 100,000—the price is SGD 105,417. This bond is trading at a premium above par value because the coupon rate of 4% *per period* is greater than the market discount rate of 3% *per period*. Usually, those interest rates are annualized by multiplying the rate per period by the number of periods in a year. Therefore, an equivalent statement is that the bond is priced at a premium because its stated *annual* coupon rate of 8% is greater than the stated *annual* market discount rate of 6%. Interest rates, unless stated otherwise, are typically quoted as annual rates.

EXAMPLE 1

Bonds Trading at a Discount, at a Premium, and at Par

Identify whether each of the following bonds is trading at a discount, at par value, or at a premium. Calculate the prices of the bonds per 100 in par value using Equation 1. If the coupon rate is deficient or excessive compared with the market discount rate, calculate the amount of the deficiency or excess per 100 of par value.

Bond	Coupon Payment per Period	Number of Periods to Maturity	Market Discount Rate per Period
A	2	6	3%
B	6	4	4%

Bond	Coupon Payment per Period	Number of Periods to Maturity	Market Discount Rate per Period
C	5	5	5%
D	0	10	2%

Solutions:

Bond A

$$\frac{2}{(1.03)^1}+\frac{2}{(1.03)^2}+\frac{2}{(1.03)^3}+\frac{2}{(1.03)^4}+\frac{2}{(1.03)^5}+\frac{102}{(1.03)^6}=94.583$$

Bond A is trading at a discount. Its price is below par value because the coupon rate per period (2%) is less than the required yield per period (3%). The deficiency per period is the coupon rate minus the market discount rate, times the par value: (0.02 – 0.03) × 100 = –1. The present value of deficiency is –5.417, discounted using the required yield (market discount rate) per period.

$$\frac{-1}{(1.03)^1}+\frac{-1}{(1.03)^2}+\frac{-1}{(1.03)^3}+\frac{-1}{(1.03)^4}+\frac{-1}{(1.03)^5}+\frac{-1}{(1.03)^6}=-5.417$$

The amount of the deficiency can be used to calculate the price of the bond; the price is 94.583 (= 100 – 5.417).

Bond B

$$\frac{6}{(1.04)^1}+\frac{6}{(1.04)^2}+\frac{6}{(1.04)^3}+\frac{106}{(1.04)^4}=107.260$$

Bond B is trading at a premium because the coupon rate per period (6%) is greater than the market discount rate per period (4%). The excess per period is the coupon rate minus market discount rate, times the par value: (0.06 – 0.04) × 100 = +2. The present value of excess is +7.260, discounted using the required yield per period.

$$\frac{2}{(1.04)^1}+\frac{2}{(1.04)^2}+\frac{2}{(1.04)^3}+\frac{2}{(1.04)^4}=7.260$$

The price of the bond is 107.260 (= 100 + 7.260).

Bond C

$$\frac{5}{(1.05)^1}+\frac{5}{(1.05)^2}+\frac{5}{(1.05)^3}+\frac{5}{(1.05)^4}+\frac{105}{(1.05)^5}=100.000$$

Bond C is trading at par value because the coupon rate is equal to the market discount rate. The coupon payments are neither excessive nor deficient given the risk of the bond.

Bond D

$$\frac{100}{(1.02)^{10}}=82.035$$

Bond D is a zero-coupon bond, which always will trade at a discount below par value (as long as the required yield is greater than zero). The deficiency in the coupon payments is –2 per period: (0 – 0.02) × 100 = –2.

$$\frac{-2}{(1.02)^1}+\frac{-2}{(1.02)^2}+\frac{-2}{(1.02)^3}+\frac{-2}{(1.02)^4}+\frac{-2}{(1.02)^5}+$$
$$\frac{-2}{(1.02)^6}+\frac{-2}{(1.02)^7}+\frac{-2}{(1.02)^8}+\frac{-2}{(1.02)^9}+\frac{-2}{(1.02)^{10}}=-17.965$$

The price of the bond is 82.035 (= 100 – 17.965).

2.2 Yield-to-Maturity

If the market price of a bond is known, Equation 1 can be used to calculate its **yield-to-maturity** (sometimes called the redemption yield or yield-to-redemption). The yield-to-maturity is the internal rate of return on the cash flows—the uniform interest rate such that when the future cash flows are discounted at that rate, the sum of the present values equals the price of the bond. It is the *implied* market discount rate.

The yield-to-maturity is the rate of return on the bond to an investor given three critical assumptions:

1 The investor holds the bond to maturity.

2 The issuer makes all of the coupon and principal payments in the full amount on the scheduled dates. Therefore, the yield-to-maturity is the *promised* yield—the yield assuming the issuer does not default on any of the payments.

3 The investor is able to reinvest coupon payments at that same yield. This is a characteristic of an internal rate of return.

For example, suppose that a four-year, 5% annual coupon payment bond is priced at 105 per 100 of par value. The yield-to-maturity is the solution for the rate, r, in this equation:

$$105=\frac{5}{(1+r)^1}+\frac{5}{(1+r)^2}+\frac{5}{(1+r)^3}+\frac{105}{(1+r)^4}$$

Solving by trial-and-error search, or using the time-value-of-money keys on a financial calculator, obtains the result that r = 0.03634. The bond trades at a premium because its coupon rate (5%) is greater than the yield that is required by investors (3.634%).

Yields-to-maturity do not depend on the actual amount of par value in a fixed-income portfolio. For example, suppose a Japanese institutional investor owns a three-year, 2.5% semiannual payment bond having a par value of JPY100 million. The bond currently is priced at JPY98,175,677. The yield per semiannual period can be obtained by solving this equation for r:

$$98.175677=\frac{1.25}{(1+r)^1}+\frac{1.25}{(1+r)^2}+\frac{1.25}{(1+r)^3}+\frac{1.25}{(1+r)^4}+\frac{1.25}{(1+r)^5}+\frac{101.25}{(1+r)^6}$$

The yield per semiannual period turns out to be 1.571% (r = 0.01571), which can be annualized to be 3.142% (0.01571 × 2 = 0.03142). In general, a three-year, 2.5% semiannual bond for *any* amount of par value has an annualized yield-to-maturity of 3.142% if it is priced at 98.175677% of par value.

EXAMPLE 2

Yields-to-Maturity for a Premium, Discount, and Zero-Coupon Bond

Calculate the yields-to-maturity for the following bonds. The prices are stated per 100 of par value.

Bond	Coupon Payment per Period	Number of Periods to Maturity	Price
A	3.5	4	103.75
B	2.25	6	96.50
C	0	60	22.375

Solutions:

Bond A

$$103.75 = \frac{3.5}{(1+r)^1} + \frac{3.5}{(1+r)^2} + \frac{3.5}{(1+r)^3} + \frac{103.5}{(1+r)^4}, \quad r = 0.02503$$

Bond A is trading at a premium, so its yield-to-maturity per period (2.503%) must be lower than its coupon rate per period (3.5%).

Bond B

$$96.50 = \frac{2.25}{(1+r)^1} + \frac{2.25}{(1+r)^2} + \frac{2.25}{(1+r)^3} + \frac{2.25}{(1+r)^4} + \frac{2.25}{(1+r)^5} + \frac{102.25}{(1+r)^6}, \quad r = 0.02894$$

Bond B is trading at a discount, so the yield-to-maturity per period (2.894%) must be higher than the coupon rate per period (2.25%).

Bond C

$$22.375 = \frac{100}{(1+r)^{60}}, \quad r = 0.02527$$

Bond C is a zero-coupon bond trading at a significant discount below par value. Its yield-to-maturity is 2.527% per period.

2.3 Relationships between the Bond Price and Bond Characteristics

The price of a fixed-rate bond will change whenever the market discount rate changes. Four relationships about the change in the bond price given the market discount rate are:

1 The bond price is inversely related to the market discount rate. When the market discount rate increases, the bond price decreases (the inverse effect).

2 For the same coupon rate and time-to-maturity, the percentage price change is greater (in absolute value, meaning without regard to the sign of the change) when the market discount rate goes down than when it goes up (the convexity effect).

3 For the same time-to-maturity, a lower-coupon bond has a greater percentage price change than a higher-coupon bond when their market discount rates change by the same amount (the coupon effect).

4 Generally, for the same coupon rate, a longer-term bond has a greater percentage price change than a shorter-term bond when their market discount rates change by the same amount (the maturity effect).

Exhibit 1 illustrates these relationships using nine annual coupon payment bonds. The bonds have different coupon rates and times-to-maturity but otherwise are the same in terms of risk. The coupon rates are 10%, 20%, and 30% for bonds having 10, 20, and 30 years to maturity. At first, the bonds are all priced at a market discount rate of 20%. Equation 1 is used to determine the prices. Then the market discount rate is decreased by 1 percentage point, from 20% to 19%, and next, it is increased from 20% to 21%.

Exhibit 1 Relationships between Bond Prices and Bond Characteristics

				Discount Rates Go Down		Discount Rates Go Up	
Bond	Coupon Rate	Maturity	Price at 20%	Price at 19%	% Change	Price at 21%	% Change
A	10.00%	10	58.075	60.950	4.95%	55.405	−4.60%
B	20.00%	10	100.000	104.339	4.34%	95.946	−4.05%
C	30.00%	10	141.925	147.728	4.09%	136.487	−3.83%
D	10.00%	20	51.304	54.092	5.43%	48.776	−4.93%
E	20.00%	20	100.000	105.101	5.10%	95.343	−4.66%
F	30.00%	20	148.696	156.109	4.99%	141.910	−4.56%
G	10.00%	30	50.211	52.888	5.33%	47.791	−4.82%
H	20.00%	30	100.000	105.235	5.23%	95.254	−4.75%
I	30.00%	30	149.789	157.581	5.20%	142.716	−4.72%

The first relationship is that the bond price and the market discount rate move inversely. All bond prices in Exhibit 1 go up when the rates go down from 20% to 19%, and all prices go down when the rates go up from 20% to 21%. This happens because of the fixed cash flows on a fixed-rate bond. The numerators in Equation 1 do not change when the market discount rate in the denominators rises or falls. Therefore, the price (PV) moves inversely with the market discount rate (r).

The second relationship reflects the convexity effect. In Exhibit 1, the percentage price changes are calculated using this equation:

$$\%\ \text{Change} = \frac{\text{New price} - \text{Old price}}{\text{Old price}}$$

For example, when the market discount rate falls on Bond A, the price rises from 58.075 to 60.950. The percentage price increase is 4.95%.

$$\%\ \text{Change} = \frac{60.950 - 58.075}{58.075} = 0.0495$$

For each bond, the percentage price increases are greater in *absolute value* than the percentage price decreases. This implies that the relationship between bond prices and the market discount rate is not linear; instead, it is curved. It is described as being "convex." The convexity effect is shown in Exhibit 2 for a 10%, 10-year bond.

Exhibit 2 The Convex Relationship between the Market Discount Rate and the Price of a 10-Year, 10% Annual Coupon Payment Bond

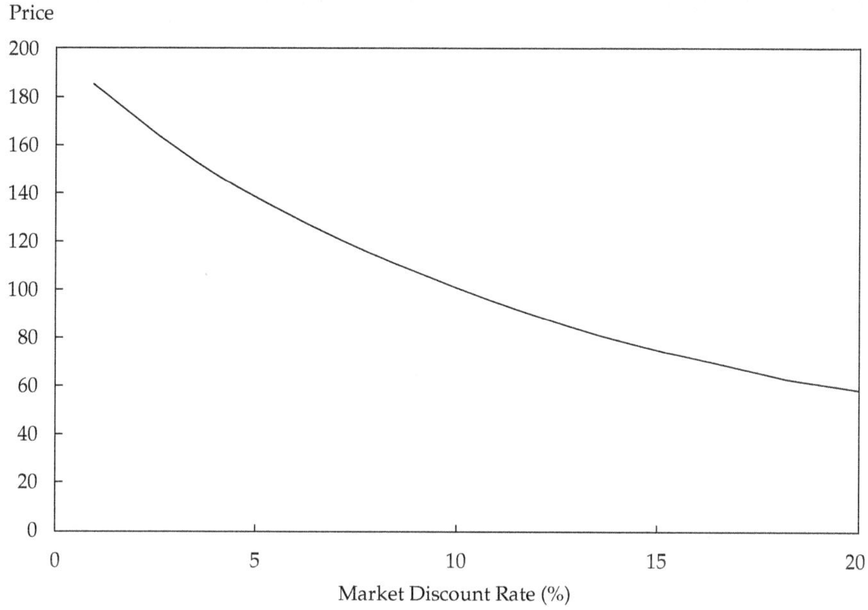

The third relationship is the coupon effect. Consider Bonds A, B, and C, which have 10 years to maturity. For both the decrease and increase in the yield-to-maturity, Bond A has a larger percentage price change than Bond B, and Bond B has a larger change than C. The same pattern holds for the 20-year and 30-year bonds. Therefore, lower-coupon bonds have more price volatility than higher-coupon bonds, other things being equal.

The fourth relationship is the maturity effect. Compare the results for Bonds A and D, for Bonds B and E, and for Bonds C and F. The 20-year bonds have greater percentage price changes than the 10-year bonds for either an increase or a decrease in the market discount rate. In general, longer-term bonds have more price volatility than shorter-term bonds, other things being equal.

There are exceptions to the maturity effect. That is why the word "generally" appears in the statement of the relationship at the beginning of this section. Compare the results in Exhibit 1 for Bonds D and G, for Bonds E and H, and for Bonds F and I. For the higher-coupon bonds trading at a premium, Bonds F and I, the usual property holds—the 30-year bonds have greater percentage price changes than the 20-year bonds. The same pattern holds for Bonds E and H, which are priced initially at par value. The exception is illustrated in the results for Bonds D and G, which are priced at a discount because the coupon rate is lower than the market discount rate. The 20-year, 10% bond has a greater percentage price change than the 30-year, 10% bond. Exceptions to the maturity effect are rare in practice. They occur only for low-coupon (but not zero-coupon), long-term bonds trading at a discount. The maturity effect always holds on zero-coupon bonds, as it does for bonds priced at par value or at a premium above par value.

One final point to note in Exhibit 1 is that Bonds B, E, and H, which have coupon rates of 20%, all trade at par value when the market discount rate is 20%. A bond having a coupon rate equal to the market discount rate is priced at par value on a coupon payment date, regardless of the number of years to maturity.

EXAMPLE 3

Bond Percentage Price Changes Based on Coupon and Time-to-Maturity

An investor is considering the following six annual coupon payment government bonds:

Bond	Coupon Rate	Time-to-Maturity	Yield-to-Maturity
A	0%	2 years	5.00%
B	5%	2 years	5.00%
C	8%	2 years	5.00%
D	0%	4 years	5.00%
E	5%	4 years	5.00%
F	8%	4 years	5.00%

1 Based on the relationships between bond prices and bond characteristics, which bond will go up in price the *most* on a percentage basis if all yields go down from 5.00% to 4.90%?

2 Based on the relationships between the bond prices and bond characteristics, which bond will go down in price the *least* on a percentage basis if all yields go up from 5.00% to 5.10%?

Solution to 1:

Bond D will go up in price the most on a percentage basis because it has the lowest coupon rate (the coupon effect) and the longer time-to-maturity (the maturity effect). There is no exception to the maturity effect in these bonds because there are no low-coupon bonds trading at a discount.

Solution to 2:

Bond C will go down in price the least on a percentage basis because it has the highest coupon rate (the coupon effect) and the shorter time-to-maturity (the maturity effect). There is no exception to the maturity effect because Bonds C and F are priced at a premium above par value.

Exhibit 2 demonstrates the impact on a bond price assuming the time-to-maturity does not change. It shows an *instantaneous* change in the market discount rate from one moment to the next.

But bond prices change as time passes even if the market discount rate remains the same. As time passes, the bondholder comes closer to receiving the par value at maturity. The **constant-yield price trajectory** illustrates the change in the price of a fixed-income bond over time. This trajectory shows the "pull to par" effect on the price of a bond trading at a premium or a discount to par value. If the issuer does not default, the price of a bond approaches par value as its time-to-maturity approaches zero.

Exhibit 3 shows the constant-yield price trajectories for 4% and 12% annual coupon payment, 10-year bonds. Both bonds have a market discount rate of 8%. The 4% bond's initial price is 73.160 per 100 of par value. The price increases each year and approaches par value as the maturity date nears. The 12% bond's initial price is 126.840, and it decreases each year, approaching par value as the maturity date nears. Both prices are "pulled to par."

Exhibit 3 Constant-Yield Price Trajectories for 4% and 12% Annual Coupon Payment, 10-Year Bonds at a Market Discount Rate of 8%

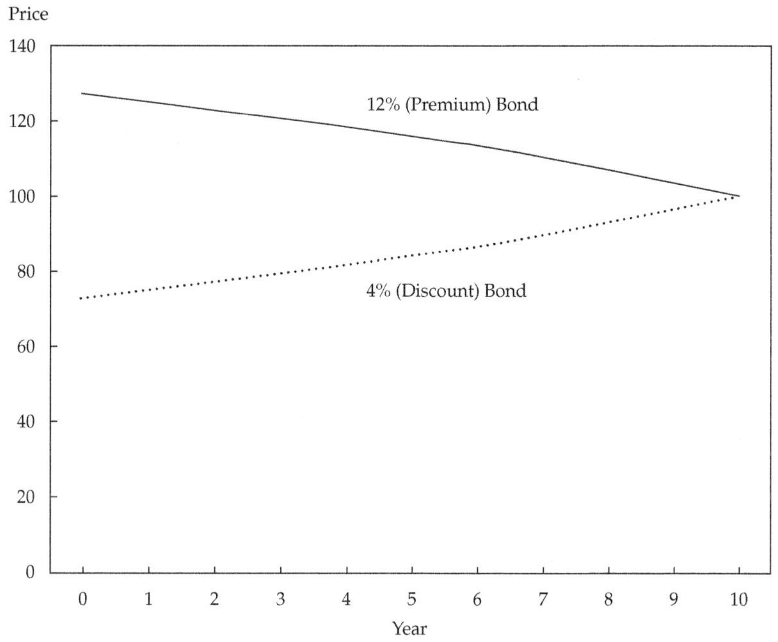

	0	1	2	3	4	5	6	7	8	9	10
Discount Bond	73.160	75.012	77.013	79.175	81.508	84.029	86.751	89.692	92.867	96.296	100.00
Premium Bond	126.84	124.98	122.98	120.82	118.49	115.97	113.24	110.30	107.13	103.70	100.00

2.4 Pricing Bonds with Spot Rates

When a fixed-rate bond is priced using the market discount rate, the same discount rate is used for each cash flow. A more fundamental approach to calculate the price of a bond is to use a sequence of market discount rates that correspond to the cash flow dates. These market discount rates are called **spot rates**. Spot rates are yields-to-maturity on zero-coupon bonds maturing at the date of each cash flow. Sometimes these are called "zero rates." Bond price (or value) determined using the spot rates is sometimes referred to as the bond's "no-arbitrage value." If a bond's price differs from its no-arbitrage value, an arbitrage opportunity exists in the absence of transaction costs.

Suppose that the one-year spot rate is 2%, the two-year spot rate is 3%, and the three-year spot rate is 4%. Then, the price of a three-year bond that makes a 5% annual coupon payment is 102.960.

$$\frac{5}{(1.02)^1} + \frac{5}{(1.03)^2} + \frac{105}{(1.04)^3} =$$

$$4.902 + 4.713 + 93.345 = 102.960$$

This three-year bond is priced at a premium above par value, so its yield-to-maturity must be less than 5%. Using Equation 1, the yield-to-maturity is 3.935%.

$$102.960 = \frac{5}{(1+r)^1} + \frac{5}{(1+r)^2} + \frac{105}{(1+r)^3}, \quad r = 0.03935$$

When the coupon and principal cash flows are discounted using the yield-to-maturity, the same price is obtained.

$$\frac{5}{(1.03935)^1} + \frac{5}{(1.03935)^2} + \frac{105}{(1.03935)^3} =$$

$$4.811 + 4.629 + 93.520 = 102.960$$

Notice that the present values of the individual cash flows discounted using spot rates differ from those using the yield-to-maturity. The present value of the first coupon payment is 4.902 when discounted at 2%, but it is 4.811 when discounted at 3.935%. The present value of the final cash flow, which includes the redemption of principal, is 93.345 at 4% and 93.520 at 3.935%. Nevertheless, the sum of the present values using either approach is 102.960.

Equation 2 is a general formula for calculating a bond price given the sequence of spot rates:

$$PV = \frac{PMT}{(1+Z_1)^1} + \frac{PMT}{(1+Z_2)^2} + \cdots + \frac{PMT + FV}{(1+Z_N)^N} \tag{2}$$

where

Z_1 = spot rate, or the zero-coupon yield, or zero rate, for Period 1

Z_2 = spot rate, or the zero-coupon yield, or zero rate, for Period 2

Z_N = spot rate, or the zero-coupon yield, or zero rate, for Period N

EXAMPLE 4

Bond Prices and Yields-to-Maturity Based on Spot Rates

Calculate the price (per 100 of par value) and the yield-to-maturity for a four-year, 3% annual coupon payment bond given the following two sequences of spot rates.

Time-to-Maturity	Spot Rates A	Spot Rates B
1 year	0.39%	4.08%
2 years	1.40%	4.01%
3 years	2.50%	3.70%
4 years	3.60%	3.50%

Solution:

Spot Rates A

$$\frac{3}{(1.0039)^1} + \frac{3}{(1.0140)^2} + \frac{3}{(1.0250)^3} + \frac{103}{(1.0360)^4} =$$

$$2.988 + 2.918 + 2.786 + 89.412 = 98.104$$

Given spot rates A, the four-year, 3% bond is priced at 98.104.

$$98.104 = \frac{3}{(1+r)^1} + \frac{3}{(1+r)^2} + \frac{3}{(1+r)^3} + \frac{103}{(1+r)^4}, \quad r = 0.03516$$

The yield-to-maturity is 3.516%.

Spot Rates B

$$\frac{3}{(1.0408)^1} + \frac{3}{(1.0401)^2} + \frac{3}{(1.0370)^3} + \frac{103}{(1.0350)^4} =$$

$$2.882 + 2.773 + 2.690 + 89.759 = 98.104$$

$$98.104 = \frac{3}{(1+r)^1} + \frac{3}{(1+r)^2} + \frac{3}{(1+r)^3} + \frac{103}{(1+r)^4}, \quad r = 0.03516$$

Given spot rates B, the four-year, 3% bond is again priced at 98.104 to yield 3.516%.

This example demonstrates that two very different sequences of spot rates can result in the same bond price and yield-to-maturity. Spot rates A are increasing for longer maturities, whereas spot rates B are decreasing.

PRICES AND YIELDS: CONVENTIONS FOR QUOTES AND CALCULATIONS

3

When investors purchase shares, they pay the quoted price. For bonds, however, there can be a difference between the quoted price and the price paid. This section explains why this difference occurs and how to calculate the quoted price and the price that will be paid. It also describes how prices are estimated for bonds that are not actively traded, and demonstrates how yield measures are calculated for fixed-rate bonds, floating-rate notes, and money market instruments.

3.1 Flat Price, Accrued Interest, and the Full Price

When a bond is between coupon payment dates, its price has two parts: the **flat price** (PV^{Flat}) and the **accrued interest** (AI). The sum of the parts is the **full price** (PV^{Full}), which also is called the invoice or "dirty" price. The flat price, which is the full price minus the accrued interest, is also called the quoted or "clean" price.

$$PV^{Full} = PV^{Flat} + AI \tag{3}$$

The flat price usually is quoted by bond dealers. If a trade takes place, the accrued interest is added to the flat price to obtain the full price paid by the buyer and received by the seller on the **settlement date**. The settlement date is when the bond buyer makes cash payment and the seller delivers the security.

The reason for using the flat price for quotation is to avoid misleading investors about the market price trend for the bond. If the full price were to be quoted by dealers, investors would see the price rise day after day even if the yield-to-maturity did not change. That is because the amount of accrued interest increases each day. Then, after the coupon payment is made, the quoted price would drop dramatically. Using the flat price for quotation avoids that misrepresentation. It is the flat price that is "pulled to par" along the constant-yield price trajectory shown in Exhibit 3.

Accrued interest is the proportional share of the next coupon payment. Assume that the coupon period has "T" days between payment dates and that "t" days have gone by since the last payment. The accrued interest is calculated using Equation 4:

$$AI = \frac{t}{T} \times PMT \tag{4}$$

where

t = number of days from the last coupon payment to the settlement date

T = number of days in the coupon period

t/T = fraction of the coupon period that has gone by since the last payment

PMT = coupon payment per period

Notice that the accrued interest part of the full price does not depend on the yield-to-maturity. Therefore, it is the flat price that is affected by a market discount rate change.

There are different conventions used in bond markets to count days. The two most common day-count conventions are actual/actual and 30/360. For the actual/actual method, the actual number of days is used, including weekends, holidays, and leap days. For example, a semiannual payment bond pays interest on 15 May and 15 November of each year. The accrued interest for settlement on 27 June would be the actual number of days between 15 May and 27 June (t = 43 days) divided by the actual number of days between 15 May and 15 November (T = 184 days), times the coupon payment. If the stated coupon rate is 4.375%, the accrued interest is 0.511209 per 100 of par value.

$$AI = \frac{43}{184} \times \frac{4.375}{2} = 0.511209$$

Day-count conventions vary from market to market. However, actual/actual is most common for government bonds.

The 30/360 day-count convention often is used on corporate bonds. It *assumes* that each month has 30 days and that a full year has 360 days. Therefore, for this method, there are assumed to be 42 days between 15 May and 27 June: 15 days between 15 May and 30 May and 27 days between 1 June and 27 June. There are assumed to be 180 days in the six-month period between 15 May and 15 November. The accrued interest on a 4.375% semiannual payment corporate bond is 0.510417 per 100 of par value.

$$AI = \frac{42}{180} \times \frac{4.375}{2} = 0.510417$$

The full price of a fixed-rate bond between coupon payments given the market discount rate per period (r) can be calculated with Equation 5:

$$PV^{Full} = \frac{PMT}{(1+r)^{1-t/T}} + \frac{PMT}{(1+r)^{2-t/T}} + \cdots + \frac{PMT + FV}{(1+r)^{N-t/T}} \quad (5)$$

This is very similar to Equation 1. The difference is that the next coupon payment (PMT) is discounted for the remainder of the coupon period, which is $1 - t/T$. The second coupon payment is discounted for that fraction plus another full period, $2 - t/T$.

Equation 5 is simplified by multiplying the numerator and denominator by the expression $(1 + r)^{t/T}$. The result is Equation 6:

$$PV^{Full} = \left[\frac{PMT}{(1+r)^1} + \frac{PMT}{(1+r)^2} + \cdots + \frac{PMT + FV}{(1+r)^N}\right] \times (1+r)^{t/T} \quad (6)$$
$$= PV \times (1+r)^{t/T}$$

An advantage to Equation 6 is that PV, the expression in the brackets, is easily obtained using the time-value-of-money keys on a financial calculator because there are N evenly spaced periods. PV here is identical to Equation 1 and is not the same as PV^{Flat}.

For example, consider a 5% semiannual coupon payment government bond that matures on 15 February 2028. Accrued interest on this bond uses the actual/actual day-count convention. The coupon payments are made on 15 February and 15 August of each year. The bond is to be priced for settlement on 14 May 2019. That date is 88 days into the 181-day period. There are actually 88 days from the last coupon on

15 February to 14 May and 181 days between 15 February and the next coupon on 15 August. The annual yield-to-maturity is stated to be 4.80%. That corresponds to a market discount rate of 2.40% per semiannual period. As of the beginning of the coupon period on 15 February 2019, there would be 18 evenly spaced semiannual periods until maturity. The first step is to solve for PV using Equation 1, whereby $PMT = 2.5$, $N = 18$, $FV = 100$, and $r = 0.0240$.

$$PV = \frac{2.5}{(1.0240)^1} + \frac{2.5}{(1.0240)^2} + \cdots + \frac{102.5}{(1.0240)^{18}} = 101.447790$$

The price of the bond would be 101.447790 per 100 of par value if its yield-to-maturity is 2.40% per period on the last coupon payment date. This is not the actual price for the bond on that date. It is a "what-if" price using the required yield that corresponds to the settlement date of 14 May 2019.

Equation 6 can be used to get the full price for the bond.

$$PV^{Full} = 101.447790 \times (1.0240)^{88/181} = 102.624323$$

The full price is 102.624323 per 100 of par value. The accrued interest is 1.215470 per 100 of par value.

$$AI = \frac{88}{181} \times 2.5 = 1.215470$$

The flat price is 101.408853 per 100 of par value.[1]

$$PV^{Flat} = PV^{Full} - AI = 102.624323 - 1.215470 = 101.408853$$

EXAMPLE 5

Calculating the Full Price, Accrued Interest, and Flat Price for a Bond

A 6% German corporate bond is priced for settlement on 18 June 2019. The bond makes semiannual coupon payments on 19 March and 19 September of each year and matures on 19 September 2030. The corporate bond uses the 30/360 day-count convention for accrued interest. Calculate the full price, the accrued interest, and the flat price per EUR100 of par value for three stated annual yields-to-maturity: (A) 5.80%, (B) 6.00%, and (C) 6.20%.

Solution:

Given the 30/360 day-count convention assumption, there are 89 days between the last coupon on 19 March 2015 and the settlement date on 18 June 2015 (11 days between 19 March and 30 March, plus 60 days for the full months of April and May, plus 18 days in June). Therefore, the fraction of the coupon period that has gone by is assumed to be 89/180. At the beginning of the period, there are 11.5 years (and 23 semiannual periods) to maturity.

---

1 Microsoft Excel users can obtain the flat price using the PRICE financial function: PRICE(DATE(2019,5,14),DATE(2028,2,15),0.05,0.048,100,2,1). The inputs are the settlement date, maturity date, annual coupon rate as a decimal, annual yield-to-maturity as a decimal, par value, number of periods in the year, and the code for the day-count (0 for 30/360, 1 for actual/actual).

(A) *Stated annual yield-to-maturity of 5.80%, or 2.90% per semiannual period:*

The price at the beginning of the period is 101.661589 per 100 of par value.

$$PV = \frac{3}{(1.0290)^1} + \frac{3}{(1.0290)^2} + \cdots + \frac{103}{(1.0290)^{23}} = 101.661589$$

The full price on 18 June is EUR103.108770.

$$PV^{Full} = 101.661589 \times (1.0290)^{89/180} = 103.108770$$

The accrued interest is EUR1.483333, and the flat price is EUR101.625437.

$$AI = \frac{89}{180} \times 3 = 1.4833333$$

$$PV^{Flat} = 103.108770 - 1.483333 = 101.625437$$

(B) *Stated annual yield-to-maturity of 6.00%, or 3.00% per semiannual period:*

The price at the beginning of the period is par value, as expected, because the coupon rate and the market discount rate are equal.

$$PV = \frac{3}{(1.0300)^1} + \frac{3}{(1.0300)^2} + \cdots + \frac{103}{(1.0300)^{23}} = 100.000000$$

The full price on 18 June is EUR101.472251.

$$PV^{Full} = 100.000000 \times (1.0300)^{89/180} = 101.472251$$

The accrued interest is EUR1.483333, and the flat price is EUR99.988918.

$$AI = \frac{89}{180} \times 3 = 1.4833333$$

$$PV^{Flat} = 101.472251 - 1.483333 = 99.988918$$

The flat price of the bond is a little below par value, even though the coupon rate and the yield-to-maturity are equal, because the accrued interest does not take into account the time value of money. The accrued interest is the interest earned by the owner of the bond for the time between the last coupon payment and the settlement date, 1.483333 per 100 of par value. However, that interest income is not received until the next coupon date. In theory, the accrued interest should be the *present value* of 1.483333. In practice, however, accounting and financial reporting need to consider issues of practicality and materiality. For those reasons, the calculation of accrued interest in practice neglects the time value of money. Therefore, compared to theory, the reported accrued interest is a little "too high" and the flat price is a little "too low." The full price, however, is correct because it is the sum of the present values of the future cash flows, discounted using the market discount rate.

(C) *Stated annual yield-to-maturity of 6.20%, or 3.10% per semiannual period:*

The price at the beginning of the period is 98.372607 per 100 of par value.

$$PV = \frac{3}{(1.0310)^1} + \frac{3}{(1.0310)^2} + \cdots + \frac{103}{(1.0310)^{23}} = 98.372607$$

The full price on 18 June is EUR99.868805.

$$PV^{Full} = 98.372607 \times (1.0310)^{89/180} = 99.868805$$

The accrued interest is EUR1.483333, and the flat price is EUR98.385472.

$$AI = \frac{89}{180} \times 3 = 1.4833333$$

$$PV^{Flat} = 99.868805 - 1.483333 = 98.385472$$

The accrued interest is the same in each case because it does not depend on the yield-to-maturity. The differences in the flat prices indicate the differences in the rate of return that is required by investors.

3.2 Matrix Pricing

Some fixed-rate bonds are not actively traded. Therefore, there is no market price available to calculate the rate of return required by investors. The same problem occurs for bonds that are not yet issued. In these situations, it is common to estimate the market discount rate and price based on the quoted or flat prices of more frequently traded comparable bonds. These comparable bonds have similar times-to-maturity, coupon rates, and credit quality. This estimation process is called **matrix pricing**.

For example, suppose that an analyst needs to value a three-year, 4% semiannual coupon payment corporate bond, Bond X. Assume that Bond X is not actively traded and that there are no recent transactions reported for this particular security. However, there are quoted prices for four corporate bonds that have very similar credit quality:

- Bond A: two-year, 3% semiannual coupon payment bond trading at a price of 98.500
- Bond B: two-year, 5% semiannual coupon payment bond trading at a price of 102.250
- Bond C: five-year, 2% semiannual coupon payment bond trading at a price of 90.250
- Bond D: five-year, 4% semiannual coupon payment bond trading at a price of 99.125

The bonds are displayed in a matrix according to the coupon rate and the time-to-maturity. This matrix is shown in Exhibit 4.

Exhibit 4 Matrix Pricing Example

	2% Coupon	3% Coupon	4% Coupon	5% Coupon
Two Years		98.500		102.250
		3.786%		3.821%
Three Years			Bond X	
Four Years				
Five Years	90.250		99.125	
	4.181%		4.196%	

In Exhibit 4, below each bond price is the yield-to-maturity. It is stated as the yield per semiannual period times two. For example, the yield-to-maturity on the two-year, 3% semiannual coupon payment corporate bond is 3.786%.

$$98.500 = \frac{1.5}{(1+r)^1} + \frac{1.5}{(1+r)^2} + \frac{1.5}{(1+r)^3} + \frac{101.5}{(1+r)^4}, \quad r = 0.01893, \quad \times 2 = 0.03786$$

Next, the analyst calculates the average yield for each year: 3.8035% for the two-year bonds and 4.1885% for the five-year bonds.

$$\frac{0.03786 + 0.03821}{2} = 0.038035$$

$$\frac{0.04181 + 0.04196}{2} = 0.041885$$

The estimated three-year market discount rate can be obtained with linear interpolation. The interpolated yield is 3.9318%.

$$0.038035 + \left(\frac{3-2}{5-2}\right) \times (0.041885 - 0.038035) = 0.039318$$

Using 3.9318% as the estimated three-year annual market discount rate, the three-year, 4% semiannual coupon payment corporate bond has an estimated price of 100.191 per 100 of par value.

$$\frac{2}{(1.019659)^1} + \frac{2}{(1.019659)^2} + \frac{2}{(1.019659)^3} + \frac{2}{(1.019659)^4} + \frac{2}{(1.019659)^5} +$$

$$\frac{102}{(1.019659)^6} = 100.191$$

Notice that 3.9318% is the stated annual rate. It is divided by two to get the yield per semiannual period: (0.039318/2 = 0.019659).

Matrix pricing also is used in underwriting new bonds to get an estimate of the **required yield spread** over the **benchmark rate**. The benchmark rate typically is the yield-to-maturity on a government bond having the same, or close to the same, time-to-maturity. The spread is the difference between the yield-to-maturity on the new bond and the benchmark rate. The yield spread is the additional compensation required by investors for the difference in the credit risk, liquidity risk, and tax status of the bond relative to the government bond. This spread is sometimes called the **spread over the benchmark**. Yield spreads are often stated in terms of basis points (bps), where one **basis point** equals one-hundredth of a percentage point. For example, if a yield-to-maturity is 2.25% and the benchmark rate is 1.50%, the yield spread is 0.75%, or 75 bps. Yield spreads are covered in more detail later in this reading.

Suppose that a corporation is about to issue a five-year bond. The corporate issuer currently has a four-year, 3% annual coupon payment debt liability on its books. The price of that bond is 102.400 per 100 of par value. This is the full price, which is the same as the flat price because the accrued interest is zero. This implies that the coupon payment has just been made and there are four full years to maturity. The four-year rate of return required by investors for this bond is 2.36%.

$$102.400 = \frac{3}{(1+r)^1} + \frac{3}{(1+r)^2} + \frac{3}{(1+r)^3} + \frac{103}{(1+r)^4}, \quad r = 0.0236$$

Suppose that there are no four-year government bonds to calculate the yield spread on this security. However, there are three-year and five-year government bonds that have yields-to-maturity of 0.75% and 1.45%, respectively. The average of the two yields-to-maturity is 1.10%, which is the estimated yield for the four-year government bond. Therefore, the estimated yield spread is 126 bps over the implied benchmark rate (0.0236 – 0.0110 = 0.0126).

There usually is a different yield spread for each maturity and for each credit rating. The term structure of "risk-free" rates, which is discussed further in Section 4, is the relationship between yields-to-maturity on "risk-free" bonds and times-to-maturity. The quotation marks around "risk-free" indicate that no bond is truly without risk. The primary component of the yield spread for many bonds is compensation for credit risk, not for time-to-maturity, and as a result, the yield spreads reflect the **term structure of credit spreads**. The term structure of credit spreads is the relationship between the spreads over the "risk-free" (or benchmark) rates and times-to-maturity. These term structures are covered in more detail in later readings.

The issuer now has an estimate of the four-year yield spread, 126 bps. This spread is a reference point for estimating the five-year spread for the newly issued bond. Suppose that the term structure of credit spreads for bonds of the corporate issuer's quality indicates that five-year spreads are about 25 bps higher than four-year spreads. Therefore, the estimated five-year required yield spread is 151 bps (0.0126 + 0.0025 = 0.0151). Given the yield-to-maturity of 1.45% on the five-year government bond, the expected market discount rate for the newly issued bond is 2.96% (0.0145 + 0.0151 = 0.0296). The corporation might set the coupon rate to be 3% and expect that the bond can be sold for a small premium above par value.

EXAMPLE 6

Using Matrix Pricing to Estimate Bond Price

An analyst needs to assign a value to an illiquid four-year, 4.5% annual coupon payment corporate bond. The analyst identifies two corporate bonds that have similar credit quality: One is a three-year, 5.50% annual coupon payment bond priced at 107.500 per 100 of par value, and the other is a five-year, 4.50% annual coupon payment bond priced at 104.750 per 100 of par value. Using matrix pricing, the estimated price of the illiquid bond per 100 of par value is *closest* to:

A 103.895.

B 104.991.

C 106.125.

Solution:

B is correct. The first step is to determine the yields-to-maturity on the observed bonds. The required yield on the three-year, 5.50% bond priced at 107.500 is 2.856%.

$$107.500 = \frac{5.50}{(1+r)^1} + \frac{5.50}{(1+r)^2} + \frac{105.50}{(1+r)^3}, \quad r = 0.02856$$

The required yield on the five-year, 4.50% bond priced at 104.750 is 3.449%.

$$104.750 = \frac{4.50}{(1+r)^1} + \frac{4.50}{(1+r)^2} + \frac{4.50}{(1+r)^3} + \frac{4.50}{(1+r)^4} + \frac{104.50}{(1+r)^5}, \quad r = 0.03449$$

The estimated market discount rate for a four-year bond having the same credit quality is the average of two required yields:

$$\frac{0.02856 + 0.03449}{2} = 0.031525$$

Given an estimated yield-to-maturity of 3.1525%, the estimated price of the illiquid four-year, 4.50% annual coupon payment corporate bond is 104.991 per 100 of par value.

$$\frac{4.50}{(1.031525)^1} + \frac{4.50}{(1.031525)^2} + \frac{4.50}{(1.031525)^3} + \frac{104.50}{(1.031525)^4} = 104.991$$

3.3 Annual Yields for Varying Compounding Periods in the Year

There are many ways to measure the rate of return on a fixed-rate bond investment. Consider a five-year, zero-coupon government bond. The purchase price today is 80. The investor receives 100 at redemption in five years. One possible yield measure is 25%—the gain of 20 divided by the amount invested, 80. However, investors want a yield measure that is *standardized* to allow for comparison between bonds that have different times-to-maturity. Therefore, yield measures typically are *annualized.* A possible annual rate for this zero-coupon bond is 5% per year—25% divided by five years. But for bonds maturing in more than one year, investors want an *annualized and compounded* yield-to-maturity. Money market rates on instruments maturing in one year or less typically are *annualized but not compounded.* They are stated on a simple interest basis. This concept is covered later in this reading.

In general, an annualized and compounded yield on a fixed-rate bond depends on the assumed number of periods in the year, which is called the **periodicity** of the annual rate. Typically, the periodicity matches the frequency of coupon payments. A bond that pays semiannual coupons has a stated annual yield-to-maturity for a periodicity of two—the rate per semiannual period times two. A bond that pays quarterly coupons has a stated annual yield for a periodicity of four—the rate per quarter times four. It is always important to know the periodicity of a stated annual rate.

The periodicity of the annual market discount rate for a zero-coupon bond is *arbitrary* because there are no coupon payments. For semiannual compounding, the annual yield-to-maturity on the five-year, zero-coupon bond priced at 80 per 100 of par value is stated to be 4.5130%. This annual rate has a periodicity of two.

$$80 = \frac{100}{(1+r)^{10}}, \quad r = 0.022565, \quad \times 2 = 0.045130$$

For quarterly compounding, the annual yield-to-maturity is stated to be 4.4880%. This annual rate has a periodicity of four.

$$80 = \frac{100}{(1+r)^{20}}, \quad r = 0.011220, \quad \times 4 = 0.044880$$

For monthly compounding, the annual yield-to-maturity is stated to be 4.4712%. This annual rate has a periodicity of 12.

$$80 = \frac{100}{(1+r)^{60}}, \quad r = 0.003726, \quad \times 12 = 0.044712$$

For annual compounding, the yield-to-maturity is stated to be 4.5640%. This annual rate has a periodicity of one.

$$80 = \frac{100}{(1+r)^{5}}, \quad r = 0.045640, \quad \times 1 = 0.045640$$

This is known as an **effective annual rate**. An effective annual rate has a periodicity of one because there is just one compounding period in the year.

In this zero-coupon bond example, 2.2565% compounded two times a year, 1.1220% compounded four times a year, and 0.3726% compounded twelve times a year are all equivalent to an effective annual rate of 4.5640%. The compounded total return is the same for each expression for the annual rate. They differ in terms of the number of compounding periods per year—that is, in terms of the *periodicity* of the annual rate. For a given pair of cash flows, the stated annual rate and the periodicity are inversely related.

The most common periodicity for USD-denominated bond yields is two because most bonds in the USD market make semiannual coupon payments. An annual rate having a periodicity of two is known as a **semiannual bond basis yield**, or **semiannual bond equivalent yield**. Therefore, a semiannual bond basis yield is the yield per semiannual period times two. It is important to remember that "semiannual bond basis yield" and "yield per semiannual period" have different meanings. For example, if a bond yield is 2% per semiannual period, its annual yield is 4% when stated on a semiannual bond basis.

An important tool used in fixed-income analysis is to convert an annual yield from one periodicity to another. These are called periodicity, or compounding, conversions. A general formula to convert an annual percentage rate for m periods per year, denoted APR_m, to an annual percentage rate for n periods per year, APR_n, is Equation 7.

$$\left(1+\frac{APR_m}{m}\right)^m = \left(1+\frac{APR_n}{n}\right)^n \quad (7)$$

For example, suppose that a three-year, 5% semiannual coupon payment corporate bond is priced at 104 per 100 of par value. Its yield-to-maturity is 3.582%, quoted on a semiannual bond basis for a periodicity of two: 0.01791 × 2 = 0.03582.

$$104 = \frac{2.5}{(1+r)^1} + \frac{2.5}{(1+r)^2} + \frac{2.5}{(1+r)^3} + \frac{2.5}{(1+r)^4} + \frac{2.5}{(1+r)^5} + \frac{102.5}{(1+r)^6}, \quad r = 0.01791$$

To compare this bond with others, an analyst converts this annualized yield-to-maturity to quarterly and monthly compounding. That entails using Equation 7 to convert from a periodicity of $m = 2$ to periodicities of $n = 4$ and $n = 12$.

$$\left(1+\frac{0.03582}{2}\right)^2 = \left(1+\frac{APR_4}{4}\right)^4, \quad APR_4 = 0.03566$$

$$\left(1+\frac{0.03582}{2}\right)^2 = \left(1+\frac{APR_{12}}{12}\right)^{12}, \quad APR_{12} = 0.03556$$

An annual yield-to-maturity of 3.582% for semiannual compounding provides the same rate of return as annual yields of 3.566% and 3.556% for quarterly and monthly compounding, respectively. A general rule for these periodicity conversions is *compounding more frequently at a lower annual rate corresponds to compounding less frequently at a higher annual rate.* This rule can be used to check periodicity conversion calculations.

Equation 7 also applies to *negative* bond yields. Government bond yields have been negative in in several countries, including Switzerland, Germany, Sweden, and Japan. For a simple example, consider a 5-year, zero-coupon bond priced at 105 (percent of par value). Its yield-to-maturity is −0.971% stated as an effective annual rate for a periodicity of 1.

$$105 = \frac{100}{(1+r)^5}, \quad r = -0.00971$$

Converting that to semiannual and monthly compounding for periodicities of 2 and 12 results in annual yields of –0.973% and –0.975%, respectively.

$$\left(1+\frac{-0.00971}{1}\right)^1=\left(1+\frac{APR_2}{2}\right)^2,\quad APR_2=-0.00973$$

$$\left(1+\frac{-0.00971}{1}\right)^1=\left(1+\frac{APR_{12}}{12}\right)^{12},\quad APR_{12}=-0.00975$$

Compounding more frequently within the year results in a lower (more negative) yield-to-maturity.

EXAMPLE 7

Yield Conversion Based on Periodicity

A five-year, 4.50% semiannual coupon payment government bond is priced at 98 per 100 of par value. Calculate the annual yield-to-maturity stated on a semiannual bond basis, rounded to the nearest basis point. Convert that annual yield to:

A an annual rate that can be used for direct comparison with otherwise comparable bonds that make *quarterly* coupon payments and

B an annual rate that can be used for direct comparison with otherwise comparable bonds that make *annual* coupon payments.

Solution:

The stated annual yield-to-maturity on a semiannual bond basis is 4.96% (0.0248 × 2 = 0.0496).

$$98=\frac{2.25}{(1+r)^1}+\frac{2.25}{(1+r)^2}+\frac{2.25}{(1+r)^3}+\frac{2.25}{(1+r)^4}+\frac{2.25}{(1+r)^5}+\frac{2.25}{(1+r)^6}+$$
$$\frac{2.25}{(1+r)^7}+\frac{2.25}{(1+r)^8}+\frac{2.25}{(1+r)^9}+\frac{102.25}{(1+r)^{10}},\quad r=0.0248$$

A Convert 4.96% from a periodicity of two to a periodicity of four:

$$\left(1+\frac{0.0496}{2}\right)^2=\left(1+\frac{APR_4}{4}\right)^4,\quad APR_4=0.0493$$

The annual percentage rate of 4.96% for compounding semiannually compares with 4.93% for compounding quarterly. That makes sense because increasing the frequency of compounding lowers the annual rate.

B Convert 4.96% from a periodicity of two to a periodicity of one:

$$\left(1+\frac{0.0496}{2}\right)^2=\left(1+\frac{APR_1}{1}\right)^1,\quad APR_1=0.0502$$

The annual rate of 4.96% for compounding semiannually compares with an effective annual rate of 5.02%. Converting from more frequent to less frequent compounding entails raising the annual percentage rate.

3.4 Yield Measures for Fixed-Rate Bonds

An important concern for quoting and calculating bond yields-to-maturity is the actual timing of the cash flows. Consider a 6% semiannual payment corporate bond that matures on 15 March 2028. Suppose that for settlement on 23 January 2020, the bond is priced at 98.5 per 100 of par value to yield 6.236% quoted on a semiannual bond basis. Its coupon payments are scheduled for 15 March and 15 September of each year. The yield calculation implicitly assumes that the payments are made on those dates. It neglects the reality that 15 March 2020 is a Sunday and 15 March 2025 is a Saturday. In fact, the coupon payments will be made to investors on the following Monday.

Yield measures that neglect weekends and holidays are quoted on what is called **street convention**. The street convention yield-to-maturity is the internal rate of return on the cash flows assuming the payments are made on the scheduled dates. This assumption simplifies bond price and yield calculations and commonly is used in practice. Sometimes the **true yield** is also quoted. The true yield-to-maturity is the internal rate of return on the cash flows using the actual calendar of weekends and bank holidays. The true yield is never higher than the street convention yield because weekends and holidays delay the time to payment. The difference is typically small, no more than a basis point or two. Therefore, the true yield is not commonly used in practice. Sometimes, a **government equivalent yield** is quoted for a corporate bond. A government equivalent yield restates a yield-to-maturity based on 30/360 day-count to one based on actual/actual. The government equivalent yield on a corporate bond can be used to obtain the spread over the government yield. Doing so keeps the yields stated on the same day-count convention basis.

Another yield measure that is commonly quoted for fixed-income bonds is the **current yield**, also called the income or running yield. The current yield is the sum of the coupon payments received over the year divided by the flat price. For example, a 10-year, 2% semiannual coupon payment bond is priced at 95 per 100 of par value. Its current yield is 2.105%.

$$\frac{2}{95} = 0.02105$$

The current yield is a crude measure of the rate of return to an investor because it neglects the frequency of coupon payments in the numerator and any accrued interest in the denominator. It focuses only on interest income. In addition to collecting and reinvesting coupon payments, the investor has a gain if the bond is purchased at a discount and is redeemed at par value. The investor has a loss if the bond is purchased at a premium and is redeemed at par value. Sometimes the **simple yield** on a bond is quoted. It is the sum of the coupon payments plus the straight-line amortized share of the gain or loss, divided by the flat price. Simple yields are used mostly to quote Japanese government bonds, known as "JGBs."

EXAMPLE 8

Comparing Yields for Different Periodicities

An analyst observes these reported statistics for two bonds.

	Bond A	Bond B
Annual Coupon Rate	8.00%	12.00%
Coupon Payment Frequency	Semiannually	Quarterly
Years to Maturity	5 Years	5 Years

(continued)

	Bond A	Bond B
Price (per 100 of par value)	90	105
Current Yield	8.889%	11.429%
Yield-to-Maturity	10.630%	10.696%

1 Confirm the calculation of the two yield measures for the two bonds.

2 The analyst believes that Bond B has a little more risk than Bond A. How much additional compensation, in terms of a higher yield-to-maturity, does a buyer of Bond B receive for bearing this risk compared with Bond A?

Solution to 1:

Current Yield for Bond A

$$\frac{8}{90} = 0.08889$$

Yield-to-Maturity for Bond A

$$90 = \frac{4}{(1+r)^1} + \frac{4}{(1+r)^2} + \cdots + \frac{104}{(1+r)^{10}}, \quad r = 0.05315, \quad \times 2 = 0.10630$$

Current Yield for Bond B

$$\frac{12}{105} = 0.11429$$

Yield-to-Maturity for Bond B

$$105 = \frac{3}{(1+r)^1} + \frac{3}{(1+r)^2} + \cdots + \frac{103}{(1+r)^{20}}, \quad r = 0.02674, \quad \times 4 = 0.10696$$

Solution to 2:

The yield-to-maturity on Bond A of 10.630% is an annual rate for compounding semiannually. The yield-to-maturity on Bond B of 10.696% is an annual rate for compounding quarterly. The difference in the yields is *not* 6.6 bps (0.10696 – 0.10630 = 0.00066). It is essential to compare the yields for the same periodicity to make a statement about relative value.

10.630% for a periodicity of two converts to 10.492% for a periodicity of four:

$$\left(1 + \frac{0.10630}{2}\right)^2 = \left(1 + \frac{APR_4}{4}\right)^4, \quad APR_4 = 0.10492$$

10.696% for a periodicity of four converts to 10.839% for a periodicity of two:

$$\left(1 + \frac{0.10696}{4}\right)^4 = \left(1 + \frac{APR_2}{2}\right)^2, \quad APR_2 = 0.10839$$

The additional compensation for the greater risk in Bond B is 20.9 bps (0.10839 – 0.10630 = 0.00209) when the yields are stated on a semiannual bond basis. The additional compensation is 20.4 bps (0.10696 – 0.10492 = 0.00204) when both are annualized for quarterly compounding.

If a fixed-rate bond contains an **embedded option**, other yield measures are used. An embedded option is part of the security and cannot be removed and sold separately. For example, a **callable bond** contains an embedded call option that gives the issuer the right to buy the bond back from the investor at specified prices on predetermined dates. The preset dates usually coincide with coupon payment dates after a **call protection** period. A call protection period is the time during which the issuer of the bond is not allowed to exercise the call option.

Suppose that a seven-year, 8% annual coupon payment bond is first callable in four years. That gives the investor four years of protection against the bond being called. After the call protection period, the issuer might exercise the call option if interest rates decrease or the issuer's credit quality improves. Those circumstances allow the issuer to refinance the debt at a lower cost of funds. The preset prices that the issuer pays if the bond is called often are at a premium above par. For example, the "call schedule" for this bond might be that it is first callable at 102 (per 100 of par value) on the coupon payment date in four years, callable at 101 in five years, and at par value on coupon payment dates thereafter.

The yield-to-maturity on this seven-year, 8% callable bond is just one of several traditional yield measures for the investment. Others are yield-to-first-call, yield-to-second-call, and so on. If the current price for the bond is 105 per 100 of par value, the yield-to-first-call in four years is 6.975%.

$$105 = \frac{8}{(1+r)^1} + \frac{8}{(1+r)^2} + \frac{8}{(1+r)^3} + \frac{8+102}{(1+r)^4}, \quad r = 0.06975$$

The yield-to-second-call in five years is 6.956%.

$$105 = \frac{8}{(1+r)^1} + \frac{8}{(1+r)^2} + \frac{8}{(1+r)^3} + \frac{8}{(1+r)^4} + \frac{8+101}{(1+r)^5}, \quad r = 0.06956$$

The yield-to-third-call is 6.953%.

$$105 = \frac{8}{(1+r)^1} + \frac{8}{(1+r)^2} + \frac{8}{(1+r)^3} + \frac{8}{(1+r)^4} + \frac{8}{(1+r)^5} + \frac{8+100}{(1+r)^6}, \quad r = 0.06953$$

Finally, the yield-to-maturity is 7.070%.

$$105 = \frac{8}{(1+r)^1} + \frac{8}{(1+r)^2} + \frac{8}{(1+r)^3} + \frac{8}{(1+r)^4} + \frac{8}{(1+r)^5} + \frac{8}{(1+r)^6} + \frac{8+100}{(1+r)^7}, \quad r = 0.07070$$

Each calculation is based on Equation 1, whereby the call price (or par value) is used for *FV*. The lowest of the sequence of yields-to-call and the yield-to-maturity is known as the **yield-to-worst**. In this case, it is the yield-to-third-call of 6.953%. The intent of this yield measure is to provide to the investor the most conservative assumption for the rate of return.

The yield-to-worst is a commonly cited yield measure for fixed-rate callable bonds used by bond dealers and investors. However, a more precise approach is to use an option pricing model and an assumption about future interest rate volatility to value the embedded call option. The value of the embedded call option is added to the flat price of the bond to get the **option-adjusted price**. The investor bears the call risk (the bond issuer has the option to call), so the embedded call option reduces the value of the bond from the investor's perspective. The investor pays a lower price for the callable bond than if it were option-free. If the bond were non-callable, its price would be higher. The option-adjusted price is used to calculate the **option-adjusted yield**. The option-adjusted yield is the required market discount rate whereby the price is adjusted for the value of the embedded option. The value of the call option is the price of the option-free bond minus the price of the callable bond.

3.5 Yield Measures for Floating-Rate Notes

Floating-rate notes are very different from a fixed-rate bond. The interest payments on a floating-rate note, which often is called a floater or an FRN, are not fixed. Instead, they vary from period to period depending on the current level of a reference interest rate. The interest payments could go up or down; that is why they "float." The intent of an FRN is to offer the investor a security that has less market price risk than a fixed-rate bond when market interest rates fluctuate. In principle, a floater has a stable price even in a period of volatile interest rates. With a traditional fixed-income security, interest rate volatility affects the price because the future cash flows are constant. With a floating-rate note, interest rate volatility affects future interest payments.

The reference rate on a floating-rate note usually is a short-term money market rate, such as three-month Libor (the London Interbank Offered Rate). The principal on the floater typically is non-amortizing and is redeemed in full at maturity. The reference rate is determined at the beginning of the period, and the interest payment is made at the end of the period. This payment structure is called "in arrears." The most common day-count conventions for calculating accrued interest on floaters are actual/360 and actual/365.

Although there are many varieties of FRNs, only the most common and traditional floaters are covered here. On these floaters, a specified yield spread is added to, or subtracted from, the reference rate. For example, the floater might reset its interest rate quarterly at three-month Libor plus 0.50%. This specified yield spread over the reference rate is called the **quoted margin** on the FRN. The role of the quoted margin is to compensate the investor for the difference in the credit risk of the issuer and that implied by the reference rate. For example, a company with a stronger credit rating than that of the banks included in Libor may be able to obtain a "sub-Libor" cost of borrowed funds, which results in a negative quoted margin. An AAA-rated company might be able to issue an FRN that pays three-month Libor minus 0.25%.

The **required margin** is the yield spread over, or under, the reference rate such that the FRN is priced at par value on a rate reset date. Suppose that a traditional floater is issued at par value and pays three-month Libor plus 0.50%. The quoted margin is 50 bps. If there is no change in the credit risk of the issuer, the required margin remains at 50 bps. On each quarterly reset date, the floater will be priced at par value. Between coupon dates, its flat price will be at a premium or discount to par value if Libor goes down or up. However, if the required margin continues to be the same as the quoted margin, the flat price is "pulled to par" as the next reset date nears. At the reset date, any change in Libor is included in the interest payment for the next period.

Changes in the required margin usually come from changes in the issuer's credit risk. Changes in liquidity or tax status also could affect the required margin. Suppose that on a reset date, the required margin goes up to 75 bps because of a downgrade in the issuer's credit rating. A floater having a quoted margin of 50 bps now pays its investors a "deficient" interest payment. This FRN will be priced at a discount below par value. The amount of the discount is the present value of the deficient future cash flows. That annuity is 25 bps per period for the remaining life of the bond. It is the difference between the required and quoted margins. If the required margin goes down from 50 bps to 40 bps, the FRN will be priced at a premium. The amount of the premium is the present value of the 10 bp annuity for the "excess" interest payment each period.

Fixed-rate and floating-rate bonds are essentially the same with respect to changes in credit risk. With fixed-rate bonds, the premium or discount arises from a difference in the fixed coupon rate and the required yield-to-maturity. With floating-rate bonds, the premium or discount arises from a difference in the fixed quoted margin and the required margin. However, fixed-rate and floating-rate bonds are very different with respect to changes in benchmark interest rates.

The valuation of a floating-rate note needs a pricing model. Equation 8 is a simplified FRN pricing model. Following market practice, the required margin is called the **discount margin**.

$$PV = \frac{\frac{(\text{Index} + QM) \times FV}{m}}{\left(1 + \frac{\text{Index} + DM}{m}\right)^1} + \frac{\frac{(\text{Index} + QM) \times FV}{m}}{\left(1 + \frac{\text{Index} + DM}{m}\right)^2} + \cdots + \frac{\frac{(\text{Index} + QM) \times FV}{m} + FV}{\left(1 + \frac{\text{Index} + DM}{m}\right)^N} \quad (8)$$

where

PV = present value, or the price of the floating-rate note
Index = reference rate, stated as an annual percentage rate
QM = quoted margin, stated as an annual percentage rate
FV = future value paid at maturity, or the par value of the bond
m = periodicity of the floating-rate note, the number of payment periods per year
DM = discount margin, the required margin stated as an annual percentage rate
N = number of evenly spaced periods to maturity

This equation is similar to Equation 1, which is the basic pricing formula for a fixed-rate bond given the market discount rate. In Equation 1, *PMT* is the coupon payment *per period*. Here, *annual* rates are used. The first interest payment is the annual rate for the period (Index + *QM*) times the par value (*FV*) and divided by the number of periods in the year (*m*). In Equation 1, the market discount rate per period (*r*) is used to discount the cash flows. Here, the discount rate per period is the reference rate plus the discount margin (Index + *DM*) divided by the periodicity (*m*).

This is a simplified FRN pricing model for several reasons. First, *PV* is for a rate reset date when there are *N* evenly spaced periods to maturity. There is no accrued interest so that the flat price is the full price. Second, the model assumes a 30/360 day-count convention so that the periodicity is an integer. Third, and most important, the same reference rate (Index) is used for all payment periods in both the numerators and denominators. More complex FRN pricing models use projected future rates for Index in the numerators and spot rates in the denominators. Therefore, the calculation for *DM* depends on the simplifying assumptions in the pricing model.

Suppose that a two-year FRN pays six-month Libor plus 0.50%. Currently, six-month Libor is 1.25%. In Equation 8, Index = 0.0125, $QM = 0.0050$, and $m = 2$. The numerators in Equation 8, ignoring the repayment of principal, are 0.875.

$$\frac{(\text{Index} + QM) \times FV}{m} = \frac{(0.0125 + 0.0050) \times 100}{2} = 0.875$$

Suppose that the yield spread required by investors is 40 bps over the reference rate, $DM = 0.0040$. The assumed discount rate per period is 0.825%.

$$\frac{\text{Index} + DM}{m} = \frac{0.0125 + 0.0040}{2} = 0.00825$$

Using Equation 8 for $N = 4$, the FRN is priced at 100.196 per 100 of par value.

$$\frac{0.875}{(1 + 0.00825)^1} + \frac{0.875}{(1 + 0.00825)^2} + \frac{0.875}{(1 + 0.00825)^3} + \frac{0.875 + 100}{(1 + 0.00825)^4} = 100.196$$

This floater is priced at a premium above par value because the quoted margin is greater than the discount margin.

A similar calculation is to estimate the discount margin given the market price of the floating-rate note. Suppose that a five-year FRN pays three-month Libor plus 0.75% on a quarterly basis. Currently, three-month Libor is 1.10%. The price of the floater is 95.50 per 100 of par value, a discount below par value because of a downgrade in the issuer's credit rating.

$$\frac{(\text{Index} + QM) \times FV}{m} = \frac{(0.0110 + 0.0075) \times 100}{4} = 0.4625$$

In Equation 8, use $PV = 95.50$ and $N = 20$.

$$95.50 = \frac{0.4625}{\left(1 + \frac{0.0110 + DM}{4}\right)^1} + \frac{0.4625}{\left(1 + \frac{0.0110 + DM}{4}\right)^2} + \cdots + \frac{0.4625 + 100}{\left(1 + \frac{0.0110 + DM}{4}\right)^{20}}$$

This has the same format as Equation 1, which can be used to solve for the market discount rate per period, $r = 0.7045\%$.

$$95.50 = \frac{0.4625}{(1 + r)^1} + \frac{0.4625}{(1 + r)^2} + \cdots + \frac{0.4625 + 100}{(1 + r)^{20}}, \quad r = 0.007045$$

This can be used to solve for $DM = 1.718\%$.

$$0.007045 = \frac{0.0110 + DM}{4}, \quad DM = 0.01718$$

If this FRN was issued at par value, investors required at that time a spread of only 75 bps over three-month Libor. Now, after the credit downgrade, investors require an *estimated* discount margin of 171.8 bps. The floater trades at a discount because the quoted margin remains fixed at 75 bps. The calculated discount margin is an estimate because it is based on a simplified FRN pricing model.

EXAMPLE 9

Calculating the Discount Margin for a Floating-Rate Note

A four-year French floating-rate note pays three-month Euribor (Euro Interbank Offered Rate, an index produced by the European Banking Federation) plus 1.25%. The floater is priced at 98 per 100 of par value. Calculate the discount margin for the floater assuming that three-month Euribor is constant at 2%. Assume the 30/360 day-count convention and evenly spaced periods.

Solution:

By assumption, the interest payment each period is 0.8125 per 100 of par value.

$$\frac{(\text{Index} + QM) \times FV}{m} = \frac{(0.0200 + 0.0125) \times 100}{4} = 0.8125$$

The discount margin can be estimated by solving for DM in this equation.

$$98 = \frac{0.8125}{\left(1 + \frac{0.0200 + DM}{4}\right)^1} + \frac{0.8125}{\left(1 + \frac{0.0200 + DM}{4}\right)^2} + \cdots + \frac{0.8125 + 100}{\left(1 + \frac{0.0200 + DM}{4}\right)^{16}}$$

The solution for the discount rate per period is 0.9478%.

$$98 = \frac{0.8125}{(1+r)^1} + \frac{0.8125}{(1+r)^2} + \cdots + \frac{0.8125 + 100}{(1+r)^{16}}, \quad r = 0.009478$$

Therefore, DM = 1.791%.

$$0.009478 = \frac{0.0200 + DM}{4}, \quad DM = 0.01791$$

The quoted margin is 125 bps over the Euribor reference rate. Using the simplified FRN pricing model, it is estimated that investors require a 179.1 bp spread for the floater to be priced at par value.

3.6 Yield Measures for Money Market Instruments

Money market instruments are short-term debt securities. They range in time-to-maturity from overnight sale and repurchase agreements (repos) to one-year bank certificates of deposit. Money market instruments also include commercial paper, government issues of less than one year, bankers' acceptances, and time deposits based on such indexes as Libor and Euribor. Money market mutual funds are a major investor in such securities. These mutual funds can invest only in certain eligible money market securities.

There are several important differences in yield measures between the money market and the bond market:

1. Bond yields-to-maturity are annualized and compounded. Yield measures in the money market are annualized but not compounded. Instead, the rate of return on a money market instrument is stated on a simple interest basis.
2. Bond yields-to-maturity can be calculated using standard time-value-of-money analysis and with formulas programmed into a financial calculator. Money market instruments often are quoted using nonstandard interest rates and require different pricing equations than those used for bonds.
3. Bond yields-to-maturity usually are stated for a common periodicity for all times-to-maturity. Money market instruments having different times-to-maturity have different periodicities for the annual rate.

In general, quoted money market rates are either **discount rates** or **add-on rates**. Although market conventions vary around the world, commercial paper, Treasury bills (a US government security issued with a maturity of one year or less), and bankers' acceptances often are quoted on a discount rate basis. Bank certificates of deposit, repos, and such indexes as Libor and Euribor are quoted on an add-on rate basis. It is important to understand that "discount rate" has a unique meaning in the money market. In general, discount rate means "interest rate used to calculate a present value"—for instance, "market discount rate" as used in this reading. In the money market, however, discount rate is a specific type of quoted rate. Some examples will clarify this point.

Equation 9 is the pricing formula for money market instruments quoted on a discount rate basis.

$$PV = FV \times \left(1 - \frac{\text{Days}}{\text{Year}} \times DR\right) \tag{9}$$

where

PV = present value, or the price of the money market instrument

FV = future value paid at maturity, or the face value of the money market instrument

Days = number of days between settlement and maturity

Year = number of days in the year

DR = discount rate, stated as an annual percentage rate

Suppose that a 91-day US Treasury bill (T-bill) with a face value of USD10 million is quoted at a discount rate of 2.25% for an assumed 360-day year. Enter FV = 10,000,000, Days = 91, Year = 360, and DR = 0.0225. The price of the T-bill is USD9,943,125.

$$PV = 10{,}000{,}000 \times \left(1 - \frac{91}{360} \times 0.0225\right) = 9{,}943{,}125$$

The unique characteristics of a money market discount rate can be examined with Equation 10, which transforms Equation 9 algebraically to isolate the DR term.

$$DR = \left(\frac{\text{Year}}{\text{Days}}\right) \times \left(\frac{FV - PV}{FV}\right) \tag{10}$$

The first term, Year/Days, is the periodicity of the annual rate. The second term reveals the odd character of a money market discount rate. The numerator, $FV - PV$, is the interest earned on the T-bill, USD56,875 (= 10,000,000 – 9,943,125), over the 91 days to maturity. However, the denominator is FV, not PV. In theory, an interest rate is the amount earned divided by the investment amount (PV)—not divided by the total return at maturity, which includes the earnings (FV). Therefore, by design, a money market discount rate *understates* the rate of return to the investor, and it *understates* the cost of borrowed funds to the issuer. That is because PV is less than FV (as long as DR is greater than zero).

Equation 11 is the pricing formula for money market instruments quoted on an add-on rate basis.

$$PV = \frac{FV}{\left(1 + \frac{\text{Days}}{\text{Year}} \times AOR\right)} \tag{11}$$

where

PV = present value, principal amount, or the price of the money market instrument

FV = future value, or the redemption amount paid at maturity including interest

Days = number of days between settlement and maturity

Year = number of days in the year

AOR = add-on rate, stated as an annual percentage rate

Suppose that a Canadian pension fund buys a 180-day banker's acceptance (BA) with a quoted add-on rate of 4.38% for a 365-day year. If the initial principal amount is CAD10 million, the redemption amount due at maturity is found by re-arranging Equation 11 and entering PV = 10,000,000, Days = 180, Year = 365, and AOR = 0.0438.

$$FV = 10{,}000{,}000 + \left(10{,}000{,}000 \times \frac{180}{365} \times 0.0438\right) = 10{,}216{,}000$$

At maturity, the pension fund receives CAD10,216,000, the principal of CAD10 million plus interest of CAD216,000. The interest is calculated as the principal times the fraction of the year times the annual add-on rate. It is added to the principal to determine the redemption amount.

Suppose that after 45 days, the pension fund sells the BA to a dealer. At that time, the quoted add-on rate for a 135-day BA is 4.17%. The sale price for the BA can be calculated using Equation 11 for FV = 10,216,000, Days = 135, Year = 365, and AOR = 0.0417. The sale price is CAD10,060,829.

$$PV = \frac{10{,}216{,}000}{\left(1 + \frac{135}{365} \times 0.0417\right)} = 10{,}060{,}829$$

The characteristics of an add-on rate can be examined with Equation 12, which transforms Equation 11 algebraically to isolate the AOR term.

$$AOR = \left(\frac{\text{Year}}{\text{Days}}\right) \times \left(\frac{FV - PV}{PV}\right) \tag{12}$$

This equation indicates that an add-on rate is a reasonable yield measure for a money market investment. The first term, Year/Days, is the periodicity of the annual rate. The second term is the interest earned, $FV - PV$, divided by PV, the amount invested.

The pension fund's rate of return on its 45-day investment in the banker's acceptance can be calculated with Equation 12. Enter Year = 365, Days = 45, FV = 10,060,829, and PV = 10,000,000. Notice that FV here is the sale price, not the redemption amount.

$$AOR = \left(\frac{365}{45}\right) \times \left(\frac{10{,}060{,}829 - 10{,}000{,}000}{10{,}000{,}000}\right) = 0.04934$$

The rate of return, stated on a 365-day add-on rate basis, is 4.934%. This result is an annual rate for a periodicity of 8.11 (= 365/45). Implicitly, this assumes that the investment can be replicated 8.11 times over the year.

Investment analysis is made difficult for money market securities because (1) some instruments are quoted on a discount rate basis and others on an add-on rate basis and (2) some are quoted for a 360-day year and others for a 365-day year. Another difference is that the "amount" of a money market instrument quoted on a discount rate basis typically is the face value paid at maturity. However, the "amount" when quoted on an add-on rate basis usually is the principal, the price at issuance. To make money market investment decisions, it is essential to compare instruments on a common basis. An example illustrates this point.

Suppose that an investor is comparing two money market instruments: (A) 90-day commercial paper quoted at a discount rate of 5.76% for a 360-day year and (B) 90-day bank time deposit quoted at an add-on rate of 5.90% for a 365-day year. Which offers the higher expected rate of return assuming that the credit risks are the same? The price of the commercial paper is 98.560 per 100 of face value, calculated using Equation 9 and entering FV = 100, Days = 90, Year = 360, and DR = 0.0576.

$$PV = 100 \times \left(1 - \frac{90}{360} \times 0.0576\right) = 98.560$$

Next, use Equation 12 to solve for the AOR for a 365-day year, whereby $Year$ = 365, $Days$ = 90, FV = 100, and PV = 98.560.

$$AOR = \left(\frac{365}{90}\right) \times \left(\frac{100 - 98.560}{98.560}\right) = 0.05925$$

The 90-day commercial paper discount rate of 5.76% converts to an add-on rate for a 365-day year of 5.925%. This converted rate is called a **bond equivalent yield**, or sometimes just an "investment yield." A bond equivalent yield is a money market rate stated on a 365-day add-on rate basis. If the risks are the same, the commercial paper offers 2.5 bps more in annual return than the bank time deposit.

EXAMPLE 10

Comparing Money Market Instruments Based on Bond Equivalent Yields

Suppose that a money market investor observes quoted rates on the following four 180-day money market instruments:

Money Market Instrument	Quotation Basis	Assumed Number of Days in the Year	Quoted Rate
A	Discount Rate	360	4.33%
B	Discount Rate	365	4.36%
C	Add-On Rate	360	4.35%
D	Add-On Rate	365	4.45%

Calculate the bond equivalent yield for each instrument. Which instrument offers the investor the highest rate of return if the credit risks are the same?

Solution:

A Use Equation 9 to get the price per 100 of par value, where $FV = 100$, $Days = 180$, Year = 360, and $DR = 0.0433$.

$$PV = 100 \times \left(1 - \frac{180}{360} \times 0.0433\right) = 97.835$$

Use Equation 12 to get the bond equivalent yield, where Year = 365, Days = 180, $FV = 100$, and $PV = 97.835$.

$$AOR = \left(\frac{365}{180}\right) \times \left(\frac{100 - 97.835}{97.835}\right) = 0.04487$$

The bond equivalent yield for Bond A is 4.487%.

B Use Equation 9 to get the price per 100 of face value, where $FV = 100$, Days = 180, Year = 365, and $DR = 0.0436$.

$$PV = 100 \times \left(1 - \frac{180}{365} \times 0.0436\right) = 97.850$$

Use Equation 12 to get the bond equivalent yield, where Year = 365, Days = 180, $FV = 100$, and $PV = 97.850$.

$$AOR = \left(\frac{365}{180}\right) \times \left(\frac{100 - 97.850}{97.850}\right) = 0.04456$$

The bond equivalent yield for Bond B is 4.456%.

C First, determine the redemption amount per 100 of principal ($PV = 100$), where Days = 180, Year = 360, and $AOR = 0.0435$.

$$FV = 100 + \left(100 \times \frac{180}{360} \times 0.0435\right) = 102.175$$

Use Equation 12 to get the bond equivalent yield, where Year = 365, Days = 180, FV = 102.175, and PV = 100.

$$AOR = \left(\frac{365}{180}\right) \times \left(\frac{102.175 - 100}{100}\right) = 0.04410$$

The bond equivalent yield for Bond C is 4.410%.

Another way to get the bond equivalent yield for Bond C is to observe that the AOR of 4.35% for a 360-day year can be obtained using Equation 12 for Year = 360, Days = 180, FV = 102.175, and PV = 100.

$$AOR = \left(\frac{360}{180}\right) \times \left(\frac{102.175 - 100}{100}\right) = 0.0435$$

Therefore, an add-on rate for a 360-day year only needs to be multiplied by the factor of 365/360 to get the 365-day year bond equivalent yield.

$$\frac{365}{360} \times 0.0435 = 0.04410$$

D The quoted rate for Bond D of 4.45% is a bond equivalent yield, which is defined as an add-on rate for a 365-day year.

If the risks of these money market instruments are the same, Bond A offers the highest rate of return on a bond equivalent yield basis, 4.487%.

The third difference between yield measures in the money market and the bond market is the periodicity of the annual rate. Because bond yields-to-maturity are computed using interest rate compounding, there is a well-defined periodicity. For instance, bond yields-to-maturity for semiannual compounding are annualized for a periodicity of two. Money market rates are computed using simple interest without compounding. In the money market, the periodicity is the number of days in the year divided by the number of days to maturity. Therefore, money market rates for different times-to-maturity have different periodicities.

Suppose that an analyst prefers to convert money market rates to a semiannual bond basis so that the rates are directly comparable to yields on bonds that make semiannual coupon payments. The quoted rate for a 90-day money market instrument is 10%, quoted as a bond equivalent yield, which means its periodicity is 365/90. Using Equation 7, the conversion is from m = 365/90 to n = 2 for $APR_{365/90}$ = 0.10.

$$\left(1 + \frac{0.10}{365/90}\right)^{365/90} = \left(1 + \frac{APR_2}{2}\right)^2, \quad APR_2 = 0.10127$$

Therefore, 10% for a periodicity of 365/90 corresponds to 10.127% for a periodicity of two. The difference is significant—12.7 bps. In general, the difference depends on the level of the annual percentage rate. When interest rates are lower, the difference between the annual rates for any two periodicities is reduced.

4 THE MATURITY STRUCTURE OF INTEREST RATES

There are many reasons why the yields-to-maturity on any two bonds are different. Suppose that the yield-to-maturity is higher on Bond X than on Bond Y. The following are some possible reasons for the difference between the yields:

- Currency—Bond X could be denominated in a currency with a higher expected rate of inflation than the currency in which Bond Y is denominated.
- Credit risk—Bond X could have a non-investment-grade rating of BB, and Bond Y could have an investment-grade rating of AA.
- Liquidity—Bond X could be illiquid, and Bond Y could be actively traded.
- Tax Status—Interest income on Bond X could be taxable, whereas interest income on Bond Y could be exempt from taxation.
- Periodicity—Bond X could make a single annual coupon payment, and its yield-to-maturity could be quoted for a periodicity of one. Bond Y could make monthly coupon payments, and its yield-to-maturity could be annualized for a periodicity of 12.

Obviously, another reason is that Bond X and Bond Y could have different times-to-maturity. This factor explaining the differences in yields is called the **maturity structure**, or **term structure**, of interest rates. It involves the analysis of yield curves, which are relationships between yields-to-maturity and times-to-maturity. There are different types of yield curves, depending on the characteristics of the underlying bonds.

In theory, maturity structure should be analyzed for bonds that have the same properties other than time-to-maturity. The bonds should be denominated in the same currency and have the same credit risk, liquidity, and tax status. Their annual rates should be quoted for the same periodicity. Also, they should have the same coupon rate so that they each have the same degree of coupon reinvestment risk. In practice, maturity structure is analyzed for bonds for which these strong assumptions rarely hold.

The ideal dataset would be yields-to-maturity on a series of *zero-coupon* government bonds for a full range of maturities. This dataset is the government bond **spot curve**, sometimes called the zero or "strip" curve (because the coupon payments are "stripped" off of the bonds). The spot, zero, or strip curve is a sequence of yields-to-maturity on zero-coupon bonds. Often, these government spot rates are interpreted as the "risk-free" yields; in this context, "risk-free" refers only to default risk. There still could be a significant amount of inflation risk to the investor, as well as liquidity risk.

A government bond spot curve is illustrated in Exhibit 5 for maturities ranging from 1 to 30 years. The annual yields are stated on a semiannual bond basis, which facilitates comparison to coupon-bearing bonds that make semiannual payments.

Exhibit 5 A Government Bond Spot Curve

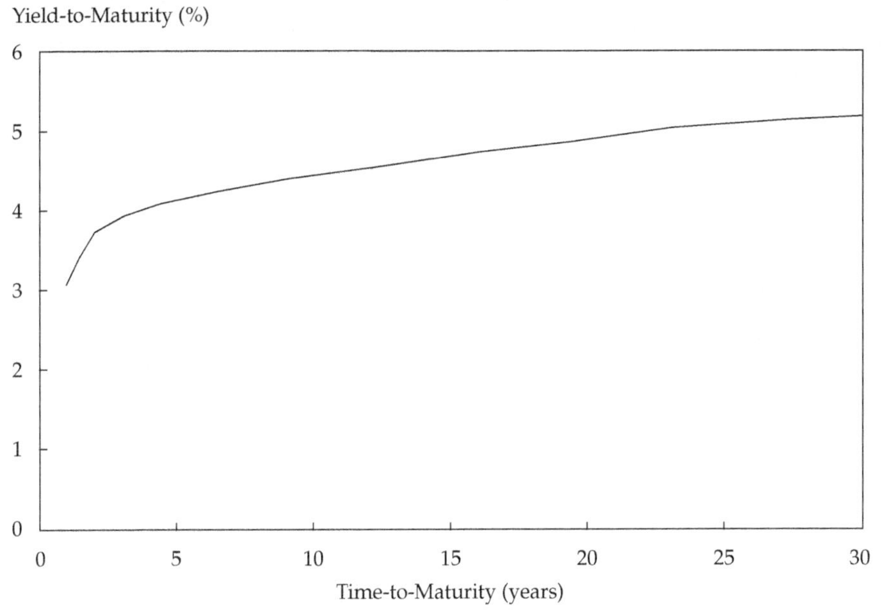

This spot curve is upward sloping and flattens for longer times-to-maturity. Longer-term government bonds usually have higher yields than shorter-term bonds. This pattern is typical under normal market conditions. Sometimes, a spot curve is downward sloping in that shorter-term yields are higher than longer-term yields. This downward sloping spot curve is called an inverted yield curve. The theories that attempt to explain the shape of the yield curve and its implications for future financial market conditions are covered in later readings.

This hypothetical spot curve is ideal for analyzing maturity structure because it best meets the "other things being equal" assumption. These government bonds presumably have the same currency, credit risk, liquidity, and tax status. Most importantly, they have no coupon reinvestment risk because there are no coupons to reinvest. However, most actively traded government and corporate bonds make coupon payments. Therefore, analysis of maturity structure usually is based on price data on government bonds that make coupon payments. These coupon bonds might not have the same liquidity and tax status. Older ("seasoned") bonds tend to be less liquid than newly issued debt because they are owned by "buy-and-hold" institutional and retail investors. Governments issue new debt for regular times-to-maturity—for instance, 5-year and 10-year bonds. The current 6-year bond could be a 10-year bond that was issued four years ago. Also, as interest rates fluctuate, older bonds are priced at a discount or premium to par value, which can lead to tax differences. In some countries, capital gains have different tax treatment than capital losses and interest income.

Analysts usually use only the most recently issued and actively traded government bonds to build a yield curve. These bonds have similar liquidity, and because they are priced closer to par value, they have fewer tax effects. A problem is that there are limited data for the full range of maturities. Therefore, it is necessary to *interpolate* between observed yields. Exhibit 6 illustrates a yield curve for a government that issues 2-year, 3-year, 5-year, 7-year, 10-year, and 30-year bonds that make semiannual coupon payments. Straight-line interpolation is used between those points on the yield curve for coupon bonds.

Exhibit 6 A Government Bond Yield Curve

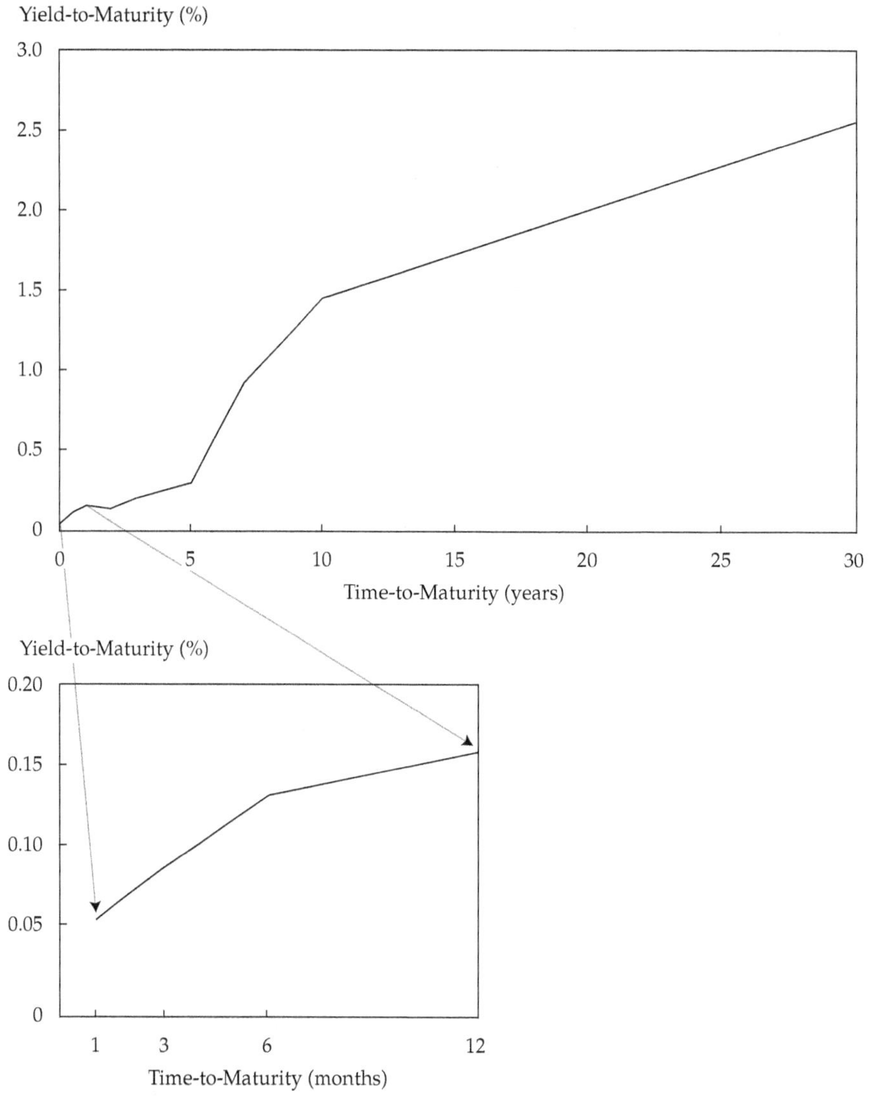

Exhibit 6 also includes yields for short-term government securities having 1 month, 3 months, 6 months, and 12 months to maturity. Although these money market instruments might have been issued and traded on a discount rate basis, they typically are reported as bond equivalent yields. It is important for the analyst to know whether they have been converted to the same periodicity as the longer-term government bonds. If not, the observed yield curve can be misleading because the number of periods in the year is not the same.

In addition to the yield curve on coupon bonds and the spot curve on zero-coupon bonds, maturity structure can be assessed using a **par curve**. A par curve is a sequence of yields-to-maturity such that each bond is priced at par value. The bonds, of course, are assumed to have the same currency, credit risk, liquidity, tax status, and annual yields stated for the same periodicity. Between coupon payment dates, the flat price (not the full price) is assumed to be equal to par value.

The par curve is obtained from a spot curve. On a coupon payment date, the following equation can be used to calculate a par rate given the sequence of spot rates.

$$100 = \frac{PMT}{\left(1+z_1\right)^1} + \frac{PMT}{\left(1+z_2\right)^2} + \cdots + \frac{PMT+100}{\left(1+z_N\right)^N} \qquad \textbf{(13)}$$

This equation is very similar to Equation 2 whereby $PV = FV = 100$. The problem is to solve for PMT algebraically. Then, $PMT/100$ is equal to the par rate *per period.*

An example illustrates the calculation of the par curve given a spot curve. Suppose the spot rates on government bonds are 5.263% for one year, 5.616% for two years, 6.359% for three years, and 7.008% for four years. These are effective annual rates. The one-year par rate is 5.263%.

$$100 = \frac{PMT+100}{\left(1.05263\right)^1}, \quad PMT = 5.263$$

The two-year par rate is 5.606%.

$$100 = \frac{PMT}{\left(1.05263\right)^1} + \frac{PMT+100}{\left(1.05616\right)^2}, \quad PMT = 5.606$$

The three-year and four-year par rates are 6.306% and 6.899%, respectively.

$$100 = \frac{PMT}{\left(1.05263\right)^1} + \frac{PMT}{\left(1.05616\right)^2} + \frac{PMT+100}{\left(1.06359\right)^3}, \quad PMT = 6.306$$

$$100 = \frac{PMT}{\left(1.05263\right)^1} + \frac{PMT}{\left(1.05616\right)^2} + \frac{PMT}{\left(1.06359\right)^3} + \frac{PMT+100}{\left(1.07008\right)^4}, \quad PMT = 6.899$$

The fixed-income securities covered so far have been **cash market securities**. Money market securities often are settled on a "same day," or "cash settlement," basis. Other securities have a difference between the trade date and the settlement date. For instance, if a government bond trades on a $T + 1$ basis, there is a one-day difference between the trade date and the settlement date. If a corporate bond trades on a $T + 3$ basis, the seller delivers the bond and the buyer makes payment in three business days. Cash markets are also called spot markets, which can be confusing because spot rate can have two meanings. It can mean the "rate on a bond traded in the spot, or cash, market." It can also mean "yield on a zero-coupon bond," which is the meaning of spot rate used in this reading.

A **forward market** is for future delivery, beyond the usual settlement time period in the cash market. Agreement to the terms for the transaction is on the trade date, but delivery of the security and payment for it is deferred to a future date. A **forward rate** is the interest rate on a bond or money market instrument traded in a forward market. For example, suppose that in the cash market, a five-year zero-coupon bond is priced at 81 per 100 of par value. Its yield-to-maturity is 4.2592%, stated on a semiannual bond basis.

$$81 = \frac{100}{\left(1+r\right)^{10}}, \quad r = 0.021296, \quad \times 2 = 0.042592$$

Suppose that a dealer agrees to deliver a five-year bond two years into the future for a price of 75 per 100 of par value. The credit risk, liquidity, and tax status of this bond traded in the forward market are the same as the one in the cash market. The forward rate is 5.8372%.

$$75 = \frac{100}{\left(1+r\right)^{10}}, \quad r = 0.029186, \quad \times 2 = 0.058372$$

The notation for forward rates is important to understand. Although finance textbook authors use varying notation, the most common market practice is to name this forward rate the "2y5y". This is pronounced "the two-year into five-year rate," or simply "the 2's, 5's." The idea is that the first number (two years) refers to the length of the forward period in years from today and the second number (five years) refers to the **tenor** of the underlying bond. The tenor is the remaining time-to-maturity for a bond (or a derivative contract). Therefore, 5.8372% is the "2y5y" forward rate for the zero-coupon bond—the five-year yield two years into the future. Note that the bond that will be a five-year zero in two years currently has seven years to maturity. In the money market, the forward rate usually refers to months. For instance, an analyst might inquire about the "1m6m" forward rate on Euribor, which is the rate on six-month Euribor one month into the future.

Implied forward rates (also known as forward yields) are calculated from spot rates. An implied forward rate is a break-even reinvestment rate. It links the return on an investment in a shorter-term zero-coupon bond to the return on an investment in a longer-term zero-coupon bond. Suppose that the shorter-term bond matures in *A* periods and the longer-term bond matures in *B* periods. The yields-to-maturity per period on these bonds are denoted z_A and z_B. The first is an *A*-period zero-coupon bond trading in the cash market. The second is a *B*-period zero-coupon cash market bond. The implied forward rate between period *A* and period *B* is denoted $IFR_{A,B-A}$. It is a forward rate on a security that starts in period *A* and ends in period *B*. Its tenor is $B - A$ periods.

Equation 14 is a general formula for the relationship between the two spot rates and the implied forward rate.

$$(1 + z_A)^A \times (1 + \text{IFR}_{A,B-A})^{B-A} = (1 + z_B)^B \quad \textbf{(14)}$$

Suppose that the yields-to-maturity on three-year and four-year zero-coupon bonds are 3.65% and 4.18%, respectively, stated on a semiannual bond basis. An analyst would like to know the "3y1y" implied forward rate, which is the implied one-year forward yield three years into the future. Therefore, $A = 6$ (periods), $B = 8$ (periods), $B - A = 2$ (periods), $z_6 = 0.0365/2$ (per period), and $z_8 = 0.0418/2$ (per period).

$$\left(1 + \frac{0.0365}{2}\right)^6 \times \left(1 + IFR_{6,2}\right)^2 = \left(1 + \frac{0.0418}{2}\right)^8, \quad IFR_{6,2} = 0.02889,$$

$$\times 2 = 0.05778$$

The "3y1y" implied forward yield is 5.778%, annualized for a periodicity of two.

Equation 14 can be used to construct a **forward curve**. A forward curve is a series of forward rates, each having the same time frame. These forward rates might be observed on transactions in the derivatives market. Often, the forward rates are implied from transactions in the cash market. Exhibit 7 displays the forward curve that is calculated from the government bond spot curve shown in Exhibit 5. These are one-year forward rates stated on a semiannual bond basis.

Exhibit 7 A Government Bond Spot Curve and Forward Curve

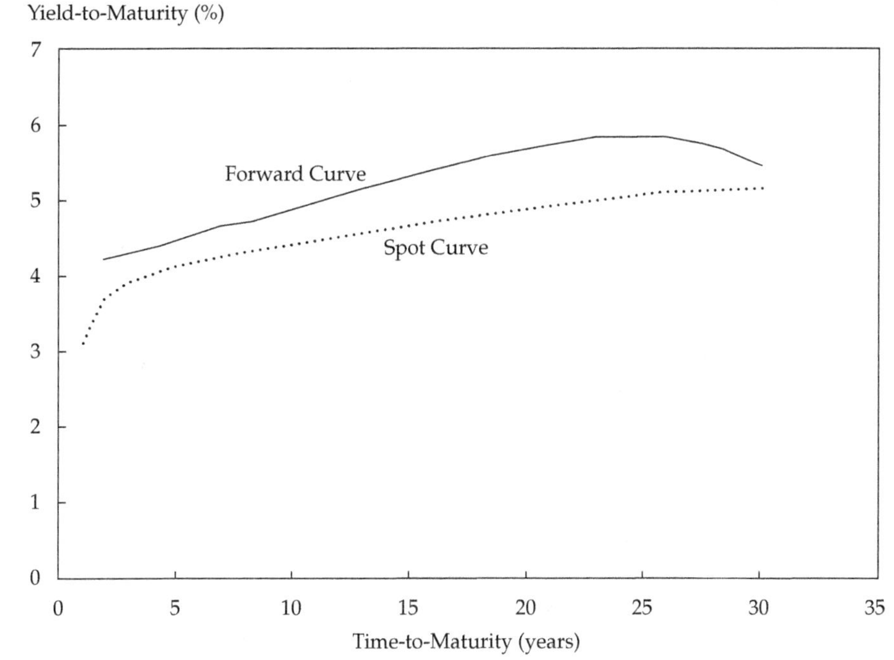

A forward rate can be interpreted as an incremental, or marginal, return for extending the time-to-maturity for an additional time period. Suppose an investor has a four-year investment horizon and is choosing between buying a three-year zero-coupon bond that is priced to yield 3.65% and a four-year zero that is priced to yield 4.18%. The incremental, or marginal, return for the fourth year is 5.778%, the "3y1y" implied forward rate. If the investor's view on future bond yields is that the one-year yield in three years is likely to be less than 5.778%, the investor might prefer to buy the four-year bond. However, if the investor's view is that the one-year yield will be more than the implied forward rate, the investor might prefer the three-year bond and the opportunity to reinvest at the expected higher rate. That explains why an implied forward rate is the *breakeven reinvestment rate.* Implied forward rates are very useful to investors as well as bond issuers in making maturity decisions.

EXAMPLE 11

Computing Forward Rates

Suppose that an investor observes these prices and yields-to-maturity on zero-coupon government bonds:

Maturity	Price	Yield-to-Maturity
1 year	97.50	2.548%
2 years	94.25	2.983%
3 years	91.75	2.891%

The prices are per 100 of par value. The yields-to-maturity are stated on a semiannual bond basis.

1 Compute the "1y1y" and "2y1y" implied forward rates, stated on a semiannual bond basis.

2 The investor has a three-year investment horizon and is choosing between (1) buying the two-year zero and reinvesting in another one-year zero in two years and (2) buying and holding to maturity the three-year zero. The investor decides to buy the two-year bond. Based on this decision, which of the following is the minimum yield-to-maturity the investor expects on one-year zeros two years from now?

A 2.548%

B 2.707%

C 2.983%

Solution to 1:

The "1y1y" implied forward rate is 3.419%. In Equation 14, A = 2 (periods), B = 4 (periods), $B - A$ = 2 (periods), z_2 = 0.02548/2 (per period), and z_4 = 0.02983/2 (per period).

$$\left(1+\frac{0.02548}{2}\right)^2 \times \left(1+IFR_{2,2}\right)^2 = \left(1+\frac{0.02983}{2}\right)^4, \quad IFR_{2,2} = 0.017095,$$

$$\times\, 2 = 0.03419$$

The "2y1y" implied forward rate is 2.707%. In Equation 14, A = 4 (periods), B = 6 (periods), $B - A$ = 2 (periods), z_4 = 0.02983/2 (per period), and z_6 = 0.02891/2 (per period).

$$\left(1+\frac{0.02983}{2}\right)^4 \times \left(1+IFR_{4,2}\right)^2 = \left(1+\frac{0.02891}{2}\right)^6, \quad IFR_{4,2} = 0.013536,$$

$$\times\, 2 = 0.02707$$

Solution to 2:

B is correct. The investor's view is that the one-year yield in two years will be greater than or equal to 2.707%.

The "2y1y" implied forward rate of 2.707% is the breakeven reinvestment rate. If the investor expects the one-year rate in two years to be less than that, the investor would prefer to buy the three-year zero. If the investor expects the one-year rate in two years to be greater than 2.707%, the investor might prefer to buy the two-year zero and reinvest the cash flow.

The forward curve has many applications in fixed-income analysis. Forward rates are used to make maturity choice decisions. They are used to identify arbitrage opportunities between transactions in the cash market for bonds and in derivatives markets. Forward rates are important in the valuation of derivatives, especially interest rate swaps and options. Those applications for the forward curve are covered in other readings.

Forward rates can be used to value a fixed-income security in the same manner as spot rates because they are interconnected. The spot curve can be calculated from the forward curve, and the forward curve can be calculated from the spot curve. Either curve can be used to value a fixed-rate bond. An example will illustrate this process.

Suppose the current forward curve for one-year rates is the following:

Time Period	Forward Rate
0y1y	1.88%
1y1y	2.77%
2y1y	3.54%
3y1y	4.12%

These are annual rates stated for a periodicity of one. They are effective annual rates. The first rate, the "0y1y," is the one-year spot rate. The others are one-year forward rates. Given these rates, the spot curve can be calculated as the *geometric average* of the forward rates.

The two-year implied spot rate is 2.3240%.

$$(1.0188 \times 1.0277) = (1 + z_2)^2, z_2 = 0.023240$$

The following are the equations for the three-year and four-year implied spot rates.

$$(1.0188 \times 1.0277 \times 1.0354) = (1 + z_3)^3, z_3 = 0.027278$$

$$(1.0188 \times 1.0277 \times 1.0354 \times 1.0412) = (1 + z_4)^4, z_4 = 0.030741$$

The three-year implied spot rate is 2.7278%, and the four-year spot rate is 3.0741%.

Suppose that an analyst needs to value a four-year, 3.75% annual coupon payment bond that has the same risks as the bonds used to obtain the forward curve. Using the implied spot rates, the value of the bond is 102.637 per 100 of par value.

$$\frac{3.75}{(1.0188)^1} + \frac{3.75}{(1.023240)^2} + \frac{3.75}{(1.027278)^3} + \frac{103.75}{(1.030741)^4} = 102.637$$

The bond also can be valued using the forward curve.

$$\frac{3.75}{(1.0188)} + \frac{3.75}{(1.0188 \times 1.0277)} + \frac{3.75}{(1.0188 \times 1.0277 \times 1.0354)} + \frac{103.75}{(1.0188 \times 1.0277 \times 1.0354 \times 1.0412)} = 102.637$$

YIELD SPREADS 5

A yield spread, in general, is the difference in yield between different fixed income securities. This section describes a number of yield spread measures.

5.1 Yield Spreads over Benchmark Rates

In fixed-income security analysis, it is important to understand *why* bond prices and yields-to-maturity change. To do this, it is useful to separate a yield-to-maturity into two components: the **benchmark** and the **spread**. The benchmark yield for a fixed-income security with a given time-to-maturity is the base rate, often a government bond yield. The spread is the difference between the yield-to-maturity and the benchmark.

The reason for this separation is to distinguish between macroeconomic and microeconomic factors that affect the bond price and, therefore, its yield-to-maturity. The benchmark captures the macroeconomic factors: the expected rate of inflation in the currency in which the bond is denominated, general economic growth and the business cycle, foreign exchange rates, and the impact of monetary and fiscal policy. Changes in those factors impact all bonds in the market, and the effect is seen mostly in changes in the benchmark yield. The spread captures the microeconomic factors specific to the bond issuer and the bond itself: credit risk of the issuer and changes in the quality rating on the bond, liquidity and trading in comparable securities, and the tax status of the bond. It should be noted, however, that general yield spreads across issuers can widen and narrow with changes in macroeconomic factors.

Exhibit 8 illustrates the building blocks of the yield-to-maturity, starting with the benchmark and the spread. The benchmark is often called the risk-free rate of return. Also, the benchmark can be broken down into the expected real rate and the expected inflation rate in the economy. The yield spread is called the risk premium over the "risk-free" rate of return. The risk premium provides the investor with compensation for the credit and liquidity risks, and possibly the tax impact of holding a specific bond.

Exhibit 8 Yield-to-Maturity Building Blocks

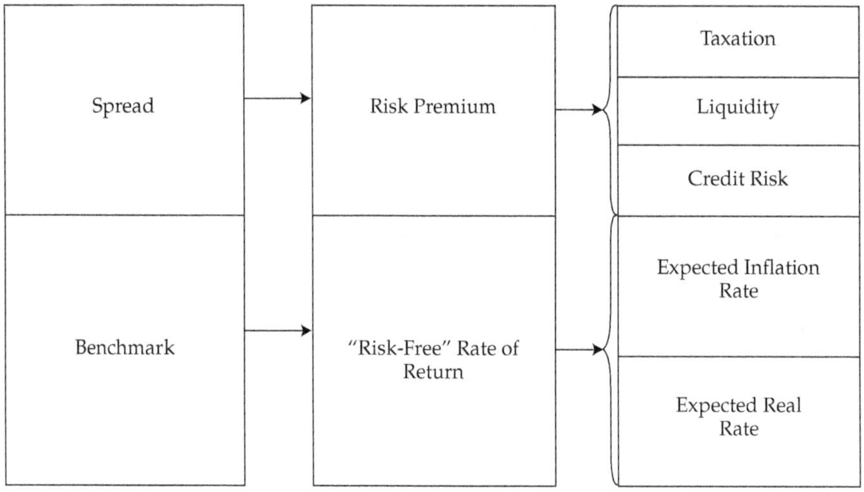

The benchmark varies across financial markets. Fixed-rate bonds often use a government benchmark security with the same time-to-maturity as, or the closest time-to-maturity to, the specified bond. This benchmark is usually the most recently issued government bond and is called the **on-the-run** security. The on-the-run government bond is the most actively traded security and has a coupon rate closest to the current market discount rate for that maturity. That implies that it is priced close to par value. Seasoned government bonds are called **off-the-run**. On-the-run bonds typically trade at slightly lower yields-to-maturity than off-the-run bonds having the same or similar times-to-maturity because of differences in demand for the securities and, sometimes, differences in the cost of financing the government security in the repo market.

A frequently used benchmark for floating-rate notes has long been Libor. As a composite interbank rate, it is not a risk-free rate. The yield spread over a specific benchmark is referred to as the **benchmark spread** and is usually measured in basis points. If no benchmark exists for a specific bond's tenor or a bond has an unusual maturity, interpolation is used to derive an implied benchmark. Also, bonds with very long tenors are priced over the longest available benchmark bond. For example, 100-year bonds (often called "century bonds") in the United States are priced over the 30-year US Treasury benchmark rate.

In the United Kingdom, the United States, and Japan, the benchmark rate for fixed-rate bonds is a government bond yield. The yield spread in basis points over an actual or interpolated government bond is known as the **G-spread**. The spread over a government bond is the return for bearing greater credit, liquidity, and other risks relative to the sovereign bond. Euro-denominated corporate bonds are priced over a EUR interest rate swap benchmark. For example, a newly issued five-year EUR bond might be priced at a rate of "mid-swaps" plus 150 bps, where "mid-swaps" is the average of the bid and offered swap rates. The yield spread is over a five-year EUR swap rate rather than a government benchmark. Note that the government bond yield or swap rate used as the benchmark for a specific corporate bond will change over time as the remaining time-to-maturity changes.

The yield spread of a specific bond over the standard swap rate in that currency of the same tenor is known as the **I-spread** or **interpolated spread** to the swap curve. This yield spread over Libor allows comparison of bonds with differing credit and liquidity risks against an interbank lending benchmark. Issuers often use the Libor spread to determine the relative cost of fixed-rate bonds versus floating-rate alternatives, such as an FRN or commercial paper. Investors use the Libor spread as a measure of a bond's credit risk. Whereas a standard interest rate swap involves an exchange of fixed for floating cash flows based on a floating index, an **asset swap** converts the periodic fixed coupon of a specific bond to a Libor plus or minus a spread. If the bond is priced close to par, this conversion approximates the price of a bond's credit risk over the Libor index. Exhibit 9 illustrates these yield spreads using the Bloomberg Fixed Income Relative Value (FIRV) page.

This example is for the 3.75% Apple bond that matures on 13 November 2047. The spreads are in the top-left corner of the page. The bond's flat asked price was 96.461 per 100 of par value on 12 July 2018, and its yield-to-maturity was 3.955%. On that date, the yield spread over a particular Treasury benchmark was 104 bps. Its G-spread over an interpolated government bond yield was also 104 bps. These two spreads sometimes differ by a few basis points, especially if the benchmark maturity differs from that of the underlying bond. The bond's I-spread was 109 bps. That Libor spread was a little larger than the G-spread because 30-year Treasury yields were slightly higher than 30-year Libor swap rates at that time. The use of these spreads in investor strategies will be covered in more detail in later readings. In general, an analyst will track these spreads relative to their averages and historical highs and lows in an attempt to identify relative value.

5.2 Yield Spreads over the Benchmark Yield Curve

A yield curve shows the relationship between yields-to-maturity and times-to-maturity for securities with the same risk profile. For example, the government bond yield curve is the relationship between the yields of on-the-run government bonds and their times-to-maturity. The swap yield curve shows the relationship between fixed Libor swap rates and their times-to-maturity.

Each of these yield curves represents the term structure of benchmark interest rates, whether for "risk-free" government yields or "risky" fixed swap rates. Benchmark yield curves tend to be upward-sloping because investors typically demand a premium for holding longer-term securities. In general, investors face greater price risk for a given change in yield for longer-term bonds. This topic is covered further in the reading "Understanding Fixed-Income Risk and Return." The term structure of interest rates is dynamic, with short-term rates driven by central bank policy and longer-term rates affected by long-term growth and inflation expectations.

Isolating credit risk over varying times-to-maturity gives rise to a term structure of credit spreads that is distinct for each borrower. The G-spread and I-spread each use the same discount rate for each cash flow. Another approach is to calculate a constant yield spread over a government (or interest rate swap) spot curve instead. This spread is known as the **zero volatility spread (Z-spread)** of a bond over the benchmark rate. In Exhibit 9, the Z-spread for the Apple bond was reported to be 107 bps.

The Z-spread over the benchmark spot curve can be calculated with Equation 15:

$$PV = \frac{PMT}{(1 + z_1 + Z)^1} + \frac{PMT}{(1 + z_2 + Z)^2} + \cdots + \frac{PMT + FV}{(1 + z_N + Z)^N} \quad (15)$$

The benchmark spot rates—z_1, z_2, ..., z_N—are derived from the government yield curve (or from fixed rates on interest rate swaps). Z is the Z-spread per period and is the same for all time periods. In Equation 15, N is an integer, so the calculation is on

Exhibit 9 Bloomberg FIRV Page for the 3.75% Apple Bond

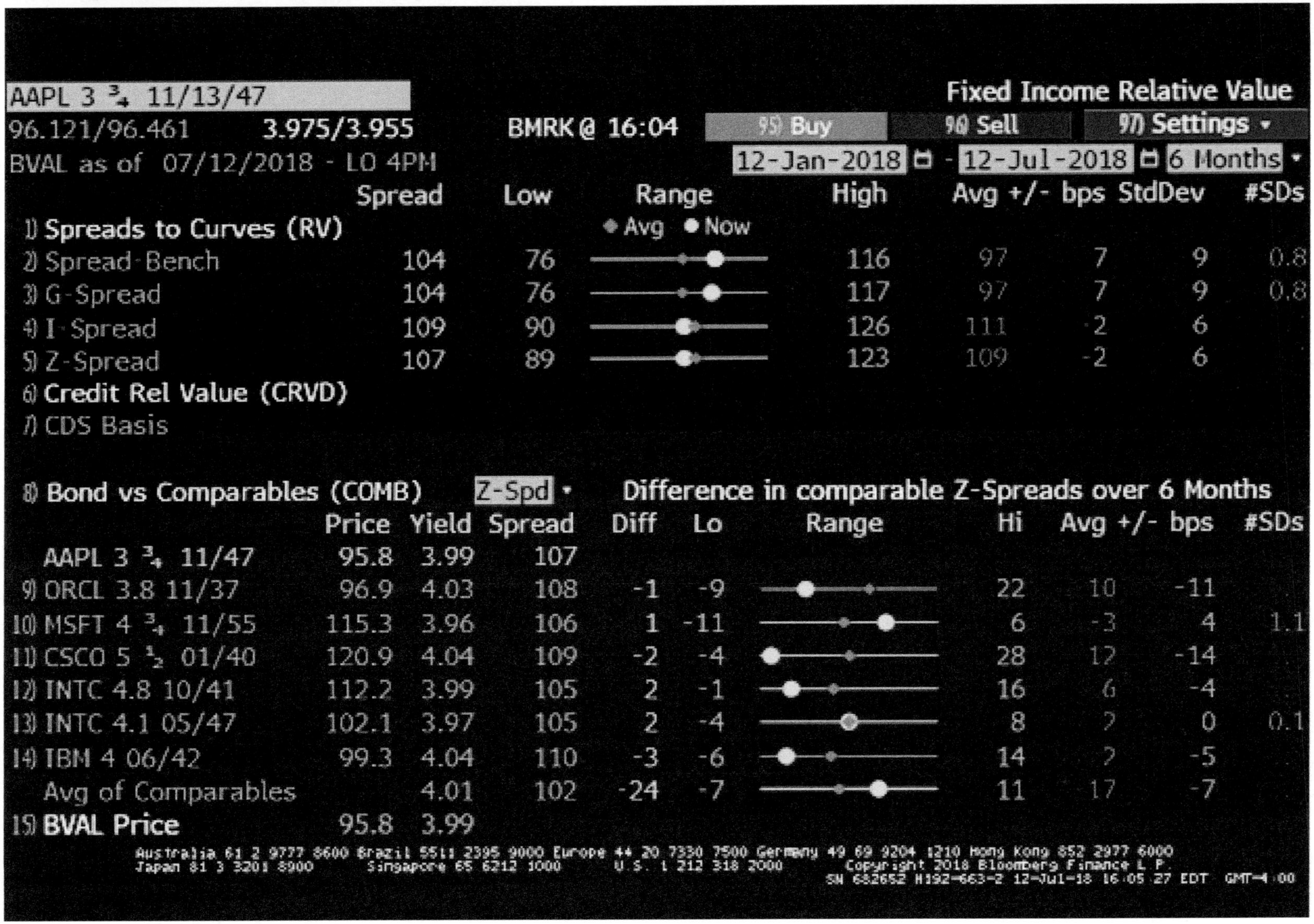

a coupon date when the accrued interest is zero. Sometimes, the Z-spread is called the "static spread" because it is constant (and has zero volatility). In practice, the Z-spread is usually calculated in a spreadsheet using a goal seek function or similar solver function.

The Z-spread is also used to calculate the **option-adjusted spread** (OAS) on a callable bond. The OAS, like the option-adjusted yield, is based on an option-pricing model and an assumption about future interest rate volatility. Then, the value of the embedded call option, which is stated in basis points per year, is subtracted from the yield spread. In particular, it is subtracted from the Z-spread:

OAS = Z-spread – Option value (in basis points per year)

This important topic is covered in later readings.

EXAMPLE 12

The G-Spread and the Z-Spread

A 6% annual coupon corporate bond with two years remaining to maturity is trading at a price of 100.125. The two-year, 4% annual payment government benchmark bond is trading at a price of 100.750. The one-year and two-year government spot rates are 2.10% and 3.635%, respectively, stated as effective annual rates.

1 Calculate the G-spread, the spread between the yields-to-maturity on the corporate bond and the government bond having the same maturity.

2 Demonstrate that the Z-spread is 234.22 bps.

Solution to 1:

The yield-to-maturity for the corporate bond is 5.932%.

$$100.125 = \frac{6}{(1+r)^1} + \frac{106}{(1+r)^2},\quad r = 0.05932$$

The yield-to-maturity for the government benchmark bond is 3.605%.

$$100.750 = \frac{4}{(1+r)^1} + \frac{104}{(1+r)^2},\quad r = 0.03605$$

The G-spread is 232.7 bps: 0.05932 – 0.03605 = 0.02327.

Solution to 2:

Solve for the value of the corporate bond using z_1 = 0.0210, z_2 = 0.03635, and Z = 0.023422:

$$\frac{6}{(1+0.0210+0.023422)^1} + \frac{106}{(1+0.03635+0.023422)^2}$$

$$= \frac{6}{(1.044422)^1} + \frac{106}{(1.059772)^2} = 100.125$$

SUMMARY

This reading covers the principles and techniques that are used in the valuation of fixed-rate bonds, as well as floating-rate notes and money market instruments. These building blocks are used extensively in fixed-income analysis. The following are the main points made in the reading:

- The market discount rate is the rate of return required by investors given the risk of the investment in the bond.
- A bond is priced at a premium above par value when the coupon rate is greater than the market discount rate.
- A bond is priced at a discount below par value when the coupon rate is less than the market discount rate.
- The amount of any premium or discount is the present value of the "excess" or "deficiency" in the coupon payments relative to the yield-to-maturity.
- The yield-to-maturity, the internal rate of return on the cash flows, is the implied market discount rate given the price of the bond.
- A bond price moves inversely with its market discount rate.
- The relationship between a bond price and its market discount rate is convex.
- The price of a lower-coupon bond is more volatile than the price of a higher-coupon bond, other things being equal.
- Generally, the price of a longer-term bond is more volatile than the price of shorter-term bond, other things being equal. An exception to this phenomenon can occur on low-coupon (but not zero-coupon) bonds that are priced at a discount to par value.
- Assuming no default, premium and discount bond prices are "pulled to par" as maturity nears.
- A spot rate is the yield-to-maturity on a zero-coupon bond.
- A yield-to-maturity can be approximated as a weighted average of the underlying spot rates.
- Between coupon dates, the full (or invoice, or "dirty") price of a bond is split between the flat (or quoted, or "clean") price and the accrued interest.
- Flat prices are quoted to not misrepresent the daily increase in the full price as a result of interest accruals.
- Accrued interest is calculated as a proportional share of the next coupon payment using either the actual/actual or 30/360 methods to count days.
- Matrix pricing is used to value illiquid bonds by using prices and yields on comparable securities having the same or similar credit risk, coupon rate, and maturity.
- The periodicity of an annual interest rate is the number of periods in the year.
- A yield quoted on a semiannual bond basis is an annual rate for a periodicity of two. It is the yield per semiannual period times two.
- The general rule for periodicity conversions is that compounding more frequently at a lower annual rate corresponds to compounding less frequently at a higher annual rate.
- Street convention yields assume payments are made on scheduled dates, neglecting weekends and holidays.

- The current yield is the annual coupon payment divided by the flat price, thereby neglecting as a measure of the investor's rate of return the time value of money, any accrued interest, and the gain from buying at a discount and the loss from buying at a premium.
- The simple yield is like the current yield but includes the straight-line amortization of the discount or premium.
- The yield-to-worst on a callable bond is the lowest of the yield-to-first-call, yield-to-second-call, and so on, calculated using the call price for the future value and the call date for the number of periods.
- The option-adjusted yield on a callable bond is the yield-to-maturity after adding the theoretical value of the call option to the price.
- A floating-rate note (floater, or FRN) maintains a more stable price than a fixed-rate note because interest payments adjust for changes in market interest rates.
- The quoted margin on a floater is typically the specified yield spread over or under the reference rate, which often is Libor.
- The discount margin on a floater is the spread required by investors, and to which the quoted margin must be set, for the FRN to trade at par value on a rate reset date.
- Money market instruments, having one year or less time-to-maturity, are quoted on a discount rate or add-on rate basis.
- Money market discount rates understate the investor's rate of return (and the borrower's cost of funds) because the interest income is divided by the face value or the total amount redeemed at maturity, and not by the amount of the investment.
- Money market instruments need to be converted to a common basis for analysis.
- A money market bond equivalent yield is an add-on rate for a 365-day year.
- The periodicity of a money market instrument is the number of days in the year divided by the number of days to maturity. Therefore, money market instruments with different times-to-maturity have annual rates for different periodicities.
- In theory, the maturity structure, or term structure, of interest rates is the relationship between yields-to-maturity and times-to-maturity on bonds having the same currency, credit risk, liquidity, tax status, and periodicity.
- A spot curve is a series of yields-to-maturity on zero-coupon bonds.
- A frequently used yield curve is a series of yields-to-maturity on coupon bonds.
- A par curve is a series of yields-to-maturity assuming the bonds are priced at par value.
- In a cash market, the delivery of the security and cash payment is made on a settlement date within a customary time period after the trade date—for example, "$T + 3$."
- In a forward market, the delivery of the security and cash payment is made on a predetermined future date.
- A forward rate is the interest rate on a bond or money market instrument traded in a forward market.
- An implied forward rate (or forward yield) is the breakeven reinvestment rate linking the return on an investment in a shorter-term zero-coupon bond to the return on an investment in a longer-term zero-coupon bond.
- An implied forward curve can be calculated from the spot curve.

- Implied spot rates can be calculated as geometric averages of forward rates.
- A fixed-income bond can be valued using a market discount rate, a series of spot rates, or a series of forward rates.
- A bond yield-to-maturity can be separated into a benchmark and a spread.
- Changes in benchmark rates capture macroeconomic factors that affect all bonds in the market—inflation, economic growth, foreign exchange rates, and monetary and fiscal policy.
- Changes in spreads typically capture microeconomic factors that affect the particular bond—credit risk, liquidity, and tax effects.
- Benchmark rates are usually yields-to-maturity on government bonds or fixed rates on interest rate swaps.
- A G-spread is the spread over or under a government bond rate, and an I-spread is the spread over or under an interest rate swap rate.
- A G-spread or an I-spread can be based on a specific benchmark rate or on a rate interpolated from the benchmark yield curve.
- A Z-spread (zero-volatility spread) is based on the entire benchmark spot curve. It is the constant spread that is added to each spot rate such that the present value of the cash flows matches the price of the bond.
- An option-adjusted spread (OAS) on a callable bond is the Z-spread minus the theoretical value of the embedded call option.

PRACTICE PROBLEMS

1 A portfolio manager is considering the purchase of a bond with a 5.5% coupon rate that pays interest annually and matures in three years. If the required rate of return on the bond is 5%, the price of the bond per 100 of par value is *closest* to:

A 98.65.

B 101.36.

C 106.43.

2 A bond with two years remaining until maturity offers a 3% coupon rate with interest paid annually. At a market discount rate of 4%, the price of this bond per 100 of par value is *closest* to:

A 95.34.

B 98.00.

C 98.11.

3 An investor who owns a bond with a 9% coupon rate that pays interest semiannually and matures in three years is considering its sale. If the required rate of return on the bond is 11%, the price of the bond per 100 of par value is *closest* to:

A 95.00.

B 95.11.

C 105.15.

4 A bond offers an annual coupon rate of 4%, with interest paid semiannually. The bond matures in two years. At a market discount rate of 6%, the price of this bond per 100 of par value is *closest* to:

A 93.07.

B 96.28.

C 96.33.

5 A bond offers an annual coupon rate of 5%, with interest paid semiannually. The bond matures in seven years. At a market discount rate of 3%, the price of this bond per 100 of par value is *closest* to:

A 106.60.

B 112.54.

C 143.90.

6 A zero-coupon bond matures in 15 years. At a market discount rate of 4.5% per year and assuming annual compounding, the price of the bond per 100 of par value is *closest* to:

A 51.30.

B 51.67.

C 71.62.

7 Consider the following two bonds that pay interest annually:

Bond	Coupon Rate	Time-to-Maturity
A	5%	2 years
B	3%	2 years

At a market discount rate of 4%, the price difference between Bond A and Bond B per 100 of par value is *closest* to:

A 3.70.

B 3.77.

C 4.00.

The following information relates to Questions 8 and 9

Bond	Price	Coupon Rate	Time-to-Maturity
A	101.886	5%	2 years
B	100.000	6%	2 years
C	97.327	5%	3 years

8 Which bond offers the lowest yield-to-maturity?

A Bond A

B Bond B

C Bond C

9 Which bond will *most likely* experience the smallest percent change in price if the market discount rates for all three bonds increase by 100 basis points?

A Bond A

B Bond B

C Bond C

---

10 Suppose a bond's price is expected to increase by 5% if its market discount rate decreases by 100 basis points. If the bond's market discount rate increases by 100 basis points, the bond price is *most likely* to change by:

A 5%.

B less than 5%.

C more than 5%.

The following information relates to Questions 11 and 12

Bond	Coupon Rate	Maturity (years)
A	6%	10
B	6%	5
C	8%	5

All three bonds are currently trading at par value.

11 Relative to Bond C, for a 200 basis point decrease in the required rate of return, Bond B will *most likely* exhibit a(n):

A equal percentage price change.

B greater percentage price change.

C smaller percentage price change.

12 Which bond will *most likely* experience the greatest percentage change in price if the market discount rates for all three bonds increase by 100 basis points?

A Bond A

B Bond B

C Bond C

---

13 An investor considers the purchase of a 2-year bond with a 5% coupon rate, with interest paid annually. Assuming the sequence of spot rates shown below, the price of the bond is *closest* to:

Time-to-Maturity	Spot Rates
1 year	3%
2 years	4%

A 101.93.

B 102.85.

C 105.81.

14 A 3-year bond offers a 10% coupon rate with interest paid annually. Assuming the following sequence of spot rates, the price of the bond is *closest* to:

Time-to-Maturity	Spot Rates
1 year	8.0%
2 years	9.0%
3 years	9.5%

A 96.98.

B 101.46.

C 102.95.

The following information relates to Questions 15–17

Bond	Coupon Rate	Time-to-Maturity	Time-to-Maturity	Spot Rates
X	8%	3 years	1 year	8%
Y	7%	3 years	2 years	9%
Z	6%	3 years	3 years	10%

All three bonds pay interest annually.

15 Based upon the given sequence of spot rates, the price of Bond X is *closest* to:

A 95.02.

B 95.28.

C 97.63.

16 Based upon the given sequence of spot rates, the price of Bond Y is *closest* to:

A 87.50.

B 92.54.

C 92.76.

17 Based upon the given sequence of spot rates, the yield-to-maturity of Bond Z is *closest* to:

A 9.00%.

B 9.92%.

C 11.93%

---

18 Bond dealers *most* often quote the:

A flat price.

B full price.

C full price plus accrued interest.

The following information relates to Questions 19–21

Bond G, described in the exhibit below, is sold for settlement on 16 June 2020.

Annual Coupon	5%
Coupon Payment Frequency	Semiannual
Interest Payment Dates	10 April and 10 October
Maturity Date	10 October 2022
Day Count Convention	30/360
Annual Yield-to-Maturity	4%

19 The full price that Bond G settles at on 16 June 2020 is *closest* to:

A 102.36.

B 103.10.

C 103.65.

20 The accrued interest per 100 of par value for Bond G on the settlement date of 16 June 2020 is *closest* to:

A 0.46.

B 0.73.

C 0.92.

21 The flat price for Bond G on the settlement date of 16 June 2020 is *closest* to:

A 102.18.

B 103.10.

C 104.02.

---

22 Matrix pricing allows investors to estimate market discount rates and prices for bonds:

A with different coupon rates.

B that are not actively traded.

C with different credit quality.

23 When underwriting new corporate bonds, matrix pricing is used to get an estimate of the:

A required yield spread over the benchmark rate.

B market discount rate of other comparable corporate bonds.

C yield-to-maturity on a government bond having a similar time-to-maturity.

24 A bond with 20 years remaining until maturity is currently trading for 111 per 100 of par value. The bond offers a 5% coupon rate with interest paid semiannually. The bond's annual yield-to-maturity is *closest* to:

A 2.09%.

B 4.18%.

C 4.50%.

25 The annual yield-to-maturity, stated for with a periodicity of 12, for a 4-year, zero-coupon bond priced at 75 per 100 of par value is *closest* to:

A 6.25%.

B 7.21%.

C 7.46%.

26 A 5-year, 5% semiannual coupon payment corporate bond is priced at 104.967 per 100 of par value. The bond's yield-to-maturity, quoted on a semiannual bond basis, is 3.897%. An analyst has been asked to convert to a monthly periodicity. Under this conversion, the yield-to-maturity is *closest to*:

A 3.87%.

B 4.95%.

C 7.67%.

The following information relates to Questions 27–30

A bond with 5 years remaining until maturity is currently trading for 101 per 100 of par value. The bond offers a 6% coupon rate with interest paid semiannually. The bond is first callable in 3 years, and is callable after that date on coupon dates according to the following schedule:

End of Year	Call Price
3	102
4	101
5	100

27 The bond's annual yield-to-maturity is *closest* to:

A 2.88%.

B 5.77%.

C 5.94%.

28 The bond's annual yield-to-first-call is *closest* to:

A 3.12%.

B 6.11%.

C 6.25%.

29 The bond's annual yield-to-second-call is *closest* to:

A 2.97%.

B 5.72%.

C 5.94%.

30 The bond's yield-to-worst is *closest* to:

A 2.88%.

B 5.77%.

C 6.25%.

---

31 A two-year floating-rate note pays 6-month Libor plus 80 basis points. The floater is priced at 97 per 100 of par value. Current 6-month Libor is 1.00%. Assume a 30/360 day-count convention and evenly spaced periods. The discount margin for the floater in basis points (bps) is *closest* to:

A 180 bps.

B 236 bps.

C 420 bps.

32 An analyst evaluates the following information relating to floating rate notes (FRNs) issued at par value that have 3-month Libor as a reference rate:

Floating Rate Note	Quoted Margin	Discount Margin
X	0.40%	0.32%
Y	0.45%	0.45%
Z	0.55%	0.72%

Based only on the information provided, the FRN that will be priced at a premium on the next reset date is:

A FRN X.

B FRN Y.

C FRN Z.

33 A 365-day year bank certificate of deposit has an initial principal amount of USD 96.5 million and a redemption amount due at maturity of USD 100 million. The number of days between settlement and maturity is 350. The bond equivalent yield is *closest* to:

A 3.48%.

B 3.65%.

C 3.78%.

34 The bond equivalent yield of a 180-day banker's acceptance quoted at a discount rate of 4.25% for a 360-day year is *closest* to:

A 4.31%.

B 4.34%.

C 4.40%.

35 Which of the following statements describing a par curve is *incorrect*?

A A par curve is obtained from a spot curve.

B All bonds on a par curve are assumed to have different credit risk.

C A par curve is a sequence of yields-to-maturity such that each bond is priced at par value.

36 A yield curve constructed from a sequence of yields-to-maturity on zero-coupon bonds is the:

A par curve.

B spot curve.

C forward curve.

37 The rate, interpreted to be the incremental return for extending the time-to-maturity of an investment for an additional time period, is the:

A add-on rate.

B forward rate.

C yield-to-maturity.

The following information relates to Questions 38 and 39

Time Period	Forward Rate
"0y1y"	0.80%
"1y1y"	1.12%
"2y1y"	3.94%
"3y1y"	3.28%
"4y1y"	3.14%

All rates are annual rates stated for a periodicity of one (effective annual rates).

38 The 3-year implied spot rate is *closest* to:

A 1.18%.

B 1.94%.

C 2.28%.

39 The value per 100 of par value of a two-year, 3.5% coupon bond, with interest payments paid annually, is *closest* to:

A 101.58.

B 105.01.

C 105.82.

---

40 The spread component of a specific bond's yield-to-maturity is *least likely* impacted by changes in:

A its tax status.

B its quality rating.

C inflation in its currency of denomination.

41 The yield spread of a specific bond over the standard swap rate in that currency of the same tenor is *best* described as the:

A I-spread.

B Z-spread.

C G-spread.

The following information relates to Question 42

Bond	Coupon Rate	Time-to-Maturity	Price
UK Government Benchmark Bond	2%	3 years	100.25
UK Corporate Bond	5%	3 years	100.65

Both bonds pay interest annually. The current three-year EUR interest rate swap benchmark is 2.12%.

42 The G-spread in basis points (bps) on the UK corporate bond is *closest* to:

A 264 bps.

B 285 bps.

C 300 bps.

---

43 A corporate bond offers a 5% coupon rate and has exactly 3 years remaining to maturity. Interest is paid annually. The following rates are from the benchmark spot curve:

Time-to-Maturity	Spot Rate
1 year	4.86%
2 years	4.95%
3 years	5.65%

The bond is currently trading at a Z-spread of 234 basis points. The value of the bond is *closest to*:

A 92.38.

B 98.35.

C 106.56.

44 An option-adjusted spread (OAS) on a callable bond is the Z-spread:

A over the benchmark spot curve.

B minus the standard swap rate in that currency of the same tenor.

C minus the value of the embedded call option expressed in basis points per year.

SOLUTIONS

1 B is correct. The bond price is closest to 101.36. The price is determined in the following manner:

$$PV = \frac{PMT}{(1+r)^1} + \frac{PMT}{(1+r)^2} + \frac{PMT + FV}{(1+r)^3}$$

where:

PV = present value, or the price of the bond
PMT = coupon payment per period
FV = future value paid at maturity, or the par value of the bond
r = market discount rate, or required rate of return per period

$$PV = \frac{5.5}{(1+0.05)^1} + \frac{5.5}{(1+0.05)^2} + \frac{5.5 + 100}{(1+0.05)^3}$$

$PV = 5.24 + 4.99 + 91.13 = 101.36$

2 C is correct. The bond price is closest to 98.11. The formula for calculating the price of this bond is:

$$PV = \frac{PMT}{(1+r)^1} + \frac{PMT + FV}{(1+r)^2}$$

where:

PV = present value, or the price of the bond
PMT = coupon payment per period
FV = future value paid at maturity, or the par value of the bond
r = market discount rate, or required rate of return per period

$$PV = \frac{3}{(1+0.04)^1} + \frac{3 + 100}{(1+0.04)^2} = 2.88 + 95.23 = 98.11$$

3 A is correct. The bond price is closest to 95.00. The bond has six semiannual periods. Half of the annual coupon is paid in each period with the required rate of return also being halved. The price is determined in the following manner:

$$PV = \frac{PMT}{(1+r)^1} + \frac{PMT}{(1+r)^2} + \frac{PMT}{(1+r)^3} + \frac{PMT}{(1+r)^4} + \frac{PMT}{(1+r)^5} + \frac{PMT + FV}{(1+r)^6}$$

where:

PV = present value, or the price of the bond
PMT = coupon payment per period
FV = future value paid at maturity, or the par value of the bond
r = market discount rate, or required rate of return per period

$$PV = \frac{4.5}{(1+0.055)^1} + \frac{4.5}{(1+0.055)^2} + \frac{4.5}{(1+0.055)^3} + \frac{4.5}{(1+0.055)^4} + \frac{4.5}{(1+0.055)^5} + \frac{4.5+100}{(1+0.055)^6}$$

$PV = 4.27 + 4.04 + 3.83 + 3.63 + 3.44 + 75.79 = 95.00$

4 B is correct. The bond price is closest to 96.28. The formula for calculating this bond price is:

$$PV = \frac{PMT}{(1+r)^1} + \frac{PMT}{(1+r)^2} + \frac{PMT}{(1+r)^3} + \frac{PMT + FV}{(1+r)^4}$$

where:

PV = present value, or the price of the bond
PMT = coupon payment per period
FV = future value paid at maturity, or the par value of the bond
r = market discount rate, or required rate of return per period

$$PV = \frac{2}{(1+0.03)^1} + \frac{2}{(1+0.03)^2} + \frac{2}{(1+0.03)^3} + \frac{2+100}{(1+0.03)^4}$$

$PV = 1.94 + 1.89 + 1.83 + 90.62 = 96.28$

5 B is correct. The bond price is closest to 112.54. The formula for calculating this bond price is:

$$PV = \frac{PMT}{(1+r)^1} + \frac{PMT}{(1+r)^2} + \frac{PMT}{(1+r)^3} + \cdots + \frac{PMT + FV}{(1+r)^{14}}$$

where:

PV = present value, or the price of the bond
PMT = coupon payment per period
FV = future value paid at maturity, or the par value of the bond
r = market discount rate, or required rate of return per period

$$PV = \frac{2.5}{(1+0.015)^1} + \frac{2.5}{(1+0.015)^2} + \frac{2.5}{(1+0.015)^3} + \cdots + \frac{2.5}{(1+0.015)^{13}} + \frac{2.5+100}{(1+0.015)^{14}}$$

$PV = 2.46 + 2.43 + 2.39 + \ldots + 2.06 + 83.21 = 112.54$

6 B is correct. The price of the zero-coupon bond is closest to 51.67. The price is determined in the following manner:

$$PV = \frac{100}{(1+r)^N}$$

where:

PV = present value, or the price of the bond
r = market discount rate, or required rate of return per period
N = number of evenly spaced periods to maturity

$$PV = \frac{100}{(1 + 0.045)^{15}}$$

$$PV = 51.67$$

7 B is correct. The price difference between Bonds A and B is closest to 3.77. One method for calculating the price difference between two bonds with an identical term to maturity is to use the following formula:

$$PV = \frac{PMT}{(1 + r)^1} + \frac{PMT}{(1 + r)^2}$$

where:

PV = price difference
PMT = coupon difference per period
r = market discount rate, or required rate of return per period

In this case the coupon difference is (5% – 3%), or 2%.

$$PV = \frac{2}{(1 + 0.04)^1} + \frac{2}{(1 + 0.04)^2} = 1.92 + 1.85 = 3.77$$

8 A is correct. Bond A offers the lowest yield-to-maturity. When a bond is priced at a premium above par value the yield-to-maturity (YTM), or market discount rate is less than the coupon rate. Bond A is priced at a premium, so its YTM is below its 5% coupon rate. Bond B is priced at par value so its YTM is equal to its 6% coupon rate. Bond C is priced at a discount below par value, so its YTM is above its 5% coupon rate.

9 B is correct. Bond B will most likely experience the smallest percent change in price if market discount rates increase by 100 basis points. A higher-coupon bond has a smaller percentage price change than a lower-coupon bond when their market discount rates change by the same amount (the coupon effect). Also, a shorter-term bond generally has a smaller percentage price change than a longer-term bond when their market discount rates change by the same amount (the maturity effect). Bond B will experience a smaller percent change in price than Bond A because of the coupon effect. Bond B will also experience a smaller percent change in price than Bond C because of the coupon effect and the maturity effect.

10 B is correct. The bond price is most likely to change by less than 5%. The relationship between bond prices and market discount rate is not linear. The percentage price change is greater in absolute value when the market discount rate goes down than when it goes up by the same amount (the convexity effect). If a 100 basis point decrease in the market discount rate will cause the price of the bond to increase by 5%, then a 100 basis point increase in the market discount rate will cause the price of the bond to decline by an amount less than 5%.

11 B is correct. Generally, for two bonds with the same time-to-maturity, a lower coupon bond will experience a greater percentage price change than a higher coupon bond when their market discount rates change by the same amount. Bond B and Bond C have the same time-to-maturity (5 years); however, Bond B offers a lower coupon rate. Therefore, Bond B will likely experience a greater percentage change in price in comparison to Bond C.

12 A is correct. Bond A will likely experience the greatest percent change in price due to the coupon effect and the maturity effect. For two bonds with the same time-to-maturity, a lower-coupon bond has a greater percentage price change than a higher-coupon bond when their market discount rates change by the same amount. Generally, for the same coupon rate, a longer-term bond has a greater percentage price change than a shorter-term bond when their market discount rates change by the same amount. Relative to Bond C, Bond A and Bond B both offer the same lower coupon rate of 6%; however, Bond A has a longer time-to-maturity than Bond B. Therefore, Bond A will likely experience the greater percentage change in price if the market discount rates for all three bonds increase by 100 basis points.

13 A is correct. The bond price is closest to 101.93. The price is determined in the following manner:

$$PV = \frac{PMT}{(1+Z_1)^1} + \frac{PMT + FV}{(1+Z_2)^2}$$

where:

PV = present value, or the price of the bond
PMT = coupon payment per period
FV = future value paid at maturity, or the par value of the bond
Z_1 = spot rate, or the zero-coupon yield, for Period 1
Z_2 = spot rate, or the zero-coupon yield, for Period 2

$$PV = \frac{5}{(1+0.03)^1} + \frac{5+100}{(1+0.04)^2}$$

$PV = 4.85 + 97.08 = 101.93$

14 B is correct. The bond price is closest to 101.46. The price is determined in the following manner:

$$PV = \frac{PMT}{(1+Z_1)^1} + \frac{PMT}{(1+Z_2)^2} + \frac{PMT + FV}{(1+Z_3)^3}$$

where:

PV = present value, or the price of the bond
PMT = coupon payment per period
FV = future value paid at maturity, or the par value of the bond
Z_1 = spot rate, or the zero-coupon yield, or zero rate, for period 1
Z_2 = spot rate, or the zero-coupon yield, or zero rate, for period 2
Z_3 = spot rate, or the zero-coupon yield, or zero rate, for period 3

$$PV = \frac{10}{(1+0.08)^1} + \frac{10}{(1+0.09)^2} + \frac{10+100}{(1+0.095)^3}$$

$PV = 9.26 + 8.42 + 83.78 = 101.46$

15 B is correct. The bond price is closest to 95.28. The formula for calculating this bond price is:

$$PV = \frac{PMT}{(1 + Z_1)^1} + \frac{PMT}{(1 + Z_2)^2} + \frac{PMT + FV}{(1 + Z_3)^3}$$

where:

PV = present value, or the price of the bond
PMT = coupon payment per period
FV = future value paid at maturity, or the par value of the bond
Z_1 = spot rate, or the zero-coupon yield, or zero rate, for period 1
Z_2 = spot rate, or the zero-coupon yield, or zero rate, for period 2
Z_3 = spot rate, or the zero-coupon yield, or zero rate, for period 3

$$PV = \frac{8}{(1 + 0.08)^1} + \frac{8}{(1 + 0.09)^2} + \frac{8 + 100}{(1 + 0.10)^3}$$

$PV = 7.41 + 6.73 + 81.14 = 95.28$

16 C is correct. The bond price is closest to 92.76. The formula for calculating this bond price is:

$$PV = \frac{PMT}{(1 + Z_1)^1} + \frac{PMT}{(1 + Z_2)^2} + \frac{PMT + FV}{(1 + Z_3)^3}$$

where:

PV = present value, or the price of the bond
PMT = coupon payment per period
FV = future value paid at maturity, or the par value of the bond
Z_1 = spot rate, or the zero-coupon yield, or zero rate, for period 1
Z_2 = spot rate, or the zero-coupon yield, or zero rate, for period 2
Z_3 = spot rate, or the zero-coupon yield, or zero rate, for period 3

$$PV = \frac{7}{(1 + 0.08)^1} + \frac{7}{(1 + 0.09)^2} + \frac{7 + 100}{(1 + 0.10)^3}$$

$PV = 6.48 + 5.89 + 80.39 = 92.76$

17 B is correct. The yield-to-maturity is closest to 9.92%. The formula for calculating the price of Bond Z is:

$$PV = \frac{PMT}{(1 + Z_1)^1} + \frac{PMT}{(1 + Z_2)^2} + \frac{PMT + FV}{(1 + Z_3)^3}$$

where:

PV = present value, or the price of the bond
PMT = coupon payment per period
FV = future value paid at maturity, or the par value of the bond
Z_1 = spot rate, or the zero-coupon yield, or zero rate, for period 1
Z_2 = spot rate, or the zero-coupon yield, or zero rate, for period 2
Z_3 = spot rate, or the zero-coupon yield, or zero rate, for period 3

$$PV = \frac{6}{(1 + 0.08)^1} + \frac{6}{(1 + 0.09)^2} + \frac{6 + 100}{(1 + 0.10)^3}$$

$$PV = 5.56 + 5.05 + 79.64 = 90.25$$

Using this price, the bond's yield-to-maturity can be calculated as:

$$PV = \frac{PMT}{(1 + r)^1} + \frac{PMT}{(1 + r)^2} + \frac{PMT + FV}{(1 + r)^3}$$

$$90.25 = \frac{6}{(1 + r)^1} + \frac{6}{(1 + r)^2} + \frac{6 + 100}{(1 + r)^3}$$

$r = 9.92\%$

18 A is correct. Bond dealers usually quote the flat price. When a trade takes place, the accrued interest is added to the flat price to obtain the full price paid by the buyer and received by the seller on the settlement date. The reason for using the flat price for quotation is to avoid misleading investors about the market price trend for the bond. If the full price were to be quoted by dealers, investors would see the price rise day after day even if the yield-to-maturity did not change. That is because the amount of accrued interest increases each day. Then after the coupon payment is made the quoted price would drop dramatically. Using the flat price for quotation avoids that misrepresentation. The full price, flat price plus accrued interest, is not usually quoted by bond dealers. Accrued interest is included in not added to the full price and bond dealers do not generally quote the full price.

19 B is correct. The bond's full price is 103.10. The price is determined in the following manner:

As of the beginning of the coupon period on 10 April 2020, there are 2.5 years (5 semiannual periods) to maturity. These five semiannual periods occur on 10 October 2020, 10 April 2021, 10 October 2021, 10 April 2022 and 10 October 2022.

$$PV = \frac{PMT}{(1 + r)^1} + \frac{PMT}{(1 + r)^2} + \frac{PMT}{(1 + r)^3} + \frac{PMT}{(1 + r)^4} + \frac{PMT + FV}{(1 + r)^5}$$

where:

PV = present value

PMT = coupon payment per period

FV = future value paid at maturity, or the par value of the bond

r = market discount rate, or required rate of return per period

$$PV = \frac{2.5}{(1 + 0.02)^1} + \frac{2.5}{(1 + 0.02)^2} + \frac{2.5}{(1 + 0.02)^3} + \frac{2.5}{(1 + 0.02)^4} + \frac{2.5 + 100}{(1 + 0.02)^5}$$

$$PV = 2.45 + 2.40 + 2.36 + 2.31 + 92.84 = 102.36$$

The accrued interest period is identified as 66/180. The number of days between 10 April 2020 and 16 June 2020 is 66 days based on the 30/360 day count convention. (This is 20 days remaining in April + 30 days in May + 16 days in June = 66 days total). The number of days between coupon periods is assumed to be 180 days using the 30/360 day convention.

$$PV^{Full} = PV \times (1 + r)^{66/180}$$

$$PV^{Full} = 102.36 \times (1.02)^{66/180} = 103.10$$

20 C is correct. The accrued interest per 100 of par value is closest to 0.92. The accrued interest is determined in the following manner: The accrued interest period is identified as 66/180. The number of days between 10 April 2020 and 16 June 2020 is 66 days based on the 30/360 day count convention. (This is 20 days remaining in April + 30 days in May + 16 days in June = 66 days total). The number of days between coupon periods is assumed to be 180 days using the 30/360 day convention.

$$\text{Accrued interest} = \frac{t}{T} \times PMT$$

where:

t = number of days from the last coupon payment to the settlement date

T = number of days in the coupon period

t/T = fraction of the coupon period that has gone by since the last payment

PMT = coupon payment per period

$$\text{Accrued interest} = \frac{66}{180} \times \frac{5.00}{2} = 0.92$$

21 A is correct. The flat price of 102.18 is determined by subtracting the accrued interest (from question 20) from the full price (from question 19).

$$PV^{Flat} = PV^{Full} - \text{Accrued Interest}$$

$$PV^{Flat} = 103.10 - 0.92 = 102.18$$

22 B is correct. For bonds not actively traded or not yet issued, matrix pricing is a price estimation process that uses market discount rates based on the quoted prices of similar bonds (similar times-to-maturity, coupon rates, and credit quality).

23 A is correct. Matrix pricing is used in underwriting new bonds to get an estimate of the required yield spread over the benchmark rate. The benchmark rate is typically the yield-to-maturity on a government bond having the same, or close to the same, time-to-maturity. The spread is the difference between the yield-to-maturity on the new bond and the benchmark rate. The yield spread is the additional compensation required by investors for the difference in the credit risk, liquidity risk, and tax status of the bond relative to the government bond.

In matrix pricing, the market discount rates of comparable bonds and the yield-to-maturity on a government bond having a similar time-to-maturity are not estimated. Rather they are known and used to estimate the required yield spread of a new bond.

24 B is correct. The formula for calculating this bond's yield-to-maturity is:

$$PV = \frac{PMT}{(1+r)^1} + \frac{PMT}{(1+r)^2} + \frac{PMT}{(1+r)^3} + \cdots + \frac{PMT}{(1+r)^{39}} + \frac{PMT + FV}{(1+r)^{40}}$$

where:

PV = present value, or the price of the bond
PMT = coupon payment per period
FV = future value paid at maturity, or the par value of the bond
r = market discount rate, or required rate of return per period

$$111 = \frac{2.5}{(1+r)^1} + \frac{2.5}{(1+r)^2} + \frac{2.5}{(1+r)^3} + \cdots + \frac{2.5}{(1+r)^{39}} + \frac{2.5 + 100}{(1+r)^{40}}$$

$$r = 0.0209$$

To arrive at the annualized yield-to-maturity, the semiannual rate of 2.09% must be multiplied by two. Therefore, the yield-to-maturity is equal to 2.09% × 2 = 4.18%.

25 B is correct. The annual yield-to-maturity, stated for a periodicity of 12, is 7.21%. It is calculated as follows:

$$PV = \frac{FV}{(1+r)^N}$$

$$75 = \left(\frac{100}{(1+r)^{4\times12}}\right)$$

$$\frac{100}{75} = (1+r)^{48}$$

$$1.33333 = (1 + r)^{48}$$

$$[1.33333]^{1/48} = [(1 + r)^{48}]^{1/48}$$

$$1.33333^{02083} = (1 + r)$$

$$1.00601 = (1 + r)$$

$$1.00601 - 1 = r$$

$$0.00601 = r$$

$r \times 12 = 0.07212$, or approximately 7.21%

26 A is correct. The yield-to-maturity, stated for a periodicity of 12 (monthly periodicity), is 3.87%. The formula to convert an annual percentage rate (annual yield-to-maturity) from one periodicity to another is as follows:

$$\left(1 + \frac{APR_m}{m}\right)^m = \left(1 + \frac{APR_n}{n}\right)^n$$

$$\left(1 + \frac{0.03897}{2}\right)^2 = \left(1 + \frac{APR_{12}}{12}\right)^{12}$$

$$(1.01949)^2 = \left(1 + \frac{APR_{12}}{12}\right)^{12}$$

$$1.03935 = \left(1 + \frac{APR_{12}}{12}\right)^{12}$$

$$(1.03935)^{1/12} = \left[\left(1 + \frac{APR_{12}}{12}\right)^{12}\right]^{1/12}$$

$$1.00322 = \left(1 + \frac{APR_{12}}{12}\right)$$

$$1.00322 - 1 = \left(\frac{APR_{12}}{12}\right)$$

$APR_{12} = 0.00322 \times 12 = 0.03865$, or approximately 3.87%.

27 B is correct. The yield-to-maturity is 5.77%. The formula for calculating this bond's yield-to-maturity is:

$$PV = \frac{PMT}{(1+r)^1} + \frac{PMT}{(1+r)^2} + \frac{PMT}{(1+r)^3} + \cdots + \frac{PMT}{(1+r)^9} + \frac{PMT + FV}{(1+r)^{10}}$$

where:

PV = present value, or the price of the bond
PMT = coupon payment per period
FV = future value paid at maturity, or the par value of the bond
r = market discount rate, or required rate of return per period

$$101 = \frac{3}{(1+r)^1} + \frac{3}{(1+r)^2} + \frac{3}{(1+r)^3} + \cdots + \frac{3}{(1+r)^9} + \frac{3 + 100}{(1+r)^{10}}$$

$r = 0.02883$

To arrive at the annualized yield-to-maturity, the semiannual rate of 2.883% must be multiplied by two. Therefore, the yield-to-maturity is equal to 2.883% × 2 = 5.77% (rounded).

28 C is correct. The yield-to-first-call is 6.25%. Given the first call date is exactly three years away, the formula for calculating this bond's yield-to-first-call is:

$$PV = \frac{PMT}{(1+r)^1} + \frac{PMT}{(1+r)^2} + \frac{PMT}{(1+r)^3} + \cdots + \frac{PMT}{(1+r)^5} + \frac{PMT + FV}{(1+r)^6}$$

where:

PV = present value, or the price of the bond
PMT = coupon payment per period
FV = call price paid at call date
r = market discount rate, or required rate of return per period

$$101 = \frac{3}{(1+r)^1} + \frac{3}{(1+r)^2} + \frac{3}{(1+r)^3} + \cdots + \frac{3}{(1+r)^5} + \frac{3+102}{(1+r)^6}$$

$r = 0.03123$

To arrive at the annualized yield-to-first-call, the semiannual rate of 3.123% must be multiplied by two. Therefore, the yield-to-first-call is equal to 3.123% × 2 = 6.25% (rounded).

29 C is correct. The yield-to-second-call is 5.94%. Given the second call date is exactly four years away, the formula for calculating this bond's yield-to-second-call is:

$$PV = \frac{PMT}{(1+r)^1} + \frac{PMT}{(1+r)^2} + \frac{PMT}{(1+r)^3} + \cdots + \frac{PMT}{(1+r)^7} + \frac{PMT + FV}{(1+r)^8}$$

where:

PV = present value, or the price of the bond
PMT = coupon payment per period
FV = call price paid at call date
r = market discount rate, or required rate of return per period

$$101 = \frac{3}{(1+r)^1} + \frac{3}{(1+r)^2} + \frac{3}{(1+r)^3} + \cdots \frac{3}{(1+r)^7} + \frac{3+101}{(1+r)^8}$$

$r = 0.0297$

To arrive at the annualized yield-to-second-call, the semiannual rate of 2.97% must be multiplied by two. Therefore, the yield-to-second-call is equal to 2.97% × 2 = 5.94%.

30 B is correct. The yield-to-worst is 5.77%. The bond's yield-to-worst is the lowest of the sequence of yields-to-call and the yield-to-maturity. From above, we have the following yield measures for this bond:

Yield-to-first-call: 6.25%

Yield-to-second-call: 5.94%

Yield-to-maturity: 5.77%

Thus, the yield-to-worst is 5.77%.

31 B is correct. The discount or required margin is 236 basis points. Given the floater has a maturity of two years and is linked to 6-month Libor, the formula for calculating discount margin is:

$$PV = \frac{\frac{(\text{Index} + QM) \times FV}{m}}{\left(1 + \frac{\text{Index} + DM}{m}\right)^1} + \frac{\frac{(\text{Index} + QM) \times FV}{m}}{\left(1 + \frac{\text{Index} + DM}{m}\right)^2} + \cdots + \frac{\frac{(\text{Index} + QM) \times FV}{m} + FV}{\left(1 + \frac{\text{Index} + DM}{m}\right)^4}$$

where:

PV = present value, or the price of the floating-rate note = 97
Index = reference rate, stated as an annual percentage rate = 0.01
QM = quoted margin, stated as an annual percentage rate = 0.0080

FV = future value paid at maturity, or the par value of the bond = 100

m = periodicity of the floating-rate note, the number of payment periods per year = 2

DM = discount margin, the required margin stated as an annual percentage rate

Substituting given values in:

$$97 = \frac{\frac{(0.01 + 0.0080) \times 100}{2}}{\left(1 + \frac{0.01 + DM}{2}\right)^1} + \frac{\frac{(0.01 + 0.0080) \times 100}{2}}{\left(1 + \frac{0.01 + DM}{2}\right)^2} + \cdots + \frac{\frac{(0.01 + 0.0080) \times 100}{2} + 100}{\left(1 + \frac{0.01 + DM}{2}\right)^4}$$

$$97 = \frac{0.90}{\left(1 + \frac{0.01 + DM}{2}\right)^1} + \frac{0.90}{\left(1 + \frac{0.01 + DM}{2}\right)^2} + \frac{0.90}{\left(1 + \frac{0.01 + DM}{2}\right)^3} + \frac{0.90 + 100}{\left(1 + \frac{0.01 + DM}{2}\right)^4}$$

To calculate DM, begin by solving for the discount rate per period:

$$97 = \frac{0.90}{(1 + r)^1} + \frac{0.90}{(1 + r)^2} + \frac{0.90}{(1 + r)^3} + \frac{0.90 + 100}{(1 + r)^4}$$

$r = 0.0168$

Now, solve for DM:

$$\frac{0.01 + DM}{2} = 0.0168$$

$DM = 0.0236$

The discount margin for the floater is equal to 236 basis points.

32 A is correct. FRN X will be priced at a premium on the next reset date because the quoted margin of 0.40% is greater than the discount or required margin of 0.32%. The premium amount is the present value of the extra or "excess" interest payments of 0.08% each quarter (0.40% – 0.32%). FRN Y will be priced at par value on the next reset date since there is no difference between the quoted and discount margins. FRN Z will be priced at a discount since the quoted margin is less than the required margin.

33 C is correct. The bond equivalent yield is closest to 3.78%. It is calculated as:

$$AOR = \left(\frac{\text{Year}}{\text{Days}}\right) \times \left(\frac{FV - PV}{PV}\right)$$

where:

PV = present value, principal amount, or the price of the money market instrument

FV = future value, or the redemption amount paid at maturity including interest

Days = number of days between settlement and maturity

Year = number of days in the year

AOR = add-on rate, stated as an annual percentage rate (also, called bond equivalent yield).

$$AOR = \left(\frac{365}{350}\right) \times \left(\frac{100 - 96.5}{96.5}\right)$$

$$AOR = 1.04286 \times 0.03627$$

$$AOR = 0.03783 \text{ or approximately } 3.78\%$$

34 C is correct. The bond equivalent yield is closest to 4.40%. The present value of the banker's acceptance is calculated as:

$$PV = FV \times \left(1 - \frac{\text{Days}}{\text{Year}} \times DR\right)$$

where:

PV = present value, or price of the money market instrument
FV = future value paid at maturity, or face value of the money market instrument
Days = number of days between settlement and maturity
Year = number of days in the year
DR = discount rate, stated as an annual percentage rate

$$PV = 100 \times \left(1 - \frac{\text{Days}}{\text{Year}} \times DR\right)$$

$$PV = 100 \times \left(1 - \frac{180}{360} \times 0.0425\right)$$

$$PV = 100 \times (1 - 0.02125)$$

$$PV = 100 \times 0.97875$$

$$PV = 97.875$$

The bond equivalent yield (AOR) is calculated as:

$$AOR = \left(\frac{\text{Year}}{\text{Days}}\right) \times \left(\frac{FV - PV}{PV}\right)$$

where:

PV = present value, principal amount, or the price of the money market instrument
FV = future value, or the redemption amount paid at maturity including interest
Days = number of days between settlement and maturity
Year = number of days in the year
AOR = add-on rate (bond equivalent yield), stated as an annual percentage rate

$$AOR = \left(\frac{365}{180}\right) \times \left(\frac{100 - PV}{PV}\right)$$

$$AOR = \left(\frac{365}{180}\right) \times \left(\frac{100 - 97.875}{97.875}\right)$$

$$AOR = 2.02778 \times 0.02171$$

$$AOR = 0.04402, \text{ or approximately } 4.40\%$$

Note that the PV is calculated using an assumed 360-day year and the AOR (bond equivalent yield) is calculated using a 365-day year.

35 B is correct. All bonds on a par curve are assumed to have similar, not different, credit risk. Par curves are obtained from spot curves and all bonds used to derive the par curve are assumed to have the same credit risk, as well as the same periodicity, currency, liquidity, tax status, and annual yields. A par curve is a sequence of yields-to-maturity such that each bond is priced at par value.

36 B is correct. The spot curve, also known as the strip or zero curve, is the yield curve constructed from a sequence of yields-to-maturities on zero-coupon bonds. The par curve is a sequence of yields-to-maturity such that each bond is priced at par value. The forward curve is constructed using a series of forward rates, each having the same timeframe.

37 B is correct. The forward rate can be interpreted to be the incremental or marginal return for extending the time-to-maturity of an investment for an additional time period. The add-on rate (bond equivalent yield) is a rate quoted for money market instruments such as bank certificates of deposit and indexes such as Libor and Euribor. Yield-to-maturity is the internal rate of return on the bond's cash flows—the uniform interest rate such that when the bond's future cash flows are discounted at that rate, the sum of the present values equals the price of the bond. It is the implied market discount rate.

38 B is correct. The 3 year implied spot rate is closest to 1.94%. It is calculated as the geometric average of the one-year forward rates:

$$(1.0080 \times 1.0112 \times 1.0394) = (1 + z_3)^3$$

$$1.05945 = (1 + z_3)^3$$

$$[1.05945]^{1/3} = [(1 + z_3)^3]^{1/3}$$

$$1.01944 = 1 + z_3$$

$$1.01944 - 1 = z_3$$

$$0.01944 = z_3,\ z_3 = 1.944\% \text{ or approximately } 1.94\%$$

39 B is correct. The value per 100 of par value is closest to105.01. Using the forward curve, the bond price is calculated as follows:

$$\frac{3.5}{1.0080} + \frac{103.5}{(1.0080 \times 1.0112)} = 3.47 + 101.54 = 105.01$$

40 C is correct. The spread component of a specific bond's yield-to-maturity is least likely impacted by changes in inflation of its currency of denomination. The effect of changes in macroeconomic factors, such as the expected rate of inflation in the currency of denomination, is seen mostly in changes in the benchmark yield. The spread or risk premium component is impacted by microeconomic factors specific to the bond and bond issuer including tax status and quality rating.

41 A is correct. The I-spread, or interpolated spread, is the yield spread of a specific bond over the standard swap rate in that currency of the same tenor. The yield spread in basis points over an actual or interpolated government bond is known as the G-spread. The Z-spread (zero-volatility spread) is the constant spread such that is added to each spot rate such that the present value of the cash flows matches the price of the bond.

42 B is correct. The G-spread is closest to 285 bps. The benchmark rate for UK fixed-rate bonds is the UK government benchmark bond. The Euro interest rate spread benchmark is used to calculate the G-spread for Euro-denominated corporate bonds, not UK bonds. The G-spread is calculated as follows:

Yield-to-maturity on the UK corporate bond:

$$100.65 = \frac{5}{(1+r)^1} + \frac{5}{(1+r)^2} + \frac{105}{(1+r)^3},\ r = 0.04762 \text{ or } 476 \text{ bps}$$

Yield-to-maturity on the UK government benchmark bond:

$$100.25 = \frac{2}{(1+r)^1} + \frac{2}{(1+r)^2} + \frac{102}{(1+r)^3},\ r = 0.01913 \text{ or } 191 \text{ bps}$$

The G-spread is 476 – 191 = 285 bps.

43 A is correct. The value of the bond is closest to 92.38. The calculation is:

$$PV = \frac{PMT}{(1+z_1+Z)^1} + \frac{PMT}{(1+z_2+Z)^2} + \frac{PMT+FV}{(1+z_3+Z)^3}$$

$$= \frac{5}{(1+0.0486+0.0234)^1} + \frac{5}{(1+0.0495+0.0234)^2} + \frac{105}{(1+0.0565+0.0234)^3}$$

$$= \frac{5}{1.0720} + \frac{5}{1.15111} + \frac{105}{1.25936} = 4.66 + 4.34 + 83.38 = 92.38$$

44 C is correct. The option value in basis points per year is subtracted from the Z-spread to calculate the option-adjusted spread (OAS). The Z-spread is the constant yield spread over the benchmark spot curve. The I-spread is the yield spread of a specific bond over the standard swap rate in that currency of the same tenor.

READING

45

Introduction to Asset-Backed Securities

by Frank J. Fabozzi, PhD, CPA, CFA

Frank J. Fabozzi, PhD, CPA, CFA, is at EDHEC Business School (France).

LEARNING OUTCOMES

Mastery	The candidate should be able to:
☐	a. explain benefits of securitization for economies and financial markets;
☐	b. describe securitization, including the parties involved in the process and the roles they play;
☐	c. describe typical structures of securitizations, including credit tranching and time tranching;
☐	d. describe types and characteristics of residential mortgage loans that are typically securitized;
☐	e. describe types and characteristics of residential mortgage-backed securities, including mortgage pass-through securities and collateralized mortgage obligations, and explain the cash flows and risks for each type;
☐	f. define prepayment risk and describe the prepayment risk of mortgage-backed securities;
☐	g. describe characteristics and risks of commercial mortgage-backed securities;
☐	h. describe types and characteristics of non-mortgage asset-backed securities, including the cash flows and risks of each type;
☐	i. describe collateralized debt obligations, including their cash flows and risks.

INTRODUCTION

1

Previous readings examined risk characteristics of various fixed-income instruments and the relationships among maturity, coupon, and interest rate changes. This reading introduces an additional level of complexity—that of fixed-income instruments created through a process known as **securitization**. This process involves transferring ownership of assets from the original owners into a special legal entity. The special legal entity then issues securities backed by these assets, and the assets' cash flows are used to pay interest and repay the principal owed to the holders of the securities. These securities are referred to generically as **asset-backed securities** (ABS); the pool of securitized assets from which the ABS's cash flows are generated is called the collateral. Assets that are used to create ABS are called **securitized assets**. These assets are typically loans and receivables and include, among others, residential mortgage loans (mortgages), commercial mortgages, automobile (auto) loans, student loans, bank loans, accounts receivables, and credit card receivables. Advances and innovations in securitization have led to securities backed, or collateralized, by all kinds of income-yielding assets, including airport landing slots and toll roads.

This reading discusses the benefits of securitization, describes securitization, and explains the investment characteristics of different types of ABS. The terminology regarding ABS varies by jurisdiction. **Mortgage-backed securities** (MBS) are ABS backed by a pool of mortgages, and a distinction is sometimes made between MBS and ABS backed by non-mortgage assets. This distinction is common in the United States, for example, where typically the term "mortgage-backed securities" refers to securities backed by high-quality real estate mortgages and the term "asset-backed securities" refers to securities backed by other types of assets. Because the US ABS market is the largest in the world, much of the discussion and many examples in this reading refer to the United States. Note, however, that many non-US investors hold US ABS, including MBS, in their portfolios.

To underline the importance of securitization from a macroeconomic perspective, Section 2 discusses of the benefits of securitization for economies and financial markets. In Section 3, the reading describes securitization and identifies the parties involved in the process and their roles. Section 3 also discusses typical structures of securitizations, including credit tranching and time tranching. Sections 4–6 discuss securities backed by mortgages for real estate property. Many types of residential mortgage designs around the world are described in Section 4. Sections 5 and 6 focus on residential MBS and commercial MBS, respectively. Section 7 discusses ABS based on two types of non-mortgage loans that are typically securitized throughout the world: auto loans and credit card receivables. Collateralized debt obligations are covered in Section 8. Section 9 concludes the reading with a summary.

2 BENEFITS OF SECURITIZATION FOR ECONOMIES AND FINANCIAL MARKETS

The securitization of pools of loans and receivables into multiple securities provides economies and financial markets with a number of benefits.

Traditionally, the purchase of such assets as houses and autos has been financed by loans originated by financial institutions, such as commercial banks. For investors to gain exposure to these loans, they must hold some combination of deposits, debt, or common equity issued by banks. This creates an additional intermediary (that is, the bank) between the borrowers and the investors. In addition, by being constrained to hold bank deposits and securities, investors cannot gain exposure to loans only; they are also affected by economic risks undertaken in other bank activities.

Securitization solves a number of these problems. It allows investors to achieve more direct legal claims on loans and portfolios of receivables and enables these investors to tailor interest rate and credit risk exposures to suit their needs. Because of disintermediation (that is, lessening the role of intermediaries), the costs paid by borrowers can be effectively lowered while the risk-adjusted returns to investors can be enhanced. At the same time, banks can improve their profitability by increasing loan origination and the related fees. They can lend more than they would be able to lend if they were able to engage in only those activities they could finance themselves with their own deposits, debt, and equity. By allowing banks to increase the amount of funds available to lend, securitization ultimately benefits individuals, governments, and companies that need to borrow.

Securitization also has benefits for investors. Securitization enables financial innovation, which allows investors to access securities with profiles that match their risk, return, and maturity needs that are otherwise not directly available. For example, a pension fund with a long-term horizon can gain access to long-term real estate loans by investing in residential MBS without having to invest in bank bonds or stocks. Although few institutional or individual investors are willing to make or purchase real estate loans, auto loans, or credit card receivables directly, they may invest in a security backed by such loans or receivables. The ABS that are created by pooling these loans and receivables have characteristics similar to those of a standard bond and do not require the specialized resources and expertise needed to originate, monitor, and collect the payments from the underlying loans and receivables. As a result, investors can add to their portfolios exposure to the risk–return characteristics provided by a wider range of assets if they so desire. Note that in many countries, the sale of ABS and similar instruments is restricted to investors who meet certain qualifications, such as those pertaining to net worth.

Securitization allows for the creation of tradable securities with better liquidity than that of the original loans on the bank's balance sheet. In making loans and receivables tradable, securitization makes financial markets more efficient. It also improves liquidity, which reduces liquidity risk in the financial system. How securitization improves liquidity will become clear when securitization is described in more detail in Section 3.

An important benefit of securitization for companies is that ABS provide an alternative means of funding operations that can be considered alongside bond, preferred equity, and common equity issuance. Companies that originate loans and receivables that can be securitized often compare the funding costs associated with each of these sources of financing and choose the optimal one. As discussed in Section 3.4, securitization is often cheaper than a corporate bond issue secured by the same collateral as the securitization.

For these reasons, securitization is beneficial to economies and financial markets, and many sovereign governments throughout the world have embraced securitization. For example, the Italian government has used securitization since the late 1990s for privatizing public assets. In emerging markets, securitization is widely used. For example, in South America, companies and banks with high credit ratings have used securitization to sell receivables on exports, such as oil, to lower their funding costs.

Although securitization brings many benefits to economies, it is not without risks, and some of these risks are widely attributed to have precipitated the turmoil in financial markets during 2007–2009. Broadly, those risks fall into two categories: risks that relate primarily to the timing of the ABS's cash flows, such as contraction risk and extension risk, and risks related to the inherent credit risk of the loans and receivables backing the ABS. This reading describes these risks and also discusses some of the structures used to mitigate them as well as redistribute them.

HOW SECURITIZATION WORKS

3

When assets are securitized, several legal and regulatory conditions must be satisfied. A number of parties participate in the process to facilitate the transaction and ensure these conditions are met. In this section, a typical securitization is described by way of a hypothetical example. The example describes the parties involved in a securitization and their roles. It also introduces the typical structures of securitizations, such as credit tranching and time tranching.

3.1 An Example of a Securitization

Mediquip, a hypothetical company, is a manufacturer of medical equipment that ranges in cost from US$50,000 to US$300,000. The majority of Mediquip's sales are made through loans granted by the company to its customers, and the medical equipment serves as collateral for the loans. These loans, which represent an asset to Mediquip, have maturities of five years and carry a fixed interest rate. They are fully amortizing with monthly payments; that is, the borrowers make equal payments each month consisting of interest payment and principal repayment. The total principal repaid from the 60 loan payments (12 months × 5 years) is such that the amount borrowed is fully repaid at the end of the term.

Mediquip's credit department makes the decision about whether to extend credit to customers and services the loans that are made. Loan servicing refers to administering any aspect of a loan, including collecting payments from borrowers, notifying borrowers who may be delinquent, and recovering and disposing of the medical equipment if the borrower does not make the scheduled payments by a specified time. If one of its customers defaults, Mediquip can seize the medical equipment and sell it to try to recoup the remaining principal on the loan. Although the servicer of such loans need not be the originator of the loans, the assumption in this example is that Mediquip is the servicer.

The following is an illustration of how these loans can be securitized. Assume that Mediquip has US$200 million of loans. This amount is shown on Mediquip's balance sheet as an asset. Assume also that Mediquip wants to raise US$200 million, which happens to be the amount of the loans. Because Mediquip's treasurer is aware of the potentially lower funding costs of securitization, he decides to raise the US$200 million by securitizing the loans on the medical equipment rather than by issuing corporate bonds.

To do so, Mediquip sets up a separate legal entity called Medical Equipment Trust (MET), to which it sells the loans on the medical equipment. Such a legal entity is referred to as a **special purpose entity** (SPE) and sometimes also called a special purpose vehicle (SPV) or a special purpose company. The legal form of the SPE varies by jurisdiction, but in almost all cases, the ultimate owner of the loans—MET in our example—is legally independent and is considered bankruptcy remote from the seller of the loans. Setting up a separate legal entity ensures that if Mediquip, the originator of the loans, files for bankruptcy, the loans backing the ABS that are issued by MET are secure within the SPE and creditors of Mediquip have no claim on them. Note that in some jurisdictions, the SPE may, in turn, transfer the loans to a trust or a limited company.

A securitization is diagramed in Exhibit 1. The SPE set up by Mediquip is called MET. The top of Exhibit 1 reflects Mediquip's business model as described above—that is, the sale of medical equipment financed by loans (first oval). Mediquip sells to MET US$200 million of loans (second oval) and receives from MET US$200 million in cash (third oval); in this simplified example, the costs associated with the securitization are ignored. MET issues and sells securities that are backed by the pool of securitized loans (fourth oval) and receives cash (fifth oval). These securities are the ABS mentioned earlier, and the US$200 million of loans represent the collateral. The periodic cash payments that are received from the collateral—that is, the monthly payments made by Mediquip's customers that include both interest payment and principal repayment (sixth oval)—are used to make the periodic cash payments to the security holders—the investors who bought the ABS (seventh oval).

Exhibit 1 Mediquip's Securitization

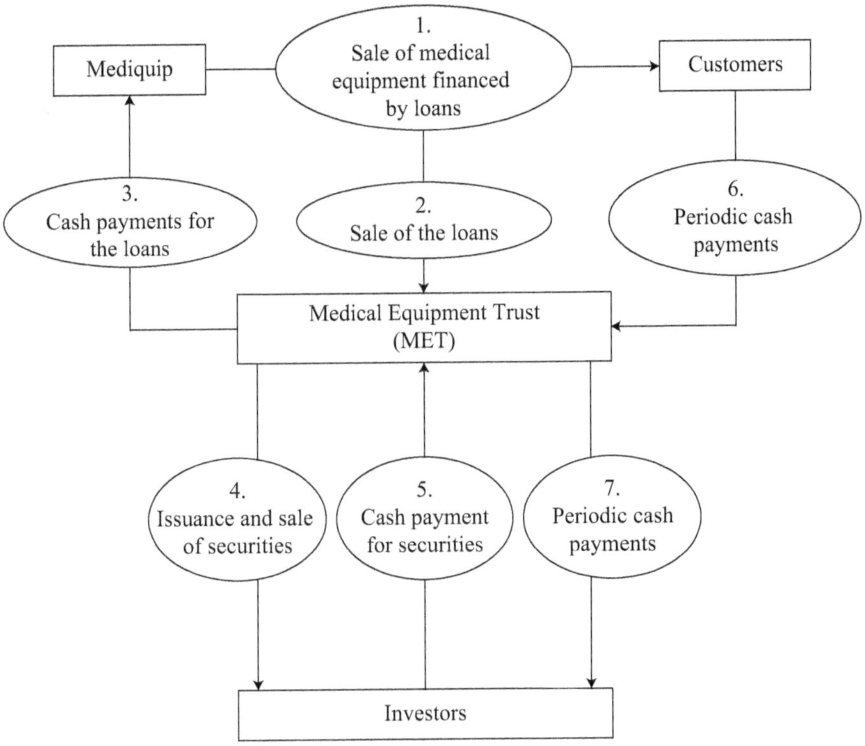

3.2 Parties to a Securitization and Their Roles

Securitization requires the publication of a prospectus, a document that contains information about the securitization.[1] The three main parties to a securitization are:

- the seller of the collateral, sometimes called the depositor (Mediquip in our example);
- the SPE that purchases the loans or receivables and uses them as collateral to issue the ABS—MET in our example. (The SPE is often referred to as the issuer in the prospectus because it is the entity that issues the securities; it may also be called the trust if the SPE is set up as a trust); and
- the servicer of the loans (Mediquip in our example).

Other parties are also involved in a securitization: independent accountants, lawyers/attorneys, trustees, underwriters, rating agencies, and financial guarantors. All these parties, including the servicer when it is different from the seller of the collateral, are referred to as third parties to the securitization.

A significant amount of legal documentation is involved in a securitization. Lawyers/attorneys are responsible for preparing the legal documents. An important legal document is the purchase agreement between the seller of the collateral and the SPE, which

1 To be more precise, in the United States, a "base prospectus" and a "supplementary prospectus" are typically filed with the Securities and Exchange Commission. The base prospectus provides definitions, information about the parties to the securitization, and certain information about securities to be offered in the future—the types of assets that may be securitized, the types of structures that will be used, and the types of credit enhancement (the last two are discussed in Section 5.3). The supplementary prospectus provides the details of a specific securitization.

sets forth the representations and warranties that the seller makes about the assets sold. These representations and warranties assure investors about the quality of the assets, an important consideration when assessing the risks associated with the ABS.

Another important legal document is the prospectus, which describes the structure of the securitization, including the priority and amount of payments to be made to the servicer, administrators, and the ABS holders. Securitizations often use several forms of credit enhancements, which are documented in the prospectus. Credit enhancements are provisions that are used to reduce the credit risk of a bond issue. They include (1) internal credit enhancements, such as subordination, overcollateralization and reserve accounts, and (2) external credit enhancements, such as financial guarantees by banks or insurance companies, letters of credit, and cash collateral accounts. Securitizations often use subordination, which is further discussed in Section 4. Prior to the 2007–2009 credit crisis, many securitizations included financial guarantees by a third party. The most common third-party financial guarantors are monoline insurance companies or monoline insurers. A monoline insurer is a private insurance company whose business is restricted to providing guarantees for financial instruments such as ABS. Following the financial difficulties and downgrading of the major monoline insurers as a result of the financial crisis that began in the mortgage market in mid-2007, few structures in recent years have used financial guarantees from a monoline insurer.

A trustee or trustee agent is typically a financial institution with trust powers that safeguards the assets after they have been sold to the SPE, holds the funds due to the ABS holders until they are paid, and provides periodic information to the ABS holders. The information is provided in the form of remittance reports, which may be issued monthly, quarterly, or as agreed to in the terms of the prospectus.

Underwriters and rating agencies perform the same functions in a securitization as they do in a standard bond offering.

EXAMPLE 1

A Used Luxury Auto Securitization

Used Luxury Auto (ULA) is a hypothetical company that has established a nationwide business in buying used luxury autos and then refurbishing them with the latest in electronic equipment (for instance, UBS ports and rear-view cameras). ULA Corp then sells these autos in the retail market, often financing the sales with promissory notes from the buyers via its ULA Credit Corp.

The following information is taken from a theoretical filing by ULA with the Securities and Exchange Commission for a securitization:

Issuer: ULA Trust 2020

Seller and Servicer: ULA Credit Corp

Notes:

$500,000,000 4.00% ULA Trust contract-backed Class A notes, rated AAA

$250,000,000 4.80% ULA Trust contract-backed Class B notes, rated A

Contracts: The assets underlying the notes are fixed-rate promissory notes relating to the purchase of used automobiles refurbished by ULA Corp.

1 The collateral for this securitization is:

A ULA Trust contract-backed Class A and Class B notes.

B Used automobiles refurbished by ULA Corp.

C Fixed-rate promissory notes relating to the purchase of used automobiles refurbished by ULA Corp.

2 The special purpose entity in this securitization is:

A ULA Corp.

B ULA Credit Corp.

C ULA Trust 2020.

3 ULA Credit Corp is responsible for:

A selling the collateral to the SPE and collecting payments from borrowers on the underlying promissory notes.

B refurbishing the used motorcycles and collecting payments from borrowers on the underlying promissory notes.

C selling the contract-backed Class A and Class B notes to investors and making the cash interest and principal payments to them.

Solution to 1:

C is correct. The collateral is the pool of securitized assets from which the cash flows will be generated. It is the debt obligations that have been securitized. These contracts are the loans, called promissory notes, provided to purchasers of the used automobiles that were refurbished by ULA Corp.

Solution to 2:

C is correct. ULA Trust 2020 is the issuer of the ABS and, thus, the SPE. The SPE purchases the contracts that become the collateral from ULA Corp, the automobile refurbisher, but it is ULA Credit Corp that originates the loans and is, therefore, the seller of the collateral. ULA Credit Corp. is also the servicer of the debt obligations.

Solution to 3:

A is correct. ULA Credit Corp is the seller of the collateral, the promissory notes. As the servicer, it is responsible for collecting payments from borrowers, notifying borrowers who may be delinquent, and if necessary, recovering and disposing of the automobile if the borrower defaults.

3.3 Structure of a Securitization

A simple securitization may involve the sale of only one class of bond or ABS. Let us call this class Bond Class A. Returning to the Mediquip and MET example, MET may raise US$200 million by issuing 200,000 certificates for Bond Class A with a par value of US$1,000 per certificate. Thus, each certificate holder is entitled to 1/200,000 of the payments from the collateral after payment of servicing and other administrative fees; what these fees represent is discussed in Section 5.1.1.

The structure of the securitization is often more complicated than a single class of ABS. As mentioned earlier, it is common for securitizations to include a form of internal credit enhancement called **subordination**, also referred to as **credit tranching**. In such a structure, there is more than one bond class or tranche, and the bond classes differ as to how they will share any losses resulting from defaults of the borrowers whose loans are in the collateral. The bond classes are classified as senior bond classes or subordinated bond classes—hence, the reason this structure is also referred to as a senior/subordinated structure. The subordinated bond classes are sometimes called "non-senior bond classes" or "junior bond classes." They function as credit protection for the more senior bond classes; that is, losses are realized by the subordinated bond classes before any losses are realized by the senior bond classes. This type of protection is also commonly referred to as a "waterfall" structure because of the cascading flow of payments between bond classes in the event of default.

For example, suppose MET issues two bond classes with a total par value of US$200 million: Bond Class A, the senior bond class, with a par value of US$120 million, and Bond Class B, the subordinated bond class, with a par value of US$80 million. In this senior/subordinated structure, also referred to as credit tranching, Bond Class B will absorb losses up to US$80 million. Thus, as long as defaults by Mediquip's customers do not exceed US$80 million, Bond Class A will be fully repaid its US$120 million. The purpose of this structure is to redistribute the credit risk associated with the collateral. The creation of a set of bond classes allows investors to choose the level of credit risk that they prefer to bear.

More than one subordinated bond class may be created. Suppose MET issues the following structure:

Bond Class	Par Value (US$ millions)
A (senior)	180
B (subordinated)	14
C (subordinated)	6
Total	200

In this structure, Bond Class A is the senior bond class whereas both Bond Class B and Bond Class C are subordinated bond classes from the perspective of Bond Class A. The rules for the distribution of losses are as follows. All losses on the collateral are absorbed by Bond Class C before any losses are realized by Bond Class B and then Bond Class A. Consequently, if the losses on the collateral do not exceed US$6 million, no losses will be realized by Bond Class A or Bond Class B. If the losses exceed US$6 million, Bond Class B must absorb the losses up to an additional US$14 million. For example, if the total loss on the collateral is US$16 million, Bond Class C loses its entire par value of US$6 million and Bond Class B realizes a loss of US$10 million of its par value of US$14 million. Bond Class A does not realize any loss in this scenario. Clearly, Bond Class A realizes a loss only if the total loss on the collateral exceeds US$20 million.

The structure of a securitization may also allow the redistribution of another type of risk, called "prepayment risk," among bond classes. **Prepayment risk** is the uncertainty that the cash flows will be different from the scheduled cash flows as set forth in the loan agreement because of the borrowers' ability to alter payments, usually to take advantage of interest rate movements. For example, when interest rates decline, borrowers tend to pay off part or all of their loans and refinance at lower interest rates. The creation of bond classes that possess different expected maturities is referred to as **time tranching** and is further discussed in Section 5.2.

It is possible, and quite common, for a securitization to have structures with both credit tranching and time tranching.

EXAMPLE 2

Bond Classes and Tranching

Return to the ULA securitization described in Example 1. Based on the information provided, the form of credit enhancement that the transaction *most likely* includes is:

A time tranching.

B credit tranching.

C a financial guarantee.

Solution:

B is correct. The ULA securitization includes two bond classes: Class A and Class B. Each bond class has a fixed but different interest rate; the interest rate increases from 4.00% for Class A notes to 4.80% for Class B notes. Thus, it is likely that the transaction has credit tranching and that the two bond classes display a senior/subordinated structure, with Class A notes being senior to Class B notes, the subordinated bond class. As the credit risk increases from the Class A notes to the Class B notes, so does the interest rate to reflect the additional compensation investors require for bearing the additional credit risk. The information provided does not give any indication of either time tranching or a financial guarantee.

3.4 Key Role of the Special Purpose Entity

The SPE plays a pivotal role in securitization. In fact, the setup of a legal entity that plays the same role as an SPE in terms of protecting the rights of ABS holders is a prerequisite in any country that wants to allow securitization. Indeed, without a provision in a country's legal system for the equivalent of an SPE, the benefits of using securitization by an entity seeking to raise funds would not exist. Let us explain why by returning to our example involving Mediquip and MET.

Assume that Mediquip has a credit rating from a credit-rating agency, such as Standard & Poor's, Moody's Investors Service, or Fitch Ratings. A credit rating reflects the opinion of a credit-rating agency about the creditworthiness of an entity and/or the debt securities the entity issues. Suppose that the credit rating assigned to Mediquip is BB or Ba2. Such a credit rating means that Mediquip is below what is referred to as an investment-grade credit rating.

Assume again that Mediquip's treasurer wants to raise US$200 million and is contemplating doing so by issuing a five-year corporate bond rather than by securitizing the loans. The treasurer is, of course, concerned about the funding cost and would like the lowest possible interest rate available relative to some benchmark interest rate. The difference between the interest rate paid on the five-year corporate bond and the benchmark interest rate is the spread. The spread reflects the compensation investors require for buying the corporate bond, which is riskier than the bonds issued at the benchmark interest rate. The major factor affecting the spread is the issuer's credit rating—hence, the reason the spread is called a "credit spread."

Another factor that will influence the credit spread is whether the bond is backed by collateral. A corporate bond that has collateral is often referred to as a secured bond. The collateral usually reduces the credit spread, making the credit spread of a secured bond lower than that of an otherwise identical unsecured bond. In our example, Mediquip's treasurer can use the loans on the medical equipment as collateral for the secured corporate bond issue. Thus, if Mediquip issues a five-year corporate bond to raise US$200 million, the credit spread will reflect its credit rating primarily and the collateral slightly. We will soon explain why the collateral affects the credit spread only slightly.

Now suppose that instead of using the loans as collateral for a secured corporate bond issue, Mediquip sells the loan contracts in an arm's length transaction to MET, the SPE. After the sale is completed, it is MET, not Mediquip, that legally owns them. As a result, if Mediquip is forced into bankruptcy while the loans are still outstanding, Mediquip's creditors cannot recover them because they are legally owned by another entity. Note that it is possible, however, that transfers made to bankruptcy-remote vehicles can be challenged as fraudulent conveyances and potentially unwound. The legal implication of setting up MET is that investors contemplating the purchase of any bond class backed by the cash flows from the pool of loans on the medical equipment will evaluate the credit risk associated with collecting the payments due on the receivables independently of Mediquip's credit rating.

Credit ratings are assigned to each of the various bond classes created in the securitization. They depend on the quality of the collateral—that is, how the rating agencies evaluate the credit risk of the pool of securitized loans or receivables. Depending on the structure of the securitization, each bond class receives a credit rating that reflects its credit risk, and some of the bond classes may have a better credit rating than the company that is seeking to raise funds. As a consequence, in aggregate, the funding cost of a securitization may be lower than that of a corporate bond issue. Access to lower funding cost is a key role of the SPE in a securitization.

A fair question is why a securitization can be cheaper than a corporate bond issue secured by the same collateral as the securitization. The reason is that the SPE would not be affected by the bankruptcy of the seller of the collateral. As mentioned above, the assets belong to the SPE, not to the entity that sold the assets to the SPE. In the United States and other countries, when a company is liquidated, creditors receive distributions based on the absolute priority rule to the extent that assets are available. The absolute priority rule is the principle that senior creditors are paid in full before subordinated creditors are paid anything. The absolute priority rule also guarantees the seniority of creditors relative to equity holders.

Whereas the absolute priority rule generally holds in liquidations, it has not always been upheld by the courts in reorganizations. Thus, although investors in the debt of a company may believe they have priority over the equity holders and priority over other classes of creditors, the actual outcome of a reorganization may be far different from the terms stated in the debt agreement; that is, there is no assurance that if the corporate bond has collateral, the rights of the bondholders will be respected. For this reason, the credit spread for a corporate bond backed by collateral does not decrease dramatically.

In the case of a securitization, the courts have in most jurisdictions no discretion to change seniority because the bankruptcy of a company does not affect the SPE. The rules set forth in the legal document, which describes how losses are to be absorbed by each bond class, are unaffected by the company's bankruptcy. This important decoupling of the credit risk of the entity needing funds from the bond classes issued by the SPE explains why the SPE's legal role is critical.

The SPE is bankruptcy remote from the seller of the collateral, which means that the bankruptcy of the seller of the collateral will not affect the holders of securities issued by the SPE and backed by the collateral. The security holders face credit risk only to the extent that the borrowers whose claims the SPE has purchased default on their loans. The SPE's ability to make cash payments to the security holders remains intact as long as the borrowers make the interest payments and/or the principal repayments on their loans.

However, all countries do not have the same legal framework. Impediments have arisen in some countries with respect to the issuance of ABS because the concept of trust law is not as well developed globally as it is in the United States and many other developed countries.[2] Thus, investors should be aware of the legal considerations that apply in the jurisdictions where they purchase ABS.

---

2 In many EU countries, the creditors are protected in the recognition of the securitization as a true sale. The SPE has full legal ownership of the securitized assets, which are de-recognized from the seller's balance sheet. In the event of default of the originator/servicer, the SPE can appoint a substitute company to the service role and continue to pay bondholders from the income stream of the securitized assets without the other creditors of the initial originator/servicer being able to have any recourse or claim to these assets.

EXAMPLE 3

Special Purpose Entity and Bankruptcy

Agnelli Industries (Agnelli), a manufacturer of industrial machine tools based in Bergamo, Italy, has €500 million of corporate bonds outstanding. These bonds have a credit rating below investment grade. Agnelli has €400 million of receivables on its balance sheet that it would like to securitize. The receivables represent payments Agnelli expects to receive for machine tools it has sold to various customers in Europe. Agnelli sells the receivables to Agnelli Trust, a special purpose entity. Agnelli Trust then issues ABS, backed by the pool of receivables, with the following structure:

Bond Class	Par Value (€ millions)
A (senior)	280
B (subordinated)	60
C (subordinated)	60
Total	400

Bond Class A is given an investment-grade credit rating by the credit-rating agencies.

1 Why does Bond Class A have a higher credit rating than the corporate bonds?

2 If Agnelli Industries files for bankruptcy after the issuance of the asset-backed security:

A Bond Classes A, B, and C will be unaffected.

B Bond Classes A, B, and C will lose their entire par value.

C losses will be realized by Bond Class C first, then by Bond Class B, and then by Bond Class A.

3 If one of Agnelli's customers defaults on its €60 million loan:

A Bond Classes A, B, and C will realize losses of €20 million each.

B Bond Class C will realize losses of €60 million, but Bond Classes A and B will be unaffected.

C Bond Classes B and C will realize losses of €30 million each, but Bond Class A will be unaffected.

Solution to 1:

Bond Class A are issued by Agnelli Trust, an SPE that is bankruptcy remote from Agnelli. Thus, the investors who hold Agnelli's bonds and/or common shares have no legal claim on the cash flows from the securitized receivables that are the collateral for the ABS. As long as Agnelli's customers make the interest payments and/or principal repayments on their loans, Agnelli Trust will be able to make cash payments to the ABS investors. Because of the credit tranching, even if some of Agnelli's customers were to default on their loans, the losses would be realized by the subordinated Bond Classes B and C before any losses are realized by the senior Bond Class A. The credit risk associated with Bond Class A is, therefore, lower than that of Bond Classes B and C and the corporate bonds, justifying the investment-grade credit rating.

Solution to 2:

A is correct. The ABS have been issued by Agnelli Trust, an SPE that is bankruptcy remote from Agnelli. If the securitization is viewed as resulting in a true sale, the fact that Agnelli files for bankruptcy does not affect the ABS holders. These ABS holders face credit risk only to the extent that Agnelli's customers who bought the machine tools do not make the obligatory payments on their loans. As long as the customers continue to make payments, all three bond classes will receive their expected cash flows. These cash flows are completely and legally independent of anything that happens to Agnelli itself.

Solution to 3:

B is correct. The rules for the distribution of losses are as follows. All losses on the collateral are absorbed by Bond Class C before any losses are realized by Bond Class B and then Bond Class A. Consequently, if the losses on the collateral are €60 million, which is the par value of Bond Class C, Bond Class C loses its entire par value, but Bond Classes A and B are unaffected.

4 RESIDENTIAL MORTGAGE LOANS

Before describing the various types of residential mortgage-backed securities, this section briefly discusses the fundamental features of the underlying assets: residential mortgage loans. The mortgage designs described in this section are those that are typically securitized.

A **mortgage loan**, or simply **mortgage**, is a loan secured by the collateral of some specified real estate property that obliges the borrower (often someone wishing to buy a home) to make a predetermined series of payments to the lender (often initially a bank or mortgage company). The mortgage gives the lender the right to foreclose on the loan if the borrower defaults; that is, a **foreclosure** allows the lender to take possession of the mortgaged property and then sell it in order to recover funds toward satisfying the debt obligation.

Typically, the amount of the loan advanced to buy the property is less than the property's purchase price. The borrower makes a down payment, and the amount borrowed is the difference between the property's purchase price and the down payment. When the loan is first taken out, the borrower's equity in the property is equal to the down payment. Over time, as the market value of the property changes, the borrower's equity also changes. It also changes as the borrower makes mortgage payments that include principal repayment.

The ratio of the amount of the mortgage to the property's value is called the **loan-to-value ratio** (LTV). The lower the LTV, the higher the borrower's equity. From the lender's perspective, the higher the borrower's equity, the less likely the borrower is to default. Moreover, the lower the LTV, the more protection the lender has for recovering the amount loaned if the borrower does default and the lender repossesses and sells the property.

In the United States, market participants typically identify two types of mortgages based on the credit quality of the borrower: prime loans and subprime loans. Generally, for a loan to be considered prime, the borrower must be viewed as having high credit quality; that is, the borrower must have strong employment and credit histories, income sufficient to pay the loan obligation, and substantial equity in the underlying property. If the borrower has lower credit quality or if the loan is not a first lien on the property (that is, a party other than the current potential lender has a prior claim on the underlying property), the loan is treated as subprime.

Throughout the world, there are a considerable number of mortgage designs. Mortgage design means the specification of (1) the maturity of the loan, (2) how the interest rate is determined, (3) how the principal is to be repaid (that is, the amortization schedule), (4) whether the borrower has the option to prepay and, in such cases, whether any prepayment penalties might be imposed, and (5) the rights of the lender in a foreclosure.

4.1 Maturity

In the United States, the typical maturity of a mortgage ranges from 15 to 30 years. For most countries in Europe, a residential mortgage typically has a maturity between 20 and 40 years, but in some countries, such as France and Spain, it can be as long as 50 years. Japan is an extreme case; the maturity of a mortgage can be 100 years.[3] Note that what is called the term of a mortgage means the number of years to maturity.

4.2 Interest Rate Determination

The interest rate on a mortgage is called the **mortgage rate**, **contract rate**, or **note rate**. How the mortgage rate is determined varies considerably among countries. The four basic ways that the mortgage rate can be specified are as follows:

- *Fixed rate:* The mortgage rate remains the same during the life of the mortgage. The United States and France have a high proportion of this type of interest rate determination. Although fixed-rate mortgages are not the dominant form in Germany, they do exist there.
- *Adjustable or variable rate:* The mortgage rate is reset periodically—daily, weekly, monthly, or annually. The determination of the new mortgage rate for an adjustable-rate mortgage (ARM) at the reset date may be based on some reference rate or index (in which case, it is called an indexed-referenced ARM) or a rate determined at the lender's discretion (in which case, it is called a reviewable ARM). Residential mortgages in Australia, Ireland, South Korea, Spain, and the United Kingdom are dominated by adjustable-rate mortgages. In Australia, Ireland, and the United Kingdom, the reviewable ARM is standard. In South Korea and Spain, the indexed-referenced ARM is the norm. Canada and the United States have ARMs that are typically tied to an index or reference rate, although this type of mortgage rate is not the dominant form of interest rate determination. An important feature of an ARM is that it will usually have a maximum interest rate by which the mortgage rate can change at a reset date and a maximum interest rate that the mortgage rate can reach during the mortgage's life.
- *Initial period fixed rate:* The mortgage rate is fixed for some initial period and is then adjusted. The adjustment may call for a new fixed rate or for a variable rate. When the adjustment calls for a fixed rate, the mortgage is referred to as a rollover or renegotiable mortgage. This mortgage design is dominant in Canada, Denmark, Germany, the Netherlands, and Switzerland. When the mortgage

3 The term of residential mortgages is usually in line with the age of the borrower at the end of the loan maturity period, with the borrower's retirement age being a usual upper limit.

starts out with a fixed rate and then switches to an adjustable rate after a specified initial term, the mortgage is referred to as a hybrid mortgage. Hybrid mortgages are popular in the United Kingdom.

- *Convertible*: The mortgage rate is initially either a fixed rate or an adjustable rate. At some point, the borrower has the option to convert the mortgage to a fixed rate or an adjustable rate for the remainder of the mortgage's life. Almost half of the mortgages in Japan are convertible.

4.3 Amortization Schedule

In most countries, residential mortgages are **amortizing loans**. The amortization of a loan means the gradual reduction of the amount borrowed over time. Assuming no prepayments are made by the borrower, the periodic mortgage payments made by the borrower consist of interest payments and scheduled principal repayments. The scheduled principal repayment is the amount of reduction of the outstanding mortgage balance and is thus referred to as the amortization. As discussed in a previous reading, there are two types of amortizing loans: fully amortizing loans and partially amortizing loans. In a fully amortizing loan, the sum of all the scheduled principal repayments during the mortgage's life is such that when the last mortgage payment is made, the loan is fully repaid. Most residential mortgages in the United States are fully amortizing loans. In a partially amortizing loan, the sum of all the scheduled principal repayments is less than the amount borrowed. The last payment that has to be made is then the unpaid mortgage balance, and that last payment is said to be a "balloon" payment.

If no scheduled principal repayment is specified for a certain number of years, the loan is said to be an **interest-only mortgage**. Interest-only mortgages have been available in Australia, Denmark, Finland, France, Germany, Greece, Ireland, the Netherlands, Portugal, South Korea, Spain, Switzerland, and the United Kingdom. Interest-only mortgages also have been available to a limited extent in the United States. A special type of interest-only mortgage is one in which there are no scheduled principal repayments over the entire life of the loan. In this case, the balloon payment is equal to the original loan amount. These mortgages, referred to as "interest-only lifetime mortgages" or "bullet mortgages," have been available in Denmark, the Netherlands, and the United Kingdom.

4.4 Prepayment Options and Prepayment Penalties

A prepayment is any payment toward the repayment of principal that is in excess of the scheduled principal repayment. A mortgage may entitle the borrower to prepay all or part of the outstanding mortgage principal prior to the scheduled due date when the principal must be repaid. This contractual provision is referred to as a **prepayment option** or an **early repayment option**. From the lender's or investor's viewpoint, the effect of a prepayment option is that the amount and timing of the cash flows from a mortgage cannot be known with certainty. This risk was referred to as prepayment risk in Section 3. Prepayment risk affects all mortgages that allow prepayment, not just the level-payment, fixed-rate, fully amortizing mortgages.

The mortgage may stipulate some sort of monetary penalty when a borrower prepays within a certain time period after the mortgage is originated, and this time period may extend for the full life of the loan. Such mortgage designs are referred to as **prepayment penalty mortgages**. The purpose of the prepayment penalty is to compensate the lender for the difference between the contract rate and the prevailing mortgage rate if the borrower prepays when interest rates decline. Hence, the prepayment penalty is effectively a mechanism that provides for yield maintenance for the lender. The method for calculating the penalty varies. Prepayment penalty mortgages are common in Europe. Although the proportion of prepayment penalty mortgages in the United States is small, they do exist.

4.5 Rights of the Lender in a Foreclosure

A mortgage can be a recourse loan or a non-recourse loan. When the borrower fails to make the contractual loan payments, the lender can repossess the property and sell it, but the proceeds received from the sale of the property may be insufficient to recoup the losses. In a **recourse loan**, the lender has a claim against the borrower for the shortfall between the amount of the outstanding mortgage balance and the proceeds received from the sale of the property. In a **non-recourse loan**, the lender does not have such a claim and thus can look only to the property to recover the outstanding mortgage balance. In the United States, recourse is typically determined by the state, and residential mortgages are non-recourse loans in many states. In contrast, residential mortgages in most European countries are recourse loans.

The recourse/non-recourse feature of a mortgage has implications for projecting the likelihood of defaults by borrowers, particularly in the case of what is sometimes called "underwater mortgages"—that is, mortgages for which the value of the property has declined below the amount owed by the borrower. For example, in the United States, where mortgages are typically non-recourse, the borrower may have an incentive to default on an underwater mortgage and allow the lender to foreclose on the property, even if resources are available to continue to make mortgage payments. This type of default by a borrower is referred to as a "strategic default." A strategic default, however, has negative consequences for the borrower, who will then have a lower credit score and a reduced ability to borrow in the future. Thus, not all borrowers faced with underwater mortgages will default. In countries where residential mortgages are recourse loans, a strategic default is less likely because the lender can seek to recover the shortfall from the borrower's other assets and/or income.

Now that the basics of a residential mortgage have been set out, we can turn our attention to how these mortgages are securitized—that is, transformed into MBS. In the following sections, we focus on the US residential mortgage sector because it is the largest in the world and many non-US investors hold US MBS in their portfolios.

EXAMPLE 4

Residential Mortgage Designs

1 In an interest-only mortgage, the borrower:

- A does not have to repay the principal as long as she pays the interest.
- B does not have to make principal repayments for a certain number of years, after which she starts paying down the original loan amount.
- C does not have to make principal repayments over the entire life of the mortgage and pays down the original loan amount as a balloon payment.

2 A bank advertises a mortgage with the following interest rate: 2.99% (12-month Euribor + 2.50%), resetting once a year. The mortgage is *most likely*:

- A a hybrid mortgage.
- B an adjustable-rate mortgage.
- C an initial period fixed-rate mortgage.

3 If the borrower fails to make the contractual mortgage payments on a non-recourse mortgage, the lender:

A cannot foreclose the property.

B can only recover the outstanding mortgage balance through the sale of the property.

C can recover the outstanding mortgage balance through the sale of the property and the borrower's other assets and/or income.

Solution to 1:

B is correct. In an interest-only mortgage, there is no scheduled principal repayment for a certain number of years, so the borrower starts paying down the original loan amount only after an initial period of interest-only payments. Some, but not all, interest-only mortgages do not have scheduled principal repayments over the entire life of the loan. These mortgages are called interest-only lifetime mortgages or bullet mortgages, and they require the borrower to pay back the original loan amount at maturity.

Solution to 2:

B is correct. An adjustable-rate mortgage is one for which the mortgage rate is typically based on some reference rate or index (indexed-referenced ARM) or a rate determined at the lender's discretion (reviewable ARM) and is reset periodically. A mortgage rate of 12-month Euribor + 2.50%, resetting once per year, suggests that the mortgage is an index-referenced ARM. The 2.99% rate is the current mortgage rate (that is, 12-month Euribor of 0.49% + 2.50%) and should not be taken as an indication that it is a fixed-rate, initial period fixed-rate, or hybrid mortgage.

Solution to 3:

B is correct. In the case of a non-recourse mortgage, the lender can foreclose the property if the borrower fails to make the contractual mortgage payments. However, the lender can use only the proceeds from the property to recover the outstanding mortgage balance.

5 RESIDENTIAL MORTGAGE-BACKED SECURITIES

The bonds created from the securitization of mortgages related to the purchase of residential properties are residential mortgage-backed securities (RMBS). In such countries as the United States, Canada, Japan, and South Korea, a distinction is often made between securities that are guaranteed by the government or a quasi-government entity and securities that are not. Quasi-government entities are usually created by governments to perform various functions for them. Examples of quasi-government entities include government-sponsored enterprises (GSEs) such as Fannie Mae (previously the Federal National Mortgage Association) and Freddie Mac (previously the Federal Home Loan Mortgage Corporation) in the United States and the Japan Housing Finance Agency (JHF).

In the United States, securities backed by residential mortgages are divided into three sectors: (1) those guaranteed by a federal agency, (2) those guaranteed by a GSE, and (3) those issued by private entities and that are not guaranteed by a federal agency or a GSE. The first two sectors are referred to as **agency RMBS**, and the third sector as **non-agency RMBS**. A significant amount of space in this section is devoted to US agency and non-agency RMBS because these securities represent a large sector of the investment-grade bond market and are included in the portfolios of many US as well as non-US investors.

Agency RMBS include securities issued by federal agencies, such as the Government National Mortgage Association, popularly referred to as Ginnie Mae. This entity is a federally related institution because it is part of the US Department of Housing and Urban Development. As a result, the RMBS that it guarantees carry the full faith and credit of the US government with respect to timely payment of interest and repayment of principal.

Agency RMBS also include RMBS issued by GSEs, such as Fannie Mae and Freddie Mac. RMBS issued by GSEs do not carry the full faith and credit of the US government.[4] Agency RMBS issued by GSEs differ from non-agency RMBS in two ways. First, the credit risk of the RMBS issued by Fannie Mae and Freddie Mac is reduced by the guarantee of the GSE itself, which charges a fee for insuring the issue. In contrast, non-agency RMBS use credit enhancements to reduce credit risk, which is further discussed in Section 5.3. The second way in which RMBS issued by GSEs differ from non-agency RMBS is with regard to the pool of securitized loans. For a loan to be included in a pool of loans backing an agency RMBS, it must meet specific underwriting standards established by various government agencies. These standards set forth the maximum size of the loan, the loan documentation required, the maximum loan-to-value ratio, and whether or not insurance is required. If a loan satisfies the underwriting standards for inclusion as collateral for an agency RMBS, it is called a "conforming mortgage." If a loan fails to satisfy the underwriting standards, it is called a "non-conforming mortgage."

This section starts with a discussion of agency RMBS, which include mortgage pass-through securities and collateralized mortgage obligations. We then discuss non-agency RMBS.[5]

5.1 Mortgage Pass-Through Securities

A **mortgage pass-through security** is a security created when one or more holders of mortgages form a pool of mortgages and sell shares or participation certificates in the pool. A pool can consist of several thousand or only a few mortgages. When a mortgage is included in a pool of mortgages that is used as collateral for a mortgage pass-through security, the mortgage is said to be securitized.

5.1.1 *Characteristics*

The cash flows of a mortgage pass-through security depend on the cash flows of the underlying pool of mortgages. The cash flows consist of monthly mortgage payments representing interest, the scheduled repayment of principal, and any prepayments. Cash payments are made to security holders each month. Neither the amount nor the timing of the cash flows from the pool of mortgages, however, is necessarily identical to that of the cash flow passed through to the security holders. In fact, the monthly cash flows of a mortgage pass-through security are less than the monthly cash flow of the underlying pool of mortgages by an amount equal to the servicing and other administrative fees.

4 In September 2008, both GSEs were placed in conservatorship. In a conservatorship, a judge appoints an entity to take charge of the financial affairs of another entity. As of 2018, they are still in US government conservatorship.

5 A popular bond market index, the Bloomberg Barclays US Aggregate Bond Index, has a sector called the "mortgage sector." In the mortgage sector, Bloomberg Barclays includes only agency RMBS that are mortgage pass-through securities.

The servicing fee is the charge related to servicing the mortgages. Servicing involves collecting monthly payments from borrowers, forwarding proceeds to owners of the loan, sending payment notices to borrowers, reminding borrowers when payments are overdue, maintaining records of the outstanding mortgage balance, initiating foreclosure proceedings if necessary, and providing tax information to borrowers when applicable. The servicing fee is typically a portion of the mortgage rate. The other administrative fees are those charged by the issuer or financial guarantor of the mortgage pass-through security for guaranteeing the issue.

A mortgage pass-through security's coupon rate is called the **pass-through rate**. The pass-through rate is lower than the mortgage rate on the underlying pool of mortgages by an amount equal to the servicing and other administrative fees. The pass-through rate that the investor receives is said to be "net interest" or "net coupon."

Not all of the mortgages that are included in a pool of securitized mortgages have the same mortgage rate and the same maturity. Consequently, for each mortgage pass-through security, a **weighted average coupon rate** (WAC) and a **weighted average maturity** (WAM) are determined. The WAC is calculated by weighting the mortgage rate of each mortgage in the pool by the percentage of the outstanding mortgage balance relative to the outstanding amount of all the mortgages in the pool. Similarly, the WAM is calculated by weighting the remaining number of months to maturity of each mortgage in the pool by the outstanding mortgage balance relative to the outstanding amount of all the mortgages in the pool. Example 5 illustrates the calculation of the WAC and WAM.

EXAMPLE 5

Weighted Average Coupon Rate and Weighted Average Maturity

Assume that a pool includes three mortgages with the following characteristics:

Mortgage	Outstanding Mortgage Balance (US$)	Coupon Rate (%)	Number of Months to Maturity
1	1,000	5.1	34
2	3,000	5.7	76
3	6,000	5.3	88

The outstanding amount of three mortgages is US$10,000. Thus, the weights of Mortgages 1, 2, and 3 are 10%, 30%, and 60 %, respectively.

The WAC is:

$$10\% \times 5.1\% + 30\% \times 5.7\% + 60\% \times 5.3\% = 5.4\%$$

The WAM is:

$$10\% \times 34 + 30\% \times 76 + 60\% \times 88 = 79 \text{ months}$$

5.1.2 *Prepayment Risk*

An investor who owns mortgage pass-through securities does not know what the future cash flows will be because these future cash flows depend on actual prepayments. As we noted earlier, this risk is called prepayment risk. This prepayment risk has two components: contraction risk and extension risk, both of which largely reflect changes in the general level of interest rates.

Contraction risk is the risk that when interest rates decline, actual prepayments will be higher than forecasted because homeowners will refinance at now-available lower interest rates. Thus, a security backed by mortgages will have a shorter maturity than was anticipated at the time of purchase. Holding a security whose maturity becomes shorter when interest rates decline has two adverse consequences for investors. First, investors must reinvest the proceeds at lower interest rates. Second, if the security is prepayable or callable, its price appreciation is not as great as that of an otherwise identical bond that does not have a prepayment or call option.

In contrast, **extension risk** is the risk that when interest rates rise, prepayments will be lower than forecasted because homeowners are reluctant to give up the benefits of a contractual interest rate that now looks low. As a result, a security backed by mortgages will typically have a longer maturity than was anticipated at the time of purchase. From the investors' perspective, the value of the security has fallen because the higher interest rates translate into a lower price for the security, and the income investors receive (and can potentially reinvest) is typically limited to the interest payment and scheduled principal repayments.

5.1.3 *Prepayment Rate Measures*

In describing prepayments, market participants refer to the prepayment rate or prepayment speed. The two key prepayment rate measures are the single monthly mortality rate (SMM), a monthly measure, and its corresponding annualized rate, the conditional prepayment rate (CPR).

The SMM reflects the dollar amount of prepayment for the month as a fraction of the balance on the mortgage after accounting for the scheduled principal repayment for the month. It is calculated as follows:

$$\text{SMM} = \frac{\text{Prepayment for the month}}{\begin{pmatrix}\text{Beginning outstanding mortgage balance for the month} \\ -\ \text{Scheduled principal repayment for the month}\end{pmatrix}} \quad (1)$$

Note that the SMM is typically expressed as a percentage.

When market participants describe the assumed prepayment for a pool of residential mortgages, they refer to the annualized SMM, which is the CPR. A CPR of 6%, for example, means that approximately 6% of the outstanding mortgage balance at the beginning of the year is expected to be prepaid by the end of the year.

A key factor in the valuation of a mortgage pass-through security and other products derived from a pool of mortgages is forecasting the future prepayment rate. This task involves prepayment modeling. Prepayment modeling uses characteristics of the mortgage pool and other factors to develop a statistical model for forecasting future prepayments.

In the United States, market participants describe prepayment rates in terms of a prepayment pattern or benchmark over the life of a mortgage pool. This pattern is the Public Securities Association (PSA) prepayment benchmark, which is produced by the Securities Industry and Financial Markets Association (SIFMA). The PSA prepayment benchmark is expressed as a series of monthly prepayment rates. Based on historical patterns, it assumes that prepayment rates are low for newly originated mortgages and then speed up as the mortgages become seasoned. Slower or faster prepayment rates are then referred to as some percentage of the PSA prepayment benchmark. Rather than going into the details of the PSA prepayment benchmark, this discussion will rely on some PSA assumptions. What is important to remember is that the standard for the PSA model is 100 PSA; that is, at 100 PSA, investors can expect prepayments to follow the PSA prepayment benchmark—for example, an increase of prepayment rates of 0.20% for the first 30 months until they peak at 6% in Month 30.

A PSA assumption greater than 100 PSA means that prepayments are assumed to be faster than the standard model. In contrast, a PSA assumption lower than 100 PSA means that prepayments are assumed to be slower than the standard model.

5.1.4 *Cash Flow Construction*

Let us see how to construct the monthly cash flow for a hypothetical mortgage pass-through security. We assume the following:

- The underlying pool of mortgages has a par value of US$800 million.
- The mortgages are fixed-rate, level-payment, and fully amortizing loans.
- The WAC for the mortgages in the pool is 6%.
- The WAM for the mortgages in the pool is 357 months.
- The pass-through rate is 5.5%.

Exhibit 2 shows the cash flows to the mortgage pass-through security holders for selected months assuming a prepayment rate of 165 PSA. The SMM in Column 3 and mortgage payments in Column 4 are given. The net interest payment in Column 5 is the amount available to pay security holders after servicing and other administrative fees. This amount is equal to the beginning outstanding mortgage balance in Column 2 multiplied by the pass-through rate of 5.5% and then divided by 12. The scheduled principal repayment in Column 6 is the difference between the mortgage payment in Column 4 and the gross interest payment. The gross interest payment is equal to the beginning outstanding mortgage balance in Column 2 multiplied by the WAC of 6% and then divided by 12. The prepayment in Column 7 is calculated by applying Equation 1, using the SMM provided in Column 3, the beginning outstanding mortgage balance in Column 2, and the scheduled principal repayment in Column 6.[6] The total principal repayment in Column 8 is the sum of the scheduled principal repayment in Column 6 and the prepayments in Column 7. Subtracting this amount from the beginning outstanding mortgage balance for the month gives the beginning outstanding mortgage balance for the following month. Finally, the projected cash flow for this mortgage pass-through security in Column 9 is the sum of the net interest payment in Column 5 and the total principal repayment in Column 8.

Exhibit 2 Monthly Cash Flow to Bondholders for a US$800 Million Mortgage Pass-Through Security with a WAC of 6.0%, a WAM of 357 Months, and a Pass-Through Rate of 5.5%, Assuming a Prepayment Rate of 165 PSA

(1)	(2)	(3)	(4)	(5)	(6)	(7)	(8)	(9)
Month	Beginning Outstanding Mortgage Balance (US$)	SMM (%)	Mortgage Payment (US$)	Net Interest Payment (US$)	Scheduled Principal Repayment (US$)	Prepayment (US$)	Total Principal Repayment (US$)	Projected Cash Flow (US$)
1	800,000,000	0.111	4,810,844	3,666,667	810,844	884,472	1,695,316	5,361,982
2	798,304,684	0.139	4,805,520	3,658,896	813,996	1,104,931	1,918,927	5,577,823
3	796,385,757	0.167	4,798,862	3,650,101	816,933	1,324,754	2,141,687	5,791,788
⋮								

6 The SMM in Column 3 is rounded, which results in some rounding error in the calculation of the prepayments in Column 7 and, thus, of the total principal repayments and the projected cash flows in Columns 8 and 9, respectively.

Exhibit 2 (Continued)

(1) Month	(2) Beginning Outstanding Mortgage Balance (US$)	(3) SMM (%)	(4) Mortgage Payment (US$)	(5) Net Interest Payment (US$)	(6) Scheduled Principal Repayment (US$)	(7) Prepayment (US$)	(8) Total Principal Repayment (US$)	(9) Projected Cash Flow (US$)
29	674,744,235	0.865	4,184,747	3,092,578	811,026	5,829,438	6,640,464	9,733,042
30	668,103,771	0.865	4,148,550	3,062,142	808,031	5,772,024	6,580,055	9,642,198
⋮								
100	326,937,929	0.865	2,258,348	1,498,466	623,659	2,822,577	3,446,236	4,944,702
101	323,491,693	0.865	2,238,814	1,482,670	621,355	2,792,788	3,414,143	4,896,814
⋮								
200	103,307,518	0.865	947,322	473,493	430,784	889,871	1,320,655	1,794,148
201	101,986,863	0.865	939,128	467,440	429,193	878,461	1,307,654	1,775,094
⋮								
300	19,963,930	0.865	397,378	91,501	297,559	170,112	467,670	559,172
301	19,496,260	0.865	393,941	89,358	296,460	166,076	462,536	551,893
⋮								
356	484,954	0.865	244,298	2,223	241,873	2,103	243,976	246,199
357	240,978	0.865	242,185	1,104	240,980	0	240,980	242,084

Note: Since the WAM is 357 months, the underlying mortgage pool is seasoned an average of three months, and therefore based on a 165 PSA, the CPR is 0.132% in month 1 (seasoned month 4), and the pool seasons at 6% in month 27.

5.1.5 *Weighted Average Life*

A standard practice in the bond market is to refer to the maturity of a bond. This practice is not followed for MBS because principal repayments (scheduled principal repayments and prepayments) are made over the life of the security. Although an MBS has a "legal maturity," which is the date when the last scheduled principal repayment is due, the legal maturity does not reveal much about the actual principal repayments and the interest rate risk associated with the MBS. For example, a 30-year, option-free, corporate bond and an MBS with a 30-year legal maturity with the same coupon rate are not equivalent in terms of interest rate risk. Effective duration can be calculated for both the corporate bond and the MBS to assess the sensitivity of the securities to interest rate movements. But a measure widely used by market participants for MBS is the **weighted average life** or simply the **average life** of the MBS. This measure gives investors an indication of how long they can expect to hold the MBS before it is paid off assuming interest rates stay at current levels and, thus, expected prepayments are realized. In other words, the average life of the MBS is the convention-based average time to receipt of all the projected principal repayments (scheduled principal repayments and projected prepayments).

A mortgage pass-through security's average life depends on the prepayment assumption, as illustrated in the following table. This table provides the average life of the mortgage pass-through security used in Exhibit 2 for various prepayment rates. Note that at the assumed prepayment rate of 165 PSA, the mortgage pass-through security has an average life of 8.6 years. The average life extends when the prepayment rate goes down and contracts rapidly as the prepayment rate goes up. So, at a prepayment rate of 600 PSA, the average life of the mortgage pass-through security is only 3.2 years.

PSA assumption	100	125	165	250	400	600
Average life (years)	11.2	10.1	8.6	6.4	4.5	3.2

EXAMPLE 6

Mortgage Pass-Through Securities

1 A non-conforming mortgage:

A cannot be used as collateral in a mortgage-backed security.

B does not satisfy the underwriting standards for inclusion as collateral for an agency residential mortgage-backed security.

C does not give the lender a claim against the borrower for the shortfall between the amount of the outstanding mortgage balance and the proceeds from the sale of the property in the event that the borrower defaults on the mortgage.

2 The monthly cash flows of a mortgage pass-through security *most likely*:

A are constant.

B change when interest rates decline.

C are equal to the cash flows of the underlying pool of mortgages.

3 A prepayment rate of 80 PSA means that investors can expect:

A 80% of the par value of the mortgage pass-through security to be repaid prior to the security's maturity.

B 80% of the borrowers whose mortgages are included in the collateral backing the mortgage pass-through security to prepay their mortgages.

C the prepayment rate of the mortgages included in the collateral backing the mortgage pass-through security to be 80% of the monthly prepayment rates forecasted by the PSA model.

4 All else being equal, when interest rates decline:

A investors in mortgage pass-through securities face extension risk.

B the weighted average maturity of a mortgage pass-through security lengthens.

C the increase in the price of a mortgage pass-through security is less than the increase in the price of an otherwise identical bond with no prepayment option.

Solution to 1:

B is correct. A non-conforming mortgage is one that does not satisfy the underwriting standards for inclusion as collateral for an agency RMBS. The standards specify the maximum size of the loan, the loan documentation required, the maximum loan-to-value ratio, and whether or not insurance is required for the loans in the pool.

Solution to 2:

B is correct. The monthly cash flows of a mortgage pass-through security depend on the cash flows of the underlying pool of mortgages, but their amount and timing cannot be known with certainty because of prepayments. When interest rates decline, borrowers are likely to prepay all or part of their outstanding mortgage balance, which will affect the monthly cash flows of the mortgage pass-through security. Remember that the fees related to servicing and guaranteeing the mortgages reduce the monthly cash flows of a mortgage pass-through security relative to those of the underlying pool of mortgages.

Solution to 3:

C is correct. A prepayment rate of 80 PSA means that investors can expect the prepayment rate of the mortgages included in the collateral backing the mortgage pass-through security to be 80% of the monthly prepayment rates forecasted by the PSA model. For example, if the PSA model forecasts an increase in prepayment rates of 0.20% for the first 30 months until they peak at 6% in Month 30, 80 PSA would assume an increase in prepayment rates of 0.16% (80% × 0.20%) for the first 30 months until they peak at 4.80% (80% × 6%) in Month 30. Thus, investors can expect slower prepayments than the PSA prepayment benchmark.

Solution to 4:

C is correct. When interest rates decline, the prepayment rate on a mortgage pass-through security goes up because homeowners refinance at now-available lower interest rates. As a result, investors face contraction risk; that is, they receive payments faster than anticipated. Investors who decide to retain the security face the prospect of having to reinvest those payments at relatively low interest rates. Investors who decide to sell the security would have to do so at a price lower than that of an otherwise identical bond with no prepayment option and thus no prepayment risk.

5.2 Collateralized Mortgage Obligations

As noted in the previous section, prepayment risk is an important consideration when investing in mortgage pass-through securities. Some institutional investors are concerned with extension risk and others with contraction risk. The structuring of a securitization can help redistribute the cash flows of mortgage-related products (mortgage pass-through securities or pools of loans) to different bond classes or tranches, which leads to the creation of securities that have different exposures to prepayment risk and thus different risk–return patterns relative to the mortgage-related product from which they were created.

When the cash flows of mortgage-related products are redistributed to various tranches, the resulting securities are called **collateralized mortgage obligations** (CMOs). The mortgage-related products from which the cash flows are obtained are considered the collateral. Note that in contrast to a mortgage pass-through security, the collateral is not a pool of mortgages but a mortgage pass-through security. In fact, in practice, the collateral is usually a pool of mortgage pass-through securities—hence the reason market participants sometimes use the terms "collateral" and "mortgage pass-through securities" interchangeably.

The creation of a CMO cannot eliminate or change prepayment risk; it can only distribute the various forms of this risk among different bond classes. The CMO's major financial innovation is that securities can be created to closely satisfy the asset/liability needs of institutional investors, thereby broadening the appeal of mortgage-backed products.

A wide range of CMO structures exists. The major ones are reviewed in the following subsections.

5.2.1 *Sequential-Pay CMO Structures*

The first CMOs were structured so that each tranche would be retired sequentially. Such structures are called "sequential-pay CMOs." The rule for the monthly distribution of the principal repayments (scheduled principal repayment plus prepayments) to the tranches in this structure is as follows. First, distribute all principal payments to Tranche 1 until the principal balance for Tranche 1 is zero. After Tranche 1 is paid off, distribute all principal payments to Tranche 2 until the principal balance for Tranche 2 is zero. And so on.

To illustrate a sequential-pay CMO, let us use a hypothetical transaction called CMO-01. Assume that the collateral for CMO-01 is the mortgage pass-through security described in Exhibit 2 in Section 5.1.4. Recall that the total par value of the collateral is US$800 million, the pass-through coupon rate is 5.5%, the WAC is 6%, and the WAM is 357 months. From this US$800 million of collateral, four tranches are created, as shown in Exhibit 3. In this simple structure, the coupon rate is the same for each tranche and also the same as the mortgage pass-through security's coupon rate. This feature is for simplicity; typically, the coupon rate varies by tranche.[7]

Exhibit 3 CMO-01: Sequential-Pay CMO Structure with Four Tranches

Tranche	Par Amount (US$ millions)	Coupon Rate (%)
A	389	5.5
B	72	5.5
C	193	5.5
D	146	5.5
Total	800	

Payment rules: *For payment of monthly coupon interest:* Disburse monthly coupon interest to each tranche on the basis of the amount of principal outstanding for each tranche at the beginning of the month. *For disbursement of principal payments:* Disburse principal payments to Tranche A until it is completely paid off. After Tranche A is completely paid off, disburse principal payments to Tranche B until it is completely paid off. After Tranche B is completely paid off, disburse principal payments to Tranche C until it is completely paid off. After Tranche C is completely paid off, disburse principal payments to Tranche D until it is completely paid off.

Remember that a CMO is created by redistributing the cash flows—interest payments and principal repayments—to the various tranches on the basis of a set of payment rules. The payment rules at the bottom of Exhibit 3 describe how the cash flows

7 Keep in mind that the coupon rate for a tranche is affected by the term structure of interest rates (that is, basically, the yield curve). Typically, yield increases as maturity increases. A CMO has tranches with different average lives. Usually, the longer the average life, the higher the coupon rate should be. So, in the hypothetical four-tranche sequential-pay structure shown in Exhibit 3, Tranche A might have a 4.2% coupon rate, Tranche B a 4.8% coupon rate, Tranche C a 5.2% coupon rate, and Tranche D a 5.5% coupon rate. In any event, investors evaluate each tranche on the basis of its perceived risk and price it accordingly. Consequently, investors pay a price for the tranche that reflects the yield they expect to receive given the specific coupon rate. Separately, the difference between the coupon rate paid by the underlying pool of mortgages net of servicing and other administrative fees (that is, the net coupon—5.5% in our example) and the coupon rate paid to each of the tranches that has a coupon rate of less than the net coupon is used to create securities called "structured interest-only tranches." A discussion of these tranches is beyond the scope of this reading.

from the mortgage pass-through security are to be distributed to the four tranches. CMO-01 has separate rules for the interest payment and the principal repayment, the latter being the sum of the scheduled principal repayment and the prepayments.

Although the payment rules for the distribution of the principal repayments are known, the precise amount of the principal repayment in each month is not. This amount will depend on the cash flow of the collateral, which depends on the actual prepayment rate of the collateral. The assumed prepayment rate (165 PSA in Exhibit 2) allows determining only the projected, not the actual, cash flow.

Consider what has been accomplished by creating the sequential-pay CMO-01 structure. Earlier, we saw that with a prepayment rate of 165 PSA, the mortgage pass-through security's average life was 8.6 years. Exhibit 4 reports the average life of the collateral and the four tranches assuming various actual prepayment rates. Note that the four tranches have average lives that are shorter or longer than the collateral, thereby attracting investors who have preferences for different average lives. For example, a pension fund that needs cash only after a few years because it expects a significant increase in the number of retirements after that time may opt for a tranche with a longer average life.

Exhibit 4 Average Life of the Collateral and the Four Tranches of CMO-01 for Various Actual Prepayment Rates

Prepayment	Average Life (years)				
Rate	**Collateral**	**Tranche A**	**Tranche B**	**Tranche C**	**Tranche D**
100 PSA	11.2	4.7	10.4	15.1	24.0
125 PSA	10.1	4.1	8.9	13.2	22.4
165 PSA	8.6	3.4	7.3	10.9	19.8
250 PSA	6.4	2.7	5.3	7.9	15.2
400 PSA	4.5	2.0	3.8	5.3	10.3
600 PSA	3.2	1.6	2.8	3.8	7.0

A major problem that remains is the considerable variability of the average lives of the tranches. How this problem can be handled is shown in the next section, but at this point, note that some protection against prepayment risk is provided for each tranche. The protection arises because prioritizing the distribution of principal (that is, establishing the payment rule for the principal repayment) effectively protects the shorter-term tranche (A in this structure) against extension risk. This protection must come from somewhere; it actually comes from the longer-term tranches. Similarly, Tranches C and D provide protection against extension risk for Tranches A and B. At the same time, Tranches C and D benefit because they are provided protection against contraction risk; this protection comes from Tranches A and B. Thus, the sequential-pay CMO-01 structure allows investors concerned about extension risk to invest in Tranches A or B and those concerned about contraction risk to invest in Tranches C or D.

5.2.2 *CMO Structures Including Planned Amortization Class and Support Tranches*

A common structure in CMOs is to include **planned amortization class (PAC) tranches**, which offer greater predictability of the cash flows as long as the prepayment rate is within a specified band over the collateral's life. Remember that the creation of an MBS, whether it is a mortgage pass-through or a CMO, cannot make prepayment risk disappear. So where does the reduction of prepayment risk (both extension risk and contraction risk) that PAC tranches offer investors come from? The answer is that it comes from the existence of non-PAC tranches, called **support tranches** or companion tranches. The structure of the CMO makes the support tranches absorb prepayment risk first. Because PAC tranches have limited (but not complete) protection against both extension risk and contraction risk, they are said to provide two-sided prepayment protection.

The greater predictability of the cash flows for the PAC tranches occurs because a principal repayment schedule must be satisfied. As long as the prepayment rate is within the specified band, called the PAC band, all prepayment risk is absorbed by the support tranche. If the collateral prepayments are slower than forecasted, the support tranches do not receive any principal repayment until the PAC tranches receive their scheduled principal repayment. This rule reduces the extension risk of the PAC tranches. Similarly, if the collateral prepayments are faster than forecasted, the support tranches absorb any principal repayments in excess of the scheduled principal repayments. This rule reduces the contraction risk of the PAC tranches. Even if the prepayment rate is outside the PAC band, prepayment risk is first absorbed by the support tranche. Thus, the key to the prepayment protection that PAC tranches offer investors is the amount of support tranches outstanding. If the support tranches are paid off quickly because of faster-than-expected prepayments, they no longer provide any protection for the PAC tranches.

Support tranches expose investors to the highest level of prepayment risk. Therefore, investors must be particularly careful in assessing the cash flow characteristics of support tranches in order to reduce the likelihood of adverse portfolio consequences resulting from prepayments.

To illustrate how to create CMO structures including PAC and support tranches, we use again the US$800 million mortgage pass-through security described in Exhibit 2 in Section 5.1.4, with a pass-through coupon rate of 5.5%, a WAC of 6%, and a WAM of 357 months as collateral. The creation of PAC tranches requires the specification of two PSA prepayment rates: a *lower* PSA prepayment assumption and an *upper* PSA prepayment assumption. The lower and upper PSA prepayment assumptions are called the "initial PAC collar" or the "initial PAC band." The PAC collar for a CMO is typically dictated by market conditions. In our example, we assume that the lower and upper PSA prepayment assumptions are 100 PSA and 250 PSA, respectively, so the initial PAC collar is 100–250 PSA.

Exhibit 5 shows a CMO structure called CMO-02 that contains only two tranches: a 5.5% coupon PAC tranche created assuming an initial PAC collar of 100–250 PSA and a support tranche.

Exhibit 5 CMO-02: CMO Structure with One PAC Tranche and One Support Tranche

Tranche	Par Amount (US$ million)	Coupon Rate (%)
P (PAC)	487.6	5.5
S (support)	312.4	5.5
Total	800.0	

Payment rules: *For payment of monthly coupon interest:* Disburse monthly coupon interest to each tranche on the basis of the amount of principal outstanding for each tranche at the beginning of the month. *For disbursement of principal payments:* Disburse principal payments to Tranche P on the basis of its schedule of principal repayments. Tranche P has priority with respect to current and future principal payments to satisfy the schedule. Any excess principal payments in a month over the amount necessary to satisfy the schedule for Tranche P are paid to Tranche S. When Tranche S is completely paid off, all principal payments are to be made to Tranche P regardless of the schedule.

Exhibit 6 reports the average life of the PAC and support tranches in CMO-02 assuming various actual prepayment rates. Note that between 100 PSA and 250 PSA, the average life of the PAC tranche is constant at 7.7 years. At slower or faster PSA rates, however, the schedule is broken and the average life changes—extending when the prepayment rate is less than 100 PSA and contracting when it is greater than 250 PSA. Even so, there is much less variability for the average life of the PAC tranche compared with that of the support tranche.

Exhibit 6 Average Life of the PAC Tranche and the Support Tranche of CMO-02 for Various Actual Prepayment Rates and an Initial PAC Collar of 100–250 PSA

	Average Life (years)	
Prepayment Rate	**PAC Tranche (P)**	**Support Tranche (S)**
50 PSA	10.2	24.9
75 PSA	8.6	22.7
100 PSA	7.7	20.0
165 PSA	7.7	10.7
250 PSA	7.7	3.3
400 PSA	5.5	1.9
600 PSA	4.0	1.4

Most CMO structures including PAC and support tranches have more than one PAC tranche. A sequence of six PAC tranches (that is, PAC tranches paid off in sequence as specified by a principal repayment schedule) is not uncommon. For example, consider CMO-03 in Exhibit 7, which contains four sequential PAC tranches (P-A, P-B, P-C, and P-D) and one support tranche. The total par amount of the PAC and support tranches is the same as for CMO-02 in Exhibit 5. The difference is that instead of one PAC tranche with a schedule, there are four PAC tranches with schedules. As described in the payment rules, the PAC tranches are paid off in sequence.

Exhibit 7 CMO-03: CMO Structure with Sequential PAC Tranches and One Support Tranche

Tranche	Par Amount (US$ million)	Coupon Rate (%)
P-A (PAC)	287.6	5.5
P-B (PAC)	90.0	5.5
P-C (PAC)	60.0	5.5
P-D (PAC)	50.0	5.5

(continued)

Exhibit 7 (Continued)

Tranche	Par Amount (US$ million)	Coupon Rate (%)
S (support)	312.4	5.5
Total	800.0	

Payment rules: *For payment of monthly coupon interest:* Disburse monthly coupon interest to each tranche on the basis of the amount of principal outstanding for each tranche at the beginning of the month. *For disbursement of principal payments:* Disburse principal payments to Tranche P-A on the basis of its schedule of principal repayments. Tranche P-A has priority with respect to current and future principal payments to satisfy the schedule. Any excess principal payments in a month over the amount necessary to satisfy the schedule while P-A is outstanding is paid to Tranche S. Once P-A is paid off, disburse principal payments to Tranche P-B on the basis of its schedule of principal repayments. Tranche P-B has priority with respect to current and future principal payments to satisfy the schedule. Any excess principal payments in a month over the amount necessary to satisfy the schedule while P-B is outstanding are paid to Tranche S. The same rule applies for P-C and P-D. When Tranche S is completely paid off, all principal payments are to be made to the outstanding PAC tranches regardless of the schedule.

5.2.3 *Other CMO Structures*

Often, there is a demand for tranches that have a floating rate. Although the collateral pays a fixed rate, it is possible to create a tranche with a floating rate. This is done by constructing a floater and an inverse floater combination from any of the fixed-rate tranches in the CMO structure. Because the floating-rate tranche pays a higher rate when interest rates go up and the inverse floater pays a lower rate when interest rates go up, they offset each other. Thus, a fixed-rate tranche can be used to satisfy the demand for a floating-rate tranche.

In a similar vein, other types of tranches to satisfy the various needs of investors are possible.

EXAMPLE 7

Collateralized Mortgage Obligations

1 A collateralized mortgage obligation:

A eliminates prepayment risk.

B is created from a pool of conforming loans.

C redistributes various forms of prepayment risk among different bond classes.

2 The variability in the average life of the PAC tranche of a CMO relative to the average life of the mortgage pass-through securities from which the CMO is created is:

A lower.

B the same.

C higher.

3 Referring to Exhibit 7, the tranche of CMO-03 that is *most suitable* for an investor concerned about contraction risk is:

A P-A (PAC).

B P-D (PAC).

C S (support).

4 The tranche of a collateralized mortgage obligation that is *most suitable* for an investor who expects a fall in interest rates is:

A a fixed-rate tranche.

B an inverse floating-rate tranche.

C a PAC tranche.

5 The investment that is *most suitable* for an investor who is willing and able to accept significant prepayment risk is:

A a mortgage pass-through security.

B the support tranche of a collateralized mortgage obligation.

C the inverse floating-rate tranche of a collateralized mortgage obligation.

Solution to 1:

C is correct. CMOs are created by redistributing the cash flows of mortgage-related products, including mortgage pass-through securities, to different bond classes or tranches on the basis of a set of payment rules.

Solution to 2:

A is correct. The purpose of creating different bond classes in a CMO is to provide a risk–return profile that is more suitable to investors than the risk-return profile of the mortgage pass-through securities from which the CMO is created. The PAC tranche has considerably less variability in average life than the mortgage pass-through securities. In contrast, the support tranche has more variability in average life than the mortgage pass-through securities.

Solution to 3:

B is correct. Contraction risk is the risk that when interest rates decline, prepayments will be higher than expected and the security's maturity will become shorter than was anticipated at the time of purchase. PAC tranches offer investors protection against contraction risk (and extension risk). The PAC tranche that is most suitable for an investor concerned about contraction risk is P-D because it is the latest-payment PAC tranche; that is, any principal repayments in excess of the scheduled principal repayments are absorbed sequentially by the support tranche, then P-A, P-B, and, finally, P-D.

Solution to 4:

B is correct. The tranche of a CMO that is most suitable for an investor who expects a fall in interest rates is an inverse floating-rate tranche. The inverse floater pays a coupon rate that is inversely related to prevailing interest rates. Thus, if interest rates fall, the CMO's coupon rate will rise.

Solution to 5:

B is correct. The investment that is most suitable to an investor who is willing and able to accept significant prepayment risk is the support tranche of a collateralized mortgage obligation. Because the PAC tranche has a stable average life at prepayment rates within the PAC band, all prepayment risk is absorbed by the support tranche for prepayment rates within the band. Even at rates outside the PAC band, prepayment risk is first absorbed by the support tranche. Investors will be compensated for bearing prepayment risk in the sense that, if properly priced, the support tranche will have a higher expected rate of return than the PAC tranche.

5.3 Non-agency Residential Mortgage-Backed Securities

Agency RMBS are those issued by Ginnie Mae, Fannie Mae, and Freddie Mac. RMBS issued by any other entity are non-agency RMBS. Entities that issue non-agency RMBS are typically thrift institutions, commercial banks, and private conduits. Private conduits may purchase non-conforming mortgages, pool them, and then sell mortgage pass-through securities whose collateral is the underlying pool of non-conforming mortgages. Because they are not guaranteed by the government or by a GSE, credit risk is an important consideration when investing in non-agency RMBS.

Non-agency RMBS share many features and structuring techniques with agency CMOs. However, because non-agency RMBS are not guaranteed by the US government or by a GSE that can provide protection against losses in the pool, some form of internal or external credit enhancement is necessary to make these securities attractive to investors. These credit enhancements allow investors to reduce credit risk or transfer credit risk between bond classes, thus enabling investors to choose the risk–return profile that best suits their needs. Credit enhancements also play an important role in obtaining favorable credit ratings, which make non-agency RMBS more marketable to investors. The level of credit enhancement is usually determined relative to a specific credit rating desired by the issuer for a security. Note that one of the consequences of the 2007–2009 credit crisis has been an overall increase in the level of credit enhancement.

As mentioned in Section 3.3, subordination, or credit tranching, is a common form of credit enhancement. The subordination levels (that is, the amount of credit protection for a bond class) are set at the time of issuance. However, the subordination levels change over time, as voluntary prepayments and defaults occur. To protect investors in non-agency RMBS, a securitization is designed to keep the amount of credit enhancement from deteriorating over time. If the credit enhancement for senior tranches deteriorates because of poor performance of the collateral, a mechanism called the "shifting interest mechanism" locks out subordinated bond classes from receiving payments for a period of time. Many non-agency RMBS also include other credit enhancements, such as overcollateralization and reserve accounts.

When forecasting the future cash flows of non-agency RMBS, investors must consider two important components. The first is the assumed default rate for the collateral. The second is the recovery rate, because even though the collateral may default, not all of the outstanding mortgage balance may be lost. The repossession and subsequent sale of the recovered property may provide cash flows that will be available to pay bondholders. That amount is based on the assumed amount that will be recovered.

The focus in Section 5 is on securities backed by a pool of residential mortgages. The next section discusses securities backed by a pool of commercial mortgages.

6 COMMERCIAL MORTGAGE-BACKED SECURITIES

Commercial mortgage-backed securities (CMBS) are backed by a pool of commercial mortgages on income-producing property, such as multifamily properties (e.g., apartment buildings), office buildings, industrial properties (including warehouses), shopping centers, hotels, and health care facilities (e.g., senior housing care facilities). The collateral is a pool of commercial loans that were originated either to finance a commercial purchase or to refinance a prior mortgage obligation.

6.1 Credit Risk

In the United States and other countries where commercial mortgages are non-recourse loans, the lender can look only to the income-producing property backing the loan for interest payments and principal repayments. If a default occurs, the lender can foreclose the commercial property but it can only use the proceeds from the sale of that property to recover the principal outstanding, and it has no recourse to the borrower's other assets and/or income for any unpaid balance. The lender must view each property individually, and lenders evaluate each property using measures that have been found useful in assessing credit risk.

Two measures that have been found to be key indicators of potential credit performance are the loan-to-value ratio (LTV), which was discussed in Section 4, and the debt-service-coverage (DSC) ratio, sometimes referred to as DSCR. The DSC ratio is equal to the property's annual net operating income (NOI) divided by the debt service (that is, the annual amount of interest payments and principal repayments). The NOI is defined as the rental income reduced by cash operating expenses and a non-cash replacement reserve reflecting the depreciation of the property over time. A DSC ratio that exceeds 1.0 indicates that the cash flows from the property are sufficient to cover the debt service while maintaining the property in its initial state of repair. The higher the DSC ratio, the more likely it is that the borrower will be able to meet debt-servicing requirements from the property's cash flows.

6.2 CMBS Structure

A credit-rating agency determines the level of credit enhancement necessary to achieve a desired credit rating. For example, if specific loan-to-value and DSC ratios are needed and those ratios cannot be met at the loan level, subordination is used to achieve the desired credit rating.

Interest on the principal outstanding is paid to all tranches. Losses arising from loan defaults are charged against the outstanding principal balance of the CMBS tranche with the lowest priority. This tranche may not be rated by credit-rating agencies; in this case, this unrated tranche is called the "first-loss piece," "residual tranche," or "equity tranche." The total loss charged includes the amount previously advanced and the actual loss incurred in the sale of the loan's underlying property.

Two characteristics that are usually specific to CMBS structures are the presence of a call protection and a balloon maturity provision.

6.2.1 *Call Protection*

A critical investment feature that distinguishes CMBS from RMBS is the protection against early prepayments available to investors' known as a **call protection**. An investor in an RMBS is exposed to considerable prepayment risk because the borrower has the right to prepay a loan, in whole or in part, before the scheduled principal repayment date. As explained in Section 4.4, a borrower in the United States usually does not pay any penalty for prepayment. The discussion of CMOs highlighted how investors can purchase certain types of tranches (e.g., sequential-pay and PAC tranches) to modify or reduce prepayment risk.

With CMBS, investors have considerable call protection. In fact, it is this protection that results in CMBS trading in the market more like corporate bonds than like RMBS. The call protection comes either at the structure level or at the loan level. Structural call protection is achieved when CMBS are structured to have sequential-pay tranches, by credit rating. A lower-rated tranche cannot be paid down until the higher-rated tranche is completely retired, so the AAA rated bonds must be paid off before the AA rated bonds are, and so on. Principal losses resulting from defaults, however, are affected from the bottom of the structure upward.

At the loan level, four mechanisms offer investors call protection:

- A prepayment lockout, which is a contractual agreement that prohibits any prepayments during a specified period of time.
- Prepayment penalty points, which are predetermined penalties that a borrower who wants to refinance must pay to do so—a point is equal to 1% of the outstanding loan balance.
- A yield maintenance charge, also called a "make-whole charge," which is a penalty paid by the borrower that makes refinancing solely to get a lower mortgage rate uneconomical for the borrower. In its simplest terms, a yield maintenance charge is designed to make the lender indifferent as to the timing of prepayments.
- Defeasance, for which the borrower provides sufficient funds for the servicer to invest in a portfolio of government securities that replicates the cash flows that would exist in the absence of prepayments. The cash payments that must be met by the borrower are projected on the basis of the terms of the loan. Then, a portfolio of government securities is constructed in such a way that the interest payments and the principal repayments from the portfolio will be sufficient to pay off each obligation when it comes due. When the last obligation is paid off, the value of the portfolio is zero (that is, there are no funds remaining). The cost of assembling such a portfolio is the cost of defeasing the loan that must be repaid by the issuer.[8]

6.2.2 *Balloon Maturity Provision*

Many commercial loans backing CMBS are balloon loans that require a substantial principal repayment at maturity of the loan. If the borrower fails to make the balloon payment, the borrower is in default. The lender may extend the loan over a period of time called the "workout period." In doing so, the lender may modify the original terms of the loan and charge a higher interest rate, called the "default interest rate," during the workout period.

The risk that a borrower will not be able to make the balloon payment because either the borrower cannot arrange for refinancing or cannot sell the property to generate sufficient funds to pay off the outstanding principal balance is called "balloon risk." Because the life of the loan is extended by the lender during the workout period, balloon risk is a type of extension risk.

EXAMPLE 8

An Example of a Commercial Mortgage-Backed Security

The following information is taken from a filing with the US Securities and Exchange Commission about a CMBS issued in April 2013 by Citigroup Commercial Mortgage Trust 2013-GCJ11. The collateral for this CMBS was a pool of 72 fixed-rate mortgages secured by first liens (first claims) on various types of commercial, multifamily, and manufactured housing community properties.

8 This portfolio strategy for paying off liabilities is used by insurance companies. In the United States, it has also been used by municipal bond issuers; the resulting bonds are referred to as "pre-refunded bonds."

Classes of Offered Certificates	Initial Principal Amount (US$)	Initial Pass-Through Rate (%)
A-1	75,176,000	0.754
A-2	290,426,000	1.987
A-3	150,000,000	2.815
A-4	236,220,000	3.093
A-AB	92,911,000	2.690
X-A	948,816,000	1.937
A-S	104,083,000	3.422
B	75,423,000	3.732
C	42,236,000	

The filing included the following statements:

If you acquire Class B certificates, then your rights to receive distributions of amounts collected or advanced on or in respect of the mortgage loans will be subordinated to those of the holders of the Class A-1, Class A-2, Class A-3, Class A-4, Class A-AB, Class X-A, and Class A-S certificates. If you acquire Class C certificates, then your rights to receive distributions of amounts collected or advanced on or in respect of the mortgage loans will be subordinated to those of the holders of the Class B certificates and all other classes of offered certificates.

"Prepayment Penalty Description" or "Prepayment Provision" means the number of payments from the first due date through and including the maturity date for which a mortgage loan is, as applicable, (i) locked out from prepayment, (ii) provides for payment of a prepayment premium or yield maintenance charge in connection with a prepayment, (iii) permits defeasance.

1 Based on the information provided, this CMBS:

A did not include any credit enhancement.

B included an internal credit enhancement.

C included an external credit enhancement.

2 Based on the information provided, investors in this CMBS had prepayment protection at:

A the loan level.

B the structure level.

C both the loan and structure levels.

3 Defeasance can be *best* described as:

A a predetermined penalty that a borrower who wants to refinance must pay to do so.

B a contractual agreement that prohibits any prepayments during a specified period of time.

C funds that the borrower must provide to replicate the cash flows that would exist in the absence of prepayments.

4 A risk that investors typically face when holding CMBS is:

A call risk

B balloon risk.

C contraction risk.

5 The credit risk of a commercial mortgage-backed security is lower:

A the lower the DSC ratio and the lower the LTV.

B the lower the DSC ratio and the higher the LTV.

C the higher the DSC ratio and the lower the LTV.

Solution to 1:

B is correct. The CMBS included a senior/subordinated structure, which is a form of internal credit enhancement. Class B provided protection for all of the bond classes listed above it. Similarly, Class C provided protection for all other bond classes, including Class B; it was the first-loss piece, also called the residual tranche or equity tranche. Note that because it was the residual tranche, Class C had no specific pass-through rate. Investors in Class C will have priced it on the basis of some expected residual rate of return, but they could have done better or worse than expected depending on how interest rate movements and default rates affected the performance of the other tranches.

Solution to 2:

C is correct. This CMBS offered investors prepayment protection at both the structure and loan levels. The structural call protection was achieved thanks to the sequential-pay tranches. At the loan level, the CMBS included three of the four types of call protection—namely, a prepayment lockout, a yield maintenance charge, and defeasance.

Solution to 3:

C is correct. Defeasance is a call protection at the loan level that requires the borrower to provide sufficient funds for the servicer to invest in a portfolio of government securities that replicates the cash flows that would exist in the absence of prepayments.

Solution to 4:

B is correct. Because many commercial loans backing CMBS require a balloon payment, investors in CMBS typically face balloon risk—that is, the risk that if the borrower cannot arrange for refinancing or cannot sell the property to make the balloon payment, the CMBS may extend in maturity because the lender has to wait to obtain the outstanding principal until the borrower can make the balloon amount. Balloon risk is a type of extension risk.

Solution to 5:

C is correct. The DSC ratio and the LTV are key indicators of potential credit performance and thus allow investors to assess the credit risk of a CMBS. The DSC ratio is equal to the property's annual NOI divided by the annual amount of interest payments and principal repayments. So the higher the DSC ratio, the lower the CMBS's credit risk. The LTV is equal to the amount of the mortgage divided by the property's value. So the lower the LTV, the lower the CMBS's credit risk.

To this point, this reading has addressed the securitization of real estate property, both residential and commercial. Section 7 discusses the securitization of debt obligations in which the underlying asset is not real estate.

NON-MORTGAGE ASSET-BACKED SECURITIES

7

Numerous types of non-mortgage assets have been used as collateral in securitization. The largest in most countries are auto loan and lease receivables, credit card receivables, personal loans, and commercial loans. What is important to keep in mind is that, regardless of the type of asset, ABS that are not guaranteed by a government or a quasi-government entity are subject to credit risk.

ABS can be categorized on the basis of the way the collateral repays—that is, whether the collateral is amortizing or non-amortizing. Traditional residential mortgages and auto loans are examples of amortizing loans. The cash flows for an amortizing loan include interest payments, scheduled principal repayments and any prepayments, if permissible. If the loan has no schedule for paying down the principal, it is a non-amortizing loan. Because a non-amortizing loan does not involve scheduled principal repayments, an ABS backed by non-amortizing loans is not affected by prepayment risk. Credit card receivable ABS are an example of ABS backed by non-amortizing loans.

Consider an ABS backed by a pool of 1,000 amortizing loans with a total par value of US$100 million. Over time, some of the loans will be paid off; the amounts received from the scheduled principal repayment and any prepayments will be distributed to the bond classes on the basis of the payment rule. Consequently, over time, the number of loans in the collateral will drop from 1,000 and the total par value will fall to less than US$100 million.

Now, what happens if the collateral of the ABS is 1,000 non-amortizing loans? Some of these loans will be paid off in whole or in part before the maturity of the ABS. When those loans are paid off, what happens depends on whether the loans were paid off during the lockout period or after it. The lockout period or revolving period is the period during which the principal repaid is reinvested to acquire additional loans with a principal equal to the principal repaid. The reinvestment in new loans can result in the collateral including more or less than 1,000 loans, but the loans will still have a total par value of US$100 million. When the lockout period is over, any principal that is repaid will not be used to reinvest in new loans but will instead be distributed to the bond classes.

This reading cannot cover all types of non-mortgage ABS. It focuses on the two popular non-mortgage ABS in most countries: auto loan ABS and credit card receivable ABS.

7.1 Auto Loan ABS

Auto loan ABS are backed by auto loans and lease receivables. The focus in this section is on the largest type of auto securitizations—that is, auto loan-backed securities. In some countries, auto loan-backed securities represent the largest or second largest sector of the securitization market.

The cash flows for auto loan-backed securities consist of scheduled monthly payments (that is, interest payments and scheduled principal repayments) and any prepayments. For securities backed by auto loans, prepayments result from sales and trade-ins requiring full payoff of the loan, repossession and subsequent resale of autos, insurance proceeds received upon loss or destruction of autos, and early payoffs of the loans.

All auto loan-backed securities have some form of credit enhancement, often a senior/subordinated structure. In addition, many auto loan-backed securities come with overcollateralization and a reserve account, often an excess spread account. Recall from a previous reading that the excess spread, sometimes called excess interest cash flow, is an amount that can be retained and deposited into a reserve account and that can serve as a first line of protection against losses.

To illustrate the typical structure of auto loan-backed securities, let us use the example of securities issued by Fideicomiso Financiero Autos VI. The collateral was a pool of 827 auto loans denominated in Argentine pesos (ARS). The loans were originated by BancoFinansur. The structure of the securitization included three bond classes:

Bond Class	Outstanding Principal Balance (ARS)
Class A Floating-Rate Debt Securities	22,706,000
Class B Floating-Rate Debt Securities	1,974,000
Certificates	6,008,581
Total	30,658,245

The certificates provided credit protection for Class B, and Class B provides credit protection for Class A. Further credit enhancement came from overcollateralization and the presence of an excess spread account. The reference rate for the floating-rate debt securities was BADLAR (Buenos Aires Deposits of Large Amount Rate), the benchmark rate for loans in Argentina. This reference rate is the average rate on 30-day deposits of at least ARS1 million. For Class A, the interest rate was BADLAR plus 450 bps, with a minimum rate of 18% and a maximum rate of 26%; for Class B, it was BADLAR plus 650 bps, with 20% and 28% as the minimum and maximum rates, respectively.

EXAMPLE 9

An Example of an Auto Loan ABS

The following information is from the prospectus supplement for US$877,670,000 of auto loan ABS issued by AmeriCredit Automobile Receivables Trust 2013–4:

> The collateral for this securitization is a pool of sub-prime automobile loan contracts secured for new and used automobiles and light-duty trucks and vans.
>
> The issuing entity will issue seven sequential-pay classes of asset-backed notes pursuant to the indenture. The notes are designated as the "Class A-1 Notes," the "Class A-2 Notes," the "Class A-3 Notes," the "Class B Notes," the "Class C Notes," the "Class D Notes," and the "Class E Notes." The Class A-1 Notes, the Class A-2 Notes, and the Class A-3 Notes are the "Class A Notes." The Class A Notes, the Class B Notes, the Class C Notes, and the Class D Notes are being offered by this prospectus supplement and are sometimes referred to as the publicly offered notes. The Class E Notes are not being offered by this prospectus supplement and will initially be retained by the depositor or an affiliate of the depositor. The Class E Notes are sometimes referred to as the privately placed notes.
>
> Each class of notes will have the initial note principal balance, interest rate, and final scheduled distribution date listed in the following tables:

Publicly Offered Notes			
Class	Initial Note Principal Balance (US$)	Interest Rate (%)	Final Scheduled Distribution Date
A-1 (senior)	168,000,000	0.25	8 August 2014
A-2 (senior)	279,000,000	0.74	8 November 2016
A-3 (senior)	192,260,000	0.96	9 April 2018
B (subordinated)	68,870,000	1.66	10 September 2018
C (subordinated)	85,480,000	2.72	9 September 2019
D (subordinated)	84,060,000	3.31	8 October 2019

Privately Placed Notes			
Class	Initial Note Principal Balance (US$)	Interest Rate (%)	Final Scheduled Distribution Date
E (subordinated)	22,330,000	4.01	8 January 2021

Interest on each class of notes will accrue during each interest period at the applicable interest rate.

The overcollateralization amount represents the amount by which the aggregate principal balance of the automobile loan contracts exceeds the principal balance of the notes. On the closing date, the initial amount of overcollateralization is approximately US$49,868,074 or 5.25% of the aggregate principal balance of the automobile loan contracts as of the cutoff date.

On the closing date, 2.0% of the expected initial aggregate principal balance of the automobile loan contracts will be deposited into the reserve account, which is approximately US$18,997,361.

1 The reference to sub-prime meant that:

A the asset-backed notes were rated below investment grade.

B the automobile (auto) loan contracts were made to borrowers who did not have or could not document strong credit.

C some of the auto loan contracts were secured by autos of low quality that may have been difficult to sell in case the borrower defaults.

2 Based on the information provided, if on the first distribution date there were losses on the loans of US$10 million:

A none of the classes of notes will have incurred losses.

B Class E notes will have incurred losses of US$10 million.

C Classes B, C, D, and E will have incurred losses pro rata of their initial note principal balances.

3 Based on the information provided, if the first loss on the loans was US$40 million over and above the protection provided by the internal credit enhancements and occurred in January 2014, which class(es) of notes realized losses?

A Class E and then Class D

B Each class of subordinated notes in proportion to its principal balance

C Class E and then each class of subordinated notes in proportion to its principal balance

Solution to 1:

B is correct. A subprime loan is one granted to borrowers with lower credit quality, who have typically experienced prior credit difficulties or who cannot otherwise document strong credit.

Solution to 2:

A is correct. The amount of the loss (US$10 million) was lower than the combined amount of overcollateralization and the reserve account (US$49,868,074 + US$18,997,361 = US$68,865,435). Therefore, none of the classes of notes will have incurred losses.

Solution to 3:

A is correct. Once the amount of losses exceeds the amount of protection provided by the overcollateralization and the reserve account, losses are absorbed by the bond classes. Because it was a sequential-pay structure, Class E notes were the first ones to absorb losses, up to the principal amount of US$22,330,000. It meant that there was still US$17,670,000 to be absorbed by another bond class, which would have been the Class D notes.

7.2 Credit Card Receivable ABS

When a purchase is made on a credit card, the issuer of the credit card (the lender) extends credit to the cardholder (the borrower). Credit cards are issued by banks, credit card companies, retailers, and travel and entertainment companies. At the time of purchase, the cardholder agrees to repay the amount borrowed (that is, the cost of the item purchased) plus any applicable finance charges. The amount that the cardholder agrees to pay the issuer of the credit card is a receivable from the perspective of the issuer of the credit card. Credit card receivables are used as collateral for the issuance of credit card receivable ABS.

For a pool of credit card receivables, the cash flows consist of finance charges collected, fees, and principal repayments. Finance charges collected represent the periodic interest the credit card borrower is charged on the unpaid balance after the grace period. The interest rate may be fixed or floating. The floating rate may be capped; that is, it may have an upper limit because some countries have usury rate laws that impose a cap on interest rates. Fees include late payment fees and any annual membership fees.

Interest is paid to holders of credit card receivable ABS periodically (e.g., monthly, quarterly, or semiannually). As noted earlier, the collateral of credit card receivable ABS is a pool of non-amortizing loans. These loans have lockout periods during which the cash flows that are paid out to security holders are based only on finance charges collected and fees. When the lockout period is over, the principal that is repaid by the cardholders is no longer reinvested but instead is distributed to investors.

Some provisions in credit card receivable ABS require early amortization of the principal if specific events occur. Such provisions are referred to as "early amortization" or "rapid amortization" provisions and are included to safeguard the credit quality of the issue. The only way the principal cash flows can be altered is by the triggering of the early amortization provision.

To illustrate the typical structure of credit card receivable ABS, consider the GE Capital Credit Card Master Note Trust Series 2013-1 issued in March 2013. The originator of the credit card receivables was GE Capital Retail Bank, now known as Synchrony Bank, and the servicer was GE Capital Corporation. The collateral was a pool of credit card receivables from several private-label and co-branded credit card issuers, including JCPenney, Lowe's Home Improvement, Sam's Club, Walmart, Gap, and Chevron. The structure of the US$969,085,000 securitization was as follows: Class A notes for US$800,000,000, Class B notes for US$100,946,373, and Class C notes for US$68,138,802. Thus, the issue had a senior/subordinate structure. The Class A notes were the senior notes and were rated Aaa by Moody's and AAA by Fitch. The Class B notes were rated A2 by Moody's and A+ by Fitch. The Class C notes were rated Baa2 by Moody's and BBB+ by Fitch.

EXAMPLE 10

Credit Card Receivable ABS vs. Auto Loan ABS

Credit card receivable asset-backed securities (ABS) differ from auto loan ABS in the following way:

A credit card loans are recourse loans, whereas auto loans are non-recourse loans.

B the collateral for credit card receivable-backed securities is a pool of non-amortizing loans, whereas the collateral for auto loan ABS is a pool of amortizing loans.

C credit card receivable-backed securities have regular principal repayments, whereas auto loan ABS include a lockout period during which the cash proceeds from principal repayments are reinvested in additional loan receivables.

Solution:

B is correct. A main difference between credit card receivable ABS and auto loan ABS is the type of loans that back the securities. For credit card receivable ABS, the collateral is a pool of non-amortizing loans. During the lockout period, the cash proceeds from principal repayments are reinvested in additional credit card receivables. When the lockout period is over, principal repayments are used to pay off the outstanding principal. For auto loan-backed securities, the collateral is a pool of amortizing loans. Security holders receive regular principal repayments. As a result, the outstanding principal balance declines over time.

8 COLLATERALIZED DEBT OBLIGATIONS

Collateralized debt obligation (CDO) is a generic term used to describe a security backed by a diversified pool of one or more debt obligations: CDOs backed by corporate and emerging market bonds are collateralized bond obligations (CBOs); CDOs backed by leveraged bank loans are collateralized loan obligations (CLOs); CDOs backed by ABS, RMBS, CMBS, and other CDOs are structured finance CDOs; CDOs backed by a portfolio of credit default swaps for other structured securities are synthetic CDOs.

8.1 CDO Structure

A CDO involves the creation of an SPE. In a CDO, there is a need for a CDO manager, also called "**collateral manager**," to buy and sell debt obligations for and from the CDO's collateral (that is, the portfolio of assets) to generate sufficient cash flows to meet the obligations to the CDO bondholders.

The funds to purchase the collateral assets for a CDO are obtained from the issuance of debt obligations. These debt obligations are bond classes or tranches and include senior bond classes, mezzanine bond classes (that is, bond classes with credit ratings between senior and subordinated bond classes), and subordinated bond classes, often referred to as the residual or equity tranches. The motivation for investors to invest in senior or mezzanine bond classes is to earn a potentially higher yield than that on a comparably rated corporate bond by gaining exposure to debt products that they may not otherwise be able to purchase. Investors in equity tranches have the potential to earn an equity-type return, thereby offsetting the increased risk from investing in the subordinated class. The key to whether or not a CDO is viable is whether a structure can be created that offers a competitive return for the subordinated tranche.

The basic economics of the CDO is that the funds are raised by the sale of the bond classes and the CDO manager invests those funds in assets. The CDO manager seeks to earn a rate of return higher than the aggregate cost of the bond classes. The return in excess of what is paid out to the bond classes accrues to the holders of the equity tranche and to the CDO manager. In other words, a CDO is a leveraged transaction in which those who invest in the equity tranche use borrowed funds (the bond classes issued) to generate a return above the funding cost.

As with ABS, each CDO bond class is structured to provide a specific level of risk for investors. The CDO is constructed so as to impose restrictions on the CDO manager via various tests and limits that must be satisfied for the CDO to meet investors' varying risk appetites while still providing adequate protection for the senior bond class. If the CDO manager fails pre-specified tests, a provision is triggered that requires the payoff of the principal to the senior bond class until the tests are satisfied. This process effectively deleverages the CDO because the cheapest funding source for the CDO, the senior bond class, is reduced.

The ability of the CDO manager to make the interest payments and principal repayments depends on the performance of the collateral. The proceeds to meet the obligations to the CDO bond classes can come from one or more of the following sources: interest payments from collateral assets, maturing of collateral assets, and sale of collateral assets. The cash flows and credit risks of a CDO are best illustrated by an example.

8.2 An Example of a CDO Transaction

Although various motivations may prompt a sponsor to create a CDO, the following example uses a CDO for which the purpose is to capture what market participants mistakenly label a CDO arbitrage transaction. The term "arbitrage" is not used here in the traditional sense—that is, a risk-free transaction that earns an expected positive net profit but requires no net investment of money. In this context, arbitrage is used in a loose sense to describe a transaction in which the motivation is to capture a spread between the return that could potentially be earned on the collateral and the funding cost.

To understand the structure of a CDO transaction and its risks, consider the following US$100 million issue:

Tranche	Par Value (US$ million)	Coupon Rate
Senior	80	Libor[a] + 70 bps
Mezzanine	10	10-year US Treasury rate + 200 bps
Equity	10	—

[a] Libor is the dollar London Interbank Offered Rate.

Suppose that the collateral consists of bonds that all mature in 10 years and that the coupon rate for every bond is the 10-year US Treasury rate plus 400 bps. Because the collateral pays a fixed rate (the 10-year US Treasury rate plus 400 bps) but the senior tranche requires a floating-rate payment (Libor plus 70 bps), the CDO manager enters into an interest rate swap agreement with another party. An interest rate swap is simply an agreement to periodically exchange interest payments. The payments are calculated based on a notional amount. This amount is not exchanged between the two parties but is simply used to determine the amount of interest payment for each party. By construction, the notional amount of the interest rate swap is the par value of the senior tranche—that is, US$80 million in this example. Let us suppose that through the interest rate swap, the CDO manager agrees to do the following: (1) pay a fixed rate each year equal to the 10-year US Treasury rate plus 100 bps and (2) receive Libor.

Assume that the 10-year US Treasury rate at the time this CDO is issued is 7%. Now, consider the annual cash flow for the first year. First, let us look at the collateral. Assuming no default, the collateral will pay an interest rate equal to the 10-year US Treasury rate of 7% plus 400 bps—that is, 11%. So, the interest payment is 11% × US$100,000,000 = US$11,000,000.

Now, let us determine the interest that must be paid to the senior and mezzanine tranches. For the senior tranche, the interest payment is US$80,000,000 × (Libor + 70 bps). For the mezzanine tranche, the coupon rate is the 10-year US Treasury rate plus 200 bps—that is, 9%. So, the interest payment for the mezzanine tranche is 9% × US$10,000,000 = US$900,000.

Finally, consider the interest rate swap. In this agreement, the CDO manager agreed to pay the swap counterparty the 10-year US Treasury rate plus 100 bps—that is, 8%—based on a notional amount of US$80 million. So, the amount paid to the swap counterparty is 8% × US$80,000,000 = US$6,400,000 the first year. The amount received from the swap counterparty is Libor based on a notional amount of US$80 million—that is, Libor × US$80,000,000.

All of this information can now be put together. The cash inflows for the CDO are

Interest from collateral	$11,000,000
Interest from swap counterparty	$80,000,000 × Libor
Total interest received	$11,000,000 + $80,000,000 × Libor

The cash outflows for the CDO are

Interest to senior tranche	$80,000,000	× (Libor + 70 bps)
Interest to mezzanine tranche	$900,000	
Interest to swap counterparty	$6,400,000	
Total interest paid	$7,300,000	+ $80,000,000 × (Libor + 70 bps)

Netting the total interest received ($11,000,000 + $80,000,000 × Libor) and the total interest paid ($7,300,000 + $80,000,000 × [Libor + 70 bps]) leaves a net interest of $3,700,000 – $80,000,000 × 70 bps = US$3,140,000. From this amount, any fees—including the CDO manager's fees—must be paid. The balance is then the amount available to pay the equity tranche. Suppose the CDO manager's fees are US$640,000. The cash flow available to the equity tranche for the first year is US$2.5 million ($3,140,000 – $640,000). Because the equity tranche has a par value of US$10 million and is assumed to be sold at par, the annual return is 25%.

Obviously, some simplifying assumptions have been made in this example. For instance, it is assumed that no defaults would occur. Furthermore, it is assumed that all of the securities purchased by the CDO manager are non-callable and, thus, that the coupon rate would not decline because of securities being called. Despite these simplifying assumptions, the example does demonstrate the economics of an arbitrage CDO transaction, the need for the use of an interest rate swap, and how the equity tranche will realize a return.

In practice, CDOs are subject to risks that investors should be aware of. For example, in the case of defaults in the collateral, there is a risk that the manager will fail to earn a return sufficient to pay off the investors in the senior and mezzanine tranches, resulting in a loss for these investors. Investors in the equity tranche risk the loss of their entire investment. Even if payments are made to these investors, the return they realize may not be the return expected at the time of purchase.

Moreover, after some period, the CDO manager must begin repaying principal to the senior and mezzanine tranches. The interest rate swap must be structured to take this requirement into account because the entire amount of the senior tranche is not outstanding for the life of the collateral.

EXAMPLE 11

Collateralized Debt Obligations

An additional risk of an investment in an arbitrage collateralized debt obligation relative to an investment in an asset-backed security is:

A the default risk on the collateral assets.

B the risk that the CDO manager fails to earn a return sufficient to pay off the investors in the senior and the mezzanine tranches.

C the risk due to the mismatch between the collateral making fixed-rate payments and the bond classes making floating-rate payments.

Solution:

B is correct. In addition to the risks associated with investments in ABS, such as the default risk on the collateral assets and the risk due to the potential mismatch between the collateral making fixed-rate payments and the bond classes making floating-rate payments, investors in CDOs face the risk that the CDO manager fails to earn a return sufficient to pay off the investors in the senior and the mezzanine tranches. With an ABS, the cash flows from the collateral are used to pay off the holders of the bond classes without the active management of the collateral—that is, without a manager altering the composition of the debt obligations in the pool that is backing the securitization. In contrast, in an arbitrage CDO, a CDO manager buys and sells debt obligations with the dual purpose of not only paying off the holders of the bond classes but also generating an attractive/competitive return for the equity tranche and for the manager.

SUMMARY

- Securitization involves pooling debt obligations, such as loans or receivables, and creating securities backed by the pool of debt obligations called asset-backed securities (ABS). The cash flows of the debt obligations are used to make interest payments and principal repayments to the holders of the ABS.

- Securitization has several benefits. It allows investors direct access to liquid investments and payment streams that would be unattainable if all the financing were performed through banks. It enables banks to increase loan originations at economic scales greater than if they used only their own in-house loan portfolios. Thus, securitization contributes to lower costs of borrowing for entities raising funds, higher risk-adjusted returns to investors, and greater efficiency and profitability for the banking sector.
- The parties to a securitization include the seller of the collateral (pool of loans), the servicer of the loans, and the special purpose entity (SPE). The SPE is bankruptcy remote, which plays a pivotal role in the securitization.
- A common structure in a securitization is subordination, which leads to the creation of more than one bond class or tranche. Bond classes differ as to how they will share any losses resulting from defaults of the borrowers whose loans are in the collateral. The credit ratings assigned to the various bond classes depend on how the credit-rating agencies evaluate the credit risks of the collateral and any credit enhancements.
- The motivation for the creation of different types of structures is to redistribute prepayment risk and credit risk efficiently among different bond classes in the securitization. Prepayment risk is the uncertainty that the actual cash flows will be different from the scheduled cash flows as set forth in the loan agreements because borrowers may choose to repay the principal early to take advantage of interest rate movements.
- Because of the SPE, the securitization of a company's assets may include some bond classes that have better credit ratings than the company itself or its corporate bonds. Thus, the company's funding cost is often lower when raising funds through securitization than when issuing corporate bonds.
- A mortgage is a loan secured by the collateral of some specified real estate property that obliges the borrower to make a predetermined series of payments to the lender. The cash flow of a mortgage includes (1) interest, (2) scheduled principal payments, and (3) prepayments (any principal repaid in excess of the scheduled principal payment).
- The various mortgage designs throughout the world specify (1) the maturity of the loan; (2) how the interest rate is determined (i.e., fixed rate versus adjustable or variable rate); (3) how the principal is repaid (i.e., whether the loan is amortizing and if it is, whether it is fully amortizing or partially amortizing with a balloon payment); (4) whether the borrower has the option to prepay and if so, whether any prepayment penalties might be imposed; and (5) the rights of the lender in a foreclosure (i.e., whether the loan is a recourse or non-recourse loan).
- In the United States, there are three sectors for securities backed by residential mortgages: (1) those guaranteed by a federal agency (Ginnie Mae) whose securities are backed by the full faith and credit of the US government, (2) those guaranteed by a GSE (e.g., Fannie Mae and Freddie Mac) but not by the US government, and (3) those issued by private entities that are not guaranteed by a federal agency or a GSE. The first two sectors are referred to as agency residential mortgage-backed securities (RMBS), and the third sector as non-agency RMBS.
- A mortgage pass-through security is created when one or more holders of mortgages form a pool of mortgages and sell shares or participation certificates in the pool. The cash flow of a mortgage pass-through security depends on the

cash flow of the underlying pool of mortgages and consists of monthly mortgage payments representing interest, the scheduled repayment of principal, and any prepayments, net of servicing and other administrative fees.

- Market participants measure the prepayment rate using two measures: the single monthly mortality rate (SMM) and its corresponding annualized rate—namely, the conditional prepayment rate (CPR). For MBS, a measure widely used by market participants to assess is the weighted average life or simply the average life of the MBS.
- Market participants use the Public Securities Association (PSA) prepayment benchmark to describe prepayment rates. A PSA assumption greater than 100 PSA means that prepayments are assumed to occur faster than the benchmark, whereas a PSA assumption lower than 100 PSA means that prepayments are assumed to occur slower than the benchmark.
- Prepayment risk includes two components: contraction risk and extension risk. The former is the risk that when interest rates decline, the security will have a shorter maturity than was anticipated at the time of purchase because homeowners will refinance at the new, lower interest rates. The latter is the risk that when interest rates rise, fewer prepayments will occur than what was anticipated at the time of purchase because homeowners are reluctant to give up the benefits of a contractual interest rate that now looks low.
- The creation of a collateralized mortgage obligation (CMO) can help manage prepayment risk by distributing the various forms of prepayment risk among different classes of bondholders. The CMO's major financial innovation is that the securities created more closely satisfy the asset/liability needs of institutional investors, thereby broadening the appeal of mortgage-backed products.
- The most common types of CMO tranches are sequential-pay tranches, planned amortization class (PAC) tranches, support tranches, and floating-rate tranches.
- Non-agency RMBS share many features and structuring techniques with agency CMOs. However, they typically include two complementary mechanisms. First, the cash flows are distributed by rules that dictate the allocation of interest payments and principal repayments to tranches with various degrees of priority/seniority. Second, there are rules for the allocation of realized losses, which specify that subordinated bond classes have lower payment priority than senior classes.
- In order to obtain favorable credit ratings, non-agency RMBS and non-mortgage ABS often require one or more credit enhancements. The most common forms of internal credit enhancement are senior/subordinated structures, reserve funds, and overcollateralization. In external credit enhancement, credit support in the case of defaults resulting in losses in the pool of loans is provided in the form of a financial guarantee by a third party to the transaction.
- Commercial mortgage-backed securities (CMBS) are securities backed by a pool of commercial mortgages on income-producing property.
- Two key indicators of the potential credit performance of CMBS are the debt-service-coverage (DSC) ratio and the loan-to-value ratio (LTV). The DSC ratio is the property's annual net operating income divided by the debt service.
- CMBS have considerable call protection, which allows CMBS to trade in the market more like corporate bonds than like RMBS. This call protection comes in two forms: at the structure level and at the loan level. The creation of sequential-pay tranches is an example of call protection at the structure level. At the loan level, four mechanisms offer investors call protection: prepayment lockouts, prepayment penalty points, yield maintenance charges, and defeasance.

- ABS are backed by a wide range of asset types. The most popular non-mortgage ABS are auto loan ABS and credit card receivable ABS. The collateral is amortizing for auto loan ABS and non-amortizing for credit card receivable ABS. As with non-agency RMBS, these ABS must offer credit enhancement to be appealing to investors.
- A collateralized debt obligation (CDO) is a generic term used to describe a security backed by a diversified pool of one or more debt obligations (e.g., corporate and emerging market bonds, leveraged bank loans, ABS, RMBS, and CMBS).
- A CDO involves the creation of an SPE. The funds necessary to pay the bond classes come from a pool of loans that must be serviced. A CDO requires a collateral manager to buy and sell debt obligations for and from the CDO's portfolio of assets to generate sufficient cash flows to meet the obligations of the CDO bondholders and to generate a fair return for the equity holders.
- The structure of a CDO includes senior, mezzanine, and subordinated/equity bond classes.

PRACTICE PROBLEMS

1 Securitization is beneficial for banks because it:

A repackages bank loans into simpler structures.

B increases the funds available for banks to lend.

C allows banks to maintain ownership of their securitized assets.

2 Securitization benefits financial markets by:

A increasing the role of intermediaries.

B establishing a barrier between investors and originating borrowers.

C allowing investors to tailor credit risk and interest rate risk exposures to meet their individual needs.

3 A benefit of securitization is the:

A reduction in disintermediation.

B simplification of debt obligations.

C creation of tradable securities with greater liquidity than the original loans.

4 Securitization benefits investors by:

A providing more direct access to a wider range of assets.

B reducing the inherent credit risk of pools of loans and receivables.

C eliminating cash flow timing risks of an ABS, such as contraction and extension risks.

5 In a securitization, the special purpose entity (SPE) is responsible for the:

A issuance of the asset-backed securities.

B collection of payments from the borrowers.

C recovery of underlying assets from delinquent borrowers.

6 In a securitization, the collateral is initially sold by the:

A issuer.

B depositor.

C underwriter.

7 A special purpose entity issues asset-backed securities in the following structure.

Bond Class	Par Value (€ millions)
A (senior)	200
B (subordinated)	20
C (subordinated)	5

At which of the following amounts of default in par value would Bond Class A experience a loss?

A €20 million

B €25 million

C €26 million

8 In a securitization, time tranching provides investors with the ability to choose between:

A extension and contraction risks.

B senior and subordinated bond classes.

C fully amortizing and partially amortizing loans.

9 The creation of bond classes with a waterfall structure for sharing losses is referred to as:

A time tranching.

B credit tranching.

C overcollateralization.

10 Which of the following statements related to securitization is correct?

A Time tranching addresses the uncertainty of a decline in interest rates.

B Securitizations are rarely structured to include both credit tranching and time tranching.

C Junior and senior bond classes differ in that junior classes can only be paid off at the bond's set maturity.

11 A goal of securitization is to:

A separate the seller's collateral from its credit ratings.

B uphold the absolute priority rule in bankruptcy reorganizations.

C account for collateral's primary influence on corporate bond credit spreads.

12 The last payment in a partially amortizing residential mortgage loan is *best* referred to as a:

A waterfall.

B principal repayment.

C balloon payment.

13 If a mortgage borrower makes prepayments without penalty to take advantage of falling interest rates, the lender will *most likely* experience:

A extension risk.

B contraction risk.

C yield maintenance.

14 Which of the following characteristics of a residential mortgage loan would *best* protect the lender from a strategic default by the borrower?

A Recourse

B A prepayment option

C Interest-only payments

15 William Marolf obtains a 5 million EUR mortgage loan from Bank Nederlandse. A year later the principal on the loan is 4 million EUR and Marolf defaults on the loan. Bank Nederlandse forecloses, sells the property for 2.5 million EUR, and is entitled to collect the 1.5 million EUR shortfall, from Marolf. Marolf *most likely* had a:

A bullet loan.

B recourse loan.

C non-recourse loan.

16 Fran Martin obtains a non-recourse mortgage loan for $500,000. One year later, when the outstanding balance of the mortgage is $490,000, Martin cannot make his mortgage payments and defaults on the loan. The lender forecloses on the loan and sells the house for $315,000. What amount is the lender entitled to claim from Martin?

A $0.

B $175,000.

C $185,000.

17 A ballloon payment equal to a mortgage's original loan amount is a characteristic of a:

A bullet mortgage.

B fully amortizing mortgage.

C partially amortizing mortgage.

18 Which of the following statements is correct concerning mortgage loan defaults?

A A non-recourse jurisdiction poses higher default risks for lenders.

B In a non-recourse jurisdiction, strategic default will not affect the defaulting borrower's future access to credit.

C When a recourse loan defaults, the mortgaged property is the lender's sole source for recovery of the outstanding mortgage balance.

19 Which of the following describes a typical feature of a non-agency residential mortgage-backed security (RMBS)?

A Senior/subordinated structure

B A pool of conforming mortgages as collateral

C A guarantee by a government-sponsored enterprise

20 If interest rates increase, an investor who owns a mortgage pass-through security is *most likely* affected by:

A credit risk.

B extension risk.

C contraction risk.

21 Which of the following is *most likely* an advantage of collateralized mortgage obligations (CMOs)? CMOs can

A eliminate prepayment risk.

B be created directly from a pool of mortgage loans.

C meet the asset/liability requirements of institutional investors.

22 The longest-term tranche of a sequential-pay CMO is *most likely* to have the lowest:

A average life.

B extension risk.

C contraction risk.

23 The tranches in a collateralized mortgage obligation (CMO) that are *most likely* to provide protection for investors against both extension and contraction risk are:

A planned amortization class (PAC) tranches.

B support tranches.

C sequential-pay tranches.

24 Support tranches are *most* appropriate for investors who are:

A concerned about their exposure to extension risk.

B concerned about their exposure to concentration risk.

C willing to accept prepayment risk in exchange for higher returns.

25 In the context of mortgage-backed securities, a conditional prepayment rate (CPR) of 8% means that approximately 8% of the outstanding mortgage pool balance at the beginning of the year is expected to be prepaid:

A in the current month.

B by the end of the year.

C over the life of the mortgages.

26 For a mortgage pass-through security, which of the following risks *most likely* increases as interest rates decline?

A Balloon

B Extension

C Contraction

27 Compared with the weighted average coupon rate of its underlying pool of mortgages, the pass-through rate on a mortgage pass-through security is:

A lower.

B the same.

C higher.

28 The single monthly mortality rate (SMM) *most likely:*

A increases as extension risk rises.

B decreases as contraction risk falls.

C stays fixed over time when the standard prepayment model remains at 100 PSA.

29 Credit risk is an important consideration for commercial mortgage-backed securities (CMBS) if the CMBS are backed by mortgage loans that:

A are non-recourse.

B have call protection.

C haveprepayment penalty points.

30 Which commercial mortgage-backed security (CMBS) characteristic causes a CMBS to trade more like a corporate bond than a residential mortgage-backed security (RMBS)?

A Call protection

B Internal credit enhancement

C Debt-service coverage ratio level

31 A commercial mortgage-backed security (CMBS) does not meet the debt-to-service coverage at the loan level necessary to achieve a desired credit rating. Which of the following features would *most likely* improve the credit rating of the CMBS?

A Subordination

B Call protection

C Balloon payments

32 If a default occurs in a non-recourse commercial mortgage-backed security (CMBS), the lender will *most likely*:

A recover prepayment penalty points paid by the borrower to offset losses.

B use only the proceeds received from the sale of the property to recover losses.

C initiate a claim against the borrower for any shortfall resulting from the sale of the property.

33 Which of the following investments is least subject to prepayment risk?

A Auto loan receivable–backed securities

B Commercial mortgage-backed securities (CMBSs)

C Non-agency residential mortgage-backed securities (RMBSs)

34 An excess spread account incorporated into a securitization is designed to limit:

A credit risk.

B extension risk.

C contraction risk.

35 Which of the following *best* describes the cash flow that owners of credit card receivable asset-backed securities receive during the lockout period?

A No cash flow

B Only principal payments collected

C Only finance charges collected and fees

36 Which type of asset-backed security is not affected by prepayment risk?

A Auto loan ABSs

B Residential MBSs

C Credit card receivable ABSs

37 In auto loan ABSs, the form of credit enhancement that *most likely* serves as the first line of loss protection is the:

A excess spread account.

B sequential pay structure.

C proceeds from repossession sales.

38 In credit card receivable ABSs, principal cash flows can be altered only when the:

A lockout period expires.

B excess spread account is depleted.

C early amortization provision is triggered.

39 The CDO tranche with a credit rating status between senior and subordinated bond classes is called the:

A equity tranche.

B residual tranche.

C mezzanine tranche.

40 The key to a CDO's viability is the creation of a structure with a competitive return for the:

A senior tranche.

B mezzanine tranche.

C subordinated tranche.

41 When the collateral manager fails pre-specified risk tests, a CDO is:

A deleveraged by reducing the senior bond class.

B restructured to reduce its most expensive funding source.

C liquidated by paying off the bond classes in order of seniority.

42 Collateralized mortgage obligations (CMOs) are designed to:

A eliminate contraction risk in support tranches.

B distribute prepayment risk to various tranches.

C eliminate extension risk in planned amortization tranches.

SOLUTIONS

1 B is correct. Securitization increases the funds available for banks to lend because it allows banks to remove loans from their balance sheets and issue bonds that are backed by those loans. Securitization repackages relatively simple debt obligations, such as bank loans, into more complex, not simpler, structures. Securitization involves transferring ownership of assets from the original owner—in this case, the banks—into a special legal entity. As a result, banks do not maintain ownership of the securitized assets.

2 C is correct. By removing the wall between ultimate investors and originating borrowers, investors can achieve better legal claims on the underlying mortgages and portfolios of receivables. This transparency allows investors to tailor interest rate risk and credit risk to their specific needs.

3 C is correct. Securitization allows for the creation of tradable securities with greater liquidity than the original loans on a bank's balance sheet. Securitization results in lessening the roles of intermediaries, which increases disintermediation. Securitization is a process in which relatively simple debt obligations, such as loans, are repackaged into more complex structures.

4 A is correct. Securitization allows investors to achieve more direct legal claims on loans and portfolios of receivables. As a result, investors can add to their portfolios exposure to the risk–return characteristics provided by a wider range of assets.

B is incorrect because securitization does not reduce credit risk but, rather, provides a structure to mitigate and redistribute the inherent credit risks of pools of loans and receivables.

C is incorrect because securitization does not eliminate the timing risks associated with ABS cash flows but, rather, provides a structure to mitigate and redistribute those risks, such as contraction risk and extension risk.

5 A is correct. In a securitization, the special purpose entity (SPE) is the special legal entity responsible for the issuance of the asset-backed securities. The servicer, not the SPE, is responsible for both the collection of payments from the borrowers and the recovery of underlying assets if the borrowers default on their loans.

6 B is correct. In a securitization, the loans or receivables are initially sold by the depositor to the special purpose entity (SPE) that uses them as collateral to issue the ABS.

A is incorrect because the SPE, often referred to as the issuer, is the purchaser of the collateral rather than the seller of the collateral.

C is incorrect because the underwriter neither sells nor purchases the collateral in a securitization. The underwriter performs the same functions in a securitization as it does in a standard bond offering.

7 C is correct. The first €25 (€5 + €20) million in default are absorbed by the subordinated classes (C and B). The senior Class A bonds will only experience a loss when defaults exceed €25 million.

8 A is correct. Time tranching is the process in which a set of bond classes or tranches is created that allow investors a choice in the type of prepayment risk, extension or contraction, that they prefer to bear. Senior and subordinated bond classes are used in credit tranching. Credit tranching structures allow investors to choose the amount of credit risk that they prefer to bear. Fully and partially amortizing loans are two types of amortizing loans.

9 B is correct. Credit tranching is a form of credit enhancement called subordination in which bond classes or tranches differ as to how they will share losses resulting from defaults of the borrowers whose loans are part of the collateral. This type of protection is commonly referred to as a waterfall structure because of the cascading flow of payments between bond classes in the event of default.

A is incorrect because time tranching involves the creation of bond classes that possess different expected maturities rather than bond classes that differ as to how credit losses will be shared. Time tranching involves the redistribution of prepayment risk, whereas credit tranching involves the redistribution of credit risk.

C is incorrect because although overcollateralization is a form of internal credit enhancement similar to subordination, it is the amount by which the principal amount of the pool of collateral exceeds the principal balance of the securities issued and backed by the collateral pool. Losses are absorbed first by the amount of overcollateralization and then according to the credit tranching structure.

10 A is correct. Time tranching is the creation of bond classes that possess different expected maturities so that prepayment risk can be redistributed among bond classes. When loan agreements provide borrowers the ability to alter payments, in the case of declining interest rates, this prepayment risk increases because borrowers tend to pay off part or all of their loans and refinance at lower interest rates.

B is incorrect because it is possible, and quite common, for a securitization to have structures with both credit tranching and time tranching.

C is incorrect because the subordinated structures of junior and senior bond classes differ as to how they will share any losses relative to defaults of the borrowers whose loans are in the collateral pool. Junior classes offer protection for senior classes, with losses first realized by the former. The classes are not distinguished by scheduled repayment terms but, rather, by a loss sharing hierarchy in the event of borrower default.

11 A is correct. The legal implication of a special purpose entity (SPE), a prerequisite for securitization, is that investors contemplating the purchase of bond classes backed by the assets of the SPE will evaluate the credit risk of those assets independently from the credit rating of the entity that sold the assets to the SPE. This separation of the seller's collateral from its credit rating provides the opportunity for the SPE to access a lower aggregate funding cost than what the seller might otherwise obtain.

B is incorrect because the absolute priority rule, under which senior creditors are paid in full before subordinated creditors, has not always been upheld in bankruptcy reorganizations. There is no assurance that if a corporate bond has collateral, the rights of the bondholders will be respected. It is this uncertainty that creates the dominant influence of credit ratings over collateral in credit spreads.

C is incorrect because corporate bond credit spreads will reflect the seller's credit rating primarily and the collateral slightly. Securitization separates the seller's collateral from its credit rating, effectively altering the influence of collateral on the credit spread.

12 C is correct. In a partially amortizing loan, the sum of all the scheduled principal repayments is less than the amount borrowed. The last payment is for the remaining unpaid mortgage balance and is called the "balloon payment."

13 B is correct. Contraction risk is the risk that when interest rates decline, actual prepayments will be higher than forecasted. Extension risk is the risk that when interest rates rise, prepayments will be lower than forecasted. Yield maintenance results from prepayment penalties; the lender is protected from loss in yield by the imposition of prepayment penalties.

14 A is correct. In a recourse loan, the lender has a claim against the borrower for the shortfall between the amount of the mortgage balance outstanding and the proceeds received from the sale of the property. A prepayment option is a benefit to the borrower and would thus not offer protection to the lender. An interest-only mortgage requires no principal repayment for a number of years and will not protect the lender from strategic default by the borrower.

15 B is correct. Bank Nederlandse has a claim against Marolf for 1.5 million EUR, the shortfall between the amount of the mortgage balance outstanding and the proceeds received from the sale of the property. This indicates that the mortgage loan is a recourse loan. The recourse/non-recourse feature indicates the rights of a lender in foreclosure. If Marolf had a non-recourse loan, the bank would have only been entitled to the proceeds from the sale of the underlying property, or 2.5 million EUR. A bullet loan is a special type of interest-only mortgage for which there are no scheduled principal payments over the entire term of the loan. Since the unpaid balance is less than the original mortgage loan, it is unlikely that Marolf has an interest only mortgage.

16 A is correct. Because the loan has a non-recourse feature, the lender can only look to the underlying property to recover the outstanding mortgage balance and has no further claim against the borrower. The lender is simply entitled to foreclose on the home and sell it.

17 A is correct. A bullet mortgage is a special type of interest-only mortgage in which there are no scheduled principal repayments over the entire life of the loan. At maturity, a balloon payment is required equal to the original loan amount.

B is incorrect because with a fully amortizing mortgage, the sum of all the scheduled principal repayments during the mortgage's life is such that when the last mortgage payment is made, the loan is fully repaid, with no balloon payment required.

C is incorrect because with a partially amortizing mortgage, the sum of all the scheduled principal repayments is less than the amount borrowed, resulting in a balloon payment equal to the unpaid mortgage balance (rather than the original loan amount).

18 A is correct. In non-recourse loan jurisdictions, the borrower may have an incentive to default on an underwater mortgage and allow the lender to foreclose on the property because the lender has no claim against the borrower for the shortfall. For this reason, such defaults, known as strategic defaults, are more likely in non-recourse jurisdictions and less likely in recourse jurisdictions, where the lender does have a claim against the borrower for the shortfall.

B is incorrect because strategic defaults in non-recourse jurisdictions do have negative consequences for the defaulting borrowers in the form of a lower credit score and a reduced ability to borrow in the future. These negative consequences can be a deterrent in the incidence of underwater mortgage defaults.

C is incorrect because when a recourse loan defaults, the lender can look to both the property and the borrower to recover the outstanding mortgage balance. In a recourse loan, the lender has a claim against the borrower for the shortfall between the amount of the outstanding mortgage balance and the proceeds received from the sale of the property.

19 A is correct. Non-agency RMBS are credit enhanced, either internally or externally, to make the securities more attractive to investors. The most common forms of internal credit enhancements are senior/subordinated structures, reserve accounts, and overcollateralization. Conforming mortgages are used as collateral for agency (not non-agency) mortgage pass-through securities. An agency RMBS, rather than a non-agency RMBS, issued by a GSE (government sponsored enterprise), is guaranteed by the respective GSE.

20 B is correct. Extension risk is the risk that when interest rate rise, fewer prepayments will occur. Homeowners will be reluctant to give up the benefit of a contractual interest rate that is lower. As a result, the mortgage pass-through security becomes longer in maturity than anticipated at the time of purchase.

21 C is correct. Using CMOs, securities can be created to closely satisfy the asset/liability needs of institutional investors. The creation of a CMO cannot eliminate prepayment risk; it can only distribute the various forms of this risk among various classes of bondholders. The collateral of CMOs are mortgage-related products, not the mortgages themselves.

22 C is correct. For a CMO with multiple sequential-pay tranches, the longest-term tranche will have the lowest contraction (prepayments greater than forecasted) risk because of the protection against this risk offered by the other tranches. The longest-term tranche is likely to have the highest average life and extension risk because it is the last tranche repaid in a sequential-pay tranche.

23 A is correct. PAC tranches have limited (but not complete) protection against both extension risk and contraction risk. This protection is provided by the support tranches. A sequential-pay tranche can protect against either extension risk or contraction risk but not both of these risks. The CMO structure with sequential-pay tranches allows investors concerned about extension risk to invest in shorter-term tranches and those concerned about contraction risk to invest in the longer-term tranches.

24 C is correct. The greater predictability of cash flows provided in the planned amortization class (PAC) tranches comes at the expense of support tranches. As a result, investors in support tranches are exposed to higher extension risk and contraction risk than investors in PAC tranches. Investors will be compensated for bearing this risk because support tranches have a higher expected return than PAC tranches.

25 B is correct. CPR is an annualized rate, which indicates the percentage of the outstanding mortgage pool balance at the beginning of the year that is expected to be prepaid by the end of the year.

26 C is correct. When interest rates decline, a mortgage pass-through security is subject to contraction risk. Contraction risk is the risk that when interest rates decline, actual prepayments will be higher than forecasted because borrowers will refinance at now-available lower interest rates. Thus, a security backed by mortgages will have a shorter maturity than was anticipated when the security was purchased.

27 A is correct. The coupon rate of a mortgage pass-through security is called the pass-through rate, whereas the mortgage rate on the underlying pool of mortgages is calculated as a weighted average coupon rate (WAC). The pass-through rate is lower than the WAC by an amount equal to the servicing fee and other administrative fees.

28 B is correct. The SMM is a monthly measure of the prepayment rate or prepayment speed. Contraction risk is the risk that when interest rates decline, actual prepayments will be higher than forecast. So if contraction risk falls, prepayments are likely to be lower than forecast, which would imply a decrease in the SMM.

A is incorrect because the SMM is a monthly measure of the prepayment rate or prepayment speed. Extension risk is the risk that when interest rates rise, actual prepayments will be lower than forecast. So if extension risk rises, prepayments are likely to be lower than forecast, which would imply a decrease, not an increase, in the SMM.

C is incorrect because at 100 PSA, investors can expect prepayments to follow the PSA prepayment benchmark. Based on historical patterns, the PSA standard model assumes that prepayment rates are low for newly initiated mortgages and then speed up as mortgages season. Thus, 100 PSA does not imply that the SMM remains the same but, rather, implies that it will vary over the life of the mortgage.

29 A is correct. If commercial mortgage loans are non-recourse loans, the lender can only look to the income-producing property backing the loan for interest and principal repayment. If there is a default, the lender looks to the proceeds from the sale of the property for repayment and has no recourse against the borrower for any unpaid mortgage loan balance. Call protection and prepayment penalty points protect against prepayment risk.

30 A is correct. With CMBS, investors have considerable call protection. An investor in a RMBS is exposed to considerable prepayment risk, but with CMBS, call protection is available to the investor at the structure and loan level. The call protection results in CMBS trading in the market more like a corporate bond than a RMBS. Both internal credit enhancement and the debt-service-coverage (DSC) ratio address credit risk, not prepayment risk.

31 A is correct. If specific ratios of debt to service coverage are needed, and those ratios cannot be met at the loan level, subordination is used to achieve the desired credit rating. Call protection protects investors against prepayment risk. Balloon payments increase the risk of the underlying loans.

32 B is correct. In a non-recourse CMBS, the lender can look only to the income-producing property backing the loan for interest and principal repayment. If a default occurs, the lender can use only the proceeds from the sale of the property for repayment and has no recourse to the borrower for any unpaid balance.

33 B is correct. A critical feature that differentiates CMBSs from RMBSs is the call protection provided to investors. An investor in a RMBS is exposed to considerable prepayment risk because the borrower has the right to prepay the loan before maturity. CMBSs provide investors with considerable call protection that comes either at the structure level or at the loan level.

34 A is correct. An excess spread account, sometimes called excess interest cash flow, is a form of internal credit enhancement that limits credit risk. It is an amount that can be retained and deposited into a reserve account and that can serve as a first line of protection against losses. An excess spread account does not limit prepayment risk, extension, or contraction.

35 C is correct. During the lockout period, the cash flow that is paid out to owners of credit card receivable asset-backed securities is based only on finance charges collected and fees.

36 C is correct. Because credit card receivable ABSs are backed by non-amortizing loans that do not involve scheduled principal repayments, they are not affected by prepayment risk.

A is incorrect because auto loan ABSs are affected by prepayment risk since they are backed by amortizing loans involving scheduled principal repayments.

B is incorrect because residential MBSs are affected by prepayment risk since they are backed by amortizing loans involving scheduled principal repayments.

37 A is correct. In addition to a senior/subordinated (sequential pay) structure, many auto loan ABSs are structured with additional credit enhancement in the form of overcollateralization and a reserve account, often an excess spread account. The excess spread is an amount that can be retained and deposited into a reserve account that can serve as a first line of protection against losses.

B is incorrect because in an auto loan ABS, losses are typically applied against the excess spread account and the amount of overcollateralization before the waterfall loss absorption of the sequential pay structure.

C is incorrect because in auto loan ABSs, proceeds from the repossession and resale of autos are prepayment cash flows rather than a form of credit enhancement for loss protection.

38 C is correct. In credit card receivable ABSs, the only way the principal cash flows can be altered is by triggering the early amortization provision. Such provisions are included in the ABS structure to safeguard the credit quality of the issue.

A is incorrect because expiration of the lockout period does not result in the alteration of principal cash flows but instead defines when principal repayments are distributed to the ABS investors. During the lockout period, principal repayments by cardholders are reinvested. When the lockout period expires, principal repayments by cardholders are distributed to investors.

B is incorrect because the excess spread account is a credit enhancement for loss absorption. When the excess spread account is depleted, losses are applied against the overcollateralization amount followed by the senior/subordinated structure. The only way principal cash flows can be altered is by triggering the early amortization provision.

39 C is correct. The mezzanine tranche consists of bond classes with credit ratings between senior and subordinated bond classes.

A is incorrect because the equity tranche falls within and carries the credit rating applicable to the subordinated bond classes.

B is incorrect because the residual tranche falls within and carries the credit ratings applicable to the subordinated bond classes.

40 C is correct. The key to whether a CDO is viable is whether a structure can be created that offers a competitive return for the subordinated tranche (often referred to as the residual or equity tranche). Investors in a subordinated tranche typically use borrowed funds (the bond classes issued) to generate a return above the funding cost.

A is incorrect because the viability of a CDO depends on a structure that offers a competitive return for the subordinated tranche rather than the senior tranche.

B is incorrect because the viability of a CDO depends on a structure that offers a competitive return for the subordinated tranche rather than the mezzanine tranche.

41 A is correct. When the collateral manager fails pre-specified tests, a provision is triggered that requires the payoff of the principal to the senior class until the tests are satisfied. This reduction of the senior class effectively deleverages the CDO because the CDO's cheapest funding source is reduced.

42 B is correct. CMOs are designed to redistribute cash flows of mortgage-related products to different bond classes or tranches through securitization. Although CMOs do not eliminate prepayment risk, they distribute prepayment risk among various classes of bondholders.

FIXED INCOME

STUDY SESSION 15

Fixed Income (2)

This study session examines the fundamental elements underlying bond returns and risks with a specific focus on interest rate and credit risk. Duration, convexity, and other key measures for assessing a bond's sensitivity to interest rate risk are introduced. An explanation of credit risk and the use of credit analysis for risky bonds concludes the session.

READING ASSIGNMENTS

Reading 46	Understanding Fixed-Income Risk and Return by James F. Adams, PhD, CFA, and Donald J. Smith, PhD
Reading 47	Fundamentals of Credit Analysis by Christopher L. Gootkind, CFA

READING

46

Understanding Fixed-Income Risk and Return

by James F. Adams, PhD, CFA, and Donald J. Smith, PhD

James F. Adams, PhD, CFA, is at J.P. Morgan (USA). Donald J. Smith, PhD, is at Boston University Questrom School of Business (USA).

LEARNING OUTCOMES

Mastery	*The candidate should be able to:*
☐	a. calculate and interpret the sources of return from investing in a fixed-rate bond;
☐	b. define, calculate, and interpret Macaulay, modified, and effective durations;
☐	c. explain why effective duration is the most appropriate measure of interest rate risk for bonds with embedded options;
☐	d. define key rate duration and describe the use of key rate durations in measuring the sensitivity of bonds to changes in the shape of the benchmark yield curve;
☐	e. explain how a bond's maturity, coupon, and yield level affect its interest rate risk;
☐	f. calculate the duration of a portfolio and explain the limitations of portfolio duration;
☐	g. calculate and interpret the money duration of a bond and price value of a basis point (PVBP);
☐	h. calculate and interpret approximate convexity and distinguish between approximate and effective convexity;
☐	i. estimate the percentage price change of a bond for a specified change in yield, given the bond's approximate duration and convexity;
☐	j. describe how the term structure of yield volatility affects the interest rate risk of a bond;
☐	k. describe the relationships among a bond's holding period return, its duration, and the investment horizon;
☐	l. explain how changes in credit spread and liquidity affect yield-to-maturity of a bond and how duration and convexity can be used to estimate the price effect of the changes.

1 INTRODUCTION

It is important for analysts to have a well-developed understanding of the risk and return characteristics of fixed-income investments. Beyond the vast worldwide market for publicly and privately issued fixed-rate bonds, many financial assets and liabilities with known future cash flows may be evaluated using the same principles. The starting point for this analysis is the yield-to-maturity, or internal rate of return on future cash flows, which was introduced in the fixed-income valuation reading. The return on a fixed-rate bond is affected by many factors, the most important of which is the receipt of the interest and principal payments in the full amount and on the scheduled dates. Assuming no default, the return is also affected by changes in interest rates that affect coupon reinvestment and the price of the bond if it is sold before it matures. Measures of the price change can be derived from the mathematical relationship used to calculate the price of the bond. The first of these measures (duration) estimates the change in the price for a given change in interest rates. The second measure (convexity) improves on the duration estimate by taking into account the fact that the relationship between price and yield-to-maturity of a fixed-rate bond is not linear.

Section 2 uses numerical examples to demonstrate the sources of return on an investment in a fixed-rate bond, which includes the receipt and reinvestment of coupon interest payments and the redemption of principal if the bond is held to maturity. The other source of return is capital gains (and losses) on the sale of the bond prior to maturity. Section 2 also shows that fixed-income investors holding the same bond can have different exposures to interest rate risk if their investment horizons differ. Discussion of credit risk, although critical to investors, is postponed to Section 5 so that attention can be focused on interest rate risk.

Section 3 provides a thorough review of bond duration and convexity, and shows how the statistics are calculated and used as measures of interest rate risk. Although procedures and formulas exist to calculate duration and convexity, these statistics can be approximated using basic bond-pricing techniques and a financial calculator. Commonly used versions of the statistics are covered, including Macaulay, modified, effective, and key rate durations. The distinction is made between risk measures that are based on changes in the bond's yield-to-maturity (i.e., *yield* duration and convexity) and on benchmark yield curve changes (i.e., *curve* duration and convexity).

Section 4 returns to the issue of the investment horizon. When an investor has a short-term horizon, duration (and convexity) are used to estimate the change in the bond price. In this case, yield volatility matters. In particular, bonds with varying times-to-maturity have different degrees of yield volatility. When an investor has a long-term horizon, the interaction between coupon reinvestment risk and market price risk matters. The relationship among interest rate risk, bond duration, and the investment horizon is explored.

Section 5 discusses how the tools of duration and convexity can be extended to credit and liquidity risks and highlights how these different factors can affect a bond's return and risk.

A summary of key points and practice problems in the CFA Institute multiple-choice format conclude the reading.

2 SOURCES OF RETURN

An investor in a fixed-rate bond has three sources of return: (1) receipt of the promised coupon and principal payments on the scheduled dates, (2) reinvestment of coupon payments, and (3) potential capital gains or losses on the sale of the bond prior to maturity. In this section, it is assumed that the issuer makes the coupon and principal payments as scheduled. This reading focuses primarily on interest rate risk (the risk that interest rates will change), which affects the reinvestment of coupon payments and the market price if the bond is sold prior to maturity. Credit risk is considered later in this reading and is the primary subject of the reading "Fundamentals of Credit Analysis."

When a bond is purchased at a premium or a discount, it adds another aspect to the rate of return. Recall from the reading on fixed-income valuation that a discount bond offers the investor a "deficient" coupon rate, or one below the market discount rate. The amortization of the discount in each period brings the return in line with the market discount rate as the bond's carrying value is "pulled to par." For a premium bond, the coupon rate exceeds the market discount rate and the amortization of the premium adjusts the return to match the market discount rate. Through amortization, the bond's carrying value reaches par value at maturity.

A series of examples will demonstrate the effect of a change in interest rates on two investors' realized rate of returns. Interest rates are the rates at which coupon payments are reinvested and the market discount rates at the time of purchase and at the time of sale if the bond is not held to maturity. In Examples 1 and 2, interest rates are unchanged. The two investors, however, have different time horizons for holding the bond. Examples 3 and 4 show the impact of an increase in interest rates on the two investors' total return. Examples 5 and 6 show the impact of a decrease in interest rates. In each of the six examples, an investor initially buys a 10-year, 8% annual coupon payment bond at a price of 85.503075 per 100 of par value. The bond's yield-to-maturity is 10.40%.

$$85.503075 = \frac{8}{(1+r)^1} + \frac{8}{(1+r)^2} + \frac{8}{(1+r)^3} + \frac{8}{(1+r)^4} + \frac{8}{(1+r)^5} + \frac{8}{(1+r)^6} + \frac{8}{(1+r)^7} + \frac{8}{(1+r)^8} + \frac{8}{(1+r)^9} + \frac{108}{(1+r)^{10}}, \quad r = 0.1040$$

EXAMPLE 1

A "buy-and-hold" investor purchases a 10-year, 8% annual coupon payment bond at 85.503075 per 100 of par value and holds it until maturity. The investor receives the series of 10 coupon payments of 8 (per 100 of par value) for a total of 80, plus the redemption of principal (100) at maturity. In addition to collecting the coupon interest and the principal, the investor has the opportunity to reinvest the cash flows. If the coupon payments are reinvested at 10.40%, the future value of the coupons on the bond's maturity date is 129.970678 per 100 of par value.

$$\left[8 \times (1.1040)^9\right] + \left[8 \times (1.1040)^8\right] + \left[8 \times (1.1040)^7\right] + \left[8 \times (1.1040)^6\right] + \left[8 \times (1.1040)^5\right] + \left[8 \times (1.1040)^4\right] + \left[8 \times (1.1040)^3\right] + \left[8 \times (1.1040)^2\right] + \left[8 \times (1.1040)^1\right] + 8 = 129.970678$$

The first coupon payment of 8 is reinvested at 10.40% for nine years until maturity, the second is reinvested for eight years, and so forth. The future value of the annuity is obtained easily on a financial calculator, using 8 for the payment that is received at the end of each of the 10 periods. The amount in excess of the coupons, 49.970678 (= 129.970678 – 80), is the "interest-on-interest" gain from compounding.

The investor's total return is 229.970678, the sum of the reinvested coupons (129.970678) and the redemption of principal at maturity (100). The realized rate of return is 10.40%.

$$85.503075 = \frac{229.970678}{(1+r)^{10}}, \quad r = 0.1040$$

Example 1 demonstrates that the yield-to-maturity at the time of purchase measures the investor's rate of return under three assumptions: (1) The investor holds the bond to maturity, (2) there is no default by the issuer, and (3) the coupon interest payments are reinvested at that same rate of interest.

Example 2 considers another investor who buys the 10-year, 8% annual coupon payment bond and pays the same price. This investor, however, has a four-year investment horizon. Therefore, coupon interest is only reinvested for four years, and the bond is sold immediately after receiving the fourth coupon payment.

EXAMPLE 2

A second investor buys the 10-year, 8% annual coupon payment bond and sells the bond after four years. Assuming that the coupon payments are reinvested at 10.40% for four years, the future value of the reinvested coupons is 37.347111 per 100 of par value.

$$\left[8 \times (1.1040)^3\right] + \left[8 \times (1.1040)^2\right] + \left[8 \times (1.1040)^1\right] + 8 = 37.347111$$

The interest-on-interest gain from compounding is 5.347111 (= 37.347111 – 32). After four years, when the bond is sold, it has six years remaining until maturity. If the yield-to-maturity remains 10.40%, the sale price of the bond is 89.668770.

$$\frac{8}{(1.1040)^1} + \frac{8}{(1.1040)^2} + \frac{8}{(1.1040)^3} + \frac{8}{(1.1040)^4} +$$
$$\frac{8}{(1.1040)^5} + \frac{108}{(1.1040)^6} = 89.668770$$

The total return is 127.015881 (= 37.347111 + 89.668770) and the realized rate of return is 10.40%.

$$85.503075 = \frac{127.015881}{(1+r)^4}, \quad r = 0.1040$$

In Example 2, the investor's **horizon yield** is 10.40%. A horizon yield is the internal rate of return between the total return (the sum of reinvested coupon payments and the sale price or redemption amount) and the purchase price of the bond. The horizon yield on a bond investment is the annualized holding-period rate of return.

Example 2 demonstrates that the realized horizon yield matches the original yield-to-maturity if: (1) coupon payments are reinvested at the same interest rate as the original yield-to-maturity, and (2) the bond is sold at a price on the constant-yield price trajectory, which implies that the investor does not have any capital gains or losses when the bond is sold.

Capital gains arise if a bond is sold at a price above its constant-yield price trajectory and capital losses occur if a bond is sold at a price below its constant-yield price trajectory. This trajectory is based on the yield-to-maturity when the bond is purchased. The trajectory is shown in Exhibit 1 for a 10-year, 8% annual payment bond purchased at a price of 85.503075 per 100 of par value.

Exhibit 1 Constant-Yield Price Trajectory for a 10-Year, 8% Annual Payment Bond

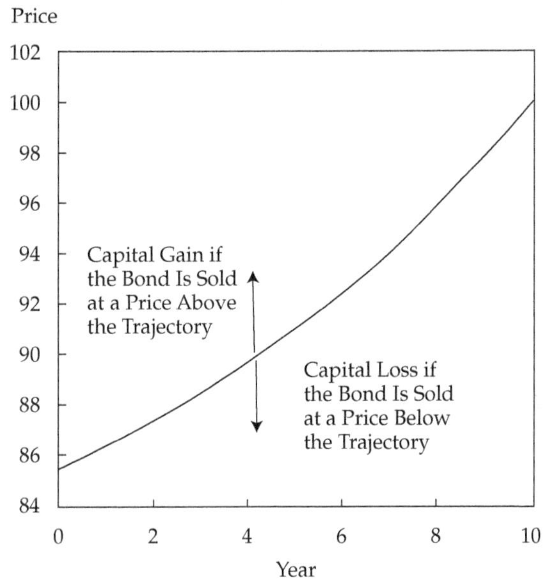

Note: Price is price per 100 of par value

A point on the trajectory represents the **carrying value** of the bond at that time. The carrying value is the purchase price plus the amortized amount of the discount if the bond is purchased at a price below par value. If the bond is purchased at a price above par value, the carrying value is the purchase price minus the amortized amount of the premium.

The amortized amount for each year is the change in the price between two points on the trajectory. The initial price of the bond is 85.503075 per 100 of par value. Its price (the carrying value) after one year is 86.393394, calculated using the original yield-to-maturity of 10.40%. Therefore, the amortized amount for the first year is 0.890319 (= 86.393394 – 85.503075). The bond price in Example 2 increases from 85.503075 to 89.668770, and that increase over the four years is movement *along* the constant-yield price trajectory. At the time the bond is sold, its carrying value is also 89.668770, so there is no capital gain or loss.

Examples 3 and 4 demonstrate the impact on investors' realized horizon yields if interest rates go up by 100 basis points (bps). The market discount rate on the bond increases from 10.40% to 11.40%. Coupon reinvestment rates go up by 100 bps as well.

EXAMPLE 3

The buy-and-hold investor purchases the 10-year, 8% annual payment bond at 85.503075. After the bond is purchased and before the first coupon is received, interest rates go up to 11.40%. The future value of the reinvested coupons at 11.40% for 10 years is 136.380195 per 100 of par value.

$$\left[8\times(1.1140)^9\right]+\left[8\times(1.1140)^8\right]+\left[8\times(1.1140)^7\right]+\left[8\times(1.1140)^6\right]+$$
$$\left[8\times(1.1140)^5\right]+\left[8\times(1.1140)^4\right]+\left[8\times(1.1140)^3\right]+\left[8\times(1.1140)^2\right]+$$
$$\left[8\times(1.1140)^1\right]+8=136.380195$$

The total return is 236.380195 (= 136.380195 + 100). The investor's realized rate of return is 10.70%.

$$85.503075=\frac{236.380195}{(1+r)^{10}},\quad r=0.1070$$

In Example 3, the buy-and-hold investor benefits from the higher coupon reinvestment rate. The realized horizon yield is 10.70%, 30 bps higher than the outcome in Example 1, when interest rates are unchanged. There is no capital gain or loss because the bond is held until maturity. The carrying value at the maturity date is par value, the same as the redemption amount.

EXAMPLE 4

The second investor buys the 10-year, 8% annual payment bond at 85.503075 and sells it in four years. After the bond is purchased, interest rates go up to 11.40%. The future value of the reinvested coupons at 11.40% after four years is 37.899724 per 100 of par value.

$$\left[8\times(1.1140)^3\right]+\left[8\times(1.1140)^2\right]+\left[8\times(1.1140)^1\right]+8=37.899724$$

The sale price of the bond after four years is 85.780408.

$$\frac{8}{(1.1140)^1}+\frac{8}{(1.1140)^2}+\frac{8}{(1.1140)^3}+\frac{8}{(1.1140)^4}+$$
$$\frac{8}{(1.1140)^5}+\frac{108}{(1.1140)^6}=85.780408$$

The total return is 123.680132 (= 37.899724 + 85.780408), resulting in a realized four-year horizon yield of 9.67%.

$$85.503075=\frac{123.680132}{(1+r)^4},\quad r=0.0967$$

In Example 4, the second investor has a lower realized rate of return compared with the investor in Example 2, in which interest rates are unchanged. The future value of reinvested coupon payments goes up by 0.552613 (= 37.899724 – 37.347111) per 100 of par value because of the higher interest rates. But there is a *capital loss* of 3.888362 (= 89.668770 – 85.780408) per 100 of par value. Notice that the capital loss is measured from the bond's carrying value, the point on the constant-yield price trajectory, and not from the original purchase price. The bond is now sold at a price below the constant-yield price trajectory. The reduction in the realized four-year horizon yield from 10.40% to 9.67% is a result of the capital loss being greater than the gain from reinvesting coupons at a higher rate, which reduces the investor's total return.

Examples 5 and 6 complete the series of rate-of-return calculations for the two investors. Interest rates decline by 100 bps. The required yield on the bond falls from 10.40% to 9.40% after the purchase of the bond. The interest rates at which the coupon payments are reinvested fall as well.

EXAMPLE 5

The buy-and-hold investor purchases the 10-year bond at 85.503075 and holds the security until it matures. After the bond is purchased and before the first coupon is received, interest rates go down to 9.40%. The future value of reinvesting the coupon payments at 9.40% for 10 years is 123.888356 per 100 of par value.

$$\left[8\times(1.0940)^9\right]+\left[8\times(1.0940)^8\right]+\left[8\times(1.0940)^7\right]+\left[8\times(1.0940)^6\right]+$$
$$\left[8\times(1.0940)^5\right]+\left[8\times(1.0940)^4\right]+\left[8\times(1.0940)^3\right]+\left[8\times(1.0940)^2\right]+$$
$$\left[8\times(1.0940)^1\right]+8=123.888356$$

The total return is 223.888356, the sum of the future value of reinvested coupons and the redemption of par value. The investor's realized rate of return is 10.10%.

$$85.503075=\frac{223.888356}{(1+r)^{10}},\quad r=0.1010$$

In Example 5, the buy-and-hold investor suffers from the lower coupon reinvestment rates. The realized horizon yield is 10.10%, 30 bps lower than the result in Example 1, when interest rates are unchanged. There is no capital gain or loss because the bond is held until maturity. Examples 1, 3, and 5 indicate that the interest rate risk for a buy-and-hold investor arises entirely from changes in coupon reinvestment rates.

EXAMPLE 6

The second investor buys the 10-year bond at 85.503075 and sells it in four years. After the bond is purchased, interest rates go down to 9.40%. The future value of the reinvested coupons at 9.40% is 36.801397 per 100 of par value.

$$\left[8\times(1.0940)^3\right]+\left[8\times(1.0940)^2\right]+\left[8\times(1.0940)^1\right]+8=36.801397$$

This reduction in future value is offset by the higher sale price of the bond, which is 93.793912 per 100 of par value.

$$\frac{8}{(1.0940)^1}+\frac{8}{(1.0940)^2}+\frac{8}{(1.0940)^3}+\frac{8}{(1.0940)^4}+$$
$$\frac{8}{(1.0940)^5}+\frac{108}{(1.0940)^6}=93.793912$$

The total return is 130.595309 (= 36.801397 + 93.793912), and the realized yield is 11.17%.

$$85.503075 = \frac{130.595309}{(1+r)^4}, \quad r = 0.1117$$

The investor in Example 6 has a capital gain of 4.125142 (= 93.793912 – 89.668770). The capital gain is measured from the carrying value, the point on the constant-yield price trajectory. That gain offsets the reduction in the future value of reinvested coupons of 0.545714 (= 37.347111 – 36.801397). The total return is higher than that in Example 2, in which the interest rate remains at 10.40%.

In these examples, interest income for the investor is the return associated with the *passage of time*. Therefore, interest income includes the receipt of coupon interest, the reinvestment of those cash flows, and the amortization of the discount from purchase at a price below par value (or the premium from purchase at a price above par value) to bring the return back in line with the market discount rate. A capital gain or loss is the return to the investor associated with the *change in the value* of the security. On the fixed-rate bond, a change in value arises from a change in the yield-to-maturity, which is the implied market discount rate. In practice, the way interest income and capital gains and losses are calculated and reported on financial statements depends on financial and tax accounting rules.

This series of examples illustrates an important point about fixed-rate bonds: The *investment horizon* is at the heart of understanding interest rate risk and return. There are two offsetting types of interest rate risk that affect the bond investor: coupon reinvestment risk and market price risk. The future value of reinvested coupon payments (and, in a portfolio, the principal on bonds that mature before the horizon date) *increases* when interest rates go up and *decreases* when rates go down. The sale price on a bond that matures after the horizon date (and thus needs to be sold) *decreases* when interest rates go up and *increases* when rates go down. Coupon reinvestment risk matters more when the investor has a long-term horizon relative to the time-to-maturity of the bond. For instance, a buy-and-hold investor only has coupon reinvestment risk. Market price risk matters more when the investor has a short-term horizon relative to the time-to-maturity. For example, an investor who sells the bond before the first coupon is received has only market price risk. Therefore, two investors holding the same bond (or bond portfolio) can have different exposures to interest rate risk if they have different investment horizons.

EXAMPLE 7

An investor buys a four-year, 10% annual coupon payment bond priced to yield 5.00%. The investor plans to sell the bond in two years once the second coupon payment is received. Calculate the purchase price for the bond and the horizon yield assuming that the coupon reinvestment rate after the bond purchase and the yield-to-maturity at the time of sale are (1) 3.00%, (2) 5.00%, and (3) 7.00%.

Solution:

The purchase price is 117.729753.

$$\frac{10}{(1.0500)^1} + \frac{10}{(1.0500)^2} + \frac{10}{(1.0500)^3} + \frac{110}{(1.0500)^4} = 117.729753$$

1 3.00%: The future value of reinvested coupons is 20.300.

$$(10 \times 1.0300) + 10 = 20.300$$

The sale price of the bond is 113.394288.

$$\frac{10}{(1.0300)^1} + \frac{110}{(1.0300)^2} = 113.394288$$

Total return: 20.300 + 113.394288 = 133.694288.

If interest rates go down from 5.00% to 3.00%, the realized rate of return over the two-year investment horizon is 6.5647%, higher than the original yield-to-maturity of 5.00%.

$$117.729753 = \frac{133.694288}{(1+r)^2}, \quad r = 0.065647$$

2 5.00%: The future value of reinvested coupons is 20.500.

$$(10 \times 1.0500) + 10 = 20.500$$

The sale price of the bond is 109.297052.

$$\frac{10}{(1.0500)^1} + \frac{110}{(1.0500)^2} = 109.297052$$

Total return: 20.500 + 109.297052 = 129.797052.

If interest rates remain 5.00% for reinvested coupons and for the required yield on the bond, the realized rate of return over the two-year investment horizon is equal to the yield-to-maturity of 5.00%.

$$117.729753 = \frac{129.797052}{(1+r)^2}, \quad r = 0.050000$$

3 7.00%: The future value of reinvested coupons is 20.700.

$$(10 \times 1.0700) + 10 = 20.700$$

The bond is sold at 105.424055.

$$\frac{10}{(1.0700)^1} + \frac{110}{(1.0700)^2} = 105.424055$$

Total return: 20.700 + 105.424055 = 126.124055.

$$117.729753 = \frac{126.124055}{(1+r)^2}, \quad r = 0.035037$$

If interest rates go up from 5.00% to 7.00%, the realized rate of return over the two-year investment horizon is 3.5037%, lower than the yield-to-maturity of 5.00%.

INTEREST RATE RISK ON FIXED-RATE BONDS

3

This section covers two commonly used measures of interest rate risk: duration and convexity. It distinguishes between risk measures based on changes in a bond's own yield to maturity (yield duration and convexity) and those that affect the bond based on changes in a benchmark yield curve (curve duration and convexity).

3.1 Macaulay, Modified, and Approximate Duration

The duration of a bond measures the sensitivity of the bond's full price (including accrued interest) to changes in the bond's yield-to-maturity or, more generally, to changes in benchmark interest rates. Duration estimates changes in the bond price assuming that variables other than the yield-to-maturity or benchmark rates are held constant. Most importantly, the time-to-maturity is unchanged. Therefore, duration measures the *instantaneous* (or, at least, same-day) change in the bond price. The accrued interest is the same, so it is the flat price that goes up or down when the full price changes. Duration is a useful measure because it represents the approximate amount of time a bond would have to be held for the market discount rate at purchase to be realized if there is a single change in interest rate. If the bond is held for the duration period, an increase from reinvesting coupons is offset by a decrease in price if interest rates increase and a decrease from reinvesting coupons is offset by an increase in price if interest rates decrease.

There are several types of bond duration. In general, these can be divided into **yield duration** and **curve duration**. Yield duration is the sensitivity of the bond price with respect to the bond's own yield-to-maturity. Curve duration is the sensitivity of the bond price (or more generally, the market value of a financial asset or liability) with respect to a benchmark yield curve. The benchmark yield curve could be the government yield curve on coupon bonds, the spot curve, or the forward curve, but in practice, the government par curve is often used. Yield duration statistics used in fixed-income analysis include Macaulay duration, modified duration, money duration, and the price value of a basis point (PVBP). A curve duration statistic often used is effective duration. Effective duration is covered in Section 3.2.

Macaulay duration is named after Frederick Macaulay, the Canadian economist who first wrote about the statistic in a book published in 1938.[1] Equation 1 is a general formula to calculate the Macaulay duration (MacDur) of a traditional fixed-rate bond.

$$\text{MacDur} = \left[\frac{\dfrac{(1-t/T)\times PMT}{(1+r)^{1-t/T}} + \dfrac{(2-t/T)\times PMT}{(1+r)^{2-t/T}} + \cdots + \dfrac{(N-t/T)\times(PMT+FV)}{(1+r)^{N-t/T}}}{\dfrac{PMT}{(1+r)^{1-t/T}} + \dfrac{PMT}{(1+r)^{2-t/T}} + \cdots + \dfrac{PMT+FV}{(1+r)^{N-t/T}}}\right] \quad (1)$$

where

t = the number of days from the last coupon payment to the settlement date

T = the number of days in the coupon period

t/T = the fraction of the coupon period that has gone by since the last payment

PMT = the coupon payment per period

FV = the future value paid at maturity, or the par value of the bond

r = the yield-to-maturity, or the market discount rate, per period

N = the number of evenly spaced periods to maturity as of the beginning of the current period

1 Frederick R. Macaulay, *Some Theoretical Problems Suggested by the Movements of Interest Rates, Bond Yields and Stock Prices in the United States since 1856* (New York: National Bureau of Economic Research, 1938).

The denominator in Equation 1 is the full price (PV^{Full}) of the bond including accrued interest. It is the present value of the coupon interest and principal payments, with each cash flow discounted by the same market discount rate, r.

$$PV^{Full} = \frac{PMT}{(1+r)^{1-t/T}} + \frac{PMT}{(1+r)^{2-t/T}} + \cdots + \frac{PMT + FV}{(1+r)^{N-t/T}} \tag{2}$$

Equation 3 combines Equations 1 and 2 to reveal an important aspect of the Macaulay duration: Macaulay duration is a weighted average of the time to receipt of the bond's promised payments, where the weights are the shares of the full price that correspond to each of the bond's promised future payments.

$$\text{MacDur} = \left\{ \begin{array}{l} (1-t/T)\left[\dfrac{\dfrac{PMT}{(1+r)^{1-t/T}}}{PV^{Full}}\right] + (2-t/T)\left[\dfrac{\dfrac{PMT}{(1+r)^{2-t/T}}}{PV^{Full}}\right] + \cdots + \\ (N-t/T)\left[\dfrac{\dfrac{PMT+FV}{(1+r)^{N-t/T}}}{PV^{Full}}\right] \end{array} \right\} \tag{3}$$

The times to receipt of cash flow measured in terms of time periods are $1 - t/T$, $2 - t/T$, ..., $N - t/T$. The weights are the present values of the cash flows divided by the full price. Therefore, Macaulay duration is measured in terms of time periods. A couple of examples will clarify this calculation.

Consider first the 10-year, 8% annual coupon payment bond used in Examples 1–6. The bond's yield-to-maturity is 10.40%, and its price is 85.503075 per 100 of par value. This bond has 10 evenly spaced periods to maturity. Settlement is on a coupon payment date so that $t/T = 0$. Exhibit 2 illustrates the calculation of the bond's Macaulay duration.

Exhibit 2 Macaulay Duration of a 10-Year, 8% Annual Payment Bond

Period	Cash Flow	Present Value	Weight	Period × Weight
1	8	7.246377	0.08475	0.0847
2	8	6.563747	0.07677	0.1535
3	8	5.945423	0.06953	0.2086
4	8	5.385347	0.06298	0.2519
5	8	4.878032	0.05705	0.2853
6	8	4.418507	0.05168	0.3101
7	8	4.002271	0.04681	0.3277
8	8	3.625245	0.04240	0.3392
9	8	3.283737	0.03840	0.3456
10	108	40.154389	0.46963	4.6963
		85.503075	1.00000	7.0029

The first two columns of Exhibit 2 show the number of periods to the receipt of the cash flow and the amount of the payment per 100 of par value. The third column is the present value of the cash flow. For example, the final payment is 108 (the last coupon payment plus the redemption of principal) and its present value is 40.154389.

$$\frac{108}{(1.1040)^{10}} = 40.154389$$

The sum of the present values is the full price of the bond. The fourth column is the weight, the share of total market value corresponding to each cash flow. The final payment of 108 per 100 of par value is 46.963% of the bond's market value.

$$\frac{40.154389}{85.503075} = 0.46963$$

The sum of the weights is 1.00000. The fifth column is the number of periods to the receipt of the cash flow (the first column) multiplied by the weight (the fourth column). The sum of that column is 7.0029, which is the Macaulay duration of this 10-year, 8% annual coupon payment bond. This statistic is sometimes reported as 7.0029 *years,* although the time frame is not needed in most applications.

Now consider an example *between* coupon payment dates. A 6% semiannual payment corporate bond that matures on 14 February 2027 is purchased for settlement on 11 April 2019. The coupon payments are 3 per 100 of par value, paid on 14 February and 14 August of each year. The yield-to-maturity is 6.00% quoted on a street-convention semiannual bond basis. The full price of this bond comprises the flat price plus accrued interest. The flat price for the bond is 99.990423 per 100 of par value. The accrued interest is calculated using the 30/360 method to count days. This settlement date is 57 days into the 180-day semiannual period, so $t/T = 57/180$. The accrued interest is 0.950000 (= 57/180 × 3) per 100 of par value. The full price for the bond is 100.940423 (= 99.990423 + 0.950000). Exhibit 3 shows the calculation of the bond's Macaulay duration.

Exhibit 3 Macaulay Duration of an Eight-Year, 6% Semiannual Payment Bond Priced to Yield 6.00%

Period	Time to Receipt	Cash Flow	Present Value	Weight	Time × Weight
1	0.6833	3	2.940012	0.02913	0.019903
2	1.6833	3	2.854381	0.02828	0.047601
3	2.6833	3	2.771244	0.02745	0.073669
4	3.6833	3	2.690528	0.02665	0.098178
5	4.6833	3	2.612163	0.02588	0.121197
6	5.6833	3	2.536080	0.02512	0.142791
7	6.6833	3	2.462214	0.02439	0.163025
8	7.6833	3	2.390499	0.02368	0.181959
9	8.6833	3	2.320873	0.02299	0.199652
10	9.6833	3	2.253275	0.02232	0.216159
11	10.6833	3	2.187645	0.02167	0.231536
12	11.6833	3	2.123927	0.02104	0.245834
13	12.6833	3	2.062065	0.02043	0.259102
14	13.6833	3	2.002005	0.01983	0.271389
15	14.6833	3	1.943694	0.01926	0.282740

Exhibit 3 (Continued)

Period	Time to Receipt	Cash Flow	Present Value	Weight	Time × Weight
16	15.6833	103	64.789817	0.64186	10.066535
			100.940423	1.00000	12.621268

There are 16 semiannual periods to maturity between the last coupon payment date of 14 February 2019 and maturity on 14 February 2027. The time to receipt of cash flow in semiannual periods is in the second column: 0.6833 = 1 – 57/180, 1.6833 = 2 – 57/180, etc. The cash flow for each period is in the third column. The annual yield-to-maturity is 6.00%, so the yield per semiannual period is 3.00%. When that yield is used to get the present value of each cash flow, the full price of the bond is 100.940423, the sum of the fourth column. The weights, which are the shares of the full price corresponding to each cash flow, are in the fifth column. The Macaulay duration is the sum of the items in the sixth column, which is the weight multiplied by the time to receipt of each cash flow. The result, 12.621268, is the Macaulay duration on an eight-year, 6% semiannual payment bond for settlement on 11 April 2019 measured in *semiannual periods*. Similar to coupon rates and yields-to-maturity, duration statistics invariably are annualized in practice. Therefore, the Macaulay duration typically is reported as 6.310634 *years* (= 12.621268/2).[2] (Such precision for the duration statistic is not needed in practice. Typically, "6.31 years" is enough. The full precision is shown here to illustrate calculations.)

Another approach to calculating the Macaulay duration is to use a closed-form equation derived using calculus and algebra. Equation 4 is a general closed-form formula for determining the Macaulay duration of a fixed-rate bond, where c is the coupon rate per period (PMT/FV).[3]

$$\text{MacDur} = \left\{\frac{1+r}{r} - \frac{1+r+\left[N \times (c-r)\right]}{c \times \left[(1+r)^N - 1\right] + r}\right\} - (t/T) \tag{4}$$

The Macaulay duration of the 10-year, 8% annual payment bond is calculated by entering $r = 0.1040$, $c = 0.0800$, $N = 10$, and $t/T = 0$ into Equation 4.

$$\text{MacDur} = \frac{1+0.1040}{0.1040} - \frac{1+0.1040+\left[10 \times (0.0800 - 0.1040)\right]}{0.0800 \times \left[(1+0.1040)^{10} - 1\right] + 0.1040} = 7.0029$$

Therefore, the weighted average time to receipt of the interest and principal payments that will result in realization of the initial market discount rate on this 10-year bond is 7.00 years.

2 Microsoft Excel users can obtain the Macaulay duration using the DURATION financial function: DURATION(DATE(2019,4,11),DATE(2027,2,14),0.06,0.06,2,0). The inputs are the settlement date, maturity date, annual coupon rate as a decimal, annual yield-to-maturity as a decimal, periodicity, and the code for the day count (0 for 30/360, 1 for actual/actual).

3 The step-by-step derivation of this formula is in Donald J. Smith, *Bond Math: The Theory behind the Formulas*, 2nd edition (Hoboken, NJ: John Wiley & Sons, 2014).

The Macaulay duration of the 6% semiannual payment bond maturing on 14 February 2027 is obtained by entering $r = 0.0300$, $c = 0.0300$, $N = 16$, and $t/T = 57/180$ into Equation 4.

$$\text{MacDur} = \left[\frac{1+0.0300}{0.0300} - \frac{1+0.0300+\left[16\times(0.0300-0.0300)\right]}{0.0300\times\left[(1+0.0300)^{16}-1\right]+0.0300}\right] - (57/180)$$
$$= 12.621268$$

Equation 4 uses the yield-to-maturity *per period*, the coupon rate *per period*, the number of *periods* to maturity, and the fraction of the current *period* that has gone by. Its output is the Macaulay duration in terms of *periods*. It is converted to annual duration by dividing by the number of periods in the year.

The calculation of the **modified duration** (ModDur) statistic of a bond requires a simple adjustment to Macaulay duration. It is the Macaulay duration statistic divided by one plus the yield per period.

$$\text{ModDur} = \frac{\text{MacDur}}{1+r} \tag{5}$$

For example, the modified duration of the 10-year, 8% annual payment bond is 6.3432.

$$\text{ModDur} = \frac{7.0029}{1.1040} = 6.3432$$

The modified duration of the 6% semiannual payment bond maturing on 14 February 2027 is 12.253658 semiannual periods.

$$\text{ModDur} = \frac{12.621268}{1.0300} = 12.253658$$

The annualized modified duration of the bond is 6.126829 (= 12.253658/2).[4]

Although modified duration might seem to be just a Macaulay duration with minor adjustments, it has an important application in risk measurement: Modified duration provides an estimate of the percentage price change for a bond given a change in its yield-to-maturity.

$$\%\Delta PV^{Full} \approx -\text{AnnModDur} \times \Delta\text{Yield} \tag{6}$$

The percentage price change refers to the full price, including accrued interest. The AnnModDur term in Equation 6 is the *annual* modified duration, and the ΔYield term is the change in the *annual* yield-to-maturity. The ≈ sign indicates that this calculation is an estimation. The minus sign indicates that bond prices and yields-to-maturity move inversely.

If the annual yield on the 6% semiannual payment bond that matures on 14 February 2027 jumps by 100 bps, from 6.00% to 7.00%, the estimated loss in value for the bond is 6.1268%.

$$\%\Delta PV^{Full} \approx -6.126829 \times 0.0100 = -0.061268$$

If the yield-to-maturity were to drop by 100 bps to 5.00%, the estimated gain in value is also 6.1268%.

$$\%\Delta PV^{Full} \approx -6.126829 \times -0.0100 = 0.061268$$

Modified duration provides a *linear* estimate of the percentage price change. In terms of absolute value, the change is the same for either an increase or decrease in the yield-to-maturity. Recall from "Introduction to Fixed-Income Valuation" that for

4 Microsoft Excel users can obtain the modified duration using the MDURATION financial function: MDURATION(DATE(2019,4,11),DATE(2027,2,14),0.06,0.06,2,0). The inputs are the same as for the Macaulay duration in Footnote 2.

a given coupon rate and time-to-maturity, the percentage price change is greater (in absolute value) when the market discount rate goes down than when it goes up. Later in this reading, a "convexity adjustment" to duration is introduced. It improves the accuracy of this estimate, especially when a large change in yield-to-maturity (such as 100 bps) is considered.

The modified duration statistic for a fixed-rate bond is easily obtained if the Macaulay duration is already known. An alternative approach is to *approximate* modified duration directly. Equation 7 is the approximation formula for annual modified duration.

$$\text{ApproxModDur} = \frac{(PV_{-}) - (PV_{+})}{2 \times (\Delta\text{Yield}) \times (PV_0)} \tag{7}$$

The objective of the approximation is to estimate the slope of the line tangent to the price–yield curve. The slope of the tangent and the approximated slope are shown in Exhibit 4.

Exhibit 4 Approximate Modified Duration

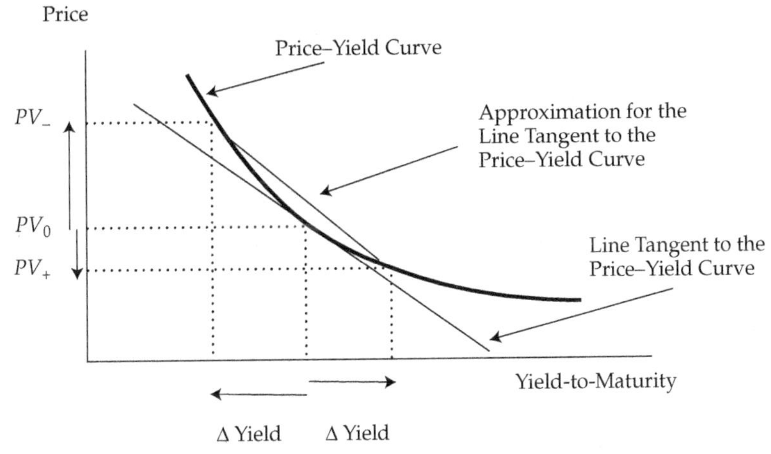

To estimate the slope, the yield-to-maturity is changed up and down by the same amount—the ΔYield. Then the bond prices given the new yields-to-maturity are calculated. The price when the yield is increased is denoted PV_{+}. The price when the yield-to-maturity is reduced is denoted PV_{-}. The original price is PV_0. These prices are the full prices, including accrued interest. The slope of the line based on PV_{+} and PV_{-} is the approximation for the slope of the line tangent to the price–yield curve. The following example illustrates the remarkable accuracy of this approximation. In fact, as ΔYield approaches zero, the approximation approaches AnnModDur.

Consider the 6% semiannual coupon payment corporate bond maturing on 14 February 2027. For settlement on 11 April 2019, the full price (PV_0) is 100.940423 given that the yield-to-maturity is 6.00%.

$$PV_0 = \left[\frac{3}{(1.03)^1} + \frac{3}{(1.03)^2} + \cdots + \frac{103}{(1.03)^{16}}\right] \times (1.03)^{57/180} = 100.940423$$

Raise the annual yield-to-maturity by five bps, from 6.00% to 6.05%. This increase corresponds to an increase in the yield-to-maturity per semiannual period of 2.5 bps, from 3.00% to 3.025% per period. The new full price (PV_+) is 100.631781.

$$PV_+ = \left[\frac{3}{(1.03025)^1} + \frac{3}{(1.03025)^2} + \cdots + \frac{103}{(1.03025)^{16}}\right] \times (1.03025)^{57/180} = 100.631781$$

Lower the annual yield-to-maturity by five bps, from 6.00% to 5.95%. This decrease corresponds to a decrease in the yield-to-maturity per semiannual period of 2.5 bps, from 3.00% to 2.975% per period. The new full price (PV_-) is 101.250227.

$$PV_- = \left[\frac{3}{(1.02975)^1} + \frac{3}{(1.02975)^2} + \cdots + \frac{103}{(1.02975)^{16}}\right] \times (1.02975)^{57/180} = 101.250227$$

Enter these results into Equation 7 for the 5 bp change in the annual yield-to-maturity, or $\Delta\text{Yield} = 0.0005$:

$$\text{ApproxModDur} = \frac{101.250227 - 100.631781}{2 \times 0.0005 \times 100.940423} = 6.126842$$

The "exact" annual modified duration for this bond is 6.126829 and the "approximation" is 6.126842—virtually identical results. Therefore, although duration can be calculated using the approach in Exhibits 2 and 3—basing the calculation on the weighted average time to receipt of each cash flow—or using the closed-form formula as in Equation 4, it can also be estimated quite accurately using the basic bond-pricing equation and a financial calculator. The Macaulay duration can be approximated as well—the approximate modified duration multiplied by one plus the yield per period.

$$\text{ApproxMacDur} = \text{ApproxModDur} \times (1 + r) \quad \textbf{(8)}$$

The approximation formulas produce results for *annualized* modified and Macaulay durations. The frequency of coupon payments and the periodicity of the yield-to-maturity are included in the bond price calculations.

EXAMPLE 8

Assume that the 3.75% US Treasury bond that matures on 15 August 2041 is priced to yield 5.14% for settlement on 15 October 2020. Coupons are paid semiannually on 15 February and 15 August. The yield-to-maturity is stated on a street-convention semiannual bond basis. This settlement date is 61 days into a 184-day coupon period, using the actual/actual day-count convention. Compute the approximate modified duration and the approximate Macaulay duration for this Treasury bond assuming a 5 bp change in the yield-to-maturity.

Solution:

The yield-to-maturity per semiannual period is 0.0257 (= 0.0514/2). The coupon payment per period is 1.875 (= 3.75/2). At the beginning of the period, there are 21 years (42 semiannual periods) to maturity. The fraction of the period that has passed is 61/184. The full price at that yield-to-maturity is 82.967530 per 100 of par value.

$$PV_0 = \left[\frac{1.875}{(1.0257)^1} + \frac{1.875}{(1.0257)^2} + \cdots + \frac{1.875}{(1.0257)^{42}}\right] \times (1.0257)^{61/184} = 82.96753$$

Raise the yield-to-maturity from 5.14% to 5.19%—therefore, from 2.57% to 2.595% per semiannual period, and the price becomes 82.411395 per 100 of par value.

$$PV_+ = \left[\frac{1.875}{(1.02595)^1} + \frac{1.875}{(1.02595)^2} + \cdots + \frac{1.875}{(1.02595)^{42}}\right] \times (1.02595)^{61/184}$$
$$= 82.411395$$

Lower the yield-to-maturity from 5.14% to 5.09%—therefore, from 2.57% to 2.545% per semiannual period, and the price becomes 83.528661 per 100 of par value.

$$PV_- = \left[\frac{1.875}{(1.02545)^1} + \frac{1.875}{(1.02545)^2} + \cdots + \frac{1.875}{(1.02545)^{42}}\right] \times (1.02545)^{61/184}$$
$$= 83.528661$$

The approximate annualized modified duration for the Treasury bond is 13.466.

$$\text{ApproxModDur} = \frac{83.528661 - 82.411395}{2 \times 0.0005 \times 82.967530} = 13.466$$

The approximate annualized Macaulay duration is 13.812.

$$\text{ApproxMacDur} = 13.466 \times 1.0257 = 13.812$$

Therefore, from these statistics, the investor knows that the weighted average time to receipt of interest and principal payments is 13.812 years (the Macaulay duration) and that the estimated loss in the bond's market value is 13.466% (the modified duration) if the market discount rate were to suddenly go up by 1% from 5.14% to 6.14%.

3.2 Effective Duration

Another approach to assess the interest rate risk of a bond is to estimate the percentage change in price given a change in a benchmark yield curve—for example, the government par curve. This estimate, which is very similar to the formula for approximate modified duration, is called the **effective duration**. The effective duration of a bond is the sensitivity of the bond's price to a change in a benchmark yield curve. The formula to calculate effective duration (EffDur) is Equation 9.

$$\text{EffDur} = \frac{(PV_-) - (PV_+)}{2 \times (\Delta\text{Curve}) \times (PV_0)} \quad (9)$$

The difference between approximate modified duration and effective duration is in the denominator. Modified duration is a *yield duration* statistic in that it measures interest rate risk in terms of a change in the bond's own yield-to-maturity (ΔYield). Effective duration is a *curve duration* statistic in that it measures interest rate risk in terms of a parallel shift in the benchmark yield curve (ΔCurve).

Effective duration is essential to the measurement of the interest rate risk of a complex bond, such as a bond that contains an embedded call option. The duration of a callable bond is *not* the sensitivity of the bond price to a change in the yield-to-worst (i.e., the lowest of the yield-to-maturity, yield-to-first-call, yield-to-second-call, and so forth). The problem is that future cash flows are uncertain because they are contingent on future interest rates. The issuer's decision to call the bond depends on the ability to refinance the debt at a lower cost of funds. In brief, a callable bond does not have a well-defined internal rate of return (yield-to-maturity). Therefore, yield duration statistics, such as modified and Macaulay durations, do not apply; effective duration is the appropriate duration measure.

The specific option-pricing models that are used to produce the inputs to effective duration for a callable bond are covered in later readings. However, as an example, suppose that the full price of a callable bond is 101.060489 per 100 of par value. The option-pricing model inputs include (1) the length of the call protection period, (2) the schedule of call prices and call dates, (3) an assumption about credit spreads over benchmark yields (which includes any liquidity spread as well), (4) an assumption about future interest rate volatility, and (5) the level of market interest rates (e.g., the government par curve). The analyst then holds the first four inputs constant and raises and lowers the fifth input. Suppose that when the government par curve is raised and lowered by 25 bps, the new full prices for the callable bond from the model are 99.050120 and 102.890738, respectively. Therefore, PV_0 = 101.060489, PV_+ = 99.050120, PV_- = 102.890738, and ΔCurve = 0.0025. The effective duration for the callable bond is 7.6006.

$$\text{EffDur} = \frac{102.890738 - 99.050120}{2 \times 0.0025 \times 101.060489} = 7.6006$$

This curve duration measure indicates the bond's sensitivity to the benchmark yield curve—in particular, the government par curve—assuming no change in the credit spread. In practice, a callable bond issuer might be able to exercise the call option and obtain a lower cost of funds if (1) benchmark yields fall and the credit spread over the benchmark is unchanged or (2) benchmark yields are unchanged and the credit spread is reduced (e.g., because of an upgrade in the issuer's rating). A pricing model can be used to determine a "credit duration" statistic—that is, the sensitivity of the bond price to a change in the credit spread. On a traditional fixed-rate bond, modified duration estimates the percentage price change for a change in the benchmark yield and/or the credit spread. For bonds that do not have a well-defined internal rate of return because the future cash flows are not fixed—for instance, callable bonds and floating-rate notes—pricing models are used to produce different statistics for changes in benchmark interest rates and for changes in credit risk.

Another fixed-income security for which yield duration statistics, such as modified and Macaulay durations, are not relevant is a mortgage-backed bond. These securities arise from a residential (or commercial) loan portfolio securitization. The key point for measuring interest rate risk on a mortgage-backed bond is that the cash flows are contingent on homeowners' ability to refinance their debt at a lower rate. In effect, the homeowners have call options on their mortgage loans.

A practical consideration in using effective duration is in setting the change in the benchmark yield curve. With approximate modified duration, accuracy is improved by choosing a smaller yield-to-maturity change. But the pricing models for more-complex securities, such as callable and mortgage-backed bonds, include assumptions about the behavior of the corporate issuers, businesses, or homeowners. Rates typically need to change by a minimum amount to affect the decision to call a bond or refinance a mortgage loan because issuing new debt involves transaction costs. Therefore, estimates of interest rate risk using effective duration are not necessarily improved by choosing a smaller change in benchmark rates. Effective duration has become an important tool in the financial analysis of not only traditional bonds but also financial liabilities. Example 9 demonstrates such an application of effective duration.

EXAMPLE 9

Defined-benefit pension schemes typically pay retirees a monthly amount based on their wage level at the time of retirement. The amount could be fixed in nominal terms or indexed to inflation. These programs are referred to as "defined-benefit pension plans" when US GAAP or IFRS accounting standards are used. In Australia, they are called "superannuation funds."

A British defined-benefit pension scheme seeks to measure the sensitivity of its retirement obligations to market interest rate changes. The pension scheme manager hires an actuarial consultancy to model the present value of its liabilities under three interest rate scenarios: (1) a base rate of 5%, (2) a 100 bp increase in rates, up to 6%, and (3) a 100 bp drop in rates, down to 4%.

The actuarial consultancy uses a complex valuation model that includes assumptions about employee retention, early retirement, wage growth, mortality, and longevity. The following chart shows the results of the analysis.

Interest Rate Assumption	Present Value of Liabilities
4%	GBP973.5 million
5%	GBP926.1 million
6%	GBP871.8 million

Compute the effective duration of the pension scheme's liabilities.

Solution:

PV_0 = 926.1, PV_+ = 871.8, PV_- = 973.5, and ΔCurve = 0.0100. The effective duration of the pension scheme's liabilities is 5.49.

$$\text{EffDur} = \frac{973.5 - 871.8}{2 \times 0.0100 \times 926.1} = 5.49$$

This effective duration statistic for the pension scheme's liabilities might be used in asset allocation decisions to decide the mix of equity, fixed income, and alternative assets.

Although effective duration is the most appropriate interest rate risk measure for bonds with embedded options, it also is useful with traditional bonds to supplement the information provided by the Macaulay and modified yield durations. Exhibit 5 displays the Bloomberg Yield and Spread (YAS) Analysis page for the 2.875% US Treasury note that matures on 15 May 2028.

Exhibit 5 Bloomberg YAS Page for the 2.875% US Treasury Note

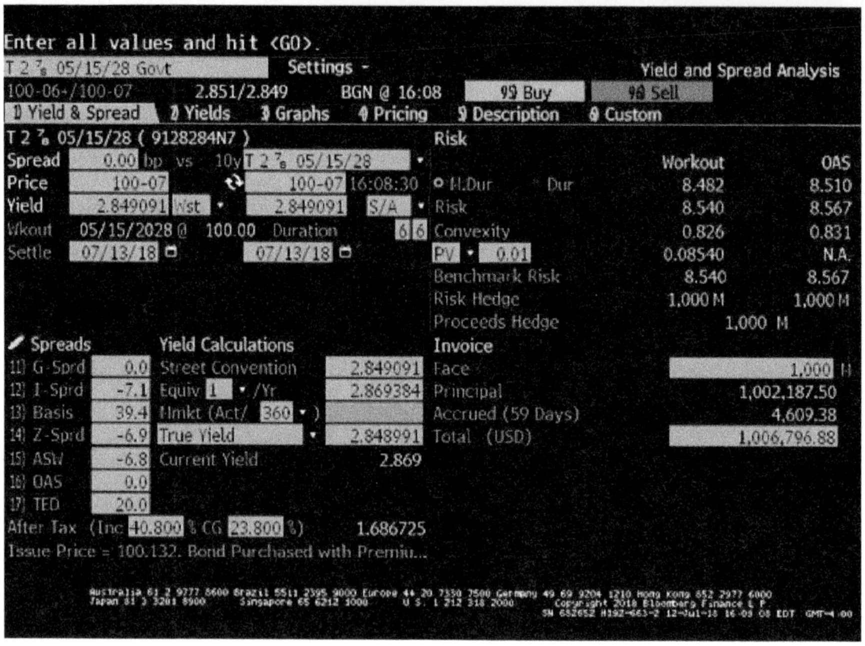

Used with permission of Bloomberg Businessweek Copyright © 2018. All rights reserved.

In Exhibit 5, the quoted (flat) asked price for the bond is 100-07, which is equal to 100 and 7 32nds per 100 of par value for settlement on 13 July 2018. Most bond prices are stated in decimals, but US Treasuries are usually quoted in fractions. As a decimal, the flat price is 100.21875. The accrued interest uses the actual/actual day-count method. That settlement date is 59 days into a 184-day semiannual coupon payment period. The accrued interest is 0.4609375 per 100 of par value (= 59/184 × 0.02875/2 × 100). The full price of the bond is 100.679688. The yield-to-maturity of the bond is 2.849091%, stated on a street-convention semiannual bond basis.

The modified duration for the bond is shown in Exhibit 5 to be 8.482, which is the conventional *yield* duration statistic. Its *curve* duration, however, is 8.510, which is the price sensitivity with respect to changes in the US Treasury par curve. On Bloomberg, the effective duration is called the "OAS duration" because it is based on the option-pricing model that is also used to calculate the option-adjusted spread. The small difference arises because the government yield curve is not flat. When the par curve is shifted in the model, the government spot curve is also shifted, although not in the same "parallel" manner. Therefore, the change in the bond price is not exactly the same as it would be if its own yield-to-maturity changed by the same amount as the change in the par curve. In general, the modified duration and effective duration on a traditional option-free bond are not identical. The difference narrows when the yield curve is flatter, the time-to-maturity is shorter, and the bond is priced closer to par value (so that the difference between the coupon rate and the yield-to-maturity is smaller). The modified duration and effective duration on an option-free bond are identical only in the rare circumstance of an absolutely flat yield curve.

3.3 Key Rate Duration

Above, the effective duration for a sample callable bond was calculated as:

$$\text{EffDur} = \frac{102.890738 - 99.050120}{2 \times 0.0025 \times 101.060489} = 7.6006$$

This duration measure indicates the bond's sensitivity to the benchmark yield curve assuming that all yields change by the same amount. "Key rate" duration provides further insight into a bond's sensitivity to changes in the benchmark yield curve. A **key rate duration** (or **partial duration**) is a measure of a bond's sensitivity to a change in the benchmark yield curve at a specific maturity segment. In contrast to effective duration, key rate durations help identify "shaping risk" for a bond—that is, a bond's sensitivity to changes in the shape of the benchmark yield curve (e.g., the yield curve becoming steeper or flatter).

The previous illustration of effective duration assumed a parallel shift of 25 bps at all maturities. However, the analyst may want to know how the price of the callable bond is expected to change if benchmark rates at short maturities (say up to 2 years) shifted up by 25 bps but longer maturity benchmark rates remained unchanged. This scenario would represent a flattening of the yield curve, given that the yield curve is upward sloping. Using key rate durations, the expected price change would be approximately equal to minus the key rate duration for the short maturity segment times the 0.0025 interest rate shift at that segment. Of course, for parallel shifts in the benchmark yield curve, key rate durations will indicate the same interest rate sensitivity as effective duration.

3.4 Properties of Bond Duration

The Macaulay and modified yield duration statistics for a traditional fixed-rate bond are functions of the input variables: the coupon rate or payment per period, the yield-to-maturity per period, the number of periods to maturity (as of the beginning of the period), and the fraction of the period that has gone by. The properties of bond duration are obtained by changing one of these variables while holding the others constant. Because duration is the basic measure of interest rate risk on a fixed-rate bond, these properties are important to understand.

The closed-form formula for Macaulay duration, presented as Equation 4 and again here, is useful in demonstrating the characteristics of the bond duration statistic.

$$\text{MacDur} = \left\{ \frac{1+r}{r} - \frac{1+r+\left[N \times (c-r)\right]}{c \times \left[(1+r)^N - 1\right] + r} \right\} - (t/T)$$

The same characteristics hold for modified duration. Consider first the fraction of the period that has gone by (t/T). Macaulay and modified durations depend on the day-count basis used to obtain the yield-to-maturity. The duration of a bond that uses the actual/actual method to count days is slightly different from that of an otherwise comparable bond that uses the 30/360 method. The key point is that for a constant yield-to-maturity (r), the expression in braces is unchanged as time passes during the period. Therefore, the Macaulay duration decreases smoothly as t goes from $t = 0$ to $t = T$, which creates a "saw-tooth" pattern. This pattern for a typical fixed-rate bond is illustrated in Exhibit 6.

Exhibit 6 Macaulay Duration between Coupon Payments with a Constant Yield-to-Maturity

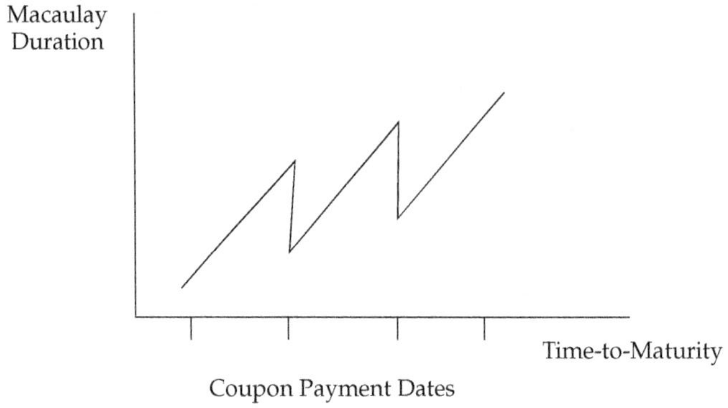

As times passes during the coupon period (moving from right to left in the diagram), the Macaulay duration declines smoothly and then jumps upward after the coupon is paid.

The characteristics of bond duration related to changes in the coupon rate, the yield-to-maturity, and the time-to-maturity are illustrated in Exhibit 7.

Exhibit 7 Properties of the Macaulay Yield Duration

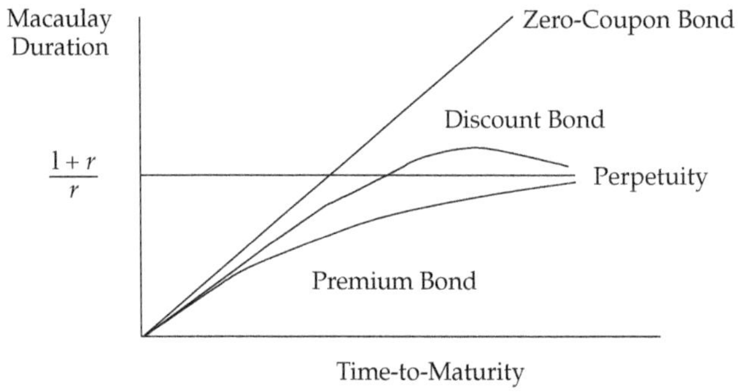

Exhibit 7 shows the graph for coupon payment dates when $t/T = 0$, thus not displaying the saw-tooth pattern between coupon payments. The relationship between the Macaulay duration and the time-to-maturity for a zero-coupon bond is the 45-degree line: MacDur = N when $c = 0$ (and $t/T = 0$). Therefore, the Macaulay duration of a zero-coupon bond is its time-to-maturity.

A **perpetuity** or perpetual bond, which also is called a consol, is a bond that does not mature. There is no principal to redeem. The investor receives a fixed coupon payment forever, unless the bond is callable. Non-callable perpetuities are rare, but they have an interesting Macaulay duration: MacDur = $(1 + r)/r$ as N approaches infinity. In effect, the second expression within the braces approaches zero as the number of periods to maturity increases because N in the numerator is a coefficient but N in the denominator is an exponent and the denominator increases faster than the numerator as N grows larger.

Typical fixed-rate coupon bonds with a stated maturity date are portrayed in Exhibit 7 as the premium and discount bonds. The usual pattern is that longer times-to-maturity correspond to higher Macaulay duration statistics. This pattern always holds for bonds trading at par value or at a premium above par. In Equation 4, the second expression within the braces is a positive number for premium and par bonds.

The numerator is positive because the coupon rate (c) is greater than or equal to the yield-to-maturity (r), whereas the denominator is always positive. Therefore, the Macaulay duration is always less than $(1 + r)/r$, and it approaches that threshold from below as the time-to-maturity increases.

The curious result displayed in Exhibit 7 is in the pattern for discount bonds. Generally, the Macaulay duration increases for a longer time-to-maturity. But at some point when the time-to-maturity is high enough, the Macaulay duration exceeds $(1 + r)/r$, reaches a maximum, and then approaches the threshold from above. In Equation 4, such a pattern develops when the number of periods (N) is large and the coupon rate (c) is below the yield-to-maturity (r). Then the numerator of the second expression within the braces can become negative. The implication is that on long-term discount bonds, the interest rate risk can actually be less than on a shorter-term bond, which explains why the word "generally" is needed in describing the maturity effect for the relationship between bond prices and yields-to-maturity. Generally, for the same coupon rate, a longer-term bond has a greater percentage price change than a shorter-term bond when their yields-to-maturity change by the same amount. The exception is when the longer-term bond actually has a lower duration statistic.

Coupon rates and yields-to-maturity are both inversely related to the Macaulay duration. In Exhibit 7, for the same time-to-maturity and yield-to-maturity, the Macaulay duration is higher for a zero-coupon bond than for a low-coupon bond trading at a discount. Also, the low-coupon bond trading at a discount has a higher duration than a high-coupon bond trading at a premium. Therefore, all else being equal, a lower-coupon bond has a higher duration and more interest rate risk than a higher-coupon bond. The same pattern holds for the yield-to-maturity. A higher yield-to-maturity reduces the weighted average of the time to receipt of cash flow. More weight is on the cash flows received in the near term, and less weight is on the cash flows received in the more-distant future periods if those cash flows are discounted at a higher rate.

In summary, the Macaulay and modified duration statistics for a fixed-rate bond depend primarily on the coupon rate, yield-to-maturity, and time-to-maturity. A higher coupon rate or a higher yield-to-maturity reduces the duration measures. A longer time-to-maturity *usually* leads to a higher duration. It *always* does so for a bond priced at a premium or at par value. But if the bond is priced at a discount, a longer time-to-maturity *might* lead to a lower duration. This situation only occurs if the coupon rate is low (but not zero) relative to the yield and the time-to-maturity is long.

EXAMPLE 10

A hedge fund specializes in investments in emerging market sovereign debt. The fund manager believes that the implied default probabilities are too high, which means that the bonds are viewed as "cheap" and the credit spreads are too high. The hedge fund plans to take a position on one of these available bonds.

Bond	Time-to-Maturity	Coupon Rate	Price	Yield-to-Maturity
(A)	10 years	10%	58.075279	20%
(B)	20 years	10%	51.304203	20%
(C)	30 years	10%	50.210636	20%

The coupon payments are annual. The yields-to-maturity are effective annual rates. The prices are per 100 of par value.

1 Compute the approximate modified duration of each of the three bonds using a 1 bp change in the yield-to-maturity and keeping precision to six decimals (because approximate duration statistics are very sensitive to rounding).
2 Which of the three bonds is expected to have the highest percentage price increase if the yield-to-maturity on each decreases by the same amount—for instance, by 10 bps from 20% to 19.90%?

Solution to 1:

Bond A:

$PV_0 = 58.075279$

$PV_+ = 58.047598$

$$\frac{10}{(1.2001)^1} + \frac{10}{(1.2001)^2} + \cdots + \frac{110}{(1.2001)^{10}} = 58.047598$$

$PV_- = 58.102981$

$$\frac{10}{(1.1999)^1} + \frac{10}{(1.1999)^2} + \cdots + \frac{110}{(1.1999)^{10}} = 58.102981$$

The approximate modified duration of Bond A is 4.768.

$$\text{ApproxModDur} = \frac{58.102981 - 58.047598}{2 \times 0.0001 \times 58.075279} = 4.768$$

Bond B:

$PV_0 = 51.304203$

$PV_+ = 51.277694$

$$\frac{10}{(1.2001)^1} + \frac{10}{(1.2001)^2} + \cdots + \frac{110}{(1.2001)^{20}} = 51.277694$$

$PV_- = 51.330737$

$$\frac{10}{(1.1999)^1} + \frac{10}{(1.1999)^2} + \cdots + \frac{110}{(1.1999)^{20}} = 51.330737$$

The approximate modified duration of Bond B is 5.169.

$$\text{ApproxModDur} = \frac{51.330737 - 51.277694}{2 \times 0.0001 \times 51.304203} = 5.169$$

Bond C:

$PV_0 = 50.210636$

$PV_+ = 50.185228$

$$\frac{10}{(1.2001)^1} + \frac{10}{(1.2001)^2} + \cdots + \frac{110}{(1.2001)^{30}} = 50.185228$$

$PV_- = 50.236070$

$$\frac{10}{(1.1999)^1} + \frac{10}{(1.1999)^2} + \cdots + \frac{110}{(1.1999)^{30}} = 50.236070$$

The approximate modified duration of Bond C is 5.063.

$$\text{ApproxModDur} = \frac{50.236070 - 50.185228}{2 \times 0.0001 \times 50.210636} = 5.063$$

Solution to 2:

Despite the significant differences in times-to-maturity (10, 20, and 30 years), the approximate modified durations on the three bonds are fairly similar (4.768, 5.169, and 5.063). Because the yields-to-maturity are so high, the additional time to receipt of interest and principal payments on the 20- and 30-year bonds have low weight. Nevertheless, Bond B, with 20 years to maturity, has the highest modified duration. If the yield-to-maturity on each is decreased by the same amount—for instance, by 10 bps, from 20% to 19.90%—Bond B would be expected to have the highest percentage price increase because it has the highest modified duration. This example illustrates the relationship between the Macaulay duration and the time-to-maturity on discount bonds in Exhibit 7. The 20-year bond has a higher duration than the 30-year bond.

Callable bonds require the use of effective duration because Macaulay and modified yield duration statistics are not relevant. The yield-to-maturity for callable bonds is not well-defined because future cash flows are uncertain. Exhibit 8 illustrates the impact of the change in the benchmark yield curve (ΔCurve) on the price of a callable bond price compared with that on a comparable non-callable bond. The two bonds have the same credit risk, coupon rate, payment frequency, and time-to-maturity. The vertical axis is the bond price. The horizontal axis is a particular benchmark yield—for instance, a point on the par curve for government bonds.

Exhibit 8 Interest Rate Risk Characteristics of a Callable Bond

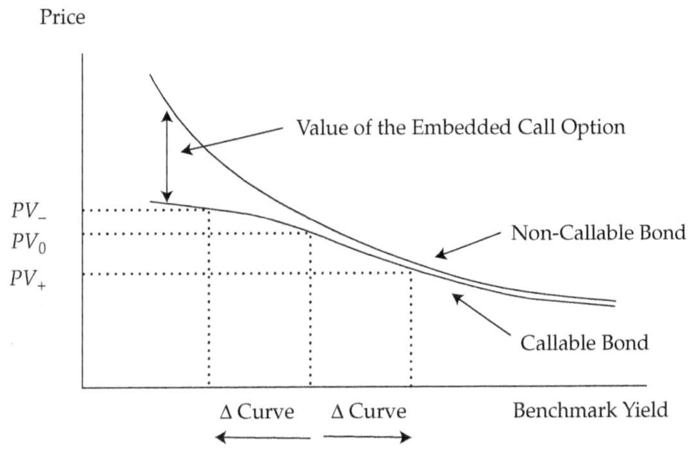

As shown in Exhibit 8, the price of the non-callable bond is always greater than that of the callable bond with otherwise identical features. The difference is the value of the embedded call option. Recall that the call option is an option to the issuer and not the holder of the bond. When interest rates are high compared with the coupon rate, the value of the call option is low. When rates are low, the value of the call option is much greater because the issuer is more likely to exercise the option to refinance the debt at a lower cost of funds. The investor bears the "call risk" because if the bond is called, the investor must reinvest the proceeds at a lower interest rate.

Exhibit 8 shows the inputs for calculating the effective duration of the callable bond. The entire benchmark curve is raised and lowered by the same amount, ΔCurve. The key point is that when benchmark yields are high, the effective durations of the callable and non-callable bonds are very similar. Although the exhibit does not illustrate it, the slopes of the lines tangent to the price–yield curve are about the same in such a situation. But when interest rates are low, the effective duration of the callable bond is lower than that of the otherwise comparable non-callable bond. That is because the callable bond price does not increase as much when benchmark yields fall. The slope of the line tangent to the price–yield curve would be flatter. The presence of the call option limits price appreciation. Therefore, an embedded call option reduces the effective duration of the bond, especially when interest rates are falling and the bond is more likely to be called. The lower effective duration can also be interpreted as a shorter expected life—the weighted average of time to receipt of cash flow is reduced.

Exhibit 9 considers another embedded option—a put option.

Exhibit 9 Interest Rate Risk Characteristics of a Putable Bond

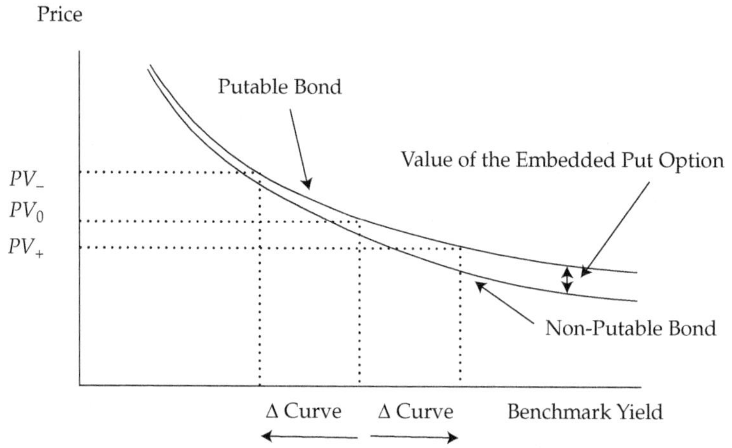

A putable bond allows the investor to sell the bond back to the issuer prior to maturity, usually at par value, which protects the investor from higher benchmark yields or credit spreads that otherwise would drive the bond to a discounted price. Therefore, the price of a putable bond is always higher than that of an otherwise comparable non-putable bond. The price difference is the value of the embedded put option.

An embedded put option reduces the effective duration of the bond, especially when rates are rising. If interest rates are low compared with the coupon rate, the value of the put option is low and the impact of a change in the benchmark yield on the bond's price is very similar to the impact on the price of a non-putable bond. But when benchmark interest rates rise, the put option becomes more valuable to the investor. The ability to sell the bond at par value limits the price depreciation as rates rise. In summary, the presence of an embedded option reduces the sensitivity of the bond price to changes in the benchmark yield curve, assuming no change in credit risk.

3.5 Duration of a Bond Portfolio

Similar to equities, bonds are typically held in a portfolio. There are two ways to calculate the duration of a bond portfolio: (1) the weighted average of time to receipt of the *aggregate* cash flows, and (2) the weighted average of the individual bond durations that comprise the portfolio. The first method is the theoretically correct approach, but it is difficult to use in practice. The second method is commonly used by fixed-income portfolio managers, but it has its own limitations. The differences in these two methods to compute portfolio duration can be examined with a numerical example.

Suppose an investor holds the following portfolio of two *zero-coupon* bonds:

Bond	Maturity	Price	Yield	Macaulay Duration	Modified Duration	Par Value	Market Value	Weight
(X)	1 year	98.00	2.0408%	1	0.980	10,000,000	9,800,000	0.50
(Y)	30 years	9.80	8.0503%	30	27.765	100,000,000	9,800,000	0.50

The prices are per 100 of par value. The yields-to-maturity are effective annual rates. The total market value for the portfolio is 19,600,000. The portfolio is evenly weighted in terms of market value between the two bonds.

The first approach views the portfolio as a series of aggregated cash flows. Its **cash flow yield** is 7.8611%. A cash flow yield is the internal rate of return on a series of cash flows, usually used on a complex security such as a mortgage-backed bond (using projected cash flows based on a model of prepayments as a result of refinancing) or a portfolio of fixed-rate bonds. It is the solution for r in the following equation.

$$19{,}600{,}000 = \frac{10{,}000{,}000}{(1+r)^1} + \frac{0}{(1+r)^2} + \cdots + \frac{0}{(1+r)^{29}} + \frac{100{,}000{,}000}{(1+r)^{30}}, \quad r = 0.078611$$

The Macaulay duration of the portfolio in this approach is the weighted average of the times to receipt of aggregated cash flow. The cash flow yield is used to obtain the weights. This calculation is similar to Equation 1, and the portfolio duration is 16.2825.

$$\text{MacDur} = \left[\frac{\dfrac{1 \times 10{,}000{,}000}{(1.078611)^1} + \dfrac{30 \times 100{,}000{,}000}{(1.078611)^{30}}}{\dfrac{10{,}000{,}000}{(1.078611)^1} + \dfrac{100{,}000{,}000}{(1.078611)^{30}}}\right] = 16.2825$$

There are just two future cash flows in the portfolio—the redemption of principal on the two zero-coupon bonds. In more complex portfolios, a series of coupon and principal payments may occur on some dates, with an aggregated cash flow composed of coupon interest on some bonds and principal on those that mature.

The modified duration of the portfolio is the Macaulay duration divided by one plus the cash flow yield per period (here, the periodicity is 1).

$$\text{ModDur} = \frac{16.2825}{1.078611} = 15.0958$$

The modified duration for the portfolio is 15.0958. That statistic indicates the percentage change in the market value given a change in the cash flow yield. If the cash flow yield increases or decreases by 100 bps, the market value of the portfolio is expected to decrease or increase by about 15.0958%.

Although this approach is theoretically correct, it is difficult to use in practice. First, the cash flow yield is not commonly calculated for bond portfolios. Second, the amount and timing of future coupon and principal payments are uncertain if the portfolio contains callable or putable bonds or floating-rate notes. Third, interest rate risk is usually expressed as a change in benchmark interest rates, not as a change in the cash flow yield. Fourth, the change in the cash flow yield is not necessarily the same amount as the change in the yields-to-maturity on the individual bonds. For instance, if the yields-to-maturity on the two zero-coupon bonds in this portfolio both increase or decrease by 10 bps, the cash flow yield increases or decreases by only 9.52 bps.

In practice, the second approach to portfolio duration is commonly used. The Macaulay and modified durations for the portfolio are calculated as the weighted average of the statistics for the individual bonds. The shares of overall portfolio market value are the weights. This weighted average is an approximation of the theoretically correct portfolio duration, which is obtained using the first approach. This approximation becomes more accurate when the differences in the yields-to-maturity on the bonds in the portfolio are smaller. When the yield curve is flat, the two approaches produce the same portfolio duration.

Given the equal "50/50" weights in this simple numerical example, this version of portfolio duration is easily computed.

$$\text{Average Macaulay duration} = (1 \times 0.50) + (30 \times 0.50) = 15.50$$

$$\text{Average modified duration} = (0.980 \times 0.50) + (27.765 \times 0.50) = 14.3725$$

Note that 0.980 = 1/1.020404 and 27.765 = 30/1.080503. An advantage of the second approach is that callable bonds, putable bonds, and floating-rate notes can be included in the weighted average using the effective durations for these securities.

The main advantage to the second approach is that it is easily used as a measure of interest rate risk. For instance, if the yields-to-maturity on the bonds in the portfolio increase by 100 bps, the estimated drop in the portfolio value is 14.3725%. However, this advantage also indicates a limitation: This measure of portfolio duration implicitly assumes a **parallel shift** in the yield curve. A parallel yield curve shift implies that all rates change by the same amount in the same direction. In reality, interest rate changes frequently result in a steeper or flatter yield curve. Yield volatility is discussed later in this reading.

EXAMPLE 11

An investment fund owns the following portfolio of three fixed-rate government bonds:

	Bond A	Bond B	Bond C
Par value	EUR25,000,000	EUR25,000,000	EUR50,000,000
Coupon rate	9%	11%	8%
Time-to-maturity	6 years	8 years	12 years
Yield-to-maturity	9.10%	9.38%	9.62%
Market value	EUR24,886,343	EUR27,243,887	EUR44,306,787
Macaulay duration	4.761	5.633	7.652

The total market value of the portfolio is EUR96,437,017. Each bond is on a coupon date so that there is no accrued interest. The market values are the full prices given the par value. Coupons are paid semiannually. The yields-to-maturity are stated on a semiannual bond basis, meaning an annual rate for a periodicity of 2. The Macaulay durations are annualized.

1 Calculate the average (annual) modified duration for the portfolio using the shares of market value as the weights.

2 Estimate the percentage loss in the portfolio's market value if the (annual) yield-to-maturity on each bond goes up by 20 bps.

Solution to 1:

The average (annual) modified duration for the portfolio is 6.0495.

$$\left(\frac{4.761}{1+\frac{0.0910}{2}} \times \frac{24{,}886{,}343}{96{,}437{,}017}\right) + \left(\frac{5.633}{1+\frac{0.0938}{2}} \times \frac{27{,}243{,}887}{96{,}437{,}017}\right) +$$

$$\left(\frac{7.652}{1+\frac{0.0962}{2}} \times \frac{44{,}306{,}787}{96{,}437{,}017}\right) = 6.0495$$

Note that the annual modified duration for each bond is the annual Macaulay duration, which is given, divided by one plus the yield-to-maturity per semi-annual period.

Solution to 2:

The estimated decline in market value if each yield rises by 20 bps is 1.21%: $-6.0495 \times 0.0020 = -0.0121$.

3.6 Money Duration of a Bond and the Price Value of a Basis Point

Modified duration is a measure of the *percentage price change* of a bond given a change in its yield-to-maturity. A related statistic is **money duration**. The money duration of a bond is a measure of the *price change* in units of the currency in which the bond is denominated. The money duration can be stated per 100 of par value or in terms of the actual position size of the bond in the portfolio. In the United States, money duration is commonly called "dollar duration."

Money duration (MoneyDur) is calculated as the annual modified duration times the full price (PV^{Full}) of the bond, including accrued interest.

$$\text{MoneyDur} = \text{AnnModDur} \times PV^{Full} \quad (10)$$

The estimated change in the bond price in currency units is calculated using Equation 11, which is very similar to Equation 6. The difference is that for a given change in the annual yield-to-maturity (ΔYield), modified duration estimates the percentage price change and money duration estimates the change in currency units.

$$\Delta PV^{Full} \approx -\text{MoneyDur} \times \Delta\text{Yield} \quad (11)$$

For a theoretical example of money duration, consider the 6% semiannual coupon payment bond that matures on 14 February 2027 and is priced to yield 6.00% for settlement on 11 April 2019. The full price of the bond is 100.940423 per 100 of par value, and the annual modified duration is 6.1268. Suppose that a Nairobi based life insurance company has a position in the bond for a par value of KES100,000,000. The market value of the investment is KES 100,940,423. The money duration of this bond is KES 618,441,784 (= 6.1268 × KES 100,940,423). Therefore, if the yield-to-maturity rises by 100 bps—from 6.00% to 7.00%—the expected loss is approximately KES 6,184,418 (= KES 618,441,784 × 0.0100). On a percentage basis, that expected loss is approximately 6.1268%. The "convexity adjustment" introduced in the next section makes these estimates more accurate.

Another version of money duration is the **price value of a basis point** (PVBP) for the bond. The PVBP is an estimate of the change in the full price given a 1 bp change in the yield-to-maturity. The PVBP can be calculated using a formula similar to that for the approximate modified duration. Equation 12 is the formula for the PVBP.

$$\text{PVBP} = \frac{(PV_-) - (PV_+)}{2} \quad (12)$$

PV_- and PV_+ are the full prices calculated by decreasing and increasing the yield-to-maturity by 1 bp. The PVBP is also called the "PV01," standing for the "price value of an 01"or "present value of an 01," where "01" means 1 bp. In the United States, it is commonly called the "DV01," or the "dollar value of a 01." A related statistic, sometimes called a "basis point value" (or BPV), is the money duration times 0.0001 (1 bp).

For a numerical example of the PVBP calculation, consider the 2.875% semiannual coupon payment US Treasury note that matures on 15 May 2028. In Exhibit 5, the PVBP for the Treasury note is shown to be 0.08540. Its yield-to-maturity is 2.849091%, and the settlement date is 59 days into a 184-day period. To confirm this result, calculate the new prices by increasing and decreasing the yield-to-maturity. First, increase the yield by 1 bp (0.01%), from 2.849091% to 2.859091%, to solve for a PV_+ of 100.594327.

$$PV_+ = \left[\frac{1.4375}{\left(1+\frac{0.02859091}{2}\right)^1} + \cdots + \frac{101.4375}{\left(1+\frac{0.02859091}{2}\right)^{20}}\right] \times \left(1+\frac{0.02859091}{2}\right)^{59/184}$$
$$= 101.594327$$

Then, decrease the yield-to-maturity by 1 bp, from 2.849091% to 2.839091%, to solve for a PV_- of 100.765123.

$$PV_- = \left[\frac{1.4375}{\left(1+\frac{0.02839091}{2}\right)^1} + \cdots + \frac{101.4375}{\left(1+\frac{0.02839091}{2}\right)^{20}}\right] \times \left(1+\frac{0.02839091}{2}\right)^{59/184}$$
$$= 100.765123$$

The PVBP is obtained by substituting these results into Equation 12.

$$\text{PVBP} = \frac{100.765123 - 100.594327}{2} = 0.08540$$

Another money duration statistic reported on the Bloomberg YAS page is "risk." It is shown to be 8.540. Bloomberg's risk statistic is simply the PVBP (or PV01) times 100.

EXAMPLE 12

A life insurance company holds a USD10 million (par value) position in a 5.95% Dominican Republic bond that matures on 25 January 2027. The bond is priced (flat) at 101.996 per 100 of par value to yield 5.6511% on a street-convention semiannual bond basis for settlement on 24 July 2018. The total market value of the position, including accrued interest, is USD10,495,447, or 104.495447 per 100 of par value. The bond's (annual) Macaulay duration is 6.622.

1. Calculate the money duration per 100 in par value for the sovereign bond.
2. Using the money duration, estimate the loss on the position for each 1 bp increase in the yield-to-maturity for that settlement date.

Solution to 1:

The money duration is the annual modified duration times the full price of the bond per 100 of par value.

$$\left(\frac{6.622}{1+\frac{0.056511}{2}}\right) \times \text{USD}104.954472 = \text{USD}675.92$$

Solution to 2:

For each 1 bp increase in the yield-to-maturity, the loss is estimated to be USD 0.067592 per 100 of par value: USD 675.92 × 0.0001 = USD 0.067592.

Given a position size of USD 10 million in par value, the estimated loss per basis-point increase in the yield is USD 6,759.20. The money duration is per 100 of par value, so the position size of USD10 million is divided by USD 100.

$$\text{USD}0.067592 \times \frac{\text{USD}10{,}000{,}000}{\text{USD}100} = \text{USD}6{,}759.20$$

3.7 Bond Convexity

Modified duration measures the primary effect on a bond's percentage price change given a change in the yield-to-maturity. A secondary effect is measured by the convexity statistic, which is illustrated in Exhibit 10 for a traditional (option-free) fixed-rate bond.

Exhibit 10 Convexity of a Traditional (Option-Free) Fixed-Rate Bond

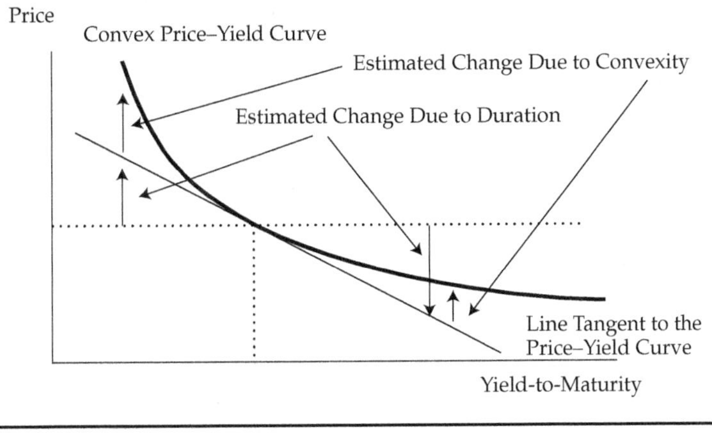

The true relationship between the bond price and the yield-to-maturity is the curved (convex) line shown in Exhibit 10. This curved line shows the actual bond price given its market discount rate. Duration (in particular, money duration) estimates the change in the bond price along the straight line that is tangent to the curved line. For small yield-to-maturity changes, there is little difference between the lines. But for larger changes, the difference becomes significant.

The convexity statistic for the bond is used to improve the estimate of the percentage price change provided by modified duration alone. Equation 13 is the convexity-adjusted estimate of the percentage change in the bond's full price.[5]

$$\%\Delta PV^{Full} \approx$$

$$(-\text{AnnModDur} \times \Delta\text{Yield}) + \left[\frac{1}{2} \times \text{AnnConvexity} \times (\Delta\text{Yield})^2\right] \quad (13)$$

The first bracketed expression, the "first-order" effect, is the same as Equation 6. The (annual) modified duration, AnnModDur, is multiplied by the change in the (annual) yield-to-maturity, ΔYield. The second bracketed expression, the "second-order" effect, is the **convexity adjustment**. The convexity adjustment is the annual convexity statistic, AnnConvexity, times one-half, multiplied by the change in the yield-to-maturity *squared.* This additional term is a positive amount on a traditional (option-free) fixed-rate bond for either an increase or decrease in the yield. In Exhibit 10, this amount adds to the linear estimate provided by the duration alone, which brings the adjusted estimate very close to the actual price on the curved line. But it still is an estimate, so the ≈ sign is used.

Similar to the Macaulay and modified durations, the annual convexity statistic can be calculated in several ways. It can be calculated using tables, such as Exhibits 2 and 3. It also is possible to derive a closed-form equation for the convexity of a fixed-rate bond on and between coupon payment dates using calculus and algebra.[6] But like modified duration, convexity can be approximated with accuracy. Equation 14 is the formula for the approximate convexity statistic, ApproxCon.

$$\text{ApproxCon} = \frac{(PV_-) + (PV_+) - [2 \times (PV_0)]}{(\Delta\text{Yield})^2 \times (PV_0)} \quad (14)$$

This equation uses the same inputs as Equation 7 for ApproxModDur. The new price when the yield-to-maturity is increased is PV_+. The new price when the yield is decreased by the same amount is PV_-. The original price is PV_0. These are the full prices, including accrued interest, for the bond.

The accuracy of this approximation can be demonstrated with the special case of a zero-coupon bond. The absence of coupon payments simplifies the interest rate risk measures. The Macaulay duration of a zero-coupon bond is $N - t/T$ in terms of periods to maturity. The exact convexity statistic of a zero-coupon bond, also in terms of periods, is calculated with Equation 15.

$$\text{Convexity (of a zero-coupon bond)} = \frac{[N - (t/T)] \times [N + 1 - (t/T)]}{(1 + r)^2} \quad (15)$$

N is the number of periods to maturity as of the beginning of the current period, t/T is the fraction of the period that has gone by, and r is the yield-to-maturity per period.

For an example of this calculation, consider a long-term, zero-coupon US Treasury bond. The bond's Bloomberg YAS page is shown in Exhibit 11.

5 Readers who have studied calculus will recognize this equation as the first two terms of a Taylor series expansion. The first term, the modified duration, includes the first derivative of the bond price with respect to a change in the yield. The second term, the convexity, includes the second derivative.

6 The step-by-step derivation of this formula is in Donald J. Smith, *Bond Math: The Theory behind the Formulas*, 2nd edition (Hoboken, NJ: John Wiley & Sons, 2014).

Exhibit 11 Bloomberg YAS Page for the Zero-Coupon US Treasury Bond

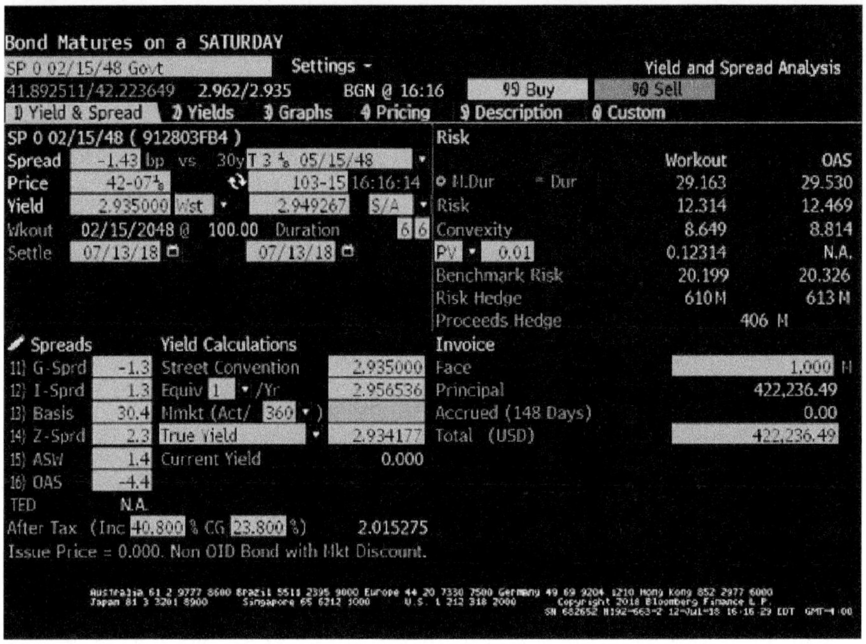

The bond matures on 15 February 2048 and its asked price was 42.223649 per 100 of par value for settlement on 13 July 2018. Its yield-to-maturity was 2.935% stated on a street-convention semiannual bond basis. Even though it is a zero-coupon bond, its yield-to-maturity is based on the actual/actual day-count convention. That settlement date was 148 days into a 181-day period. The annual modified duration was 29.163.

For this bond, $N = 60$, $t/T = 148/181$, and $r = 0.02935/2$. Entering these variables into Equation 15 produces a convexity of 3,459.45 in terms of semiannual periods.

$$\frac{\left[60-(148/181)\right]\times\left[60+1-(148/181)\right]}{\left(1+\dfrac{0.02935}{2}\right)^{2}} = 3{,}459.45$$

As with the other statistics, convexity is annualized in practice and for use in the convexity adjustment in Equation 13. It is divided by the periodicity *squared.* The yield-to-maturity on this zero-coupon bond is stated on a semiannual bond basis, meaning a periodicity of 2. Therefore, the annualized convexity statistic is 864.9.

$$\frac{3{,}459.45}{4} = 864.9$$

For example, suppose that the yield-to-maturity is expected to fall by 10 bps, from 2.935% to 2.835%. Given the (annual) modified duration of 29.163 and (annual) convexity of 864.9, the expected percentage price gain is 2.9595%.

$$\begin{aligned}\%\Delta PV^{Full} &\approx \left[-29.163\times -0.0010\right]+\left[\frac{1}{2}\times 864.9\times(-0.0010)^{2}\right]\\ &= 0.029163 + 0.000432\\ &= 0.029595\end{aligned}$$

Modified duration alone (under)estimates the gain to be 2.9163%. The convexity adjustment adds 4.32 bps.

The long-term, zero-coupon bond of Exhibit 11 demonstrates the difference between *yield* duration and convexity and *curve* duration and convexity, even on an option-free bond. Its modified duration is 29.163, whereas its effective duration is 29.530. Its yield convexity is reported on the Bloomberg page to be 8.649, and its effective convexity is 8.814. (Note that Bloomberg scales the convexity statistics by dividing by 100.) In general, the differences are heightened when the benchmark yield curve is not flat, when the bond has a long time-to-maturity, and the bond is priced at a significant discount or premium.

To obtain the ApproxCon for this long-term, zero-coupon bond, calculate PV_0, PV_+, and PV_- for yields-to-maturity of 2.935%, 2.945%, and 2.925%, respectively. For this exercise, ΔYield = 0.0001.

$$PV_0 = \frac{100}{\left(1+\frac{0.02935}{2}\right)^{60}} \times \left(1+\frac{0.02935}{2}\right)^{148/181} = 42.223649$$

$$PV_+ = \frac{100}{\left(1+\frac{0.02945}{2}\right)^{60}} \times \left(1+\frac{0.02945}{2}\right)^{148/181} = 42.100694$$

$$PV_- = \frac{100}{\left(1+\frac{0.02925}{2}\right)^{60}} \times \left(1+\frac{0.02925}{2}\right)^{148/181} = 42.346969$$

Using these results, first calculate ApproxModDur using Equation 7 to confirm that these inputs are correct. In Exhibit 11, modified duration is stated to be 29.163.

$$\text{ApproxModDur} = \frac{42.346969 - 42.100694}{2 \times 0.0001 \times 42.223649} = 29.163$$

Using Equation 14, ApproxCon is 864.9.

$$\text{ApproxCon} = \frac{42.346969 + 42.100694 - (2 \times 42.223649)}{(0.0001)^2 \times 42.223649} = 864.9$$

This result, 864.9, is an approximation for *annualized* convexity. The number of periods in the year is included in the price calculations. This approximation in this example is the same as the "exact" result using the closed-form equation for the special case of the zero-coupon bond. Any small difference is not likely to be meaningful for practical applications.

Because this is an individual zero-coupon bond, it is easy to calculate the new price if the yield-to-maturity does go down by 50 bps, to 2.435%.

$$\frac{100}{\left(1+\frac{0.02435}{2}\right)^{60}} \times \left(1+\frac{0.02435}{2}\right)^{148/181} = 48.860850$$

Therefore, the actual percentage price increase is 15.7192%.

$$\frac{48.860850 - 42.223649}{42.223649} = 0.157192$$

The convexity-adjusted estimate is 15.6626%.

$$\%\Delta PV^{Full} \approx (-29.163 \times -0.0050) + \left[\frac{1}{2} \times 864.9 \times (-0.0050)^2\right]$$
$$= 0.145815 + 01010811$$
$$= 0.156626$$

EXAMPLE 13

An Italian bank holds a large position in a 7.25% annual coupon payment corporate bond that matures on 4 April 2034. The bond's yield-to-maturity is 7.44% for settlement on 27 June 2019, stated as an effective annual rate. That settlement date is 83 days into the 360-day year using the 30/360 method of counting days.

1 Calculate the full price of the bond per 100 of par value.
2 Calculate the approximate modified duration and approximate convexity using a 1 bp increase and decrease in the yield-to-maturity.
3 Calculate the estimated convexity-adjusted percentage price change resulting from a 100 bp increase in the yield-to-maturity.
4 Compare the estimated percentage price change with the actual change, assuming the yield-to-maturity jumps to 8.44% on that settlement date.

Solutions:

There are 15 years from the beginning of the current period on 4 April 2019 to maturity on 4 April 2034.

1 The full price of the bond is 99.956780 per 100 of par value.

$$PV_0 = \left[\frac{7.25}{(1.0744)^1} + \cdots + \frac{107.25}{(1.0744)^{15}}\right] \times (1.0744)^{83/360} = 99.956780$$

2 $PV_+ = 99.869964$, and $PV_- = 100.043703$.

$$PV_+ = \left[\frac{7.25}{(1.0745)^1} + \cdots + \frac{107.25}{(1.0745)^{15}}\right] \times (1.0745)^{83/360} = 99.869964$$

$$PV_- = \left[\frac{7.25}{(1.0743)^1} + \cdots + \frac{107.25}{(1.0743)^{15}}\right] \times (1.0743)^{83/360} = 100.043703$$

The approximate modified duration is 8.6907.

$$\text{ApproxModDur} = \frac{100.043703 - 99.869964}{2 \times 0.0001 \times 99.956780} = 8.6907$$

The approximate convexity is 107.157.

$$\text{ApproxCon} = \frac{100.043703 + 99.869964 - (2 \times 99.956780)}{(0.0001)^2 \times 99.956780} = 107.157$$

3 The convexity-adjusted percentage price drop resulting from a 100 bp increase in the yield-to-maturity is estimated to be 8.1555%. Modified duration alone estimates the percentage drop to be 8.6907%. The convexity adjustment adds 53.52 bps.

$$\%\Delta PV^{Full} \approx (-8.6907 \times 0.0100) + \left[\frac{1}{2} \times 107.157 \times (-0.0100)^2\right]$$
$$= -0.086907 + 0.005358$$
$$= -0.81549$$

4 The new full price if the yield-to-maturity goes from 7.44% to 8.44% on that settlement date is 91.780921.

$$PV^{Full} = \left[\frac{7.25}{(1.0844)^1} + \cdots + \frac{107.25}{(1.0844)^{15}}\right] \times (1.0844)^{83/360} = 91.780921$$

$$\%\Delta PV^{Full} = \frac{91.780921 - 99.956780}{99.956780} = -0.081794$$

The actual percentage change in the bond price is –8.1794%. The convexity-adjusted estimate is –8.1549%, whereas the estimated change using modified duration alone is –8.6907%.

The money duration of a bond indicates the first-order effect on the full price of a bond in units of currency given a change in the yield-to-maturity. The **money convexity** statistic (MoneyCon) is the second-order effect. The money convexity of the bond is the annual convexity multiplied by the full price, such that:

$$\Delta PV^{Full} \approx -(\text{MoneyDur} \times \Delta\text{Yield}) + \left[\frac{1}{2} \times \text{MoneyCon} \times (\Delta\text{Yield})^2\right] \quad (16)$$

For a money convexity example, consider again the Hong Kong–based life insurance company that has a HKD100,000,000 position in the 6.00% bond that matures on 14 February 2027. In Section 3.5, using the money duration alone, the estimated loss is HKD6,184,418 if the yield-to-maturity increases by 100 bps. The money duration for the position is HKD618,441,784. That estimation is improved by including the convexity adjustment. In Section 3.1, these inputs are calculated to obtain the approximate modified duration of 6.1268 for a 5 bp change in the yield-to-maturity (ΔYield = 0.0005): PV_0 = 100.940423, PV_+ = 100.631781, and PV_- = 101.250227. Enter these into Equation 14 to calculate the approximate convexity.

$$\text{ApproxCon} = \frac{101.250227 + 100.631781 - (2 \times 100.940423)}{(0.0005)^2 \times 100.940423} = 46.047$$

The money convexity is 46.047 times the market value of the position, HKD100,940,423. The convexity-adjusted loss given a 100 bp jump in the yield-to-maturity is HKD5,952,018.

$$-[(6.1268 \times \text{HKD}100{,}940{,}423) \times 0.0100] +$$
$$\left[\frac{1}{2} \times (46.047 \times \text{HKD}100{,}940{,}423) \times (0.0100)^2\right]$$
$$= -\text{HKD}6{,}184{,}418 + \text{HKD}232{,}400$$
$$= -\text{HKD}5{,}952{,}018$$

The factors that lead to greater convexity are the same as for duration. A fixed-rate bond with a longer time-to-maturity, a lower coupon rate, and a lower yield-to-maturity has greater convexity than a bond with a shorter time-to-maturity, a higher coupon rate, and a higher yield-to-maturity. Another factor is the dispersion of cash flows, meaning the degree to which payments are spread out over time. If two bonds have the same duration, the one that has the greater dispersion of cash flows has the greater convexity. The positive attributes of greater convexity for an investor are shown in Exhibit 12.

Exhibit 12 The Positive Attributes of Greater Bond Convexity on a Traditional (Option-Free) Bond

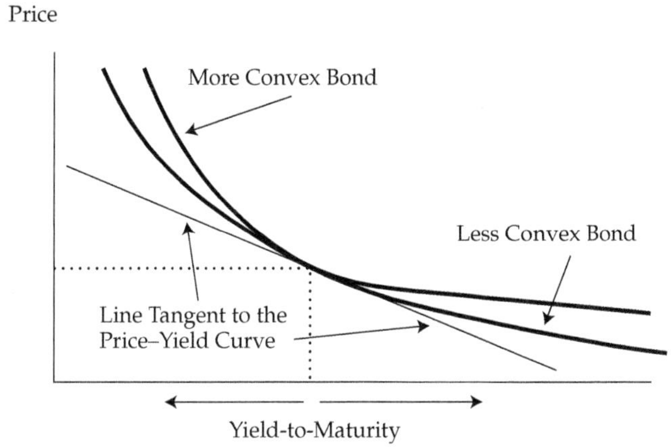

The two bonds in Exhibit 12 are assumed to have the same price, yield-to-maturity, and modified duration. Therefore, they share the same line tangent to their price–yield curves. The benefit of greater convexity occurs when their yields-to-maturity change. For the same decrease in yield-to-maturity, the more convex bond *appreciates more* in price. And for the same increase in yield-to-maturity, the more convex bond *depreciates less* in price. The conclusion is that the more convex bond outperforms the less convex bond in both bull (rising price) and bear (falling price) markets. This conclusion assumes, however, that this positive attribute is not "priced into" the bond. To the extent that it is included, the more convex bond would have a higher price (and lower yield-to-maturity). That does not diminish the value of convexity. It only suggests that the investor has to pay for it. As economists say, "There is no such thing as a free lunch."

EXAMPLE 14

The investment manager for a UK defined-benefit pension scheme is considering two bonds about to be issued by a large life insurance company. The first is a 30-year, 4% semiannual coupon payment bond. The second is a 100-year, 4% semiannual coupon payment "century" bond. Both bonds are expected to trade at par value at issuance.

Calculate the approximate modified duration and approximate convexity for each bond using a 5 bp increase and decrease in the annual yield-to-maturity. Retain accuracy to six decimals per 100 of par value.

Solution:

In the calculations, the yield per semiannual period goes up by 2.5 bps to 2.025% and down by 2.5 bps to 1.975%. The 30-year bond has an approximate modified duration of 17.381 and an approximate convexity of 420.80.

$$PV_+ = \frac{2}{(1.02025)^1} + \cdots + \frac{102}{(1.02025)^{60}} = 99.136214$$

$$PV_- = \frac{2}{(1.01975)^1} + \cdots + \frac{102}{(1.01975)^{60}} = 100.874306$$

$$\text{ApproxModDur} = \frac{100.874306 - 99.136214}{2 \times 0.0005 \times 100} = 17.381$$

$$\text{ApproxCon} = \frac{100.874306 + 99.136214 - (2 \times 100)}{(0.0005)^2 \times 100} = 420.80$$

The 100-year century bond has an approximate modified duration of 24.527 and an approximate convexity of 1,132.88.

$$PV_+ = \frac{2}{(1.02025)^1} + \cdots + \frac{102}{(1.02025)^{200}} = 98.787829$$

$$PV_- = \frac{2}{(1.01975)^1} + \cdots + \frac{102}{(1.01975)^{200}} = 101.240493$$

$$\text{ApproxModDur} = \frac{101.240493 - 98.787829}{2 \times 0.0005 \times 100} = 24.527$$

$$\text{ApproxCon} = \frac{101.240493 + 98.787829 - (2 \times 100)}{(0.0005)^2 \times 100} = 1{,}132.88$$

The century bond offers a higher modified duration—24.527 compared with 17.381—and a much greater degree of convexity—1,132.88 compared with 420.80.

In the same manner that the primary, or first-order, effect of a shift in the benchmark yield curve is measured by effective duration, the secondary, or second-order, effect is measured by **effective convexity**. The effective convexity of a bond is a *curve convexity* statistic that measures the secondary effect of a change in a benchmark yield curve. A pricing model is used to determine the new prices when the benchmark curve is shifted upward (PV_+) and downward (PV_-) by the same amount (ΔCurve). These changes are made holding other factors constant—for example, the credit spread. Then, Equation 17 is used to calculate the effective convexity (EffCon) given the initial price (PV_0).

$$\text{EffCon} = \frac{[(PV_-) + (PV_+)] - [2 \times (PV_0)]}{(\Delta\text{Curve})^2 \times (PV_0)} \quad (17)$$

This equation is very similar to Equation 14, for approximate *yield* convexity. The difference is that in Equation 14, the denominator includes the change in the yield-to-maturity squared, $(\Delta\text{Yield})^2$. Here, the denominator includes the change in the benchmark yield curve squared, $(\Delta\text{Curve})^2$.

Consider again the callable bond example in Section 3.2. It is assumed that an option-pricing model is used to generate these callable bond prices: PV_0 = 101.060489, PV_+ = 99.050120, PV_- = 102.890738, and ΔCurve = 0.0025. The effective duration for the callable bond is 7.6006.

$$\text{EffDur} = \frac{102.890738 - 99.050120}{2 \times 0.0025 \times 101.060489} = 7.6006$$

Using these inputs in Equation 17, the effective convexity is –285.17.

$$\text{EffCon} = \frac{102.890738 + 99.050120 - (2 \times 101.060489)}{(0.0025)^2 \times 101.060489} = -285.17$$

Negative convexity, which could be called "concavity," is an important feature of callable bonds. Putable bonds, on the other hand, always have positive convexity. As a second-order effect, effective convexity indicates the change in the first-order effect (i.e., effective duration) as the benchmark yield curve is changed. In Exhibit 8, as the benchmark yield goes down, the slope of the line tangent to the curve for the non-callable bond steepens, which indicates positive convexity. But the slope of the line tangent to the callable bond flattens as the benchmark yield goes down. Technically, it reaches an inflection point, which is when the effective convexity shifts from positive to negative.

In summary, when the benchmark yield is high and the value of the embedded call option is low, the callable and the non-callable bonds experience very similar effects from interest rate changes. They both have positive convexity. But as the benchmark yield is reduced, the curves diverge. At some point, the callable bond moves into the range of negative convexity, which indicates that the embedded call option has more value to the issuer and is more likely to be exercised. This situation limits the potential price appreciation of the bond arising from lower interest rates, whether because of a lower benchmark yield or a lower credit spread.

Another way to understand why a callable bond can have negative convexity is to rearrange Equation 17.

$$\text{EffCon} = \frac{\left[(PV_-) - (PV_0)\right] - \left[(PV_0) - (PV_+)\right]}{(\Delta\text{Curve})^2 \times (PV_0)}$$

In the numerator, the first bracketed expression is the increase in price when the benchmark yield curve is lowered. The second expression is the decrease in price when the benchmark yield curve is raised. On a non-callable bond, the increase is always larger than the decrease (in absolute value). This result is the "convexity effect" for the relationship between bond prices and yields-to-maturity. On a callable bond, the increase can be smaller than the decrease (in absolute value). That creates negative convexity, as illustrated in Exhibit 8.

4 INTEREST RATE RISK AND THE INVESTMENT HORIZON

This section explores the effect of yield volatility on the investment horizon, and on the interaction between the investment horizon, market price risk, and coupon reinvestment risk.

4.1 Yield Volatility

An important aspect in understanding the interest rate risk and return characteristics of an investment in a fixed-rate bond is the time horizon. This section considers a short-term horizon. A primary concern for the investor is the change in the price of the bond given a sudden (i.e., same-day) change in its yield-to-maturity. The accrued interest does not change, so the impact of the change in the yield is on the flat price of the bond. Section 4.2 considers a long-term horizon. The reinvestment of coupon interest then becomes a key factor in the investor's horizon yield.

Bond duration is the primary measure of risk arising from a change in the yield-to-maturity. Convexity is the secondary risk measure. In the discussion of the impact on the bond price, the phrase "for a *given* change in the yield-to-maturity" is used repeatedly. For instance, the given change in the yield-to-maturity could be 1 bp, 25 bps, or 100 bps. In comparing two bonds, it is assumed that the "given change" is the same for both securities. When the government bond par curve is shifted up or down by the same amount to calculate effective duration and effective convexity, the events are described as "parallel" yield curve shifts. Because yield curves are rarely (if ever) straight lines, this shift may also be described as a "shape-preserving" shift to the yield curve. The key assumption is that all yields-to-maturity under consideration rise or fall by the same amount across the curve.

Although the assumption of a parallel shift in the yield curve is common in fixed-income analysis, it is not always realistic. In reality, the shape of the yield curve changes based on factors affecting the supply and demand of shorter-term versus longer-term securities. In fact, the term structure of bond yields (also called the "term structure of interest rates") is typically upward sloping. However, the **term structure of yield volatility** may have a different shape depending on a number of factors. The term structure of yield volatility is the relationship between the volatility of bond yields-to-maturity and times-to-maturity.

For example, a central bank engaging in expansionary monetary policy might cause the yield curve to steepen by reducing short-term interest rates. But this policy might cause greater *volatility* in short-term bond yields-to-maturity than in longer-term bonds, resulting in a downward-sloping term structure of yield volatility. Longer-term bond yields are mostly determined by future inflation and economic growth expectations. Those expectations often tend to be less volatile.

The importance of yield volatility in measuring interest rate risk is that bond price changes are products of two factors: (1) the impact *per* basis-point change in the yield-to-maturity and (2) the *number* of basis points in the yield-to-maturity change. The first factor is duration or the combination of duration and convexity, and the second factor is the yield volatility. For example, consider a 5-year bond with a modified duration of 4.5 and a 30-year bond with a modified duration of 18.0. Clearly, for a *given* change in yield-to-maturity, the 30-year bond represents more much more interest rate risk to an investor who has a short-term horizon. In fact, the 30-year bond appears to have *four times* the risk given the ratio of the modified durations. But that assumption neglects the possibility that the 30-year bond might have half the yield volatility of the 5-year bond.

Equation 13, restated here, summarizes the two factors.

$$\%\Delta PV^{Full} \approx (-\text{AnnModDur} \times \Delta\text{Yield}) + \left[\frac{1}{2} \times \text{AnnConvexity} \times (\Delta\text{Yield})^2\right]$$

The estimated percentage change in the bond price depends on the modified duration and convexity as well as on the yield-to-maturity change. Parallel shifts between two bond yields and along a benchmark yield curve are common assumptions in fixed-income analysis. However, an analyst must be aware that non-parallel shifts frequently occur in practice.

EXAMPLE 15

A fixed-income analyst is asked to rank three bonds in terms of interest rate risk. Interest rate risk here means the potential price decrease on a percentage basis given a sudden change in financial market conditions. The increases in the yields-to-maturity represent the "worst case" for the scenario being considered.

Bond	Modified Duration	Convexity	ΔYield
A	3.72	12.1	25 bps
B	5.81	40.7	15 bps
C	12.39	158.0	10 bps

The modified duration and convexity statistics are annualized. ΔYield is the increase in the annual yield-to-maturity. Rank the bonds in terms of interest rate risk.

Solution:

Calculate the estimated percentage price change for each bond:

Bond A:

$$(-3.72 \times 0.0025) + \left[\frac{1}{2} \times 12.1 \times (0.0025)^2\right] = -0.009262$$

Bond B:

$$(-5.81 \times 0.0015) + \left[\frac{1}{2} \times 40.7 \times (0.0015)^2\right] = -0.008669$$

Bond C:

$$(-12.39 \times 0.0010) + \left[\frac{1}{2} \times 158.0 \times (0.0010)^2\right] = -0.012311$$

Based on these assumed changes in the yield-to-maturity and the modified duration and convexity risk measures, Bond C has the highest degree of interest rate risk (a potential loss of 1.2311%), followed by Bond A (a potential loss of 0.9262%) and Bond B (a potential loss of 0.8669%).

4.2 Investment Horizon, Macaulay Duration, and Interest Rate Risk

Although short-term interest rate risk is a concern to some investors, other investors have a long-term horizon. Day-to-day changes in bond prices cause *unrealized* capital gains and losses. Those unrealized gains and losses might need to be accounted for in financial statements. This section considers a long-term investor concerned only with the total return over the investment horizon. Therefore, interest rate risk is important to this investor. The investor faces coupon reinvestment risk as well as market price risk if the bond needs to be sold prior to maturity.

Earlier, we discussed examples of interest rate risk using a 10-year, 8% annual coupon payment bond that is priced at 85.503075 per 100 of par value. The bond's yield-to-maturity is 10.40%. A key result in Example 3 is that an investor with a 10-year time horizon is concerned only with coupon reinvestment risk. This situation assumes, of course, that the issuer makes all of the coupon and principal payments as scheduled. The buy-and-hold investor has a higher total return if interest rates rise (see Example 3) and a lower total return if rates fall (see Example 5). The investor in

Examples 4 and 6 has a four-year horizon. This investor faces market price risk in addition to coupon reinvestment risk. In fact, the market price risk dominates because this investor has a higher total return if interest rates fall (see Example 6) and a lower return if rates rise (see Example 4).

Now, consider a third investor who has a seven-year time horizon. If interest rates remain at 10.40%, the future value of reinvested coupon interest is 76.835787 per 100 of par value.

$$\left[8 \times (1.1040)^6\right] + \left[8 \times (1.1040)^5\right] + \left[8 \times (1.1040)^4\right] + \left[8 \times (1.1040)^3\right] +$$
$$\left[8 \times (1.1040)^2\right] + \left[8 \times (1.1040)^1\right] + 8 = 76.835787$$

The bond is sold for a price of 94.073336, assuming that the bond stays on the constant-yield price trajectory and continues to be "pulled to par."

$$\frac{8}{(1.1040)^1} + \frac{8}{(1.1040)^2} + \frac{108}{(1.1040)^3} = 94.073336$$

The total return is 170.909123 (= 76.835787 + 94.073336) per 100 of par value, and the horizon yield, as expected, is 10.40%.

$$85.503075 = \frac{170.909123}{(1+r)^7}, \quad r = 0.1040$$

Following Examples 3 and 4, assume that the yield-to-maturity on the bond rises to 11.40%. Also, coupon interest is now reinvested each year at 11.40%. The future value of reinvested coupons becomes 79.235183 per 100 of par value.

$$\left[8 \times (1.1140)^6\right] + \left[8 \times (1.1140)^5\right] + \left[8 \times (1.1140)^4\right] + \left[8 \times (1.1140)^3\right] +$$
$$\left[8 \times (1.1140)^2\right] + \left[8 \times (1.1140)^1\right] + 8 = 79.235183$$

After receiving the seventh coupon payment, the bond is sold. There is a capital loss because the price, although much higher than at purchase, is below the constant-yield price trajectory.

$$\frac{8}{(1.1140)^1} + \frac{8}{(1.1140)^2} + \frac{108}{(1.1140)^3} = 91.748833$$

The total return is 170.984016 (= 79.235183 + 91.748833) per 100 of par value and the holding-period rate of return is 10.407%.

$$85.503075 = \frac{170.984016}{(1+r)^7}, \quad r = 0.10407$$

Following Examples 5 and 6, assume that the coupon reinvestment rates and the bond yield-to-maturity fall to 9.40%. The future value of reinvested coupons is 74.512177.

$$\left[8 + (1.0940)^6\right] + \left[8 + (1.0940)^5\right] + \left[8 + (1.0940)^4\right] + \left[8 + (1.0940)^3\right] +$$
$$\left[8 + (1.0940)^2\right] + \left[8 + (1.0940)^1\right] + 8 = 74.52177$$

The bond is sold at a capital gain because the price is above the constant-yield price trajectory.

$$\frac{8}{(1.0940)^1} + \frac{8}{(1.0940)^2} + \frac{108}{(1.0940)^3} = 96.481299$$

The total return is 170.993476 (= 74.512177 + 96.481299) per 100 of par value, and the horizon yield is 10.408%.

$$85.503075 = \frac{170.993476}{(1 + r)^7}, \quad r = 0.10408$$

These results are summarized in the following table to reveal the remarkable outcome: The total returns and horizon yields are virtually the same. The investor with the 7-year horizon, unlike those having a 4- or 10-year horizon, achieves the same holding-period rate of return whether interest rates rise, fall, or remain the same. Note that the terms "horizon yield" and "holding-period rate of return" are used interchangeably in this reading. Sometimes "horizon yield" refers to yields on bonds that need to be sold at the end of the investor's holding period.

Interest Rate	Future Value of Reinvested Coupon	Sale Price	Total Return	Horizon Yield
9.40%	74.512177	96.481299	170.993476	10.408%
10.40%	76.835787	94.073336	170.909123	10.400%
11.40%	79.235183	91.748833	170.984016	10.407%

This particular bond was chosen as an example to demonstrate an important property of Macaulay duration: For a particular assumption about yield volatility, Macaulay duration indicates the investment horizon for which coupon reinvestment risk and market price risk offset each other. In Section 3.1, the Macaulay duration of this 10-year, 8% annual payment bond is calculated to be 7.0029 years. This is one of the applications for duration in which "years" is meaningful and in which Macaulay duration is used rather than modified duration. The particular assumption about yield volatility is that there is a one-time "parallel" shift in the yield curve that occurs before the next coupon payment date. Exhibit 13 illustrates this property of bond duration, assuming that the bond is initially priced at par value.

Exhibit 13 Interest Rate Risk, Macaulay Duration, and the Investment Horizon

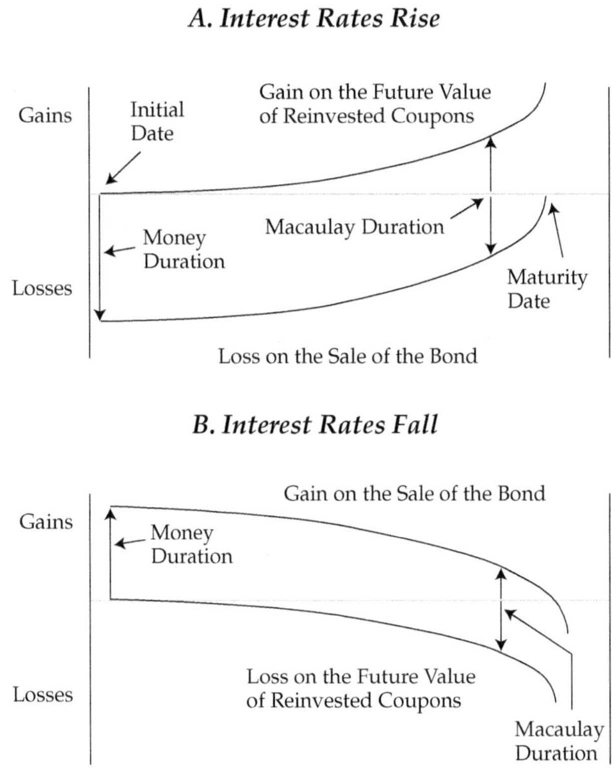

As demonstrated in Panel A of Exhibit 13, when interest rates rise, duration measures the immediate drop in value. In particular, the money duration indicates the change in price. Then as time passes, the bond price is "pulled to par." The gain in the future value of reinvested coupons starts small but builds over time as more coupons are received. The curve indicates the additional future value of reinvested coupons because of the higher interest rate. At some point in the lifetime of the bond, those two effects offset each other and the gain on reinvested coupons is equal to the loss on the sale of the bond. That point in time is the Macaulay duration statistic.

The same pattern is displayed in the Panel B when interest rates fall, which leads to a reduction in the bond yield and the coupon reinvestment rate. There is an immediate jump in the bond price, as measured by the money duration, but then the "pull to par" effect brings the price down as time passes. The impact from reinvesting at a lower rate starts small but then becomes more significant over time. The loss on reinvested coupons is with respect to the future value if interest rates had not fallen. Once again, the bond's Macaulay duration indicates the point in time when the two effects offset each other and the gain on the sale of the bond matches the loss on coupon reinvestment.

The earlier numerical example and Exhibit 13 allow for a statement of the general relationships among interest rate risk, the Macaulay duration, and the investment horizon.

1 When the investment horizon is greater than the Macaulay duration of a bond, coupon reinvestment risk dominates market price risk. The investor's risk is to lower interest rates.

2 When the investment horizon is equal to the Macaulay duration of a bond, coupon reinvestment risk offsets market price risk.

3 When the investment horizon is less than the Macaulay duration of the bond, market price risk dominates coupon reinvestment risk. The investor's risk is to higher interest rates.

In the numerical example, the Macaulay duration of the bond is 7.0 years. Statement 1 reflects the investor with the 10-year horizon; Statement 2, the investor with the 7-year horizon; and Statement 3, the investor with the 4-year horizon.

The difference between the Macaulay duration of a bond and the investment horizon is called the **duration gap**. The duration gap is a bond's Macaulay duration minus the investment horizon. The investor with the 10-year horizon has a negative duration gap and currently is at risk of lower rates. The investor with the 7-year horizon has a duration gap of zero and currently is hedged against interest rate risk. The investor with the 4-year horizon has a positive duration gap and currently is at risk of higher rates. The word "currently" is important because interest rate risk is connected to an *immediate* change in the bond's yield-to-maturity and the coupon reinvestment rates. As time passes, the investment horizon is reduced and the Macaulay duration of the bond also changes. Therefore, the duration gap changes as well.

EXAMPLE 16

An investor plans to retire in 10 years. As part of the retirement portfolio, the investor buys a newly issued, 12-year, 8% annual coupon payment bond. The bond is purchased at par value, so its yield-to-maturity is 8.00% stated as an effective annual rate.

1 Calculate the approximate Macaulay duration for the bond, using a 1 bp increase and decrease in the yield-to-maturity and calculating the new prices per 100 of par value to six decimal places.

2 Calculate the duration gap at the time of purchase.

3 Does this bond at purchase entail the risk of higher or lower interest rates? Interest rate risk here means an immediate, one-time, parallel yield curve shift.

Solution to 1:

The approximate modified duration of the bond is 7.5361. $PV_0 = 100$, $PV_+ = 99.924678$, and $PV_- = 100.075400$.

$$PV_+ = \frac{8}{(1.0801)^1} + \cdots + \frac{108}{(1.0801)^{12}} = 99.924678$$

$$PV_- = \frac{8}{(1.0799)^1} + \cdots + \frac{108}{(1.0799)^{12}} = 100.075400$$

$$\text{ApproxModDur} = \frac{100.075400 - 99.924678}{2 \times 0.0001 \times 100} = 7.5361$$

The approximate Macaulay duration is 8.1390 (= 7.5361 × 1.08).

Solution to 2:

Given an investment horizon of 10 years, the duration gap for this bond at purchase is negative: 8.1390 – 10 = –1.8610.

Solution to 3:

A negative duration gap entails the risk of lower interest rates. To be precise, the risk is an immediate, one-time, parallel, downward yield curve shift because coupon reinvestment risk dominates market price risk. The loss from reinvesting coupons at a rate lower than 8% is larger than the gain from selling the bond at a price above the constant-yield price trajectory.

5 CREDIT AND LIQUIDITY RISK

The focus of this reading is to demonstrate how bond duration and convexity estimate the bond price change, either in percentage terms or in units of currency, given an assumed yield-to-maturity change. This section addresses the *source* of the change in the yield-to-maturity. In general, the yield-to-maturity on a corporate bond is composed of a government *benchmark* yield and a *spread* over that benchmark. A change in the bond's yield-to-maturity can originate in either component or a combination of the two.

The key point is that for a traditional (option-free) fixed-rate bond, the same duration and convexity statistics apply for a change in the benchmark yield as for a change in the spread. The "building blocks" approach from "Introduction to Fixed-Income Valuation" shows that these yield-to-maturity changes can be broken down further. A change in the benchmark yield can arise from a change in either the expected inflation rate or the expected real rate of interest. A change in the spread can arise from a change in the credit risk of the issuer or in the liquidity of the bond. Therefore, for a fixed-rate bond, the "inflation duration," the "real rate duration," the "credit duration," and the "liquidity duration" are all the same number. The inflation duration would indicate the change in the bond price if expected inflation were to change by a certain amount. In the same manner, the real rate duration would indicate the bond price change if the real rate were to go up or down. The credit duration and liquidity duration would indicate the price sensitivity that would arise from changes in those building blocks in the yield-to-maturity. A bond with a modified duration of 5.00 and a convexity of 32.00 will appreciate in value by about 1.26% if its yield-to-maturity goes down by 25 bps: $(-5.00 \times -0.0025) + [1/2 \times 32.00 \times (-0.0025)^2] = +\ 0.0126$, regardless of the *source* of the yield-to-maturity change.

Suppose that the yield-to-maturity on a corporate bond is 6.00%. If the benchmark yield is 4.25%, the spread is 1.75%. An analyst believes that credit risk makes up 1.25% of the spread and liquidity risk, the remaining 0.50%. Credit risk includes the probability of default as well as the recovery of assets if default does occur. A credit rating downgrade or an adverse change in the ratings outlook for a borrower reflects a higher risk of default. Liquidity risk refers to the transaction costs associated with selling a bond. In general, a bond with greater frequency of trading and a higher volume of trading provides fixed-income investors with more opportunity to purchase or sell the security and thus has less liquidity risk. In practice, there is a difference between the *bid* (or purchase) and the *offer* (or sale) price. This difference depends on the type of bond, the size of the transaction, and the time of execution, among other factors. For instance, government bonds often trade at just a few basis points between the purchase and sale prices. More thinly traded corporate bonds can have a much wider difference between the bid and offer prices.

The problem for a fixed-income analyst is that it is rare for the changes in the components of the overall yield-to-maturity to occur in isolation. In practice, the analyst is concerned with the *interaction* between changes in benchmark yields and spreads, between changes in expected inflation and the expected real rate, and between changes in credit and liquidity risk. For example, during a financial crisis, a "flight to quality" can cause government benchmark yields to fall as credit spreads widen. An unexpected credit downgrade on a corporate bond can result in greater credit as well as liquidity risk.

EXAMPLE 17

The (flat) price on a fixed-rate corporate bond falls one day from 92.25 to 91.25 per 100 of par value because of poor earnings and an unexpected ratings downgrade of the issuer. The (annual) modified duration for the bond is 7.24. Which of the following is *closest* to the estimated change in the credit spread on the corporate bond, assuming benchmark yields are unchanged?

A 15 bps
B 100 bps
C 108 bps

Solution:

Given that the price falls from 92.25 to 91.25, the percentage price decrease is 1.084%.

$$\frac{91.25 - 92.25}{92.25} = -0.01084$$

Given an annual modified duration of 7.24, the change in the yield-to-maturity is 14.97 bps.

$$-0.01084 \approx -7.24 \times \Delta\text{Yield}, \Delta\text{Yield} = 0.001497$$

Therefore, the answer is A. The change in price reflects a credit spread increase on the bond of about 15 bps.

SUMMARY

This reading covers the risk and return characteristics of fixed-rate bonds. The focus is on the widely used measures of interest rate risk—duration and convexity. These statistics are used extensively in fixed-income analysis. The following are the main points made in the reading:

- The three sources of return on a fixed-rate bond purchased at par value are: (1) receipt of the promised coupon and principal payments on the scheduled dates, (2) reinvestment of coupon payments, and (3) potential capital gains, as well as losses, on the sale of the bond prior to maturity.
- For a bond purchased at a discount or premium, the rate of return also includes the effect of the price being "pulled to par" as maturity nears, assuming no default.
- The total return is the future value of reinvested coupon interest payments and the sale price (or redemption of principal if the bond is held to maturity).
- The horizon yield (or holding period rate of return) is the internal rate of return between the total return and purchase price of the bond.
- Coupon reinvestment risk increases with a higher coupon rate and a longer reinvestment time period.

- Capital gains and losses are measured from the carrying value of the bond and not from the purchase price. The carrying value includes the amortization of the discount or premium if the bond is purchased at a price below or above par value. The carrying value is any point on the constant-yield price trajectory.
- Interest income on a bond is the return associated with the passage of time. Capital gains and losses are the returns associated with a change in the value of a bond as indicated by a change in the yield-to-maturity.
- The two types of interest rate risk on a fixed-rate bond are coupon reinvestment risk and market price risk. These risks offset each other to a certain extent. An investor gains from higher rates on reinvested coupons but loses if the bond is sold at a capital loss because the price is below the constant-yield price trajectory. An investor loses from lower rates on reinvested coupon but gains if the bond is sold at a capital gain because the price is above the constant-yield price trajectory.
- Market price risk dominates coupon reinvestment risk when the investor has a short-term horizon (relative to the time-to-maturity on the bond).
- Coupon reinvestment risk dominates market price risk when the investor has a long-term horizon (relative to the time-to-maturity)—for instance, a buy-and-hold investor.
- Bond duration, in general, measures the sensitivity of the full price (including accrued interest) to a change in interest rates.
- Yield duration statistics measuring the sensitivity of a bond's full price to the bond's own yield-to-maturity include the Macaulay duration, modified duration, money duration, and price value of a basis point.
- Curve duration statistics measuring the sensitivity of a bond's full price to the benchmark yield curve are usually called "effective durations."
- Macaulay duration is the weighted average of the time to receipt of coupon interest and principal payments, in which the weights are the shares of the full price corresponding to each payment. This statistic is annualized by dividing by the periodicity (number of coupon payments or compounding periods in a year).
- Modified duration provides a linear estimate of the percentage price change for a bond given a change in its yield-to-maturity.
- Approximate modified duration approaches modified duration as the change in the yield-to-maturity approaches zero.
- Effective duration is very similar to approximate modified duration. The difference is that approximate modified duration is a yield duration statistic that measures interest rate risk in terms of a change in the bond's own yield-to-maturity, whereas effective duration is a curve duration statistic that measures interest rate risk assuming a parallel shift in the benchmark yield curve.
- Key rate duration is a measure of a bond's sensitivity to a change in the benchmark yield curve at specific maturity segments. Key rate durations can be used to measure a bond's sensitivity to changes in the shape of the yield curve.
- Bonds with an embedded option do not have a meaningful internal rate of return because future cash flows are contingent on interest rates. Therefore, effective duration is the appropriate interest rate risk measure, not modified duration.
- The effective duration of a traditional (option-free) fixed-rate bond is its sensitivity to the benchmark yield curve, which can differ from its sensitivity to its own yield-to-maturity. Therefore, modified duration and effective duration on a traditional (option-free) fixed-rate bond are not necessarily equal.

- During a coupon period, Macaulay and modified durations decline smoothly in a "saw-tooth" pattern, assuming the yield-to-maturity is constant. When the coupon payment is made, the durations jump upward.
- Macaulay and modified durations are inversely related to the coupon rate and the yield-to-maturity.
- Time-to-maturity and Macaulay and modified durations are *usually* positively related. They are *always* positively related on bonds priced at par or at a premium above par value. They are *usually* positively related on bonds priced at a discount below par value. The exception is on long-term, low-coupon bonds, on which it is possible to have a lower duration than on an otherwise comparable shorter-term bond.
- The presence of an embedded call option reduces a bond's effective duration compared with that of an otherwise comparable non-callable bond. The reduction in the effective duration is greater when interest rates are low and the issuer is more likely to exercise the call option.
- The presence of an embedded put option reduces a bond's effective duration compared with that of an otherwise comparable non-putable bond. The reduction in the effective duration is greater when interest rates are high and the investor is more likely to exercise the put option.
- The duration of a bond portfolio can be calculated in two ways: (1) the weighted average of the time to receipt of *aggregate* cash flows and (2) the weighted average of the durations of individual bonds that compose the portfolio.
- The first method to calculate portfolio duration is based on the cash flow yield, which is the internal rate of return on the aggregate cash flows. It cannot be used for bonds with embedded options or for floating-rate notes.
- The second method is simpler to use and quite accurate when the yield curve is relatively flat. Its main limitation is that it assumes a parallel shift in the yield curve in that the yields on all bonds in the portfolio change by the same amount.
- Money duration is a measure of the price change in terms of units of the currency in which the bond is denominated.
- The price value of a basis point (PVBP) is an estimate of the change in the full price of a bond given a 1 bp change in the yield-to-maturity.
- Modified duration is the primary, or first-order, effect on a bond's percentage price change given a change in the yield-to-maturity. Convexity is the secondary, or second-order, effect. It indicates the change in the modified duration as the yield-to-maturity changes.
- Money convexity is convexity times the full price of the bond. Combined with money duration, money convexity estimates the change in the full price of a bond in units of currency given a change in the yield-to-maturity.
- Convexity is a positive attribute for a bond. Other things being equal, a more convex bond appreciates in price more than a less convex bond when yields fall and depreciates less when yields rise.
- Effective convexity is the second-order effect on a bond price given a change in the benchmark yield curve. It is similar to approximate convexity. The difference is that approximate convexity is based on a yield-to-maturity change and effective convexity is based on a benchmark yield curve change.
- Callable bonds have negative effective convexity when interest rates are low. The increase in price when the benchmark yield is reduced is less in absolute value than the decrease in price when the benchmark yield is raised.

- The change in a bond price is the product of: (1) the impact per basis-point change in the yield-to-maturity and (2) the number of basis points in the yield change. The first factor is estimated by duration and convexity. The second factor depends on yield volatility.
- The investment horizon is essential in measuring the interest rate risk on a fixed-rate bond.
- For a particular assumption about yield volatility, the Macaulay duration indicates the investment horizon for which coupon reinvestment risk and market price risk offset each other. The assumption is a one-time parallel shift to the yield curve in which the yield-to-maturity and coupon reinvestment rates change by the same amount in the same direction.
- When the investment horizon is greater than the Macaulay duration of the bond, coupon reinvestment risk dominates price risk. The investor's risk is to lower interest rates. The duration gap is negative.
- When the investment horizon is equal to the Macaulay duration of the bond, coupon reinvestment risk offsets price risk. The duration gap is zero.
- When the investment horizon is less than the Macaulay duration of the bond, price risk dominates coupon reinvestment risk. The investor's risk is to higher interest rates. The duration gap is positive.
- Credit risk involves the probability of default and degree of recovery if default occurs, whereas liquidity risk refers to the transaction costs associated with selling a bond.
- For a traditional (option-free) fixed-rate bond, the same duration and convexity statistics apply if a change occurs in the benchmark yield or a change occurs in the spread. The change in the spread can result from a change in credit risk or liquidity risk.
- In practice, there often is interaction between changes in benchmark yields and in the spread over the benchmark.

PRACTICE PROBLEMS

1 A "buy-and-hold" investor purchases a fixed-rate bond at a discount and holds the security until it matures. Which of the following sources of return is *least likely* to contribute to the investor's total return over the investment horizon, assuming all payments are made as scheduled?

A Capital gain

B Principal payment

C Reinvestment of coupon payments

2 Which of the following sources of return is *most likely* exposed to interest rate risk for an investor of a fixed-rate bond who holds the bond until maturity?

A Capital gain or loss

B Redemption of principal

C Reinvestment of coupon payments

3 An investor purchases a bond at a price above par value. Two years later, the investor sells the bond. The resulting capital gain or loss is measured by comparing the price at which the bond is sold to the:

A carrying value.

B original purchase price.

C original purchase price value plus the amortized amount of the premium.

The following information relates to Problems 4–6

An investor purchases a nine-year, 7% annual coupon payment bond at a price equal to par value. After the bond is purchased and before the first coupon is received, interest rates increase to 8%. The investor sells the bond after five years. Assume that interest rates remain unchanged at 8% over the five-year holding period.

4 Per 100 of par value, the future value of the reinvested coupon payments at the end of the holding period is *closest* to:

A 35.00.

B 40.26.

C 41.07.

5 The capital gain/loss per 100 of par value resulting from the sale of the bond at the end of the five-year holding period is *closest* to a:

A loss of 8.45.

B loss of 3.31.

C gain of 2.75.

6 Assuming that all coupons are reinvested over the holding period, the investor's five-year horizon yield is *closest* to:

A 5.66%.

B 6.62%.

C 7.12%.

---

7 An investor buys a three-year bond with a 5% coupon rate paid annually. The bond, with a yield-to-maturity of 3%, is purchased at a price of 105.657223 per 100 of par value. Assuming a 5-basis point change in yield-to-maturity, the bond's approximate modified duration is *closest* to:

A 2.78.

B 2.86.

C 5.56.

8 Which of the following statements about duration is correct? A bond's:

A effective duration is a measure of yield duration.

B modified duration is a measure of curve duration.

C modified duration cannot be larger than its Macaulay duration (assuming a positive yield-to-maturity).

9 An investor buys a 6% annual payment bond with three years to maturity. The bond has a yield-to-maturity of 8% and is currently priced at 94.845806 per 100 of par. The bond's Macaulay duration is *closest* to:

A 2.62.

B 2.78.

C 2.83.

10 The interest rate risk of a fixed-rate bond with an embedded call option is *best* measured by:

A effective duration.

B modified duration.

C Macaulay duration.

11 Which of the following is *most* appropriate for measuring a bond's sensitivity to shaping risk?

A key rate duration

B effective duration

C modified duration

12 A Canadian pension fund manager seeks to measure the sensitivity of her pension liabilities to market interest rate changes. The manager determines the present value of the liabilities under three interest rate scenarios: a base rate of 7%, a 100 basis point increase in rates up to 8%, and a 100 basis point drop in rates down to 6%. The results of the manager's analysis are presented below:

Interest Rate Assumption	Present Value of Liabilities
6%	CAD 510.1 million
7%	CAD 455.4 million
8%	CAD 373.6 million

The effective duration of the pension fund's liabilities is *closest* to:

A 1.49.

B 14.99.

C 29.97.

13 Which of the following statements about Macaulay duration is correct?

A A bond's coupon rate and Macaulay duration are positively related.

B A bond's Macaulay duration is inversely related to its yield-to-maturity.

C The Macaulay duration of a zero-coupon bond is less than its time-to-maturity.

14 Assuming no change in the credit risk of a bond, the presence of an embedded put option:

A reduces the effective duration of the bond.

B increases the effective duration of the bond.

C does not change the effective duration of the bond.

15 A bond portfolio consists of the following three fixed-rate bonds. Assume annual coupon payments and no accrued interest on the bonds. Prices are per 100 of par value.

Bond	Maturity	Market Value	Price	Coupon	Yield-to-Maturity	Modified Duration
A	6 years	170,000	85.0000	2.00%	4.95%	5.42
B	10 years	120,000	80.0000	2.40%	4.99%	8.44
C	15 years	100,000	100.0000	5.00%	5.00%	10.38

The bond portfolio's modified duration is *closest* to:

A 7.62.

B 8.08.

C 8.20.

16 A limitation of calculating a bond portfolio's duration as the weighted average of the yield durations of the individual bonds that compose the portfolio is that it:

A assumes a parallel shift to the yield curve.

B is less accurate when the yield curve is less steeply sloped.

C is not applicable to portfolios that have bonds with embedded options.

17 Using the information below, which bond has the *greatest* money duration per 100 of par value assuming annual coupon payments and no accrued interest?

Bond	Time-to-Maturity	Price Per 100 of Par Value	Coupon Rate	Yield-to-Maturity	Modified Duration
A	6 years	85.00	2.00%	4.95%	5.42
B	10 years	80.00	2.40%	4.99%	8.44
C	9 years	85.78	3.00%	5.00%	7.54

A Bond A

B Bond B

C Bond C

18 A bond with exactly nine years remaining until maturity offers a 3% coupon rate with annual coupons. The bond, with a yield-to-maturity of 5%, is priced at 85.784357 per 100 of par value. The estimated price value of a basis point for the bond is *closest* to:

A 0.0086.

B 0.0648.

C 0.1295.

19 The "second-order" effect on a bond's percentage price change given a change in yield-to-maturity can be *best* described as:

A duration.

B convexity.

C yield volatility.

20 A bond is currently trading for 98.722 per 100 of par value. If the bond's yield-to-maturity (YTM) rises by 10 basis points, the bond's full price is expected to fall to 98.669. If the bond's YTM decreases by 10 basis points, the bond's full price is expected to increase to 98.782. The bond's approximate convexity is *closest* to:

A 0.071.

B 70.906.

C 1,144.628.

21 A bond has an annual modified duration of 7.020 and annual convexity of 65.180. If the bond's yield-to-maturity decreases by 25 basis points, the expected percentage price change is *closest* to:

A 1.73%.

B 1.76%.

C 1.78%.

22 A bond has an annual modified duration of 7.140 and annual convexity of 66.200. The bond's yield-to-maturity is expected to increase by 50 basis points. The expected percentage price change is *closest* to:

A −3.40%.

B −3.49%.

C −3.57%.

23 Which of the following statements relating to yield volatility is *most* accurate? If the term structure of yield volatility is downward sloping, then:

A short-term rates are higher than long-term rates.

B long-term yields are more stable than short-term yields.

C short-term bonds will always experience greater price fluctuation than long-term bonds.

24 The holding period for a bond at which the coupon reinvestment risk offsets the market price risk is *best* approximated by:

A duration gap.

B modified duration.

C Macaulay duration.

25 When the investor's investment horizon is less than the Macaulay duration of the bond she owns:

A the investor is hedged against interest rate risk.

B reinvestment risk dominates, and the investor is at risk of lower rates.

C market price risk dominates, and the investor is at risk of higher rates.

26 An investor purchases an annual coupon bond with a 6% coupon rate and exactly 20 years remaining until maturity at a price equal to par value. The investor's investment horizon is eight years. The approximate modified duration of the bond is 11.470 years. The duration gap at the time of purchase is *closest* to:

A −7.842.

B 3.470.

C 4.158.

27 A manufacturing company receives a ratings upgrade and the price increases on its fixed-rate bond. The price increase was *most likely* caused by a(n):

A decrease in the bond's credit spread.

B increase in the bond's liquidity spread.

C increase of the bond's underlying benchmark rate.

SOLUTIONS

1 A is correct. A capital gain is least likely to contribute to the investor's total return. There is no capital gain (or loss) because the bond is held to maturity. The carrying value of the bond at maturity is par value, the same as the redemption amount. When a fixed-rate bond is held to its maturity, the investor receives the principal payment at maturity. This principal payment is a source of return for the investor. A fixed-rate bond pays periodic coupon payments, and the reinvestment of these coupon payments is a source of return for the investor. The investor's total return is the redemption of principal at maturity and the sum of the reinvested coupons.

2 C is correct. Because the fixed-rate bond is held to maturity (a "buy-and-hold" investor), interest rate risk arises entirely from changes in coupon reinvestment rates. Higher interest rates increase income from reinvestment of coupon payments, and lower rates decrease income from coupon reinvestment. There will not be a capital gain or loss because the bond is held until maturity. The carrying value at the maturity date is par value, the same as the redemption amount. The redemption of principal does not expose the investor to interest rate risk. The risk to a bond's principal is credit risk.

3 A is correct. Capital gains (losses) arise if a bond is sold at a price above (below) its constant-yield price trajectory. A point on the trajectory represents the carrying value of the bond at that time. That is, the capital gain/loss is measured from the bond's carrying value, the point on the constant-yield price trajectory, and not from the original purchase price. The carrying value is the original purchase price plus the amortized amount of the discount if the bond is purchased at a price below par value. If the bond is purchased at a price above par value, the carrying value is the original purchase price minus (not plus) the amortized amount of the premium. The amortized amount for each year is the change in the price between two points on the trajectory.

4 C is correct. The future value of reinvested cash flows at 8% after five years is closest to 41.07per 100 of par value.

$$\left[7 \times (1.08)^4\right] + \left[7 \times (1.08)^3\right] + \left[7 \times (1.08)^2\right] + \left[7 \times (1.08)^1\right] + 7 = 41.0662$$

The 6.07 difference between the sum of the coupon payments over the five-year holding period (35) and the future value of the reinvested coupons (41.07) represents the "interest-on-interest" gain from compounding.

5 B is correct. The capital loss is closest to 3.31 per 100 of par value. After five years, the bond has four years remaining until maturity and the sale price of the bond is 96.69, calculated as:

$$\frac{7}{(1.08)^1} + \frac{7}{(1.08)^2} + \frac{7}{(1.08)^3} + \frac{107}{(1.08)^4} = 96.69$$

The investor purchased the bond at a price equal to par value (100). Because the bond was purchased at a price equal to its par value, the carrying value is par value. Therefore, the investor experienced a capital loss of 96.69 – 100 = –3.31.

6 B is correct. The investor's five-year horizon yield is closest to 6.62%. After five years, the sale price of the bond is 96.69 (from problem 5) and the future value of reinvested cash flows at 8% is 41.0662 (from problem 4) per 100 of par value. The total return is 137.76 (= 41.07 + 96.69), resulting in a realized five-year horizon yield of 6.62%:

$$100.00 = \frac{137.76}{(1+r)^5}, \quad r = 0.0662$$

7 A is correct. The bond's approximate modified duration is closest to 2.78. Approximate modified duration is calculated as:

$$\text{ApproxModDur} = \frac{(PV_-) - (PV_+)}{2 \times (\Delta\text{Yield}) \times (PV_0)}$$

Lower yield-to-maturity by 5 bps to 2.95%:

$$PV_- = \frac{5}{(1+0.0295)^1} + \frac{5}{(1+0.0295)^2} + \frac{5+100}{(1+0.0295)^3} = 105.804232$$

Increase yield-to-maturity by 5 bps to 3.05%:

$$PV_+ = \frac{5}{(1+0.0305)^1} + \frac{5}{(1+0.0305)^2} + \frac{5+100}{(1+0.0305)^3} = 105.510494$$

$$PV_0 = 105.657223, \ \Delta\text{Yield} = 0.0005$$

$$\text{ApproxModDur} = \frac{105.804232 - 105.510494}{2 \times 0.0005 \times 105.657223} = 2.78$$

8 C is correct. A bond's modified duration cannot be larger than its Macaulay duration assuming a positive yield-to-maturity. The formula for modified duration is:

$$\text{ModDur} = \frac{\text{MacDur}}{1+r}$$

where r is the bond's yield-to-maturity per period. Therefore, ModDur will typically be less than MacDur.

Effective duration is a measure of curve duration. Modified duration is a measure of yield duration.

9 C is correct. The bond's Macaulay duration is closest to 2.83. Macaulay duration (MacDur) is a weighted average of the times to the receipt of cash flow. The weights are the shares of the full price corresponding to each coupon and principal payment.

Period	Cash Flow	Present Value	Weight	Period × Weight
1	6	5.555556	0.058575	0.058575
2	6	5.144033	0.054236	0.108472
3	106	84.146218	0.887190	2.661570
		94.845806	1.000000	2.828617

Thus, the bond's Macaulay duration (MacDur) is 2.83.

Alternatively, Macaulay duration can be calculated using the following closed-form formula:

$$\text{MacDur} = \left\{\frac{1+r}{r} - \frac{1+r+\left[N \times (c-r)\right]}{c \times \left[(1+r)^N - 1\right] + r}\right\} - (t/T)$$

$$\text{MacDur} = \left\{\frac{1.08}{0.08} - \frac{1.08+\left[3 \times (0.06-0.08)\right]}{0.06 \times \left[(1.08)^3 - 1\right] + 0.08}\right\} - 0$$

$$\text{MacDur} = 13.50 - 10.67 = 2.83$$

10 A is correct. The interest rate risk of a fixed-rate bond with an embedded call option is best measured by effective duration. A callable bond's future cash flows are uncertain because they are contingent on future interest rates. The issuer's decision to call the bond depends on future interest rates. Therefore, the yield-to-maturity on a callable bond is not well defined. Only effective duration, which takes into consideration the value of the call option, is the appropriate interest rate risk measure. Yield durations like Macaulay and modified durations are not relevant for a callable bond because they assume no changes in cash flows when interest rates change.

11 A is correct. Key rate duration is used to measure a bond's sensitivity to a shift at one or more maturity segments of the yield curve which result in a change to yield curve shape. Modified and effective duration measure a bond's sensitivity to parallel shifts in the entire curve.

12 B is correct. The effective duration of the pension fund's liabilities is closest to 14.99. The effective duration is calculated as follows:

$$\text{EffDur} = \frac{(PV_-) - (PV_+)}{2 \times (\Delta\text{Curve}) \times (PV_0)}$$

$PV_0 = 455.4$, $PV_+ = 373.6$, $PV_- = 510.1$, and $\Delta\text{Curve} = 0.0100$.

$$\text{EffDur} = \frac{510.1 - 373.6}{2 \times 0.0100 \times 455.4} = 14.99$$

13 B is correct. A bond's yield-to-maturity is inversely related to its Macaulay duration: The higher the yield-to-maturity, the lower its Macaulay duration and the lower the interest rate risk. A higher yield-to-maturity decreases the weighted average of the times to the receipt of cash flow, and thus decreases the Macaulay duration.

A bond's coupon rate is inversely related to its Macaulay duration: The lower the coupon, the greater the weight of the payment of principal at maturity. This results in a higher Macaulay duration. Zero-coupon bonds do not pay periodic coupon payments; therefore, the Macaulay duration of a zero-coupon bond is its time-to-maturity.

14 A is correct. The presence of an embedded put option reduces the effective duration of the bond, especially when rates are rising. If interest rates are low compared with the coupon rate, the value of the put option is low and the impact of the change in the benchmark yield on the bond's price is very similar to the impact on the price of a non-putable bond. But when benchmark interest rates rise, the put option becomes more valuable to the investor. The ability to

sell the bond at par value limits the price depreciation as rates rise. The presence of an embedded put option reduces the sensitivity of the bond price to changes in the benchmark yield, assuming no change in credit risk.

15 A is correct. The portfolio's modified duration is closest to 7.62.Portfolio duration is commonly estimated as the market-value-weighted average of the yield durations of the individual bonds that compose the portfolio.

The total market value of the bond portfolio is 170,000 + 120,000 + 100,000 = 390,000.

The portfolio duration is 5.42 × (170,000/390,000) + 8.44 × (120,000/390,000) + 10.38 × (100,000/390,000) = 7.62.

16 A is correct. A limitation of calculating a bond portfolio's duration as the weighted average of the yield durations of the individual bonds is that this measure implicitly assumes a parallel shift to the yield curve (all rates change by the same amount in the same direction). In reality, interest rate changes frequently result in a steeper or flatter yield curve. This approximation of the "theoretically correct" portfolio duration is *more* accurate when the yield curve is flatter (less steeply sloped). An advantage of this approach is that it can be used with portfolios that include bonds with embedded options. Bonds with embedded options can be included in the weighted average using the effective durations for these securities.

17 B is correct. Bond B has the greatest money duration per 100 of par value. Money duration (MoneyDur) is calculated as the annual modified duration (AnnModDur) times the full price (PV^{Full}) of the bond including accrued interest. Bond B has the highest money duration per 100 of par value.

$$\text{MoneyDur} = \text{AnnModDur} \times PV^{Full}$$

$$\text{MoneyDur of Bond A} = 5.42 \times 85.00 = 460.70$$

$$\text{MoneyDur of Bond B} = 8.44 \times 80.00 = 675.20$$

$$\text{MoneyDur of Bond C} = 7.54 \times 85.78 = 646.78$$

18 B is correct. The PVBP is closest to 0.0648. The formula for the price value of a basis point is:

$$\text{PVBP} = \frac{(PV_-) - (PV_+)}{2}$$

where:

PVBP = price value of a basis point

PV_- = full price calculated by lowering the yield-to-maturity by one basis point

PV_+ = full price calculated by raising the yield-to-maturity by one basis point

Lowering the yield-to-maturity by one basis point to 4.99% results in a bond price of 85.849134:

$$PV_- = \frac{3}{(1+0.0499)^1} + \cdots + \frac{3+100}{(1+0.0499)^9} = 85.849134$$

Increasing the yield-to-maturity by one basis point to 5.01% results in a bond price of 85.719638:

$$PV_+ = \frac{3}{(1+0.0501)^1} + \cdots + \frac{3+100}{(1+0.0501)^9} = 85.719638$$

$$\text{PVBP} = \frac{85.849134 - 85.719638}{2} = 0.06475$$

Alternatively, the PVBP can be derived using modified duration:

$$\text{ApproxModDur} = \frac{(PV_-) - (PV_+)}{2 \times (\Delta\text{Yield}) \times (PV_0)}$$

$$\text{ApproxModDur} = \frac{85.849134 - 85.719638}{2 \times 0.0001 \times 85.784357} = 7.548$$

$$\text{PVBP} = 7.548 \times 85.784357 \times 0.0001 = 0.06475$$

19 B is correct. Convexity measures the "second order" effect on a bond's percentage price change given a change in yield-to-maturity. Convexity adjusts the percentage price change estimate provided by modified duration to better approximate the true relationship between a bond's price and its yield-to-maturity which is a curved line (convex).

Duration estimates the change in the bond's price along the straight line that is tangent to this curved line ("first order" effect). Yield volatility measures the magnitude of changes in the yields along the yield curve.

20 B is correct. The bond's approximate convexity is closest to 70.906. Approximate convexity (ApproxCon) is calculated using the following formula:

$$\text{ApproxCon} = [PV_- + PV_+ - (2 \times PV_0)]/(\Delta\text{Yield}^2 \times PV_0)$$

where:

PV_- = new price when the yield-to-maturity is decreased

PV_+ = new price when the yield-to-maturity is increased

PV_0 = original price

ΔYield = change in yield-to-maturity

$\text{ApproxCon} = [98.782 + 98.669 - (2 \times 98.722)]/(0.001^2 \times 98.722) = 70.906$

21 C is correct. The expected percentage price change is closest to 1.78%. The convexity-adjusted percentage price change for a bond given a change in the yield-to-maturity is estimated by:

$$\%\Delta PV^{Full} \approx [-\text{AnnModDur} \times \Delta\text{Yield}] + [0.5 \times \text{AnnConvexity} \times (\Delta\text{Yield})^2]$$

$\%\Delta PV^{Full} \approx [-7.020 \times (-0.0025)] + [0.5 \times 65.180 \times (-0.0025)^2] = 0.017754$, or 1.78%

22 B is correct. The expected percentage price change is closest to −3.49%. The convexity-adjusted percentage price change for a bond given a change in the yield-to-maturity is estimated by:

$$\%\Delta PV^{Full} \approx [-\text{AnnModDur} \times \Delta\text{Yield}] + [0.5 \times \text{AnnConvexity} \times (\Delta\text{Yield})^2]$$

$\%\Delta PV^{Full} \approx [-7.140 \times 0.005] + [0.5 \times 66.200 \times (0.005)^2] = -0.034873$, or −3.49%

23 B is correct. If the term structure of yield volatility is downward-sloping, then short-term bond yields-to-maturity have greater volatility than for long-term bonds. Therefore, long-term yields are more stable than short-term yields. Higher volatility in short-term rates does not necessarily mean that the level of short-term rates is higher than long-term rates. With a downward-sloping term structure of yield volatility, short-term bonds will not always experience greater price fluctuation than long-term bonds. The estimated percentage change in a bond price depends on the modified duration and convexity as well as on the yield-to-maturity change.

24 C is correct. When the holder of a bond experiences a one-time parallel shift in the yield curve, the Macaulay duration statistic identifies the number of years necessary to hold the bond so that the losses (or gains) from coupon reinvestment offset the gains (or losses) from market price changes. The duration gap is the difference between the Macaulay duration and the investment horizon. Modified duration approximates the percentage price change of a bond given a change in its yield-to-maturity.

25 C is correct. The duration gap is equal to the bond's Macaulay duration minus the investment horizon. In this case, the duration gap is positive, and price risk dominates coupon reinvestment risk. The investor risk is to higher rates.

The investor is hedged against interest rate risk if the duration gap is zero; that is, the investor's investment horizon is equal to the bond's Macaulay duration. The investor is at risk of lower rates only if the duration gap is negative; that is, the investor's investment horizon is greater than the bond's Macaulay duration. In this case, coupon reinvestment risk dominates market price risk.

26 C is correct. The duration gap is closest to 4.158. The duration gap is a bond's Macaulay duration minus the investment horizon. The approximate Macaulay duration is the approximate modified duration times one plus the yield-to-maturity. It is 12.158 (= 11.470 × 1.06).

Given an investment horizon of eight years, the duration gap for this bond at purchase is positive: 12.158 – 8 = 4.158. When the investment horizon is less than the Macaulay duration of the bond, the duration gap is positive, and price risk dominates coupon reinvestment risk.

27 A is correct. The price increase was most likely caused by a decrease in the bond's credit spread. The ratings upgrade most likely reflects a lower expected probability of default and/or a greater level of recovery of assets if default occurs. The decrease in credit risk results in a smaller credit spread. The increase in the bond price reflects a decrease in the yield-to-maturity due to a smaller credit spread. The change in the bond price was not due to a change in liquidity risk or an increase in the benchmark rate.

READING

47

Fundamentals of Credit Analysis

by Christopher L. Gootkind, CFA

Christopher L. Gootkind, CFA, is at Loomis Sayles & Company, LP (USA).

LEARNING OUTCOMES

Mastery	*The candidate should be able to:*
☐	**a.** describe credit risk and credit-related risks affecting corporate bonds;
☐	**b.** describe default probability and loss severity as components of credit risk;
☐	**c.** describe seniority rankings of corporate debt and explain the potential violation of the priority of claims in a bankruptcy proceeding;
☐	**d.** distinguish between corporate issuer credit ratings and issue credit ratings and describe the rating agency practice of "notching";
☐	**e.** explain risks in relying on ratings from credit rating agencies;
☐	**f.** explain the four Cs (Capacity, Collateral, Covenants, and Character) of traditional credit analysis;
☐	**g.** calculate and interpret financial ratios used in credit analysis;
☐	**h.** evaluate the credit quality of a corporate bond issuer and a bond of that issuer, given key financial ratios of the issuer and the industry;
☐	**i.** describe factors that influence the level and volatility of yield spreads;
☐	**j.** explain special considerations when evaluating the credit of high yield, sovereign, and non-sovereign government debt issuers and issues.

The author would like to thank several of his Fixed Income Research colleagues at Loomis, Sayles & Company for their assistance with this reading: Paul Batterton, CFA, Diana Moskowitz, CFA, Diana Monteith, Shannon O'Mara, CFA, and Laura Sarlo, CFA.

1 INTRODUCTION

With bonds outstanding worth many trillions of US dollars, the debt markets play a critical role in the global economy. Companies and governments raise capital in the debt market to fund current operations; buy equipment; build factories, roads, bridges, airports, and hospitals; acquire assets, and so on. By channeling savings into productive investments, the debt markets facilitate economic growth. Credit analysis has a crucial function in the debt capital markets—efficiently allocating capital by properly assessing credit risk, pricing it accordingly, and repricing it as risks change. How do fixed-income investors determine the riskiness of that debt, and how do they decide what they need to earn as compensation for that risk?

This reading covers basic principles of credit analysis, which may be broadly defined as the process by which credit risk is evaluated. Readers will be introduced to the definition of credit risk, the interpretation of credit ratings, the four Cs of traditional credit analysis, and key financial measures and ratios used in credit analysis. The reading explains, among other things, how to compare bond issuer creditworthiness within a given industry as well as across industries and how credit risk is priced in the bond market.

The reading focuses primarily on analysis of corporate debt; however, credit analysis of sovereign and non-sovereign, particularly municipal, government bonds will also be addressed. Structured finance, a segment of the debt markets that includes securities backed by pools of assets, such as residential and commercial mortgages as well as other consumer loans, will not be covered here.

The key components of credit risk—default probability and loss severity—are introduced in the next section along with such credit-related risks as spread risk, credit migration risk, and liquidity risk. Section 3 discusses the relationship between credit risk and the capital structure of the firm. Credit ratings and the role of credit rating agencies are addressed in Section 4. Section 5 focuses on the process of analyzing the credit risk of corporations, whereas Section 6 examines the impact of credit spreads on risk and return. Special considerations applicable to the analysis of (i) high-yield (low-quality) corporate bonds and (ii) government bonds are presented in Section 7. Section 8 gives a brief summary, and a set of review questions concludes the reading.

2 CREDIT RISK

Credit risk is the risk of loss resulting from the borrower (issuer of debt) failing to make full and timely payments of interest and/or principal. Credit risk has two components. The first is known as **default risk**, or **default probability**, which is the probability that a borrower defaults—that is, fails to meet its obligation to make full and timely payments of principal and interest, according to the terms of the debt security. The second component is **loss severity** (also known as "loss given default") in the event of default—that is, the portion of a bond's value (including unpaid interest) an investor loses. A default can lead to losses of various magnitudes. In most instances, in the event of default, bondholders will recover some value, so there will not be a total loss on the investment. Thus, credit risk is reflected in the distribution of potential losses that may arise if the investor is not paid in full and on time. Although it is sometimes important to consider the entire distribution of potential losses and their respective probabilities,[1] it is often convenient to summarize the risk with a single default probability and loss severity and to focus on the **expected loss**:

Expected loss = Default probability × Loss severity given default

The loss severity, and hence the expected loss, can be expressed as either a monetary amount (e.g., €450,000) or as a percentage of the principal amount (e.g., 45 percent). The latter form of expression is generally more useful for analysis because it is independent of the amount of investment. Loss severity is often expressed as (1 – Recovery rate), where the recovery rate is the percentage of the principal amount recovered in the event of default.

Because default risk (default probability) is quite low for most high-quality debt issuers, bond investors tend to focus primarily on assessing this probability and devote less effort to assessing the potential loss severity arising from default. However, as an issuer's default risk rises, investors will focus more on what the recovery rate might be in the event of default. This issue will be discussed in more detail later. Important credit-related risks include the following:

- **Spread risk**. Corporate bonds and other "credit-risky" debt instruments typically trade at a yield premium, or spread, to bonds that have been considered "default-risk free," such as US Treasury bonds or German government bonds. Yield spreads, expressed in basis points, widen based on two primary factors: (1) a decline in an issuer's creditworthiness, sometimes referred to as credit migration or downgrade risk, and (2) an increase in **market liquidity risk**. These two risks are separate but frequently related.
- **Credit migration risk** or **downgrade risk**. This is the risk that a bond issuer's creditworthiness deteriorates, or migrates lower, leading investors to believe the risk of default is higher and thus causing the yield spreads on the issuer's bonds to widen and the price of its bonds to fall. The term "downgrade" refers to action by the major bond rating agencies, whose role will be covered in more detail in Section 4.
- **Market liquidity risk**. This is the risk that the price at which investors can actually transact—buying or selling—may differ from the price indicated in the market. To compensate investors for the risk that there may not be sufficient market liquidity for them to buy or sell bonds in the quantity they desire, the spread or yield premium on corporate bonds includes a market liquidity component, in addition to a credit risk component. Unlike stocks, which trade on exchanges, most markets bonds trade primarily over the counter, through broker–dealers trading for their own accounts. Their ability and willingness to make markets, as reflected in the bid–ask spread, is an important determinant of market liquidity risk. The two main issuer-specific factors that affect market liquidity risk are (1) the size of the issuer (that is, the amount of publicly traded debt an issuer has outstanding) and (2) the credit quality of the issuer. In general, the less debt an issuer has outstanding, the less frequently its debt trades, and thus the higher the market liquidity risk. And the lower the quality of the issuer, the higher the market liquidity risk.

1 As an example, careful attention to the full distribution of potential losses is important in analyzing credit risk in structured finance products because the various tranches usually share unequally in the credit losses on the underlying loans or securities. A particular tranche typically bears none of the losses up to some level of underlying losses, then it bears all of the underlying losses until the tranche is wiped out. Losses on a "thin" tranche are very likely to be either 0 percent or 100 percent, with relatively small probabilities on intermediate loss severities. This situation is not well described by a single "average" loss severity.

During times of financial stress or crisis, such as in late 2008, market liquidity can decline sharply, causing yield spreads on corporate bonds, and other credit-risky debt, to widen and their prices to drop. Some research has been done on trying to quantify market liquidity risk,[2] and more is likely to be done in the aftermath of the financial crisis.

EXAMPLE 1

Defining Credit Risk

1 Which of the following *best* defines credit risk?
   - A The probability of default times the severity of loss given default
   - B The loss of principal and interest payments in the event of bankruptcy
   - C The risk of not receiving full interest and principal payments on a timely basis

2 Which of the following is the *best* measure of credit risk?
   - A The expected loss
   - B The severity of loss
   - C The probability of default

3 Which of the following is NOT credit or credit-related risk?
   - A Default risk
   - B Interest rate risk
   - C Downgrade or credit migration risk

Solution to 1:

C is correct. Credit risk is the risk that the borrower will not make full and timely payments.

Solution to 2:

A is correct. The expected loss captures both of the key components of credit risk: (the product of) the probability of default and the loss severity in the event of default. Neither component alone fully reflects the risk.

Solution to 3:

B is correct. Bond price changes due to general interest rate movements are not considered credit risk.

---

2 For example, see Francis A. Longstaff, Sanjay Mithal, and Eric Neis, "Corporate Yield Spreads: Default Risk or Liquidity? New Evidence from the Credit-Default Swap Market," Journal of Finance, vol. 60, no. 5, October 2005:2213–2253.

CAPITAL STRUCTURE, SENIORITY RANKING, AND RECOVERY RATES

3

The various debt obligations of a given borrower will not necessarily all have the same **seniority ranking**, or priority of payment. In this section, we will introduce the topic of an issuer's capital structure and discuss the various types of debt claims that may arise from that structure, as well as their ranking and how those rankings can influence recovery rates in the event of default.

3.1 Capital Structure

The composition and distribution across operating units of a company's debt and equity—including bank debt, bonds of all seniority rankings, preferred stock, and common equity—is referred to as its **capital structure**. Some companies and industries have straightforward capital structures, with all the debt equally ranked and issued by one main operating entity. Other companies and industries, due to their frequent acquisitions and divestitures (e.g., media companies or conglomerates) or high levels of regulation (e.g., banks and utilities), tend to have more complicated capital structures. Companies in these industries often have many different subsidiaries, or operating companies, that have their own debt outstanding and parent holding companies that also issue debt, with different levels or rankings of seniority. Similarly, the cross-border operations of multi-national corporations tend to increase the complexity of their capital structures.

3.2 Seniority Ranking

Just as borrowers can issue debt with many different maturity dates and coupons, they can also have many different rankings in terms of seniority. The ranking refers to the priority of payment, with the most senior or highest-ranking debt having the first claim on the cash flows and assets of the issuer. This level of seniority can affect the value of an investor's claim in the event of default and restructuring. Broadly, there is **secured debt** and **unsecured debt**. Secured debt means the debtholder has a direct claim—a pledge from the issuer—on certain assets and their associated cash flows. Unsecured bondholders have only a general claim on an issuer's assets and cash flow. In the event of default, unsecured debtholders' claims rank below (i.e., get paid after) those of secured creditors[3] under what's known as the **priority of claims**.

3 The term "creditors" is used throughout this reading to mean holders of debt instruments, such as bonds and bank loans. Unless specifically stated, it does not include such obligations as trade credit, tax liens, or employment-related obligations.

Exhibit 1 Seniority Ranking

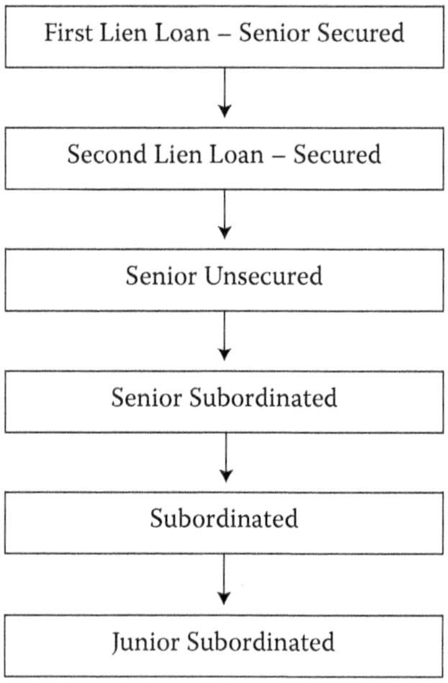

Within each category of debt, there are finer gradations of types and rankings. Within secured debt, there is first mortgage and first lien debt, which are the highest-ranked debt in terms of priority of repayment. **First mortgage debt** or loan refers to the pledge of a specific property (e.g., a power plant for a utility or a specific casino for a gaming company). **First lien debt** or loan refers to a pledge of certain assets that could include buildings but might also include property and equipment, licenses, patents, brands, and so on. There can also be **second lien**, or even third lien, secured debt, which, as the name implies, has a secured interest in the pledged assets but ranks below first lien debt in both collateral protection and priority of payment.

Within unsecured debt, there can also be finer gradations and seniority rankings. The highest-ranked unsecured debt is senior unsecured debt. It is the most common type of all corporate bonds outstanding. Other, lower-ranked debt includes **subordinated debt** and junior subordinated debt. Among the various creditor classes, these obligations have among the lowest priority of claims and frequently have little or no recovery in the event of default. That is, their loss severity can be as high as 100 percent. (See Exhibit 1 for a sample seniority ranking.) For regulatory and capital purposes, banks in Europe and the United States have issued debt and debt-like securities that rank even lower than subordinated debt[4] and are intended to provide a capital cushion in times of financial distress. Many of them did not work as intended during the financial crisis that began in 2008, and most were phased out, potentially to be replaced by more effective instruments that automatically convert to equity in certain circumstances.

There are many reasons why companies issue—and investors buy—debt with different seniority rankings. Issuers are interested in optimizing their cost of capital—finding the right mix of the various types of both debt and equity—for their industry and type of business. Issuers may offer secured debt because that is what the market (i.e., investors) may require, given a company's perceived riskiness, or because secured debt is generally lower cost due to the reduced credit risk inherent in its higher

4 These have various names such as hybrids, trust preferred, and upper and lower Tier 2 securities. In some cases, the non-payment or deferral of interest does not constitute an event of default, and in other cases, they might convert into perpetual securities—that is, securities with no maturity date.

priority of claims. Or, issuers may offer subordinated debt because (1) they believe it is less expensive than issuing equity[5] (and doesn't dilute existing shareholders) and is typically less restrictive than issuing senior debt and (2) investors are willing to buy it because they believe the yield being offered is adequate compensation for the risk they perceive. Credit risk versus return will be discussed in more detail later in the reading.

EXAMPLE 2

Seniority Ranking

The Acme Company has senior unsecured bonds as well as both first and second lien debt in its capital structure. Which ranks higher with respect to priority of claims: senior unsecured bonds or second lien debt?

Solution:

Second lien debt ranks higher than senior unsecured bonds because of its secured position.

3.3 Recovery Rates

All creditors at the same level of the capital structure are treated as one class; thus, a senior unsecured bondholder whose debt is due in 30 years has the same pro rata claim in bankruptcy as one whose debt matures in six months. This provision is referred to as bonds ranking **pari passu** ("on an equal footing") in right of payment.

Defaulted debt will often continue to be traded by investors and broker–dealers based on their assessment that either in liquidation of the bankrupt company's assets or in reorganization, the bonds will have some recovery value. In the case of reorganization, or restructuring (whether through formal bankruptcy or on a voluntary basis), new debt, equity, cash, or some combination thereof could be issued in exchange for the original defaulted debt.

As discussed, recovery rates vary by seniority of ranking in a company's capital structure, under the priority of claims treatment in bankruptcy. Over many decades, there have been enough defaults to generate statistically meaningful historical data on recovery rates by seniority ranking. Exhibit 2 provides recovery rates by seniority ranking for North American non-financial companies.[6] For example, as shown in Exhibit 2, investors on average recovered 46.9 percent of the value of senior secured debt that defaulted in 2016, but only 29.2 percent of the value of senior unsecured issues that defaulted that year.

5 Debtholders require a lower return than equity holders because they have prior claims to an issuer's cash flow and assets. That is, the cost of debt is lower than the cost of equity. In most countries, this cost differential is even greater due to the tax deductibility of interest payments.

6 The recovery rates shown for default years 2016 and 2017 should be viewed as preliminary because some of the numbers are based on the relatively small number of defaults for which final recovery had been determined at the time of the Moody's study. For example, the 2017 and 2016 subordinated recovery rates reflect only two bonds and one bond, respectively.

Exhibit 2 Average Corporate Debt Recovery Rates Measured by Ultimate Recoveries

	Emergence Year*			Default Year		
Seniority ranking	**2017**	**2016**	**1987–2017**	**2017**	**2016**	**1987–2017**
Bank loans	81.3%	72.6%	80.4%	80.2%	78.3%	80.4%
Senior secured bonds	52.3%	35.9%	62.3%	57.5%	46.9%	62.3%
Senior unsecured bonds	54.1%	11.7%	47.9%	47.4%	29.2%	47.9%
Subordinated bonds	4.5%	6.6%	28.0%	NA	8.0%	28.0%

* Emergence year is typically the year the defaulted company emerges from bankruptcy. Default year data refer to the recovery rate of debt that defaulted in that year (i.e., 2016 and 2017) or range of years (i.e., 1987–2017). Data are for North American nonfinancial companies. NA indicates not available.
Source: Moody's Investors Service, Inc.'s Ultimate Recovery Database.

There are a few things worth noting:

1 **Recovery rates can vary widely by industry**. Companies that go bankrupt in industries that are in secular decline (e.g., newspaper publishing) will most likely have lower recovery rates than those that go bankrupt in industries merely suffering from a cyclical economic downturn.

2 **Recovery rates can also vary depending on when they occur in a credit cycle.**[7] As shown in Exhibit 3, at or near the bottom of a credit cycle—which is almost always closely linked with an economic cycle—recoveries will tend to be lower than at other times in the credit cycle. This is because there will be many companies closer to, or already in, bankruptcy, causing valuations to be depressed.

7 Credit cycles describe the changing availability—and pricing—of credit. When the economy is strong or improving, the willingness of lenders to extend credit, and on favorable terms, is high. Conversely, when the economy is weak or weakening, lenders pull back, or "tighten" credit, by making it less available and more expensive. This frequently contributes to asset values, such as real estate, declining, causing further economic weakness and higher defaults. Central banks frequently survey banks to assess how "tight" or "loose" their lending standards are. This information, as well as the level and direction of corporate bond default rates, helps provide a good sense of where one is in the credit cycle.

Exhibit 3 Global Recovery Rates by Seniority Ranking, 1990–2017

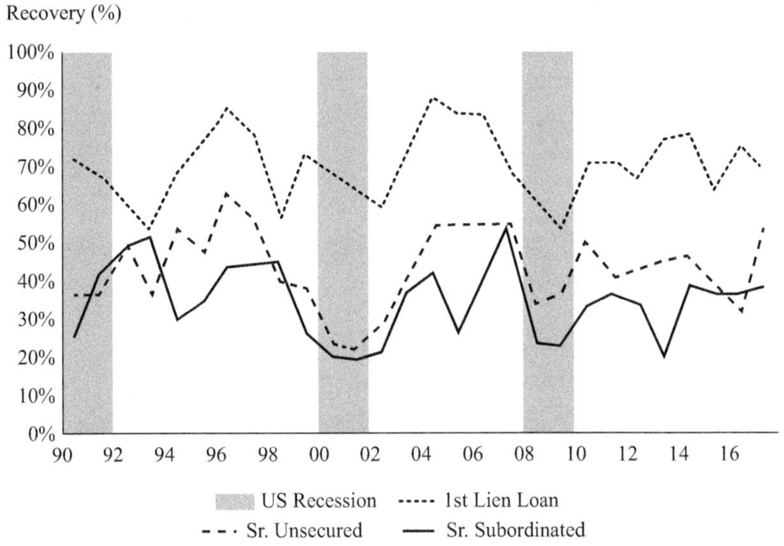

Source: Based on data from Moody's Investors Service, Inc.'s Ultimate Recovery Database.

3 **These recovery rates are averages.** In fact, there can be large variability, both across industries, as noted above, as well as across companies within a given industry. Factors might include composition and proportion of debt across an issuer's capital structure. An abundance of secured debt will lead to smaller recovery rates on lower-ranked debt.

Understanding recovery rates is important because they are a key component of credit analysis and risk. Recall that the best measure of credit risk is expected loss—that is, probability of default times loss severity given default. And loss severity equals (1 – Recovery rate). Having an idea how much one can lose in the event of default is a critical factor in valuing credit, particularly lower-quality credit, as the default risk rises.

Priority of claims: Not always absolute. The priority of claims in bankruptcy—the idea that the highest-ranked creditors get paid out first, followed by the next level, and on down, like a waterfall—is well established and is often described as "absolute." In principle, in the event of bankruptcy or liquidation:

- Creditors with a secured claim have the right to the value of that specific property before any other claim. If the value of the pledged property is less than the amount of the claim, then the difference becomes a senior unsecured claim.
- Unsecured creditors have a right to be paid in full before holders of equity interests (common and preferred shareholders) receive value on their interests.
- Senior unsecured creditors take priority over all subordinated creditors. A creditor is senior unsecured unless expressly subordinated.

In practice, however, creditors with lower seniority and even shareholders may receive some consideration without more senior creditors being paid in full. Why might this be the case? In bankruptcy, there are different classes of claimants, and all classes that are impaired (that is, receive less than full claim) get to vote to confirm the plan of reorganization. This vote is subject to the absolute priority of claims. Either by consent of the various parties or by the judge's order, however, absolute priority may not be strictly enforced in the final plan. There may be disputes over the value of various assets in the bankruptcy estate (e.g., what is a plant, or a patent portfolio, worth?) or the present value or timing of payouts. For example, what is the value of the new debt I'm receiving for my old debt of a reorganized company before it emerges from bankruptcy?

Resolution of these disputes takes time, and cases can drag on for months and years. In the meantime, during bankruptcy, substantial expenses are being incurred for legal and accounting fees, and the value of the company may be declining as key employees leave, customers go elsewhere, and so on. Thus, to avoid the time, expense, and uncertainty over disputed issues, such as the value of property in the estate, the legality of certain claims, and so forth, the various claimants have an incentive to negotiate and compromise. This frequently leads to creditors with lower seniority and other claimants (e.g., even shareholders) receiving more consideration than they are legally entitled to.

It's worth noting that in the United States, the bias is toward reorganization and recovery of companies in bankruptcy, whereas in other jurisdictions, such as the United Kingdom, the bias is toward liquidation of companies in bankruptcy and maximizing value to the banks and other senior creditors. It's also worth noting that bankruptcy and bankruptcy laws are very complex and can vary greatly by country, so it is difficult to generalize about how creditors will fare. As shown in the earlier chart, there is huge variability in recovery rates for defaulted debt. Every case is different.

EXAMPLE 3

Priority of Claims

1 Under which circumstance is a subordinated bondholder *most likely* to recover some value in a bankruptcy without a senior creditor getting paid in full? When:

   A absolute priority rules are enforced.

   B the various classes of claimants agree to it.

   C the company is liquidated rather than reorganized.

2 In the event of bankruptcy, claims at the same level of the capital structure are:

   A on an equal footing, regardless of size, maturity, or time outstanding.

   B paid in the order of maturity from shortest to longest, regardless of size or time outstanding.

   C paid on a first-in, first-out (FIFO) basis so that the longest-standing claims are satisfied first, regardless of size or maturity.

Solution to 1:

B is correct. All impaired classes get to vote on the reorganization plan. Negotiation and compromise are often preferable to incurring huge legal and accounting fees in a protracted bankruptcy process that would otherwise reduce the value of the estate for all claimants. This process may allow junior creditors (e.g., subordinated bondholders) to recover some value even though more senior creditors do not get paid in full.

Solution to 2:

A is correct. All claims at the same level of the capital structure are pari passu (on an equal footing).

RATINGS AGENCIES, CREDIT RATINGS, AND THEIR ROLE IN THE DEBT MARKETS

4

The major credit ratings agencies—Moody's Investors Service ("Moody's"), Standard & Poor's ("S&P"), and Fitch Ratings ("Fitch")—play a central, if somewhat controversial, role in the credit markets. For the vast majority of outstanding bonds, at least two of the agencies provide ratings: a symbol-based measure of the potential risk of default of a particular bond or issuer of debt. In the public and quasi-public bond markets,[8] issuers won't offer, and investors won't buy, bonds that do not carry ratings from Moody's, S&P, or Fitch. This practice applies for all types of bonds—government or sovereign, government related,[9] supranational,[10] corporate, non-sovereign government, and mortgage- and asset-backed debt. How did the ratings agencies attain such a dominant position in the credit markets? What are credit ratings, and what do they mean? How does the market use credit ratings? What are the risks of relying solely or excessively on credit ratings?

The history of the major ratings agencies goes back more than 100 years. John Moody began publishing credit analysis and opinions on US railroads in 1909. S&P published its first ratings in 1916. They have grown in size and prominence since then. Many bond investors like the fact that there are independent analysts who meet with the issuer and often have access to material, non-public information, such as financial projections that investors cannot receive, to aid in the analysis. What has also proven very attractive to investors is that credit ratings provide direct and easy comparability of the relative credit riskiness of all bond issuers, within and across industries and bond types, although there is some debate about ratings comparability across the types of bonds.[11]

Several factors have led to the near universal use of credit ratings in the bond markets and the dominant role of the major credit rating agencies. These factors include the following:

- Independent assessment of credit risk
- Ease of comparison across bond issuers, issues, and market segments
- Regulatory and statutory reliance and usage[12]
- Issuer payment for ratings[13]

8 That is, underwritten by investment banks, as opposed to privately placed on a "best efforts" basis.

9 These are government agencies or instrumentalities that may have implicit or explicit guarantees from the government. Examples include Ginnie Mae in the United States and *Pfandbriefe* in Germany.

10 Supranationals are international financial institutions, such as the International Bank for Reconstruction and Development ("World Bank"), the Asian Development Bank, and the European Investment Bank, that are established by treaty and owned by several member governments.

11 Investigations conducted after the late 2008/early 2009 financial crisis suggested that, for a given rating category, municipal bonds have experienced a lower historical incidence of default than corporate debt.

12 It is common for regulations to make reference to ratings issued by recognized credit ratings agencies. In light of the role played by the agencies in the sub-prime mortgage crisis, however, some jurisdictions (e.g., the United States) are moving to remove such references. Nonetheless, the so-called Basel III global framework for bank supervision developed beginning in 2009 retains such references.

13 The "issuer pay" model allows the distribution of ratings to a broad universe of investors and undoubtedly facilitated widespread reliance on ratings. It is controversial, however, because some believe it creates a conflict of interest among the rating agency, the investor, and the issuer. Studies suggest, however, that ratings are not biased upward and alternate payment models, such as "investor pays," have their own shortcomings, including the "free rider" problem inherent in a business where information is widely available and freely shared. So, despite its potential problems, and some calls for a new payment model, the "issuer pay" model remains entrenched in the market.

- Huge growth of debt markets
- Development and expansion of bond portfolio management and the accompanying bond indexes.

However, in the aftermath of the financial crisis of 2008–2009, when the rating agencies were blamed for contributing to the crisis with their overly optimistic ratings on securities backed by subprime mortgages, there were attempts to reduce the role and dominant positions of the major credit rating agencies. New rules, regulations, and legislation were passed to require the agencies to be more transparent, reduce conflicts of interest, and stimulate more competition. Challenging the dominance of Moody's, S&P, and Fitch, additional credit rating agencies have emerged. Some credit rating agencies that are well-established in their home markets but are not so well known globally, such as Dominion Bond Rating Service (DBRS) in Canada and Japan Credit Rating Agency (JCR) in Japan, have tried to raise their profiles. The market dominance of the biggest credit rating agencies, however, remains largely intact.

4.1 Credit Ratings

The three major global credit rating agencies—Moody's, S&P, and Fitch—use similar, symbol-based ratings that are basically an assessment of a bond issue's risk of default. Exhibit 4 shows their long-term ratings ranked from highest to lowest.[14]

Exhibit 4 Long-Term Ratings Matrix: Investment Grade vs. Non-Investment Grade

		Moody's	S&P	Fitch
Investment Grade	High-Quality Grade	Aaa	AAA	AAA
		Aa1	AA+	AA+
		Aa2	AA	AA
		Aa3	AA–	AA–
	Upper-Medium Grade	A1	A+	A+
		A2	A	A
		A3	A–	A–
	Low-Medium Grade	Baa1	BBB+	BBB+
		Baa2	BBB	BBB
		Baa3	BBB–	BBB–

14 The rating agencies also provide ratings on short-term debt instruments, such as bank deposits and commercial paper. However, they use different scales: From the highest to lowest rating, Moody's uses P-1, P-2, P-3; S&P uses A-1+, A-1, A-2, A-3; Fitch uses F-1, F-2, F-3. Below that is not prime. Short-term ratings are typically used by money market funds, with the vast majority of the instruments they own rated in the highest (or in the case of S&P, the highest or second-highest) category. These top ratings basically map to a single-A or higher long-term rating.

Exhibit 4 (Continued)

		Moody's	S&P	Fitch
Non-Investment Grade "Junk" or "High Yield"	Low Grade or Speculative Grade	Ba1	BB+	BB+
		Ba2	BB	BB
		Ba3	BB–	BB–
		B1	B+	B+
		B2	B	B
		B3	B–	B–
		Caa1	CCC+	CCC+
		Caa2	CCC	CCC
		Caa3	CCC–	CCC–
		Ca	CC	CC
		C	C	C
	Default	C	D	D

Bonds rated triple-A (Aaa or AAA) are said to be "of the highest quality, subject to the lowest level of credit risk"[15] and thus have extremely low probabilities of default. Double-A (Aa or AA) rated bonds are referred to as "high-quality grade" and are also regarded as having very low default risk. Bonds rated single-A are referred to as "upper-medium grade." Baa (Moody's) or BBB (S&P and Fitch) are called "low-medium grade." Bonds rated Baa3/BBB– or higher are called "investment grade." Bonds rated Ba1 or lower by Moody's and BB+ or lower by S&P and Fitch, respectively, have speculative credit characteristics and increasingly higher default risk. As a group, these bonds are referred to in a variety of ways: "low grade," "speculative grade," "non-investment grade," "below investment grade," "high yield," and, in an attempt to reflect the extreme level of risk, some observers refer to these bonds as "junk bonds." The D rating is reserved for securities that are already in default in S&P's and Fitch's scales. For Moody's, bonds rated C are likely, but not necessarily, in default. Generally, issuers of bonds rated investment grade are more consistently able to access the debt markets and can borrow at lower interest rates than those rated below investment grade.

In addition, rating agencies will typically provide outlooks on their respective ratings—positive, stable, or negative—and may provide other indicators on the potential direction of their ratings under certain circumstances, such as "On Review for Downgrade" or "On CreditWatch for an Upgrade."[16] It should also be noted that, in support of the ratings they publish, the rating agencies also provide extensive written commentary and financial analysis on the obligors they rate, as well as summary industry statistics.

4.2 Issuer vs. Issue Ratings

Rating agencies will typically provide both issuer and issue ratings, particularly as they relate to corporate debt. Terminology used to distinguish between issuer and issue ratings includes corporate family rating (CFR) and corporate credit rating (CCR) or issuer credit rating and issue credit rating. An issuer credit rating is meant to address

15 Moody's Investors Service, "Ratings Symbols and Definitions" (June 2018).

16 Additional detail on their respective ratings definitions, methodologies, and criteria can be found on each of the major rating agency's websites: www.moodys.com, www.standardandpoors.com, and www.fitch.com.

an obligor's overall creditworthiness—its ability and willingness to make timely payments of interest and principal on its debt. The issuer credit rating usually applies to its senior unsecured debt.

Issue ratings refer to specific financial obligations of an issuer and take into consideration such factors as ranking in the capital structure (e.g., secured or subordinated). Although **cross-default provisions**, whereby events of default such as non-payment of interest[17] on one bond trigger default on all outstanding debt,[18] implies the same default probability for all issues, specific issues may be assigned different credit ratings—higher or lower—due to a ratings adjustment methodology known as **notching**.

Notching. For the rating agencies, likelihood of default—default risk—is the primary factor in assigning their ratings. However, there are secondary factors as well. These factors include the priority of payment in the event of a default (e.g., secured versus senior unsecured versus subordinated) as well as potential loss severity in the event of default. Another factor considered by rating agencies is **structural subordination**, which can arise when a corporation with a holding company structure has debt at both its parent holding company and operating subsidiaries. Debt at the operating subsidiaries will get serviced by the cash flow and assets of the subsidiaries before funds can be passed ("upstreamed") to the holding company to service debt at that level.

Recognizing these different payment priorities, and thus the potential for higher (or lower) loss severity in the event of default, the rating agencies have adopted a notching process whereby their credit ratings on issues can be moved up or down from the issuer rating, which is usually the rating applied to its senior unsecured debt. As a general rule, the higher the senior unsecured rating, the smaller the notching adjustment will be. The reason behind this is that the higher the rating, the lower the perceived risk of default, so the need to "notch" the rating to capture the potential difference in loss severity is greatly reduced. For lower-rated credits, however, the risk of default is greater and thus the potential difference in loss from a lower (or higher) priority ranking is a bigger consideration in assessing an issue's credit riskiness. Thus, the rating agencies will typically apply larger rating adjustments. For example, S&P applies the following notching guidelines:

> A key principle is that investment-grade ratings focus more on timeliness, while non-investment grade ratings give additional weight to recovery. For example, subordinated debt can be rated up to two notches below a noninvestment grade corporate credit rating, but one notch at most if the corporate credit rating is investment grade. Conversely, ... the 'AAA' rating category need not be notched at all, while at the 'CCC' level the gaps may widen.
>
> The rationale for this convention is straightforward: as default risk increases, the concern over what can be recovered takes on greater relevance and, therefore, greater rating significance. Accordingly, the ultimate recovery aspect of ratings is given more weight as one moves down the rating spectrum.[19]

---

17 This issue will be covered in greater detail in the section on covenants.

18 Nearly all bonds have a cross-default provision. Rare exceptions to this cross-default provision include the deeply subordinated, debt-like securities referenced earlier in this reading.

19 Standard & Poor's, "Rating The Issue," in *Corporate Ratings Criteria 2008* (New York: Standard and Poor's, 2008):65.

Exhibit 5 is an example of S&P's notching criteria, as applied to Infor Software Parent LLC, Inc. (Infor). Infor is a US-based global software and services company whose corporate credit rating from S&P is B–. Note how the company's senior secured bonds are rated B, whereas its senior unsecured bonds are rated two notches lower at CCC+ and its holding company debt is rated even one notch lower at CCC.

Exhibit 5 Infor S&P Ratings Detail (as of December 2018)

Corporate credit rating	B–/Stable
Senior secured (3 issues)	B
Senior unsecured (2 issues)	CCC+
Holding company debt (1 issue)	CCC

Source: Standard & Poor's Financial Services, LLC.

4.3 Risks in Relying on Agency Ratings

The dominant position of the rating agencies in the global debt markets, and the near-universal use of their credit ratings on debt securities, suggests that investors believe they do a good job assessing credit risk. In fact, with a few exceptions (e.g., too high ratings on US subprime mortgage-backed securities issued in the mid-2000s, which turned out to be much riskier than expected), their ratings have proved quite accurate as a relative measure of default risk. For example, Exhibit 6 shows historical S&P one-year global corporate default rates by rating category for the 20 year period from 1998 to 2017.[20]

Exhibit 6 Global Corporate Annual Default Rates by Rating Category (%)

	AAA	AA	A	BBB	BB	B	CCC/C
1998	0.00	0.00	0.00	0.41	0.82	4.63	42.86
1999	0.00	0.17	0.18	0.20	0.95	7.29	33.33
2000	0.00	0.00	0.27	0.37	1.16	7.70	35.96
2001	0.00	0.00	0.27	0.34	2.96	11.53	45.45
2002	0.00	0.00	0.00	1.01	2.89	8.21	44.44
2003	0.00	0.00	0.00	0.23	0.58	4.07	32.73
2004	0.00	0.00	0.08	0.00	0.44	1.45	16.18
2005	0.00	0.00	0.00	0.07	0.31	1.74	9.09
2006	0.00	0.00	0.00	0.00	0.30	0.82	13.33
2007	0.00	0.00	0.00	0.00	0.20	0.25	15.24
2008	0.00	0.38	0.39	0.49	0.81	4.09	27.27
2009	0.00	0.00	0.22	0.55	0.75	10.94	49.46
2010	0.00	0.00	0.00	0.00	0.58	0.86	22.62
2011	0.00	0.00	0.00	0.07	0.00	1.67	16.30
2012	0.00	0.00	0.00	0.00	0.03	1.57	27.52
2013	0.00	0.00	0.00	0.00	0.10	1.64	24.50

(continued)

20 S&P uses a static pool methodology here. It measures the percentage of issues that defaulted in a given calendar year based on how they were rated at the beginning of the year.

Exhibit 6 (Continued)

	AAA	AA	A	BBB	BB	B	CCC/C
2014	0.00	0.00	0.00	0.00	0.00	0.78	17.42
2015	0.00	0.00	0.00	0.00	0.16	2.40	26.51
2016	0.00	0.00	0.00	0.00	0.47	3.70	33.17
2017	0.00	0.00	0.00	0.00	0.08	0.98	26.23
Mean	0.00	0.03	0.07	0.19	0.69	3.82	27.98
Max	0.00	0.38	0.39	1.01	2.96	11.53	45.45
Min	0.00	0.00	0.00	0.00	0.00	0.25	9.09

Source: Based on data from Standard & Poor's Financial Services, LLC.

As Exhibit 6 shows, the highest-rated bonds have extremely low default rates. With very few exceptions, the lower the rating, the higher the annual rate of default, with bonds rated CCC and lower experiencing the highest default rates by far.

There are limitations and risks, however, to relying on credit rating agency ratings, including the following:

- **Credit ratings can change over time**. Over a long time period (e.g., many years), credit ratings can migrate—move up or down—significantly from what they were at the time of bond issuance. Using Standard & Poor's data, Exhibit 7 shows the average three-year migration (or "transition") by rating from 1981 to 2017. Note that the higher the credit rating, the greater the ratings stability. Even for AAA rated credits, however, only about 65 percent of the time did ratings remain in that rating category over a three-year period. (Of course, AAA rated credits can have their ratings move in only one direction—down.) A very small fraction of AAA rated credits became non-investment grade or defaulted within three years. For single-B rated credits, only 41 percent of the time did ratings remain in that rating category over three-year periods. This observation about how credit ratings can change over time isn't meant to be a criticism of the rating agencies. It is meant to demonstrate that creditworthiness can and does change—up or down—and that bond investors should not assume an issuer's credit rating will remain the same from time of purchase through the entire holding period.

Exhibit 7 Average Three-Year Global Corporate Transition Rates, 1981–2017 (%)

From/To	AAA	AA	A	BBB	BB	B	CCC/C	D	NR*
AAA	65.48	22.09	2.35	0.32	0.19	0.08	0.11	0.13	9.24
AA	1.21	66.14	18.53	2.06	0.35	0.22	0.03	0.12	11.33
A	0.06	4.07	68.85	11.72	1.30	0.44	0.09	0.25	13.21
BBB	0.02	0.28	8.42	64.66	7.11	1.64	0.30	0.87	16.70
BB	0.01	0.06	0.51	11.08	47.04	11.58	1.25	3.96	24.51

Exhibit 7 (Continued)

From/To	AAA	AA	A	BBB	BB	B	CCC/C	D	NR*
B	0.00	0.03	0.21	0.78	10.23	41.46	4.67	12.57	30.05
CCC/C	0.00	0.00	0.14	0.61	1.63	16.86	10.54	40.65	29.57

* NR means not rated—that is, certain corporate issuers were no longer rated by S&P. This could occur for a variety of reasons, including issuers paying off their debt and no longer needing ratings.
Source: 2017 Annual Global Corporate Default Study, p.53.

- **Credit ratings tend to lag the market's pricing of credit risk.** Bond prices and credit spreads frequently move more quickly because of changes in perceived creditworthiness than rating agencies change their ratings (or even outlooks) up or down. Bond prices and relative valuations can move every day, whereas bond ratings, appropriately, don't change that often. Even over long time periods, however, credit ratings can badly lag changes in bond prices. Exhibit 8 shows the price and Moody's rating of a bond from US automaker Ford Motor Company before, during, and after the financial crisis in 2008. Note how the bond's price moved down sharply well before Moody's downgraded its credit rating—multiple times—and also how the bond's price began to recover—and kept recovering—well before Moody's upgraded its credit rating on Ford debt.

Exhibit 8 Historical Example: Ford Motor Company Senior Unsecured Debt: Price vs. Moody's Rating 2005–2011

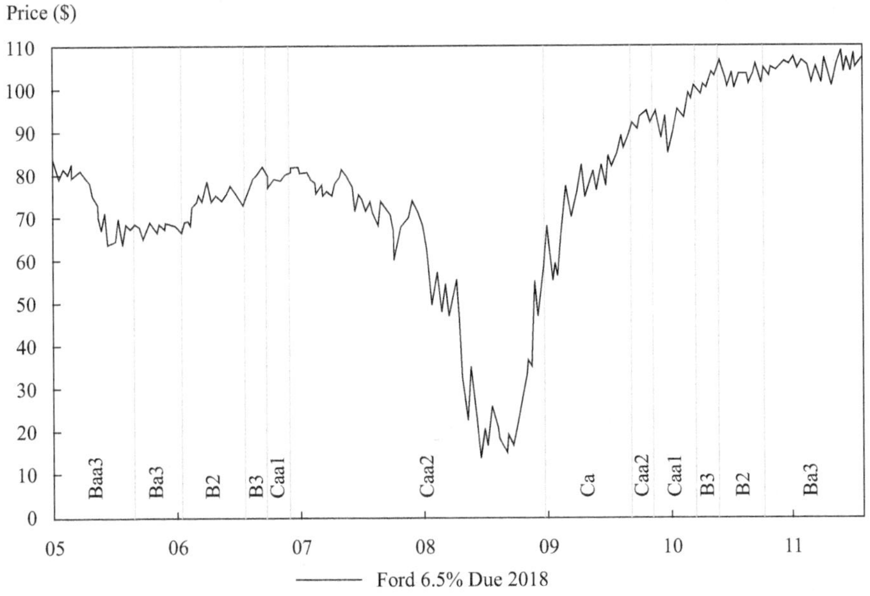

Sources: Data based on Bloomberg Finance L.P. and Moody's Investors Service.

Moreover, particularly for certain speculative-grade credits, two bonds with similar ratings may trade at very different valuations. This is partly a result of the fact that credit ratings primarily try to assess the risk of default, whereas for low-quality credits, the market begins focusing more on expected loss (default probability times loss severity). So, bonds from two separate issuers with comparable (high) risk of default but different recovery rates may have similar ratings but trade at significantly different dollar prices.[21]

Thus, bond investors who wait for rating agencies to change their ratings before making buy and sell decisions in their portfolios may be at risk of underperforming other investors who make portfolio decisions in advance of—or not solely based on—rating agency changes.

- **Rating agencies may make mistakes.** The mis-rating of billions of dollars of subprime-backed mortgage securities is one example. Other historical examples include the mis-ratings of US companies Enron and WorldCom and European issuer Parmalat. Like many investors, the rating agencies did not understand the accounting fraud being committed in those companies.
- **Some risks are difficult to capture in credit ratings.** Examples include litigation risk, such as that which can affect tobacco companies, or environmental and business risks faced by chemical companies and utility power plants. This would also include the impact from natural disasters. Leveraged transactions, such as debt-financed acquisitions and large stock buybacks (share repurchases), are often difficult to anticipate and thus to capture in credit ratings.

As described, there are risks in relying on credit rating agency ratings when investing in bonds. Thus, while the credit rating agencies will almost certainly continue to play a significant role in the bond markets, it is important for investors to perform their own credit analyses and draw their own conclusions regarding the credit risk of a given debt issue or issuer.

EXAMPLE 4

Credit Ratings

1 Using the S&P ratings scale, investment grade bonds carry which of the following ratings?

   A AAA to EEE

   B BBB– to CCC

   C AAA to BBB–

2 Using both Moody's and S&P ratings, which of the following pairs of ratings is considered high yield, also known as "below investment grade," "speculative grade," or "junk"?

   A Baa1/BBB–

   B B3/CCC+

   C Baa3/BB+

3 What is the difference between an issuer rating and an issue rating?

   A The issuer rating applies to all of an issuer's bonds, whereas the issue rating considers a bond's seniority ranking.

   B The issuer rating is an assessment of an issuer's overall creditworthiness, whereas the issue rating is always higher than the issuer rating.

21 See Christopher L. Gootkind, "Improving Credit Risk Analysis," in *Fixed-Income Management for the 21st Century* (Charlottesville, VA: Association for Investment Management and Research, 2002).

C The issuer rating is an assessment of an issuer's overall creditworthiness, typically reflected as the senior unsecured rating, whereas the issue rating considers a bond's seniority ranking (e.g., secured or subordinated).

4 Based on the practice of notching by the rating agencies, a subordinated bond from a company with an issuer rating of BB would likely carry what rating?

A B+

B BB

C BBB–

5 The fixed-income portfolio manager you work with asked you why a bond from an issuer you cover didn't rise in price when it was upgraded by Fitch from B+ to BB. Which of the following is the *most likely* explanation?

A Bond prices never react to rating changes.

B The bond doesn't trade often so the price hasn't adjusted to the rating change yet.

C The market was expecting the rating change, and so it was already "priced in" to the bond.

6 Amalgamated Corp. and Widget Corp. each have bonds outstanding with similar coupons and maturity dates. Both bonds are rated B2, B–, and B by Moody's, S&P, and Fitch, respectively. The bonds, however, trade at very different prices—the Amalgamated bond trades at €89, whereas the Widget bond trades at €62. What is the *most likely* explanation of the price (and yield) difference?

A Widget's credit ratings are lagging the market's assessment of the company's credit deterioration.

B The bonds have similar risks of default (as reflected in the ratings), but the market believes the Amalgamated bond has a higher expected loss in the event of default.

C The bonds have similar risks of default (as reflected in the ratings), but the market believes the Widget bond has a higher expected recovery rate in the event of default.

Solution to 1:

C is correct.

Solution to 2:

B is correct. Note that issuers with ratings such as Baa3/BB+ (answer C) are called "crossovers" because one rating is investment grade (the Moody's rating of Baa3) and the other is high yield (the S&P rating of BB+).

Solution to 3:

C is correct.

Solution to 4:

A is correct. The subordinated bond would have its rating notched lower than the company's BB rating, probably by two notches, reflecting the higher weight given to loss severity for below-investment-grade credits.

Solution to 5:

C is correct. The market was anticipating the rating upgrade and had already priced it in. Bond prices often do react to rating changes, particularly multi-notch ones. Even if bonds don't trade, their prices adjust based on dealer quotations given to bond pricing services.

Solution to 6:

A is correct. Widget's credit ratings are probably lagging behind the market's assessment of its deteriorating creditworthiness. Answers B and C both state the situation backwards. If the market believed that the Amalgamated bond had a higher expected loss given default, then that bond would be trading at a lower, not a higher, price. Similarly, if the market believed that the Widget bond had a higher expected recovery rate in the event of default, then that bond would be trading at a higher, not a lower, price.

5 TRADITIONAL CREDIT ANALYSIS: CORPORATE DEBT SECURITIES

The goal of credit analysis is to assess an issuer's ability to satisfy its debt obligations, including bonds and other indebtedness, such as bank loans. These debt obligations are contracts, the terms of which specify the interest rate to be paid, the frequency and timing of payments, the maturity date, and the covenants that describe the permissible and required actions of the borrower. Because corporate bonds are contracts, enforceable by law, credit analysts generally assume an issuer's willingness to pay and concentrate instead on assessing its ability to pay. Thus, the main focus in credit analysis is to understand a company's ability to generate cash flow over the term of its debt obligations. In so doing, analysts must assess both the credit quality of the company and the fundamentals of the industry in which the company operates. Traditional credit analysis considers the sources, predictability, and sustainability of cash generated by a company to service its debt obligations. This section will focus on corporate credit analysis; in particular, it will emphasize non-financial companies. Financial institutions have very different business models and funding profiles from industrial and utility companies.

5.1 Credit Analysis vs. Equity Analysis: Similarities and Differences

The above description of credit analysis suggests credit and equity analyses should be very similar; in many ways, they are. There are motivational differences, however, between equity and fixed-income investors that are an important aspect of credit analysis. Strictly speaking, management works for the shareholders of a company. Its primary objective is to maximize the value of the company for its owners. In contrast, management's legal duty to its creditors—including bondholders—is to meet the terms of the governing contracts. Growth in the value of a corporation from rising profits and cash flow accrues to the shareholders, while the best outcome for bondholders is to receive full, timely payment of interest and repayment of principal when due. Conversely, shareholders are more exposed to the decline in value if a company's earnings and cash flow decline because bondholders have a prior claim on cash flow and assets. But if a company's earnings and cash flow decline to the extent that it can no longer make its debt payments, then bondholders are at risk of loss as well.

In summary, in exchange for a prior claim on cash flow and assets, bondholders do not share in the growth in value of a company (except to the extent that its creditworthiness improves) but have downside risk in the event of default. In contrast, shareholders have theoretically unlimited upside opportunity, but in the event of default, their investment is typically wiped out before the bondholders suffer a loss. This is very similar to the type of payoff patterns seen in financial options. In fact, in recent years, credit risk models, have been developed based on the insights of option pricing theory. Although it is beyond the scope of this present introduction to the subject, it is an expanding area of interest to both institutional investors and rating agencies.

Thus, although the analysis is similar in many respects for both equity and credit, equity analysts are interested in the strategies and investments that will increase a company's value and grow earnings per share. They then compare that earnings and growth potential with that of other companies in a given industry. Credit analysts will look more at the downside risk by measuring and assessing the sustainability of a company's cash flow relative to its debt levels and interest expense. Importantly for credit analysts, the balance sheet will show the composition of an issuer's debt—the overall amount, how much is coming due and when, and the distribution by seniority ranking. In general, equity analysts will focus more on income and cash flow statements, whereas credit analysts tend to focus more on the balance sheet and cash flow statements.

5.2 The Four Cs of Credit Analysis: A Useful Framework

Traditionally, many analysts evaluated creditworthiness based on what is often called the "four Cs of credit analysis":[22]

- Capacity
- Collateral
- Covenants
- Character

Capacity refers to the ability of the borrower to make its debt payments on time; this is the focus of this section. **Collaterals** refers to the quality and value of the assets supporting the issuer's indebtedness. **Covenants** are the terms and conditions of lending agreements that the issuer must comply with. **Character** refers to the quality of management. Each of these will now be covered in greater detail.

5.2.1 *Capacity*

Capacity is the ability of a borrower to service its debt. To determine that, credit analysis, in a process similar to equity analysis, starts with industry analysis and then turns to examination of the specific issuer (company analysis).

22 There is no unique list of Cs. In addition to those listed here, one may see "capital" and/or "conditions" on a particular author's list of four (or five) Cs. Conditions typically refers to overall economic conditions. Capital refers to the company's accumulated capital and its specific capital assets and is essentially subsumed within the categories of capacity and collateral. Keep in mind that the list of Cs is a convenient way to summarize the important aspects of the analysis, not a checklist to be applied mechanically.

Industry structure. A useful framework for analyzing industry structure was developed by business school professor and consultant Michael Porter.[23] The framework considers the effects of five competitive forces on an industry:

1 **Threat of entry.** Threat of entry depends on the extent of barriers to entry and the expected response from incumbents to new entrants. Industries with high entry barriers tend to be more profitable and have lower credit risk than industries with low entry barriers because incumbents do not need to hold down prices or take other steps to deter new entrants. High entry barriers can take many forms, including high capital investment, such as in aerospace; large, established distribution systems, such as in auto dealerships; patent protection, such as in technology or pharmaceutical industries; or a high degree of regulation, such as in utilities.

2 **Power of suppliers.** An industry that relies on just a few suppliers tends to be less profitable and to have greater credit risk than an industry that has multiple suppliers. Industries and companies with just a few suppliers have limited negotiating power to keep the suppliers from raising prices, whereas industries that have many suppliers can play them off against each other to keep prices in check.

3 **Power of buyers/customers.** Industries that rely heavily on just a few main customers have greater credit risk because the negotiating power lies with the buyers. For example, a toolmaker that sells 50 percent of its products to one large global retailer has limited negotiating power with its principal customer.

4 **Threat of substitutes.** Industries (and companies) that offer products and services that provide great value to their customers, and for which there are not good or cost-competitive substitutes, typically have strong pricing power, generate substantial cash flows, and represent less credit risk than other industries or companies. Certain (patent-protected) drugs are an example. Over time, however, disruptive technologies and inventions can increase substitution risk. For example, years ago, airplanes began displacing many trains and steamships. Newspapers were considered to have a nearly unassailable market position until television and then the internet became substitutes for how people received news and information. Over time, recorded music has shifted from records to tapes, to compact discs, to mp3s and other forms of digital media.

5 **Rivalry among existing competitors.** Industries with strong rivalry—because of numerous competitors, slow industry growth, or high barriers to exit—tend to have less cash flow predictability and, therefore, higher credit risk than industries with less competition. Regulation can affect the extent of rivalry and competition. For example, regulated utilities typically have a monopoly position in a given market, which results in relatively stable and predictable cash flows.

It is important to consider how companies in an industry generate revenues and earn profits. Is it an industry with high fixed costs and capital investment or one with modest fixed costs? These structures generate revenues and earn profits in very different ways. Two examples of industries with high fixed costs, also referred to as "having high operating leverage," are airlines and hotels. Many of their operating costs are fixed—running a hotel, flying a plane—so they cannot easily cut costs. If an insufficient number of people stay at a hotel or fly in a plane, fixed operating costs may not be covered and losses may result. With higher occupancy of a hotel or plane, revenues are higher, and it is more likely that fixed costs will be covered and profits earned.

23 Porter, Michael E. 2008. "The Five Competitive Forces That Shape Strategy." *Harvard Business Review*, vol. 86, no. 1:78–93.

Industry fundamentals. After understanding an industry's structure, the next step is to assess its fundamentals, including its sensitivity to macroeconomic factors, its growth prospects, its profitability, and its business need—or lack thereof—for high credit quality. Judgments about these can be made by looking at the following:

- *Cyclical or non-cyclical.* This is a crucial assessment because industries that are cyclical—that is, have greater sensitivity to broader economic performance—have more volatile revenues, margins, and cash flows and thus are inherently riskier than non-cyclical industries. Consumer product and health care companies are typically considered non-cyclical, whereas auto and steel companies can be very cyclical. Companies in cyclical industries should carry lower levels of debt relative to their ability to generate cash flow over an economic cycle than companies in less-cyclical or non-cyclical industries.
- *Growth prospects.* Although growth is typically a greater focus for equity analysts than for credit analysts, bond investors have an interest in growth as well. Industries that have little or no growth tend to consolidate via mergers and acquisitions. Depending upon how these are financed (e.g., using stock or debt) and the economic benefits (or lack thereof) of the merger, they may or may not be favorable to corporate bond investors. Weaker competitors in slow-growth industries may begin to struggle financially, adversely affecting their creditworthiness.
- *Published industry statistics.* Analysts can get an understanding of an industry's fundamentals and performance by researching statistics that are published by and available from a number of different sources, including the rating agencies, investment banks, industry publications, and frequently, government agencies.

Company fundamentals. Following analysis of an industry's structure and fundamentals, the next step is to assess the fundamentals of the company: the corporate borrower. Analysts should examine the following:

- Competitive position
- Track record/operating history
- Management's strategy and execution
- Ratios and ratio analysis

Competitive position. Based on their knowledge of the industry structure and fundamentals, analysts assess a company's competitive position within the industry. What is its market share? How has it changed over time: Is it increasing, decreasing, holding steady? Is it well above (or below) its peers? How does it compare with respect to cost structure? How might it change its competitive position? What sort of financing might that require?

Track record/Operating history. How has the company performed over time? It's useful to go back several years and analyze the company's financial performance, perhaps during times of both economic growth and contraction. What are the trends in revenues, profit margins, and cash flow? Capital expenditures represent what percent of revenues? What are the trends on the balance sheet—use of debt versus equity? Was this track record developed under the current management team? If not, when did the current management team take over?

Management's strategy and execution. What is management's strategy for the company: to compete and to grow? Does it make sense, and is it plausible? How risky is it, and how differentiated is it from its industry peers? Is it venturing into unrelated businesses? Does the analyst have confidence in management's ability to execute? What is management's track record, both at this company and at previous ones? Credit analysts also want to know and understand how management's strategy will affect its balance sheet. Does management plan to manage the balance sheet prudently, in a manner that doesn't adversely affect bondholders? Analysts can learn about management's strategy from reading comments, discussion, and analysis that are included with financial statements filed with appropriate regulators, listening to conference calls about earnings or other big announcements (e.g., acquisitions), going to company websites to find earnings releases and copies of slides of presentations at various industry conferences, visiting and speaking with the company, and so on.

EXAMPLE 5

Industry and Company Analysis

1 Given a hotel company, a chemical company, and a consumer products company, which is *most likely* to be able to support a high debt load over an economic cycle?

  A The hotel company, because people need a place to stay when they travel.

  B The chemical company, because chemicals are a key input to many products.

  C The consumer products company, because consumer products are typically resistant to recessions.

2 Heavily regulated monopoly companies, such as utilities, often carry high debt loads. Which of the following statements about such companies is *most* accurate?

  A Regulators require them to carry high debt loads.

  B They generate strong and stable cash flows, enabling them to support high levels of debt.

  C They are not very profitable and need to borrow heavily to maintain their plant and equipment.

3 XYZ Corp. manufactures a commodity product in a highly competitive industry in which no company has significant market share and where there are low barriers to entry. Which of the following *best* describes XYZ's ability to take on substantial debt?

  A Its ability is very limited because companies in industries with those characteristics generally cannot support high debt loads.

  B Its ability is high because companies in industries with those characteristics generally have high margins and cash flows that can support significant debt.

  C We don't have enough information to answer the question.

Solution to 1:

C is correct. Consumer products companies are considered non-cyclical, whereas hotel and chemical companies are more cyclical and thus more vulnerable to economic downturns.

Solution to 2:

B is correct. Because such monopolies' financial returns are generally dictated by the regulators, they generate consistent cash flows and are, therefore, able to support high debt levels.

Solution to 3:

A is correct. Companies in industries with those characteristics typically have low margins and limited cash flow and thus cannot support high debt levels.

Ratios and ratio analysis. To provide context to the analysis and understanding of a company's fundamentals—based on the industry in which it operates, its competitive position, its strategy and execution—a number of financial measures derived from the company's principal financial statements are examined. Credit analysts calculate a number of ratios to assess the financial health of a company, identify trends over time, and compare companies across an industry to get a sense of relative creditworthiness. Note that typical values of these ratios vary widely from one industry to another because of different industry characteristics previously identified: competitive structure, economic cyclicality, regulation, and so on.

We will categorize the key credit analysis measures into three different groups:

- Profitability and cash flow
- Leverage
- Coverage

Profitability and cash flow measures. It is from profitability and cash flow generation that companies can service their debt. Credit analysts typically look at operating profit margins and operating income to get a sense of a company's underlying profitability and see how it varies over time. Operating income is defined as operating revenues minus operating expenses and is commonly referred to as "earnings before interest and taxes" (EBIT). Credit analysts focus on EBIT because it is useful to determine a company's performance prior to costs arising from its capital structure (i.e., how much debt it carries versus equity). And "before taxes" is used because interest expense is paid before income taxes are calculated.

There are several measures of cash flow used in credit analysis; some are more conservative than others because they make certain adjustments for cash that gets used in managing and maintaining the business or in making payments to shareholders. The cash flow measures and leverage and coverage ratios discussed below are non-IFRS in the sense that they do not have official IFRS definitions; the concepts, names, and definitions given should be viewed as one usage among several possible, in most cases.

- **Earnings before interest, taxes, depreciation, and amortization (EBITDA).** EBITDA is a commonly used measure of cash flow that takes operating income and adds back depreciation and amortization expense because those are non-cash items. This is a somewhat crude measure of cash flow because it excludes certain cash-related expenses of running a business, such as capital expenditures and changes in (non-cash) working capital. Thus, despite its popularity as a cash flow measure, analysts look at other measures in addition to EBITDA.
- **Funds from operations (FFO).** Standard & Poor's defines funds from operations as net income from continuing operations plus depreciation, amortization, deferred income taxes, and other non-cash items.[24]

---

24 The funds from operations differs only slightly from the better known cash flow from operations in that it excludes working capital changes. The idea behind using FFO in credit analysis is to take out the near-term swings and seasonality in working capital that can potentially distort the amount of operating cash flow a business is generating. Over time, the working capital swings are expected to even out. Analysts tend to look at both FFO and cash flow from operations, particularly for businesses with large working capital swings (e.g., very cyclical manufacturing companies).

- **Free cash flow before dividends (FCF before dividends).**[25] This measures excess cash flow generated by the company (excluding non-recurring items) before payments to shareholders or that could be used to pay down debt or pay dividends. It can be calculated as net income (excluding non-recurring items) plus depreciation and amortization minus increase (plus decrease) in non-cash working capital minus capital expenditures. This is, depending upon the treatment of dividends and interest in the cash flow statement, approximated by the cash flow from operating activities minus capital expenditures. Companies that have negative free cash flow before payments to shareholders will be consuming cash they have or will need to rely on additional financing—from banks, bond investors, or equity investors. This obviously represents higher credit risk.
- **Free cash flow after dividends (FCF after dividends).** This measure just takes free cash flow before dividends and subtracts dividend payments. If this number is positive, it represents cash that could be used to pay down debt or build up cash on the balance sheet. Either action may be viewed as deleveraging, which is favorable from a credit risk standpoint. Some credit analysts will calculate net debt by subtracting balance sheet cash from total debt, although they shouldn't assume the cash will be used to pay down debt. Actual debt paid down from free cash flow is a better indicator of deleveraging. Some analysts will also deduct stock buybacks to get the "truest" measure of free cash flow that can be used to de-lever on either a gross or net debt basis; however, others view stock buybacks (share repurchases) as more discretionary and as having less certain timing than dividends, and thus treat those two types of shareholder payments differently when calculating free cash flow.

Leverage ratios. There are a few measures of leverage used by credit analysts. The most common are the debt/capital, debt/EBITDA, and measures of funds or cash flows/debt ratios. Note that many analysts adjust a company's reported debt levels for debt-like liabilities, such as underfunded pensions and other retiree benefits, as well as operating leases. When adjusting for leases, analysts will typically add back the imputed interest or rent expense to various cash flow measures.

- **Debt/capital**. Capital is calculated as total debt plus shareholders equity. This ratio shows the percent of a company's capital base that is financed with debt. A lower percentage of debt indicates lower credit risk. This traditional ratio is generally used for investment-grade corporate issuers. Where goodwill or other intangible assets are significant (and subject to obsolescence, depletion, or impairment), it is often informative to also compute the debt to capital ratio after assuming a write-down of the after-tax value of such assets.
- **Debt/EBITDA.** This ratio is a common leverage measure. Analysts use it on a "snapshot" basis, as well as to look at trends over time and at projections and to compare companies in a given industry. Rating agencies often use it as a trigger for rating actions, and banks reference it in loan covenants. A higher ratio indicates more leverage and thus higher credit risk. Note that this ratio can be very volatile for companies with high cash flow variability, such as those in cyclical industries and with high operating leverage (fixed costs).

25 This is similar to free cash flow to the firm (FCFF), referred to in the Level I CFA Program reading "Understanding Cash Flow Statements."

- **FFO/debt.** Credit rating agencies often use this leverage ratio. They publish key median and average ratios, such as this one, by rating category so analysts can get a sense of why an issuer is assigned a certain credit rating, as well as where that rating may migrate based on changes to such key ratios as this one. A higher ratio indicates greater ability to pay debt by funds from operations.
- **FCF after dividends/debt.** A higher ratio indicates that a greater amount of debt can be paid off from free cash flow after dividend payments.

Coverage ratios. Coverage ratios measure an issuer's ability to meet—to "cover"—its interest payments. The two most common are the EBITDA/interest expense and EBIT/interest expense ratios.

- **EBITDA/interest expense.** This measurement of interest coverage is a bit more liberal than the one that uses EBIT because it does not subtract out the impact of (non-cash) depreciation and amortization expense. A higher ratio indicates higher credit quality.
- **EBIT/interest expense.** Because EBIT does not include depreciation and amortization, it is considered a more conservative measure of interest coverage. This ratio is now used less frequently than EBITDA/interest expense.

Exhibit 9 is an example of key average credit ratios by rating category for industrial companies over the 12-month period 3Q2017–3Q2018, as calculated by Bloomberg Barclays Indices, using public company data.[26]

Exhibit 9 Industrial Comparative Ratio Analysis

Credit Rating	EBITDA Margin (%)	Return on Capital (%)	EBIT Interest Coverage (x)	EBITDA Interest Coverage (x)	FFO/Debt (%)	Free Operations Cash Flow/Debt (%)	Debt/ EBITDA (x)	Debt/Debt plus Equity (%)
Aaa								
US	66.4	6.5	4.2	21.3	51.9	43.5	−0.2	43.3
Aa								
US	21.9	10.8	15.4	45.0	109.9	58.1	1.2	50.6
A								
US	26.0	13.5	13.3	18.9	49.1	31.8	1.8	51.2
Baa								
US	23.9	11.5	7.2	NA	40.7	20.3	3.9	49.4
Ba								
US	21.7	3.5	4.6	NA	27.7	11.0	4.1	64.0
B								
US	21.2	3.7	2.5	NA	20.3	1.8	5.2	69.3

(continued)

26 Note there are only a few AAA-rated corporations remaining, so the small sample size can skew the average ratios of a few key credit metrics. That said, it should be clear that, overall, higher-rated issuers have stronger credit metrics.

Exhibit 9 (Continued)

Credit Rating	EBITDA Margin (%)	Return on Capital (%)	EBIT Interest Coverage (x)	EBITDA Interest Coverage (x)	FFO/Debt (%)	Free Operations Cash Flow/Debt (%)	Debt/ EBITDA (x)	Debt/Debt plus Equity (%)
Caa								
US	16.0	0.2	−0.6	1.3	10.0	−6.6	9.3	95.3

Notes: As of 19 December 2018.
Source: Bloomberg Barclays Indices.

Comments on issuer liquidity. An issuer's access to liquidity is also an important consideration in credit analysis. Companies with high liquidity represent lower credit risk than those with weak liquidity, other factors being equal. The financial crisis of 2008–2009 showed that access to liquidity via the debt and equity markets should not be taken for granted, particularly for companies that do not have strong balance sheets or steady operating cash flow.

When assessing an issuer's liquidity, credit analysts tend to look at the following:

- **Cash on the balance sheet.** Cash holdings provide the greatest assurance of having sufficient liquidity to make promised payments.
- **Net working capital.** The big US automakers used to have enormous negative working capital, despite having high levels of cash on the balance sheet. This proved disastrous when the financial crisis hit in 2008 and the economy contracted sharply. Auto sales—and thus revenues—fell, the auto companies cut production, and working capital consumed billions of dollars in cash as accounts payable came due when the companies most needed liquidity.
- **Operating cash flow.** Analysts will project this figure out a few years and consider the risk that it may be lower than expected.
- **Committed bank lines.** Committed but untapped lines of credit provide contingent liquidity in the event that the company is unable to tap other, potentially cheaper, financing in the public debt markets.
- **Debt coming due and committed capital expenditures in the next one to two years.** Analysts will compare the sources of liquidity with the amount of debt coming due as well as with committed capital expenditures to ensure that companies can repay their debt and still invest in the business if the capital markets are somehow not available.

As will be discussed in more detail in the section on special considerations for high-yield credits, issuer liquidity is a bigger consideration for high-yield companies than for investment grade companies.

EXAMPLE 6

Mallinckrodt PLC (Mallinckrodt) is an Ireland-incorporated specialty pharmaceutical company. As a credit analyst, you have been asked to assess its creditworthiness—on its own, compared to a competitor in its overall industry, and compared with a similarly rated company in a different industry. Using the financial statements provided in Exhibits 10 through 12 for the three years ending 31 December 2015, 2016, and 2017, address the following:

1 Calculate Mallinckrodt's operating profit margin, EBITDA, and free cash flow after dividends. Comment on what these measures indicate about Mallinckrodt's profitability and cash flow.

2 Determine Mallinckrodt's leverage ratios: debt/EBITDA, debt/capital, free cash flow after dividends/debt. Comment on what these leverage ratios indicate about Mallinckrodt's creditworthiness.

3 Calculate Mallinckrodt's interest coverage using both EBIT and EBITDA. Comment on what these coverage ratios indicate about Mallinckrodt's creditworthiness.

4 Using the credit ratios provided in Exhibit 11 on Johnson & Johnson, compare the creditworthiness of Mallinckrodt relative to Johnson & Johnson.

5 Compare the Exhibit 12 credit ratios of Luxembourg-based ArcelorMittal, one of the world's largest global steelmakers, with those of Mallinckrodt. Comment on the volatility of the credit ratios of the two companies. Which company looks to be more cyclical? What industry factors might explain some of the differences? In comparing the creditworthiness of these two companies, what other factors might be considered to offset greater volatility of credit ratios?

Exhibit 10a Mallinckrodt PLC Financial Statements

Consolidated Statements of Operations

	Year End Sept. 30*	Years Ended Dec. 31	
(Dollars in millions, except per share amounts)	**2015**	**2016**	**2017**
Net revenues	**2,923.1**	**3,399.5**	**3,221.6**
Operating expenses:			
Cost of sales	1,300.2	1,549.6	1,565.3
Research and development	203.3	267.0	277.3
Selling, general and administrative expenses	1,023.8	1,070.3	920.9
Restructuring charges, net	45.0	33.0	31.2
Non-restructuring impairment charges	—	231.2	63.7
Gain on divestiture and license	(3.0)	—	(56.9)
Total operating expenses	**2,569.3**	**3,151.1**	**2,801.5**
Operating income	**353.8**	**248.4**	**420.1**
Other (expense) income:			
Interest expense	(255.6)	(378.1)	(369.1)
Interest income	1.0	1.6	4.6
Other income (expense), net	8.1	(3.5)	6.0

(continued)

Exhibit 10a (Continued)

Consolidated Statements of Operations

(Dollars in millions, except per share amounts)	Year End Sept. 30* 2015	Years Ended Dec. 31 2016	2017
Total other (expense) income, net	**(246.5)**	**(380.0)**	**(358.5)**
Income before income taxes and non-controlling interest	**107.3**	**(131.6)**	**61.6**
Provision (Benefit) for income taxes	(129.3)	(340.0)	(1,709.6)
Net income	**236.6**	**208.4**	**1,771.2**
Income from discontinued operations, net of income taxes	88.1	71.0	363.2
Net income attributable to common shareholders	**324.7**	**279.4**	**2,134.4**

* *Note*: Mallinckrodt changed their fiscal year end from September 30 to December 31.
Source: Company Filings, Loomis, Sayles & Company.

Exhibit 10b Mallinckrodt PLC Financial Statements

Consolidated Balance Sheets

(Dollars in millions)	Year End Sept. 30* 2015	Years Ended Dec. 31 2016	2017
ASSETS			
Current Assets:			
Cash and cash equivalents	365.9	342.0	1,260.9
Accounts receivable	489.6	431.0	445.8
Inventories	262.1	350.7	340.4
Deferred income taxes	139.2	—	—
Prepaid expenses and other current assets	194.4	131.9	84.1
Notes receivable	—	—	154.0
Current assets held for sale	394.9	310.9	—
Total current assets	**1,846.1**	**1,566.5**	**2,285.2**
Property, plant and equipment, net	793.0	881.5	966.8
Goodwill	3,649.4	3,498.1	3,482.7
Intangible assets, net	9,666.3	9,000.5	8,375.0
Other assets	225.7	259.7	171.2
Long-term assets held for sale	223.6	—	—

Exhibit 10b (Continued)

Consolidated Balance Sheets

(Dollars in millions)	Year End Sept. 30* 2015	Years Ended Dec. 31 2016	2017
Total Assets	**16,404.1**	**15,206.3**	**15,280.9**
LIABILITIES AND EQUITY			
Current Liabilities:			
Current maturities of long-term debt	22.0	271.2	313.7
Accounts payable	116.8	112.1	113.3
Accrued payroll and payroll-related costs	95.0	76.1	98.5
Accrued interest	80.2	68.7	57.0
Income taxes payable	—	101.7	15.8
Accrued and other current liabilities	486.1	557.1	452.1
Current liabilities held for sale	129.3	120.3	-
Total current liabilities	**929.4**	**1,307.2**	**1,050.4**
Long-term debt	6,474.3	5,880.8	6,420.9
Pension and postretirement benefits	114.2	136.4	67.1
Environmental liabilities	73.3	73.0	73.2
Deferred income taxes	3,117.5	2,398.1	689.0
Other income tax liabilities	121.3	70.4	94.1
Other liabilities	209.0	356.1	364.2
Long-term liabilities held for sale	53.9	—	—
Total Liabilities	**11,092.9**	**10,222.0**	**8,758.9**
Shareholders' Equity:			
Ordinary shares	23.5	23.6	18.4
Ordinary shares held in treasury at cost	(109.7)	(919.8)	(1,564.7)
Additional paid-in capital	5,357.6	5,424.0	5,492.6
Retained earnings	38.9	529.0	2,588.6
Accumulated other comprehensive income	0.9	(72.5)	(12.9)
Total Shareholders' Equity	5,311.2	4,984.3	6,522.0
Total Liabilities and Shareholders' Equity	16,404.1	15,206.3	15,280.9

Source: Company Filings, Loomis, Sayles & Company

Exhibit 10c Mallinckrodt PLC Financial Statements

Consolidated Statements of Cash Flow

(Dollars in millions)	Year End Sept. 30* 2015	Years Ended Dec. 31 2016	2017
Cash Flows From Operating Activities:			
Net income (loss)	324.7	279.4	2134.4
Depreciation and amortization	672.5	831.7	808.3
Share-based compensation	117.0	45.4	59.2
Deferred income taxes	(191.6)	(528.3)	−1744.1
Non-cash impairment charges	—	231.2	63.7
Inventory provisions	—	8.5	34.1
Gain on disposal of discontinued operations	—	1.7	−418.1
Other non-cash items	(25.5)	45.5	−21.4
Change in working capital	33.4	153.7	−188.8
Net cash from operating activities	**930.5**	**1,068.8**	**727.3**
Cash Flows From Investing Activities:			
Capital expenditures	(148.0)	(199.1)	−186.1
Acquisitions and intangibles, net of cash acquired	(2,154.7)	(247.2)	−76.3
Proceeds from divestitures, net of cash	-	3.0	576.9
Other	3.0	(4.9)	3.9
Net cash from investing activities	**(2,299.7)**	**(448.2)**	**318.4**
Cash Flows From Financing Activities:			
Issuance of external debt	3,010.0	226.3	1465
Repayment of external debt and capital leases	(1,848.4)	(525.7)	−917.2
Debt financing costs	(39.9)	—	−12.7
Proceeds from exercise of share options	34.4	10.8	4.1
Repurchase of shares	(92.2)	(536.3)	−651.7
Other	(28.1)	(21.8)	−17.7
Net cash from financing activities	**1,035.8**	**(846.7)**	**−130.2**
Effect of currency rate changes on cash	(11.6)	(1.2)	**2.5**
Net increase (decrease) in cash and cash equivalents	(345.0)	(227.3)	918
Cash and cash equivalents at beginning of period	777.6	588.4	361.1
Cash and cash equivalents at end of period	432.6	361.1	1279.1

Source: Company Filings, Loomis, Sayles & Company

Exhibit 10d Mallinckrodt PLC Credit Ratios

	2015	2016	2017
Operating Margin	12.1%	7.3%	13.0%
Debt/EBITDA	6.3x	5.7x	5.5x
EBITDA/Interest	4.0x	2.9x	3.3x
FCF/Debt	12.0%	14.1%	8.0%
Debt/Capital	55.0%	55.2%	50.8%

Source: Company Filings, Loomis, Sayles & Company.

Exhibit 11 Johnson & Johnson's Credit Ratios

	2015	2016	2017
Operating profit margin	26.2%	29.5%	25.8%
Debt/EBITDA	0.9x	1.1x	1.4x
EBITDA/Interest	40.1x	34.4x	27.1x
FCF after dividends/Debt	81.1%	57.3%	51.4%
Debt/Capital	22.0%	28.1%	36.5%

Source: Company Filings, Loomis, Sayles & Company.

Exhibit 12 ArcelorMittal Credit Ratios

	2015	2016	2017
Operating profit margin	0.3%	5.5%	7.7%
Debt/EBITDA	5.8x	2.3x	1.6x
EBITDA/Interest	2.5x	5.0x	9.2x
FCF after dividends/Debt	–2.8%	1.9%	13.5%
Debt/Capital	41.8%	29.7%	24.0%

Source: Company Filings, Loomis, Sayles & Company.

Solutions:

1 Operating profit margin (%) = Operating income/Revenue

2015: 353.8/2,923.1 = 0.121 or 12.1 percent

2016: 248.4/3,399.5 = 0.084 or 7.3 percent

2017: 420.1/3,221.6 = 0.130 or 13.0 percent

EBITDA = Operating income + Depreciation and Amortization

2015: 353.8 + 672.5 = 1,026.3

2016: 248.4+ 831.7 = 1,080.1

2017: 420.1 + 808.3= 1,228.4

FCF after dividends = Cash flow from operations – Capital expenditures – Dividends

2015: 930.5 – 148 – 0 = 782.5

2016: 1,068.8 – 199.1 – 0 = 869.7

2017: 727.3 – 186.1 – 0 = 541.2

Operating profit margin decreased from 2015 to 2016, but increased from 2016 to 2017. Conversely, FCF after dividends increased from 2015 to 2016, but decreased from 2016 to 2017. EBITDA increased from 2015 to 2017. From 2015 to 2016, sales increased by 16.3% and operating expenses increased by 22.6%. As a result, operating profit margin decreased even though EBITDA and FCF increased. However, from 2016 to 2017, sales decreased by 5.2% and operating expenses decreased by 11.1%. As a result, operating profit margin and EBITDA increased, while FCF after dividends decreased.

2 Debt/EBITDA

Total debt = Short-term debt and Current portion of long-term debt + Long-term debt

2015: Debt: 22.0 + 6,474.3 = 6,496.3

Debt/EBITDA: 6,496.3/1,026.3 = 6.3x

2016: Debt: 271.2 + 5,880.8 = 6,152.0

Debt/EBITDA: 6,152.0/1,080.1 = 5.7x

2017: Debt: 313.7 + 6,420.9 = 6,734.6

Debt/EBITDA: 6,734.6/1,228. 4 = 5.5x

Debt/Capital (%)

Capital = Debt + Equity

2015: Capital: 6,496.3 + 5,311.2 = 11,807.5

Debt/Capital: 6,496.3/11,807.5 = 55.0 percent

2016: Capital: 6,152.0 + 4,984.3 = 11,136.3

Debt/Capital: 6,152.0/11,136.3 = 55.2 percent

2017: Capital: 6,734.6 + 6,522.0 = 13,256.6

Debt/Capital: 6,734.6/13,256.6 = 50.8 percent

FCF after dividends/Debt (%)

2015: 782.5/6,496.3 = 12.0 percent

2016: 869.7/6,152 = 14.1 percent

2017: 541.2/6734.6 = 8.0 percent

Although the debt/EBITDA and debt/capital ratios improved between 2015 and 2017, the "FCF after dividends/Debt" ratio deteriorated significantly as cash flow from operations declined as a result of the loss taken on disposal of discontinued operations. Given that the loss is most likely a non-recurring event, Mallinckrodt's creditworthiness likely improved over the 2015 to 2017 period.

3 EBIT/Interest expense

2015: 353.8/255.6 = 1.4x

2016: 248.4/378.1 = 0.7x

2017: 420.1/369.1 = 1.1x

EBITDA/Interest expense

2015: 1,026.3/255.6 = 4.0x

2016: 1,080.1/378.1= 2.9x

2017: 1,228.4/369.1 = 3.3x

Based on these coverage ratios, Mallinckrodt's creditworthiness declined from 2015 to 2016, then showed modest improvement in 2017. The 2017 coverage ratios are still weaker than the 2015 coverage ratios, indicating that growth in EBIT and EBITDA are not keeping pace with the rising interest expense.

4 Johnson & Johnson (J&J) has a higher operating profit margin, better leverage ratios—lower Debt/EBITDA, higher FCF after dividends/debt over the three years, lower debt/capital, and better interest coverage as measured by EBITDA/interest. Collectively, those ratios suggest J&J has higher credit quality than Mallinckrodt.

5 Mallinckrodt has both a higher and a less volatile operating profit margin than ArcelorMittal (Arcelor). However, while Mallinckrodt's leverage ratios have been deteriorating, Arcelor's have been improving. Based on the volatility of its cash flow and operating profit margin, Arcelor appears to be a much more cyclical credit. However, with its meaningfully lower debt levels, one could expect Arcelor to have a higher credit rating.

A steelmaker likely has a significant amount of long-term assets financed by debt. It is a highly competitive industry with little ability to distinguish products from other competitors. To mitigate the impact of its more volatile credit ratios, Arcelor might maintain high levels of liquidity. Its size and global diversity may also be a "plus." Given its size, it may be able to negotiate favorable supplier and customer contracts and to keep costs down through economies of scale.

5.2.2 *Collateral*

Collateral, or asset value, analysis is typically emphasized more with lower credit quality companies. As discussed earlier, credit analysts focus primarily on probability of default, which is mostly about an issuer's ability to generate sufficient cash flow to support its debt payments, as well as its ability to refinance maturing debt. Only when the default probability rises to a sufficient level do analysts typically consider asset or collateral value in the context of loss severity in the event of default.

Analysts do think about the value and quality of a company's assets; however, these are difficult to observe directly. Factors to consider include the nature and amount of intangible assets on the balance sheet. Some assets, such as patents, are clearly valuable and can be sold if necessary to cover liabilities. Goodwill, on the other hand, is not considered a high-quality asset. In fact, sustained weak financial performance most likely implies that a company's goodwill will be written down, reinforcing its poor quality. Another factor to consider is the amount of depreciation an issuer takes relative to its capital expenditures: Low capital expenditures relative to depreciation expense could imply that management is insufficiently investing in its business, which will lead to lower-quality assets, potentially reduced future operating cash flow, and higher loss severity in the event of default.

A market-based signal that credit analysts use to impute the quality of a publicly traded company's assets, and its ability to support its debt, is equity market capitalization. For instance, a company whose stock trades below book value may have lower-quality assets than is suggested by the amount reported on the balance sheet.

As economies become more service- and knowledge-based and those types of companies issue debt, it's important to understand that these issuers rely more on human and intellectual capital than on "hard assets." In generating profits and cash flow, these companies are not as asset intensive. One example would be software companies. Another example would be investment management firms. Human- and intellectual- capital-based companies may generate a lot of cash flow, but their collateral value is questionable, unless there are patents and other types of intellectual property and "intangible capital" that may not appear directly on the balance sheet but could be valuable in the event of financial distress or default.

Regardless of the nature of the business, the key point of collateral analysis is to assess the value of the assets relative to the issuer's level—and seniority ranking—of debt.

5.2.3 *Covenants*

Covenants are meant to protect creditors while also giving management sufficient flexibility to operate its business on behalf of and for the benefit of the shareholders. They are integral to credit agreements, whether they are bonds or bank loans, and they spell out what the issuer's management is (1) obligated to do and (2) limited in doing. The former are called "affirmative covenants," whereas the latter are called "negative" or "restrictive covenants." Obligations would include such duties as making interest and principal payments and filing audited financial statements on a timely basis. Covenants might also require a company to redeem debt in the event of the company being acquired[27] or to keep the ratio of debt to EBITDA below some prescribed amount. The limitations might include a cap on the amount of cash that can be paid out to shareholders relative to earnings, or perhaps on the amount of additional secured debt that can be issued. Covenant violations are a breach of contract and can be considered default events unless they are cured in a short time or a waiver is granted.

For corporate bonds, covenants are described in the bond **prospectus**, the document that is part of a new bond issue. The prospectus describes the terms of the bond issue, as well as supporting financial statements, to help investors perform their analyses and make investment decisions as to whether or not to submit orders to buy the new bonds. Actually, the **trust deed** or **bond indenture** is the governing legal credit agreement and is typically incorporated by reference in the prospectus.

Covenants are an important but underappreciated part of credit analysis. Strong covenants protect bond investors from the possibility of management taking actions that would hurt an issuer's creditworthiness. For example, without appropriate covenants management might pay large dividends, undertake stock buybacks well in excess of free cash flow, sell the company in a leveraged buyout,[28] or take on a lot of secured debt that structurally subordinates unsecured bondholders. All of these actions would enrich shareholders at the expense of bondholders. Recall that management works for the shareholders and that bonds are contracts, with management's only real obligation to creditors being to uphold the terms of the contract. The inclusion of covenants in the contract is intended to protect bondholders.

The bond-buying investor base is very large and diverse, particularly for investment-grade debt. It includes institutional investors such as insurance companies, investment management firms, pension funds, mutual funds, hedge funds, sovereign wealth funds, and so on. Although there are some very large institutional investors, the buyer base is fragmented and does not—and legally cannot—act as a syndicate. Thus, bondholders are generally not able to negotiate strong covenants on most new bond issues.

---

27 This is often referred to as a "change of control" covenant.

28 A leveraged buyout (LBO) is an acquisition of a company by private investors using high levels of debt and relatively little equity.

Covenants on new bond issues tend to be stronger during weak economic or market conditions because investors seek more protection during such times. There are a few organized institutional investor groups focused on strengthening covenants: the Credit Roundtable[29] in the United States and the European Model Covenant Initiative in the United Kingdom.

Covenant language is often very technical and written in "legalese," so it can be helpful to have an in-house person with a legal background to review and interpret the specific covenant terms and wording. One might also use a third-party service specializing in covenant analysis, such as Covenant Review.[30]

We will go into more detail on specific covenants in the section on special considerations for high-yield bonds.

5.2.4 *Character*

The character of a corporate borrower can be difficult to observe. The analysis of character as a factor in credit analysis dates to when loans were made to companies owned by individuals. Most corporate bond issuers are now publicly owned by shareholders or privately owned by pools of capital, such as private equity firms. Management often has little ownership in a corporation, so analysis and assessment of character is different than it would be for owner-managed firms. Credit analysts can make judgments about management's character in the following ways:

- An assessment of the soundness of management's strategy.
- Management's track record in executing past strategies, particularly if they led to bankruptcy or restructuring. A company run by executives whose prior positions/ventures resulted in significant distress might still be able to borrow in the debt markets, but it would likely have to borrow on a secured basis and/or pay a higher rate of interest.
- Use of aggressive accounting policies and/or tax strategies. Examples might include using a significant amount of off-balance-sheet financing, capitalizing versus immediately expensing items, recognizing revenue prematurely, and/or frequently changing auditors. These are potential warning flags to other behaviors or actions that may adversely impact an issuer's creditworthiness.
- Any history of fraud or malfeasance—a major warning flag to credit analysts.
- Previous poor treatment of bondholders—for example, management actions that resulted in major credit rating downgrades. These actions might include a debt-financed acquisition, a large special dividend to shareholders, or a major debt-financed stock buyback program.

EXAMPLE 7

The Four Cs

1 Which of the following would not be a bond covenant?

  A The issuer must file financial statements with the bond trustee on a timely basis.

  B The company can buy back as much stock as it likes.

  C If the company offers security to any creditors, it must offer security to this bond issue.

29 See www.creditroundtable.org.
30 See www.covenantreview.com.

2 Why should credit analysts be concerned if a company's stock trades below book value?

A It means the company is probably going bankrupt.

B It means the company will probably incur lots of debt to buy back its undervalued stock.

C It's a signal that the company's asset value on its balance sheet may be impaired and have to be written down, suggesting less collateral protection for creditors.

3 If management is of questionable character, how can investors incorporate this assessment into their credit analysis and investment decisions?

A They can choose not to invest based on the increased credit risk.

B They can insist on getting collateral (security) and/or demand a higher return.

C They can choose not to invest or insist on additional security and/or higher return.

Solution to 1:

B is correct. Covenants describe what the borrower is (1) obligated to do or (2) limited in doing. It's the absence of covenants that would permit a company to buy back as much stock as it likes. A requirement that the company offer security to this bond issue if it offers security to other creditors (answer C) is referred to as a "negative pledge."

Solution to 2:

C is correct.

Solution to 3:

C is correct. Investors can always say no if they are not comfortable with the credit risk presented by a bond or issuer. They may also decide to lend to a borrower with questionable character only on a secured basis and/or demand a higher return for the perceived higher risk.

6 CREDIT RISK VS. RETURN: YIELDS AND SPREADS

The material in this section applies to all bonds subject to credit risk. For simplicity, in what follows all such bonds are sometimes referred to as "corporate" bonds.

As in other types of investing, taking more risk in credit offers higher potential return, but with more volatility and less certainty of earning that return. Using credit ratings as a proxy for risk, Exhibit 13 shows the composite yield to maturity[31] for bonds of all maturities within each rating category in the US and European bond markets according to Bloomberg Barclays, one of the largest providers of fixed-income market indexes.

31 High-yield bonds are often quoted on a "yield to call" (YTC) or "yield to worst" (YTW) basis because so many of them are callable before maturity, whereas most investment-grade bonds are non-callable, or at least callable at such punitive premiums that issuers are not likely to exercise that option.

Exhibit 13 Corporate Yields by Rating Category (%)

Bloomberg Barclays Indices	Investment Grade				Non-Investment Grade			
	AAA	AA	A	BBB	BB	B	CCC	CC–D
US	3.63	3.52	3.86	4.35	5.14	6.23	8.87	19.51
Pan European*	1.25	0.76	1.18	1.67	2.92	5.63	8.78	54.95

Data as of 30 September 2018.
* Pan European yields may be "artificially low" due to the ECB's extraordinary corporate bond Quantitative Easing (QE) Program.
Source: Bloomberg Barclays Indices.

Note that the lower the credit quality, the higher the quoted yield. The realized yield, or return, will almost always be different because of changes in interest rates and the credit-related risks discussed earlier. For example, in the aggregate credit losses will "eat up" some of the yield premium offered by lower-quality bonds versus higher-quality credits. Trailing 12-month returns by credit rating category, and the volatility (standard deviation) of those returns, are shown in Exhibit 14.

Exhibit 14 US Credit Trailing 12-Month Returns by Rating Category, 31 December 1996–30 September 2018

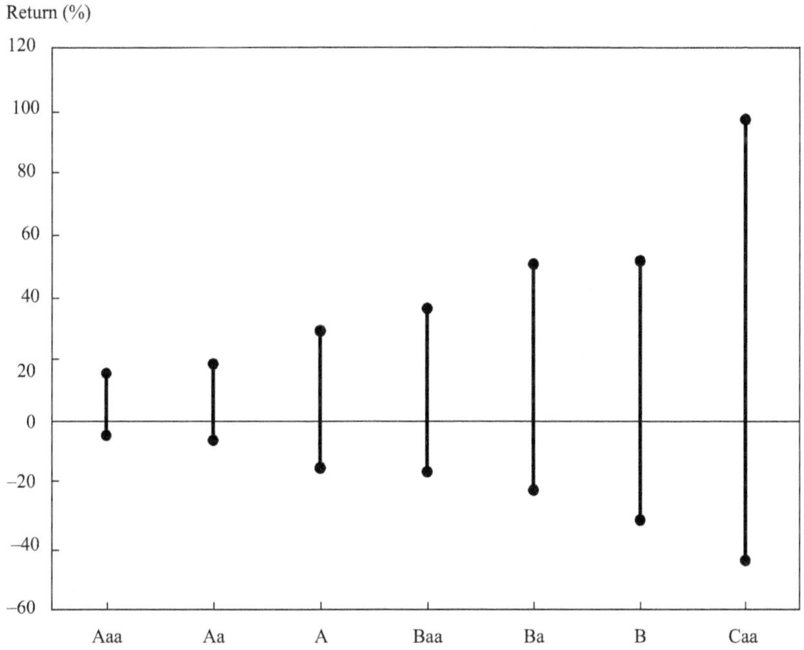

	Aaa	Aa	A	Baa	Ba	B	Caa
Avg. Return:	4.82%	5.60%	5.78%	6.53%	7.98%	6.79%	8.26%
Max. Return:	16.08%	19.30%	29.39%	36.43%	50.80%	52.10%	97.47%
Min. Return:	–4.17%	–5.47%	–14.98%	–15.70%	–22.12%	–31.47%	–44.35%
Avg. Volatility:	3.43%	4.14%	4.76%	5.15%	5.75%	7.13%	11.00%

Source: Bloomberg Barclays Indices, Loomis Sayles.

As shown in the exhibit, the higher the credit risk, the greater the return potential and the higher the volatility of that return. This pattern is consistent with other types of investing that involves risk and return (although average returns on single-B rated bonds appear anomalous in this example).

For extremely liquid bonds that are deemed to have virtually no default risk (e.g., German government bonds, or *Bunds*), the yield is a function of real interest rates plus an expected inflation rate and a maturity premium. Of course, those factors are present in corporate bonds as well. In addition, the yield on corporate bonds will include a liquidity premium and a credit spread intended to compensate investors for these additional risks as well as for the expected level of credit losses. Thus, the yield on a corporate bond can be decomposed as

Yield on corporate bond = Real risk-free interest rate + Expected inflation rate + Maturity premium + Liquidity premium + Credit spread

Changes in any of these components will alter the yield, price, and return on the bond.

Investors in corporate bonds focus primarily on the yield spread relative to a comparable, default-free bond, which is composed of the liquidity premium and the credit spread:

Yield spread = Liquidity premium + Credit spread

The market's willingness to bear risk will affect each of these components. In general, however, it is not possible to directly observe the market's assessment of the components separately—analysts can only observe the total yield spread.

Spreads on all corporate bonds can be affected by a number of factors, with lower-quality issuers typically experiencing greater spread volatility. These factors, which are frequently linked, include the following:

- **Credit cycle.** As the credit cycle improves, credit spreads will narrow. Conversely, a deteriorating credit cycle will cause credit spreads to widen. Spreads are tightest at or near the top of the credit cycle, when financial markets believe risk is low, whereas they are widest at or near the bottom of the credit cycle, when financial markets believe risk is high.
- **Broader economic conditions.** Not surprisingly, weakening economic conditions will push investors to desire a greater risk premium and drive overall credit spreads wider. Conversely, a strengthening economy will cause credit spreads to narrow because investors anticipate credit measures will improve due to rising corporate cash flow, thus reducing the risk of default.
- **Financial market performance overall, including equities.** In weak financial markets, credit spreads will widen, whereas in strong markets, credit spreads will narrow. In a steady, low-volatility environment, credit spreads will typically also narrow, as investors tend to "reach for yield."
- **Broker–dealers' willingness to provide sufficient capital for market making.** Bonds trade primarily over the counter, so investors need broker–dealers to commit capital for market-making purposes. During the financial crisis in 2008–2009, several large broker–dealer counterparties either failed or were taken over by another. This, combined with financial and regulatory stresses faced by virtually all the other broker–dealers, greatly reduced the total capital

available for making markets and the willingness to buy/sell credit-risky bonds. Future regulatory reform may well lead to persistent or even permanent reductions in broker-provided capital.

- **General market supply and demand.** In periods of heavy new issue supply, credit spreads will widen if there is insufficient demand. In periods of high demand for bonds, spreads will move tighter.

Each of the first four factors played a role during the financial crisis of 2008–2009, causing spreads to widen dramatically, as shown in Exhibit 15, before narrowing sharply as governments intervened and markets stabilized. This is shown in two panels—one for investment grade, another for high yield—because of the much greater spread volatility in high-yield bonds, particularly CCC rated credits. This spread volatility is reflected in the different spread ranges on the y-axes. OAS is option-adjusted spread, which incorporates the value of the embedded call option in certain corporate bonds that issuers have the right to exercise before maturity.[32]

32 The details of valuing bonds with embedded options and the calculation of OAS are covered in Level II of the CFA Program curriculum.

Exhibit 15 US Investment-Grade and High-Yield Corporate Spreads

A. Investment-Grade Corporate Spreads

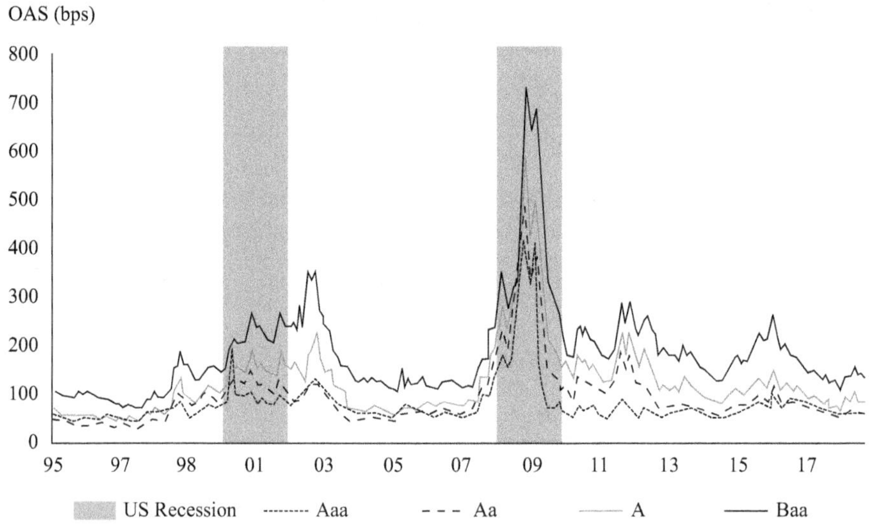

B. High-Yield Corporate Spreads

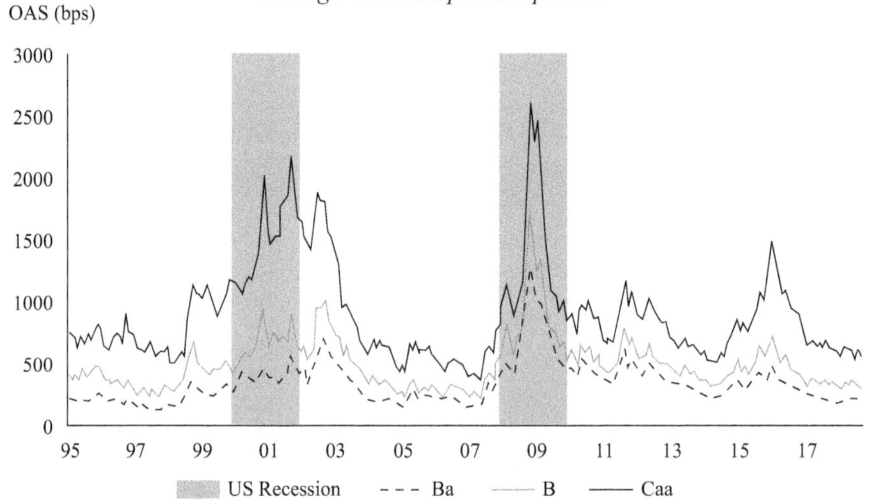

Sources: Bloomberg Barclays Indices and Loomis, Sayles & Company.

EXAMPLE 8

Yield Spreads

1 Which bonds are likely to exhibit the greatest spread volatility?

  A Bonds from issuers rated AA

  B Bonds from issuers rated BB

  C Bonds from issuers rated A

2 If investors become increasingly worried about the economy—say, as shown by declining stock prices—what is the *most likely* impact on credit spreads?

A There will be no change to credit spreads. They aren't affected by equity markets.

B Narrower spreads will occur. Investors will move out of equities into debt securities.

C Wider spreads will occur. Investors are concerned about weaker creditworthiness.

Solution to 1:

B is correct. Lower-quality bonds exhibit greater spread volatility than higher-quality bonds. All of the factors that affect spreads—the credit cycle, economic conditions, financial performance, market-making capacity, and supply/demand conditions—will tend to have a greater impact on the pricing of lower-quality credits.

Solution to 2:

C is correct. Investors will require higher yields as compensation for the credit deterioration—including losses—that is likely to occur in a weakening economy.

We have discussed how yield spreads on credit-risky debt obligations, such as corporate bonds, can fluctuate based on a number of factors, including changes in the market's view of issuer-specific or idiosyncratic risk. The next question to ask is how these spread changes affect the price of and return on these bonds.

Although bond investors do concern themselves with default risks, recall that the probability of default for higher-quality bonds is typically very low: For investment-grade bonds, annual defaults are nearly always well below 1 percent (recall Exhibit 6). On the other hand, default rates can be very high for lower-quality issuers, although they can vary widely depending upon the credit cycle, among other things. What most investors in investment-grade debt focus on more than default risk is spread risk—that is, the effect on prices and returns from changes in spreads.

The price impact from spread changes is driven by two main factors: the modified duration (price sensitivity with respect to changes in interest rates) of the bond and the magnitude of the spread change. The effect on return to the bondholder depends on the holding period used for calculating the return.

The simplest example is that of a small, instantaneous change in the yield spread. In this case, the price impact, i.e., the percentage change in price (including accrued interest), can be approximated by

$$\text{Price impact} \approx -\text{MDur} \times \Delta\text{Spread}$$

where MDur is the modified duration. The negative sign in this equation reflects the fact that because bond prices and yields move in opposite directions, narrower spreads have a positive impact on bond prices and thus returns, whereas wider spreads have a negative impact on bond returns. Note that if the spread change is expressed in basis points, then the price impact will also be in basis points, whereas if the spread change is expressed as a decimal, the price impact will also be expressed as a decimal. Either way, the result is easily re-expressed as a percent.

For larger spread changes (and thus larger yield changes), the impact of convexity needs to be incorporated into the approximation:

$$\text{Price impact} \approx -(\text{MDur} \times \Delta\text{Spread}) + \tfrac{1}{2}\text{Cvx} \times (\Delta\text{Spread})^2$$

In this case, one must be careful to ensure that convexity (denoted by Cvx) is appropriately scaled to be consistent with the way the spread change is expressed. In general, for bonds without embedded options, one can scale convexity so that it has the same order of magnitude as the duration squared and then express the spread change as a decimal. For example, for a bond with duration of 5.0 and reported convexity of 0.235, one would re-scale convexity to 23.5 before applying the formula. For a 1 percent (i.e., 100 bps) increase in spread, the result would be

Price impact = $(-5.0 \times 0.01) + ½ \times 23.5 \times (0.01)^2 = -0.048825$ or -4.8825 percent

The price impact of instantaneous spread changes is illustrated in Exhibit 16 using two bonds from British Telecom, the UK telecommunications company. The bonds, denominated in British pounds, are priced to provide a certain spread over British government bonds (gilts) of a similar maturity. From the starting spread, in increments of 25 bps and for both wider and narrower spreads, the new price and actual return for each spread change are calculated. In addition, the exhibit shows the approximate returns with and without the convexity term. As can be seen, the approximation using only duration is reasonably accurate for small spread changes but for larger changes, the convexity term generally provides a meaningful improvement.

Exhibit 16 Impact of Duration on Price for a Given Change in Spread

Issuer: British Telecom, 5.75%, 07/12/2028

Price: £122.978	Modified Duration: 7.838	Spread to Gilt Curve: 150.7 b.p.
Accrued interest: 0.958	Convexity: 77.2	YTM (conv): 3.16

	Scenarios								
Spread Δ (b.p.)	−100	−75	−50	−25	0	25	50	75	100
Spread (b.p.)	50.7	75.7	100.7	125.7	150.7	175.7	200.7	225.7	250.7
Price (£)	131.62	129.12	126.68	124.29	122.98	119.69	117.47	115.30	113.18
Price + Accrued (£)	132.58	130.08	127.64	125.25	123.94	120.65	118.43	116.26	114.14
Price Δ (£)	8.64	6.14	3.70	1.31	0.00	−3.29	−5.51	−7.68	−9.80
Return (%)									
Actual	6.97%	4.96%	2.99%	1.06%	0.00%	−2.65%	−4.44%	−6.20%	−7.91%
Approx: Dur only	7.84%	5.88%	3.92%	1.96%	0.00%	−1.96%	−3.92%	−5.88%	−7.84%
Approx: Dur & Cvx	8.22%	6.10%	4.02%	1.98%	0.00%	−1.94%	−3.82%	−5.66%	−7.45%

Issuer: British Telecom, 3.625%, 21/11/2047

Price: £94.244	Modified Duration: 17.144	Spread to Gilt Curve: 210.8 b.p.
Accrued interest: 2.185	Convexity: 408.4	YTM (conv): 4.11

	Scenarios								
Spread Δ (b.p.)	−100	−75	−50	−25	0	25	50	75	100
Spread (b.p.)	110.8	135.8	160.8	185.8	210.8	235.8	260.8	285.8	310.8
Price (£)	111.28	106.38	101.77	97.41	93.24	89.41	85.75	82.30	79.04
Price + Accrued (£)	113.47	108.57	103.96	99.60	95.43	91.60	87.94	84.48	81.22
Price Δ (£)	18.04	13.14	8.53	4.17	0.00	−3.83	−7.49	−10.95	−14.21
Return (%)									
Actual	18.90%	13.77%	8.93%	4.37%	0.00%	−4.02%	−7.85%	−11.47%	−14.89%

Exhibit 16 (Continued)

	Scenarios								
Approx: Dur only	17.14%	12.86%	8.57%	4.29%	0.00%	−4.29%	−8.57%	−12.86%	−17.14%
Approx: Dur & Cvx	19.19%	14.01%	9.08%	4.41%	0.00%	−4.16%	−8.06%	−11.71%	−15.10%

Source: Bloomberg Finance, L.P. (settle date is 13 December 2018).

Note that the price change for a given spread change is higher for the longer-duration bond—in this case, the 2047 maturity British Telecom bond—than for the shorter-duration, 2028 maturity British Telecom bond. Longer-duration corporate bonds are referred to as having "higher spread sensitivity"; that is, their prices, and thus returns, are more volatile with respect to changes in spread. It is essentially the same concept as duration for any bond: The longer the duration of a bond, the greater the price volatility for a given change in interest rates/yields.

In addition, investors want to be compensated for the fact that the further time one is from a bond's maturity (i.e., the longer the bond), the greater the uncertainty about an issuer's future creditworthiness. Based on credit analysis, an investor might be confident that an issuer's risk of default is relatively low in the near term; however, looking many years into the future, the investor's uncertainty grows because of factors that are increasingly difficult, if not impossible, to forecast (e.g., poor management strategy or execution, technological obsolescence, natural or man-made disasters, corporate leveraging events). This increase in credit risk over time can be seen in Exhibit 17. Note that in this Standard & Poor's study,[33] one-year default rates for the 2017 issuance pool are 0 percent for all rating categories of BB or higher. The three-year default rates for bonds issued in 2015 are materially higher, and the observed defaults include bonds originally rated up to BBB (i.e., low investment grade). The 5-year default rates for bonds issued in 2013 are higher than the 3-year default rates, and the defaults also includes bonds initially rated as high as BBB. In addition to the risk of default rising over time, the data also show quite conclusively that the lower the credit rating, the higher the risk of default. Finally, note the very high risk of default for bonds rated CCC or lower over all time horizons. This is consistent with Exhibit 7 earlier in the reading, which showed significant three-year ratings variability ("migration"), with much of the migration to lower credit ratings (i.e., higher risk of default).

Exhibit 17 Default Rate by Rating Category (%) (Non-financials)

Credit Rating	1 Year (2017 pool)	3 Year (2015 pool)	10 Year (2013 pool)
AAA	0.00	0.00	0.00
AA	0.00	0.00	0.00
A	0.00	0.00	0.00
BBB	0.00	0.08	0.27
BB	0.10	2.46	3.33

(continued)

33 From S&P, "2010 Annual Global Corporate Default Study and Ratings Transitions," Standard & Poor's report (5 April 2018).

Exhibit 17 (Continued)

Credit Rating	1 Year (2017 pool)	3 Year (2015 pool)	10 Year (2013 pool)
B	0.95	10.11	12.90
CCC/C	27.15	41.43	44.70

Source: Based on data from S&P, "2017 Annual Global Corporate Default Study and Ratings Transitions," Standard & Poor's report (30 March 2011).

It is also worth noting that bid–ask spreads (in yield terms) translate into higher transaction costs for longer-duration bonds; investors want to be compensated for that as well. For these reasons, spread curves (often called **credit curves**), like yield curves, are typically upward sloping. That is, longer-maturity bonds of a given issuer typically trade at wider spreads than shorter-maturity bonds to their respective comparable-maturity government bonds.[34] Exhibit 18, using the US telecommunications company AT&T as a historical example, shows the upward-sloping credit curve by plotting the yields of its bonds versus their maturity. (As a large and frequent issuer, AT&T has many bonds outstanding across the yield curve.)

Exhibit 18 Historical Example: AT&T Credit Curve vs. US Treasury Curve

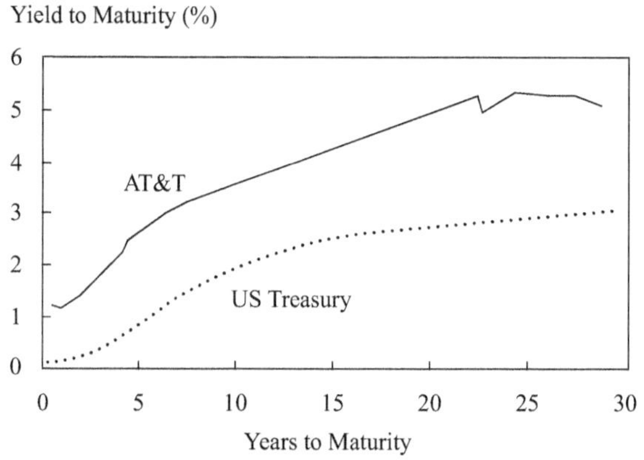

Source: Based on data from Bloomberg Finance, L.P., as of 5 October 2011.

34 There are some exceptions to this—bonds that trade at a high premium price over par due to having coupons that are well above the bond's yield to maturity and bonds that trade at distressed levels due to credit concerns. Many investors are averse to paying high premium prices for bonds that have credit risk because of the greater potential price decline—towards a recovery price in the event of default—from a credit-adverse event. Thus, high-coupon intermediate-maturity bonds can trade at similar or wider spreads to longer-maturity bonds. For distressed credits, the high risk of default causes all bonds for a given issuer to migrate toward the same expected recovery price. In this case, the shorter-maturity and shorter-duration bonds will have a higher quoted yield to maturity, and wider spread, than the longer-maturity and longer-duration bonds. This follows from the price impact formulas. The shorter the duration, the higher the yield (including spread) must go to bring the price down to a given expected recovery price.

EXAMPLE 9

Price Impact

Calculate the price impact on a 10-year corporate bond with a 4.75 percent coupon priced at 100, with an instantaneous 50 bps widening in spread due to the issuer's announcement that it was adding substantial debt to finance an acquisition, (which resulted in a two-notch downgrade by the rating agencies). The bond has a modified duration of 7.9 and its convexity is 74.9.

Solution:

The impact from the 50 bps spread widening is:

$$\begin{aligned}\text{Price impact} &\approx -(\text{MDur} \times \Delta\text{Spread}) + \tfrac{1}{2}\,\text{Cvx} \times (\Delta\text{Spread})^2 \\ &= -(0.0050 \times 7.9) + (0.5 \times 74.9) \times (0.0050)^2 \\ &= -0.0386, \text{ or } -3.86 \text{ percent}\end{aligned}$$

Because yields and bond prices move in opposite directions, the wider spread caused the bond price to fall. Using a bond-pricing calculator, the exact return is −3.85 percent, so this approximation was very accurate.

In summary, spread changes can have a significant impact on the price and performance of credit-risky bonds over a given holding period, and the higher the modified duration of the bond(s), the greater the price impact from changes in spread. Wider spreads hurt bond performance, whereas narrower spreads help bond performance. For bond investors who actively manage their portfolios (i.e., don't just buy bonds and hold them to maturity), forecasting spread changes and expected credit losses on both individual bonds and their broader portfolios is an important strategy for enhancing investment performance.

SPECIAL CONSIDERATIONS OF HIGH-YIELD, SOVEREIGN, AND NON-SOVEREIGN CREDIT ANALYSIS 7

Thus far, we have focused primarily on basic principles of credit analysis and investing with emphasis on higher-quality, investment-grade corporate bonds. Although many of these principles are applicable to other credit-risky segments of the bond market, there are some differences in credit analysis that need to be considered. This section focuses on special considerations in evaluating the credit of debt issuers from the following three market segments: high-yield corporate bonds, sovereign bonds, and non-sovereign government bonds.

7.1 High Yield

Recall that high-yield, or non-investment-grade, corporate bonds are those rated below Baa3/BBB− by the major rating agencies. These bonds are sometimes referred to as "junk bonds" because of the higher risk inherent in their weak balance sheets and/or poor or less-proven business prospects.

There are many reasons companies are rated below investment grade, including

- Highly leveraged capital structure
- Weak or limited operating history

- Limited or negative free cash flow
- Highly cyclical business
- Poor management
- Risky financial policies
- Lack of scale and/or competitive advantages
- Large off-balance-sheet liabilities
- Declining industry (e.g., newspaper publishing)

Companies with weak balance sheets and/or business profiles have lower margin for error and greater risk of default relative to higher-quality investment-grade names. And the higher risk of default means more attention must be paid to recovery analysis (or loss severity, in the event of default). Consequently, high-yield analysis typically is more in-depth than investment-grade analysis and thus has special considerations. This includes the following:

- Greater focus on issuer liquidity and cash flow
- Detailed financial projections
- Detailed understanding and analysis of the debt structure
- Understanding of an issuer's corporate structure
- Covenants
- Equity-like approach to high yield analysis

Liquidity. Liquidity—that is, having cash and/or the ability to generate or raise cash—is important to all issuers. It is absolutely critical for high-yield companies. Investment-grade companies typically have substantial cash on their balance sheets, generate a lot of cash from operations relative to their debt (or else they wouldn't be investment grade!), and/or are presumed to have alternate sources of liquidity, such as bank lines and commercial paper.[35] For these reasons, investment-grade companies can more easily roll over (refinance) maturing debt. On the other hand, high-yield companies may not have those options available. For example, there is no high-yield commercial paper market, and bank credit facilities often carry tighter restrictions for high-yield companies. Both bad company-specific news and difficult financial market conditions can lead to high-yield companies being unable to access the debt markets. And although the vast majority of investment-grade corporate debt issuers have publicly traded equity and can thus use that equity as a financing option, many high-yield companies are privately held and thus don't have access to public equity markets.

Thus, issuer liquidity is a key focus in high-yield analysis. Sources of liquidity, from strongest to weakest, are the following:

1 Cash on the balance sheet
2 Working capital
3 Operating cash flow
4 Bank credit facilities
5 Equity issuance
6 Asset sales

35 Commercial paper (CP) is short-term funding—fewer than 270 days—used by many large, investment-grade corporations on a daily basis. In practice, issuance of CP requires solid, long-term, investment-grade ratings, mostly A rated or better, with a much smaller market for BBB rated companies.

Cash on the balance sheet is easy to see and self-evident as a source for repaying debt.[36] As mentioned earlier in this reading, working capital can be a large source or use of liquidity, depending on its amount, its use in a company's cash-conversion cycle, and its role in a company's operations. Operating cash flow is a ready source of liquidity as sales turn to receivables, which turn to cash over a fairly short time period. Bank lines, or credit facilities, can be an important source of liquidity, though there may be some covenants relating to the use of the bank lines which are crucial to know and will be covered a little later. Equity issuance may not be a reliable source of liquidity because an issuer is private or because of poor market conditions if a company does have publicly traded equity. Asset sales are the least reliable source of liquidity because both the potential value and the actual time of closing can be highly uncertain.

The amount of these liquidity sources should be compared with the amount and timing of upcoming debt maturities. A large amount of debt coming due in the next 6–12 months alongside low sources of liquidity will be a warning flag for bond investors and could push an issuer into default because investors may choose not to buy new bonds intended to pay off the existing debt. Insufficient liquidity—that is, running out of cash or no longer having access to external financing to refinance or pay off existing debt—is the principal reason issuers default. Although liquidity is important for industrial companies, it is an absolute necessity for financial firms, as seen in the case of Lehman Brothers and other troubled firms during the financial crisis of 2008. Financial institutions are highly levered and often highly dependent on funding longer-term assets with short-term term liabilities.

Financial Projections. Because high-yield companies have less room for error, it's important to forecast, or project, future earnings and cash flow out several years, perhaps including several scenarios, to assess whether the issuer's credit profile is stable, improving, or declining and thus whether it needs other sources of liquidity or is at risk of default. Ongoing capital expenditures and working capital changes should be incorporated as well. Special emphasis should be given to realistic "stress" scenarios that could expose a borrower's vulnerabilities.

Debt Structure. High-yield companies tend to have many layers of debt in their capital structures, with varying levels of seniority and, therefore, different potential recovery rates in the event of default. (Recall the historical table of default recovery rates based on seniority in Exhibit 2.) A high-yield issuer will often have at least some of the following types of obligations in its debt structure:

- (Secured) Bank debt[37]
- Second lien debt
- Senior unsecured debt
- Subordinated debt, which may include convertible bonds[38]
- Preferred stock[39]

---

36 Note that some cash may be "trapped" in other countries for certain tax, business, or regulatory reasons, and may not be easily accessible, or repatriation—bringing the money back to the home country—could trigger cash tax payments.

37 Because of the higher risk of default, in most instances bank debt will be secured for high-yield issuers.

38 Convertible bonds are debt instruments that give holders the option to convert to a fixed number of shares of common stock. They can be at any level of the capital structure but are frequently issued as senior subordinated debt.

39 Preferred stock has elements of both debt and equity. It typically receives a fixed payment like a bond does and has higher priority of claims than common stock. As a type of equity, however, it is subordinated to debt.

The lower the ranking in the debt structure, the lower the credit rating and the lower the expected recovery in the event of default. In exchange for these associated higher risks, investors will normally demand higher yields.

As discussed in Section 5, a standard leverage calculation used by credit analysts is debt/EBITDA and is quoted as a multiple (e.g., "5.2x levered"). For an issuer with several layers of debt with different expected recovery rates, high-yield analysts should calculate leverage at each level of the debt structure. Example 10 shows calculations of gross leverage, as measured by Debt/EBITDA, at each level of the debt structure and net leverage for the entire debt structure. Gross leverage calculations do not adjust debt for cash on hand. Net leverage adjusts debt by subtracting cash from total debt.

EXAMPLE 10

Debt Structure and Leverage

Hexion Inc. is a specialty chemical company. It has a complicated, high-yield debt structure, consisting of first lien debt (loans and bonds), secured bonds, second lien bonds, and senior unsecured debt, due to a series of mergers as well as a leveraged buyout in 2005. Exhibit 19 is a simplified depiction of the company's debt structure, as well as some key credit-related statistics.

Exhibit 19 Hexion Inc. Debt and Leverage Structure as of Year-End 2017

Financial Information ($ millions)	
Cash	$115
Total debt	$3,668
Net debt	$3,553
Interest expense	$329
EBITDA	$365

Debt Structure ($ millions)	
First lien debt (loans and bonds)	$2,607
Secured bonds	$225
Second lien bonds	$574
Senior unsecured bonds	$263
TOTAL DEBT	$3,669

Source: Company Filings, Loomis Sayles & Company.

Using the information provided, address the following:

1 Calculate gross leverage, as measured by Debt/EBITDA, through each level of debt, including total debt.

2 Calculate the net leverage, as measured by (Debt – Cash)/EBITDA, for the total debt structure.

3 Why might Hexion have so much secured debt relative to unsecured debt (both senior and subordinated)? (Note: This question draws on concepts from earlier sections.)

Solutions to 1 and 2:

	Gross Leverage (Debt/EBITDA)	Net Leverage (Debt – Cash)/ EBITDA
Secured debt leverage		
(First lien + Secured debt)/EBITDA		
(2,607 + 225)/365	7.8x	
Second Lien Leverage		
(First lien + Secured debt + Second lien debt)/EBITDA		
(2,607 + 225 + 574)/365	9.3x	
Total leverage (includes unsecured)		
(Total debt/EBITDA)		
3,669/365	10.1x	
Net leverage (leverage net of cash through entire debt structure)		
(Total debt – Cash)/EBITDA		9.7x

Solution to 3:

Hexion might have that much secured debt because (1) it was less expensive than issuing additional unsecured debt on which investors would have demanded a higher yield and/or (2) given the riskiness of the business (chemicals are a cyclical business)), the high leverage of the business model, and the riskiness of the balance sheet (lots of debt from a leveraged buyout), investors would only be willing to lend the company money on a secured basis.

High-yield companies that have a lot of secured debt (typically bank debt) relative to unsecured debt are said to have a "top-heavy" capital structure. With this structure, there is less capacity to take on more bank debt in the event of financial stress. Along with the often more stringent covenants associated with bank debt and its generally shorter maturity compared with other types of debt, this means that these issuers are more susceptible to default, as well as to lower recovery for the various less secured creditors.

Corporate Structure. Many debt-issuing corporations, including high-yield companies, utilize a holding company structure with a parent and several operating subsidiaries. Knowing where an issuer's debt resides (parent versus subsidiaries) and how cash can move from subsidiary to parent ("upstream") and vice versa ("downstream") are critical to the analysis of high-yield issuers.

In a holding company structure, the parent owns stock in its subsidiaries. Typically, the parent doesn't generate much of its own earnings or cash flow but instead receives dividends from its subsidiaries. The subsidiaries' dividends are generally paid out of earnings after they satisfy of all their other obligations, such as debt payments. To the extent that their earnings and cash flow are weak, subsidiaries may be limited in their ability to pay dividends to the parent. Moreover, subsidiaries that carry a lot of their own debt may have restrictions or limitations on how much cash they can provide to the parent via dividends or in another way, such as through an intercompany loan. These restrictions and limitations on cash moving between parent and subsidiaries can have a major impact on their respective abilities to meet their debt obligations. The parent's reliance on cash flow from its subsidiaries means the parent's debt is structurally subordinated to the subsidiaries' debt and thus will usually have a lower recovery rating in default.

For companies with very complex holding companies, there may also be one or more intermediate holding companies, each carrying their own debt, and in some cases, they may not own 100 percent of the subsidiaries' stock. This structure is sometimes seen in high-yield companies that have been put together through many mergers and acquisitions or that were part of a leveraged buyout.[40]

Exhibit 20 shows the capital structure of Infor, Inc. (Infor), a high-yield software and services company highlighted earlier as an example of the credit rating agency notching process. Infor's capital structure consists of a parent company that has debt—in this case, convertible senior notes—as well as a subsidiary with multiple layers of outstanding debt by seniority.

Exhibit 20 Infor's Capital Structure

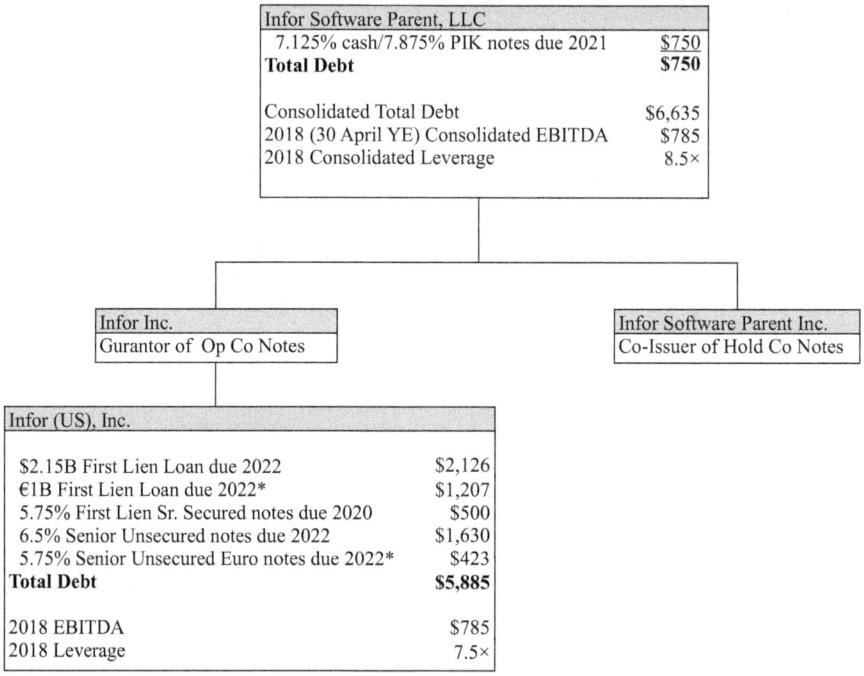

* Conversion from Euro to USD.
Source: Company filing; Loomis, Sayles & Company.

Thus, high-yield investors should analyze and understand an issuer's corporate structure, including the distribution of debt between the parent and its subsidiaries. Leverage ratios should be calculated at each of the debt-issuing entities, as well as on a consolidated basis.

40 For holding companies with complex corporate structures, such as multiple subsidiaries with their own capital structures, a default in one subsidiary may not trigger a cross-default. Astute analysts will look for that in indentures and other legal documentation.

Also important is that although the debt of an operating subsidiary may be "closer to" and better secured by particular assets of the subsidiary, the credit quality of a parent company might still be higher. The parent company could, while being less directly secured by any particular assets, still benefit from the diversity and availability of all the cash flows in the consolidated system. In short, credit quality is not simply an automatic analysis of debt provisions and liens.

Covenant Analysis. As discussed earlier, analysis of covenants is very important for all bonds. It is especially important for high-yield credits because of their reduced margin of safety. Key covenants for high-yield issuers may include the following:

- Change of control put
- Restricted payments
- Limitations on liens and additional indebtedness
- Restricted versus unrestricted subsidiaries

Under the **change of control put**, in the event of an acquisition (a "change of control"), bondholders have the right to require the issuer to buy back their debt (a "put option"), often at par or at some small premium to par value. This covenant is intended to protect creditors from being exposed to a weaker, more indebted borrower as a result of acquisition. For investment-grade issuers, this covenant typically has a two-pronged test: acquisition of the borrower and a consequent downgrade to a high-yield rating.

The **restricted payments** covenant is meant to protect creditors by limiting how much cash can be paid out to shareholders over time. The restricted payments "basket" is typically sized relative to an issuer's cash flow and debt outstanding—or is being raised—and is an amount that can grow with retained earnings or cash flow, giving management more flexibility to make pay-outs.

The **limitations on liens** covenant is meant to put limits on how much secured debt an issuer can have. This covenant is important to unsecured creditors who are structurally subordinated to secured creditors; the higher the amount of debt that is layered ahead of them, the less they stand to recover in the event of default.

With regard to **restricted versus unrestricted subsidiaries**, issuers may classify certain of their subsidiaries as restricted and others as unrestricted as it pertains to offering guarantees for their holding company debt. These subsidiary guarantees can be very useful to holding company creditors because they put their debt on equal standing (pari passu) with debt at the subsidiaries instead of with structurally subordinated debt. Restricted subsidiaries should be thought of as those that are designated to help service parent-level debt, typically through guarantees. They tend to be an issuer's larger subsidiaries and have significant assets, such as plants and other facilities, and/or cash flow. There may be tax or legal (e.g., country of domicile) reasons why certain subsidiaries are restricted while others are not. Analysts should carefully read the definitions of restricted versus unrestricted subsidiaries in the indenture because sometimes the language is so loosely written that the company can reclassify subsidiaries from one type to another with a simple vote by a board of directors or trustees.

For high-yield investors, it is also important to know what covenants are in an issuer's bank credit agreements. These agreements are typically filed with the securities commission in the country where the loan document was drafted. Bank covenants can be more restrictive than bond covenants and may include so-called **maintenance covenants**, such as leverage tests, whereby the ratio of, say, debt/EBITDA may not exceed "x" times. In the event a covenant is breached, the bank is likely to block further loans under the agreement until the covenant is cured. If not cured, the bank may accelerate full payment of the facility, triggering a default.

Equity-like approach to high-yield analysis. High-yield bonds are sometimes thought of as a "hybrid" between higher-quality bonds, such as investment-grade corporate debt, and equity securities. Their more volatile price and spread movements are less influenced by interest rate changes than are higher-quality bonds, and they show greater correlation with movements in equity markets. Indeed, as shown in Exhibit 21, historical returns on high-yield bonds and the standard deviation of those returns fall somewhere between investment-grade bonds and equities.

Exhibit 21 US Trailing 12-Month Returns by Asset Class, 31 December 1988–30 September 2018

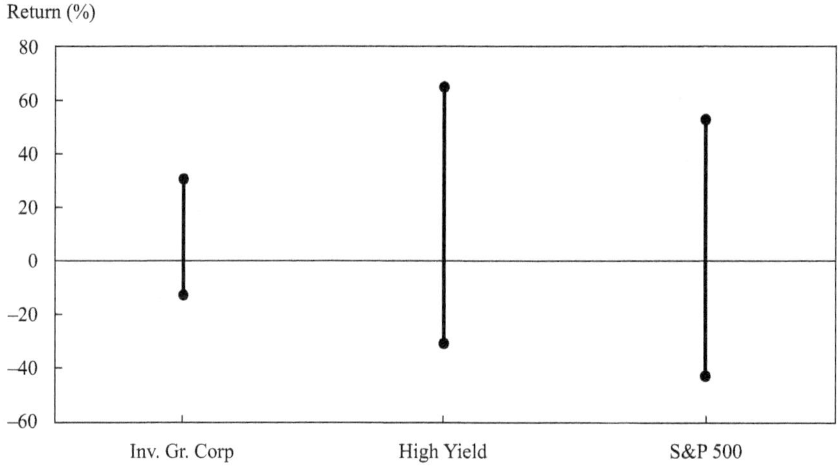

	Inv. Gr. Corp	High Yield	S&P 500
Avg. Return:	7.00%	8.86%	11.39%
Max. Return:	31.07%	64.95%	53.62%
Min. Return:	−13.82%	−31.23%	−43.32%
Avg. Volatility:	4.71%	6.79%	12.91%

Sources: Bloomberg Barclays Indices, Haver Analytics, and Loomis, Sayles & Company.

Consequently, an equity market-like approach to analyzing a high-yield issuer can be useful. One approach is to calculate an issuer's enterprise value. Enterprise value (EV) is usually calculated by adding equity market capitalization and total debt and then subtracting excess cash.[41,42] Enterprise value is a measure of what a business is worth (before any takeover premium) because an acquirer of the company would have to either pay off or assume the debt and it would receive the acquired company's cash.

Bond investors like using EV because it shows the amount of equity "cushion" beneath the debt. It can also give a sense of (1) how much more leverage management might attempt to put on a company in an effort to increase equity returns or (2) how likely—and how expensive—a credit-damaging leveraged buyout might be. Similar to how stock investors look at equity multiples, bond investors may calculate and compare EV/EBITDA and debt/EBITDA across several issuers as part of their analysis. Narrow differences between the EV/EBITDA and debt/EBITDA ratios for a given issuer indicate a small equity cushion and, therefore, potentially higher risk for bond investors.

41 Excess cash takes total cash and subtracts any negative working capital.

42 Unlike the vast majority of investment-grade companies, many high-yield issuers do not have publicly traded equity. For those issuers, one can use comparable public company equity data to estimate EV.

7.2 Sovereign Debt

Governments around the world issue debt to help finance their general operations, including current expenses such as wages for government employees, and investments in long-term assets such as infrastructure and education. Government bonds in developed countries have traditionally been viewed as the default risk-free rate off of which all other credits are priced. Fiscal challenges in developed countries exacerbated by the 2008 global financial crisis ("GFC") and 2011–2012 eurocrisis, however, have called into question the notion of a "risk-free rate," even for some of the highest-quality government borrowers. As their capital markets have developed, an increasing number of sovereign governments have been able to issue debt in foreign markets (generally denominated in a currency other than that of the sovereign government, often the US dollar or euro) as well as debt in the domestic market (issued in the sovereign government's own currency). Generally, sovereign governments with weak currencies can only access foreign debt markets by issuing bonds in foreign currencies that are viewed to be safer stores of value. Debt issued in the domestic market is somewhat easier to service because the debt is typically denominated in the country's own currency, subject to its own laws, and money can be printed to service the sovereign government's domestic debt. Twenty years ago, many emerging market countries[43] could only issue debt in foreign markets because a domestic market did not exist. Today, many are able to issue debt domestically and have successfully built yield curves of domestic bonds across the maturity spectrum. All sovereign governments are best able to service foreign and domestic debt if they run "twin surpluses"—that is, a government budget surplus as well as a current account surplus.

Despite ongoing financial globalization and the development of domestic bond markets, sovereign government defaults occur. Defaults are often precipitated by such events as war, political upheaval, major currency devaluation, a sharp deterioration in trade, or dramatic price declines in a country's key commodity exports. Default risks for some developed countries escalated after 2009 as government revenues dropped precipitously following the financial crisis of 2008, expenditures surged, and financial markets focused on the long-term sustainability of public finances, given aging populations and rising social security needs. Some of the weaker and more highly indebted members of the eurozone became unable to access the debt markets at economical rates and had to seek loans from the International Monetary Fund (IMF) and the European Union. These weaker governments had previously been able to borrow at much lower rates because of their membership in the European Union and adoption of the euro. Intra-eurozone yield spreads widened and countries were shut out of markets, however, as the global financial crisis exacted a high toll on their public finances and, in some cases, their banking systems, which became contingent liabilities for the sovereigns. In Ireland, the government guaranteed most bank liabilities, undermining the country's own fiscal metrics .

Like corporate analysis, sovereign credit analysis is based on a combination of qualitative and quantitative factors. Ultimately, the two key issues for sovereign analysis are: 1) a government's ability to pay, and 2) its willingness to pay. Willingness to pay is important because, due to the principle of sovereign immunity, investors are generally unable to force a sovereign to pay its debts. Sovereign immunity prevents governments from being sued. To date, global initiatives aimed at creating a mechanism for orderly sovereign restructurings and defaults have not found traction.

---

43 There is no commonly accepted definition of emerging market countries. The World Bank considers GDP/Capita to be a useful measure, with below-average GDP/Capita likely indicating an emerging market. Other factors include the degree of openness and maturity of the economy, as well as a country's political stability.

To illustrate the most important considerations in sovereign credit analysis, we present a basic framework for evaluating sovereign credit and assigning sovereign debt ratings.[44] The framework highlights the specific characteristics analysts should expect in a high-quality sovereign credit. Some of these are self-explanatory (e.g., absence of corruption). For others, a brief rationale and/or range of values is included to clarify interpretation. Most, but not all, of these items are included in rating agency Standard & Poor's methodology.

Institutional and economic profile

- *Institutional assessment*
  - Institutions' ability to deliver sound public finances and balanced economic growth
  - Effectiveness and predictability of policymaking institutions
  - Track record of managing previous political, economic, and/or financial crises
  - Ability and willingness to implement reforms to address fiscal challenges
  - Transparent and accountable institutions with low perceived level of corruption
  - Independence of statistical offices and media
  - Checks and balances between institutions
  - Unbiased enforcement of contracts and respect for rule of law and property rights
  - Debt repayment culture
  - Potential external and domestic security risks
- *Economic assessment*
  - Income per capita: More prosperous countries generally have a broader and deeper tax base with which to support debt.
  - Trend growth prospects: Creditworthiness is supported by sustainable and durable trend growth across business cycles.
  - Diversity and stability of growth: Sovereigns exposed to economic concentration are more vulnerable. A narrow economy tends to show higher volatility in growth and can impair a government's balance sheet.

Flexibility and performance profile

- *External assessment*
  - Status of currency: Sovereigns that control a reserve currency or a very actively traded currency are able to use their own currency in many international transactions and are less vulnerable to adverse shifts in global investor portfolios.
  - External liquidity: Countries with a substantial supply of foreign currency (foreign exchange reserves plus current account receipts) relative to projected funding needs in foreign currency (current account payments plus debt maturities) are less vulnerable to interruption of external liquidity.

---

44 This outline was developed from the detailed exposition of Standard & Poor's methodology given in "Sovereign Rating Methodology," December 2017.

  - External debt: Countries with low foreign debt relative to current account receipts are better able to service their foreign debt. This is similar to a coverage ratio for a corporation.
- *Fiscal assessment*
  - Fiscal performance and flexibility: Trend change in net general government debt as a percent of GDP: Stable or declining debt as a percent of GDP indicates a strong credit; a rising ratio can prove unsustainable and is, therefore, a sign of diminishing creditworthiness.
  - Long-term fiscal trends: Perceived willingness and ability to increase revenue or cut expenditure to ensure debt service.
  - Debt burden and structure: Net general government debt of less than 30 percent is good; more than 100 percent is poor. General government interest expense as a percent of revenue: Less than 5 percent is good; greater than 15 percent is poor.
  - Ability to access funding, manage both the amortization profile and contingent liabilities arising from financial sector, public enterprises, and guarantees.
- *Monetary assessment*
  - Ability to use monetary policy tailored to domestic economic objectives (e.g., growth) to address imbalances or shocks.
  - Exchange rate regime: Sovereigns with a reserve currency have the most flexibility. A freely floating currency allows maximum effectiveness for monetary policy. A fixed-rate regime limits effectiveness and flexibility. A hard peg, such as a currency board or monetary union, affords no independent monetary policy.
  - Credibility of monetary policy: Measured by track record of low and stable inflation. Credible monetary policy is supported by an operationally and legally independent central bank with a clear mandate. The central bank's ability to be a lender of last resort to the financial system also enhances stability.
  - Confidence in the central bank provides a foundation for confidence in the currency as a store of value and for the central bank to effectively manage policy through a crisis.
  - Most effective policy transmission occurs in systems with sound banking systems and well -developed domestic capital markets including active money market and corporate bond markets, such that policymakers credibly enact policy relying on market-based policy tools (e.g., open market operations) over administrative policy tools (e.g., reserve requirements).

In light of a sovereign government's various powers—taxation, regulation, monetary policy, and ultimately, the sovereign's ability to "print money" to repay debt—within its own economy, it is virtually always at least as good a credit in its domestic currency as it is in foreign currency. Thus, credit rating agencies often distinguish between domestic and foreign bonds, with domestic bond ratings sometimes one notch higher. Of course, if a sovereign government were to rely heavily on printing money to repay debt, it would fuel high inflation or hyperinflation and increase default risk on domestic debt as well.[45]

45 According to Reinhart and Rogoff in their book *This Time is Different*, between 1800 and 2009 there have been more than 250 defaults on foreign sovereign debt and at least 68 defaults on domestic debt. Reinhart and Rogoff use a broader definition of default that includes very high levels of inflation (more than 20 percent).

EXAMPLE 11

Sovereign Debt

Exhibit 22 shows several key sovereign statistics for Portugal.

Exhibit 22 Key Sovereign Statistics for Portugal

€ (billions), except where noted	2006	2008	2010	2012	2014	2015	2016	2017
Nominal GDP	160.3	171.2	172.6	168.4	173.1	179.8	186.5	194.6
Population (millions)	10.6	10.6	10.6	10.5	10.4	10.3	10.3	10.3
Unemployment (%)	8.6	8.5	12	15.6	13.9	12.4	11.1	8.9
Exports as share GDP (%)	22.2	22.6	21.3	26.8	27.8	27.6	26.8	28.3
Current account as share GDP (%)	−10.7	−12.6	−10	−2.1	0.2	0.3	0.7	0.6
Government revenues	64.8	70.7	71.8	72.2	77.2	78.8	79.9	83.1
Government expenditures	71.4	77.1	88.7	81.7	89.6	86.7	83.5	88.9
Budget balance (surplus/deficit)	−6.5	−6.4	−16.9	−9.5	−12.4	−7.9	−3.6	−5.8
Government interest payments	4.2	5.3	5.2	8.2	8.5	8.2	7.8	7.4
Primary balance (surplus/deficit)	−2.2	−1.1	−11.7	−1.3	−3.9	0.3	4.2	1.6
Government debt	102.4	123.1	161.3	212.6	226	231.5	241	242.8
Interest rate on new debt (%)	3.9	4.5	5.4	3.4	3.8	2.4	3.2	3.1

Sources: Haver Analytics, Eurostat, and Instituto Nacional de Estatistica (Portugal).

1 Calculate the government debt/GDP ratio for Portugal for the years 2014–2017 as well as for the years 2006, 2008, 2010, and 2012

2 Calculate GDP/Capita for the same periods.

3 Based on those calculations, as well as other data from Exhibit 22, what can you say about Portugal's credit trend?

Solutions to 1 and 2:

	2006	2008	2010	2012	2014	2015	2016	2017
Gross Government Debt/GDP	64%	72%	93%	126%	131%	129%	129%	125%
GDP/Capita	15,123	16,151	16,283	16,038	16,644	17,456	18,107	18,893

Solution to 3:

The credit trend is stabilizing. Government debt/GDP is declining ever so slightly after peaking in 2014. The government is running a modest budget deficit with a primary balance that is in surplus for the past three years. Portugal is running a very small current account surplus, reducing its reliance on external funding, and has increased its exports as a share of GDP. Unemployment, while still fairly high, has fallen in the past several years. Interest payments on government debt have started to decline, both as a percentage of GDP and in absolute terms. The interest rate on new government debt has stabilized, perhaps benefitting from the European Central Bank's quantitative easing policies. Taken together, there are strong indications that the Portuguese government's credit situation has stabilized and may be expected to improve further if current trends are sustained.

7.3 Non-Sovereign Government Debt

Sovereigns are the largest issuers of government debt but non-sovereign—sometimes called sub-sovereign or local—governments and the quasi-government entities that are created by governments issue bonds as well. The non-sovereign or local governments include governments of states, provinces, regions and cities. For example, the City of Tokyo (Tokyo Metropolitan Government) has debt outstanding, as does the Lombardy region in Italy, the City of Buenos Aires in Argentina, and the State of California in the United States. Local government bonds may be referred to as municipal bonds.

However, when people talk about municipal bonds, they are usually referring to US municipal bonds, which represent one of the largest bond markets. As of year-end 2017, the US municipal bond market was approximately $3.9 trillion in size, roughly 9 percent of the total US bond market.[46] The US municipal bond market is composed of both tax-exempt[47] and, to a lesser extent, taxable bonds issued by state and city governments and their agencies. Municipal borrowers may also issue bonds on behalf of private entities, such as non-profit colleges or hospitals. Historically, for any given rating category, these bonds have much lower default rates than corporate bonds with the same ratings. For example, according to Moody's Investors Service, the 10-year average cumulative default rate from 1970 through 2017 was 0.17 percent for municipal bonds, compared with a 10.24 percent 10-year average cumulative default rate for all corporate debt.[48]

The majority of local government bonds, including municipal bonds, are either general obligation bonds or revenue bonds. General obligation (GO) bonds are unsecured bonds issued with the full faith and credit of the issuing non-sovereign government. These bonds are supported by the taxing authority of the issuer. Revenue bonds are issued for specific project financing (e.g., financing for a new sewer system, a toll road, bridge, hospital, a sports arena, etc.).

The credit analysis of GO bonds has some similarities to sovereign debt analysis (e.g., the ability to levy and collect taxes and fees to help service debt) but also some differences. For example, almost without exception, US municipalities must balance their operating budgets (i.e., exclusive of long-term capital projects) annually. Non-sovereign governments are unable to use monetary policy the way many sovereigns can.

The economic analysis of non-sovereign government GO bonds, including US municipal bonds, focuses on employment, per capita income (and changes in it over time), per capita debt (and changes in it over time), the tax base (depth, breadth, diversification, stability, etc.), demographics, and net population growth, as well as an analysis of whether the area represented by the non-sovereign government has the infrastructure and location to attract and support new jobs. Analysis should look at the volatility and variability of revenues during times of both economic strength and weakness. An overreliance on one or two types of tax revenue—particularly a volatile one, such as capital gains taxes or sales taxes—can signal increased credit risk. Pensions and other post-retirement obligations may not show up directly on the non-sovereign government's balance sheet, and many of these entities have underfunded pensions that

46 Securities Industry and Financial Markets Association (SIFMA) Outstanding U.S. Bond Market Data", as of 2Q 2018, (2017).

47 Tax exempt refers to the fact that interest received on these bonds is not subject to US federal income taxes and, in many cases, is exempt for in-state residents from state and city income taxes as well.

48 Moody's Investors Service, "US Municipal Bond Defaults and Recoveries, 1970–2017."

need to be addressed. Adding the unfunded pension and post-retirement obligations to the debt reveals a more realistic picture of the issuer's debt and longer-term obligations. The relative ease or difficulty in managing the annual budgeting process and the government's ability to operate consistently within its budget are also important credit analysis considerations.

Disclosure by non-sovereign governments varies widely, with some of the smaller issuers providing limited financial information. Reporting requirements are inconsistent, so the financial reports may not be available for six months or more after the closing of a reporting period.

Exhibit 23 compares several key debt statistics from two of the larger states in the United States: Illinois and Texas. Illinois has the lowest credit ratings of any of the states, whereas Texas has one of the highest. Note the higher debt burden (and lower ranking) across several measures: Total debt, Debt/Capita, Debt/Personal income, and debt as a percent of state GDP. When including net pension liabilities of government employees and retirees, the debt burdens are even greater, especially in the case of Illinois. What is not shown here is that Illinois also has a higher tax burden and greater difficulty balancing its budget on an annual basis than Texas does.

Exhibit 23 Municipal Debt Comparison: Illinois vs. Texas

	Illinois	Texas
Ratings:		
Moody's	Baa3	Aaa
S&P	BBB–	AAA
Fitch	BBB	AAA
Unemployment rate (%)*	4.20	3.70
Median Household Income ($)**	$61,229	$57,051
Debt burden, net ($/rank)***		
Total (millions)	37,374 (5)	11,603 (13)
Per capita	2,919 (6)	410 (42)
As a percent of 2016 personal income	5.60 (5)	0.90 (42)
As a percent of 2016 GDP	4.70 (6)	0.73 (42)
ANPL, net ($/rank)****		
Total (millions)	250,136 (1)	140,253 (3)
Per capita	19,539 (1)	4,955 (19)
As a percent of 2017 personal income	37.00 (1)	10.60 (19)
As a percent of 2017 GDP	30.50 (1)	8.30 (20)

* *Source:* Bureau of Labor Statistics, data as of October 2018.
** *Source:* US Census Bureau, data as of 2017.
*** *Source:* Moody's Investor Services, Inc., debt data as of 2017.
**** *Source:* Moody's Investor Services, Inc., adjusted net pension liability data as of 2017.

Revenue bonds, which are issued to finance a specific project, have a higher degree of risk than GO bonds because they are dependent on a single source of revenue. The analysis of these bonds is a combination of an analysis of the project and the finances around the particular project. The project analysis focuses on the need and projected utilization of the project, as well as on the economic base supporting the project. The financial analysis has some similarities to the analysis of a corporate bond in that it is focused on operating results, cash flow, liquidity, capital structure, and the ability to service and repay the debt. A key credit measure for revenue-backed non-sovereign government bonds is the debt-service-coverage (DSC) ratio, which measures how much revenue is available to cover debt payments (principal and interest) after operating expenses. Many revenue bonds have a minimum DSC ratio covenant; the higher the DSC ratio, the stronger the creditworthiness.

SUMMARY

In this reading, we introduced readers to the basic principles of credit analysis. We described the importance of the credit markets and credit and credit-related risks. We discussed the role and importance of credit ratings and the methodology associated with assigning ratings, as well as the risks of relying on credit ratings. The reading covered the key components of credit analysis and the financial measure used to help assess creditworthiness.

We also discussed risk versus return when investing in credit and how spread changes affect holding period returns. In addition, we addressed the special considerations to take into account when doing credit analysis of high-yield companies, sovereign borrowers, and non-sovereign government bonds.

- Credit risk is the risk of loss resulting from the borrower failing to make full and timely payments of interest and/or principal.
- The key components of credit risk are risk of default and loss severity in the event of default. The product of the two is expected loss. Investors in higher-quality bonds tend not to focus on loss severity because default risk for those securities is low.
- Loss severity equals (1 – Recovery rate).
- Credit-related risks include downgrade risk (also called credit migration risk) and market liquidity risk. Either of these can cause yield spreads—yield premiums—to rise and bond prices to fall.
- Downgrade risk refers to a decline in an issuer's creditworthiness. Downgrades will cause its bonds to trade with wider yield spreads and thus lower prices.
- Market liquidity risk refers to a widening of the bid–ask spread on an issuer's bonds. Lower-quality bonds tend to have greater market liquidity risk than higher-quality bonds, and during times of market or financial stress, market liquidity risk rises.
- The composition of an issuer's debt and equity is referred to as its "capital structure." Debt ranks ahead of all types of equity with respect to priority of payment, and within the debt component of the capital structure, there can be varying levels of seniority.
- With respect to priority of claims, secured debt ranks ahead of unsecured debt, and within unsecured debt, senior debt ranks ahead of subordinated debt. In the typical case, all of an issuer's bonds have the same probability of default due to cross-default provisions in most indentures. Higher priority of claim implies higher recovery rate—lower loss severity—in the event of default.

- For issuers with more complex corporate structures—for example, a parent holding company that has operating subsidiaries—debt at the holding company is structurally subordinated to the subsidiary debt, although the possibility of more diverse assets and earnings streams from other sources could still result in the parent having higher effective credit quality than a particular subsidiary.
- Recovery rates can vary greatly by issuer and industry. They are influenced by the composition of an issuer's capital structure, where in the economic and credit cycle the default occurred, and what the market's view of the future prospects are for the issuer and its industry.
- The priority of claims in bankruptcy is not always absolute. It can be influenced by several factors, including some leeway accorded to bankruptcy judges, government involvement, or a desire on the part of the more senior creditors to settle with the more junior creditors and allow the issuer to emerge from bankruptcy as a going concern, rather than risking smaller and delayed recovery in the event of a liquidation of the borrower.
- Credit rating agencies, such as Moody's, Standard & Poor's, and Fitch, play a central role in the credit markets. Nearly every bond issued in the broad debt markets carries credit ratings, which are opinions about a bond issue's creditworthiness. Credit ratings enable investors to compare the credit risk of debt issues and issuers within a given industry, across industries, and across geographic markets.
- Bonds rated Aaa to Baa3 by Moody's and AAA to BBB– by Standard & Poor's (S&P) and/or Fitch (higher to lower) are referred to as "investment grade." Bonds rated lower than that—Ba1 or lower by Moody's and BB+ or lower by S&P and/or Fitch—are referred to as "below investment grade" or "speculative grade." Below-investment-grade bonds are also called "high-yield" or "junk" bonds.
- The rating agencies rate both issuers and issues. Issuer ratings are meant to address an issuer's overall creditworthiness—its risk of default. Ratings for issues incorporate such factors as their rankings in the capital structure.
- The rating agencies will notch issue ratings up or down to account for such factors as capital structure ranking for secured or subordinated bonds, reflecting different recovery rates in the event of default. Ratings may also be notched due to structural subordination.
- There are risks in relying too much on credit agency ratings. Creditworthiness may change over time, and initial/current ratings do not necessarily reflect the creditworthiness of an issuer or bond over an investor's holding period. Valuations often adjust before ratings change, and the notching process may not adequately reflect the price decline of a bond that is lower ranked in the capital structure. Because ratings primarily reflect the probability of default but not necessarily the severity of loss given default, bonds with the same rating may have significantly different expected losses (default probability times loss severity). And like analysts, credit rating agencies may have difficulty forecasting certain credit-negative outcomes, such as adverse litigation, leveraging corporate transactions, and such low probability/high severity events as earthquakes and hurricanes.
- The role of corporate credit analysis is to assess the company's ability to make timely payments of interest and to repay principal at maturity.
- Credit analysis is similar to equity analysis. It is important to understand, however, that bonds are contracts and that management's duty to bondholders and other creditors is limited to the terms of the contract. In contrast,

management's duty to shareholders is to act in their best interest by trying to maximize the value of the company—perhaps even at the expense of bondholders at times.

- Credit analysts tend to focus more on the downside risk given the asymmetry of risk/return, whereas equity analysts focus more on upside opportunity from earnings growth, and so on.
- The "4 Cs" of credit—capacity, collateral, covenants, and character—provide a useful framework for evaluating credit risk.
- Credit analysis focuses on an issuer's ability to generate cash flow. The analysis starts with an industry assessment—structure and fundamentals—and continues with an analysis of an issuer's competitive position, management strategy, and track record.
- Credit measures are used to calculate an issuer's creditworthiness, as well as to compare its credit quality with peer companies. Key credit ratios focus on leverage and interest coverage and use such measures as EBITDA, free cash flow, funds from operations, interest expense and balance sheet debt.
- An issuer's ability to access liquidity is also an important consideration in credit analysis.
- The higher the credit risk, the greater the offered/required yield and potential return demanded by investors. Over time, bonds with more credit risk offer higher returns but with greater volatility of return than bonds with lower credit risk.
- The yield on a credit-risky bond comprises the yield on a default risk–free bond with a comparable maturity plus a yield premium, or "spread," that comprises a credit spread and a liquidity premium. That spread is intended to compensate investors for credit risk—risk of default and loss severity in the event of default—and the credit-related risks that can cause spreads to widen and prices to decline—downgrade or credit migration risk and market liquidity risk.

  $$\text{Yield spread} = \text{Liquidity premium} + \text{Credit spread}.$$

- In times of financial market stress, the liquidity premium can increase sharply, causing spreads to widen on all credit-risky bonds, with lower-quality issuers most affected. In times of credit improvement or stability, however, credit spreads can narrow sharply as well, providing attractive investment returns.
- Credit curves—the plot of yield spreads for a given bond issuer across the yield curve—are typically upward sloping, with the exception of high premium-priced bonds and distressed bonds, where credit curves can be inverted because of the fear of default, when all creditors at a given ranking in the capital structure will receive the same recovery rate without regard to debt maturity.
- The impact of spread changes on holding period returns for credit-risky bonds are a product of two primary factors: the basis point spread change and the sensitivity of price to yield as reflected by (end-of-period) modified duration and convexity. Spread narrowing enhances holding period returns, whereas spread widening has a negative impact on holding period returns. Longer-duration bonds have greater price and return sensitivity to changes in spread than shorter-duration bonds.

  $$\text{Price impact} \approx -(\text{MDur} \times \Delta\text{Spread}) + \tfrac{1}{2}\text{Cvx} \times (\Delta\text{Spread})^2$$

- For high-yield bonds, with their greater risk of default, more emphasis should be placed on an issuer's sources of liquidity, as well as on its debt structure and corporate structure. Credit risk can vary greatly across an issuer's debt structure depending on the seniority ranking. Many high-yield companies have complex capital structures, resulting in different levels of credit risk depending on where the debt resides.

- Covenant analysis is especially important for high-yield bonds. Key covenants include payment restrictions, limitation on liens, change of control, coverage maintenance tests (often limited to bank loans), and any guarantees from restricted subsidiaries. Covenant language can be very technical and legalistic, so it may help to seek legal or expert assistance.
- An equity-like approach to high-yield analysis can be helpful. Calculating and comparing enterprise value with EBITDA and debt/EBITDA can show a level of equity "cushion" or support beneath an issuer's debt.
- Sovereign credit analysis includes assessing both an issuer's ability and willingness to pay its debt obligations. Willingness to pay is important because, due to sovereign immunity, a sovereign government cannot be forced to pay its debts.
- In assessing sovereign credit risk, a helpful framework is to focus on five broad areas: (1) institutional effectiveness and political risks, (2) economic structure and growth prospects, (3) external liquidity and international investment position, (4) fiscal performance, flexibility, and debt burden, and (5) monetary flexibility.
- Among the characteristics of a high-quality sovereign credit are the absence of corruption and/or challenges to political framework; governmental checks and balances; respect for rule of law and property rights; commitment to honor debts; high per capita income with stable, broad-based growth prospects; control of a reserve or actively traded currency; currency flexibility; low foreign debt and foreign financing needs relative to receipts in foreign currencies; stable or declining ratio of debt to GDP; low debt service as a percent of revenue; low ratio of net debt to GDP; operationally independent central bank; track record of low and stable inflation; and a well-developed banking system and active money market.
- Non-sovereign or local government bonds, including municipal bonds, are typically either general obligation bonds or revenue bonds.
- General obligation (GO) bonds are backed by the taxing authority of the issuing non-sovereign government. The credit analysis of GO bonds has some similarities to sovereign analysis—debt burden per capita versus income per capita, tax burden, demographics, and economic diversity. Underfunded and "off-balance-sheet" liabilities, such as pensions for public employees and retirees, are debt-like in nature.
- Revenue-backed bonds support specific projects, such as toll roads, bridges, airports, and other infrastructure. The creditworthiness comes from the revenues generated by usage fees and tolls levied.

PRACTICE PROBLEMS

1 The risk that a bond's creditworthiness declines is *best* described by:

A credit migration risk.

B market liquidity risk.

C spread widening risk.

2 Stedsmart Ltd and Fignermo Ltd are alike with respect to financial and operating characteristics, except that Stedsmart Ltd has less publicly traded debt outstanding than Fignermo Ltd. Stedsmart Ltd is *most likely* to have:

A no market liquidity risk.

B lower market liquidity risk.

C higher market liquidity risk.

3 In the event of default, the recovery rate of which of the following bonds would *most likely* be the highest?

A First mortgage debt

B Senior unsecured debt

C Junior subordinate debt

4 During bankruptcy proceedings of a firm, the priority of claims was not strictly adhered to. Which of the following is the *least likely* explanation for this outcome?

A Senior creditors compromised.

B The value of secured assets was less than the amount of the claims.

C A judge's order resulted in actual claims not adhering to strict priority of claims.

5 A fixed income analyst is *least likely* to conduct an independent analysis of credit risk because credit rating agencies:

A may at times mis-rate issues.

B often lag the market in pricing credit risk.

C cannot foresee future debt-financed acquisitions.

6 If goodwill makes up a large percentage of a company's total assets, this *most likely* indicates that:

A the company has low free cash flow before dividends.

B there is a low likelihood that the market price of the company's common stock is below book value.

C a large percentage of the company's assets are not of high quality.

7 In order to analyze the **collateral** of a company a credit analyst should assess the:

A cash flows of the company.

B soundness of management's strategy.

C value of the company's assets in relation to the level of debt.

8 In order to determine the **capacity** of a company, it would be *most* appropriate to analyze the:

A company's strategy.

B growth prospects of the industry.

C aggressiveness of the company's accounting policies.

9 A credit analyst is evaluating the credit worthiness of three companies: a construction company, a travel and tourism company, and a beverage company. Both the construction and travel and tourism companies are cyclical, whereas the beverage company is non-cyclical. The construction company has the highest debt level of the three companies. The highest credit risk is *most likely* exhibited by the:

A construction company.

B beverage company.

C travel and tourism company.

10 Based on the information provided in Exhibit 1, the EBITDA interest coverage ratio of Adidas AG is *closest* to:

A 7.91x.

B 10.12x.

C 12.99x.

Exhibit 1 Adidas AG Excerpt from Consolidated Income Statement in a given year (€ in millions)

Gross profit	5,730
Royalty and commission income	100
Other operating income	110
Other operating expenses	5,046
Operating profit	894
Interest income	25
Interest expense	113
Income before taxes	806
Income taxes	238
Net income	568

Additional information:
Depreciation and amortization: €249 million

Source: Adidas AG Annual Financial Statements, December 2010

11 The following information is from the annual report of Adidas AG for December 2010:

- Depreciation and amortization: €249 million
- Total assets: €10,618 million
- Total debt: €1,613 million
- Shareholders' equity: €4,616 million

The debt/capital ratio of Adidas AG is *closest* to:

A 15.19%.

B 25.90%.

C 34.94%.

12 Funds from operations (FFO) of Pay Handle Ltd increased in 2011. In 2011 the total debt of the company remained unchanged, while additional common shares were issued. Pay Handle Ltd's ability to service its debt in 2011, as compared to 2010, *most likely*:

A improved.

B worsened.

C remained the same.

13 Based on the information in Exhibit 2, Grupa Zywiec SA's credit risk is *most likely*:

A lower than the industry.

B higher than the industry.

C the same as the industry.

Exhibit 2 European Food, Beverage, and Tobacco Industry and Grupa Zywiec SA Selected Financial Ratios for 2010

	Total debt/Total capital (%)	FFO/Total debt (%)	Return on capital (%)	Total debt/ EBITDA (x)	EBITDA interest coverage (x)
Grupa Zywiec SA	47.1	77.5	19.6	1.2	17.7
Industry Median	**42.4**	**23.6**	**6.55**	**2.85**	**6.45**

14 Based on the information in Exhibit 3, the credit rating of Davide Campari-Milano S.p.A. is *most likely*:

A lower than Associated British Foods plc.

B higher than Associated British Foods plc.

C the same as Associated British Foods plc.

Exhibit 3 European Food, Beverage, and Tobacco Industry; Associated British Foods plc; and Davide Campari-Milano S.p.A Selected Financial Ratios, 2010

Company	Total debt/total capital (%)	FFO/total debt (%)	Return on capital (%)	Total debt/EBITDA (x)	EBITDA interest coverage (x)
Associated British Foods plc	0.2	84.3	0.1	1.0	13.9
Davide Campari-Milano S.p.A.	42.9	22.9	8.2	3.2	3.2
European Food, Beverage, and Tobacco Median	**42.4**	**23.6**	**6.55**	**2.85**	**6.45**

15 Holding all other factors constant, the *most likely* effect of low demand and heavy new issue supply on bond yield spreads is that yield spreads will:

A widen.

B tighten.

C not be affected.

16 Credit risk of a corporate bond is *best* described as the:

A risk that an issuer's creditworthiness deteriorates.

B probability that the issuer fails to make full and timely payments.

C risk of loss resulting from the issuer failing to make full and timely payments.

17 The risk that the price at which investors can actually transact differs from the quoted price in the market is called:

A spread risk.

B credit migration risk.

C market liquidity risk.

18 Loss severity is *best* described as the:

A default probability multiplied by the loss given default.

B portion of a bond's value recovered by bondholders in the event of default.

C portion of a bond's value, including unpaid interest, an investor loses in the event of default.

19 The two components of credit risk are default probability and:

A spread risk.

B loss severity.

C market liquidity risk.

20 For a high-quality debt issuer with a large amount of publicly traded debt, bond investors tend to devote *most* effort to assessing the issuer's:

A default risk.

B loss severity.

C market liquidity risk.

21 The expected loss for a given debt instrument is estimated as the product of default probability and:

A (1 + Recovery rate).

B (1 – Recovery rate).

C 1/(1 + Recovery rate).

22 The priority of claims for senior subordinated debt is:

A lower than for senior unsecured debt.

B the same as for senior unsecured debt.

C higher than for senior unsecured debt.

23 A senior unsecured credit instrument holds a higher priority of claims than one ranked as:

A mortgage debt.

B second lien loan.

C senior subordinated.

24 In a bankruptcy proceeding, when the absolute priority of claims is enforced:

A senior subordinated creditors rank above second lien holders.

B preferred equity shareholders rank above unsecured creditors.

C creditors with a secured claim have the first right to the value of that specific property.

25 In the event of default, which of the following is *most likely* to have the highest recovery rate?

A Second lien

B Senior unsecured

C Senior subordinated

26 The process of moving credit ratings of different issues up or down from the issuer rating in response to different payment priorities is *best* described as:

A notching.

B structural subordination.

C cross-default provisions.

27 The factor considered by rating agencies when a corporation has debt at both its parent holding company and operating subsidiaries is *best* referred to as:

A credit migration risk.

B corporate family rating.

C structural subordination.

28 Which type of security is *most likely* to have the same rating as the issuer?

A Preferred stock

B Senior secured bond

C Senior unsecured bond

29 Which of the following corporate debt instruments has the highest seniority ranking?

A Second lien

B Senior unsecured

C Senior subordinated

30 An issuer credit rating usually applies to a company's:

A secured debt.

B subordinated debt.

C senior unsecured debt.

31 The rating agency process whereby the credit ratings on issues are moved up or down from the issuer rating *best* describes:

A notching.

B pari passu ranking.

C cross-default provisions.

32 The notching adjustment for corporate bonds rated Aa2/AA is *most likely*:

A larger than the notching adjustment for corporate bonds rated B2/B.

B the same as the notching adjustment for corporate bonds rated B2/B.

C smaller than the notching adjustment for corporate bonds rated B2/B.

33 Which of the following statements about credit ratings is *most accurate*?

A Credit ratings can migrate over time.

B Changes in bond credit ratings precede changes in bond prices.

C Credit ratings are focused on expected loss rather than risk of default.

34 Which industry characteristic *most likely* has a positive effect on a company's ability to service debt?

A Low barriers to entry in the industry

B High number of suppliers to the industry

C Broadly dispersed market share among large number of companies in the industry

35 When determining the capacity of a borrower to service debt, a credit analyst should begin with an examination of:

A industry structure.

B industry fundamentals.

C company fundamentals.

36 Which of the following accounting issues should *mostly likely* be considered a character warning flag in credit analysis?

A Expensing items immediately

B Changing auditors infrequently

C Significant off-balance-sheet financing

37 In credit analysis, capacity is *best* described as the:

A quality of management.

B ability of the borrower to make its debt payments on time.

C quality and value of the assets supporting an issuer's indebtedness.

38 Among the Four Cs of credit analysis, the recognition of revenue prematurely *most likely* reflects a company's:

A character.

B covenants.

C collateral.

Use the following Exhibit for Questions 39 and 40

Exhibit 4 Industrial Comparative Ratio Analysis, Year 20XX

	EBITDA Margin (%)	Return on Capital (%)	EBIT/ Interest Expense (×)	EBITDA/ Interest Expense (×)	Debt/ EBITDA (×)	Debt/ Capital (%)
Company A	25.1	25.0	15.9	19.6	1.6	35.2
Company B	29.6	36.3	58.2	62.4	0.5	15.9
Company C	21.8	16.6	8.9	12.4	2.5	46.3

39 Based on only the leverage ratios in Exhibit 4, the company with the *highest* credit risk is:

A Company A.

B Company B.

C Company C.

40 Based on only the coverage ratios in Exhibit 4, the company with the *highest* credit quality is:

- **A** Company A.
- **B** Company B.
- **C** Company C.

Use the following Exhibits for Questions 41 and 42

Exhibit 5 Consolidated Income Statement (£ millions)

	Company X	Company Y
Net revenues	50.7	83.7
Operating expenses	49.6	70.4
Operating income	1.1	13.3
Interest income	0.0	0.0
Interest expense	0.6	0.8
Income before income taxes	0.5	12.5
Provision for income taxes	–0.2	–3.5
Net income	0.3	9.0

Exhibit 6 Consolidated Balance Sheets (£ millions)

	Company X	Company Y
ASSETS		
Current assets	10.3	21.9
Property, plant, and equipment, net	3.5	20.1
Goodwill	8.3	85.0
Other assets	0.9	5.1
Total assets	23.0	132.1
LIABILITIES AND SHAREHOLDERS' EQUITY		
Current liabilities		
Accounts payable and accrued expenses	8.4	16.2
Short-term debt	0.5	8.7

(continued)

Exhibit 6 (Continued)

	Company X	Company Y
Total current liabilities	8.9	24.9
Long-term debt	11.7	21.1
Other non-current liabilities	1.1	22.1
Total liabilities	21.7	68.1
Total shareholders' equity	1.3	64.0
Total liabilities and shareholders' equity	23.0	132.1

Exhibit 7 Consolidated Statements of Cash Flow (£ millions)

	Company X	Company Y
CASH FLOWS FROM OPERATING ACTIVITIES		
Net income	0.3	9.0
Depreciation	1.0	3.8
Goodwill impairment	2.0	1.6
Changes in working capital	0.0	−0.4
Net cash provided by operating activities	3.3	14.0
CASH FLOWS FROM INVESTING ACTIVITIES		
Additions to property and equipment	−1.0	−4.0
Additions to marketable securities	−0.1	0.0
Proceeds from sale of property and equipment	0.2	2.9
Proceeds from sale of marketable securities	0.3	0.0
Net cash used in investing activities	−0.6	−1.1
CASH FLOWS FROM FINANCING ACTIVITIES		
Repurchase of common stock	−1.5	−4.0
Dividends to shareholders	−0.3	−6.1
Change in short-term debt	0.0	−3.4
Additions to long-term debt	3.9	3.9
Reductions in long-term debt	−3.4	−2.5
Net cash – financing activities	−1.3	−12.1

Exhibit 7 (Continued)

	Company X	Company Y
NET INCREASE IN CASH AND CASH EQUIVALENTS	1.4	0.8

41 Based on Exhibits 5–7, in comparison to Company X, Company Y has a higher:

A debt/capital ratio.

B debt/EBITDA ratio.

C free cash flow after dividends/debt ratio.

42 Based on Exhibits 5–7, in comparison to Company Y, Company X has greater:

A leverage.

B interest coverage.

C operating profit margin.

---

43 Credit yield spreads *most likely* widen in response to:

A high demand for bonds.

B weak performance of equities.

C strengthening economic conditions.

44 The factor that *most likely* results in corporate credit spreads widening is:

A an improving credit cycle.

B weakening economic conditions.

C a period of high demand for bonds.

45 Credit spreads are *most likely* to widen:

A in a strengthening economy.

B as the credit cycle improves.

C in periods of heavy new issue supply and low borrower demand.

46 Which of the following factors in credit analysis is more important for general obligation non-sovereign government debt than for sovereign debt?

A Per capita income

B Power to levy and collect taxes

C Requirement to balance an operating budget

47 In contrast to high-yield credit analysis, investment-grade analysis is *more likely* to rely on:

A spread risk.

B an assessment of bank credit facilities.

C matching of liquidity sources to upcoming debt maturities.

48 Which of the following factors would *best* justify a decision to avoid investing in a country's sovereign debt?

A Freely floating currency

B A population that is not growing

C Suitable checks and balances in policymaking

SOLUTIONS

1 A is correct. Credit migration risk or downgrade risk refers to the risk that a bond issuer's creditworthiness may deteriorate or migrate lower. The result is that investors view the risk of default to be higher, causing the spread on the issuer's bonds to widen.

2 C is correct. Market liquidity risk refers to the risk that the price at which investors transact may be different from the price indicated in the market. Market liquidity risk is increased by (1) less debt outstanding and/or (2) a lower issue credit rating. Because Stedsmart Ltd is comparable to Fignermo Ltd except for less publicly traded debt outstanding, it should have higher market liquidity risk.

3 A is correct. First mortgage debt is senior secured debt and has the highest priority of claims. First mortgage debt also has the highest expected recovery rate. First mortgage debt refers to the pledge of specific property. Neither senior unsecured nor junior subordinate debt has any claims on specific assets.

4 B is correct. Whether or not secured assets are sufficient for the claims against them does not influence priority of claims. Any deficiency between pledged assets and the claims against them becomes senior unsecured debt and still adheres to the guidelines of priority of claims.

5 C is correct. Both analysts and ratings agencies have difficulty foreseeing future debt-financed acquisitions.

6 C is correct. Goodwill is viewed as a lower quality asset compared with tangible assets that can be sold and more easily converted into cash.

7 C is correct. The value of assets in relation to the level of debt is important to assess the collateral of the company; that is, the quality and value of the assets that support the debt levels of the company.

8 B is correct. The growth prospects of the industry provide the analyst insight regarding the capacity of the company.

9 A is correct. The construction company is both highly leveraged, which increases credit risk, and in a highly cyclical industry, which results in more volatile earnings.

10 B is correct. The interest expense is €113 million and EBITDA = Operating profit + Depreciation and amortization = €894 + 249 million = €1,143 million. EBITDA interest coverage = EBITDA/Interest expense = 1,143/113 = 10.12 times.

11 B is correct. Total debt is €1,613 million with Total capital = Total debt + Shareholders' equity = €1,613 + 4,616 = €6,229 million. The Debt/Capital ratio = 1,613/6,229 = 25.90%.

12 A is correct. If the debt of the company remained unchanged but FFO increased, more cash is available to service debt compared to the previous year. Additionally, the debt/capital ratio has improved. It would imply that the ability of Pay Handle Ltd to service their debt has improved.

13 A is correct. Based on four of the five credit ratios, Grupa Zywiec SA's credit quality is superior to that of the industry.

14 A is correct. Davide Campari-Milano S.p.A. has more financial leverage and less interest coverage than Associated British Foods plc, which implies greater credit risk.

15 A is correct. Low demand implies wider yield spreads, while heavy supply will widen spreads even further.

16 C is correct. Credit risk is the risk of loss resulting from the borrower failing to make full and timely payments of interest and/or principal.

17 C is correct. Market liquidity risk is the risk that the price at which investors can actually transact—buying or selling—may differ from the price indicated in the market.

18 C is correct. Loss severity is the portion of a bond's value (including unpaid interest) an investor loses in the event of default.

19 B is correct. The two components of credit risk are default probability and loss severity. In the event of default, loss severity is the portion of a bond's value (including unpaid interest) an investor loses. A and C are incorrect because spread and market liquidity risk are credit-related risks, not components of credit risk.

20 A is correct. Credit risk has two components: default risk and loss severity. Because default risk is quite low for most high-quality debt issuers, bond investors tend to focus more on this likelihood and less on the potential loss severity.

21 B is correct. The expected loss for a given debt instrument is the default probability multiplied by the loss severity given default. The loss severity is often expressed as (1 – Recovery rate).

22 A is correct. Senior subordinated debt is ranked lower than senior unsecured debt and thus has a lower priority of payment.

23 C is correct. The highest-ranked unsecured debt is senior unsecured debt. Lower-ranked debt includes senior subordinated debt. A and B are incorrect because mortgage debt and second lien loans are secured and higher ranked.

24 C is correct. According to the absolute priority of claims, in the event of bankruptcy, creditors with a secured claim have the right to the value of that specific property before any other claim.

25 A is correct. A second lien has a secured interest in the pledged assets. Second lien debt ranks higher in priority of payment than senior unsecured and senior subordinated debt and thus would most likely have a higher recovery rate.

26 A is correct. Notching is the process for moving ratings up or down relative to the issuer rating when rating agencies consider secondary factors, such as priority of claims in the event of a default and the potential loss severity.

27 C is correct. Structural subordination can arise when a corporation with a holding company structure has debt at both its parent holding company and operating subsidiaries. Debt at the operating subsidiaries is serviced by the cash flow and assets of the subsidiaries before funds are passed to the parent holding company.

28 C is correct. The issuer credit rating usually applies to its senior unsecured debt.

29 A is correct. Second lien debt is secured debt, which is senior to unsecured debt and to subordinated debt.

30 C is correct. An issuer credit rating usually applies to its senior unsecured debt.

31 A is correct. Recognizing different payment priorities, and thus the potential for higher (or lower) loss severity in the event of default, the rating agencies have adopted a notching process whereby their credit ratings on issues can be moved up or down from the issuer rating (senior unsecured).

32 C is correct. As a general rule, the higher the senior unsecured rating, the smaller the notching adjustment. Thus, for corporate bonds rated Aa2/AA, the rating agencies will typically apply smaller rating adjustments, or notches, to the related issue.

33 A is correct. Credit migration is the risk that a bond issuer's creditworthiness deteriorates, or migrates lower. Over time, credit ratings can migrate significantly from what they were at the time a bond was issued. An investor should not assume that an issuer's credit rating will remain the same from the time of purchase through the entire holding period.

34 B is correct. An industry with a high number of suppliers reduces the suppliers' negotiating power, thus helping companies control expenses and aiding in the servicing of debt.

35 A is correct. Credit analysis starts with industry structure—for example, by looking at the major forces of competition, followed by an analysis of industry fundamentals—and then turns to examination of the specific issuer.

36 C is correct. Credit analysts can make judgments about management's character by evaluating the use of aggressive accounting policies, such as timing revenue recognition. This activity is a potential warning flag for other behaviors or actions that may adversely affect an issuer's creditworthiness.

37 B is correct. Capacity refers to the ability of a borrower to service its debt. Capacity is determined through credit analysis of an issuer's industry and of the specific issuer.

38 A is correct. Credit analysts can make judgments about management's character in a number of ways, including by observing its use of aggressive accounting policies and/or tax strategies. An example of this aggressiveness is recognizing revenue prematurely.

39 C is correct. The debt/capital and debt/EBITDA ratios are used to assess a company's leverage. Higher leverage ratios indicate more leverage and thus higher credit risk. Company C's debt/capital (46.3%) and debt/EBITDA (2.5×) leverage ratios are higher than those for Companies A and B.

40 B is correct. The EBITDA/interest expense and EBIT/interest expense ratios are coverage ratios. Coverage ratios measure an issuer's ability to meet its interest payments. A higher ratio indicates better credit quality. Company B's EBITDA/interest expense (62.4×) and EBIT/interest expense (58.2×) coverage ratios are higher than those for Companies A and C.

41 C is correct because Company Y has a higher ratio of free cash flow after dividends to debt than Company X, not lower, as shown in the following table.

$$\text{Free cash flow after dividends as a \% of debt} = \frac{\text{FCF after dividends}}{\text{Debt}}$$

	Company X	Company Y
Cash flow from operations	£3.3	£14.0
Less		
Net capital expenditures	–0.8	–1.1
Dividends	–0.3	–6.1
Free cash flow after dividends	£2.2	£6.8
Debt	£12.2	£29.8

(continued)

	Company X	Company Y
Free cash flow after dividends as a % of debt	(2.2/12.2) × 100	(6.8/29.8) × 100
Free cash flow after dividends as a % of debt	18.0%	22.8%

A is incorrect. Company Y has a lower debt/capital ratio than Company X, as shown in the following table.

$$\text{Debt divided by Capital (\%)} = \frac{\text{Debt}}{(\text{Debt} + \text{Equity})}$$

	Company X	Company Y
Debt	£12.2	£29.8
Capital		
Debt	12.2	29.8
+ Equity	1.3	64.0
Capital	£13.5	£93.8
Debt/Capital (%)	(12.2/13.5) × 100	(29.8/93.8) × 100
Debt/Capital (%)	90.4%	31.8%

B is incorrect because Company Y has a lower debt/EBITDA ratio than Company Y, not higher, as shown in the following table.

	Company X	Company Y
Operating income	£1.1	£13.3
EBIT	£1.1	£13.3
plus		
Depreciation	1.0	3.8
Amortization	0.0	0.0
EBITDA	£2.1	£17.1
Debt	£12.2	£29.8
Debt/EBITDA	12.2/2.1	29.8/17.1
Debt/EBITDA	5.81	1.74

42 A is correct. Compared with Company Y, based on both their debt/capital ratios and their ratios of free cash flow after dividends to debt, which are measures of leverage commonly used in credit analysis, Company X is more highly leveraged, as shown in the following table.

$$\text{Debt divided by Capital (\%)} = \frac{\text{Debt}}{(\text{Debt} + \text{Equity})}$$

	Company X	Company Y
Debt	£2.2	£29.8

	Company X	Company Y
Capital		
Debt	2.2	29.8
+ Equity	4.3	64.0
Capital	£6.5	£93.8
Debt/Capital (%)	(12.2/13.5) × 100	(29.8/93.8) × 100
Debt/Capital (%)	90.4%	31.8%

$$\text{Free cash flow after dividends as a \% of debt} = \frac{\text{FCF after dividends}}{\text{Debt}}$$

	Company X	Company Y
Cash flow from operations	£3.3	£14.0
Less		
Net capital expenditures	–0.8	–1.1
Dividends	–0.3	–6.1
Free cash flow after dividends	£2.2	£6.8
Debt	£12.2	£29.8
Free cash flow after dividends as a % of debt	(2.2/12.2) × 100	(6.8/29.8) × 100
Free cash flow after dividends as a % of debt	18.0%	22.8%

43 B is correct. In weak financial markets, including weak markets for equities, credit spreads will widen.

44 B is correct. Weakening economic conditions will push investors to desire a greater risk premium and drive overall credit spreads wider.

45 C is correct. In periods of heavy new issue supply, credit spreads will widen if demand is insufficient.

46 C is correct. Non-sovereign governments typically must balance their operating budgets and lack the discretion to use monetary policy as many sovereigns can.

47 A is correct. Most investors in investment-grade debt focus on spread risk—that is, the effect of changes in spreads on prices and returns—while in high-yield analysis, the focus on default risk is relatively greater.

48 B is correct. Among the most important considerations in sovereign credit analysis is growth and age distribution of population. A relatively young and growing population contributes to growth in GDP and an expanding tax base and relies less on social services, pensions, and health care relative to an older population.

Derivatives

STUDY SESSION

Study Session 16	Derivatives

TOPIC LEVEL LEARNING OUTCOME

The candidate should be able to demonstrate a working knowledge of the analysis of derivatives, including forwards, futures, options, and swaps.

Derivatives—financial instruments whose prices are derived from the value of some underlying asset—have become increasingly important for managing financial risk, exploiting investment opportunities, and creating synthetic asset class exposure. As in other security markets, arbitrage and market efficiency play a critical role in establishing prices for these securities.

DERIVATIVES

STUDY SESSION 16

Derivatives

This study session builds the conceptual framework for understanding the basic derivatives and derivative markets. Essential features and valuation concepts for forward commitments such as forwards, futures, and swaps and contingent claims such as options are introduced.

READING ASSIGNMENTS

Reading 48	Derivative Markets and Instruments by Don M. Chance, PhD, CFA
Reading 49	Basics of Derivative Pricing and Valuation by Don M. Chance, PhD, CFA

READING

48

Derivative Markets and Instruments

by Don M. Chance, PhD, CFA

Don M. Chance, PhD, CFA, is at Louisiana State University (USA).

LEARNING OUTCOMES

Mastery	The candidate should be able to:
☐	a. define a derivative and distinguish between exchange-traded and over-the-counter derivatives;
☐	b. contrast forward commitments with contingent claims;
☐	c. define forward contracts, futures contracts, options (calls and puts), swaps, and credit derivatives and compare their basic characteristics;
☐	d. determine the value at expiration and profit from a long or a short position in a call or put option;
☐	e. describe purposes of, and controversies related to, derivative markets;
☐	f. explain arbitrage and the role it plays in determining prices and promoting market efficiency.

INTRODUCTION

1

Equity, fixed-income, currency, and commodity markets are facilities for trading the basic assets of an economy. Equity and fixed-income securities are claims on the assets of a company. Currencies are the monetary units issued by a government or central bank. Commodities are natural resources, such as oil or gold. These underlying assets are said to trade in **cash markets** or **spot markets** and their prices are sometimes referred to as **cash prices** or **spot prices**, though we usually just refer to them as stock prices, bond prices, exchange rates, and commodity prices. These markets exist around the world and receive much attention in the financial and mainstream media. Hence, they are relatively familiar not only to financial experts but also to the general population.

Somewhat less familiar are the markets for **derivatives**, which are financial instruments that derive their values from the performance of these basic assets. This reading is an overview of derivatives. Subsequent readings will explore many aspects of derivatives and their uses in depth. Among the questions that this first reading will address are the following:

- What are the defining characteristics of derivatives?
- What purposes do derivatives serve for financial market participants?
- What is the distinction between a forward commitment and a contingent claim?
- What are forward and futures contracts? In what ways are they alike and in what ways are they different?
- What are swaps?
- What are call and put options and how do they differ from forwards, futures, and swaps?
- What are credit derivatives and what are the various types of credit derivatives?
- What are the benefits of derivatives?
- What are some criticisms of derivatives and to what extent are they well founded?
- What is arbitrage and what role does it play in a well-functioning financial market?

This reading is organized as follows. Section 2 explores the definition and uses of derivatives and establishes some basic terminology. Section 3 describes derivatives markets. Section 4 categorizes and explains types of derivatives. Sections 5 and 6 discuss the benefits and criticisms of derivatives, respectively. Section 7 introduces the basic principles of derivative pricing and the concept of arbitrage. Section 8 provides a summary.

2 DERIVATIVES: DEFINITIONS AND USES

The most common definition of a derivative reads approximately as follows:

> *A derivative is a financial instrument that derives its performance from the performance of an underlying asset.*

This definition, despite being so widely quoted, can nonetheless be a bit troublesome. For example, it can also describe mutual funds and exchange-traded funds, which would never be viewed as derivatives even though they derive their values from the values of the underlying securities they hold. Perhaps the distinction that best characterizes derivatives is that they usually *transform* the performance of the underlying asset before paying it out in the derivatives transaction. In contrast, with the exception of expense deductions, mutual funds and exchange-traded funds simply pass through the returns of their underlying securities. This transformation of performance is typically understood or implicit in references to derivatives but rarely makes its way into the formal definition. In keeping with customary industry practice, this characteristic will be retained as an implied, albeit critical, factor distinguishing derivatives from mutual funds and exchange-traded funds and some other straight pass-through instruments. Also, note that the idea that derivatives take their *performance* from an underlying asset encompasses the fact that derivatives take their value and certain other characteristics from the underlying asset. Derivatives strategies perform in ways that are derived from the underlying and the specific features of derivatives.

Derivatives are similar to insurance in that both allow for the transfer of risk from one party to another. As everyone knows, insurance is a financial contract that provides protection against loss. The party bearing the risk purchases an insurance policy, which transfers the risk to the other party, the insurer, for a specified period of time. The risk itself does not change, but the party bearing it does. Derivatives allow for this same type of transfer of risk. One type of derivative in particular, the put option, when combined with a position exposed to the risk, functions almost exactly like insurance, but all derivatives can be used to protect against loss. Of course, an insurance contract must specify the underlying risk, such as property, health, or life. Likewise, so do derivatives. As noted earlier, derivatives are associated with an underlying asset. As such, the so-called "underlying asset" is often simply referred to as the **underlying**, whose value is the source of risk. In fact, the underlying need not even be an asset itself. Although common derivatives underlyings are equities, fixed-income securities, currencies, and commodities, other derivatives underlyings include interest rates, credit, energy, weather, and even other derivatives, all of which are not generally thought of as assets. Thus, like insurance, derivatives pay off on the basis of a source of risk, which is often, but not always, the value of an underlying asset. And like insurance, derivatives have a definite life span and expire on a specified date.

Derivatives are created in the form of legal contracts. They involve two parties—the buyer and the seller (sometimes known as the writer)—each of whom agrees to do something for the other, either now or later. The buyer, who purchases the derivative, is referred to as the **long** or the holder because he owns (holds) the derivative and holds a long position. The seller is referred to as the **short** because he holds a short position.[1]

A derivative contract always defines the rights and obligations of each party. These contracts are intended to be, and almost always are, recognized by the legal system as commercial contracts that each party expects to be upheld and supported in the legal system. Nonetheless, disputes sometimes arise, and lawyers, judges, and juries may be required to step in and resolve the matter.

There are two general classes of derivatives. Some provide the ability to lock in a price at which one might buy or sell the underlying. Because they force the two parties to transact in the future at a previously agreed-on price, these instruments are called **forward commitments**. The various types of forward commitments are called forward contracts, futures contracts, and swaps. Another class of derivatives provides *the right but not the obligation* to buy or sell the underlying at a pre-determined price. Because the choice of buying or selling versus doing nothing depends on a particular random outcome, these derivatives are called **contingent claims**. The primary contingent claim is called an **option**. The types of derivatives will be covered in more detail later in this reading and in considerably more depth later in the curriculum.

The existence of derivatives begs the obvious question of what purpose they serve. If one can participate in the success of a company by holding its equity, what reason can possibly explain why another instrument is required that takes its value from the performance of the equity? Although equity and other fundamental markets exist and usually perform reasonably well without derivative markets, it is possible that derivative markets can *improve* the performance of the markets for the underlyings. As you will see later in this reading, that is indeed true in practice.

Derivative markets create beneficial opportunities that do not exist in their absence. Derivatives can be used to create strategies that cannot be implemented with the underlyings alone. For example, derivatives make it easier to go short, thereby benefiting from a decline in the value of the underlying. In addition, derivatives, in and

1 In the financial world, the *long* always benefits from an increase in the value of the instrument he owns, and the *short* always benefits from a decrease in the value of the instrument he has sold. Think of the long as having possession of something and the short as having incurred an obligation to deliver that something.

of themselves, are characterized by a relatively high degree of leverage, meaning that participants in derivatives transactions usually have to invest only a small amount of their own capital relative to the value of the underlying. As such, small movements in the underlying can lead to fairly large movements in the amount of money made or lost on the derivative. Derivatives generally trade at lower transaction costs than comparable spot market transactions, are often more liquid than their underlyings, and offer a simple, effective, and low-cost way to transfer risk. For example, a shareholder of a company can reduce or even completely eliminate the market exposure by trading a derivative on the equity. Holders of fixed-income securities can use derivatives to reduce or completely eliminate interest rate risk, allowing them to focus on the credit risk. Alternatively, holders of fixed-income securities can reduce or eliminate the credit risk, focusing more on the interest rate risk. Derivatives permit such adjustments easily and quickly. These features of derivatives are covered in more detail later in this reading.

The types of performance transformations facilitated by derivatives allow market participants to practice more effective risk management. Indeed, the entire field of derivatives, which at one time was focused mostly on the instruments themselves, is now more concerned with the *uses* of the instruments. Just as a carpenter uses a hammer, nails, screws, a screwdriver, and a saw to build something useful or beautiful, a financial expert uses derivatives to manage risk. And just as it is critically important that a carpenter understand how to use these tools, an investment practitioner must understand how to properly use derivatives. In the case of the carpenter, the result is building something useful; in the case of the financial expert, the result is managing financial risk. Thus, like tools, derivatives serve a valuable purpose but like tools, they must be used carefully.

The practice of risk management has taken a prominent role in financial markets. Indeed, whenever companies announce large losses from trading, lending, or operations, stories abound about how poorly these companies managed risk. Such stories are great attention grabbers and a real boon for the media, but they often miss the point that risk management does not guarantee that large losses will not occur. Rather, **risk management** *is the process by which an organization or individual defines the level of risk it wishes to take, measures the level of risk it is taking, and adjusts the latter to equal the former.* Risk management never offers a guarantee that large losses will not occur, and it does not eliminate the possibility of total failure. To do so would typically require that the amount of risk taken be so small that the organization would be effectively constrained from pursuing its primary objectives. Risk taking is inherent in all forms of economic activity and life in general. The possibility of failure is never eliminated.

EXAMPLE 1

Characteristics of Derivatives

1 Which of the following is the best example of a derivative?
   - A A global equity mutual fund
   - B A non-callable government bond
   - C A contract to purchase Apple Computer at a fixed price

2 Which of the following is **not** a characteristic of a derivative?
   - A An underlying
   - B A low degree of leverage
   - C Two parties—a buyer and a seller

3 Which of the following statements about derivatives is **not** true?
   A They are created in the spot market.
   B They are used in the practice of risk management.
   C They take their values from the value of something else.

Solution to 1:

C is correct. Mutual funds and government bonds are not derivatives. A government bond is a fundamental asset on which derivatives might be created, but it is not a derivative itself. A mutual fund can technically meet the definition of a derivative, but as noted in the reading, derivatives transform the value of a payoff of an underlying asset. Mutual funds merely pass those payoffs through to their holders.

Solution to 2:

B is correct. All derivatives have an underlying and must have a buyer and a seller. More importantly, derivatives have high degrees of leverage, not low degrees of leverage.

Solution to 3:

A is correct. Derivatives are used to practice risk management and they take (derive) their values from the value of something else, the underlying. They are not created in the spot market, which is where the underlying trades.

Note also that risk management is a dynamic and ongoing process, reflecting the fact that the risk assumed can be difficult to measure and is constantly changing. As noted, derivatives are tools, indeed *the* tools that make it easier to manage risk. Although one can trade stocks and bonds (the underlyings) to adjust the level of risk, it is almost always more effective to trade derivatives.

Risk management is addressed more directly elsewhere in the CFA curriculum, but the study of derivatives necessarily entails the concept of risk management. In an explanation of derivatives, the focus is usually on the instruments and it is easy to forget the overriding objective of managing risk. Unfortunately, that would be like a carpenter obsessed with his hammer and nails, forgetting that he is building a piece of furniture. It is important to always try to keep an eye on the objective of managing risk.

THE STRUCTURE OF DERIVATIVE MARKETS 3

Having an understanding of equity, fixed-income, and currency markets is extremely beneficial—indeed, quite necessary—in understanding derivatives. One could hardly consider the wisdom of using derivatives on a share of stock if one did not understand the equity markets reasonably well. As you likely know, equities trade on organized exchanges as well as in over-the-counter (OTC) markets. These exchange-traded equity markets—such as the Deutsche Börse, the Tokyo Stock Exchange, and the New York Stock Exchange and its Eurex affiliate—are formal organizational structures that bring buyers and sellers together through market makers, or dealers, to facilitate transactions. Exchanges have formal rule structures and are required to comply with all securities laws.

OTC securities markets operate in much the same manner, with similar rules, regulations, and organizational structures. At one time, the major difference between OTC and exchange markets for securities was that the latter brought buyers and sellers together in a physical location, whereas the former facilitated trading strictly in an electronic manner. Today, these distinctions are blurred because many organized securities exchanges have gone completely to electronic systems. Moreover, OTC securities markets can be formally organized structures, such as NASDAQ, or can merely refer to informal networks of parties who buy and sell with each other, such as the corporate and government bond markets in the United States.

The derivatives world also comprises organized exchanges and OTC markets. Although the derivatives world is also moving toward less distinction between these markets, there are clear differences that are important to understand.

3.1 Exchange-Traded Derivatives Markets

Derivative instruments are created and traded either on an exchange or on the OTC market. Exchange-traded derivatives are standardized, whereas OTC derivatives are customized. To standardize a derivative contract means that its terms and conditions are precisely specified by the exchange and there is very limited ability to alter those terms. For example, an exchange might offer trading in certain types of derivatives that expire only on the third Friday of March, June, September, and December. If a party wanted the derivative to expire on any other day, it would not be able to trade such a derivative on that exchange, nor would it be able to persuade the exchange to create it, at least not in the short run. If a party wanted a derivative on a particular entity, such as a specific stock, that party could trade it on that exchange only if the exchange had specified that such a derivative could trade. Even the magnitudes of the contracts are specified. If a party wanted a derivative to cover €150,000 and the exchange specified that contracts could trade only in increments of €100,000, the party could do nothing about it if it wanted to trade that derivative on that exchange.

This standardization of contract terms facilitates the creation of a more liquid market for derivatives. If all market participants know that derivatives on the euro trade in 100,000-unit lots and that they all expire only on certain days, the market functions more effectively than it would if there were derivatives with many different unit sizes and expiration days competing in the same market at the same time. This standardization makes it easier to provide liquidity. Through designated market makers, derivatives exchanges guarantee that derivatives can be bought and sold.[2]

The cornerstones of the exchange-traded derivatives market are the market makers (or dealers) and the speculators, both of whom typically own memberships on the exchange.[3] The market makers stand ready to buy at one price and sell at a higher price. With standardization of terms and an active market, market makers are often able to buy and sell almost simultaneously at different prices, locking in small, short-term profits—a process commonly known as scalping. In some cases, however, they are unable to do so, thereby forcing them to either hold exposed positions or find other parties with whom they can trade and thus lay off (get rid of) the risk. This is when speculators come in. Although speculators are market participants who are willing to take risks, it is important to understand that being a speculator does not mean the reckless assumption of risk. Although speculators will take large losses at

2 It is important to understand that merely being able to buy and sell a derivative, or even a security, does not mean that liquidity is high and that the cost of liquidity is low. Derivatives exchanges guarantee that a derivative can be bought and sold, but they do not guarantee the price. The ask price (the price at which the market maker will sell) and the bid price (the price at which the market maker will buy) can be far apart, which they will be in a market with low liquidity. Hence, such a market can have liquidity, loosely defined, but the cost of liquidity can be quite high. The factors that can lead to low liquidity for derivatives are similar to those for securities: little trading interest and a high level of uncertainty.

3 Exchanges are owned by their *members*, whose memberships convey the right to trade. In addition, some exchanges are themselves publicly traded corporations whose members are shareholders, and there are also non-member shareholders.

times, good speculators manage those risks by watching their exposures, absorbing market information, and observing the flow of orders in such a manner that they are able to survive and profit. Often, speculators will hedge their risks when they become uncomfortable.

Standardization also facilitates the creation of a clearing and settlement operation. **Clearing** refers to the process by which the exchange verifies the execution of a transaction and records the participants' identities. **Settlement** refers to the related process in which the exchange transfers money from one participant to the other or from a participant to the exchange or vice versa. This flow of money is a critical element of derivatives trading. Clearly, there would be no confidence in markets in which money is not efficiently collected and disbursed. Derivatives exchanges have done an excellent job of clearing and settlement, especially in comparison to securities exchanges. Derivatives exchanges clear and settle all contracts overnight, whereas most securities exchanges require two business days.

The clearing and settlement process of derivative transactions also provides a credit guarantee. If two parties engage in a derivative contract on an exchange, one party will ultimately make money and the other will lose money. Derivatives exchanges use their clearinghouses to provide a guarantee to the winning party that if the loser does not pay, the clearinghouse will pay the winning party. The clearinghouse is able to provide this credit guarantee by requiring a cash deposit, usually called the **margin bond** or **performance bond**, from the participants to the contract. Derivatives clearinghouses manage these deposits, occasionally requiring additional deposits, so effectively that they have never failed to pay in the nearly 100 years they have existed. We will say more about this process later and illustrate how it works.

Exchange markets are said to have **transparency**, which means that full information on all transactions is disclosed to exchanges and regulatory bodies. All transactions are centrally reported within the exchanges and their clearinghouses, and specific laws require that these markets be overseen by national regulators. Although this would seem a strong feature of exchange markets, there is a definite cost. Transparency means a loss of privacy: National regulators can see what transactions have been done. Standardization means a loss of flexibility: A participant can do only the transactions that are permitted on the exchange. Regulation means a loss of both privacy and flexibility. It is not that transparency or regulation is good and the other is bad. It is simply a trade-off.

Derivatives exchanges exist in virtually every developed (and some emerging market) countries around the world. Some exchanges specialize in derivatives and others are integrated with securities exchanges.

Although there have been attempts to create somewhat non-standardized derivatives for trading on an exchange, such attempts have not been particularly successful. Standardization is a critical element by which derivatives exchanges are able to provide their services. We will look at this point again when discussing the alternative to standardization: customized OTC derivatives.

3.2 Over-the-Counter Derivatives Markets

The OTC derivatives markets comprise an informal network of market participants that are willing to create and trade virtually any type of derivative that can legally exist. The backbone of these markets is the set of dealers, which are typically banks. Most of these banks are members of a group called the International Swaps and Derivatives Association (ISDA), a worldwide organization of financial institutions that engage in derivative transactions, primarily as dealers. As such, these markets are sometimes called *dealer markets*. Acting as principals, these dealers informally agree to buy and sell various derivatives. It is *informal* because the dealers are not obligated to do so. Their participation is based on a desire to profit, which they do by purchasing at one price and selling at a higher price. Although it might seem that a dealer who can "buy low, sell high" could make money easily, the process in practice is not that simple. Because OTC instruments are not standardized, a dealer cannot expect to buy a derivative at one price and simultaneously sell it to a different party who happens to want to buy the same derivative at the same time and at a higher price.

To manage the risk they assume by buying and selling customized derivatives, OTC derivatives dealers typically hedge their risks by engaging in alternative but similar transactions that pass the risk on to other parties. For example, if a company comes to a dealer to buy a derivative on the euro, the company would effectively be transferring the risk of the euro to the dealer. The dealer would then attempt to lay off (get rid of) that risk by engaging in an alternative but similar transaction that would transfer the risk to another party. This hedge might involve another derivative on the euro or it might simply be a transaction in the euro itself. Of course, that begs the question of why the company could not have laid off the risk itself and avoided the dealer. Indeed, some can and do, but laying off risk is not simple. Unable to find identical offsetting transactions, dealers usually have to find *similar* transactions with which they can lay off the risk. Hedging one derivative with a different kind of derivative on the same underlying is a similar but not identical transaction. It takes specialized knowledge and complex models to be able to do such transactions effectively, and dealers are more capable of doing so than are ordinary companies. Thus, one might think of a dealer as a middleman, a sort of financial wholesaler using its specialized knowledge and resources to facilitate the transfer of risk. In the same manner that one could theoretically purchase a consumer product from a manufacturer, a network of specialized middlemen and retailers is often a more effective method.

Because of the customization of OTC derivatives, there is a tendency to think that the OTC market is less liquid than the exchange market. That is not necessarily true. Many OTC instruments can easily be created and then essentially offset by doing the exact opposite transaction, often with the same party. For example, suppose Corporation A buys an OTC derivative from Dealer B. Before the expiration date, Corporation A wants to terminate the position. It can return to Dealer B and ask to sell a derivative with identical terms. Market conditions will have changed, of course, and the value of the derivative will not be the same, but the transaction can be conducted quite easily with either Corporation A or Dealer B netting a gain at the expense of the other. Alternatively, Corporation A could do this transaction with a different dealer, the result of which would remove exposure to the underlying risk but would leave two transactions open and some risk that one party would default to the other. In contrast to this type of OTC liquidity, some exchange-traded derivatives have very little trading interest and thus relatively low liquidity. Liquidity is always driven by trading interest, which can be strong or weak in both types of markets.

OTC derivative markets operate at a lower degree of regulation and oversight than do exchange-traded derivative markets. In fact, until around 2010, it could largely be said that the OTC market was essentially unregulated. OTC transactions could be executed with only the minimal oversight provided through laws that regulated the parties themselves, not the specific instruments. Following the financial crisis of 2007–2009, new regulations began to blur the distinction between OTC and exchange-listed markets. In both the United States (the Wall Street Reform and Consumer Protection Act of 2010, commonly known as the Dodd–Frank Act) and Europe (the Regulation of the European Parliament and of the Council on OTC Derivatives, Central Counterparties, and Trade Repositories), regulations are changing the characteristics of OTC markets. In general, world policy-makers have advanced an agenda to make global derivatives markets more resilient and robust, pursuing increased transparency and lowered systemic risk.

When the full implementation of these new laws takes place, a number of OTC transactions will have to be cleared through central clearing agencies, information on most OTC transactions will need to be reported to regulators, and entities that operate in the OTC market will be more closely monitored. There are, however, quite a few exemptions that cover a significant percentage of derivative transactions. Clearly, the degree of OTC regulation, although increasing in recent years, is still lighter than that of exchange-listed market regulation. Many transactions in OTC markets will retain a degree of privacy with lower transparency, and most importantly, the OTC markets will remain considerably more flexible than the exchange-listed markets.

EXAMPLE 2

Exchange-Traded versus Over-the-Counter Derivatives

1 Which of the following characteristics is **not** associated with exchange-traded derivatives?
   - **A** Margin or performance bonds are required.
   - **B** The exchange guarantees all payments in the event of default.
   - **C** All terms except the price are customized to the parties' individual needs.

2 Which of the following characteristics is associated with over-the-counter derivatives?
   - **A** Trading occurs in a central location.
   - **B** They are more regulated than exchange-listed derivatives.
   - **C** They are less transparent than exchange-listed derivatives.

3 Market makers earn a profit in both exchange and over-the-counter derivatives markets by:
   - **A** charging a commission on each trade.
   - **B** a combination of commissions and markups.
   - **C** buying at one price, selling at a higher price, and hedging any risk.

4 Which of the following statements *most* accurately describes exchange-traded derivatives relative to over-the-counter derivatives? Exchange-traded derivatives are more likely to have:
   - **A** greater credit risk.
   - **B** standardized contract terms.
   - **C** greater risk management uses.

Solution to 1:

C is correct. Exchange-traded contracts are standardized, meaning that the exchange determines the terms of the contract except the price. The exchange guarantees against default and requires margins or performance bonds.

Solution to 2:

C is correct. OTC derivatives have a lower degree of transparency than exchange-listed derivatives. Trading does not occur in a central location but, rather, is quite dispersed. Although new national securities laws are tightening the regulation of OTC derivatives, the degree of regulation is less than that of exchange-listed derivatives.

Solution to 3:

C is correct. Market makers buy at one price (the bid), sell at a higher price (the ask), and hedge whatever risk they otherwise assume. Market makers do not charge a commission. Hence, A and B are both incorrect.

Solution to 4:

B is correct. Standardization of contract terms is a characteristic of exchange-traded derivatives. A is incorrect because credit risk is well-controlled in exchange markets. C is incorrect because the risk management uses are not limited by being traded over the counter.

4 TYPES OF DERIVATIVES

As previously stated, derivatives fall into two general classifications: forward commitments and contingent claims. The factor that distinguishes forward commitments from contingent claims is that forward commitments *obligate* the parties to engage in a transaction at a future date on terms agreed upon in advance, whereas contingent claims provide one party the *right but not the obligation* to engage in a future transaction on terms agreed upon in advance.

4.1 Forward Commitments

Forward commitments are contracts entered into at one point in time that require both parties to engage in a transaction at a later point in time (the expiration) on terms agreed upon at the start. The parties establish the identity and quantity of the underlying, the manner in which the contract will be executed or settled when it expires, and the fixed price at which the underlying will be exchanged. This fixed price is called the **forward price**.

As a hypothetical example of a forward contract, suppose that today Markus and Johannes enter into an agreement that Markus will sell his BMW to Johannes for a price of €30,000. The transaction will take place on a specified date, say, 180 days from today. At that time, Markus will deliver the vehicle to Johannes's home and Johannes will give Markus a bank-certified check for €30,000. There will be no recourse, so if the vehicle has problems later, Johannes cannot go back to Markus for compensation. It should be clear that both Markus and Johannes must do their due diligence and carefully consider the reliability of each other. The car could have serious quality issues and Johannes could have financial problems and be unable to pay the €30,000. Obviously, the transaction is essentially unregulated. Either party could renege on his obligation, in response to which the other party could go to court, provided a formal contract exists and is carefully written. Note finally that one of the two parties is likely to end up gaining and the other losing, depending on the secondary market price of this type of vehicle at expiration of the contract.

This example is quite simple but illustrates the essential elements of a forward contract. In the financial world, such contracts are very carefully written, with legal provisions that guard against fraud and require extensive credit checks. Now let us take a deeper look at the characteristics of forward contracts.

4.1.1 *Forward Contracts*

The following is the formal definition of a forward contract:

A forward contract is an over-the-counter derivative contract in which two parties agree that one party, the buyer, will purchase an underlying asset from the other party, the seller, at a later date at a fixed price they agree on when the contract is signed.

In addition to agreeing on the price at which the underlying asset will be sold at a later date, the two parties also agree on several other matters, such as the specific identity of the underlying, the number of units of the underlying that will be delivered, and where the future delivery will occur. These are important points but relatively minor in this discussion, so they can be left out of the definition to keep it uncluttered.

As noted earlier, a forward contract is a commitment. Each party agrees that it will fulfill its responsibility at the designated future date. Failure to do so constitutes a default and the non-defaulting party can institute legal proceedings to enforce performance. It is important to recognize that although either party could default to the other, only one party at a time can default. The party owing the greater amount could default to the other, but the party owing the lesser amount cannot default because its claim on the other party is greater. The amount owed is always based on the net owed by one party to the other.

To gain a better understanding of forward contracts, it is necessary to examine their payoffs. As noted, forward contracts—and indeed all derivatives—take (derive) their payoffs from the performance of the underlying asset. To illustrate the payoff of a forward contract, start with the assumption that we are at time $t = 0$ and that the forward contract expires at a later date, time $t = T$.[4] The spot price of the underlying asset at time 0 is S_0 and at time T is S_T. Of course, when we initiate the contract at time 0, we do not know what S_T will ultimately be. Remember that the two parties, the buyer and the seller, are going long and short, respectively.

At time $t = 0$, the long and the short agree that the short will deliver the asset to the long at time T for a price of $F_0(T)$. The notation $F_0(T)$ denotes that this value is established at time 0 and applies to a contract expiring at time T. $F_0(T)$ is the forward price.

So, let us assume that the buyer enters into the forward contract with the seller for a price of $F_0(T)$, with delivery of one unit of the underlying asset to occur at time T. Now, let us roll forward to time T, when the price of the underlying is S_T. The long is obligated to pay $F_0(T)$, for which he receives an asset worth S_T. If $S_T > F_0(T)$, it is clear that the transaction has worked out well for the long. He paid $F_0(T)$ and receives something of greater value. Thus, the contract effectively pays off $S_T - F_0(T)$ to the long, which is the value of the contract at expiration. The short has the mirror image of the long. He is required to deliver the asset worth S_T and accept a smaller amount, $F_0(T)$. The contract has a payoff for him of $F_0(T) - S_T$, which is negative. Even if the asset's value, S_T, is less than the forward price, $F_0(T)$, the payoffs are still $S_T - F_0(T)$ for the long and $F_0(T) - S_T$ for the short. We can consolidate these results by writing the short's payoff as the negative of the long's, $-[S_T - F_0(T)]$, which serves as a useful reminder that the long and the short are engaged in a zero-sum game, which is a type of competition in which one participant's gains are the other's losses. Although both lose a modest amount in the sense of both having some costs to engage in the transaction, these costs are relatively small and worth ignoring for our purposes at this time. In addition, it is worthwhile to note how derivatives transform the performance

4 Such notations as $t = 0$ and $t = T$ are commonly used in explaining derivatives. To indicate that $t = 0$ simply means that we initiate a contract at an imaginary time designated like a counter starting at zero. To indicate that the contract expires at $t = T$ simply means that at some future time, designated as T, the contract expires. Time T could be a certain number of days from now or a fraction of a year later or T years later. We will be more specific in later readings that involve calculations. For now, just assume that $t = 0$ and $t = T$ are two dates—the initiation and the expiration—of the contract.

of the underlying. The gain from owning the underlying would be $S_T - S_0$, whereas the gain from owning the forward contract would be $S_T - F_0(T)$. Both figures are driven by S_T, the price of the underlying at expiration, but they are not the same.

For an example, a buyer enters a forward contract to buy gold at a price of $F_0(T)$ = \$1,312.90 per ounce four months from now. The spot price of gold is S_0 = \$1,207.40 per ounce. Four months in the future, the price of the underlying gold is S_T = \$1,275.90 per ounce. The buyer's gain from the forward contract, the payoff from the contract, is the value of gold (at maturity) less the forward price: $S_T - F_0(T)$ = 1,275.90 – 1,312.90 = –\$37.00 per ounce. Because the value of gold when the contract matures is less than the forward price, $S_T < F_0(T)$, the buyer has incurred a loss. Notably, the forward contract seller has a contract payoff, +\$37.00, that is the negative of that of the contract buyer. The gain on owning the underlying, which is $S_T - S_0$ = 1,275.90 – 1,207.40 = \$68.40, differs from the gain (–\$37.00) on the forward contract.

The buyer also enters a forward contract to buy oil at a price of $F_0(T)$ = \$71.86 per barrel four months from now. The spot price of oil is S_0 = \$71.11 per barrel. Four months in the future, the price of the underlying oil is S_T = \$80.96 per barrel. The buyer's gain from the forward contract, the payoff from the contract, is the value of oil less the forward price: $S_T - F_0(T)$ = 80.96 – 71.86 = \$9.10 per barrel. Unlike the forward contract on gold above, because the value of oil when the contract matures is greater than the forward price, $S_T > F_0(T)$, the buyer of the forward contract realizes a gain.

Exhibit 1 illustrates the payoffs from both buying and selling a forward contract.

Exhibit 1 Payoffs from a Forward Contract

A. Payoff from Buying = $S_T - F_0(T)$

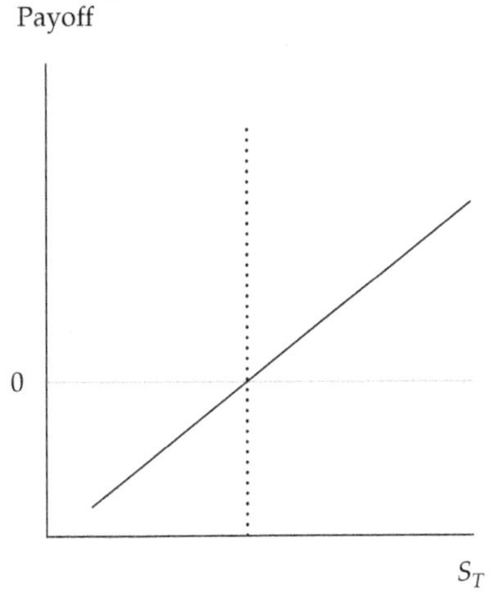

B. Payoff from Selling = $-[S_T - F_0(T)]$

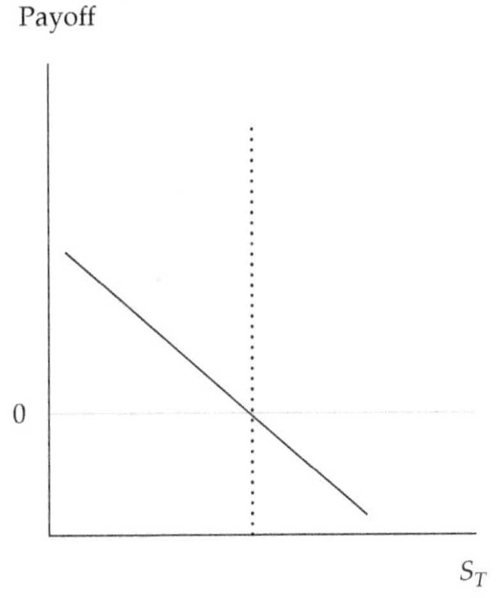

The long hopes the price of the underlying will rise above the forward price, $F_0(T)$, whereas the short hopes the price of the underlying will fall below the forward price. Except in the extremely rare event that the underlying price at T equals the forward price, there will ultimately be a winner and a loser.

An important element of forward contracts is that no money changes hands between parties when the contract is initiated. Unlike in the purchase and sale of an asset, there is no value exchanged at the start. The buyer does not pay the seller some money and obtain something. In fact, forward contracts have zero value at the start. They are neither assets nor liabilities. As you will learn in later readings, their values will deviate from zero later as prices move. Forward contracts will almost always have non-zero values at expiration.

As noted previously, the primary purpose of derivatives is for risk management. Although the uses of forward contracts are covered in depth later in the curriculum, there are a few things to note here about the purposes of forward contracts. It should be apparent that locking in the future buying or selling price of an underlying asset can be extremely attractive for some parties. For example, an airline anticipating the purchase of jet fuel at a later date can enter into a forward contract to buy the fuel at a price agreed upon when the contract is initiated. In so doing, the airline has hedged its cost of fuel. Thus, forward contracts can be structured to create a perfect hedge, providing an assurance that the underlying asset can be bought or sold at a price known when the contract is initiated. Likewise, speculators, who ultimately assume the risk laid off by hedgers, can make bets on the direction of the underlying asset without having to invest the money to purchase the asset itself.

Finally, forward contracts need not specifically settle by delivery of the underlying asset. They can settle by an exchange of cash. These contracts—called **non-deliverable forwards** (NDFs), **cash-settled forwards**, or **contracts for differences**—have the same economic effect as do their delivery-based counterparts. For example, for a physical delivery contract, if the long pays $F_0(T)$ and receives an asset worth S_T, the contract is worth $S_T - F_0(T)$ to the long at expiration. A non-deliverable forward contract would have the short simply pay cash to the long in the amount of $S_T - F_0(T)$. The long would not take possession of the underlying asset, but if he wanted the asset, he could purchase it in the market for its current price of S_T. Because he received a cash settlement in the amount of $S_T - F_0(T)$, in buying the asset the long would have to pay out only $S_T - [S_T - F_0(T)]$, which equals $F_0(T)$. Thus, the long could acquire the asset, effectively paying $F_0(T)$, exactly as the contract promised. Transaction costs do make cash settlement different from physical delivery, but this point is relatively minor and can be disregarded for our purposes here.

As previously mentioned, forward contracts are OTC contracts. There is no formal forward contract exchange. Nonetheless, there are exchange-traded variants of forward contracts, which are called futures contracts or just futures.

4.1.2 *Futures*

Futures contracts are specialized versions of forward contracts that have been standardized and that trade on a futures exchange. By standardizing these contracts and creating an organized market with rules, regulations, and a central clearing facility, the futures markets offer an element of liquidity and protection against loss by default.

Formally, a futures contract is defined as follows:

> *A futures contract is a standardized derivative contract created and traded on a futures exchange in which two parties agree that one party, the buyer, will purchase an underlying asset from the other party, the seller, at a later date and at a price agreed on by the two parties when the contract is initiated and in which there is a daily settling of gains and losses and a credit guarantee by the futures exchange through its clearinghouse.*

First, let us review what standardization means. Recall that in forward contracts, the parties customize the contract by specifying the underlying asset, the time to expiration, the delivery and settlement conditions, and the quantity of the underlying, all according to whatever terms they agree on. These contracts are not traded on an exchange. As noted, the regulation of OTC derivatives markets is increasing, but these contracts are not subject to the traditionally high degree of regulation that applies to securities and futures markets. Futures contracts first require the existence of a futures exchange, a legally recognized entity that provides a market for trading these contracts. Futures exchanges are highly regulated at the national level in all countries. These exchanges specify that only certain contracts are authorized for trading. These contracts have specific underlying assets, times to expiration, delivery and settlement conditions, and quantities. The exchange offers a facility in the form of a physical location and/or an electronic system as well as liquidity provided by authorized market makers.

Probably the most important distinctive characteristic of futures contracts is the daily settlement of gains and losses and the associated credit guarantee provided by the exchange through its clearinghouse. When a party buys a futures contract, it commits to purchase the underlying asset at a later date and at a price agreed upon when the contract is initiated. The counterparty (the seller) makes the opposite commitment, an agreement to sell the underlying asset at a later date and at a price agreed upon when the contract is initiated. The agreed-upon price is called the **futures price**. Identical contracts trade on an ongoing basis at different prices, reflecting the passage of time and the arrival of new information to the market. Thus, as the futures price changes, the parties make and lose money. Rising (falling) prices, of course, benefit (hurt) the long and hurt (benefit) the short. At the end of each day, the clearinghouse engages in a practice called **mark to market**, also known as the **daily settlement**. The clearinghouse determines an average of the final futures trades of the day and designates that price as the **settlement price**. All contracts are then said to be *marked to the settlement price*. For example, if the long purchases the contract during the day at a futures price of £120 and the settlement price at the end of the day is £122, the long's account would be marked for a gain of £2. In other words, the long has made a profit of £2 and that amount is credited to his account, with the money coming from the account of the short, who has lost £2. Naturally, if the futures price decreases, the long loses money and is charged with that loss, and the money is transferred to the account of the short.[5]

The account is specifically referred to as a **margin** account. Of course, in equity markets, margin accounts are commonly used, but there are significant differences between futures margin accounts and equity margin accounts. Equity margin accounts involve the extension of credit. An investor deposits part of the cost of the stock and borrows the remainder at a rate of interest. With futures margin accounts, both parties deposit a required minimum sum of money, but the remainder of the price is not borrowed. This required margin is typically less than 10% of the futures price, which is considerably less than in equity margin trading. In the example above, let us assume that the required margin is £10, which is referred to as the **initial margin**. Both the long and the short put that amount into their respective margin accounts. This money is deposited there to support the trade, not as a form of equity, with the remaining amount borrowed. There is no formal loan created as in equity markets. A futures margin is more of a performance bond or good faith deposit, terms that were previously mentioned. It is simply an amount of money put into an account that covers possible future losses.

Associated with each initial margin is another figure called the **maintenance margin**. The maintenance margin is the amount of money that each participant must maintain in the account after the trade is initiated, and it is always significantly lower than the initial margin. Let us assume that the maintenance margin in this example is £6. If the buyer's account is marked to market with a credit of £2, his margin balance moves to £12, while the seller's account is charged £2 and his balance moves to £8. The clearinghouse then compares each participant's balance with the maintenance margin. At this point, both participants more than meet the maintenance margin.

Let us say, however, that the price continues to move in the long's favor and, therefore, against the short. A few days later, assume that the short's balance falls to £4, which is below the maintenance margin requirement of £6. The short will then get a **margin call**, which is a request to deposit additional funds. The amount that the short has to deposit, however, is *not* the £2 that would bring his balance up to the maintenance margin. Instead, the short must deposit enough funds to bring the balance up to the initial margin. So, the short must come up with £6. The purpose of this rule is to get the party's position significantly above the minimum level and provide some breathing room. If the balance were brought up only to the maintenance level, there

5 The actual amount of money charged and credited depends on the contract size and the number of contracts. A price of £120 might actually refer to a contract that has a standard size of £100,000. Thus, £120 might actually mean 120% of the standard size, or £120,000. In addition, the parties are likely to hold more than one contract. Hence, the gain of £2 referred to in the text might really mean £2,000 (122% minus 120% times the £100,000 standard size) times the number of contracts held by the party.

would likely be another margin call soon. A party can choose not to deposit additional funds, in which case the party would be required to close out the contract as soon as possible and would be responsible for any additional losses until the position is closed.

As with forward contracts, neither party pays any money to the other when the contract is initiated. Value accrues as the futures price changes, but at the end of each day, the mark-to-market process settles the gains and losses, effectively resetting the value for each party to zero.

The clearinghouse moves money between the participants, crediting gains to the winners and charging losses to the losers. By doing this on a daily basis, the gains and losses are typically quite small, and the margin balances help ensure that the clearinghouse will collect from the party losing money. As an extra precaution, in fast-moving markets, the clearinghouse can make margin calls during the day, not just at the end of the day. Yet there still remains the possibility that a party could default. A large loss could occur quickly and consume the entire margin balance, with additional money owed.[6] If the losing party cannot pay, the clearinghouse provides a guarantee that it will make up the loss, which it does by maintaining an insurance fund. If that fund were depleted, the clearinghouse could levy a tax on the other market participants, though that has never happened.

Some futures contracts contain a provision limiting price changes. These rules, called **price limits**, establish a band relative to the previous day's settlement price, within which all trades must occur. If market participants wish to trade at a price above the upper band, trading stops, which is called **limit up**, until two parties agree on a trade at a price lower than the upper limit. Likewise, if market participants wish to trade at a price below the lower band, which is called **limit down**, no trade can take place until two parties agree to trade at a price above the lower limit. When the market hits these limits and trading stops, it is called **locked limit**. Typically, the exchange rules provide for an expansion of the limits the next day. These price limits, which may be somewhat objectionable to proponents of free markets, are important in helping the clearinghouse manage its credit exposure. Just because two parties wish to trade a futures contract at a price beyond the limits does not mean they should be allowed to do so. The clearinghouse is a third participant in the contract, guaranteeing to each party that it ensures against the other party defaulting. Therefore, the clearinghouse has a vested interest in the price and considerable exposure. Sharply moving prices make it more difficult for the clearinghouse to collect from the parties losing money.

Most participants in futures markets buy and sell contracts, collecting their profits and incurring their losses, with no ultimate intent to make or take delivery of the underlying asset. For example, the long may ultimately sell her position before expiration. When a party re-enters the market at a later date but before expiration and engages in the opposite transaction—a long selling her previously opened contract or a short buying her previously opened contract—the transaction is referred to as an offset. The clearinghouse marks the contract to the current price relative to the previous settlement price and closes out the participant's position.

At any given time, the number of outstanding contracts is called the **open interest**. Each contract counted in the open interest has a long and a corresponding short. The open interest figure changes daily as some parties open up new positions, while other parties offset their old positions. It is theoretically possible that all longs and shorts

6 For example, let us go back to when the short had a balance of £4, which is £2 below the maintenance margin and £6 below the initial margin. The short will get a margin call, but suppose he elects not to deposit additional funds and requests that his position be terminated. In a fast-moving market, the price might increase more than £4 before his broker can close his position. The remaining balance of £4 would then be depleted, and the short would be responsible for any additional losses.

offset their positions before expiration, leaving no open interest when the contract expires, but in practice there is nearly always some open interest at expiration, at which time there is a final delivery or settlement.

When discussing forward contracts, we noted that a contract could be written such that the parties engage in physical delivery or cash settlement at expiration. In the futures markets, the exchange specifies whether physical delivery or cash settlement applies. In physical delivery contracts, the short is required to deliver the underlying asset at a designated location and the long is required to pay for it. Delivery replaces the mark-to-market process on the final day. It also ensures an important principle that you will use later: *The futures price converges to the spot price at expiration.* Because the short delivers the actual asset and the long pays the current spot price for it, the futures price at expiration has to be the spot price at that time. Alternatively, a futures contract initiated right at the instant of expiration is effectively a spot transaction and, therefore, the futures price at expiration must equal the spot price. Following this logic, in cash settlement contracts, there is a final mark to market, with the futures price formally set to the spot price, thereby ensuring automatic convergence.

In discussing forward contracts, we described the process by which they pay off as the spot price at expiration minus the forward price, $S_T - F_0(T)$, the former determined at expiration and the latter agreed upon when the contract is initiated. Futures contracts basically pay off the same way, but there is a slight difference. Let us say the contract is initiated on Day 0 and expires on Day T. The intervening days are designated Days 1, 2, ..., T. The initial futures price is designated $f_0(T)$ and the daily settlement prices on Days 1, 2, ..., T are designated $f_1(T), f_2(T), ..., f_T(T)$. There are, of course, futures prices within each trading day, but let us focus only on the settlement prices for now. For simplicity, let us assume that the long buys at the settlement price on Day 0 and holds the position all the way to expiration. Through the mark-to-market process, the cash flows to the account of the long will be

$$f_1(T) - f_0(T) \text{ on Day 1}$$
$$f_2(T) - f_1(T) \text{ on Day 2}$$
$$f_3(T) - f_2(T) \text{ on Day 3}$$
$$\ldots$$
$$f_T(T) - f_{T-1}(T) \text{ on Day } T$$

These add up to

$$f_T(T) - f_0(T) \text{ on Day } T.$$

And because of the convergence of the final futures price to the spot price,

$$f_T(T) - f_0(T) = S_T - f_0(T),$$

which is the same as with forward contracts.[7] Note, however, that the timing of these profits is different from that of forwards. Forward contracts realize the full amount, $S_T - f_0(T)$, at expiration, whereas futures contracts realize this amount in parts on a day-to-day basis. Naturally, the time value of money principle says that these are not equivalent amounts of money. But the differences tend to be small, particularly in low-interest-rate environments, some of these amounts are gains and some are losses, and most futures contracts have maturities of less than a year.

But the near equivalence of the profits from a futures and a forward contract disguises an important distinction between these types of contracts. In a forward contact, with the entire payoff made at expiration, a loss by one party can be large enough to trigger a default. Hence, forward contracts are subject to default and require careful

7 Because of this equivalence, we will not specifically illustrate the profit graphs of futures contracts. You can generally treat them the same as those of forwards, which were shown in Exhibit 1.

consideration of the credit quality of the counterparties. Because futures contracts settle gains and collect losses daily, the amounts that could be lost upon default are much smaller and naturally give the clearinghouse much greater flexibility to manage the credit risk it assumes.

Unlike forward markets, futures markets are highly regulated at the national level. National regulators are required to approve new futures exchanges and even new contracts proposed by existing exchanges as well as changes in margin requirements, price limits, and any significant changes in trading procedures. Violations of futures regulations can be subject to governmental prosecution. In addition, futures markets are far more transparent than forward markets. Futures prices, volume, and open interest are widely reported and easily obtained. Futures prices of nearby expiring contracts are often used as proxies for spot prices, particularly in decentralized spot markets, such as gold, which trades in spot markets all over the world.

In spite of the advantages of futures markets over forward markets, forward markets also have advantages over futures markets. Transparency is not always a good thing. Forward markets offer more privacy and fewer regulatory encumbrances. In addition, forward markets offer more flexibility. With the ability to tailor contracts to the specific needs of participants, forward contracts can be written exactly the way the parties want. In contrast, the standardization of futures contracts makes it more difficult for participants to get exactly what they want, even though they may get close substitutes. Yet, futures markets offer a valuable credit guarantee.

Like forward markets, futures markets can be used for hedging or speculation. For example, a jewelry manufacturer can buy gold futures, thereby hedging the price it will have to pay for one of its key inputs. Although it is more difficult to construct a futures strategy that hedges perfectly than to construct a forward strategy that does so, futures offer the benefit of the credit guarantee. It is not possible to argue that futures are better than forwards or vice versa. Market participants always trade off advantages against disadvantages. Some participants prefer futures, and some prefer forwards. Some prefer one over the other for certain risks and the other for other risks. Some might use one for a particular risk at a point in time and a different instrument for the same risk at another point in time. The choice is a matter of taste and constraints.

The third and final type of forward commitment we will cover is swaps. They go a step further in committing the parties to buy and sell something at a later date: They obligate the parties to a sequence of multiple purchases and sales.

4.1.3 *Swaps*

The concept of a swap is that two parties exchange (swap) a series of cash flows. One set of cash flows is variable or floating and will be determined by the movement of an underlying asset or rate. The other set of cash flows can be variable and determined by a different underlying asset or rate, or it can be fixed. Formally, a swap is defined as follows:

> *A swap is an over-the-counter derivative contract in which two parties agree to exchange a series of cash flows whereby one party pays a variable series that will be determined by an underlying asset or rate and the other party pays either (1) a variable series determined by a different underlying asset or rate or (2) a fixed series.*

As with forward contracts, swap contracts also contain other terms—such as the identity of the underlying, the relevant payment dates, and the payment procedure—that are negotiated between the parties and written into the contract. A swap is a bit more like a forward contract than a futures contract in that it is an OTC contract, so it is privately negotiated and subject to default. Nonetheless, the similarities between futures and forwards apply to futures and swaps and, indeed, combinations of futures contracts expiring at different dates are often compared to swaps.

As with forward contracts, either party can default but only one party can default at a particular time. The money owed is always based on the net owed by one party to the other. Hence, the party owing the lesser amount cannot default to the party owing the greater amount. Only the latter can default, and the amount it owes is the net of what it owes and what is owed to it, which is also true with forwards.

Swaps are relatively young financial instruments, having been created only in the early 1980s. Thus, it may be somewhat surprising to learn that the swap is the most widely used derivative, a likely result of its simplicity and embracement by the corporate world. The most common swap is the **fixed-for-floating interest rate swap**. In fact, this type of swap is so common that it is often called a "plain vanilla swap" or just a "vanilla swap," owing to the notion that vanilla ice cream is considered plain (albeit tasty).

Let us examine a scenario in which the vanilla interest rate swap is frequently used. Suppose a corporation borrows from a bank at a floating rate. It would prefer a fixed rate, which would enable it to better anticipate its cash flow needs in making its interest payments.[8] The corporation can effectively convert its floating-rate loan to a fixed-rate loan by adding a swap, as shown in Exhibit 2.

Exhibit 2 Using an Interest Rate Swap to Convert a Floating-Rate Loan to a Fixed-Rate Loan

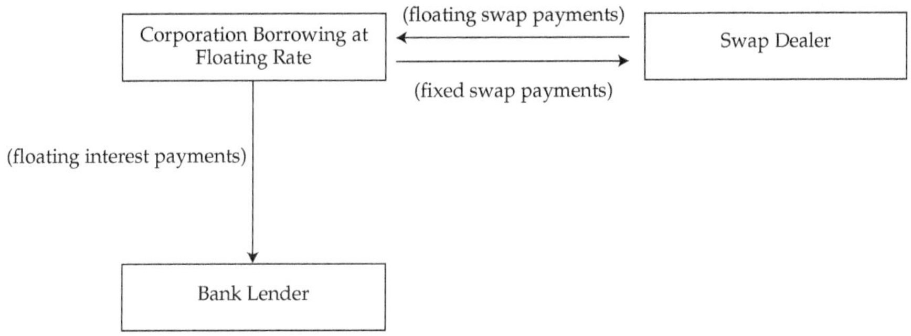

The interest payments on the loan are tied to a specific floating rate. For a dollar-based loan, that rate has historically been US dollar Libor.[9] The payments would be based on the rate from the Libor market on a specified reset date times the loan balance times a factor reflecting the number of days in the current interest calculation period. The actual payment is made at a later date. Thus, for a loan balance of, say, $10 million with monthly payments, the rate might be based on Libor on the first business day of the month, with interest payable on the first business day of the next month, which is the next reset date, and calculated as $10 million times the rate times 30/360. The 30/360 convention, an implicit assumption of 30 days in a month, is common but only one of many interest calculation conventions used in the financial world. Often, "30" is replaced by the exact number of days since the last interest payment. The use of a 360-day year is a common assumption in the financial world, which originated in the pre-calculator days when an interest rate could be multiplied by a number like 30/360, 60/360, 90/360, etc., more easily than if 365 were used.

8 Banks prefer to make floating-rate loans because their own funding is typically short term and at floating rates. Thus, their borrowing rates reset frequently, giving them a strong incentive to pass that risk on to their customers through floating-rate loans.

9 Libor is being phased out, as the panel of banks will no longer be required to submit quotations after 2021. In anticipation of this, market participants and regulators have been working to develop alternative reference rates.

Whatever the terms of the loan are, the terms of the swap are typically set to match those of the loan. Thus, a Libor-based loan with monthly payments based on the 30/360 convention would be matched with a swap with monthly payments based on Libor and the 30/360 convention and the same reset and payment dates. Although the loan has an actual balance (the amount owed by borrower to creditor), the swap does not have such a balance owed by one party to the other. Thus, it has no principal, but it does have a balance of sorts, called the **notional principal**, which ordinarily matches the loan balance. A loan with only one principal payment, the final one, will be matched with a swap with a fixed notional principal. An amortizing loan, which has a declining principal balance, will be matched with a swap with a pre-specified declining notional principal that matches the loan balance.

As with futures and forwards, no money changes hands at the start; thus, the value of a swap when initiated must be zero. The fixed rate on the swap is determined by a process that forces the value to zero, a procedure that will be covered later in the curriculum. As market conditions change, the value of a swap will deviate from zero, being positive to one party and negative to the other.

As with forward contracts, swaps are subject to default, but because the notional amount of a swap is not typically exchanged, the credit risk of a swap is much less than that of a loan.[10] The only money passing from one party to the other is the net difference between the fixed and floating interest payments. In fact, the parties do not even pay each other. Only one party pays the other, as determined by the net of the greater amount owed minus the lesser amount. This does not mean that swaps are not subject to a potentially large amount of credit risk. At a given point in time, one party could default, effectively owing the value of all remaining payments, which could substantially exceed the value that the non-defaulting party owes to the defaulting party. Thus, there is indeed credit risk in a swap. This risk must be managed by careful analysis before the transaction and by the potential use of such risk-mitigating measures as collateral.

There are also interest rate swaps in which one party pays on the basis of one interest rate and the other party pays on the basis of a different interest rate. For example, one party might make payments at Libor, whereas the other might make payments on the basis of the U. S. Treasury bill rate. The difference between Libor and the T-bill rate, often called the TED spread (T-bills versus Eurodollar), is a measure of the credit risk premium of London banks, which have historically borrowed short term at Libor, versus that of the U. S. government, which borrows short term at the T-bill rate. This transaction is called a basis swap. There are also swaps in which the floating rate is set as an average rate over the period, in accordance with the convention for many loans. Some swaps, called overnight indexed swaps, are tied to a Fed funds–type rate, reflecting the rate at which banks borrow overnight. As we will cover later, there are many other different types of swaps that are used for a variety of purposes. The plain vanilla swap is merely the simplest and most widely used.

Because swaps, forwards, and futures are forward commitments, they can all accomplish the same thing. One could create a series of forwards or futures expiring at a set of dates that would serve the same purpose as a swap. Although swaps are better suited for risks that involve multiple payments, at its most fundamental level, a swap is more or less just a series of forwards and, acknowledging the slight differences discussed above, more or less just a series of futures.

10 It is possible that the notional principal will be exchanged in a currency swap, whereby each party makes a series of payments to the other in different currencies. Whether the notional principal is exchanged depends on the purpose of the swap. This point will be covered later in the curriculum. At this time, you should see that it would be fruitless to exchange notional principals in an interest rate swap because that would mean each party would give the other the same amount of money when the transaction is initiated and re-exchange the same amount of money when the contract terminates.

EXAMPLE 3

Forward Contracts, Futures Contracts, and Swaps

1 Which of the following characterizes forward contracts and swaps but **not** futures?
   - A They are customized.
   - B They are subject to daily price limits.
   - C Their payoffs are received on a daily basis.

2 Which of the following distinguishes forwards from swaps?
   - A Forwards are OTC instruments, whereas swaps are exchange traded.
   - B Forwards are regulated as futures, whereas swaps are regulated as securities.
   - C Swaps have multiple payments, whereas forwards have only a single payment.

3 Which of the following occurs in the daily settlement of futures contracts?
   - A Initial margin deposits are refunded to the two parties.
   - B Gains and losses are reported to other market participants.
   - C Losses are charged to one party and gains credited to the other.

Solution to 1:

A is correct. Forwards and swaps are OTC contracts and, therefore, are customized. Futures are exchange traded and, therefore, are standardized. Some futures contracts are subject to daily price limits and their payoffs are received daily, but these characteristics are not true for forwards and swaps.

Solution to 2:

C is correct. Forwards and swaps are OTC instruments and both are regulated as such. Neither is regulated as a futures contract or a security. A swap is a series of multiple payments at scheduled dates, whereas a forward has only one payment, made at its expiration date.

Solution to 3:

C is correct. Losses and gains are collected and distributed to the respective parties. There is no specific reporting of these gains and losses to anyone else. Initial margin deposits are not refunded and, in fact, additional deposits may be required.

This material completes our introduction to forward commitments. All forward commitments are firm contracts. The parties are required to fulfill the obligations they agreed to. The benefit of this rigidity is that neither party pays anything to the other when the contract is initiated. If one party needs some flexibility, however, it can get it by agreeing to pay the other party some money when the contract is initiated. When the contract expires, the party who paid at the start has some flexibility in deciding whether to buy the underlying asset at the fixed price. Thus, that party did not actually agree to do anything. It had a choice. This is the nature of contingent claims.

4.2 Contingent Claims

A **contingent claim** is a derivative in which the outcome or payoff is dependent on the outcome or payoff of an underlying asset. Although this characteristic is also associated with forward commitments, a contingent claim has come to be associated with a *right*, but not an *obligation*, to make a final payment contingent on the performance of the underlying. Given that the holder of the contingent claim has a choice, the term *contingent claim* has become synonymous with the term *option*. The holder has a choice of whether or not to exercise the option. This choice creates a payoff that transforms the underlying payoff in a more pronounced manner than does a forward, futures, or swap. Those instruments provide linear payoffs: As the underlying goes up (down), the derivative gains (loses). The further up (down) the underlying goes, the more the derivative gains (loses). Options are different in that they limit losses in one direction. In addition, options can pay off as the underlying goes down. Hence, they transform the payoffs of the underlying into something quite different.

4.2.1 *Options*

We might say that an option, as a contingent claim, grants the right but not the obligation to buy an asset at a later date and at a price agreed on when the option is initiated. But there are so many variations of options that we cannot settle on this statement as a good formal definition. For one thing, options can also grant the right to sell instead of the right to buy. Moreover, they can grant the right to buy or sell earlier than at expiration. So, let us see whether we can combine these points into an all-encompassing definition of an option.

> *An option is a derivative contract in which one party, the buyer, pays a sum of money to the other party, the seller or writer, and receives the right to either buy or sell an underlying asset at a fixed price either on a specific expiration date or at any time prior to the expiration date.*

Unfortunately, even that definition does not cover every unique aspect of options. For example, options can be created in the OTC market and customized to the terms of each party, or they can be created and traded on options exchanges and standardized. As with forward contracts and swaps, customized options are subject to default, are less regulated, and are less transparent than exchange-traded derivatives. Exchange-traded options are protected against default by the clearinghouse of the options exchange and are relatively transparent and regulated at the national level. As noted in the definition above, options can be terminated early or at their expirations. When an option is terminated, either early or at expiration, the holder of the option chooses whether to exercise it. If he exercises it, he either buys or sells the underlying asset, but he does not have both rights. The right to buy is one type of option, referred to as a **call** or **call option**, whereas the right to sell is another type of option, referred to as a **put** or **put option**. With one very unusual and advanced exception that we do not cover, an option is either a call or a put, and that point is made clear in the contract.

An option is also designated as exercisable early (before expiration) or only at expiration. Options that can be exercised early are referred to as **American-style**. Options that can be exercised only at expiration are referred to as **European-style**. *It is extremely important that you do not associate these terms with where these options are traded.* Both types of options trade on all continents.

As with forwards and futures, an option can be exercised by physical delivery or cash settlement, as written in the contract. For a call option with physical delivery, upon exercise the underlying asset is delivered to the call buyer, who pays the call seller the exercise price. For a put option with physical delivery, upon exercise the put buyer delivers the underlying asset to the put seller and receives the strike price. For a cash settlement option, exercise results in the seller paying the buyer the cash equivalent value as if the asset were delivered and paid for.

The fixed price at which the underlying asset can be purchased is called the **exercise price** (also called the "strike price," the "strike," or the "striking price"). This price is somewhat analogous to the forward price because it represents the price at which the underlying will be purchased or sold if the option is exercised. The forward price, however, is set in the pricing of the contract such that the contract value at the start is zero. The strike price of the option is chosen by the participants. The actual price or value of the option is an altogether different concept.

As noted, the buyer pays the writer a sum of money called the **option premium**, or just the "premium." It represents a fair price of the option, and in a well-functioning market, it would be the value of the option. Consistent with everything we know about finance, it is the present value of the cash flows that are expected to be received by the holder of the option during the life of the option. At this point, we will not get into how this price is determined, but you will learn that later. For now, there are some fundamental concepts you need to understand, which form a basis for understanding how options are priced and why anyone would use an option.

Because the option buyer (the long) does not have to exercise the option, beyond the initial payment of the premium, there is no obligation of the long to the short. Thus, only the short can default, which would occur if the long exercises the option and the short fails to do what it is supposed to do. Thus, in contrast to forwards and swaps, in which either party could default to the other, default in options is possible only from the short to the long.

Ruling out the possibility of default for now, let us examine what happens when an option expires. Using the same notation used previously, let S_T be the price of the underlying at the expiration date, T, and X be the exercise price of the option. Remember that a call option allows the holder, or long, to pay X and receive the underlying. It should be obvious that the long would exercise the option at expiration if S_T is greater than X, meaning that the underlying value is greater than what he would pay to obtain the underlying. Otherwise, he would simply let the option expire. Thus, on the expiration date, the option is described as having a payoff of $Max(0,S_T - X)$.

Because the holder of the option would be entitled to exercise it and claim this amount, it also represents the value of the option at expiration. Let us denote that value as c_T. Thus,

$$c_T = Max(0,S_T - X) \qquad \text{(payoff to the call buyer),}$$

which is read as "take the maximum of either zero or $S_T - X$." For example, suppose you buy a call option with an exercise price of 50 and an expiration of three months for a premium of 1.50 when the stock is trading at 45. At expiration, consider the outcomes when the stock's price is 45, 50, or 55. The buyer's payoffs would be:

For $S_T = 45$, payoff $= c_T = Max(0,S_T - X) = Max(0,45 - 50) = \text{Max}(0, -5) = 0$.

For $S_T = 50$, payoff $= c_T = Max(0,S_T - X) = Max(0,50 - 50) = \text{Max}(0, 0) = 0$.

For $S_T = 55$, payoff $= c_T = Max(0,S_T - X) = Max(0,55 - 50) = \text{Max}(0, 5) = 5$.

Thus, if the underlying value exceeds the exercise price ($S_T > X$), then the option value is positive and equal to $S_T - X$. The call option is then said to be **in the money**. If the underlying value is less than the exercise price ($S_T < X$), then $S_T - X$ is negative; zero is greater than a negative number, so the option value would be zero. When the underlying value is less than the exercise price, the call option is said to be **out of the money**. When $S_T = X$, the call option is said to be **at the money**, although at the money is, for all practical purposes, out of the money because the value is still zero.

This payoff amount is also the value of the option at expiration. It represents value because it is what the option is worth at that point. If the holder of the option sells it to someone else an instant before expiration, it should sell for that amount because the new owner would exercise it and capture that amount. To the seller, the value of the option at that point is $-Max(0,S_T - X)$, which is negative to the seller if the option is in the money and zero otherwise.

Using the payoff value and the price paid for the option, we can determine the profit from the strategy, which is denoted with the Greek symbol Π. Let us say the buyer paid c_0 for the option at time 0. Then the profit is

$$\Pi = Max(0,S_T - X) - c_0 \quad \text{(profit to the call buyer),}$$

Continuing with the example with underlying prices at expiration of 45, 50, or 55, the call buyer's profit would be:

For $S_T = 45$, profit $= Max(0,S_T - X) - c_0 = Max(0,45 - 50) - 1.50 = -1.50$.

For $S_T = 50$, profit $= Max(0,S_T - X) - c_0 = Max(0,50 - 50) - 1.50 = -1.50$.

For $S_T = 55$, profit $= Max(0,S_T - X) - c_0 = Max(0,55 - 50) - 1.50 = 3.50$.

To the seller, who received the premium at the start, the payoff is

$$-c_T = -Max(0,S_T - X) \quad \text{(payoff to the call seller),}$$

At expiration, the call seller's payoffs are:

For $S_T = 45$, payoff $= -c_T = -Max(0,S_T - X) = -Max(0,45 - 50) = 0$.

For $S_T = 50$, payoff $= -c_T = -Max(0,S_T - X) = -Max(0,50 - 50) = 0$.

For $S_T = 55$, payoff $= -c_T = -Max(0,S_T - X) = -Max(0,55 - 50) = -5$.

The call seller's profit is

$$\Pi = -Max(0,S_T - X) + c_0 \quad \text{(profit to the call seller),}$$

Finally, at expiration, the call seller's profit for each underlying price at expiration are:

For $S_T = 45$, profit $= -Max(0,S_T - X) + c_0 = -Max(0,45 - 50) + 1.50 = 1.50$.

For $S_T = 50$, profit $= -Max(0,S_T - X) + c_0 = -Max(0,50 - 50) + 1.50 = 1.50$.

For $S_T = 55$, profit $= -Max(0,S_T - X) + c_0 = -Max(0,55 - 50) + 1.50 = -3.50$.

For any given price at expiration, the call seller's payoff or profit is equal to the negative of the call buyer's payoff or profit.

EXAMPLE 4

Call Option Payoffs and Profit at Expiration

Consider a call option selling for \$7 in which the exercise price is \$100 and the price of the underlying is \$98.

1 Determine the value at expiration and the profit for a call buyer under the following outcomes:

   A The price of the underlying at expiration is \$102.

   B The price of the underlying at expiration is \$94.

2 Determine the value at expiration and the profit for a call seller under the following outcomes:

   A The price of the underlying at expiration is \$91.

   B The price of the underlying at expiration is \$101.

Solution to 1:

A If the price of the underlying at expiration is \$102,

$$\text{The call buyer's value at expiration} = c_T = Max(0,S_T - X)$$
$$= Max(0,102 - 100) = \$2.$$
$$\text{The call buyer's profit} = \Pi = c_T - c_0 = 2 - 7 = -\$5.$$

B If the price of the underlying at expiration is \$94,

$$\text{The call buyer's value at expiration} = c_T = Max(0,S_T - X)$$
$$= Max(0,94 - 100) = \$0.$$
$$\text{The call buyer's profit} = \Pi = c_T - c_0 = 0 - 7 = -\$7.$$

Solution to 2:

A If the price of the underlying at expiration is \$91,

$$\text{The call seller's value at expiration} = -c_T = -Max(0,S_T - X)$$
$$= -Max(0,91 - 100) = \$0.$$
$$\text{The call seller's profit} = \Pi = -c_T + c_0 = 0 + 7 = \$7$$

B If the price of the underlying at expiration is \$101,

$$\text{The call seller's value at expiration} = -c_T = -Max(0,S_T - X)$$
$$= -Max(0,101 - 100) = -\$1.$$
$$\text{The call seller's profit} = \Pi = -c_T + c_0 = -1 + 7 = \$6.$$

Exhibit 3 illustrates the payoffs and profits to the call buyer and seller as graphical representations of these equations, with the payoff or value at expiration indicated by the dark line and the profit indicated by the light line. Note in Panel A that the buyer has no upper limit on the profit and has a fixed downside loss limit equal to the premium paid for the option. Such a condition, with limited loss and unlimited gain, is a temptation to many unsuspecting investors, but keep in mind that the graph does not indicate the frequency with which gains and losses will occur. Panel B is the mirror image of Panel A and shows that the seller has unlimited losses and limited gains. One might suspect that selling a call is, therefore, the worst investment strategy possible. Indeed, it is a risky strategy, but at this point these are only simple strategies. Other strategies can be added to mitigate the seller's risk to a substantial degree.

Exhibit 3 Payoff and Profit from a Call Option

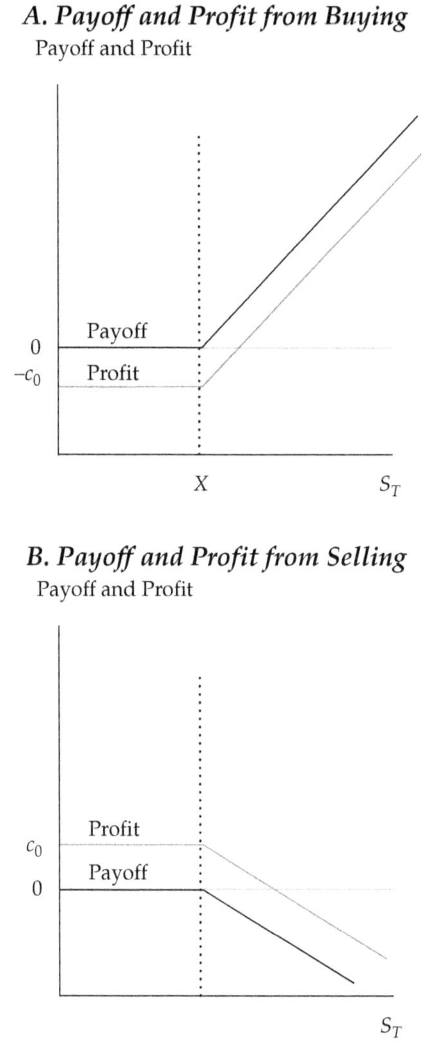

Now let us consider put options. Recall that a put option allows its holder to sell the underlying asset at the exercise price. Thus, the holder should exercise the put at expiration if the underlying asset is worth less than the exercise price ($S_T < X$). In that case, the put is said to be in the money. If the underlying asset is worth the same as the exercise price ($S_T = X$), meaning the put is at the money, or more than the exercise price ($S_T > X$), meaning the put is out of the money, the option holder would not exercise it and it would expire with zero value. Thus, the payoff to the put holder is

$$p_T = Max(0,X - S_T) \qquad \text{(payoff to the put buyer),}$$

If the put buyer paid p_0 for the put at time 0, the profit is

$$\Pi = Max(0,X - S_T) - p_0 \qquad \text{(profit to the put buyer),}$$

And for the seller, the payoff is

$$-p_T = -Max(0,X - S_T) \qquad \text{(payoff to the put seller),}$$

And the profit is

$$\Pi = -Max(0,X - S_T) + p_0 \qquad \text{(profit to the put seller),}$$

To illustrate the payoffs and profit to a put buyer and put seller, assume the put price (p_0) is 1.50, the exercise price (X) is 20.00, and the stock price at expiration (S_T) is either 18.00 or 22.00. The put buyer's payoff is:

For $S_T = 18$, payoff $= p_T = Max(0,X - S_T) = Max(0,20 - 18) = 2$.

For $S_T = 22$, payoff $= p_T = Max(0,X - S_T) = Max(0,20 - 22) = 0$.

The put buyer's profit is:

For $S_T = 18$, profit $= Max(0,X - S_T) - p_0 = Max(0,20 - 18) - 1.50 = 0.50$.

For $S_T = 22$, profit $= Max(0,X - S_T) - p_0 = Max(0,20 - 22) - 1.50 = -1.50$.

The put seller's payoff is:

For $S_T = 18$, payoff $= -p_T = -Max(0,X - S_T) = -Max(0,20 - 18) = -2$.

For $S_T = 22$, payoff $= -p_T = -Max(0,X - S_T) = -Max(0,20 - 22) = 0$.

Finally, the put seller's profit is:

For $S_T = 18$, profit $= -Max(0,X - S_T) + p_0 = -Max(0,20 - 18) + 1.50 = -0.50$.

For $S_T = 22$, profit $= -Max(0,X - S_T) + p_0 = -Max(0,20 - 22) + 1.50 = 1.50$.

For a given stock price at expiration, the put seller's payoff or profit are the negative of the put buyer's payoff or profit.

EXAMPLE 5

Put Option Payoffs and Profit at Expiration

Consider a put option selling for \$4 in which the exercise price is \$60 and the price of the underlying is \$62.

1 Determine the value at expiration and the profit for a put buyer under the following outcomes:

  A The price of the underlying at expiration is \$62.

  B The price of the underlying at expiration is \$55.

2 Determine the value at expiration and the profit for a put seller under the following outcomes:

  A The price of the underlying at expiration is \$51.

  B The price of the underlying at expiration is \$68.

Solution to 1:

A If the price of the underlying at expiration is \$62,

$$\text{The put buyer's value at expiration} = p_T = Max(0,X - S_T) = Max(0,60 - 62) = \$0.$$

$$\text{The put buyer's profit} = \Pi = p_T - p_0 = 0 - 4 = -\$4.$$

B If the price of the underlying at expiration is \$55,

$$\text{The put buyer's value at expiration} = p_T = Max(0,X - S_T) = Max(0,60 - 55) = \$5.$$

$$\text{The put buyer's profit} = \Pi = p_T - p_0 = 5 - 4 = \$1.$$

Solution to 2:

A If the price of the underlying at expiration is \$51,

$$\text{The put seller's value at expiration} = -p_T = -Max(0,X - S_T) = -Max(0,60 - 51) = -\$9.$$

$$\text{The put seller's profit} = \Pi = -p_T + p_0 = -9 + 4 = -\$5.$$

B If the price of the underlying at expiration is \$68,

$$\text{The put seller's value at expiration} = -p_T = -Max(0,X - S_T) = -Max(0,60 - 68) = \$0.$$

$$\text{The put seller's profit} = \Pi = -p_T + p_0 = 0 + 4 = \$4.$$

Exhibit 4 illustrates the payoffs and profits to the buyer and seller of a put.

Exhibit 4 Payoff and Profit from a Put Option

A. Payoff and Profit from Buying

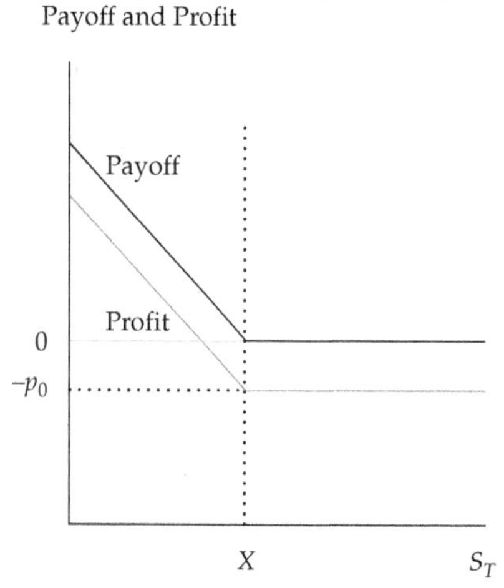

B. Payoff and Profit from Selling

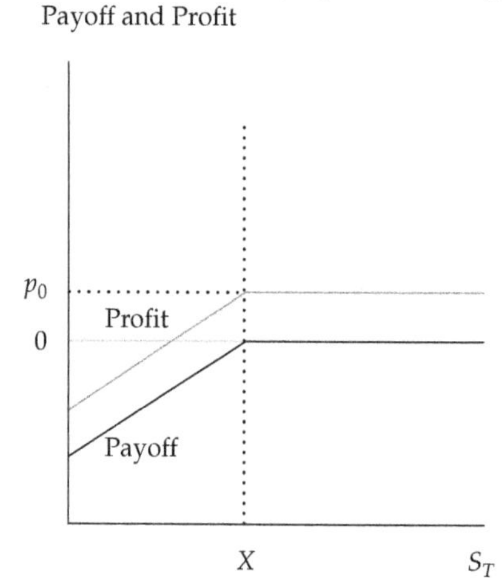

The put buyer has a limited loss, and although the gain is limited by the fact that the underlying value cannot go below zero, the put buyer does gain more the lower the value of the underlying. In this manner, we see how a put option is like insurance. Bad outcomes for the underlying trigger a payoff for both the insurance policy and the put, whereas good outcomes result only in loss of the premium. The put seller, like the insurer, has a limited gain and a loss that is larger the lower the value of the underlying. As with call options, these graphs must be considered carefully because they do not indicate the frequency with which gains and losses will occur. At this point, it should be apparent that buying a call option is consistent with a bullish point of view and buying a put option is consistent with a bearish point of view. Moreover, in contrast to forward commitments, which have payoffs that are linearly related to the payoffs of the underlying (note the straight lines in Exhibit 1), contingent claims have payoffs that are non-linear in relation to the underlying. There is linearity over a range—say, from 0 to X or from X upward or downward—but over the entire range of values for the underlying, the payoffs of contingent claims cannot be depicted with a single straight line.

We have seen only a snapshot of the payoff and profit graphs that can be created with options. Calls can be combined with puts, the underlying asset, and other calls or puts with different expirations and exercise prices to create a diverse set of payoff and profit graphs, some of which are covered later in the curriculum.

Before leaving options, let us again contrast the differences between options and forward commitments. With forward commitments, the parties agree to trade an underlying asset at a later date and at a price agreed upon when the contract is initiated. Neither party pays any cash to the other at the start. With options, the buyer pays cash to the seller at the start and receives the right, but not the obligation, to buy (if a call) or sell (if a put) the underlying asset at expiration at a price agreed upon (the exercise price) when the contract is initiated. In contrast to forwards, futures, and swaps, options do have value at the start: the premium paid by buyer to seller. That premium pays for the *right*, eliminating the *obligation*, to trade the underlying at a later date, as would be the case with a forward commitment.

Although there are numerous variations of options, most have the same essential features described here. There is, however, a distinctive family of contingent claims that emerged in the early 1990s and became widely used and, in some cases, heavily criticized. These instruments are known as credit derivatives.

4.2.2 *Credit Derivatives*

Credit risk is surely one of the oldest risks known to mankind. Human beings have been lending things to each other for thousands of years, and even the most primitive human beings must have recognized the risk of lending some of their possessions to their comrades. Until the last 20 years or so, however, the management of credit risk was restricted to simply doing the best analysis possible before making a loan, monitoring the financial condition of the borrower during the loan, limiting the exposure to a given party, and requiring collateral. Some modest forms of insurance against credit risk have existed for a number of years, but insurance can be a slow and cumbersome way of protecting against credit loss. Insurance is typically highly regulated, and insurance laws are usually very consumer oriented. Thus, credit insurance as a financial product has met with only modest success.

In the early 1990s, however, the development of the swaps market led to the creation of derivatives that would hedge credit risk. These instruments came to be known as **credit derivatives**, and they avoided many of the regulatory constraints of the traditional insurance industry. Here is a formal definition:

A credit derivative is a class of derivative contracts between two parties, a credit protection buyer and a credit protection seller, in which the latter provides protection to the former against a specific credit loss.

One of the first credit derivatives was a **total return swap**, in which the underlying is typically a bond or loan, in contrast to, say, a stock or stock index. The credit protection buyer offers to pay the credit protection seller the total return on the underlying bond. This total return consists of all interest and principal paid by the borrower plus any changes in the bond's market value. In return, the credit protection seller typically pays the credit protection buyer either a fixed or a floating rate of interest. Thus, if the bond defaults, the credit protection seller must continue to make its promised payments, while receiving a very small return or virtually no return from the credit protection buyer. If the bond incurs a loss, as it surely will if it defaults, the credit protection seller effectively pays the credit protection buyer.

Another type of credit derivative is the **credit spread option**, in which the underlying is the credit (yield) spread on a bond, which is the difference between the bond's yield and the yield on a benchmark default-free bond. As you will learn in the fixed-income material, the credit spread is a reflection of investors' perception of credit risk. Because a credit spread option requires a credit spread as the underlying, this type of derivative works only with a traded bond that has a quoted price. The credit protection buyer selects the strike spread it desires and pays the option premium to the credit protection seller. At expiration, the parties determine whether the option is in the money by comparing the bond's yield spread with the strike chosen, and if it is, the credit protection seller pays the credit protection buyer the established payoff. Thus, this instrument is essentially a call option in which the underlying is the credit spread.

A third type of credit derivative is the **credit-linked note (CLN)**. With this derivative, the credit protection buyer holds a bond or loan that is subject to default risk (the underlying reference security) and issues its own security (the credit-linked note) with the condition that if the bond or loan it holds defaults, the principal payoff on the credit-linked note is reduced accordingly. Thus, the buyer of the credit-linked note effectively insures the credit risk of the underlying reference security.

These three types of credit derivatives have had limited success compared with the fourth type of credit derivative, the **credit default swap (CDS)**. The credit default swap, in particular, has achieved much success by capturing many of the essential features of insurance while avoiding the high degree of consumer regulations that are typically associated with traditional insurance products.

In a CDS, one party—the credit protection buyer, who is seeking credit protection against a third party—makes a series of regularly scheduled payments to the other party, the credit protection seller. The seller makes no payments until a credit event occurs. A declaration of bankruptcy is clearly a credit event, but there are other types of credit events, such as a failure to make a scheduled payment or an involuntary restructuring. The CDS contract specifies what constitutes a credit event, and the industry has a procedure for declaring credit events, though that does not guarantee the parties will not end up in court arguing over whether something was or was not a credit event.

Formally, a credit default swap is defined as follows:

A credit default swap is a derivative contract between two parties, a credit protection buyer and a credit protection seller, in which the buyer makes a series of cash payments to the seller and receives a promise of compensation for credit losses resulting from the default of a third party.

A CDS is conceptually a form of insurance. Sellers of CDSs, oftentimes banks or insurance companies, collect periodic payments and are required to pay out if a loss occurs from the default of a third party. These payouts could take the form of restitution of the defaulted amount or the party holding the defaulting asset could turn it over to the CDS seller and receive a fixed amount. The most common approach is for the payout to be determined by an auction to estimate the market value of the defaulting debt. Thus, CDSs effectively provide coverage against a loss in return for the protection buyer paying a premium to the protection seller, thereby taking the form of insurance against credit loss. Although insurance contracts have certain legal characteristics that are not found in credit default swaps, the two instruments serve similar purposes and operate in virtually the same way: payments made by one party in return for a promise to cover losses incurred by the other.

Exhibit 5 illustrates the typical use of a CDS by a lender. The lender is exposed to the risk of non-payment of principal and interest. The lender lays off this risk by purchasing a CDS from a CDS seller. The lender—now the CDS buyer—promises to make a series of periodic payments to the CDS seller, who then stands ready to compensate the CDS buyer for credit losses.

Exhibit 5 Using a Credit Default Swap to Hedge the Credit Risk of a Loan

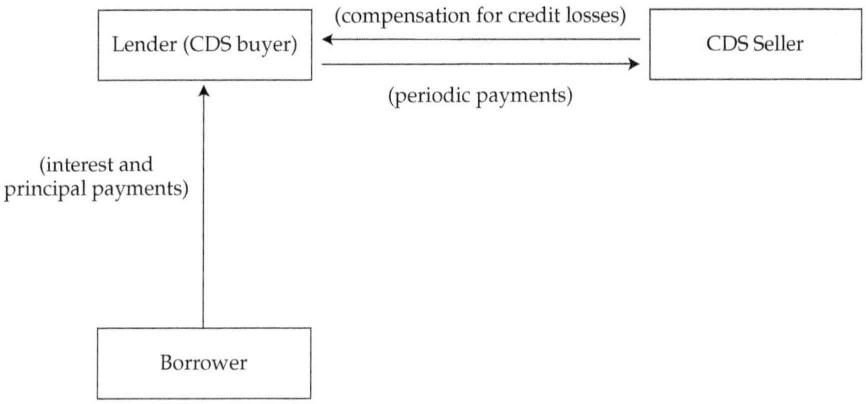

Clearly, the CDS seller is betting on the borrower's not defaulting or—more generally, as insurance companies operate—that the total payouts it is responsible for are less than the total payments collected. Of course, most insurance companies are able to do this by having reliable actuarial statistics, diversifying their risk, and selling some of the risk to other insurance companies. Actuarial statistics are typically quite solid. Average claims for life, health, and casualty insurance are well documented, and insurers can normally set premiums to cover losses and operate at a reasonable profit. Although insurance companies try to manage some of their risks at the micro level (e.g., charging smokers more for life and health insurance), most of their risk management is at the macro level, wherein they attempt to make sure their risks are not concentrated. Thus, they avoid selling too much homeowners insurance to individuals in tornado-prone areas. If they have such an exposure, they can use the reinsurance market to sell some of the risk to other companies that are not overexposed to that risk. Insurance companies attempt to diversify their risks and rely on the principle of uncorrelated risks, which plays such an important role in portfolio management. A well-diversified insurance company, like a well-diversified portfolio, should be able to earn a return commensurate with its assumed risk in the long run.

Credit default swaps should operate the same way. Sellers of CDSs should recognize when their credit risk is too concentrated. When that happens, they become buyers of CDSs from other parties or find other ways to lay off the risk. Unfortunately, during the financial crisis that began in 2007, many sellers of CDSs failed to recognize the high correlations among borrowers whose debt they had guaranteed. One well-known

CDS seller, AIG, is a large and highly successful traditional insurance company that got into the business of selling CDSs. Many of these CDSs insured against mortgages. With the growth of the subprime mortgage market, many of these CDS-insured mortgages had a substantial amount of credit risk and were often poorly documented. AIG and many other CDS sellers were thus highly exposed to systemic credit contagion, a situation in which defaults in one area of an economy ripple into another, accompanied by bank weaknesses and failures, rapidly falling equity markets, rising credit risk premiums, and a general loss of confidence in the financial system and the economy. These presumably well-diversified risks guaranteed by CDS sellers, operating as though they were insurance companies, ultimately proved to be poorly diversified. Systemic financial risks can spread more rapidly than fire, health, and casualty risks. Virtually no other risks, except those originating from wars or epidemics, spread in the manner of systemic financial risks.

Thus, to understand and appreciate the importance of the CDS market, it is necessary to recognize how that market can fail. The ability to separate and trade risks is a valuable one. Banks can continue to make loans to their customers, thereby satisfying the customers' needs, while laying off the risk elsewhere. In short, parties not wanting to bear certain risks can sell them to parties wanting to assume certain risks. If all parties do their jobs correctly, the markets and the economy work more efficiently. If, as in the case of certain CDS sellers, not everyone does a good job of managing risk, there can be serious repercussions. In the case of AIG and some other companies, taxpayer bailouts were the ultimate price paid to keep these large institutions afloat so that they could continue to provide their other critical services to consumers. The rules proposed in the new OTC derivatives market regulations—which call for greater regulation and transparency of OTC derivatives and, in particular, CDSs—have important implications for the future of this market and these instruments.

EXAMPLE 6

Options and Credit Derivatives

1 An option provides which of the following?
   - **A** Either the right to buy or the right to sell an underlying
   - **B** The right to buy and sell, with the choice made at expiration
   - **C** The obligation to buy or sell, which can be converted into the right to buy or sell

2 Which of the following is **not** a characteristic of a call option on a stock?
   - **A** A guarantee that the stock will increase
   - **B** A specified date on which the right to buy expires
   - **C** A fixed price at which the call holder can buy the stock

3 A credit derivative is which of the following?
   - **A** A derivative in which the premium is obtained on credit
   - **B** A derivative in which the payoff is borrowed by the seller
   - **C** A derivative in which the seller provides protection to the buyer against credit loss from a third party

Solution to 1:

A is correct. An option is strictly the right to buy (a call) or the right to sell (a put). It does not provide both choices or the right to convert an obligation into a right.

Solution to 2:

A is correct. A call option on a stock provides no guarantee of any change in the stock price. It has an expiration date, and it provides for a fixed price at which the holder can exercise the option, thereby purchasing the stock.

Solution to 3:

C is correct. Credit derivatives provide a guarantee against loss caused by a third party's default. They do not involve borrowing the premium or the payoff.

4.2.3 *Asset-Backed Securities*

Although these instruments are covered in more detail in the fixed-income material, we would be remiss if we failed to include them with derivatives. But we will give them only light coverage here.

As discussed earlier, derivatives take (derive) their value from the value of the underlying, as do mutual funds and exchange-traded funds (ETFs). A mutual fund or an ETF holding bonds is virtually identical to the investor holding the bonds directly. Asset-backed securities (ABSs) take this concept a step further by altering the payment streams. ABSs typically divide the payments into slices, called tranches, in which the priority of claims has been changed from equivalent to preferential. For example, in a bond mutual fund or an ETF, all investors in the fund have equal claims, and so the rate of return earned by each investor is exactly the same. If a portfolio of the same bonds were assembled into an ABS, some investors in the ABS would have claims that would supersede those of other investors. The differential nature of these claims becomes relevant when either prepayments or defaults occur.

Prepayments mostly affect only mortgages. When a portfolio of mortgages is assembled into an ABS, the resulting instrument is called a **collateralized mortgage obligation** (CMO). Commonly but not always, the credit risk has been reduced or eliminated, perhaps by a CDS, as discussed earlier. When homeowners pay off their mortgages early due to refinancing at lower rates, the holders of the mortgages suffer losses. They expected to receive a stream of returns that is now terminated. The funds that were previously earning a particular rate will now have to be invested to earn a lower rate. These losses are the mirror images of the gains homeowners make when they proudly proclaim that they refinanced their mortgages and substantially lowered their payments.

CMOs partition the claims against these mortgages into different tranches, which are typically called A, B, and C. Class C tranches bear the first wave of prepayments until that tranche has been completely repaid its full principal investment. At that point, the Class B tranche holders bear the next prepayments until they have been fully repaid. The Class A tranche holders then bear the next wave of prepayments.[11] Thus, the risk faced by the various tranche holders is different from that of a mutual fund or ETF, which would pass the returns directly through such that investors would all receive the same rates of return. Therefore, the expected returns of CMO tranches vary and are commensurate with the prepayment risk they assume. Some CMOs are also characterized by credit risk, perhaps a substantial amount, from subprime mortgages.

When bonds or loans are assembled into ABSs, they are typically called **collateralized bond obligations** (CBOs) or **collateralized loan obligations** (CLOs). These instruments (known collectively as **collateralized debt obligations**, or CDOs) do not traditionally have much prepayment risk but they do have credit risk and oftentimes

11 The reference to only three tranches is just a general statement. There are many more types of tranches. Our discussion of the three classes is for illustrative purposes only and serves to emphasize that there are high-priority claims, low-priority claims, and other claims somewhere in the middle.

a great deal of it. The CDO structure allocates this risk to tranches that are called senior, mezzanine, or junior tranches (the last sometimes called equity tranches). When defaults occur, the junior tranches bear the risk first, followed by the mezzanine tranches, and then the senior tranches. The expected returns of the tranches vary according to the perceived credit risk, with the senior tranches having the highest credit quality and the junior the lowest. Thus, the senior tranches have the lowest expected returns and the junior tranches have the highest.

An asset-backed security is formally defined as follows:

> *An asset-backed security is a derivative contract in which a portfolio of debt instruments is assembled and claims are issued on the portfolio in the form of tranches, which have different priorities of claims on the payments made by the debt securities such that prepayments or credit losses are allocated to the most-junior tranches first and the most-senior tranches last.*

ABSs seem to have only an indirect and subtle resemblance to options, but they are indeed options. They promise to make a series of returns that are typically steady. These returns can be lowered if prepayments or defaults occur. Thus, they are contingent on prepayments and defaults. Take a look again at Exhibit 4, Panel B (the profit and payoff of a short put option). If all goes well, there is a fixed return. If something goes badly, the return can be lowered, and the worse the outcome, the lower the return. Thus, holders of ABSs have effectively written put options.

This completes the discussion of contingent claims. Having now covered forward commitments and contingent claims, the final category of derivative instruments is more or less just a catch-all category in case something was missed.

4.3 Hybrids

The instruments just covered encompass all the fundamental instruments that exist in the derivatives world. Yet, the derivatives world is truly much larger than implied by what has been covered here. We have not covered and will touch only lightly on the many hybrid instruments that combine derivatives, fixed-income securities, currencies, equities, and commodities. For example, options can be combined with bonds to form either callable bonds or convertible bonds. Swaps can be combined with options to form swap payments that have upper and lower limits. Options can be combined with futures to obtain options on futures. Options can be created with swaps as the underlying to form swaptions. Some of these instruments will be covered later. For now, you should just recognize that the possibilities are almost endless.

We will not address these hybrids directly, but some are covered elsewhere in the curriculum. The purpose of discussing them here is for you to realize that derivatives create possibilities not otherwise available in their absence. This point will lead to a better understanding of why derivatives exist, a topic we will get to very shortly.

EXAMPLE 7

Forward Commitments versus Contingent Claims

1 Which of the following is **not** a forward commitment?

A An agreement to take out a loan at a future date at a specific rate

B An offer of employment that must be accepted or rejected in two weeks

C An agreement to lease a piece of machinery for one year with a series of fixed monthly payments

2 Which of the following statements is true about contingent claims?
   A Either party can default to the other.
   B The payoffs are linearly related to the performance of the underlying.
   C The most the long can lose is the amount paid for the contingent claim.

Solution to 1:

B is correct. Both A and C are commitments to engage in transactions at future dates. In fact, C is like a swap because the party agrees to make a series of future payments and in return receives temporary use of an asset whose value could vary. B is a contingent claim. The party receiving the employment offer can accept it or reject it if there is a better alternative.

Solution to 2:

C is correct. The maximum loss to the long is the premium. The payoffs of contingent claims are not linearly related to the underlying, and only one party, the short, can default.

4.4 Derivatives Underlyings

Before discussing the purposes and benefits of derivatives, we need to clarify some points that have been implied so far. We have alluded to certain underlying assets, this section will briefly discuss the underlyings more directly.

4.4.1 *Equities*

Equities are one of the most popular categories of underlyings on which derivatives are created. There are two types of equities on which derivatives exist: individual stocks and stock indexes. Derivatives on individual stocks are primarily options. Forwards, futures, and swaps on individual stocks are not widely used. Index derivatives in the form of options, forwards, futures, and swaps are very popular. Index swaps, more often called equity swaps, are quite popular and permit investors to pay the return on one stock index and receive the return on another index or a fixed rate. They can be very useful in asset allocation strategies by allowing an equity manager to increase or reduce exposure to an equity market or sector without trading the individual securities.

In addition, options on stocks are frequently used by companies as compensation and incentives for their executives and employees. These options are granted to provide incentives to work toward driving the stock price up and can result in companies paying lower cash compensation. Some companies also issue warrants, which are options sold to the public that allow the holders to exercise them and buy shares directly from the companies.

4.4.2 *Fixed-Income Instruments and Interest Rates*

Options, forwards, futures, and swaps on bonds are widely used. The problem with creating derivatives on bonds, however, is that there are almost always many issues of bonds. A single issuer, whether it is a government or a private borrower, often has more than one bond issue outstanding. For futures contracts, with their standardization requirements, this problem is particularly challenging. What does it mean to say that a futures contract is on a German bund, a US Treasury note, or a UK gilt? The most common solution to this problem is to allow multiple issues to be delivered on a single futures contract. This feature adds some interesting twists to the pricing and trading strategies of these instruments.

Until now, we have referred to the underlying as an *asset*. Yet, one of the largest derivative underlyings is not an asset. It is simply an interest rate. An interest rate is not an asset. One cannot hold an interest rate or place it on a balance sheet as an asset. Although one can hold an instrument that pays an interest rate, the rate itself is not an asset. But there are derivatives in which the rate, not the instrument that pays the rate, is the underlying. In fact, we have already covered one of these derivatives: The plain vanilla interest rate swap in which Libor is the underlying.[12] Instead of a swap, an interest rate derivative could be an option. For example, a call option on 90-day Libor with a strike of 5% would pay off if at expiration Libor exceeds 5%. If Libor is below 5%, the option simply expires unexercised.

Interest rate derivatives are the most widely used derivatives. With that in mind, we will be careful in using the expression *underlying asset* and will use the more generic *underlying*.

4.4.3 *Currencies*

Currency risk is a major factor in global financial markets, and the currency derivatives market is extremely large. Options, forwards, futures, and swaps are widely used. Currency derivatives can be complex, sometimes combining elements of other underlyings. For example, a currency swap involves two parties making a series of interest rate payments to each other in different currencies. Because interest rates and currencies are both subject to change, a currency swap has two sources of risk. Although this instrument may sound extremely complicated, it merely reflects the fact that companies operating across borders are subject to both interest rate risk and currency risk and currency swaps are commonly used to manage those risks.

4.4.4 *Commodities*

Commodities are resources, such as food, oil, and metals, that humans use to sustain life and support economic activity. Because of the economic principle of comparative advantage, countries often specialize in the production of certain resources. Thus, the commodities market is extremely large and subject to an almost unimaginable array of risks. One need only observe how the price of oil moves up as tension builds in the Middle East or how the price of orange juice rises on a forecast of cold weather in Florida.

Commodity derivatives are widely used to speculate in and manage the risk associated with commodity price movements. The primary commodity derivatives are futures, but forwards, swaps, and options are also used. The reason that futures are in the lead in the world of commodities is simply history. The first futures markets were futures on commodities. The first futures exchange, the Chicago Board of Trade, was created in 1848, and until the creation of currency futures in 1972, there were no futures on any underlying except commodities.

There has been a tendency to think of the commodities world as somewhat separate from the financial world. Commodity traders and financial traders were quite different groups. Since the creation of financial futures, however, commodity and financial traders have become relatively homogeneous. Moreover, commodities are increasingly viewed as an important asset class that should be included in investment strategies because of their ability to help diversify portfolios.

12 As you will see later, there are also futures in which the underlying is an interest rate (Eurodollar futures) and forwards in which the underlying is an interest rate (forward rate agreements, or FRAs).

4.4.5 *Credit*

As we previously discussed, credit is another underlying and quite obviously not an asset. Credit default swaps (CDSs) and collateralized debt obligations (CDOs) were discussed extensively in an earlier section. These instruments have clearly established that credit is a distinct underlying that has widespread interest from a trading and risk management perspective. In addition, to the credit of a single entity, credit derivatives are created on multiple entities. CDOs themselves are credit derivatives on portfolios of credit risks. In recent years, indexes of CDOs have been created, and instruments based on the payoffs of these CDO indexes are widely traded.

4.4.6 *Other*

This category is included here to capture some of the really unusual underlyings. One in particular is weather. Although weather is hardly an asset, it is certainly a major force in how some entities perform. For example, a ski resort needs snow, farmers need an adequate but not excessive amount of rain, and public utilities experience strains on their capacity during temperature extremes. Derivatives exist in which the payoffs are measured as snowfall, rainfall, and temperature. Although these derivatives have not been widely used—because of some complexities in pricing, among other things—they continue to exist and may still have a future. In addition, there are derivatives on electricity, which is also not an asset. It cannot be held in the traditional sense because it is created and consumed almost instantaneously. Another unusual type of derivative is based on disasters in the form of insurance claims.

Financial institutions will continue to create derivatives on all types of risks and exposures. Most of these derivatives will fail because of little trading interest, but a few will succeed. If that speaks badly of derivatives, it must be remembered that most small businesses fail, most creative ideas fail, and most people who try to become professional entertainers or athletes fail. It is the sign of a healthy and competitive system that only the very best survive.

THE SIZE OF THE DERIVATIVES MARKET

In case anyone thinks that the derivatives market is not large enough to justify studying, we should consider how big the market is. Unfortunately, gauging the size of the derivatives market is not a simple task. OTC derivatives contracts are private transactions. No reporting agency gathers data, and market size is not measured in traditional volume-based metrics, such as shares traded in the stock market. Complicating things further is the fact that derivatives underlyings include equities, fixed-income securities, interest rates, currencies, commodities, and a variety of other underlyings. All these underlyings have their own units of measurement. Hence, measuring how "big" the underlying derivatives markets are is like trying to measure how much fruit consumers purchase; the proverbial mixing of apples, oranges, bananas, and all other fruits.

The exchange-listed derivatives market reports its size in terms of volume, meaning the number of contracts traded. Exchange-listed volume, however, is an inconsistent number. For example, US Treasury bond futures contracts trade in units covering $100,000 face value. Eurodollar futures contracts trade in units covering $1,000,000 face value. Crude oil trades in 1,000-barrel (42 gallons each) units. Yet, one traded contract of each gets equal weighting in volume totals.

FIA (a global trade organization for futures, options, and centrally cleared derivatives markets) publishes detailed information about the industry. For 2017, global trading volume was 14.8 billion futures contracts, 10.4 billion options contracts, and a combined total of 25.2 billion contracts. Of nine futures instrument types, the largest three categories were interest rate futures (21.4% of global trading), equity index futures (16.9%), and currency futures (14.6%). Of nine options instrument types, the largest three categories were equity index options (48.4% of global trading), individual equity options (33.5%), and currency options (7.9%). Because options and futures contracts are typically short lived, the number of open-interest contracts is substantially less than the amount of trading volume. For the end of December 2017, open-interest futures contracts were 0.24 billion, open-interest option contracts were 0.60 billion, and the combined total was 0.84 billion contracts.

OTC volume is even more difficult to measure. There is no count of the number of contracts that trade. In fact, *volume* is an almost meaningless concept in OTC markets because any notion of volume requires a standardized size. If a customer goes to a swaps dealer and enters into a swap to hedge a \$50 million loan, there is no measure of how much volume that transaction generated. The \$50 million swap's notional principal, however, does provide a measure to some extent. Forwards, swaps, and OTC options all have notional principals, so they can be measured in that manner. Another measure of the size of the derivatives market is the market value of these contracts. As noted, forwards and swaps start with zero market value, but their market value changes as market conditions change. Options do not start with zero market value and almost always have a positive market value until expiration, when some options expire out of the money.

The OTC industry has taken both of these concepts—notional principal and market value—as measures of the size of the market. Notional principal is probably a more accurate measure. The amount of a contract's notional principal is unambiguous: It is written into the contract and the two parties cannot disagree over it. Yet, notional principal terribly overstates the amount of money actually at risk. For example, a \$50 million notional principal swap will have nowhere near \$50 million at risk. The payments on such a swap are merely the net of two opposite series of interest payments on \$50 million. The market value of such a swap is the present value of one stream of payments minus the present value of the other. This market value figure will always be well below the notional principal. Thus, market value seems like a better measure except that, unlike notional principal, it is not unambiguous. Market value requires measurement, and two parties can disagree on the market value of the same transaction.

Notional principal and market value estimates for the global OTC derivatives market are collected semi-annually by the Bank for International Settlements of Basel, Switzerland, and published on its website (http://www.bis.org/statistics/derstats.htm). At the end of 2017, notional principal was more than \$532 trillion and market value was about \$27 trillion. A figure of \$600 trillion is an almost unfathomable number and, as noted, is a misleading measure of the amount of money at risk.[13] The market value figure of \$11 trillion is a much more realistic measure, but as noted, it is less accurate, relying on estimates provided by banks. Interest rate contracts constituted 81.9% of the total notional amount outstanding. The relative sizes of the other categories were 16.4% for foreign exchange contracts and less than 2% for credit derivatives, equity-linked contracts, and commodity contracts.

The exchange-listed and OTC markets use different measures and each of those measures is subject to severe limitations. About all we can truly say for sure about the derivatives market is, "It is big."

5 THE PURPOSES AND BENEFITS OF DERIVATIVES

Economic historians know that derivatives markets have existed since at least the Middle Ages. It is unclear whether derivatives originated in the Asian rice markets or possibly in medieval trade fairs in Europe. We do know that the origin of modern futures markets is the creation of the Chicago Board of Trade in 1848. To understand why derivatives markets exist, it is useful to take a brief look at why the Chicago Board of Trade was formed.

13 To put it in perspective, it would take almost 17 million years for a clock to tick off 532 trillion seconds!

In the middle of the 19th century, midwestern America was rapidly becoming the center of agricultural production in the United States. At the same time, Chicago was evolving into a major American city, a hub of transportation and commerce. Grain markets in Chicago were the central location to which midwestern farmers brought their wheat, corn, and soybeans to sell. Unfortunately, most of these products arrived at approximately the same time of the year, September through November. The storage facilities in Chicago were strained beyond capacity. As a result, prices would fall tremendously and some farmers reportedly found it more economical to dump their grains in the Chicago River rather than transport them back to the farm. At other times of the year, prices would rise steeply. A group of businessmen saw this situation as unnecessary volatility and a waste of valuable produce. To deal with this problem, they created the Chicago Board of Trade and a financial instrument called the "to-arrive" contract. A farmer could sell a to-arrive contract at any time during the year. This contract fixed the price of the farmer's grain on the basis of delivery in Chicago at a specified later date. Grain is highly storable, so farmers can hold on to the grain and deliver it at almost any later time. This plan substantially reduced seasonal market volatility and made the markets work much better for all parties.

The traders in Chicago began to trade these contracts, speculating on movements in grain prices. Soon, it became apparent that an important and fascinating market had developed. Widespread hedging and speculative interest resulted in substantial market growth, and about 80 years later, a clearinghouse and a performance guarantee were added, thus completing the evolution of the to-arrive contract into today's modern futures contract.

Many commodities and all financial assets that underlie derivatives contracts are not seasonally produced. Hence, this initial motivation for futures markets is only a minor advantage of derivatives markets today. But there are many reasons why derivative markets serve an important and useful purpose in contemporary finance.

5.1 Risk Allocation, Transfer, and Management

Until the advent of derivatives markets, risk management was quite cumbersome. Setting the actual level of risk to the desired level of risk required engaging in transactions in the underlyings. Such transactions typically had high transaction costs and were disruptive of portfolios. In many cases, it is quite difficult to fine-tune the level of risk to the desired level. From the perspective of a risk taker, it was quite costly to buy risk because a large amount of capital would be required.

Derivatives solve these problems in a very effective way: They allow trading the risk without trading the instrument itself. For example, consider a stockholder who wants to reduce exposure to a stock. In the pre-derivatives era, the only way to do so was to sell the stock. Now, the stockholder can sell futures, forwards, calls, or swaps, or buy put options, all while retaining the stock. For a company founder, these types of strategies can be particularly useful because the founder can retain ownership and probably board membership. Many other excellent examples of the use of derivatives to transfer risk are covered elsewhere in the curriculum. The objective at this point is to establish that derivatives provide an effective method of transferring risk from parties who do not want the risk to parties who do. In this sense, risk allocation is improved within markets and, indeed, the entire global economy.

The overall purpose of derivatives is to obtain more effective risk management within companies and the entire economy. Although some argue that derivatives do not serve this purpose very well (we will discuss this point in Section 6), for now you should understand that derivatives can improve the allocation of risk and facilitate more effective risk management for both companies and economies.

5.2 Information Discovery

One of the advantages of futures markets has been described as *price discovery*. A futures price has been characterized by some experts as a revelation of some information about the future. Thus, a futures price is sometimes thought of as predictive. This statement is not strictly correct because futures prices are not really forecasts of future spot prices. They provide only a little more information than do spot prices, but they do so in a very efficient manner. The markets for some underlyings are highly decentralized and not very efficient. For example, what is gold worth? It trades in markets around the world, but probably the best place to look is at the gold futures contract expiring soonest. What is the value of the S&P 500 Index when the US markets are not open? As it turns out, US futures markets open before the US stock market opens. The S&P 500 futures price is frequently viewed as an indication of where the stock market will open.

Derivative markets can, however, convey information not impounded in spot markets. By virtue of the fact that derivative markets require less capital, information can flow into the derivative markets before it gets into the spot market. The difference may well be only a matter of minutes or possibly seconds, but it can provide the edge to astute traders.

Finally, we should note that futures markets convey another simple piece of information: What price would one accept to avoid uncertainty? If you hold a stock worth $40 and could hedge the next 12 months' uncertainty, what locked-in price should you expect to earn? As it turns out, it should be the price that guarantees the risk-free rate minus whatever dividends would be paid on the stock. Derivatives—specifically, futures, forwards, and swaps—reveal the price that the holder of an asset could take and avoid the risk.

What we have said until now applies to futures, forwards, and swaps. What about options? As you will learn later, given the underlying and the type of option (call or put), an option price reflects two characteristics of the option (exercise price and time to expiration), three characteristics of the underlying (price, volatility, and cash flows it might pay), and one general macroeconomic factor (risk-free rate). Only one of these factors, volatility, is not relatively easy to identify. But with the available models to price the option, we can infer what volatility people are using from the actual market prices at which they execute trades. That volatility, called **implied volatility**, measures the expected risk of the underlying. It reflects the volatility that investors use to determine the market price of the option. Knowing the expected risk of the underlying asset is an extremely useful piece of information. In fact, for options on broad-based market indexes, such as the S&P 500, the implied volatility is a good measure of the general level of uncertainty in the market. Some experts have even called it a measure of fear. Thus, options provide information about what investors think of the uncertainty in the market, if not their fear of it.[14]

In addition, options allow the creation of trading strategies that cannot be done by using the underlying. As the exhibits on options explained, these strategies provide asymmetrical performance: limited movement in one direction and movement in the other direction that changes with movements in the underlying.

---

14 The Chicago Board Options Exchange publishes a measure of the implied volatility of the S&P 500 Index option, which is called the VIX (volatility index). The VIX is widely followed and is cited as a measure of investor uncertainty and sometimes fear.

5.3 Operational Advantages

We noted earlier that derivatives have lower transaction costs than the underlying. The transaction costs of derivatives can be high relative to the value of the derivatives, but these costs are typically low relative to the value of the underlying. Thus, an investor who wants to take a position in, say, an equity market index would likely find it less costly to use the futures to get a given degree of exposure than to invest directly in the index to get that same exposure.

Derivative markets also typically have greater liquidity than the underlying spot markets, a result of the smaller amount of capital required to trade derivatives than to get the equivalent exposure directly in the underlying. Futures margin requirements and option premiums are quite low relative to the cost of the underlying.

One other extremely valuable operational advantage of derivative markets is the ease with which one can go short. With derivatives, it is nearly as easy to take a short position as to take a long position, whereas for the underlying asset, it is almost always much more difficult to go short than to go long. In fact, for many commodities, short selling is nearly impossible.

5.4 Market Efficiency

In the study of portfolio management, you learn that an efficient market is one in which no single investor can consistently earn returns in the long run in excess of those commensurate with the risk assumed. Of course, endless debates occur over whether equity markets are efficient. No need to resurrect that issue here, but let us proceed with the assumption that equity markets—and, in fact, most free and competitive financial markets—are reasonably efficient. This assumption does not mean that abnormal returns can never be earned, and indeed prices do get out of line with fundamental values. But competition, the relatively free flow of information, and ease of trading tend to bring prices back in line with fundamental values. Derivatives can make this process work even more rapidly.

When prices deviate from fundamental values, derivative markets offer less costly ways to exploit the mispricing. As noted earlier, less capital is required, transaction costs are lower, and short selling is easier. We also noted that as a result of these features, it is possible, indeed likely, that fundamental value will be reflected in the derivatives markets before it is restored in the underlying market. Although this time difference could be only a matter of minutes, for a trader seeking abnormal returns, a few minutes can be a valuable opportunity.

All these advantages of derivatives markets make the financial markets in general function more effectively. Investors are far more willing to trade if they can more easily manage their risk, trade at lower cost and with less capital, and go short more easily. This increased willingness to trade increases the number of market participants, which makes the market more liquid. A very liquid market may not automatically be an efficient market, but it certainly has a better chance of being one.

Even if one does not accept the concept that financial markets are efficient, it is difficult to say that markets are not more effective and competitive with derivatives. Yet, many blame derivatives for problems in the market. Let us take a look at these arguments.

6 CRITICISMS AND MISUSES OF DERIVATIVES

The history of financial markets is filled with extreme ups and downs, which are often called bubbles and crashes. Bubbles occur when prices rise for a long time and appear to exceed fundamental values. Crashes occur when prices fall rapidly. Although bubbles, if they truly exist, are troublesome, crashes are even more so because nearly everyone loses substantial wealth in a crash. A crash is then typically followed by a government study commissioned to find the causes of the crash. In the last 30 years, almost all such studies have implicated derivatives as having some role in causing the crash. Of course, because derivatives are widely used and involve a high degree of leverage, it is a given that they would be seen in a crash. It is unclear whether derivatives are the real culprit or just the proverbial smoking gun used by someone to do something wrong.

The two principal arguments against derivatives are that they are such speculative devices that they effectively permit legalized gambling and that they destabilize the financial system. Let us look at these points more closely.

6.1 Speculation and Gambling

As noted earlier, derivatives are frequently used to manage risk. In many contexts, this use involves hedging or laying off risk. Naturally, for hedging to work, there must be speculators. Someone must accept the risk. Derivatives markets are unquestionably attractive to speculators. All the benefits of derivatives draw speculators in large numbers, and indeed they should. The more speculators that participate in the market, the cheaper it is for hedgers to lay off risk. These speculators take the form of hedge funds and other professional traders who willingly accept risk that others need to shed. In recent years, the rapid growth of these types of investors has been alarming to some but almost surely has been beneficial for all investors.

Unfortunately, the general image of speculators is not a good one. Speculators are often thought to be short-term traders who attempt to exploit temporary inefficiencies, caring little about long-term fundamental values. The profits from short-term trading are almost always taxed more heavily than the profits from long-term trading, clearly targeting and in some sense punishing speculators. Speculators are thought to engage in price manipulation and to trade at extreme prices.[15] All of this type of trading is viewed more or less as just a form of gambling.

Yet, there are notable differences between gambling and speculation. Gambling typically benefits only a limited number of participants and does not generally help society as a whole. But derivatives trading brings extensive benefits to financial markets, as explained earlier, and thus does benefit society as a whole. In short, the benefits of derivatives are broad, whereas the benefits of gambling are narrow.

Nonetheless, the argument that derivatives are a form of legalized gambling will continue to be made. Speculation and gambling are certainly both forms of financial risk taking, so these arguments are not completely off base. But insurance companies speculate on loss claims, mutual funds that invest in stocks speculate on the performance of companies, and entrepreneurs go up against tremendous odds to speculate on their own ability to create successful businesses. These so-called speculators are rarely criticized for engaging in a form of legalized gambling, and indeed entrepreneurs are praised as the backbone of the economy. Really, all investment is speculative. So, why is speculation viewed as such a bad thing by so many? The answer is unclear.

15 Politicians and regulators have been especially critical of energy market speculators. Politicians, in particular, almost always blame rising oil prices on speculators, although credit is conspicuously absent for falling oil prices.

6.2 Destabilization and Systemic Risk

The arguments against speculation through derivatives often go a step further, claiming that it is not merely speculation or gambling per se but rather that it has destabilizing consequences. Opponents of derivatives claim that the very benefits of derivatives (low cost, low capital requirements, ease of going short) result in an excessive amount of speculative trading that brings instability to the market. They argue that speculators use large amounts of leverage, thereby subjecting themselves and their creditors to substantial risk if markets do not move in their hoped-for direction. Defaults by speculators can then lead to defaults by their creditors, their creditors' creditors, and so on. These effects can, therefore, be systemic and reflect an epidemic contagion whereby instability can spread throughout markets and an economy, if not the entire world. Given that governments often end up bailing out some banks and insurance companies, society has expressed concern that the risk managed with derivatives must be controlled.

This argument is not without merit. Such effects occurred in the Long-Term Capital Management fiasco of 1998 and again in the financial crisis of 2008, in which derivatives, particularly credit default swaps, were widely used by many of the problem entities. Responses to such events typically take the course of calling for more rules and regulations restricting the use of derivatives, requiring more collateral and credit mitigation measures, backing up banks with more capital, and encouraging, if not requiring, OTC derivatives to be centrally cleared like exchange-traded derivatives.

In response, however, we should note that financial crises—including the South Sea and Mississippi bubbles and the stock market crash of 1929, as well as a handful of economic calamities of the 19th and 20th centuries—have existed since the dawn of capitalism. Some of these events preceded the era of modern derivatives markets, and others were completely unrelated to the use of derivatives. Some organizations, such as Orange County, California, in 1994–1995, have proved that derivatives are not required to take on excessive leverage and nearly bring the entity to ruin. Proponents of derivatives argue that derivatives are but one of many mechanisms through which excessive risk can be taken. Derivatives may seem dangerous, and they can be if misused, but there are many ways to take on leverage that look far less harmful but can be just as risky.

Another criticism of derivatives is simply their complexity. Many derivatives are extremely complex and require a high-level understanding of mathematics. The financial industry employs many mathematicians, physicists, and computer scientists. This single fact has made many distrust derivatives and the people who work on them. It is unclear why this reason has tarnished the reputation of the derivatives industry. Scientists work on complex problems in medicine and engineering without public distrust. One explanation probably lies in the fact that scientists create models of markets by using scientific principles that often fail. To a physicist modeling the movements of celestial bodies, the science is reliable and the physicist is unlikely to misapply the science. The same science applied to financial markets is far less reliable. Financial markets are driven by the actions of people who are not as consistent as the movements of celestial bodies. When financial models fail to work as they should, the scientists are often blamed for either building models that are too complex and unable to accurately capture financial reality or misusing those models, such as using poor estimates of inputs. And derivatives, being so widely used and heavily leveraged, are frequently in the center of it all.

EXAMPLE 8

Purposes and Controversies of Derivative Markets

1 Which of the following is **not** an advantage of derivative markets?
   - A They are less volatile than spot markets.
   - B They facilitate the allocation of risk in the market.
   - C They incur lower transaction costs than spot markets.

2 Which of the following pieces of information is **not** conveyed by at least one type of derivative?
   - A The volatility of the underlying
   - B The most widely used strategy of the underlying
   - C The price at which uncertainty in the underlying can be eliminated

3 Which of the following responds to the criticism that derivatives can be destabilizing to the underlying market?
   - A Market crashes and panics have occurred since long before derivatives existed.
   - B Derivatives are sufficiently regulated that they cannot destabilize the spot market.
   - C The transaction costs of derivatives are high enough to keep their use at a minimum level.

Solution to 1:

A is correct. Derivative markets are not by nature more or less volatile than spot markets. They facilitate risk allocation by making it easier and less costly to transfer risk, and their transaction costs are lower than those of spot markets.

Solution to 2:

B is correct. Options do convey the volatility of the underlying, and futures, forwards, and swaps convey the price at which uncertainty in the underlying can be eliminated. Derivatives do not convey any information about the use of the underlying in strategies.

Solution to 3:

A is correct. Derivatives regulation is not more and is arguably less than spot market regulation, and the transaction costs of derivatives are not a deterrent to their use; in fact, derivatives are widely used. Market crashes and panics have a very long history, much longer than that of derivatives.

An important element of understanding and using derivatives is having a healthy respect for their power. Every day, we use chemicals, electricity, and fire without thinking about their dangers. We consume water and drive automobiles, both of which are statistically quite dangerous. Perhaps these risks are underappreciated, but it is more likely the case that most adults learn how to safely use chemicals, electricity, fire, water, and automobiles. Of course, there are exceptions, many of which are foolish, and foolishness is no stranger to the derivatives industry. The lesson here is that derivatives can make our financial lives better, but like chemicals, electricity, and all the rest, we need to know how to use them safely, which is why they are an important part of the CFA curriculum.

Later in the curriculum, you will learn a great deal about how derivatives are priced. At this point, we introduce the pricing of derivatives. This material not only paves the way for a deeper understanding of derivatives but also complements earlier material by helping you understand how derivatives work.

ELEMENTARY PRINCIPLES OF DERIVATIVE PRICING

7

Pricing and valuation are fundamental elements of the CFA Program. The study of fixed-income and equity securities, as well as their application in portfolio management, is solidly grounded on the principle of valuation. In valuation, the question is simple: What is something worth? Without an answer to that question, one can hardly proceed to use that *something* wisely.

Determining what a derivative is worth is similar to determining what an asset is worth. As you learn in the fixed-income and equity readings, value is the present value of future cash flows, with discounting done at a rate that reflects both the opportunity cost of money and the risk. Derivatives valuation applies that same principle but in a somewhat different way.

Think of a derivative as *attached* to an underlying. We know that the derivative *derives* its value from the value of the underlying. If the underlying's value changes, so should the value of the derivative. The underlying takes its value from the discounted present value of the expected future cash flows it offers, with discounting done at a rate reflecting the investor's risk tolerance. But if the value of the underlying is embedded in the value of the derivative, it would be double counting to discount the derivative's expected future cash flows at a risky discount rate. That effect has already been incorporated into the value of the underlying, which goes into the value of the derivative.

Derivatives usually take their values from the underlying by constructing a hypothetical combination of the derivatives and the underlyings that eliminates risk. This combination is typically called a **hedge portfolio**. With the risk eliminated, it follows that the hedge portfolio should earn the risk-free rate. A derivative's value is the price of the derivative that forces the hedge portfolio to earn the risk-free rate.

This principle of derivative valuation relies completely on the ability of an investor to hold or store the underlying asset. Let us take a look at what that means.

7.1 Storage

As noted previously, the first derivatives were agricultural commodities. Most of these commodities can be stored (i.e., held) for a period of time. Some extreme cases, such as oil and gold, which are storable for millions of years, are excellent examples of fully storable commodities. Grains, such as wheat and corn, can be stored for long but not infinite periods of time. Some commodities, such as bananas, are storable for relatively short periods of time. In the CFA Program, we are more interested in financial assets. Equities and currencies have perpetual storability, whereas bonds are storable until they mature.

Storage incurs costs. Commodity storage costs can be quite expensive. Imagine storing 1,000 kilograms of gold or a million barrels of oil. Financial assets, however, have relatively low storage costs. Some assets pay returns during storage. Stocks pay dividends and bonds pay interest. The net of payments offered minus storage costs plays a role in the valuation of derivatives.

An example earlier in this reading illustrates this point. Suppose an investor holds a dividend-paying stock and wants to eliminate the uncertainty of its selling price over a future period of time. Suppose further that the investor enters into a forward contract that commits him to deliver the stock at a later date, for which he will receive a fixed price. With uncertainty eliminated, the investor should earn the risk-free rate, but in fact, he does not. He earns more because while holding the stock, he collects dividends. Therefore, he should earn the risk-free rate *minus* the dividend yield, a concept known as the cost of carry, which will be covered in great detail in later readings. The cost of carry *plus* the dividends he earns effectively means that he makes the risk-free rate. Now, no one is claiming that this is a good way to earn the risk-free rate. There are many better ways to do that, but this strategy could be executed. There is one and only one forward price that guarantees that this strategy earns a return of the risk-free rate minus the dividend yield, or the risk-free rate after accounting for the dividends collected. If the forward price at which contracts are created does not equal this price, investors can take advantage of this discrepancy by engaging in arbitrage, which is discussed in the next section.

Forwards, futures, swaps, and options are all priced in this manner. Hence, they rely critically on the ability to store or hold the asset. Some underlyings are not storable. We previously mentioned electricity. It is produced and consumed almost instantaneously. Weather is also not storable. Fresh fish have very limited storability. Although this absence of storability may not be the reason, derivative markets in these types of underlyings have not been particularly successful, whereas those in underlyings that are more easily storable have often been successful.

The opposite of storability is the ability to go short—that is, to borrow the underlying, sell it, and buy it back later. We discussed earlier that short selling of some assets can be difficult. It is not easy to borrow oil or soybeans. There are ways around this constraint, but derivatives valuation is generally much easier when the underlying can be shorted. This point is discussed in more depth later in the curriculum.

7.2 Arbitrage

What we have been describing is the foundation of the principle of **arbitrage**. In well-functioning markets with low transaction costs and a free flow of information, the same asset cannot sell for more than one price. If it did, someone would buy it in the cheaper market and sell it in the more expensive market, earning a riskless profit. The combined actions of all parties doing this would push up the lower price and push down the higher price until they converged. For this reason, arbitrage is often referred to as the **law of one price**. Of course, for arbitrage to be feasible, the ability to purchase and sell short the asset is important.

Obviously, this rule does not apply to all markets. The same consumer good can easily sell for different prices, which is one reason why people spend so much time shopping on the internet. The costs associated with purchasing the good in the cheaper market and selling it in the more expensive market can make the arbitrage not worthwhile. The absence of information on the very fact that different prices exist would also prevent the arbitrage from occurring. Although the internet and various price-comparing websites reduce these frictions and encourage all sellers to offer competitive prices, consumer goods are never likely to be arbitragable.[16]

Financial markets, of course, are a different matter. Information on securities prices around the world is quite accessible and relatively inexpensive. Most financial markets are fairly competitive because dealers, speculators, and brokers attempt to execute

16 If the same consumer good sells for different prices in markets with a relatively free flow of information (e.g., via price-comparing websites), it still may not be possible to truly arbitrage. Buying the good at a lower price and selling it at a higher price but less than the price of the most expensive seller may not be practical, but the most expensive seller may be driven out of business. When everyone knows what everyone else is charging, the same effect of arbitrage can still occur.

trades at the best prices. Arbitrage is considered a dependable rule in the financial markets. Nonetheless, there are people who purport to make a living as arbitrageurs. How could they exist? To figure that out, first consider some examples of arbitrage.

The simplest case of an arbitrage might be for the same stock to sell at different prices in two markets. If the stock were selling at \$52 in one market and \$50 in another, an arbitrageur would buy the stock at \$50 in the one market and sell it at \$52 in the other. This trade would net an immediate \$2 profit at no risk and would not require the commitment of any of the investor's capital. This outcome would be a strong motivation for all arbitrageurs, and their combined actions would force the lower price up and the higher price down until the prices converged.

But what would be the final price? It is entirely possible that \$50 is the true fundamental value and \$52 is too high. Or \$52 could be the true fundamental value and \$50 is too low. Or the true fundamental value could lie somewhere between the two. Arbitrage does not tell us the true fundamental value. It is not an *absolute* valuation methodology, such as the discounted cash flow equity valuation model. It is a *relative* valuation methodology. It tells us the correct price of one asset or derivative *relative to* another asset or derivative.

Now, consider another situation, illustrated in Exhibit 6. Observe that we have one stock, AXE Electronics, that today is worth \$50 and one period later will be worth either \$75 or \$40. We will denote these prices as AXE = \$50, AXE^+ = \$75, and AXE^- = \$40. Another stock, BYF Technology, is today worth \$38 and one period later will be worth \$60 or \$32. Thus, BYF = \$38, BYF^+ = \$60, and BYF^- = \$32. Assume that the risk-free borrowing and lending rate is 4%. Also assume no dividends are paid on either stock during the period covered by this example.

Exhibit 6 Arbitrage Opportunity with Stock AXE, Stock BYF, and a Risk-Free Bond

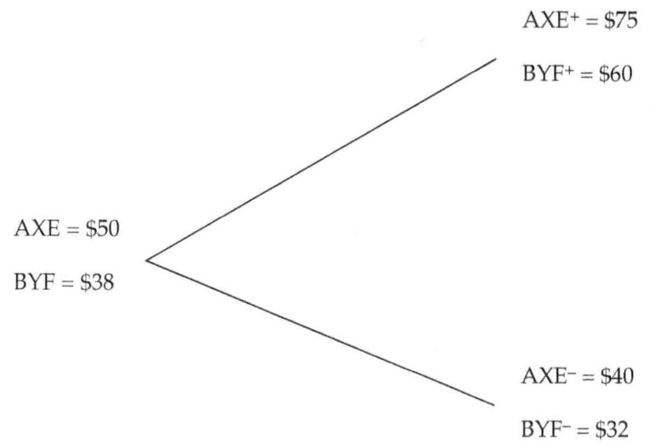

Note: The risk-free rate is 4%.

The opportunity exists to make a profit at no risk without committing any of our funds, as demonstrated in Exhibit 7. Suppose we borrow 100 shares of stock AXE, which is selling for \$50, and sell them short, thereby receiving \$5,000. We take \$4,750 and purchase 125 shares of stock BYF (125 × \$38 = \$4,750). We invest the remaining \$250 in risk-free bonds at 4%. This transaction will not require us to use any funds of our own: The short sale will be sufficient to fund the investment in BYF and leave money to invest in risk-free bonds.

Exhibit 7 Execution of Arbitrage Transaction with Stock AXE, Stock BYF, and a Risk-Free Bond

(AXE = \$50, BYF = \$38)

Sell short 100 shares of AXE for \$5,000

Buy 125 shares of BYF for \$4,750

Invest \$250 in risk-free bonds at 4%

Net investment: \$0

(AXE^+ = \$75, BYF^+ = \$60)

Sell 125 shares of BYF for \$7,500

Buy back 100 shares of AXE for \$7,500 to cover short position

Bonds are worth \$250(1.04) = \$260

Total value = \$260

(AXE^- = \$40, BYF^- = \$32)

Sell 125 shares of BYF for \$4,000

Buy back 100 shares of AXE for \$4,000 to cover short position

Bonds are worth \$250(1.04) = \$260

Total value = \$260

If the top outcome in Exhibit 7 occurs, we sell the 125 shares of BYF for 125 × \$60 = \$7,500. This amount is sufficient to buy back the 100 shares of AXE, which is selling for \$75. But we will also have the bonds, which are worth \$250 × 1.04 = \$260. If the bottom outcome occurs, we sell the 125 shares of BYF for 125 × \$32 = \$4,000—enough money to buy back the 100 shares of AXE, which is selling for \$40. Again, we will have the risk-free bonds, worth \$260. Regardless of the outcome, we end up with \$260.

Recall that we invested no money of our own and end up with a sure \$260. It should be apparent that this transaction is extremely attractive, so everyone would do it. The combined actions of multiple investors would drive down the price of AXE and/or drive up the price of BYF until an equilibrium is reached, at which point this transaction would no longer be profitable. As noted earlier, we cannot be sure of the correct fundamental price, but let us assume that BYF's price remains constant. Then AXE would fall to \$47.50. Alternatively, if we assume that AXE's price remains constant, then the price of BYF would rise to \$40. These values are obtained by noting that the prices for both outcomes occur according to the ratio 1.25 (\$75/\$60 = 1.25; \$40/\$32 = 1.25). Thus, their initial prices should be consistent with that ratio. If BYF is \$38, AXE should be \$38 × 1.25 = \$47.50. If AXE is \$50, BYF should be \$40.00 because \$40.00 × 1.25 = \$50. Of course, the two prices could settle in between. Arbitrage is only a relative pricing method. It prices the two stocks in relation to each other but does not price either on the basis of its own fundamentals.

Of course, this example is extremely simplified. Clearly, a stock price can change to more than two other prices. Also, if a given stock is at one price, another stock may be at any other price. We have created a simple case here to illustrate a point. But as you will learn later in the curriculum, when derivatives are involved, the simplification here is relatively safe. As we know, the price of a derivative is determined by the price of the underlying. Hence, when the underlying is at one particular price, the derivative's price will be determined by that price. The two assets need not be two stocks; one can be a stock and the other can be a derivative on the stock.

To see that point, consider another type of arbitrage opportunity that involves a forward contract. Recall from the previous example that at the start, AXE sells for \$50. Suppose we borrow \$50 at 4% interest by issuing a risk-free bond, use the money to buy one share of stock AXE, and simultaneously enter into a forward contract to sell this share at a price of $54 one period later. The stock will then move to either $75 or $40 in the next period. The forward contract requires that we deliver the stock and accept $54 for it. And of course, we will owe $50 × 1.04 = $52 on the loan.

Now consider the two outcomes. Regardless of the outcome, the end result is the same. The forward contract fixes the delivery price of the stock at $54:

AXE goes to $75	
Deliver stock to settle forward contract	+ $54
Pay back loan	– $52
Net	+ $2
AXE goes to $40	
Deliver stock to settle forward contract	+ $54
Pay back loan	– $52
Net	+ $2

In either case, we made $2, free and clear. In fact, we can even accommodate the possibility of more than two future prices for AXE and we will always make $2.[17] The key point is that we faced no risk and did not have to invest any of our own money, but ended up with $2, which is clearly a good trade. The $2 is an arbitrage profit. But where did it originate?

It turns out that the forward price, $54, was an inappropriate price given current market conditions. In fact, it was just an arbitrary price made up to illustrate the point. To eliminate the opportunity to earn the $2 profit, the forward price should be $52, which is equal, not coincidentally, to the amount owed on the loan. It is also no coincidence that $52 is the price of the asset increased by the rate of interest. We will cover this point later in the curriculum, but for now consider that you have just seen your first derivative pricing model.[18]

Of course, many market participants would do this transaction as long as it generated an arbitrage profit. These forces of arbitrage would either push the forward price down or the stock price up, or both, until an equilibrium is reached that eliminates the opportunity to profit at no risk with no commitment of one's own funds.

To summarize, the forces of arbitrage in financial markets assure us that the same asset cannot sell for different prices, nor can two equivalent combinations of assets that produce the same results sell for different prices. Realistically, some arbitrage opportunities can exist on a temporary basis, but they will be quickly exploited, bringing relative prices back in line with each other. Other apparent arbitrage opportunities will be too small to warrant exploiting.

Not to be naive, however, we must acknowledge that there is a large industry of people who call themselves arbitrageurs. So, how can such an industry exist if there are no opportunities for riskless profit? One explanation is that most of the arbitrage transactions are more complex than the simple examples used here. Many involve estimating information, which can result in differing opinions. Arbitrage involving options, for example, usually requires an estimate of a stock's volatility. Different

17 A good study suggestion is to try this example with any future stock price. You should get the same result, a $2 risk-free profit.

18 This illustration is the quick look at forward pricing alluded to in Section 3.1.1.

participants have different opinions about the volatility. It is quite possible that the two counterparties trading with each other believe that each is arbitraging against the other.[19]

But more importantly, the absence of arbitrage opportunities is upheld, ironically, only if participants believe that arbitrage opportunities do exist. If traders believe that no opportunities exist to earn arbitrage profits, then traders will not follow market prices and compare those prices with what they ought to be. Thus, eliminating arbitrage opportunities requires that participants be alert in watching for arbitrage opportunities. In other words, strange as it may sound, disbelief and skepticism concerning the absence of arbitrage opportunities are required for the no-arbitrage rule to be upheld.

Markets in which arbitrage opportunities are either nonexistent or quickly eliminated are relatively efficient markets. Recall that efficient markets are those in which it is not possible to consistently earn returns in excess of those that would be fair compensation for the risk assumed. Although abnormal returns can be earned in a variety of ways, arbitrage profits are definitely examples of abnormal returns. Thus, they are the most egregious violations of the principle of market efficiency.

Throughout the derivatives component of the CFA curriculum, we will use the principle of arbitrage as a dominant theme and assume that arbitrage opportunities cannot exist for any significant length of time nor can any one investor consistently capture them. Thus, prices must conform to models that assume no arbitrage. But we do not want to take the absence of arbitrage opportunities so seriously that we give up and believe that arbitrage opportunities never exist. Otherwise, they will arise and someone else will take them. Consider the rule of arbitrage a law that will be broken from time to time but one that holds far more often than not and one that should be understood and respected.

EXAMPLE 9

Arbitrage

1 Which of the following is a result of arbitrage?
  - A The law of one price
  - B The law of similar prices
  - C The law of limited profitability

2 When an arbitrage opportunity exists, what happens in the market?
  - A The combined actions of all arbitrageurs force the prices to converge.
  - B The combined actions of arbitrageurs result in a locked-limit situation.
  - C The combined actions of all arbitrageurs result in sustained profits to all.

3 Which of the following accurately defines arbitrage?
  - A An opportunity to make a profit at no risk
  - B An opportunity to make a profit at no risk and with the investment of no capital

---

19 In reality, many of the transactions that arbitrageurs do are not really arbitrage. They are quite speculative. For example, many people call themselves arbitrageurs because they buy companies that are potential takeover targets and sell the companies they think will be the buyers. This transaction is not arbitrage by any stretch of the definition. Some transactions are called "risk arbitrage," but this term is an oxymoron. As an investment professional, you should simply be prepared for such misuses of words, which simply reflect the flexibility of language.

C An opportunity to earn a return in excess of the return appropriate for the risk assumed

4 Which of the following ways best describes how arbitrage contributes to market efficiency?

A Arbitrage penalizes those who trade too rapidly.

B Arbitrage equalizes the risks taken by all market participants.

C Arbitrage improves the rate at which prices converge to their relative fair values.

Solution to 1:

A is correct. Arbitrage forces equivalent assets to have a single price. There is nothing called the law of similar prices or the law of limited profitability.

Solution to 2:

A is correct. Prices converge because of the heavy demand for the cheaper asset and the heavy supply of the more expensive asset. Profits are not sustained, and, in fact, they are eradicated as prices converge. Locked-limit is a condition in the futures market and has nothing to do with arbitrage.

Solution to 3:

B is correct. An opportunity to profit at no risk could merely describe the purchase of a risk-free asset. An opportunity to earn a return in excess of the return appropriate for the risk assumed is a concept studied in portfolio management and is often referred to as an abnormal return. It is certainly desirable but is hardly an arbitrage because it requires the assumption of risk and the investment of capital. Arbitrage is risk free and requires no capital because selling the overpriced asset produces the funds to buy the underpriced asset.

Solution to 4:

C is correct. Arbitrage imposes no penalties on rapid trading; in fact, it tends to reward those who trade rapidly to take advantage of arbitrage opportunities. Arbitrage has no effect of equalizing risk among market participants. Arbitrage does result in an acceleration of price convergence to fair values relative to instruments with equivalent payoffs.

SUMMARY

This first reading on derivatives introduces you to the basic characteristics of derivatives, including the following points:

- A derivative is a financial instrument that derives its performance from the performance of an underlying asset.
- The underlying asset, called the underlying, trades in the cash or spot markets and its price is called the cash or spot price.
- Derivatives consist of two general classes: forward commitments and contingent claims.
- Derivatives can be created as standardized instruments on derivatives exchanges or as customized instruments in the over-the-counter market.

- Exchange-traded derivatives are standardized, highly regulated, and transparent transactions that are guaranteed against default through the clearinghouse of the derivatives exchange.
- Over-the-counter derivatives are customized, flexible, and more private and less regulated than exchange-traded derivatives, but are subject to a greater risk of default.
- A forward contract is an over-the-counter derivative contract in which two parties agree that one party, the buyer, will purchase an underlying asset from the other party, the seller, at a later date and at a fixed price they agree upon when the contract is signed.
- A futures contract is similar to a forward contract but is a standardized derivative contract created and traded on a futures exchange. In the contract, two parties agree that one party, the buyer, will purchase an underlying asset from the other party, the seller, at a later date and at a price agreed on by the two parties when the contract is initiated. In addition, there is a daily settling of gains and losses and a credit guarantee by the futures exchange through its clearinghouse.
- A swap is an over-the-counter derivative contract in which two parties agree to exchange a series of cash flows whereby one party pays a variable series that will be determined by an underlying asset or rate and the other party pays either a variable series determined by a different underlying asset or rate or a fixed series.
- An option is a derivative contract in which one party, the buyer, pays a sum of money to the other party, the seller or writer, and receives the right to either buy or sell an underlying asset at a fixed price either on a specific expiration date or at any time prior to the expiration date.
- A call is an option that provides the right to buy the underlying.
- A put is an option that provides the right to sell the underlying.
- Credit derivatives are a class of derivative contracts between two parties, the credit protection buyer and the credit protection seller, in which the latter provides protection to the former against a specific credit loss.
- A credit default swap is the most widely used credit derivative. It is a derivative contract between two parties, a credit protection buyer and a credit protection seller, in which the buyer makes a series of payments to the seller and receives a promise of compensation for credit losses resulting from the default of a third party.
- An asset-backed security is a derivative contract in which a portfolio of debt instruments is assembled and claims are issued on the portfolio in the form of tranches, which have different priorities of claims on the payments made by the debt securities such that prepayments or credit losses are allocated to the most-junior tranches first and the most-senior tranches last.
- Derivatives can be combined with other derivatives or underlying assets to form hybrids.
- Derivatives are issued on equities, fixed-income securities, interest rates, currencies, commodities, credit, and a variety of such diverse underlyings as weather, electricity, and disaster claims.
- Derivatives facilitate the transfer of risk, enable the creation of strategies and payoffs not otherwise possible with spot assets, provide information about the spot market, offer lower transaction costs, reduce the amount of capital required, are easier than the underlyings to go short, and improve the efficiency of spot markets.

- Derivatives are sometimes criticized for being a form of legalized gambling and for leading to destabilizing speculation, although these points can generally be refuted.
- Derivatives are typically priced by forming a hedge involving the underlying asset and a derivative such that the combination must pay the risk-free rate and do so for only one derivative price.
- Derivatives pricing relies heavily on the principle of storage, meaning the ability to hold or store the underlying asset. Storage can incur costs but can also generate cash, such as dividends and interest.
- Arbitrage is the condition that two equivalent assets or derivatives or combinations of assets and derivatives sell for different prices, leading to an opportunity to buy at the low price and sell at the high price, thereby earning a risk-free profit without committing any capital.
- The combined actions of arbitrageurs bring about a convergence of prices. Hence, arbitrage leads to the law of one price: Transactions that produce equivalent results must sell for equivalent prices.

PRACTICE PROBLEMS

1 A derivative is *best* described as a financial instrument that derives its performance by:
  A passing through the returns of the underlying.
  B replicating the performance of the underlying.
  C transforming the performance of the underlying.
2 Derivatives are similar to insurance in that both:
  A have an indefinite life span.
  B allow for the transfer of risk from one party to another.
  C allow for the transformation of the underlying risk itself.
3 A beneficial opportunity created by the derivatives market is the ability to:
  A adjust risk exposures to desired levels.
  B generate returns proportional to movements in the underlying.
  C simultaneously take long positions in multiple highly liquid fixed-income securities.
4 Compared with exchange-traded derivatives, over-the-counter derivatives would *most likely* be described as:
  A standardized.
  B less transparent.
  C more transparent.
5 Exchange-traded derivatives are:
  A largely unregulated.
  B traded through an informal network.
  C guaranteed by a clearinghouse against default.
6 The clearing and settlement process of an exchange-traded derivatives market:
  A provides a credit guarantee.
  B provides transparency and flexibility.
  C takes longer than that of most securities exchanges.
7 Which of the following statements *best* portrays the full implementation of post-financial-crisis regulations in the OTC derivatives market?
  A Transactions are no longer private.
  B Most transactions need to be reported to regulators.
  C All transactions must be cleared through central clearing agencies.
8 A characteristic of forward commitments is that they:
  A provide linear payoffs.
  B do not depend on the outcome or payoff of an underlying asset.
  C provide one party the right to engage in future transactions on terms agreed on in advance.
9 In contrast to contingent claims, forward contracts:
  A have their prices chosen by the participants.
  B could end in default by either party.

C can be exercised by physical or cash delivery.

10 Which of the following statements *best* describes the payoff from a forward contract?

A The buyer has more to gain going long than the seller has to lose going short.

B The buyer profits if the price of the underlying at expiration exceeds the forward price.

C The gains from owning the underlying versus owning the forward contract are equivalent.

11 Which of the following statements regarding the settlement of forward contracts is correct?

A Contract settlement by cash has different economic effects from those of a settlement by delivery.

B Non-deliverable forwards and contracts for differences have distinct settlement procedures.

C At cash settlement, when the long party acquires the asset in the market, it effectively pays the forward price.

12 A futures contract is *best* described as a contract that is:

A standardized.

B subject to credit risk.

C marked to market throughout the trading day.

13 Which of the following statements explains a characteristic of futures price limits? Price limits:

A help the clearinghouse manage its credit exposure.

B can typically be expanded intra-day by willing traders.

C establish a band around the final trade of the previous day.

14 Which of the following statements describes an aspect of margin accounts for futures?

A The maintenance margin is always less than the initial margin.

B The initial margin required is typically at least 10% of the futures price.

C A margin call requires a deposit sufficient to raise the account balance to the maintenance margin.

15 Which of the following factors is shared by forwards and futures contracts?

A Timing of profits

B Flexible settlement arrangements

C Nearly equivalent profits by expiration

16 Which of the following derivatives is classified as a contingent claim?

A Futures contracts

B Interest rate swaps

C Credit default swaps

17 In contrast to contingent claims, forward commitments provide the:

A right to buy or sell the underlying asset in the future.

B obligation to buy or sell the underlying asset in the future.

C promise to provide credit protection in the event of default.

18 Which of the following derivatives provide payoffs that are non-linearly related to the payoffs of the underlying?

A Options
B Forwards
C Interest-rate swaps

19 An interest rate swap is a derivative contract in which:
A two parties agree to exchange a series of cash flows.
B the credit seller provides protection to the credit buyer.
C the buyer has the right to purchase the underlying from the seller.

20 Forward commitments subject to default are:
A forwards and futures.
B futures and interest rate swaps.
C interest rate swaps and forwards.

21 A swap is:
A more like a forward than a futures contract.
B subject to simultaneous default by both parties.
C based on an exchange of two series of fixed cash flows.

22 A plain vanilla interest rate swap is also known as:
A a basis swap.
B a fixed-for-floating swap.
C an overnight indexed swap.

23 The notional principal of a swap is:
A not exchanged in the case of an interest rate swap.
B a fixed amount whenever it is matched with a loan.
C equal to the amount owed by one swap party to the other.

24 Which of the following derivatives is *least likely* to have a value of zero at initiation of the contract?
A Futures
B Options
C Forwards

25 The buyer of an option has a contingent claim in the sense that the option creates:
A a right.
B an obligation.
C a linear payoff with respect to gains and losses of the underlying.

26 Which of the following options grants the holder the right to purchase the underlying prior to expiration?
A American-style put option
B European-style call option
C American-style call option

27 A credit derivative is a derivative contract in which the:
A clearinghouse provides a credit guarantee to both the buyer and the seller.
B seller provides protection to the buyer against the credit risk of a third party.
C the buyer and seller provide a performance bond at initiation of the contract.

28 The junior and senior tranches of an asset-backed security:

A have equivalent expected returns.

B have claims on separate underlying portfolios.

C may be differentially impacted by prepayments or credit losses.

29 In a declining interest rate environment, compared with a CMO's Class A tranche, its Class C tranche will be repaid:

A earlier.

B at the same pace.

C later.

30 For a given CDO, which of the following tranches is *most likely* to have the highest expected return?

A Equity

B Senior

C Mezzanine

31 Which of the following derivatives allows an investor to pay the return on a stock index and receive a fixed rate?

A Equity swap

B Stock warrant

C Index futures contract

32 Which of the following is *most likely* the underlying of a plain vanilla interest rate swap?

A 180-day Libor

B 10-year US Treasury bond

C Bloomberg Barclay's US Aggregate Bond Index

33 Currency swaps are:

A rarely used.

B commonly used to manage interest rate risk.

C executed by two parties making a series of interest rate payments in the same currency.

34 Which of the following statements regarding commodity derivatives is correct?

A The primary commodity derivatives are futures.

B Commodities are subject to a set of well-defined risk factors.

C Commodity traders and financial traders today are distinct groups within the financial world.

35 Compared with the underlying spot market, derivative markets are *more likely* to have:

A greater liquidity.

B higher transaction costs.

C higher capital requirements.

36 Which of the following characteristics is *least likely* to be a benefit associated with using derivatives?

A More effective management of risk

B Payoffs similar to those associated with the underlying

C Greater opportunities to go short compared with the spot market

37 Which of the following statements *best* represents information discovery in the futures market?

A The futures price is predictive.

B Information flows more slowly into the futures market than into the spot market.

C The futures market reveals the price that the holder of the asset can take to avoid uncertainty.

38 The derivative markets tend to:

A transfer liquidity from the broader financial markets.

B not reflect fundamental value after it is restored in the underlying market.

C offer a less costly way to exploit mispricing in comparison to other free and competitive financial markets.

39 Which of the following statements *most likely* contributes to the view that derivatives have some role in causing financial crashes?

A Derivatives are the primary means by which leverage and related excessive risk is brought into financial markets.

B Growth in the number of investors willing to speculate in derivatives markets leads to excessive speculative trading.

C Restrictions on derivatives, such as enhanced collateral requirements and credit mitigation measures, in the years leading up to crashes introduce market rigidity.

40 In contrast to gambling, derivatives speculation:

A has a positive public image.

B is a form of financial risk taking.

C benefits the financial markets and thus society.

41 Derivatives may contribute to financial contagion because of the:

A centrally cleared nature of OTC derivatives.

B associated significant costs and high capital requirements.

C reliance by derivatives speculators on large amounts of leverage.

42 The complex nature of derivatives has led to:

A reliable financial models of derivatives markets.

B widespread trust in applying scientific principles to derivatives.

C financial industry employment of mathematicians and physicists.

43 Which of the following is *most likely* to be a destabilizing consequence of speculation using derivatives?

A Increased defaults by speculators and creditors

B Market price swings resulting from arbitrage activities

C The creation of trading strategies that result in asymmetric performance

44 The law of one price is *best* described as:

A the true fundamental value of an asset.

B earning a risk-free profit without committing any capital.

C two assets that will produce the same cash flows in the future must sell for equivalent prices.

45 Arbitrage opportunities exist when:

A two identical assets or derivatives sell for different prices.

B combinations of the underlying asset and a derivative earn the risk-free rate.

C arbitrageurs simultaneously buy takeover targets and sell takeover acquirers.

For questions 46–49, consider a call option selling for $4 in which the exercise price is $50.

46 Determine the value at expiration and the profile for a *buyer* if the price of the underlying at expiration is $55.

A $5

B $1

C –$1

47 Determine the value at expiration and the profile for a *buyer* if the price of the underlying at expiration is $48.

A –$4

B $0

C $2

48 Determine the value at expiration and the profit for a *seller* if the price of the underling at expiration is $49.

A $4

B $0

C –$1

49 Determine the value at expiration and the profit for a *seller* if the price of the underling at expiration is $52.

A –$2

B $5

C $2

For questions 50–52, consider the following scenario:

Suppose you believe that the price of a particular underlying, currently selling at $99, is going to increase substantially in the next six months. You decide to purchase a call option expiring in six months on this underlying. The call option has an exercise price of $105 and sells for $7.

50 Determine the profit if the price of the underlying six months from now is $99.

A $6

B $0

C –$7

51 Determine the profit if the price of the underlying six months from now is $112.

A $7

B $0

C –$3

52 Determine the profit if the price of the underlying six months from now is $115.

A $0

B $3

C −$3

For questions 53–55, consider the following scenario:

Suppose you believe that the price of a particular underlying, currently selling at $99, is going to decrease substantially in the next six months. You decide to purchase a put option expiring in six months on this underlying. The put option has an exercise price of $95 and sells for $5.

53 Determine the profit for you if the price of the underlying six months from now is $100.

A $0

B $5

C −$5

54 Determine the profit for you if the price of the underlying six months from now is $95.

A $0

B $5

C −$5

55 Determine the profit for you if the price of the underlying six months from now is $85.

A $10

B $5

C $0

SOLUTIONS

1 C is correct. A derivative is a financial instrument that transforms the performance of the underlying. The transformation of performance function of derivatives is what distinguishes it from mutual funds and exchange traded funds that pass through the returns of the underlying.

A is incorrect because derivatives, in contrast to mutual funds and exchange traded funds, do not simply pass through the returns of the underlying at payout. B is incorrect because a derivative transforms rather than replicates the performance of the underlying.

2 B is correct. Insurance is a financial contract that provides protection against loss. The party bearing the risk purchases an insurance policy, which transfers the risk to the other party, the insurer, for a specified period of time. The risk itself does not change, but the party bearing it does. Derivatives allow for this same type of risk transfer.

A is incorrect because derivatives, like insurance, have a definite, as opposed to indefinite, life span and expire on a specified date.

C is incorrect because both derivatives and insurance allow for the transfer of risk from one party (the purchaser of the insurance policy or of a derivative) to another party (the insurer or a derivative seller), for a specified period of time. The risk itself does not change, but the party bearing it does.

3 A is correct. Derivatives allow market participants to practice more effective risk management, a process by which an organization, or individual, defines the level of risk it wishes to take, measures the level of risk it is taking, and adjusts the latter to equal the former.

B is incorrect because derivatives are characterized by a relatively high degree of leverage, meaning that participants in derivatives transactions usually have to invest only a small amount, as opposed to a large amount, of their own capital relative to the value of the underlying. This allows participants to generate returns that are disproportional, as opposed to proportional, to movements in the underlying.

C is incorrect because derivatives are not needed to copy strategies that can be implemented with the underlying on a standalone basis. Rather, derivatives can be used to create strategies that cannot be implemented with the underlying alone. Simultaneously taking long positions in multiple highly liquid fixed-income securities is a strategy that can be implemented with the underlying securities on a standalone basis.

4 B is correct. Over-the counter-derivatives markets are customized and mostly unregulated. As a result, over-the-counter markets are less transparent in comparison with the high degree of transparency and standardization associated with exchange-traded derivative markets.

A is incorrect because exchange-traded derivatives are standardized, whereas over-the counter derivatives are customized. C is incorrect because exchange-traded derivatives are characterized by a high degree of transparency because all transactions are disclosed to exchanges and regulatory agencies, whereas over-the-counter derivatives are relatively opaque.

5 C is correct. Exchanged-traded derivatives are guaranteed by a clearinghouse against default.

A is incorrect because traded derivatives are characterized by a relatively high degree of regulation. B is incorrect because the terms of exchange-traded derivatives terms are specified by the exchange.

6 A is correct. The clearing and settlement process of derivative transactions provides a credit guarantee.

B is incorrect because although the exchange markets are said to have transparency, they also involve standardization. That entails a loss of flexibility, with participants limited to only those transactions permitted on the exchange.

C is incorrect because derivatives exchanges clear and settle all contracts overnight, which is faster than most securities exchanges, which require two business days.

7 B is correct. With full implementation of these regulations in the OTC derivatives market, most OTC transactions need to be reported to regulators.

A is incorrect because although under full implementation of the regulations information on most OTC transactions needs to be reported to regulators, many transactions retain a degree of privacy with lower transparency.

C is incorrect because although under full implementation of new regulations a number of OTC transactions have to be cleared through central clearing agencies, there are exemptions that cover a significant percentage of derivative transactions.

8 A is correct because forward commitments provide linear payoffs.

B is incorrect because forward commitments depend on the outcome or payoff of an underlying asset.

C is incorrect because forward commitments obligate parties to make (not provide the right to engage) a final payment contingent on the performance of the underlying.

9 B is correct. In a forward contract, either party could default, whereas in a contingent claim, default is possible only from the short to the long.

A is incorrect because the forward price is set in the pricing of the contract such that the starting contract value is zero, unlike contingent claims, under which parties can select any starting value.

C is incorrect because both forward contracts and contingent claims can be settled by either physical or cash delivery.

10 B is correct. The buyer is obligated to pay the forward price $F_0(T)$ at expiration and receives an asset worth S_T, the price of the underlying. The contract effectively pays off $S_T - F_0(T)$, the value of the contract at expiration. The buyer therefore profits if $S_T > F_0(T)$.

A is incorrect because the long and the short are engaged in a zero-sum game. This is a type of competition in which one participant's gains are the other's losses, with their payoffs effectively being mirror images.

C is incorrect because although the gain from owning the underlying and the gain from owning the forward are both driven by S_T, the price of the underlying at expiration, they are not the same value. The gain from owning the underlying would be $S_T - S_0$, the change in its price, whereas the gain from owning the forward would be $S_T - F_0(T)$, the value of the forward at expiration.

11 C is correct. In the case of cash settlement, the long can acquire the asset, effectively paying the forward price, $F_0(T)$.

A is incorrect because forward contracts settled by cash or by delivery have the same economic effect.

B is incorrect because both non-deliverable forwards and contracts for differences can settle by an exchange of cash.

12 A is correct. A futures contract is a standardized derivative contract.

B is incorrect because through its clearinghouse the futures exchange provides a credit guarantee that it will make up a loss in the event a losing party cannot pay.

C is incorrect because a futures contract is marked to market at the end of each day, a process in which the futures clearinghouse determines an average of the final futures trade of the day and designates that price as the settlement price.

13 A is correct. Price limits are important in helping the clearinghouse manage its credit exposure. Sharply moving prices make it more difficult for the clearinghouse to collect from parties losing money.

B is incorrect because typically the exchange rules allow for an expansion of price limits the next day (not intra-day) if traders are willing.

C is incorrect because price limits establish a band relative to the previous day's settlement price (not final trade).

14 A is correct. The maintenance margin is always significantly lower than the initial margin.

B is incorrect because the initial margin required is typically at most (not at least) 10% of the futures price.

C is incorrect because a margin call requires a deposit large enough to bring the balance up to the initial (not maintenance) margin.

15 C is correct. Comparing the derivatives, forward and futures contracts have nearly equivalent profits by the time of expiration of the forward.

A is incorrect because the timing of profits for a futures contract is different from that of forwards. Forwards realize the full amount at expiration, whereas futures contracts realize their profit in parts on a day-to-day basis.

B is incorrect because the settlement arrangements for the forwards can be agreed on at initiation and written in the contract based on the desires of the engaged parties. However, in the case of a futures contract, the exchange (not the engaged parties) specifies whether physical delivery or cash settlement applies.

16 C is correct. A credit default swap (CDS) is a derivative in which the credit protection seller provides protection to the credit protection buyer against the credit risk of a separate party. CDS are classified as a contingent claim.

A is incorrect because futures contracts are classified as forward commitments. B is incorrect because interest rate swaps are classified as forward commitments.

17 B is correct. Forward commitments represent an obligation to buy or sell the underlying asset at an agreed upon price at a future date.

A is incorrect because the right to buy or sell the underlying asset is a characteristic of contingent claims, not forward commitments. C is incorrect because a credit default swap provides a promise to provide credit protection to the credit protection buyer in the event of a credit event such as a default or credit downgrade and is classified as a contingent claim.

18 A is correct. Options are classified as a contingent claim which provides payoffs that are non-linearly related to the performance of the underlying.

B is incorrect because forwards are classified as a forward commitment, which provides payoffs that are linearly related to the performance of the underlying. C is incorrect because interest-rate swaps are classified as a forward commitment, which provides payoffs that are linearly related to the performance of the underlying.

19 A is correct. An interest rate swap is defined as a derivative in which two parties agree to exchange a series of cash flows: One set of cash flows is variable, and the other set can be variable or fixed.

B is incorrect because a credit derivative is a derivative contract in which the credit protection seller provides protection to the credit protection buyer. C is incorrect because a call option gives the buyer the right to purchase the underlying from the seller.

20 C is correct. Interest rate swaps and forwards are over-the-counter contracts that are privately negotiated and are both subject to default. Futures contracts are traded on an exchange, which provides a credit guarantee and protection against default.

A is incorrect because futures are exchange-traded contracts which provide daily settlement of gains and losses and a credit guarantee by the exchange through its clearinghouse. B is incorrect because futures are exchange-traded contracts which provide daily settlement of gains and losses and a credit guarantee by the exchange through its clearinghouse.

21 A is correct. A swap is a bit more like a forward contract than a futures contract in that it is an OTC contract, so it is privately negotiated and subject to default.

B is incorrect because in a swap, although either party can default, only one party can do so at a particular time. Money owed is based on the net owed by one party to the other, and only the party owing the greater amount can default to the counterparty owing the lesser amount.

C is incorrect because a swap involves an exchange between parties in which at least one party pays a variable series of cash flows determined by an underlying asset or rate.

22 B is correct. A plain vanilla swap is a fixed-for-floating interest rate swap, which is the most common type of swap.

A is incorrect because a basis swap is a transaction based on the TED spread (T-bills versus Eurodollars) and is not the same as a plain vanilla swap.

C is incorrect because an overnight indexed swap is a swap that is tied to a federal funds type of rate, reflecting the rate at which banks borrow overnight, and is not the same as a plain vanilla swap.

23 A is correct. The notional principal of a swap is not exchanged in the case of an interest rate swap.

B is incorrect because an amortizing loan will be matched with a swap with a pre-specified declining (not fixed) notional principal that matches the loan balance.

C is incorrect because the notional principal is equal to the loan balance. Although the loan has an actual balance (the amount owed by the borrower to the creditor), the swap does not have such a balance owed by one swap party to the other.

24 B is correct. The buyer of the option pays the option premium to the seller of the option at the initiation of the contract. The option premium represents the value of the option, whereas futures and forwards have a value of zero at the initiation of the contract.

A is incorrect because no money changes hands between parties at the initiation of the futures contract, thus the value of the futures contract is zero at initiation. C is incorrect because no money changes hands between parties at the initiation of the forward contract, thus the value of the forward contract is zero at initiation.

25 A is correct. A contingent claim, a derivative in which the outcome or payoff depends on the outcome or payoff of an underlying asset, has come to be associated with a right, but not an obligation, to make a final payment contingent on the performance of the underlying.

B is incorrect because an option, as a contingent claim, grants the right but not the obligation to buy or sell the underlying at a later date.

C is incorrect because the holder of an option has a choice of whether to exercise the option. This choice creates a payoff that transforms the underlying payoff in a more pronounced manner than does a forward, futures, or swap, which provide linear payoffs. Options are different in that they limit losses in one direction.

26 C is correct. The right to buy the underlying is referred to as a call option. Furthermore, options that can be exercised prior to the expiration date are referred to as American-style options.

A is incorrect because a put option grants the holder the right to sell, as opposed to buy, the underlying.

B is incorrect because European-style options can only be exercised at expiration.

27 B is correct. A credit derivative is a derivative contract in which the credit protection seller provides protection to the credit protection buyer against the credit risk of a third party.

A is incorrect because the clearinghouse provides a credit guarantee to both the buyer and the seller of a futures contract, whereas a credit derivative is between two parties, in which the credit protection seller provides a credit guarantee to the credit protection buyer. C is incorrect because futures contracts require that both the buyer and the seller of the futures contract provide a cash deposit for a portion of the futures transaction into a margin account, often referred to as a performance bond or good faith deposit.

28 C is correct. An asset-backed security is a derivative contract in which a portfolio of debt instruments is assembled and claims are issued on the portfolio in the form of tranches, which have different priorities of claims on the payments made by the debt securities such that prepayments or credit losses are allocated to the most junior tranches first and the most senior tranches last.

A is incorrect because the expected returns of the tranches vary according to the perceived credit risk, with the senior tranches having the highest credit quality and the junior tranches the lowest. Thus, the senior tranches have the lowest expected returns and the junior tranches have the highest. Notably, in a bond mutual fund or an ETF, all investors in the fund have equal claims, and so the rate of return earned by each investor is the same.

B is incorrect because an asset-backed security is a derivative contract in which a single portfolio of securities is assembled and claims are issued on the portfolio in the form of tranches.

29 A is correct. Lower interest rates entice homeowners to pay off their mortgages early because they can refinance at lower rates. The most junior tranche in a CMO will bear the first wave of prepayments until that tranche has been completely repaid its full principal investment. At that point, the next tranche will bear prepayments until that tranche has been fully repaid. Therefore, the Class C tranche of a CMO will be repaid before the more senior Class A tranche.

B is incorrect because the tranches, which have different priorities of claims on the principal payments made by the underlying mortgages, will see prepayments allocated to the most junior tranches first and the most senior tranches last.

C is incorrect because the most junior tranche in a CMO will bear the first wave of prepayments until that tranche has been completely repaid its full principal investment. At that point, the next tranche will bear prepayments until that tranche has been fully repaid. Therefore, the Class C tranche will be repaid prior to, not after, the Class A tranche.

30 A is correct. The expected returns of the tranches vary according to the perceived credit risk, with the senior tranches having the highest credit quality and the junior tranches the lowest. Thus, the senior tranches have the lowest expected returns and the junior tranches have the highest. The most junior tranche is sometimes called the "equity tranche."

B is incorrect because the senior tranches in a CDO have the lowest expected returns and the junior (or equity) tranches have the highest.

C is incorrect because the senior tranches in a CDO have the lowest expected returns and the junior (or equity) tranches have the highest. A mezzanine tranche is intermediate between the senior and junior tranches.

31 A is correct. Equity swaps, also known as index swaps, are quite popular and permit investors to pay the return on one stock index and receive the return on another index or a fixed rate.

B is incorrect because warrants are options that are sold directly to the public, allowing holders to exercise and buy shares directly from the company as opposed to using stock indexes to determine returns.

C is incorrect because although index derivatives in the form of options, forwards, futures, and swaps are very popular, paying the return on a stock index and receiving a fixed rate describes an equity swap (or index swap), not a futures contract.

32 A is correct. In a plain vanilla interest rate swap, an interest rate, such as Libor, serves as the underlying. A plain vanilla interest rate swap is one of many derivatives in which a rate, not the instrument that pays the rate, is the underlying.

B is incorrect because a plain vanilla interest rate swap is one of many derivatives in which a rate, not an instrument that pays a rate, is the underlying.

C is incorrect because a plain vanilla interest rate swap is one of many derivatives in which a rate, not an instrument (or index) that pays a rate, is the underlying.

33 B is correct. Because interest rates and currencies are both subject to change, a currency swap has two sources of risk. Furthermore, companies operating across borders are subject to both interest rate risk and currency risk, and currency swaps are commonly used to manage these risks.

A is incorrect because currency risk is a major factor in global financial markets, and the currency derivatives market is extremely large, as opposed to small.

C is incorrect because a currency swap is executed by two parties making a series of interest rate payments to each other in different currencies, as opposed to the same currency.

34 A is correct. The primary commodity derivatives are futures, but forwards, swaps, and options are also used.

B is incorrect because the commodity market is extremely large and subject to an almost unimaginable array of risks.

C is incorrect because commodity and financial traders have become relatively homogeneous since the creation of financial futures. Historically, commodity traders and financial traders were quite different groups, and there used to be a tendency to think of the commodity world as somewhat separate from the financial world.

35 A is correct. Derivative markets typically have greater liquidity than the underlying spot market as a result of the lower capital required to trade derivatives compared with the underlying. Derivatives also have lower transaction costs and lower capital requirements than the underlying.

B is incorrect because transaction costs for derivatives are lower than the underlying spot market. C is incorrect because derivatives markets have lower capital requirements than the underlying spot market.

36 B is correct. One of the benefits of derivative markets is that derivatives create trading strategies not otherwise possible in the underlying spot market, thus providing opportunities for more effective risk management than simply replicating the payoff of the underlying.

A is incorrect because effective risk management is one of the primary purposes associated with derivative markets. C is incorrect because one of the operational advantages associated with derivatives is that it is easier to go short compared to the underlying spot market.

37 C is correct. The futures market reveals the price that the holder of an asset could take and avoid the risk of uncertainty.

A is incorrect because although the futures price is sometimes thought of as predictive, it provides only a little more information than does a spot price and is not really a forecast of the futures spot price.

B is incorrect because by virtue of the fact that the futures market requires less capital, information can flow into the futures market before it gets into the spot market.

38 C is correct. When prices deviate from fundamental values, derivative markets offer a less costly way to exploit mispricing in comparison to other free and competitive financial markets.

A is incorrect because derivative markets tend to transfer liquidity to (not from) the broader financial markets, because investors are far more willing to trade if they can more easily manage their risk, trade at lower cost and with less capital, and go short more easily. An increased willingness to trade leads to a more liquid market.

B is incorrect because it is likely (not unlikely) that fundamental value will be reflected in the derivative markets both before and after it is restored in the underlying market owing to lower capital requirements and transaction costs in the derivative markets.

39 B is correct. Opponents of derivatives claim that excessive speculative trading brings instability to the markets. Defaults by speculators can lead to defaults by their creditors, their creditors' creditors, and so on.

A is incorrect because derivatives are one of many mechanisms through which excessive risk can be taken. There are many ways to take on leverage that look far less harmful but can be just as risky.

C is incorrect because responses to crashes and crises typically call for more rules and regulations restricting the use of derivatives, such as requiring more collateral and credit mitigation measures. Such rules and regulations are generally implemented after a crash and are directed at limiting government bailouts of the costs from derivatives risks.

40 C is correct. Derivatives trading brings extensive benefits to financial markets (low costs, low capital requirements, ease of going short, etc.) and thus benefits society as a whole. Gambling, on the other hand, typically benefits only a limited number of participants.

A is incorrect because the general image of speculators is not a good one. Speculators are often thought to be short-term traders who attempt to exploit temporary inefficiencies, caring little about long-term fundamental values.

B is incorrect because speculation and gambling are both forms of financial risk taking.

41 C is correct. Opponents argue that speculators use large amounts of leverage, thereby subjecting themselves and their creditors to substantial risk if markets do not move in their hoped-for direction. Defaults by speculators can then lead to defaults by their creditors, their creditors' creditors, and so on. These effects can, therefore, be systemic and reflect an epidemic contagion whereby instability can spread throughout markets and an economy, if not the entire world.

A is incorrect because central clearing of OTC derivatives, similar to how exchange-traded derivatives are cleared, is intended to lessen the risk of contagion.

B is incorrect because it is derivatives' low cost and low capital requirements, not high cost and high capital requirements, that opponents point to as contributing to an excessive amount of speculative trading that brings instability to the markets.

42 C is correct. Many derivatives are extremely complex and require a high-level understanding of mathematics. As a result, the financial industry employs many mathematicians, physicists, and computer scientists.

A is incorrect because scientists create models of markets by using scientific principles that often fail. For example, to a physicist modeling the movements of celestial bodies, the science is reliable and the physicist is unlikely to misapply the science. The same science applied to financial markets is far less reliable. Financial markets are driven by the actions of people who are not as consistent as the movements of celestial bodies.

B is incorrect because the complex nature of derivatives has made many distrust, as opposed to trust, derivatives, the people who work with them, and the scientific methods they use.

43 A is correct. The benefits of derivatives, such as low transaction costs, low capital requirements, use of leverage, and the ease in which participants can go short, also can result in excessive speculative trading. These activities can lead to defaults on the part of speculators and creditors.

B is incorrect because arbitrage activities tend to bring about a convergence of prices to intrinsic value. C is incorrect because asymmetric performance is not itself destabilizing.

44 C is correct. The law of one price occurs when market participants engage in arbitrage activities so that identical assets sell for the same price in different markets.

A is incorrect because the law of one price refers to identical assets. B is incorrect because it refers to arbitrage not the law of one price.

45 A is correct. Arbitrage opportunities exist when the same asset or two equivalent combinations of assets that produce the same results sell for different prices. When this situation occurs, market participants would buy the asset in the cheaper market and simultaneously sell it in the more expensive market, thus earning a riskless arbitrage profit without committing any capital.

B is incorrect because it is not the definition of an arbitrage opportunity. C is incorrect because it is not the definition of an arbitrage opportunity.

46 B is correct. $C_T = Max(0,S_T - X) = Max(0,55 - 50) = 5$

$\Pi = C_T - C_0 = 5 - 4 = 1$

47 A is correct. $C_T = Max(0,S_T - X) = Max(0,48 - 50) = 0$

$\Pi = C_T - C_0 = 0 - 4 = -4$

48 A is correct. $-C_T = -Max(0,S_T - X) = -Max(0,49 - 50) = 0$

$\Pi = -C_T + C_0 = -0 + 4 = 4$

49 C is correct. $-C_T = -Max(0,S_T - X) = -Max(0,52 - 50) = -2$

$\Pi = -C_T + C_0 = -2 + 4 = 2$

50 C is correct. $C_T = Max(0,S_T - X) = Max(0,99 - 105) = 0$

$\Pi = C_T - C_0 = 0 - 7 = -7$

51 B is correct. $C_T = Max(0,S_T - X) = Max(0,112 - 105) = 7$

$\Pi = C_T - C_0 = 7 - 7 = 0$

Note: $112 is the breakeven price

52 B is correct. $C_T = Max(0,S_T - X) = Max(0,115 - 105) = 10$

$\Pi = C_T - C_0 = 10 - 7 = 3$

53 C is correct. $C_T = Max(0,S_T - X) = Max(0,95 - 100) = 0$

$\Pi = C_T - C_0 = 0 - 5 = -5$

54 C is correct. $C_T = Max(0,S_T - X) = Max(0,95 - 95) = 0$

$\Pi = C_T - C_0 = 0 - 5 = -5$

55 B is correct. $C_T = Max(0,S_T - X) = Max(0,95 - 85) = 10$

$\Pi = C_T - C_0 = 10 - 5 = 5$

READING

49

Basics of Derivative Pricing and Valuation

by **Don M. Chance, PhD, CFA**

Don M. Chance, PhD, CFA, is at Louisiana State University (USA).

LEARNING OUTCOMES

Mastery	*The candidate should be able to:*
□	**a.** explain how the concepts of arbitrage, replication, and risk neutrality are used in pricing derivatives;
□	**b.** distinguish between value and price of forward and futures contracts;
□	**c.** calculate a forward price of an asset with zero, positive, or negative net cost of carry;
□	**d.** explain how the value and price of a forward contract are determined at expiration, during the life of the contract, and at initiation;
□	**e.** describe monetary and nonmonetary benefits and costs associated with holding the underlying asset and explain how they affect the value and price of a forward contract;
□	**f.** define a forward rate agreement and describe its uses;
□	**g.** explain why forward and futures prices differ;
□	**h.** explain how swap contracts are similar to but different from a series of forward contracts;
□	**i.** distinguish between the value and price of swaps;
□	**j.** explain the exercise value, time value, and moneyness of an option;
□	**k.** identify the factors that determine the value of an option and explain how each factor affects the value of an option;
□	**l.** explain put–call parity for European options;
□	**m.** explain put–call–forward parity for European options;
□	**n.** explain how the value of an option is determined using a one-period binomial model;
□	**o.** explain under which circumstances the values of European and American options differ.

1 INTRODUCTION

It is important to understand how prices of derivatives are determined. Whether one is on the buy side or the sell side, a solid understanding of pricing financial products is critical to effective investment decision making. After all, one can hardly determine what to offer or bid for a financial product, or any product for that matter, if one has no idea how its characteristics combine to create value.

Understanding the pricing of financial assets is important. Discounted cash flow methods and models, such as the capital asset pricing model and its variations, are useful for determining the prices of financial assets. The unique characteristics of derivatives, however, pose some complexities not associated with assets, such as equities and fixed-income instruments. Somewhat surprisingly, however, derivatives also have some simplifying characteristics. For example, as we will see in this reading, in well-functioning derivatives markets the need to determine risk premiums is obviated by the ability to construct a risk-free hedge. Correspondingly, the need to determine an investor's risk aversion is irrelevant for derivative pricing, although it is certainly relevant for pricing the underlying.

The purpose of this reading is to establish the foundations of derivative pricing on a basic conceptual level. The following topics are covered:

- How does the pricing of the underlying asset affect the pricing of derivatives?
- How are derivatives priced using the principle of arbitrage?
- How are the prices and values of forward contracts determined?
- How are futures contracts priced differently from forward contracts?
- How are the prices and values of swaps determined?
- How are the prices and values of European options determined?
- How does American option pricing differ from European option pricing?

This reading is organized as follows. Section 2 explores two related topics, the pricing of the underlying assets on which derivatives are created and the principle of arbitrage. Section 3 describes the pricing and valuation of forwards, futures, and swaps. Section 4 introduces the pricing and valuation of options. Section 5 provides a summary.

2 FUNDAMENTAL CONCEPTS OF DERIVATIVE PRICING

In this section, we will briefly review the concepts associated with derivatives, the types of derivatives, and the pricing principles of the underlying assets. We will also look at arbitrage, a critical concept that links derivative pricing to the price of the underlying.

2.1 Basic Derivative Concepts

The definition of a derivative is as follows:

> *A derivative is a financial instrument that derives its performance from the performance of an underlying asset.*

A derivative is created as a contract between two parties, the buyer and the seller. Derivatives trade in markets around the world, which include organized exchanges, where highly standardized and regulated versions exist, and over-the-counter markets, where customized and more lightly regulated versions trade. The basic characteristics of derivatives that influence pricing are not particularly related to where the derivatives trade, but are critically dependent on the types of derivatives.

The two principal types of derivatives are forward commitments and contingent claims. A forward commitment is an obligation to engage in a transaction in the spot market at a future date at terms agreed upon today.[1] By entering into a forward commitment, a party locks in the terms of a transaction that he or she will conduct later. The word "commitment" is critical here. A forward contract is a firm obligation.

There are three types of forward commitments: forward contracts, futures contracts, and swap contracts. These contracts can be referred to more simply as forwards, futures, and swaps.

> *A* **forward contract** *is an over-the-counter derivative contract in which two parties agree that one party, the buyer, will purchase an underlying asset from the other party, the seller, at a later date at a fixed price they agree upon when the contract is signed.*

> *A* **futures contract** *is a standardized derivative contract created and traded on a futures exchange in which two parties agree that one party, the buyer, will purchase an underlying asset from the other party, the seller, at a later date at a price agreed upon by the two parties when the contract is initiated and in which there is a daily settling of gains and losses and a credit guarantee by the futures exchange through its clearinghouse.*

> *A* **swap contract** *is an over-the-counter derivative contract in which two parties agree to exchange a series of cash flows whereby one party pays a variable series that will be determined by an underlying asset or rate and the other party pays either 1) a variable series determined by a different underlying asset or rate or 2) a fixed series.*

As these definitions illustrate, forwards and futures are similar. They both establish the terms of a spot transaction that will occur at a later date. Forwards are customized, less transparent, less regulated, and subject to higher counterparty default risk. Futures are standardized, more transparent, more regulated, and generally immune to counterparty default. A swap is equivalent to a series of forward contracts, a point that will be illustrated later.

A contingent claim is a derivative in which the outcome or payoff is determined by the outcome or payoff of an underlying asset, conditional on some event occurring. Contingent claims include options, credit derivatives, and asset-backed securities. Because credit derivatives and asset-backed securities are highly specialized, this reading will focus only on options.

Recall the definition of an option:

> *An* **option** *is a derivative contract in which one party, the buyer, pays a sum of money to the other party, the seller or writer, and receives the right to either buy or sell an underlying asset at a fixed price either on a specific expiration date or at any time prior to the expiration date.*

Options can be either customized over-the-counter contracts or standardized and traded on exchanges.

---

1 Remember that the term "spot market" refers to the market in which the underlying trades. A transaction in the spot market involves a buyer paying for an asset and receiving it right away or at least within a few days, given the normal time required to settle a financial transaction.

Because derivatives take their prices from the price of the underlying, it is important to first understand how the underlying is priced. We will approach the underlying from a slightly different angle, one that emphasizes the often-subtle costs of holding the underlying, which turn out to play a major role in derivative pricing.

2.2 Pricing the Underlying

The four main types of underlying on which derivatives are based are equities, fixed-income securities/interest rates, currencies, and commodities. Equities, fixed-income securities (but not interest rates), currencies, and commodities are all assets. An interest rate is not an asset, but it can be structured as the underlying of a derivative.[2]

Consider a generic underlying asset. This asset is something of value that you can own. Some assets are financial assets, such as equities, bonds, and currencies, and some are real assets, such as commodities (e.g., gold, oil, and agricultural products) and certain physical objects (e.g., houses, automobiles, and computers).

The price of a financial asset is often determined using a present value of future cash flows approach. The value of the financial asset is the expected future price plus any interim payments such as dividends or coupon interest discounted at a rate appropriate for the risk assumed. Such a definition presumes a period of time over which an investor anticipates holding an asset, known as the holding period. The investor forecasts the price expected to prevail at the end of the holding period as well as any cash flows that are expected to be earned over the holding period. He then takes that predicted future price and expected cash flows and finds their current value by discounting them to the present. Thereby, the investor arrives at a fundamental value for the asset and will compare that value with its current market price. Based on any differential relative to the cost of trading and his confidence in his valuation model, he will make a decision about whether to trade.

2.2.1 *The Formation of Expectations*

Let us first assume that the underlying does not pay interest or dividends, nor does it have any other cash flows attributable to holding the asset. Exhibit 1 illustrates the basic idea behind the valuation process. Using a probability distribution, the investor forecasts the future over a holding period spanning time 0 to time T. The center of the distribution is the expected price of the asset at time T, which we denote as $E(S_T)$, and represents the investor's prediction of the spot price at T. The investor knows there is risk, so this prediction is imperfect—hence the reason for the probability distribution. Nonetheless, at time 0 the investor makes her best prediction of the spot price at time T, which becomes the foundation for determining what she perceives to be the value of the asset.[3]

2 This is a good example of why it is best not to use the term "underlying *asset*" when speaking of derivatives. Not all derivatives have underlying assets, but all have underlyings, some of which are not assets. Some other examples of non-asset underlyings used in derivatives are weather, insurance claims, and shipping rates. There are also some derivatives in which the underlying is another derivative.

3 The distribution shown here is symmetrical and relatively similar to a normal distribution, but this characterization is for illustrative purposes only. We are making no assumptions about symmetry or normality at this point.

Exhibit 1 The Formation of Expectations for an Asset

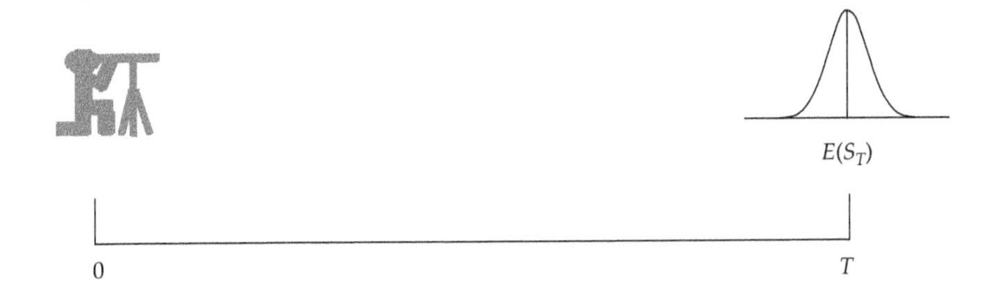

2.2.2 *The Required Rate of Return on the Underlying Asset*

To determine the value of the asset, this prediction must be converted into its price or present value. The specific procedure is to discount this expected future price, but that is the easy part. Determining the rate at which to discount the expected future price is the hard part. We use the symbol k to denote this currently unknown discount rate, which is often referred to as the required rate of return and sometimes the expected rate of return or just the expected return. At a minimum, that rate will include the risk-free rate of interest, which we denote as r. This rate represents the opportunity cost, or so-called time value of money, and reflects the price of giving up your money today in return for receiving more money later.

2.2.3 *The Risk Aversion of the Investor*

At this point, we must briefly discuss an important characteristic of investors: their degree of risk aversion. We can generally characterize three potential types of investors by how they feel about risk: risk averse, risk neutral, or risk seeking.

Risk-neutral investors are willing to engage in risky investments for which they expect to earn only the risk-free rate. Thus, they do not expect to earn a premium for bearing risk. For risk-averse investors, however, risk is undesirable, so they do not consider the risk-free rate an adequate return to compensate them for the risk. Thus, risk-averse investors require a risk premium, which is an increase in the expected return that is sufficient to justify the acceptance of risk. All things being equal, an investment with a higher risk premium will have a lower price. It is very important to understand, however, that risk premiums are not automatically earned. They are merely expectations. Actual outcomes can differ. Clearly stocks that decline in value did not earn risk premiums, even though someone obviously bought them with the expectation that they would. Nonetheless, risk premiums must exist in the long run or risk-averse investors would not accept the risk.

The third type of investor is one we must mention but do not treat as realistic. Risk seekers are those who prefer risk over certainty and will pay more to invest when there is risk, implying a negative risk premium. We almost always assume that investors prefer certainty over uncertainty, so we generally treat a risk-seeking investor as just a theoretical possibility and not a practical reality.[4]

4 People who gamble in casinos or play lotteries appear to be risk-seekers, given the advantage of the casino or the lottery organizer, but they are merely earning utility from the game itself, not necessarily from the expected financial outcome.

We will assume that investors are risk averse. To justify taking risk, risk-averse investors require a risk premium. We will use the Greek symbol λ (lambda) to denote the risk premium.[5]

2.2.4 *The Pricing of Risky Assets*

Exhibit 2 illustrates the process by which an investor obtains the current price, S_0, by discounting the expected future price of an asset with no interim cash flows, $E(S_T)$, by r (the risk-free rate) plus λ (the risk premium) over the period from 0 to T.

Exhibit 2 Discounting the Expected Future Price to Obtain the Current Price

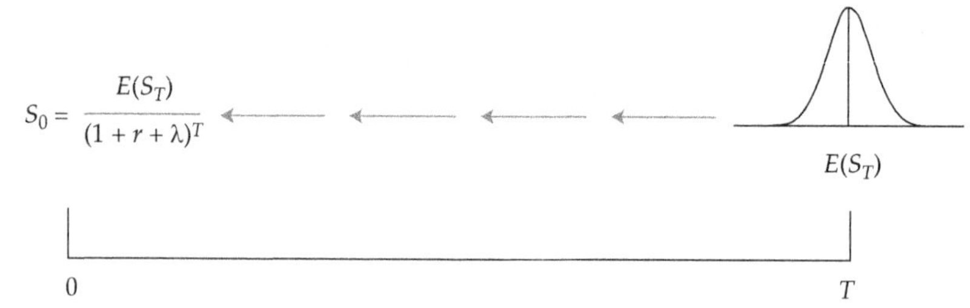

2.2.5 *Other Benefits and Costs of Holding an Asset*

Many assets generate benefits and some incur costs to their owners. Some of these costs are monetary and others are nonmonetary. The dividends paid by companies and coupon interest paid by borrowers on their bonds represent obvious benefits to the holders of these securities. With currencies representing investments that earn the risk-free rate in a foreign country, they too generate benefits in the form of interest. Barring default, interest payments on bonds and currencies are relatively certain, so we will treat them as such. Dividend payments are not certain, but dividends do tend to be fairly predictable. As such, we will make an assumption common to most derivative models that dividends are certain.[6]

There is substantial evidence that some commodities generate a benefit that is somewhat opaque and difficult to measure. This benefit is called the **convenience yield**. It represents a nonmonetary advantage of holding the asset. For most financial assets, convenience yields are either nonexistent or extremely limited. Financial assets do not possess beauty that might make a person enjoy owning them just to look at them. Convenience yields are primarily associated with commodities and generally exist as a result of difficulty in either shorting the commodity or unusually tight supplies. For example, if a commodity cannot be sold short without great difficulty or cost, the holder of the commodity has an advantage if market conditions suggest that the commodity should be sold. Also, if a commodity is in short supply, the holders of the commodity can sometimes extract a price premium that is believed by some to be higher than what would be justified in well-functioning markets. The spot price of the commodity could even be above the market's expectation of its future price, a condition that would seem to imply a negative expected return. This scenario raises the question of why anyone would want to hold the commodity if its expected return is negative. The convenience yield provides a possible explanation that attributes an

5 Although the risk-free rate is invariant with a country's economy, the risk premium varies with the amount of risk taken. Thus, while the risk-free rate is the same when applied to every investment, the risk premium is not the same for every investment.

6 Some derivative models incorporate uncertain dividends and interest, but those are beyond the scope of this introductory reading.

implied but non-financial expected return to the advantage of holding a commodity in short supply. The holder of the commodity has the ability to sell it when market conditions suggest that selling is advisable and short selling is difficult.

One cost incurred in owning commodities is the cost of storage. One could hardly own gold, oil, or wheat without incurring some costs in storing these assets. There are also costs incurred in protecting and insuring some commodities against theft or destruction. Depending on the commodity, these costs can be quite significant. For financial assets, however, the storage costs are so low that we can safely ignore them.

Finally, there is the opportunity cost of the money invested. If a person buys an asset, he forgoes interest on his money. The effect on this interest is reflected by compounding the price paid for the asset to a future value at the risk-free rate of interest. Thus, an investor who buys a stock that costs £50 in a market in which the risk-free rate is 4% will effectively have paid £50 × 1.04 = £52 a year later. Of course, the stock could be worth any value at that time, and any gain or loss should be determined in comparison to the effective price paid of £52.

As we described earlier, we determine the current price of an asset by discounting the expected future price by the sum of the risk-free rate (r) plus the risk premium (λ). When we introduce costs and benefits of holding the asset, we have to make an adjustment. With the exception of this opportunity cost of money, we will incorporate the effect of these costs and benefits by determining their value at the end of the holding period. Under the assumption that these costs and benefits are certain, we can then discount them at the risk-free rate to obtain their present value. There is a logic to doing it this way (i.e., finding their future value and discounting back to the present, as opposed to finding their present value directly). By finding their future value, we are effectively saying that the costs and benefits adjust the expected payoff at the end of the holding period. But because they are certain, we can discount their effects at the risk-free rate. So we have effectively just found their present value. The net effect is that the costs reduce the current price and the benefits increase the current price. We use the symbol θ (theta) to denote the present value of the costs and γ (gamma) as the present value of any benefits.

The net of the costs and benefits is often referred to by the term **carry**, or sometimes **cost of carry**. The holding, storing, or "carrying" of an asset is said to incur a net cost that is essentially what it takes to "carry" an asset. Exhibit 3 illustrates the effect in which the carry adjusts the price of an asset in the valuation process.

Exhibit 3 Pricing an Asset That Incurs Costs and Generates Benefits

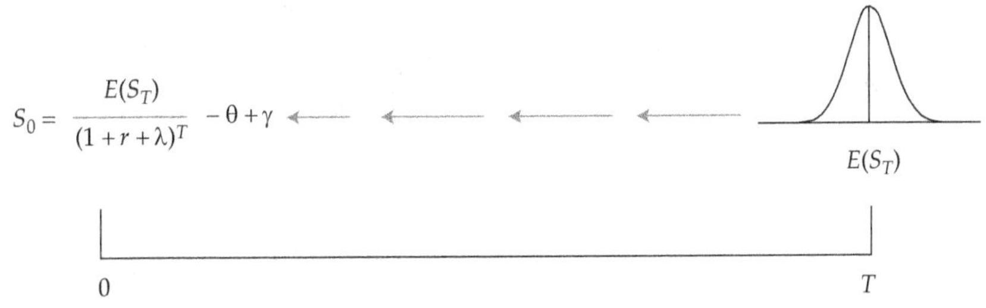

EXAMPLE 1

Pricing the Spot Asset

1 Which of the following factors does **not** affect the spot price of an asset that has no interim costs or benefits?

A The time value of money

B The risk aversion of investors

C The price recently paid by other investors

2 Which of the following does **not** represent a benefit of holding an asset?

A The convenience yield

B An optimistic expected outlook for the asset

C Dividends if the asset is a stock or interest if the asset is a bond

Solution to 1:

C is correct. The price recently paid by other investors is past information and does not affect the spot price. The time value of money and the risk aversion of investors determine the discount rate. Only current information is relevant as investors look ahead, not back.

Solution to 2:

B is correct. An optimistic forecast for the asset is not a benefit of holding the asset, but it does appear in the valuation of the asset as a high expected price at the horizon date. Convenience yields and dividends and interest are benefits of holding the asset.

To recap, although the various underlyings differ with respect to the specifics of pricing, all of them are based on expectations, risk, and the costs and benefits of holding a specific underlying. Understanding how assets are priced in the spot market is critical to understanding how derivatives are priced. To understand derivative pricing, it is necessary to establish a linkage between the derivative market and the spot market. That linkage occurs through arbitrage.

2.3 The Principle of Arbitrage

Arbitrage is a type of transaction undertaken when two assets or portfolios produce identical results but sell for different prices. If a trader buys the asset or portfolio at the cheaper price and sells it at the more expensive price, she will generate a net inflow of funds at the start. Because the two assets or portfolios produce identical results, a long position in one and a short position in the other means that at the end of the holding period, the payoffs offset. Hence, no money is gained or lost at the end of the holding period, so there is no risk. The net effect is that the arbitrageur receives money at the start and never has to pay out any money later. Such a situation amounts to free money, like walking down the street, finding money on the ground, and never having to give it up. Exhibit 4 illustrates this process for assets A and B, which have no dividends or other benefits or costs and pay off identically but sell for different prices, with $S_0^A < S_0^B$.

Exhibit 4 Executing an Arbitrage

Given: Assets A and B produce the same values at time T but at time 0, A is selling for less than B.

0	T
$S_0^A < S_0^B$:	$S_T^A = S_T^B$:
Buy A at S_0^A	Sell A for S_T^A
Sell B at S_0^B	Buy B for S_T^B
Cash flow = $S_0^B - S_0^A (> 0)$	Cash flow = $S_T^A - S_T^B (= 0)$

2.3.1 *The (In)Frequency of Arbitrage Opportunities*

When arbitrage opportunities exist, traders exploit them very quickly. The combined actions of many traders engaging in the same transaction of buying the low-priced asset or portfolio and selling the high-priced asset or portfolio results in increased demand and an increasing price for the former and decreased demand and a decreasing price for the latter. This market activity will continue until the prices converge. Assets that produce identical results can thus have only one true market price. This rule is called the "law of one price." With virtually all market participants alert for the possibility of earning such profits at no risk, it should not be surprising that arbitrage opportunities are rare.

In practice, prices need not converge precisely, or even all that quickly, because the transaction cost of exploiting an opportunity could exceed the benefit. For example, say you are walking down the sidewalk of the Champs-Élysées in Paris and notice a €1 coin on the sidewalk. You have a bad back, and it would take some effort to bend over. The transaction cost of exploiting this opportunity without any risk could exceed the benefit of the money. Some arbitrage opportunities represent such small discrepancies that they are not worth exploiting because of transaction costs.

Significant arbitrage opportunities, however, will be exploited. A significant opportunity arises from a price differential large enough to overcome the transaction costs. Any such price differential will continue to be exploited until the opportunity disappears. Thus, if you find a €10 note on the Champs-Élysées sidewalk, there is a good chance you will find it worth picking up (even with your bad back), and even if you do not pick it up, it will probably not be there for long. With enough people alert for such opportunities, only a few will arise, and the ones that do will be quickly exploited and disappear. In this manner, arbitrage makes markets work much more efficiently.

2.3.2 *Arbitrage and Derivatives*

It may be difficult to conceive of many investments that would produce identical payoffs. Even similar companies such as McDonalds and Burger King, which are in the same line of business, do not perform identically. Their performance may be correlated, but each has its own unique characteristics. For equity securities and with no derivatives involved, about the only such situation that could exist in reality is a stock that trades simultaneously in two different markets, such as Royal Dutch Shell, which trades in Amsterdam and London but is a single company. Clearly there can be only one price. If those two markets operate in different currencies, the currency-adjusted prices should be the same. Bonds issued by the same borrower are also potentially arbitrageable. All bonds of an issuer will be priced off of the term structure of interest rates. Because of this common factor, bonds of different maturities can be arbitraged against each other. But in general, two securities are unlikely to perform identically.

The picture changes, however, if we introduce derivatives. For most derivatives, the payoffs come (derive) directly from the value of the underlying at the expiration of the derivative. Although no one can predict with certainty the value of the underlying at expiration, as soon as that value is determined, the value of the derivative at expiration becomes certain. So, while the performance of McDonalds' stock may have a strong correlation to the performance of Burger King's stock, neither completely determines the other. But derivatives on McDonalds' stock and derivatives on Burger King's stock are completely determined by their respective stocks. All of the uncertainty in a derivative comes from the uncertainty in the underlying. As a result, the price of the derivative is tied to the price of the underlying. That being the case, the derivative can be used to hedge the underlying, or vice versa.

Exhibit 5 illustrates this point. When a long position in the underlying is combined with a short position in the derivative to produce a perfect hedge, all of the risk is eliminated and the position should earn the risk-free rate. If not, arbitrageurs begin to trade. If the position generates a return in excess of the risk-free rate, the arbitrageurs see an opportunity because the hedged position of the underlying (long asset and short derivative) earns more than the risk-free rate and a risk-free loan undertaken as a borrower incurs a cost equal to the risk-free rate. Therefore, implementing the hedged position and borrowing at the risk-free rate earns a return in excess of the risk-free rate, incurs a cost of the risk-free rate, and has no risk. As a result, an investor can earn excess return at no risk without committing any capital. Arbitrageurs will execute this transaction in large volumes, continuing to exploit the pricing discrepancy until market forces push prices back in line such that both risk-free transactions earn the risk-free rate.

Exhibit 5 Hedging the Underlying with a Derivative (or Vice Versa)

Out of this process, one and only one price can exist for the derivative. Otherwise, there will be an arbitrage opportunity. We typically take the underlying price as given and infer the unique derivative price that prohibits any arbitrage opportunities. Most derivatives pricing models are established on this foundation. We simply assume that no arbitrage opportunities can exist and infer the derivative price that guarantees there are no arbitrage opportunities.

2.3.3 *Arbitrage and Replication*

Because a long asset and a short derivative on the asset can be combined to produce a position equivalent to a risk-free bond, it follows that the long asset and a short risk-free asset (meaning to borrow at the risk-free rate) can be combined to produce a long derivative. Alternatively, a short derivative and the short risk-free asset can be combined to produce a short asset position. Exhibit 6 shows this process, referred to as **replication**. Replication is the creation of an asset or portfolio from another asset, portfolio, and/or derivative.

Exhibit 6 Arbitrage, Replication, and Derivatives

Long asset	+	Short derivative	=	Long risk-free asset (lending)
Long asset	+	Short risk-free asset (borrowing)	=	Long derivative
Short derivative	+	Short risk-free asset (borrowing)	=	Short asset

If all assets are correctly priced to prohibit arbitrage, however, the ability to replicate seems useless. Why would one replicate an asset or derivative if there is no cost advantage? Buying a government security to earn the risk-free rate is easier than buying the asset and selling a derivative to produce a risk-free position. At this point, that is certainly a reasonable question. As we progress through this material, however, we will relax the assumption that everything is always correctly priced and we will admit the possibility of occasional arbitrage opportunities. For example, it may be more profitable to hedge a portfolio with a derivative to produce a risk-free rate than to invest in the risk-free asset. In addition, we might find that replication can have lower transaction costs. For example, a derivative on a stock index combined with the risk-free asset [Long derivative (Stock index futures) + Long risk-free asset (Lending) = Long asset (Stock index)] can potentially replicate an index fund at lower transaction costs than buying all the securities in the index. Replication is the essence of arbitrage. The ability to replicate something with something else can be valuable to investors, either through pricing differentials, however temporary, or lower transaction costs.

2.3.4 *Risk Aversion, Risk Neutrality, and Arbitrage-Free Pricing*

Most investors are risk averse. They do not accept risk without the expectation of a return commensurate with that risk. Thus, they require risk premiums to justify the risk. One might think that this point implies a method for pricing derivatives based on the application of a risk premium to the expected payoff of the derivative and its risk. As we will describe later, this methodology is not appropriate in the pricing of derivatives.

As previously described, a derivative can be combined with an asset to produce a risk-free position. This fact does not mean that one *should* create such a combination. It merely means that one *can* do so. The derivative price is the price that guarantees the risk-free combination of the derivative and the underlying produces a risk-free return. The derivative price can then be inferred from the characteristics of the underlying, the characteristics of the derivative, and the risk-free rate. The investor's risk aversion is not a factor in determining the derivative price. Because the risk aversion of the investor is not relevant to pricing the derivative, one can just as easily obtain the derivative price by assuming that the investor is risk neutral. That means that the expected payoff of the derivative can be discounted at the risk-free rate rather than the risk-free rate plus a risk premium. Virtually all derivative pricing models ultimately take this form: discounting the expected payoff of the derivative at the risk-free rate.

The entire process of pricing derivatives is not exactly as we have described it at this point. There is an intermediate step, which entails altering the probabilities of the outcomes from the true probabilities to something called risk-neutral probabilities. We will illustrate this process later in this reading. The important point to understand is that while the risk aversion of investors is relevant to pricing assets, it is not relevant to pricing derivatives. As such, derivatives pricing is sometimes called **risk-neutral pricing**. Risk-neutral pricing uses the fact that arbitrage opportunities guarantee that a risk-free portfolio consisting of the underlying and the derivative must earn the risk-free rate. There is only one derivative price that meets that condition. Any mispricing of the derivative will lead to arbitrage transactions that drive the derivative price back to where it should be, the price that eliminates arbitrage opportunities.

The overall process of pricing derivatives by arbitrage and risk neutrality is called **arbitrage-free pricing**. We are effectively determining the price of a derivative by assuming that the market is free of arbitrage opportunities. This notion is also sometimes called the **principle of no arbitrage**. If there are no arbitrage opportunities, combinations of assets and/or derivatives that produce the same results must sell for the same price. The correct derivative price assures us that the market is free of arbitrage opportunities.

2.3.5 *Limits to Arbitrage*

As we previously described, there may be reasons to not pick up a coin lying on the ground. Likewise, some small arbitrage profits are never exploited. A bond selling for €1,000 might offer an arbitrage profit by trading a derivative on the bond and a risk-free asset at a total cost of €999, but the profit of €1 might be exceeded by the transaction costs. Such small differentials can easily remain essentially trapped within the bounds of transaction costs. In addition, arbitrage can require capital. Not everyone can borrow virtually unlimited amounts of money at what amounts to a risk-free rate. Moreover, some transactions can require additional capital to maintain positions. The corresponding gains from an offsetting position might not be liquid. Hence, on paper the position is hedged, but in practice, one position has a cash outflow while the other generates gains on paper that are realized only later. Borrowing against those future gains is not always easy.

Moreover, some apparent arbitrage transactions are not completely risk free. As you will learn later, option pricing requires knowledge of the volatility of the underlying asset, which is information that is not easy to obtain and subject to different opinions. Executing an arbitrage can entail risk if one lacks accurate information on the model inputs.

Some arbitrage positions require short-selling assets that can be difficult to short. Some securities are held only by investors who are unwilling to lend the securities and who, by policy, are not arbitrageurs themselves. Some commodities, in particular, can be difficult and costly to sell short. Hence, the arbitrage might exist in only one direction, which keeps the price from becoming seemingly too high or seemingly too low but permitting it to move virtually without limit in the opposite direction.

Arbitrage positions rely on the ultimate realization by other investors of the existence of the mispricing. For some investors, bearing these costs and risks until other investors drive the price back to its appropriate level can be nearly impossible.

The arbitrage principle is the essence of derivative pricing models. Yet, clearly there are limits to the ability of all investors to execute arbitrage transactions. In studying derivative pricing, it is important to accept the no-arbitrage rule as a paradigm, meaning a framework for analysis and understanding. Although no market experts think that arbitrage opportunities never occur, it is a common belief that finding and exploiting them is a challenging and highly competitive process that will not yield frequent success. But it is important that market participants stay alert for and exploit whatever arbitrage opportunities arise. In response, the market functions more efficiently.

EXAMPLE 2

Arbitrage

1 Which of the following *best* describes an arbitrage opportunity? It is an opportunity to:

A earn a risk premium in the short run.

B buy an asset at less than its fundamental value.

C make a profit at no risk with no capital invested.

2 What *most likely* happens when an arbitrage opportunity exists?

A Investors trade quickly and prices adjust to eliminate the opportunity.

B Risk premiums increase to compensate traders for the additional risk.

C Markets cease operations to eliminate the possibility of profit at no risk.

3 Which of the following *best* describes how derivatives are priced?

A A hedge portfolio is used that eliminates arbitrage opportunities.

B The payoff of the underlying is adjusted downward by the derivative value.

C The expected future payoff of the derivative is discounted at the risk-free rate plus a risk premium.

4 An investor who requires no premium to compensate for the assumption of risk is said to be which of the following?

A Risk seeking

B Risk averse

C Risk neutral

5 Which of the following is a limit to arbitrage?

A Clearinghouses restrict the transactions that can be arbitraged.

B Pricing models do not show whether to buy or sell the derivative.

C It may not always be possible to raise sufficient capital to engage in arbitrage.

Solution to 1:

C is correct because it is the only answer that is based on the notion of when an arbitrage opportunity exists: when two identical assets or portfolios sell for different prices. A risk premium earned in the short run can easily have occurred through luck. Buying an asset at less than fair value might not even produce a profit.

Solution to 2:

A is correct. The combined actions of traders push prices back in line to a level at which no arbitrage opportunities exist. Markets certainly do not shut down, and risk premiums do not adjust and, in fact, have no relevance to arbitrage profits.

Solution to 3:

A is correct. A hedge portfolio is formed that eliminates arbitrage opportunities and implies a unique price for the derivative. The other answers are incorrect because the underlying payoff is not adjusted by the derivative value and the discount rate of the derivative does not include a risk premium.

Solution to 4:

C is correct. Risk-seeking investors give away a risk premium because they enjoy taking risk. Risk-averse investors expect a risk premium to compensate for the risk. Risk-neutral investors neither give nor receive a risk premium because they have no feelings about risk.

Solution to 5:

C is correct. It may not always be possible to raise sufficient capital to engage in arbitrage. Clearinghouses do not restrict arbitrage. Pricing models show what the price of the derivative should be.

Thus, comparison with the market price will indicate if the derivative is overpriced and should be sold or if it is underpriced and should be purchased.

2.4 The Concept of Pricing vs. Valuation

In equity markets, analysis is undertaken with the objective of determining the value, sometimes called the fundamental value, of a stock. When a stock trades in the market for a price that differs from its fundamental value, investors will often buy or sell the stock based on the perceived mispricing. The fundamental value of a stock is typically determined by analyzing the company's financial statements, projecting its earnings and dividends, determining a discount rate based on the risk, and finding the present value of the future dividends. These steps make up the essence of dividend discount models. Other approaches include comparing the book value of a company to its market value, thereby using book value as a proxy for fundamental value, or by application of a price/earnings ratio to projected next-period earnings, or by discounting free cash flow. Each of these approaches purports to estimate the company's fundamental value, leading to the notion that a company is worth something that may or may not correspond to its price in the market.

In derivative markets, the notion of valuation as a representation of fundamental value is still a valid concept, but the terminology can be somewhat different and can lead to some confusion. Options are not a problem in this regard. They can be analyzed to determine their fundamental value, and the market price can be compared with the fundamental value. Any difference can then presumably be exploited via arbitrage. The combined actions of numerous investors should ultimately lead to the market price converging to its fundamental value, subject to the above limits to arbitrage.

The world of forwards, futures, and swaps, however, uses different terminology with respect to price and value. These contracts do not require the outlay of cash at the start the way an option, stock, or bond does. Forwards, futures, and swaps start off with values of zero. Then as the underlying moves, their values become either positive or negative. The forward, futures, or swap price is a concept that represents the fixed price or rate at which the underlying will be purchased at a later date. It is not an amount to be paid at the start. This fixed price or rate is embedded into the contract while the value will fluctuate as market conditions change. But more importantly, the value and price are not at all comparable with each other.

Consider a simple example. Suppose you own a stock priced at \$102. You have a short forward contract to sell the stock at a price of \$100 one year from now. The risk-free rate is 4%. Your position is riskless because you know that one year from now, you will sell the stock for \$100. Thus, you know you will get \$100 one year from now, which has a present value of \$100/(1.04) = \$96.15. Notice the discounting at the risk-free rate, which is appropriate because the position is riskless. Your overall position is that you own an asset worth \$102 and are short a contract worth something, and the two positions combine to have a value of \$96.15. Therefore, the forward contract must have a value of \$96.15 – \$102 = –\$5.85. Your forward contract is thus worth –\$5.85. To the party on the opposite side, it is worth +\$5.85.[7] The price of the forward contract is still \$100, which was set when you created the contract at an earlier date. As you can see, the \$100 forward price is not comparable to the \$5.85 value of the contract.

Although the forward price is fixed, any new forward contract calling for delivery of the same asset at the same time will have a different price. We will cover that point in more detail later. For now, it is important to see that your contract has a price of \$100 but a value of –\$5.85, which are two entirely different orders of magnitude. This information does not imply that the forward contract is mispriced. The value is the amount of wealth represented by owning the forward contract. The price is one of the terms the parties agreed on when they created the contract.[8] This idea applies in the same manner for futures and swaps.

PRICING AND VALUATION OF FORWARD COMMITMENTS 3

In this section, we will go into pricing forward commitments in a little more detail. Let us start by establishing that today, at time 0, we create a forward commitment that expires at time T. The value of the underlying today is S_0. At expiration the underlying value is S_T, which is not known at the initiation of the contract.

3.1 Pricing and Valuation of Forward Contracts

Previously, we noted that price and value are entirely different concepts for forward commitments. We gave an example of a forward contract with a price of \$100 but a value of –\$5.85 to the seller and +\$5.85 to the buyer. In the next subsection, we will delve more deeply into understanding these concepts of pricing and valuation for forward contracts.

3.1.1 *Pricing and Valuation of Forward Contracts at Expiration*

Recall that a forward contract specifies that one party agrees to buy the underlying from the other at the expiration date at a price agreed on at the start of the contract. Suppose that you enter into a contract with another party in which you will buy a used car from that party in one year at a price of \$10,000. Then \$10,000 is the forward price. One year later, when the contract expires, you are committed to paying \$10,000 and accepting delivery of the car. Let us say that at that time, you check the used car market and find that an identical car is worth \$10,800. How much is your forward contract worth to you at that time? It obligates you to pay \$10,000 for a car that you would otherwise have to pay \$10,800. Thus, the contract benefits you by \$800, so its value is \$800. If you were on the opposite side of the transaction, its value would be –\$800. If the market price of the car were below \$10,000, the contract would have negative value to you and the mirror image positive value to the seller.

7 This concept of the value of the forward contract as it evolves toward expiration is sometimes referred to as its mark-to-market value. The same notion is applicable to swaps. In futures, of course, contracts are automatically marked to market by the clearinghouse, and gains and losses are converted into actual cash flows from one party to the other.

8 The forward price is more like the exercise price of the option. It is the price the two parties agree will be paid at a future date for the underlying. Of course, the option has the feature that the holder need not ever pay that price, which is the case if the holder chooses not to exercise the option.

This example leads us to our first important derivative pricing result. The forward price, established at the initiation date of contract is $F_0(T)$. Let us denote the value at expiration of the forward contract as $V_T(T)$. This value is formally stated as

$$V_T(T) = S_T - F_0(T) \quad (1)$$

In words,

> *The value of a forward contract at expiration is the spot price of the underlying minus the forward price agreed to in the contract.*

In the financial world, we generally define value as the value to the long position, so the above definition is generally correct but would be adjusted if we look at the transaction from the point of view of the short party. In that case, we would multiply the value to the long party by −1 to calculate the value to the short party. Alternatively, the value to the short party is the forward price minus the spot price at expiration.

If a forward contract could be initiated right at the instant of expiration, the forward price would clearly be the spot price. Such a contract would essentially be a spot transaction.

3.1.2 *Pricing and Valuation at Initiation Date*

In Exhibit 7, we see the nature of the problem of pricing a forward contract. We are situated at time 0, facing an uncertain future. At the horizon date, time T, the underlying price will be S_T. Of course, at time 0 we do not know what S_T will turn out to be. Yet at time 0, we need to establish the forward price, $F_0(T)$, which is the price we agree to pay at time T to purchase the asset.

Exhibit 7 The Time Horizon of Forward Contracts

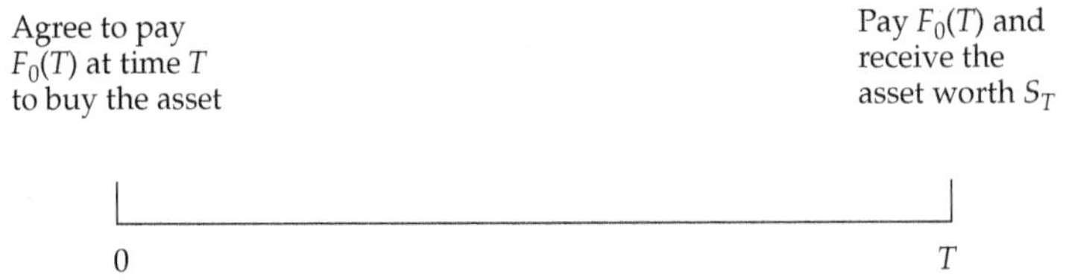

When a forward contract is initiated, neither party pays anything to the other. It is a valueless contract, neither an asset nor a liability. Therefore, its value at initiation is zero:

$$V_0(T) = 0 \quad (2)$$

The forward price that the parties agree to at the initiation date of the contract is a special price that results in the contract having zero value and prohibiting arbitrage. This is our first important result:

> *Because neither the long nor the short pays anything to the other at the initiation date of a forward contract, the value of a forward contract when initiated is zero.*

If this statement were not true and one party paid a sum of money to the other, the party receiving the money could find another party and engage in the opposite transaction, with no money paid to the other on this second contract. The two transactions would completely offset, thereby eliminating the risk. Yet, the first party would have captured some cash from the second and consequently earned an arbitrage profit because his position is completely hedged. He would walk away with money and never have to worry about paying it back. The forward price is the price the two parties agree on that generates a value of zero at the initiation date. Finding that price is actually quite easy.

Consider a very simple asset price at S_0 today that pays no dividends or interest, nor does it yield any nonfinancial benefits or incur any carrying costs. As described earlier, we can peer into the future, but at best we can make only a forecast of the price of this asset at our horizon date of time T. That forecast was previously referred to as the expected spot price at expiration, $E(S_T)$. On the surface, it might seem that pricing a forward contract would somehow involve a discounting of the expected spot price. As we said earlier, however, that is not how derivatives are priced—they are priced using arbitrage.

Suppose we hold the asset and enter into a forward contract to sell the asset at the price $F_0(T)$. It should be easy to see that we have constructed a risk-free position. We know that the asset, currently worth S_0, will be sold later at $F_0(T)$ and that this price should guarantee a risk-free return. Thus, we should find the following relationship,

$$\frac{F_0(T)}{S_0} = (1 + r)^T \tag{3}$$

We can easily solve for the forward price to obtain

$$F_0(T) = S_0(1 + r)^T \tag{4}$$

Or, in words,

> *The forward price is the spot price compounded at the risk-free rate over the life of the contract.*

There is a nice logic to this relationship. While the spot price is what someone would have to pay today to buy the asset, a forward contract locks in the purchase price at the horizon date. When that date arrives, the investor will own the asset. Instead of buying the asset today, suppose the investor uses the forward contract to guarantee that she will own the asset at the horizon date. By using the forward contract, the investor will not have committed the money, S_0, that would have forgone interest at the rate r for the period 0 to T. Notice how the risk premium on the asset does not directly appear in the pricing relationship. It does appear implicitly, because it determines the spot price paid to buy the asset. Knowing the spot price, however, eliminates the necessity of determining the risk premium. The derivatives market can simply let the spot market derive the risk premium.

As a simple example, let us say the underlying price, S_0, is £50, the risk-free rate, r, is 3%, and the contract expires in three months, meaning that $T = 3/12 = 0.25$. Then the forward price is £50(1.03)$^{0.25}$ = £50.37. Thus, the two parties would agree that the buyer will pay £50.37 to the seller in three months, and the seller will deliver the underlying to the buyer at expiration.

Now suppose the asset generates cash payments and/or benefits and incurs storage costs. As we discussed, the net cost of carry consists of the benefits, denoted as γ (dividends or interest plus convenience yield), minus the costs, denoted as θ, both of which are in present value form. To put these concepts in future value form, we simply compound them at the risk-free rate, $(\gamma - \theta)(1 + r)^T$. Because this is their value at the expiration date of the contract, we can add them to $F_0(T)$ in Equation 3, thereby restating that equation as

$$(1 + r)^T = \frac{F_0(T) + (\gamma - \theta)(1 + r)^T}{S_0}$$

The numerator is how much money we end up with at T. Rearranging, we obtain the forward price as

$$F_0(T) = (S_0 - \gamma + \theta)(1 + r)^T$$

or **(5)**

$$F_0(T) = S_0(1 + r)^T - (\gamma - \theta)(1 + r)^T$$

We see that the forward price determined using Equation 4 is reduced by the future value of any benefits and increased by the future value of any costs. In other words,

> *The forward price of an asset with benefits and/or costs is the spot price compounded at the risk-free rate over the life of the contract minus the future value of those benefits and costs.*

Again, the logic is straightforward. To acquire a position in the asset at time T, an investor could buy the asset today and hold it until time T. Alternatively, he could enter into a forward contract, committing him to buying the asset at T at the price $F_0(T)$. He would end up at T holding the asset, but the spot transaction would yield benefits and incur costs, whereas the forward transaction would forgo the benefits but avoid the costs.

Assume the benefits exceed the costs. Then the forward transaction would return less than the spot transaction. The formula adjusts the forward price downward by the expression $-(\gamma - \theta)(1 + r)^T$ to reflect this net loss over the spot transaction. In other words, acquiring the asset in the forward market would be cheaper because it forgoes benefits that exceed the costs. That does not mean the forward strategy is better. It costs less but also produces less. Alternatively, if the costs exceeded the benefits, the forward price would be higher because the forward contract avoids the costs at the expense of the lesser benefits.

Returning to our simple example, suppose the present value of the benefits is γ = £3 and the present value of the costs is θ = £4. The forward price would be £50(1.03)$^{0.25}$ – (£3 – £4)(1.03)$^{0.25}$ = £51.38. The forward price, which was £50.37 without these costs and benefits, is now higher because the carrying costs exceed the benefits.

The value of the contract when initiated is zero provided the forward price conforms to the appropriate pricing formula. To keep the analysis as simple as possible, consider the case in which the asset yields no benefits and incurs no costs. Going long the forward contract or going long the asset produces the same position at T: ownership of the asset. Nonetheless, the strategies are not equivalent. Going long the forward contract enables the investor to avoid having to pay the price of the asset, S_0, so she would collect interest on the money. Thus, the forward strategy would have a value of S_0, reflecting the investment of that much cash invested in risk-free bonds, plus the value of the forward contract. The spot strategy would have a value of S_0, reflecting the investment in the asset. These two strategies must have equal values. Hence, the value of the forward contract must be zero.

Although a forward contract has zero value at the start, it will not have zero value during its life. We now take a look at what happens during the life of the contract.

3.1.3 *Pricing and Valuation during the Life of the Contract*

We previously worked an example in which a forward contract established with a price of \$100 later has a value of –\$5.85 to the seller and +\$5.85 to the buyer. Generally we would say the value is \$5.85. We explained that with the spot price at \$102, a party that is long the asset and short the forward contract would guarantee the sale of the asset priced at \$102 at a price of \$100 in one year. The present value of \$100 in one year at 4% is \$96.15. Thus, the party guarantees that his \$102 asset will be effectively sold at a present value of \$96.15, for a present value loss of \$5.85.

In general, we can say that

The value of a forward contract is the spot price of the underlying asset minus the present value of the forward price.

Again, the logic is simple. A forward contract provides a type of synthetic position in the asset, for which we promise to pay the forward price at expiration. Thus, the value of the forward contract is the spot price of the asset minus the present value of the forward price. Let us write out this relationship using $V_t(T)$ as the value of the forward contract at time t, which is some point in time after the contract is initiated and before it expires:

$$V_t(T) = S_t - F_0(T)(1 + r)^{-(T-t)} \quad (6)$$

Note that we are working with the spot price at t, but the forward price was fixed when the contract was initiated.[9]

Now, recall the problem we worked in which the underlying had a price of £50 and the contract was initiated with a three-month life at a price of £50.37. Move one month later, so that the remaining time is two months: $T - t = 2/12 = 0.167$. Let the underlying price be £52. The value of the contract would be £52 – £50.37$(1.03)^{-0.167}$ = £1.88.

If the asset has a cost of carry, we must make only a small adjustment:

$$V_t(T) = S_t - (\gamma - \theta)(1 + r)^t - F_0(T)(1 + r)^{-(T-t)} \quad (7)$$

Note how we adjust the formula by the net of benefits minus costs. The forward contract forgoes the benefits and avoids the costs of holding the asset. Consequently, we adjust the value downward to reflect the forgone benefits and upward to reflect the avoided costs. Remember that the costs (θ) and benefits (γ) are expressed on a present value basis as of time 0. We need their value at time t. We could compound them from 0 to T and then discount them back to t by the period $T - t$, but a shorter route is to simply compound them from 0 to t. In the problem we previously worked, in which we priced the forward contract when the asset has costs and benefits, the benefits (γ) were £3 and the costs (θ) were £4, giving us a forward price of £51.38. We have now moved one month ahead, so $t = 1/12 = 0.0833$ and $T - t = 2/12 = 0.167$. Hence the value of the forward contract would be £52 – (£3 – £4)$(1.03)^{0.0833}$ – £51.38$(1.03)^{-0.167}$ = £1.88. In this case, the effect of the compounding of the net of costs and benefits (£1) over one month has no appreciable effect on the value, but that result is not a general rule.

It is important to note that although we say that Equation 7 holds during the life of the contract at some arbitrary time t, it also holds at the initiation date and at expiration. For the initiation date, we simply change t to 0 in Equation 7. Then we substitute Equation 5 for $F_0(T)$ in Equation 7, obtaining $V_0(T) = 0$, confirming that the value of a forward contract at initiation is zero. At expiration, we let $t = T$ in Equation 7 and obtain the spot price minus the forward price, as presented in Equation 1.[10]

3.1.4 *A Word about Forward Contracts on Interest Rates*

Forward contracts in which the underlying is an interest rate are called **forward rate agreements**, or FRAs. These instruments differ slightly from most other forward contracts in that the underlying is not an asset. Changes in interest rates, such as the value of an asset, are unpredictable. Moreover, virtually every company and organization is affected by the uncertainty of interest rates. Hence, FRAs are very useful devices for many companies. FRAs are forward contracts that allow participants to

9 An alternative approach to valuing a forward contract during its life is to determine the price of a new forward contract that would offset the old one. The discounted difference between the new forward price and the original forward price will lead to the same value.

10 You might be wondering whether the cost and benefit terms disappear when $t = T$. With the costs and benefits defined as those incurred over the period t to T, at expiration their value is zero by definition.

make a known interest payment at a later date and receive in return an unknown interest payment. In that way, a participant whose business will involve borrowing at a future date can hedge against an increase in interest rates by buying an FRA (the long side) and locking in a fixed payment and receiving a random payment that offsets the unknown interest payment it will make on its loan. Note that the FRA seller (the short side) is hedging against a decrease in interest rates. Also, consider that the FRA seller could be a lender wishing to lock in a fixed rate on a loan it will make at a future date.

Even though FRAs do not involve an underlying asset, they can still be combined with an underlying asset to produce a hedged position, thereby leading to fairly straightforward pricing and valuation equations. The math is a little more complex than the math for forwards on assets, but the basic ideas are the same.

FRAs have often historically been based on Libor, the London Interbank Offered Rate, which represents the rate on a Eurodollar time deposit, a loan in dollars from one London bank to another. Other rates such as Euribor (Euro Interbank Offered Rate) and Tibor (Tokyo Interbank Offered Rate) have also been used.[11] As an example, assume we are interested in going long a 30-day FRA with a fixed rate (the FRA rate) in which the underlying is 90-day Libor. A long position means that in 30 days, we will make a known interest payment and receive an interest payment corresponding to the discounted difference between 90-day Libor on that day and the FRA rate. We can either enter into a 30-day FRA on 90-day Libor or create a synthetic FRA. To do the latter, we would go long a 120-day Eurodollar time deposit and short a 30-day Eurodollar time deposit. Exhibit 8 shows the structure of this strategy. We omit some of the details here, such as how much face value we should take on the two Eurodollar transactions as well as the size of the FRA. Those technical issues are covered in more advanced material. At this time, we focus on the fact that going long over the 120-day period and short over the 30-day period leaves an investor with no exposure over the 30-day period and then converts to a position that starts 30 days from now and matures 90 days later. This synthetic position corresponds to a 30-day FRA on 90-day Libor. Exhibit 8 illustrates this point.[12]

11 Libor is being phased out, as the panel of banks will no longer be required to submit quotations after 2021. In anticipation of this, market participants and regulators have been working to develop alternative reference rates.

12 The real FRA we show appears to imply that an investor enters into a Eurodollar transaction in 30 days that matures 90 days later. This is not technically true. The investor does, however, engage in a cash settlement in 30 days that has the same value and economic form as such a transaction. Specifically, settlement at expiration of the FRA is an amount equal to the discounted difference between the underlying 90-day Libor rate on that day and the FRA rate multiplied by a notional principal amount. These details are covered in the Level II and Level III CFA Program curriculum.

Exhibit 8 Real FRA and Synthetic FRA (30-Day FRA on 90-Day Libor)

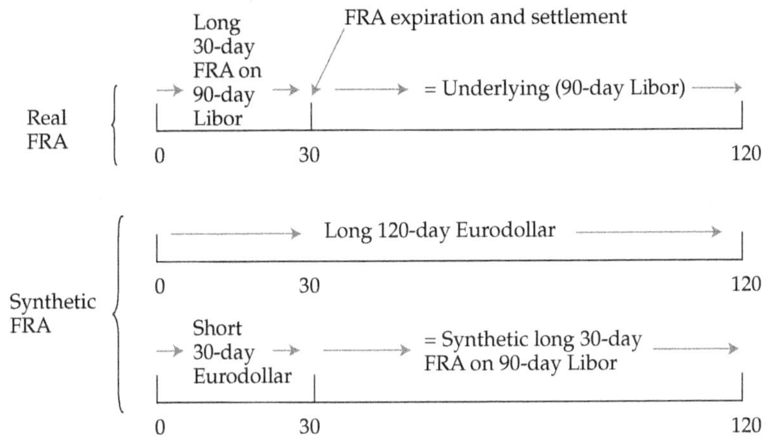

FRAs, and indeed all forward contracts relating to bonds and interest rates, are closely tied to the term structure of interest rates, a concept covered in virtually all treatments of fixed-income securities. Buying a 120-day zero-coupon bond and selling a 30-day zero-coupon bond produces a forward position in a 90-day zero-coupon bond that begins in 30 days. From that forward position, one can infer the forward rate. It would then be seen that the FRA rate *is* the forward rate, even though the derivative itself is not a forward contract on a bond.

EXAMPLE 3

Forward Contract Pricing and Valuation

1 Which of the following *best* describes the difference between the price of a forward contract and its value?

  A The forward price is fixed at the start, and the value starts at zero and then changes.

  B The price determines the profit to the buyer, and the value determines the profit to the seller.

  C The forward contract value is a benchmark against which the price is compared for the purposes of determining whether a trade is advisable.

2 Which of the following *best* describes the value of the forward contract at expiration? The value is the price of the underlying:

  A minus the forward price.

  B divided by the forward price.

  C minus the compounded forward price.

3 Which of the following factors does *not* affect the forward price?

  A The costs of holding the underlying

  B Dividends or interest paid by the underlying

  C Whether the investor is risk averse, risk seeking, or risk neutral

4 Which of the following *best* describes the forward rate of an FRA?

  A The spot rate implied by the term structure

B The forward rate implied by the term structure

C The rate on a zero-coupon bond of maturity equal to that of the forward contract

Solution to 1:

A is correct. The forward price is fixed at the start, whereas the value starts at zero and then changes. Both price and value are relevant in determining the profit for both parties. The forward contract value is not a benchmark for comparison with the price.

Solution to 2:

A is correct because the holder of the contract gains the difference between the price of the underlying and the forward price. That value can, of course, be negative, which will occur if the holder is forced to buy the underlying at a price higher than the market price.

Solution to 3:

C is correct. The costs of holding the underlying, known as carrying costs, and the dividends and interest paid by the underlying are extremely relevant to the forward price. How the investor feels about risk is irrelevant, because the forward price is determined by arbitrage.

Solution to 4:

B is correct. FRAs are based on Libor, and they represent forward rates, not spot rates. Spot rates are needed to determine forward rates, but they are not equal to forward rates. The rate on a zero-coupon bond of maturity equal to that of the forward contract describes a spot rate.

As noted, we are not covering the details of derivative pricing but rather are focusing on the intuition. At this point, we have covered the intuition of pricing forward contracts. We now move to futures contracts.

3.2 Pricing and Valuation of Futures Contracts

Futures contracts differ from forward contracts in that they have standard terms, are traded on a futures exchange, and are more heavily regulated, whereas forward contracts are typically private, customized transactions. Perhaps the most important distinction is that they are marked to market on a daily basis, meaning that the accumulated gains and losses from the previous day's trading session are deducted from the accounts of those holding losing positions and transferred to the accounts of those holding winning positions. This daily settling of gains and losses enables the futures exchange to guarantee that a party that earns a profit from a futures transaction will not have to worry about collecting the money. Thus, futures exchanges provide a credit guarantee, which is facilitated through the use of a clearinghouse. The clearinghouse collects and disburses cash flows from the parties on a daily basis, thereby settling obligations quickly before they accumulate to much larger amounts. There is no absolute assurance that a clearinghouse will not fail, but none has ever done so since the first one was created in the 1920s.

The pattern of cash flows in a futures contract is quite similar to that in a forward contract. Suppose you enter into a forward contract two days before expiration in which you agree to buy an asset at €100, the forward price. Two days later, the asset is selling for €103, and the contract expires. You therefore pay €100 and receive an asset worth €103, for a gain of €3. If the contract were cash settled, instead of involving physical delivery, you would receive €3 in cash, which you could use to defer a portion of the cost of the asset. The net effect is that you are buying the asset for €103, paying €100 plus the €3 profit on the forward contract.

Had you chosen a futures contract, the futures price at expiration would still converge to the spot price of €103. But now it would matter what the futures settlement price was on the next to last day. Let us assume that price was €99. That means on the next to last day, your account would be marked to market for a loss of €1, the price of €100 having fallen to €99. That is, you would be charged €1, with the money passed on to the opposite party. But then on the last day, your position would be marked from €99 to €103, a gain of €4. Your net would be €1 lost on the first day and €4 gained on the second for a total of €3. In both situations you gain €3, but with the forward contract, you gain it all at expiration, whereas with the futures contract, you gain it over two days. With this two-day example, the interest on the interim cash flow would be virtually irrelevant, but over longer periods and with sufficiently high interest rates, the difference in the amount of money you end up with could be noticeable.

The value of a futures contract is the accumulated gain or loss on a futures contract since its previous day's settlement. When that value is paid out in the daily settlement, the futures price is effectively reset to the settlement price and the value goes to zero. The different patterns of cash flows for forwards and futures can lead to differences in the pricing of forwards versus futures. But there are some conditions under which the pricing is the same. It turns out that if interest rates were constant, forwards and futures would have the same prices. The differential will vary with the volatility of interest rates. In addition, if futures prices and interest rates are uncorrelated, forwards and futures prices will be the same. If futures prices are positively correlated with interest rates, futures contracts are more desirable to holders of long positions than are forwards. The reason is because rising prices lead to futures profits that are reinvested in periods of rising interest rates, and falling prices leads to losses that occur in periods of falling interest rates. It is far better to receive cash flows in the interim than all at expiration under such conditions. This condition makes futures more attractive than forwards, and therefore their prices will be higher than forward prices. A negative correlation between futures prices and interest rates leads to the opposite interpretation, with forwards being more desirable than futures to the long position. The more desirable contract will tend to have the higher price.

The practical realities, however, are that the derivatives industry makes virtually no distinction between futures and forward prices.[13] Thus, we will make no distinction between futures and forward pricing, except possibly in noting some subtle issues that may arise from time to time.

EXAMPLE 4

Futures Pricing and Valuation

1 Which of the following *best* describes how futures contract payoffs differ from forward contract payoffs?

A Forward contract payoffs are larger.

B They are equal, ignoring the time value of money.

C Futures contract payoffs are larger if the underlying is a commodity.

13 At the time of this writing, many forwards (and swaps) are being processed through clearinghouses, a response to changes brought about by key legislation in several countries that was adopted following the financial crises of 2008. These OTC instruments are thus being effectively marked to market in a similar manner to the futures contracts described here. The full extent of this evolution of OTC trading through clearinghouses is not yet clear.

2 Which of the following conditions will not make futures and forward prices equivalent?

A Interest rates are constant.

B Futures prices are uncorrelated with interest rates.

C The volatility of the forward price is different from the volatility of the futures price.

3 With respect to the value of a futures contract, which of the following statements is *most* accurate? The value is the:

A futures price minus the spot price.

B present value of the expected payoff at expiration.

C accumulated gain since the previous settlement, which resets to zero upon settlement.

Solution to 1:

B is correct. Forward payoffs occur all at expiration, whereas futures payoffs occur on a day-to-day basis but would equal forward payoffs ignoring interest. Payoffs could differ, so forward payoffs are not always larger. The type of underlying is not relevant to the point of which payoff is larger.

Solution to 2:

C is correct. Constant interest rates or the condition that futures prices are uncorrelated with interest rates will make forward and futures prices equivalent. The volatility of forward and futures prices has no relationship to any difference.

Solution to 3:

C is correct. Value accumulates from the previous settlement and goes to zero when distributed.

3.3 Pricing and Valuation of Swap Contracts

Recall the structure of a forward contract, as depicted in Exhibit 7. The investor is at time 0 and needs to determine the price, $F_0(T)$, that she will agree to pay at time T to purchase the asset. This price is set such that there is no value to the contract at that time. Value can arise later as prices change, but when initiated, the contract has zero value. Neither party pays anything to the other at the start.

Now consider a swap starting at time 0 and ending at time T. We will let this swap be the type that involves a fixed payment exchanged for a floating payment. The contract specifies that the two parties will make a series of n payments at times that we will designate as 1, 2, ..., n, with the last payment occurring at time T. On each of these payment dates, the owner of the swap makes a payment of $FS_0(n, T)$ and receives a payment based on the value of the underlying at the time of each respective payment, $S_1, S_2, ..., S_n$. So from the point of view of the buyer, the sequence of cash flows from the swap is $S_1 - FS_0(n, T)$, $S_2 - FS_0(n, T)$, ..., $S_n - FS_0(n, T)$. The notation $FS_0(n, T)$ denotes the fixed payment established at time 0 for a swap consisting of n payments with the last payment at time T. We denote the time to each payment as $t_1, t_2, ..., t_n$, where $t_n = T$. This structure is shown in Exhibit 9.

Exhibit 9 Structure of Cash Flows in a Swap

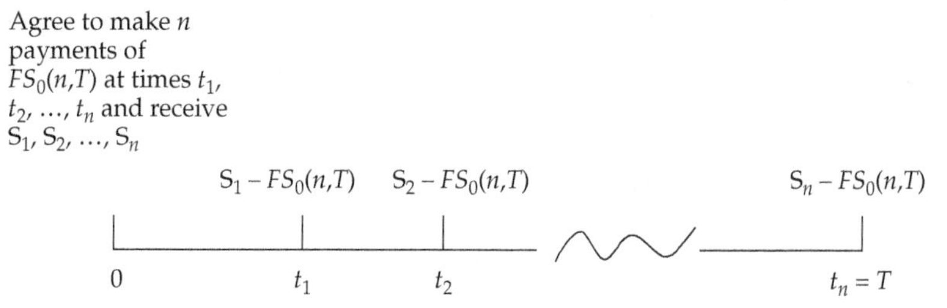

Comparing Exhibit 7 with Exhibit 9 reveals some similarities. A swap is in some sense a series of forward contracts, specifically a set of contracts expiring at various times in which one party agrees to make a fixed payment and receive a variable payment. Now consider Exhibit 10, which breaks down a swap into a series of implicit forward contracts, with the expiration of each forward contract corresponding to a swap payment date.

Exhibit 10 A Swap as a Series of Forward Contracts

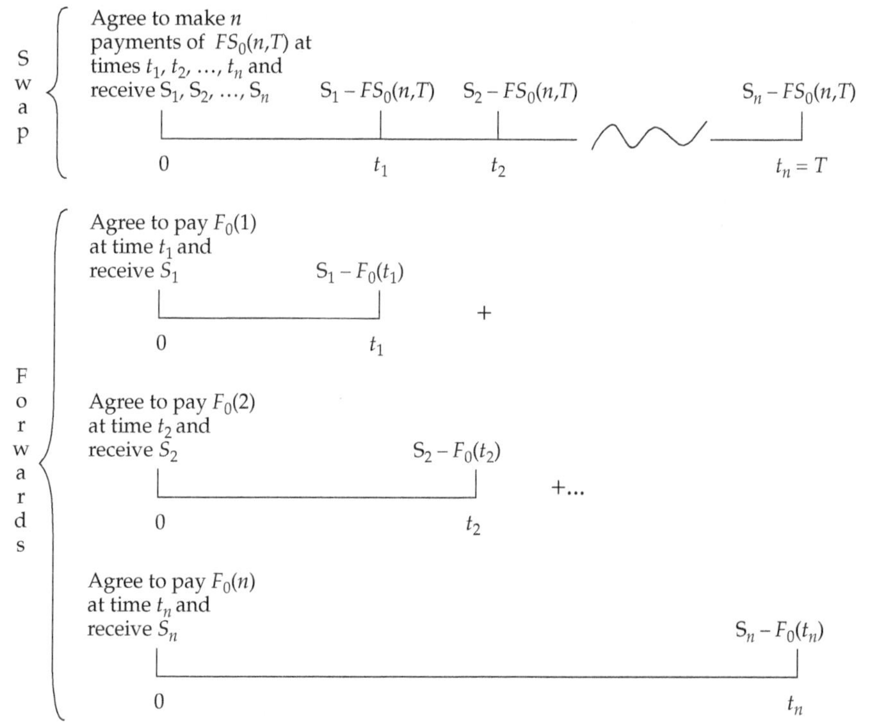

Recall from the material on forward contracts that the forward price is determined by the spot price and the net cost of carry (Equation 5), the latter being partially determined by the length of time of the contract. It should be obvious that a forward contract expiring at time t_1 will not have the same price, $F_0(t_1)$, as a forward contract expiring at time t_2, $F_0(t_2)$, and likewise for all of the implicit remaining forward contracts expiring up through time t_n. The cost of carrying an asset over different time periods will vary by the length of the time periods. In other words, the prices of the implicit forward contracts imbedded in a swap will not be equal:

$$F_0(t_1) \neq F_0(t_2) \neq \ldots \neq F_0(t_n)$$

But for a swap, all the fixed payments are equal. So, how can we equate a swap to a series of forward contracts? It turns out that we can, and in doing so, we recall a valuable point about forward pricing.

Recall that the forward price is the price that produces a zero value of the contract at the start. Zero value is essential if there is no exchange of cash flows from one party to the other. And although no exchange of cash flows is customary, it is not mandatory. The parties could agree on any forward price at the start. If the zero-value forward price were \$30 and the parties agreed on a price of \$28, it should be apparent that the buyer would be getting a great price. The seller, being rational, would require that the buyer compensate him at the start. The seller should be getting \$30 at expiration and instead will get \$28. So the buyer should compensate the seller to the amount of the present value of \$2 at expiration. If the parties agree on a price greater than \$30, similar compensation would have to be paid from seller to buyer.

A forward transaction that starts with a nonzero value is called an off-market forward. There is generally no prohibition on the use of off-market forward contracts, so two parties can engage in a series of forward contracts at whatever fixed price they so desire. Assume they agree on the price $FS_0(T)$. That is, each forward contract will be created at the fixed price that corresponds to the fixed price of a swap of the same maturity with payments made at the same dates as the series of forward contracts. That means that some of the forward contracts would have positive values and some would have negative values, but their combined values would equal zero.

Now, it sounds like that price would be hard to find, but it is not. We would not, however, go about finding it by taking random guesses. Doing so would take seemingly forever. Along the way, we would notice that some of these implicit forward contracts would have positive values and some would have negative values. If the positives outweighed the negatives, then the overall swap value would be positive, which is too high. Likewise, we might plug in a number that would produce an overall negative value, with the implicit forward contract values tending to be predominantly negative, which is too low.

Not surprisingly, we can find that price easily by appealing to the principle of arbitrage. We said that the principle of arbitrage will guide us *all the way through* derivative pricing. We will omit the details, but here is the general idea.

Suppose we buy an asset that pays the amounts $S_1, S_2, \ldots, S_n$ at times $t_1, t_2, \ldots, t_n$. These are unknown amounts. A simple example would be a floating-rate bond for which the S values represent the coupons that are unknown at the start but ultimately are determined by the evolution of interest rates. Then suppose we finance the purchase of that asset by borrowing money that we promise to repay with equal fixed payments of $FS_0(T)$. That strategy replicates the swap. As you have already learned, replication is the key to pricing.

Valuation of the swap during its life again appeals to replication and the principle of no arbitrage. We will find a way to reproduce the remaining payments on the swap with other transactions. The value of that strategy is the value of the swap.

To obtain the fixed rate on the swap or to value it later during its life, we will need information from the market for the underlying. As we previously noted, there are derivatives on bonds and interest rates, equities, currencies, and commodities. It is not possible to provide a general and simple statement of how to price swaps that covers all of these cases, but that topic is covered in advanced material.

EXAMPLE 5

Swap Pricing and Valuation

1 A swap is equivalent to a series of:

A forward contracts, each created at the swap price.

B long forward contracts, matched with short futures contracts.

C forward contracts, each created at their appropriate forward prices.

2 If the present value of the payments in a forward contract or swap is not zero, which of the following is most likely to be true?

A The contract cannot legally be created.

B The contract must be replicated by another contract with zero value.

C The party whose stream of payments to be received is greater has to pay the other party the present value difference.

Solution to 1:

A is correct. Each implicit forward contract is said to be off-market, because it is created at the swap price, not the appropriate forward price, which would be the price created in the forward market.

Solution to 2:

C is correct. The party whose stream of payments to be received is greater has to pay the other party the present value difference. Such a contract can legally be created, but the party receiving the greater present value must compensate the other party with a cash payment at the start. Replication is never required.

PRICING AND VALUATION OF OPTIONS 4

Unlike a forward, futures, or swap contract, an option is clearly an asset to the holder and a liability to the seller. The buyer of an option pays a sum of money, called the premium, and receives the right to buy (a call) or sell (a put) the underlying. The seller receives the premium and undertakes a potential obligation because the buyer has the right, but not the obligation, to exercise the option. Options are, therefore, contingent claims. Pricing the option is the same as assigning its value. Some confusion from that terminology may still arise, in that an option could trade in the market for an amount that differs from its value.

As mentioned, there are two general types of options. Calls represent the right to buy, and puts represent the right to sell. There are also two important exercise characteristics of options. American options allow exercise at any time up to the expiration, while European options allow exercise only at expiration. It is important to understand that the terms "American" and "European" have no relationship to where the options are traded. Because the right to exercise can be a complex feature of an option, European options are easier to understand, and we will focus on them first.

We will use the same notation used with forwards. We start by assuming that today is time 0, and the option expires at time T. The underlying is an asset currently priced at S_0, and at time T, its price is S_T. Of course, we do not know S_T until we get to the expiration. The option has an exercise or strike price of X. The symbols we use are as follows:

For calls,

c_0 = value (price) of European call today

c_T = value (price) of European call at expiration

C_0 = value (price) of American call today

C_T = value (price) of American call at expiration

For puts,

p_0 = value (price) of European put today
p_T = value (price) of European put at expiration
P_0 = value (price) of American put today
P_T = value (price) of American put at expiration

4.1 European Option Pricing

Recall that in studying forward contracts earlier in this reading, the first thing we learned is how a forward contract pays off at expiration. Then we backed up and determined how forward contracts are priced and valued prior to expiration. We follow that same approach for options.

4.1.1 *Value of a European Option at Expiration*

Recall that a European call option allows the holder to buy the underlying at expiration by paying the exercise price. Therefore, exercise is justified only if the value of the underlying exceeds the exercise price. Otherwise, the holder would simply let the call expire. So if the call is worth exercising ($S_T > X$), the holder pays X and receives an asset worth S_T. Thus, the option is worth $S_T - X$. If the call is not worth exercising ($S_T \leq X$), the option simply expires and is worth nothing at expiration.[14] Thus, the value of the option at expiration is the greater of either zero or the underlying price at expiration minus the exercise price, which is typically written as

$$c_T = \text{Max}(0,S_T - X) \tag{8}$$

This formula is also sometimes referred to as the **exercise value** or **intrinsic value**. In this reading, we will use the term exercise value.

Taking a simple example, if the exercise price is €40 and the underlying price is at expiration €43, the call is worth c_T = Max(€0,€43 – €40) = Max(€0,€3) = €3. If the underlying price at expiration is €39, the call is worth c_T = Max(0,€39 – €40) = Max(€0,–€1) = €0.

For puts, the holder has the right to sell the underlying at X. If the underlying is worth less than X at expiration ($X > S_T$), the put will be exercised and worth $X - S_T$ because it allowed the holder to avoid the loss in value of the asset of that amount. If the underlying is equal to or worth more than the exercise price at expiration ($S_T \geq X$), the put will simply expire with no value. So, the put is worth the greater of either zero or the exercise price minus the price of the underlying at expiration.

$$p_T = \text{Max}(0,X - S_T) \tag{9}$$

As discussed above, this formula is referred to as the exercise value or intrinsic value, and as noted, we will use the term exercise value.

Using the same example as with the call, if the underlying is €43 at expiration, the put is worth p_T = Max(€0,€40 – €43) = Max(0,–€3) = €0. If the underlying is €39 at expiration, the put is worth p_T = Max(€0,€40 – €39) = Max(€0,€1) = €1.

Thus, the holder of an option looks out into the future and sees these relationships as the payoff possibilities. That does not mean the holder knows what S_T will be, but the holder knows that all of the uncertainty of the option payoff is determined by the behavior of the underlying.

---

14 In all the remaining material, we identify conditions at expiration, such as $S_T > X$ and $S_T \leq X$. Here we merged the equality case ($S_T = X$) with the less-than case (<). We could have done it the other way around ($S_T < X$ and $S_T \geq X$), which would have had no effect on our interpretations or any calculations of option value. For convenience, in some situations we will use one specification and in some the other.

The results of this section can be restated as follows:

> *The value of a European call at expiration is the exercise value, which is the greater of zero or the value of the underlying minus the exercise price.*
>
> *The value of a European put at expiration is the exercise value, which is the greater of zero or the exercise price minus the value of the underlying.*

To understand option pricing, we have to work our way forward in a gradual manner. The next valuable steps involve using our intuition to identify some characteristics that will influence the value of the option. We might not be able to quantify their effects just yet, but we can rationalize why these factors affect the value of an option.

4.1.2 *Effect of the Value of the Underlying*

The value of the underlying is obviously a critical element in determining the value of an option. It is the uncertainty of the underlying that provides the motivation for using options. It is easy to rationalize the direction of the effect of the underlying.

A call option can be viewed as a mean of acquiring the underlying, whereas a put option can be viewed as a means of selling the underlying. Thus, a call option is logically worth more if the underlying is worth more, and a put option is logically worth more if the underlying is worth less.

The value of the underlying also forms one of the boundaries for calls. The value of a call option cannot exceed the value of the underlying. After all, a call option is only a means of acquiring the underlying. It can never give the holder more benefit than the underlying. Hence, the value of the underlying forms an upper boundary on what a call is worth. The underlying does not provide an upper or lower boundary for puts. That role is played by the exercise price, as we will see in the next section.

To recap what we learned here,

> *The value of a European call option is directly related to the value of the underlying.*
>
> *The value of a European put option is inversely related to the value of the underlying.*

4.1.3 *Effect of the Exercise Price*

The exercise price is a critical factor in determining the value of an option. The exercise price is the hurdle beyond which the underlying must go to justify exercise. For a call, the underlying must rise above the exercise price, and for a put, the underlying must fall below the exercise price, to justify exercise. When the underlying is beyond the exercise price in the appropriate direction (higher for a call, lower for a put), the option is said to be **in the money**. When the underlying is precisely at the exercise price, the option is said to be **at the money**. When the underlying has not reached the exercise price (currently lower for a call, higher for a put), the option is said to be **out of the money**. This characterization of whether the option is in-, at-, or out-of-the-money is referred to as the option's **moneyness.**

For a call option, a lower exercise price has two benefits. One is that there are more values of the underlying at expiration that are above the exercise price, meaning that there are more outcomes in which the call expires in-the-money. The other benefit is that assuming the call expires in-the-money, for any value of the underlying, the option value is greater the lower the exercise price. In other words, at expiration the underlying value S_T will be above the exercise price far more often, the lower is X. And if S_T is indeed higher than X, the payoff of $S_T - X$ is greater, the lower is X.

For puts, the effect is just the opposite. To expire in-the-money, the value of the underlying must fall below the exercise price. The higher the exercise price, the better chance the underlying has of getting below it. Likewise, if the value of the underlying does fall below the exercise price, the higher the exercise price, the greater the payoff. So, if X is higher, S_T will be below it more often, and if S_T is less than X, the payoff of $X - S_T$ is greater, the higher is X for whatever value of S_T occurs.

The exercise price also helps form an upper bound for the value of a European put. If you were holding a European put, the best outcome you could hope for is a zero value of the underlying. For equities, that would mean complete failure and dissolution of the company with shareholders receiving no final payment.[15] In that case, the put would pay $X - S_T$, but with S_T at zero, the put would pay X. If the underlying value goes to zero during the life of the European put, however, the holder cannot collect that payoff until expiration. Nonetheless, the holder would have a risk-free claim on a payoff of X at expiration. Thus, the most the put would be worth is the present value of X, meaning X discounted from expiration to the current day at the risk-free rate.[16] Although the holder cannot collect the payoff by exercising the option, he could sell it for the present value of X.

To recap these results,

The value of a European call option is inversely related to the exercise price.

The value of a European put option is directly related to the exercise price.

4.1.4 *Effect of Time to Expiration*

Logic suggests that longer-term options should be worth more than shorter-term options. That statement is usually true but not always. A call option unquestionably benefits from additional time. For example, the right to buy an asset for $50 is worth a lot more if that right is available for two years instead of one. The additional time provides further opportunity for the underlying to rise above the exercise price. Although that means there is also additional time for the underlying to fall below the exercise price, it hardly matters to the holder of the call because the loss on the downside is limited to the premium paid.

For a European put option, the additional time still provides more opportunity for the underlying price to fall below the exercise price, but with the additional risk of it rising above the exercise price mitigated by the limited loss of the premium if the put expires out-of-the-money. Thus, it sounds as if puts benefit from longer time, but that is not necessarily true. There is a subtle penalty for this additional time. Put option holders are awaiting the sale of the underlying, for which they will receive the exercise price. The longer they have to wait, the lower the present value of the payoff. For some puts, this negative effect can dwarf the positive effect. This situation occurs

---

15 You might think this point means that people who buy puts are hoping the company goes bankrupt, a seemingly morbid motivation. Yet, put buyers are often people who own the stock and buy the put for protection. This motivation is no different from owning a house and buying fire insurance. You do not want the house to burn down. If your sole motivation in buying the insurance were to make a profit on the insurance, you would want the house to burn down. This moral hazard problem illustrates why it is difficult, if not impossible, to buy insurance on a house you do not own. Likewise, executives are prohibited from owning puts on their companies' stock. Individual investors can own puts on stocks they do not own, because they cannot drive the stock price down.

16 For the put holder to truly have a risk-free claim on X at expiration, given zero value of the underlying today, the underlying value must go to zero and have no possibility of any recovery. If there is any possibility of recovery, the underlying value would not go to zero, as is often observed when a legal filing for bankruptcy is undertaken. Many equities do recover. If there were some chance of recovery but the equity value was zero, demand for the stock would be infinite, which would push the price up.

with a put the longer the time to expiration, the higher the risk-free rate of interest, and the deeper it is in-the-money. The positive effect of time, however, is somewhat more dominant.

Note that we did not mention this effect for calls. For calls, the holder is waiting to pay out money at expiration. More time lowers the value of this possible outlay. Hence, a longer time period helps call option buyers in this regard.

To recap these results,

The value of a European call option is directly related to the time to expiration.

The value of a European put option can be either directly or inversely related to the time to expiration. The direct effect is more common, but the inverse effect can prevail with a put the longer the time to expiration, the higher the risk-free rate, and the deeper it is in-the-money.

4.1.5 *Effect of the Risk-Free Rate of Interest*

We have already alluded to the effect of the risk-free rate. For call options, a longer time to expiration means that the present value of the outlay of the exercise price is lower. In other words, with a longer time to expiration, the call option holder continues to earn interest on the money that could be expended later in paying the exercise price upon exercise of the option. If the option is ultimately never exercised, this factor is irrelevant, but it remains at best a benefit and at worst has no effect. For puts, the opposite argument prevails. A longer time to expiration with a higher interest rate lowers the present value of the receipt of the exercise price upon exercise. Thus, the value today of what the put holder might receive at expiration is lower. If the put is ultimately never exercised, the risk-free rate has no effect. Thus, at best, a higher risk-free rate has no effect on the value of a put. At worst, it decreases the value of the put.

These results are summarized as follows:

The value of a European call is directly related to the risk-free interest rate.

The value of a European put is inversely related to the risk-free interest rate.

4.1.6 *Effect of Volatility of the Underlying*

In studying the pricing of equities, we are conditioned to believe that volatility has a negative effect. After all, investors like return and dislike risk. Volatility is certainly an element of risk. Therefore, volatility is bad for investors, right? Well, partially right.

First, not all volatility is bad for investors. Unsystematic volatility should be irrelevant. Investors can hold diversified portfolios. Systematic volatility is clearly undesirable, but do not think that this means that volatility should be completely avoided where possible. If volatility were universally undesirable, no one would take risks. Clearly risks have to be taken to provide opportunity for reward.

With options, volatility of the underlying is, however, universally desirable. The greater the volatility of the underlying, the more an option is worth. This seemingly counterintuitive result is easy to understand with a little explanation.

First, let us make sure we know what volatility really means. In studying asset returns, we typically represent volatility with the standard deviation of the return, which measures the variation from the average return. The S&P 500 Index has an approximate long-run volatility of around 20%. Under the assumption of a normal distribution, a standard deviation of 20% implies that about 68% of the time, the returns will be within plus or minus one standard deviation of the average. About 95% of the time, they will be within plus or minus two standard deviations of the average. About

99% of the time, they will be within plus or minus three standard deviations of the average. When the distribution is non-normal, different interpretations apply, and in some extreme cases, the standard deviation can be nearly impossible to interpret.

Standard deviation is not the only notion of volatility, however, and it is not even needed at this point. You can proceed fairly safely with a measure as simple as the highest possible value minus the lowest, known as the range. The only requirement we need right now is that the concept of volatility reflects dispersion—how high and how low the underlying can go.

So, regardless of how we measure volatility, the following conditions will hold:

1 A call option will have a higher payoff the higher the underlying is at expiration.

2 A call option will have a zero payoff if it expires with the underlying below the exercise price.

If we could impose greater volatility on the underlying, we should be able to see that in Condition 1, the payoff has a better chance of being greater because the underlying has a greater possibility of large positive returns. In Condition 2, however, the zero payoff is unaffected if we impose greater volatility. Expiring more out-of-the-money is not worse than expiring less out-of-the-money, but expiring more in-the-money is better than expiring less-in-the-money.[17]

For puts, we have

1 A put option will have a higher payoff the lower the underlying is at expiration.

2 A put option will have a zero payoff if it expires with the underlying above the exercise price.

If we could impose greater volatility, we would find that it would have a beneficial effect in (1) because a larger positive payoff would have a greater chance of occurring. In (2), the zero payoff is unaffected. The greater of the option expiring more out-of-the-money is irrelevant. Expiring more out-of-the-money is not worse than expiring less out-of-the-money.

Thus, we summarize our results in this section as

> *The value of a European call is directly related to the volatility of the underlying.*
>
> *The value of a European put is directly related to the volatility of the underlying.*

The combined effects of time and volatility give rise to the concept of the time value of an option. The **time value** of an option is the difference between the market price of the option and its intrinsic value. It represents the market valuation of the potential for higher exercise value relative to the potential for lower exercise value given the volatility of the underlying. Time value of an option is not to be confused with the time value of money, which is the notion of money later being worth less than money today as a result of the combined effects of time and interest. Time value results in an option price being greater with volatility and time but declining as expiration approaches. At expiration, no time value remains and the option is worth only its exercise value. As such, an option price is said to decay over time, a process characterized as **time value decay**, which is covered in more advanced material.

17 Think of an option expiring out-of-the-money as like it being dead. (Indeed, the option is dead.) Being "more dead" is not worse than being "less dead."

4.1.7 *Effect of Payments on the Underlying and the Cost of Carry*

We previously discussed how payments on the underlying and carrying costs enter into the determination of forward prices. They also affect option prices. Payments on the underlying refer to dividends on stocks and interest on bonds. In addition, some commodities offer a convenience yield benefit. Carrying costs include the actual physical costs of maintaining and/or storing an asset.

Let us first consider the effect of benefits. Payments of dividends and interest reduce the value of the underlying. Stocks and bonds fall in value as dividends and interest are paid. These benefits to holders of these securities do not flow to holders of options. For call option holders, this reduction is a negative factor. The price of the underlying is hurt by such payments, and call holders do not get to collect these payments. For put holders, the effect is the opposite. When the value of the underlying is reduced, put holders are helped.

Carrying costs have the opposite effect. They raise the effective cost of holding or shorting the asset. Holding call options enables an investor to participate in movements of the underlying without incurring these costs. Holding put options makes it more expensive to participate in movements in the underlying than by short selling because short sellers benefit from carrying costs, which are borne by owners of the asset.

To summarize the results from this section,

> *A European call option is worth less the more benefits that are paid by the underlying and worth more the more costs that are incurred in holding the underlying.*

> *A European put option is worth more the more benefits that are paid by the underlying and worth less the more costs that are incurred in holding the underlying.*

4.1.8 *Lowest Prices of Calls and Puts*

What we have learned so far forms a framework for understanding how European options are priced. Let us now go a step further and establish a minimum price for these options.

First, we need to look at a call option as similar to the purchase of the underlying with a portion of the purchase price financed by borrowing. If the underlying is a stock, this transaction is usually called a margin transaction. Assume that the underlying is worth S_0. Also assume that you borrow cash in the amount of the present value of X, promising to pay X back T periods later at an interest rate of r. Thus, $X/(1 + r)^T$ is the amount borrowed, and X is the amount to be paid back. Now move forward to time T and observe the price of the underlying, S_T. Upon paying back the loan, the overall strategy will be worth $S_T - X$, which can be positive or negative.

Next, consider an alternative strategy of buying a call option expiring at T with an exercise price of X, the same value as the face value of the loan. We know that the option payoffs will be $S_T - X$ if it expires in-the- money ($S_T > X$) and zero if not ($S_T \le X$). Exhibit 11 compares these two strategies.[18]

18 Note in Exhibit 11, and in others to come, that the inequality ≤ is referred to as out-of-the-money. The case of equality is technically referred to as at-the-money but the verbiage is simplified if we continue to call it out-of-the-money. It is certainly not in-the-money and at-the-money is arguably the same as out-of-the-money. Regardless of one's preference, the equality case can be attached to either of the two outcomes with no effect on our conclusions.

Exhibit 11 Call Option vs. Leveraged (Margin) Transaction

	Outcome at T	
	Call Expires Out-of-the-Money ($S_T \le X$)	Call Expires In-the-Money ($S_T > X$)
Call	0	$S_T - X$
Leveraged transaction		
Asset	S_T	S_T
Loan	$-X$	$-X$
Total	$S_T - X$	$S_T - X$

When the call expires in-the-money, both transactions produce identical payoffs. When the call expires out-of-the-money, the call value is zero, but the leveraged transaction is almost surely a loss. Its value $S_T - X$ is negative or zero at best (if S_T is exactly equal to X).

If two strategies are found to produce equivalent results in some outcomes but one produces a better result in all other outcomes, then one strategy dominates the former. Here we see that the call strategy dominates the leveraged strategy. Any strategy that dominates the other can never have a lower value at any time. Why would anyone pay more for one strategy than for another if the former will never produce a better result than the latter? Thus, the value of the call strategy, c_0, has to be worth at least the value of the leveraged transaction, S_0 (the value of the asset), minus $X/(1 + r)^T$ (the value of the loan). Hence, $c_0 \ge S_0 - X/(1 + r)^T$.

The inequality means that this statement provides the lowest price of the call, but there is one more thing we need to do. It can easily be true that $X/(1 + r)^T > S_0$. In that case, we are saying that the lowest value is a negative number, but that statement is meaningless. A call can never be worth less than zero, because its holder cannot be forced to exercise it. Thus, we tend to express this relationship as

$$c_0 \ge \text{Max}\left[0, S_0 - X/(1+r)^T\right] \quad (10)$$

which represents the greater of the value of zero or the underlying price minus the present value of the exercise price. This value becomes the lower limit of the call price.

Now consider an analogous result for puts. Suppose we want to profit from a declining price of the underlying. One way to do this is to sell the underlying short. Suppose we do that and invest cash equal to the present value of X into risk-free bonds that pay X at time T. At time T, given a price of the underlying of S_T, the short sale pays off $-S_T$, a reflection of the payment of S_T to cover the short sale. The bonds pay X. Hence, the total payoff is $X - S_T$.

Now, compare that result with the purchase of a put expiring at T with exercise price of X. If the put expires in–the-money ($S_T < X$), it is worth $X - S_T$. If it expires out-of-the-money ($S_T \ge X$), it is worth zero. Exhibit 12 illustrates the comparison of the put with the short sale and bond strategy. We see that for the in-the-money case, the put and short sale and bond strategies match each other. For the out-of-the-money case, however, the put performs better because the short sale and bond strategy pays $X - S_T$. With $S_T \ge X$, this payment amount is negative. With the put dominating the short sale and bond strategy, the put value cannot be less than the value of the short sale and bond strategy, meaning $p_0 \ge X/(1 + r)^T - S_0$. But as with calls, the right-hand side can be negative, and it hardly helps us to say that a put must sell for more than a negative number. A put can never be worth less than zero, because its owner cannot be forced to exercise it. Thus, the overall result is expressed succinctly as

$$p_0 \geq \text{Max}\left[0, X/(1+r)^T - S_0\right] \tag{11}$$

Exhibit 12 Put vs. Short Sale and Bond Purchase

	Outcome at T	
	Put Expires In-the-Money ($S_T < X$)	**Put Expires Out-of-the-Money ($S_T \geq X$)**
Put	$X - S_T$	0
Short sale and bond purchase		
Short sale	$-S_T$	$-S_T$
Bond	X	X
Total	$X - S_T$	$X - S_T$

Let us look at some basic examples. Assume the exercise price is €60, the risk-free rate is 4%, and the expiration is nine months, so $T = 9/12 = 0.75$. Consider two cases:

Underlying: S_0 = €70

Minimum call price = Max[0,€70 – €60/(1.04)$^{0.75}$] = Max(0,€11.74) = €11.74

Minimum put price = Max[0,€60/(1.04)$^{0.75}$ – €70] = Max(0,–€11.74) = €0.00

Underlying: S_0 = €50

Minimum call price = Max[0,€50 – €60/(1.04)$^{0.75}$] = Max(0,–€8.26) = €0.00

Minimum put price = Max[0,€60/(1.04)$^{0.75}$ – €50] = Max(0,€8.26) = €8.26

To recap, in this section we have established lower limits for call and put option values. Formally restating these results in words,

The lowest value of a European call is the greater of zero or the value of the underlying minus the present value of the exercise price.

The lowest value of a European put is the greater of zero or the present value of the exercise price minus the value of the underlying.

EXAMPLE 6

Basic Principles of European Option Pricing

1 Which of the following factors does *not* affect the value of a European option?

A The volatility of the underlying

B Dividends or interest paid by the underlying

C The percentage of the investor's assets invested in the option

2 Which of the following statements imply that a European call on a stock is worth more?

   A Less time to expiration

   B A higher stock price relative to the exercise price

   C Larger dividends paid by the stock during the life of the option

3 Why might a European put be worth less the longer the time to expiration?

   A The cost of waiting to receive the exercise price is higher.

   B The risk of the underlying is lower over a longer period of time.

   C The longer time to expiration means that the put is more likely to expire out-of-the-money.

4 The loss in value of an option as it moves closer to expiration is called what?

   A Time value decay

   B Volatility diminution

   C Time value of money

5 How does the minimum value of a call or put option differ from its exercise value?

   A The exercise price is adjusted for the time value of money.

   B The minimum value reflects the volatility of the underlying.

   C The underlying price is adjusted for the time value of money.

Solution to 1:

C is correct. The investor's exposure to the option is not relevant to the price one should pay to buy or ask to sell the option. Volatility and dividends or interest paid by the underlying are highly relevant to the value of the option.

Solution to 2:

B is correct. The higher the stock price and the lower the exercise price, the more valuable is the call. Less time to expiration and larger dividends reduce the value of the call.

Solution to 3:

A is correct. Although the longer time benefits the holder of the option, it also has a cost in that exercise of a longer-term put comes much later. Therefore, the receipt of the exercise price is delayed. Longer time to expiration does not lower the risk of the underlying. The longer time also does not increase the likelihood of the option expiring out-of-the-money.

Solution to 4:

A is correct. An option has time value that decays as the expiration approaches. There is no such concept as volatility diminution. Time value of money relates only to the value of money at one point in time versus another.

Solution to 5:

A is correct. The minimum value formula is the greater of zero or the difference between the underlying price and the present value of the exercise price, whereas the exercise value is the maximum of zero and the appropriate difference between the underlying price and the exercise price. Volatility does not affect the minimum price. It does not make sense to adjust the underlying price for the time value of money for the simple reason that it is already adjusted for the time value of money.

4.1.9 *Put–Call Parity*

One of the first concepts that a trader learns in options is the parity relationship between puts and calls. Even though the word "parity" means "equivalence," puts and calls are not equivalent. There is, however, a relationship between the call price and the price of its corresponding put, which we refer to as put–call parity.

Suppose Investor A owns an asset that has a current price of S_0. Assume the asset makes no cash payments and has no carrying costs. The end of the holding period is time T, at which point the asset will be worth S_T. Fearing the possibility that S_T will decline, Investor A buys a put option with an exercise price of X, which can be used to sell the asset for X at time T. This put option has a premium of p_0. Combined with the value of the asset, the investor's current position is worth $S_0 + p_0$, which is the investor's money at risk. This strategy of holding the asset and a put is sometimes called a **protective put**.

At expiration, the value of the asset is S_T. The value of the put will be either zero or $X - S_T$. If the asset increases in value such that $S_T \geq X$, then the overall position is worth S_T. The asset has performed well, and the investor will let the put expire. If the asset value declines to the point at which $S_T < X$, the asset is worth S_T, and the put is worth $X - S_T$, for a total of X. In other words, the investor would exercise the put, selling the asset for X, which exceeds the asset's current value of S_T.

This strategy seems like a reasonable and possibly quite attractive investment. Investor A receives the benefit of unlimited upside potential, with the downside performance truncated at X. Exhibit 13 shows the performance of the protective put. The graph on the left illustrates the underlying asset and the put. The graph on the right shows their combined effects.

Exhibit 13 Protective Put (Asset Plus Long Put)

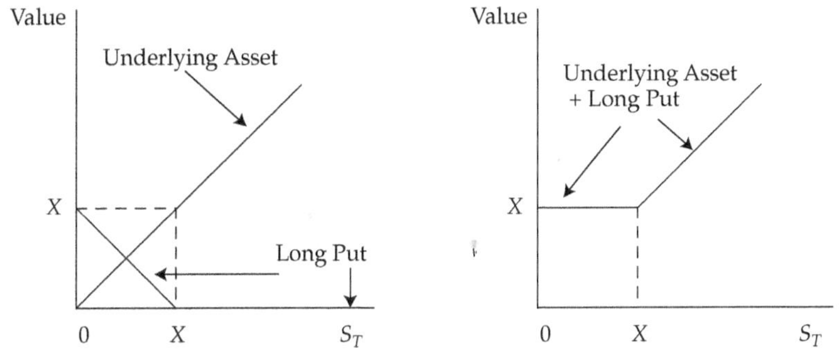

Consider Investor B, an options trader. At time 0, this investor buys a call option on this asset with an exercise price of X that expires at T and a risk-free zero-coupon bond with a face value of X that matures at T. The call costs c_0, and the bond costs the present value of X, which is $X/(1 + r)^T$. Thus, Investor B has invested funds of $c_0 + X/(1 + r)^T$. This strategy is sometimes known as a **fiduciary call**. If the underlying price exceeds the exercise price at expiration, the call will be worth $S_T - X$, and the bond will mature and pay a value of X. These values combine to equal S_T. If the underlying price does not exceed the exercise price at expiration, the call expires worthless and the bond is worth X for a combined value of X.

Exhibit 14 shows the performance of the fiduciary call. The graph on the left shows the call and bond, and the graph on the right shows the combined effects of the two strategies.

Exhibit 14 Fiduciary Call (Long Call Plus Risk-Free Bond)

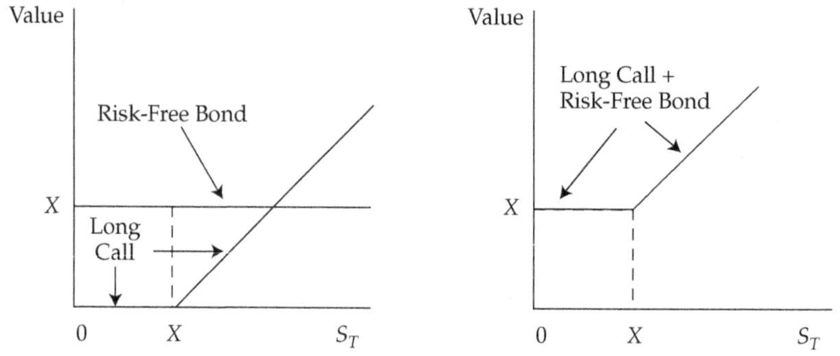

Comparing Exhibit 13 with Exhibit 14 shows that a protective put and a fiduciary call produce the same result. Exhibit 15 shows this result more directly by identifying the payoffs in the various outcomes. Recall that Investor A committed funds of $S_0 + p_0$, while Investor B committed funds of $c_0 + X/(1 + r)^T$. If both investors receive the same payoffs at time T regardless of the asset price at T, the amounts they invest at time 0 have to be the same. Thus, we require

$$S_0 + p_0 = c_0 + X/(1 + r)^T \quad (12)$$

This relationship is known as **put–call parity**.

Exhibit 15 Protective Put vs. Fiduciary Call

	Outcome at T	
	Put Expires In-the-Money ($S_T < X$)	**Call Expires In-the-Money ($S_T \geq X$)**
Protective put		
Asset	S_T	S_T
Long put	$X - S_T$	0
Total	X	S_T
Fiduciary call		
Long call	0	$S_T - X$
Risk-free bond	X	X
Total	X	S_T

For a simple example, assume call and put options with an exercise price of ¥100,000 in which the underlying is at ¥90,000 at time 0. The risk-free rate is 2% and the options expire in two months, so $T = 2/12 = 0.167$. To completely fill in the puzzle, we would need to know the put or call price, from which we could obtain the other. For now, let us write this relationship as

$$p_0 - c_0 = X/(1 + r)^T - S_0$$

The right side would be $¥100{,}000/(1.02)^{0.167} - ¥90{,}000 = ¥9{,}670$. Thus, the put price should exceed the call price by ¥9,670. Thus, if the call were priced at ¥5,000, the put price would be ¥14,670. If we knew the put price, we could obtain the call price. Put–call parity does not tell us which price is correct, and it requires knowledge of one price to get the other. Alternatively, it can tell us the difference in the put and call prices.

Put–call parity must hold, at least within transaction costs, or arbitrage opportunities would arise. For example, suppose Investor C observes market prices and finds that the left- hand side of put–call parity, $S_0 + p_0$, is less than the right-hand side, $c_0 + X/(1 + r)^T$. Thus, the put and the stock cost less than the call and the bond. Knowing that there should be equality (parity), Investor C executes an arbitrage transaction, selling the overpriced transactions (the call and the bond) and buying the underpriced transactions (the asset and the put).[19] By selling the higher priced side and buying the lower priced side, Investor C will take in more money than she will pay out, a net inflow of $c_0 + X/(1 + r)^T - (S_0 + p_0)$. At expiration, the long put and long asset will offset the short call and bond, as shown in Exhibit 16.

Exhibit 16 Put–Call Parity Arbitrage

		Outcome at T	
Transaction	**Cash Flow at Time 0**	**Put Expires In-the-Money ($S_T < X$)**	**Call Expires In-the-Money ($S_T \geq X$)**
Buy asset	$-S_0$	S_T	S_T
Buy put	$-p_0$	$X - S_T$	0
Sell call	$+c_0$	0	$-(S_T - X)$
Borrow	$+X/(1 + r)^T$	$-X$	$-X$
Total	$-S_0 - p_0 + c_0 + X/(1 + r)^T > 0$	0	0

In simple terms, if $S_T < X$, the short call expires out-of-the-money and the put is exercised to sell the asset for X. This cash, X, is then used to pay off the loan. The net effect is that no money flows in or out at T. If $S_T \geq X$, the put expires out-of-the money, and the short call is exercised, meaning that Investor C must sell the asset for X. This cash, X, is then used to pay off the loan. Again, no money flows in or out. The net effect is a perfect hedge in which no money is paid out or received at T. But there was money taken in at time 0. Taking in money today and never having to pay it out is an arbitrage profit. Arbitrage opportunities like this, however, will be noticed by many investors who will engage in the same transactions. Prices will adjust until parity is restored, whereby $S_0 + p_0 = c_0 + X/(1 + r)^T$.

19 Selling the bond is equivalent to borrowing, meaning to issue a loan.

Put–call parity provides tremendous insights into option pricing. Recall that we proved that going long the asset and long a put is equivalent to going long a call and long a risk-free bond. We can rearrange the put–call parity equation in the following ways:

$$S_0 + p_0 = c_0 + X/(1+r)^T$$
$$\Rightarrow$$
$$p_0 = c_0 - S_0 + X/(1+r)^T$$
$$c_0 = p_0 + S_0 - X/(1+r)^T$$
$$S_0 = c_0 - p_0 + X/(1+r)^T$$
$$X/(1+r)^T = S_0 + p_0 - c_0$$

By using the symbols and the signs in these versions of put–call parity, we can see several important interpretations. In the equations below, plus signs mean long and minus signs mean short:

$$p_0 = c_0 - S_0 + X/(1+r)^T \quad \Rightarrow \quad \text{long put} = \text{long call, short asset, long bond}$$
$$c_0 = p_0 + S_0 - X/(1+r)^T \quad \Rightarrow \quad \text{long call} = \text{long put, long asset, short bond}$$
$$S_0 = c_0 - p_0 + X/(1+r)^T \quad \Rightarrow \quad \text{long asset} = \text{long call, short put, long bond}$$
$$X/(1+r)^T = S_0 + p_0 - c_0 \quad \Rightarrow \quad \text{long bond} = \text{long asset, long put, short call}$$

You should be able to convince yourself of any of these points by constructing a table similar to Exhibit 15.[20]

4.1.10 *Put–Call–Forward Parity*

Recall that we demonstrated that one could create a risk-free position by going long the asset and selling a forward contract.[21] It follows that one can synthetically create a position in the asset by going long a forward contract and long a risk-free bond. Recall our put–call parity discussion and assume that Investor A creates his protective put in a slightly different manner. Instead of buying the asset, he buys a forward contract and a risk-free bond in which the face value is the forward price. Exhibit 17 shows that this strategy is a synthetic protective put. Because we showed that the fiduciary call is equivalent to the protective put, a fiduciary call has to be equivalent to a protective put with a forward contract. Exhibit 18 demonstrates this point.

Exhibit 17 Protective Put with Forward Contract vs. Protective Put with Asset

	Outcome at *T*	
	Put Expires In-the-Money ($S_T < X$)	**Put Expires Out-of-the-Money ($S_T \geq X$)**
Protective put with asset		
Asset	S_T	S_T
Long put	$X - S_T$	0
Total	X	S_T

20 As a further exercise, you might change the signs of each term in the above and provide the appropriate interpretations.
21 You might wish to review Exhibit 6.

Exhibit 17 (Continued)

	Outcome at T	
	Put Expires In-the-Money ($S_T < X$)	**Put Expires Out-of-the-Money ($S_T \geq X$)**
Protective put with forward contract		
Risk-free bond	$F_0(T)$	$F_0(T)$
Forward contract	$S_T - F_0(T)$	$S_T - F_0(T)$
Long put	$X - S_T$	0
Total	X	S_T

Exhibit 18 Protective Put with Forward Contract vs. Fiduciary Call

	Outcome at T	
	Put Expires In-the-Money ($S_T < X$)	**Call Expires In-the-Money ($S_T \geq X$)**
Protective Put with Forward Contract		
Risk-free bond	$F_0(T)$	$F_0(T)$
Forward contract	$S_T - F_0(T)$	$S_T - F_0(T)$
Long put	$X - S_T$	0
Total	X	S_T
Fiduciary Call		
Call	0	$S_T - X$
Risk-free bond	X	X
Total	X	S_T

It follows that the cost of the fiduciary call must equal the cost of the synthetic protective put, giving us what is referred to as **put–call–forward parity**,

$$F_0(T)/(1+r)^T + p_0 = c_0 + X/(1+r)^T \quad (13)$$

Returning to our put–call parity example, a forward contract on ¥90,000 expiring in two months with a 2% interest rate would have a price of ¥90,000(1.02)$^{0.167}$ = ¥90,298. Rearranging Equation 13, we have

$$p_0 - c_0 = [X - F_0(T)]/(1+r)^T$$

The right-hand side is (¥100,000 – ¥90,298)/(1.02)$^{0.167}$ = ¥9,670, which is the same answer we obtained using the underlying asset rather than the forward contract. Naturally these two models give us the same answer. They are both based on the assumption that no arbitrage is possible within the spot, forward, and options markets.

So far we have learned only how to price options in relation to other options, such as a call versus a put or a call or a put versus a forward. We need a way to price options versus their underlying.

EXAMPLE 7

Put–Call Parity

1 Which of the following statements *best* describes put–call parity?

A The put price always equals the call price.

B The put price equals the call price if the volatility is known.

C The put price plus the underlying price equals the call price plus the present value of the exercise price.

2 From put–call parity, which of the following transactions is risk-free?

A Long asset, long put, short call

B Long call, long put, short asset

C Long asset, long call, short bond

Solution to 1:

C is correct. The put and underlying make up a protective put, while the call and present value of the exercise price make up a fiduciary call. The put price equals the call price for certain combinations of interest rates, times to expiration, and option moneyness, but these are special cases. Volatility has no effect on put–call parity.

Solution to 2:

A is correct. The combination of a long asset, long put, and short call is risk free because its payoffs produce a known cash flow of the value of the exercise price. The other two combinations do not produce risk-free positions. You should work through the payoffs of these three combinations in the form of Exhibit 12.

4.2 Binomial Valuation of Options

Because the option payoff is determined by the underlying, if we know the outcome of the underlying, we know the payoff of the option. That means that the price of the underlying is the only element of uncertainty. Moreover, the uncertainty is not so much the value of the underlying at expiration as it is whether the underlying is above or below the exercise price. If the underlying is above the exercise price at expiration, the payoff is $S_T - X$ for calls and zero for puts. If the underlying is below the exercise price at expiration, the payoff is zero for calls and $X - S_T$ for puts. In other words, the payoff of the option is straightforward and known, as soon as we know whether the option expires in- or out-of-the-money. Note that for forwards, futures, and swaps, there is no such added complexity. The payoff formula is the same regardless of whether the underlying is above or below the hurdle.

As a result of this characteristic of options, derivation of an option pricing model requires the specification of a model of a random process that describes movements in the underlying. Given the entirely different nature of the payoffs above and below the exercise price, it might seem difficult to derive the option price, even if we could model movements in the underlying. Fortunately, the process is less difficult than it first appears.

At this level of treatment, we will start with a very simple model that allows only two possible movements in the underlying—one going up and one going down from where it is now. This model with two possible outcomes is called the **binomial model**. Start with the underlying at S_0, and let it go up to S_1^+ or down to S_1^-. We cannot arbitrarily set these values at just anything. We will be required to know the values of S_1^+ and S_1^-. That does not mean we know which outcome will occur. It means that we know only what the possibilities are. In doing so, we effectively know the volatility. Assume the probability of the move to S_1^+ is q and the probability of the move to S_1^- is $1 - q$. We specify the returns implied by these moves as up and down factors, u and d, where

$$u = \frac{S_1^+}{S_0},\ d = \frac{S_1^-}{S_0} \tag{14}$$

Now, consider a European call option that expires at time 1 and has an exercise price of X. Let the call prices be c_0 today and c_1^+ and c_1^- at expiration. Exhibit 19 illustrates the model. Our objective is to determine the price of the option today, meaning to determine a formula for c_0. Knowing what we know about arbitrage and the pricing of forward contracts, it would seem we could construct a risk-free portfolio involving this option.

Exhibit 19 The Binomial Option Pricing Model

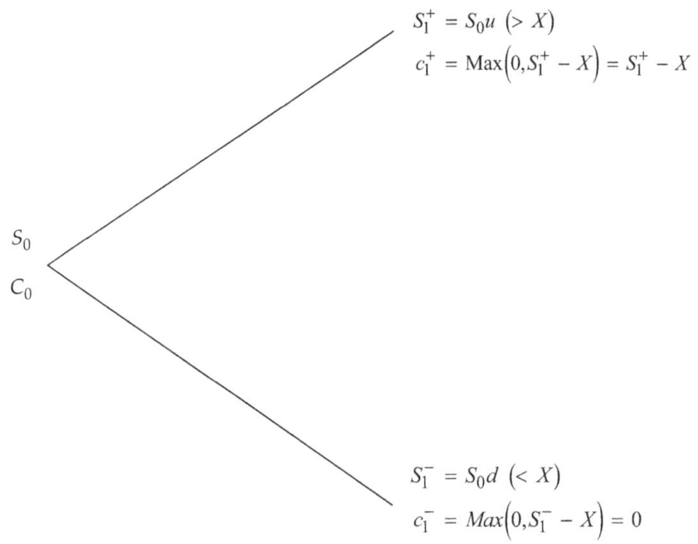

Because call options and the underlying move together, one possibility is that buying the underlying and selling a call could create a hedge. Indeed it does, but one unit of each is not the appropriate balance. Let us sell one call and hold h units of the underlying. The value h is unknown at the moment, but we will be able to determine its value. The value today of a combination of h units of the underlying and one short call is

$$V_0 = hS_0 - c_0$$

Think of V_0 as the amount of money invested. Depending on which of the two paths is taken by the underlying, the value of this portfolio at time 1 will be

$$V_1^+ = hS_1^+ - c_1^+$$

or (15)

$$V_1^- = hS_1^- - c_1^-$$

If the portfolio were hedged, then V_1^+ would equal V_1^-. We can set V_1^+ and V_1^- equal to each other and solve for the value of h that assures us that the portfolio is hedged:

$$V_1^+ = V_1^-$$
$$\Rightarrow hS_1^+ - c_1^+ = hS_1^- - c_1^- \quad (16)$$
$$\Rightarrow h = \frac{c_1^+ - c_1^-}{S_1^+ - S_1^-}$$

The values on the right-hand side are known, so we can easily calculate h. Thus, we can derive the number of units of the underlying that will perfectly hedge one unit of the short call.

We know that a perfectly hedged investment should earn the risk-free rate, r. Thus, the following statement must be true:

$$V_1^+ \text{ (or } V_1^-) = V_0(1 + r)$$

We can substitute the value of V_1^+ or V_1^- from Equation 15 into the above equation. Then we do a little algebra, which is not important to this discussion, and obtain the formula for the option price,

$$c_0 = \frac{\pi c_1^+ + (1 - \pi)c_1^-}{1 + r}$$
where
$$\pi = \frac{1 + r - d}{u - d} \quad (17)$$

Equation 17 shows that the value of the call today is a weighted average of the next two possible call prices at expiration, where the weights, π and $1 - \pi$, are given by the second formula in Equation 17.

This formula sheds a great deal of light on option pricing. Notice the following:

- The volatility of the underlying, which is reflected in the difference between S_1^+ and S_1^- and affects c_1^+ and c_1^-, is an important factor in determining the value of the option.
- The probabilities of the up and down moves, q and $1 - q$, do not appear in the formula.[22]
- The values π and $1 - \pi$ are similar to probabilities and are often called synthetic or pseudo probabilities. They produce a weighted average of the next two possible call values, a type of expected future value.
- The formula takes the form of an expected future value, the numerator, discounted at the risk-free rate.

On the first point, if volatility increases, the difference between S_1^+ and S_1^- increases, which widens the range between c_1^+ and c_1^-, leading to a higher option value. The upper payoff, c_1^+, will be larger and the lower payoff, c_1^-, will still be zero.[23] On the second point, the actual probabilities of the up and down moves do not matter. This result is because of our ability to construct a hedge and the rule of arbitrage. On the third point, the irrelevance of the actual probabilities is replaced by the relevance of a set of synthetic or pseudo probabilities, π and $1 - \pi$, which are called **risk-neutral**

22 We introduced them earlier to help make this point, but ultimately they serve no purpose.

23 Although the lower payoff is zero in this example, that will not always be the case.

probabilities. On the fourth point, these risk-neutral probabilities are used to find a synthetic expected value, which is then discounted at the risk-free rate. Thus, the option is valued as though investors are risk neutral. As we discussed extensively earlier, that is not the same as assuming that investors are risk neutral.

If the option does not trade at the specified formula, Equation 17, investors can engage in arbitrage transactions. If the option is trading too high relative to the formula, investors can sell the call, buy h shares of the underlying, and earn a return in excess of the risk-free rate, while funding the transaction by borrowing at the risk-free rate. The combined actions of arbitrageurs will result in downward pressure on the option price until it converges to the model price. If the option price is too low, buying the call, selling short h units of the asset, and investing the proceeds in risk-free bonds will generate risk-free cash that will earn more than the risk-free rate. The combined actions of arbitrageurs doing this will pressure the call price to rise until it reaches the price given by the model.

We will omit the details, but the hedge portfolio can also be constructed with puts.[24] Changing the c's to p's leads to the binomial put option pricing formula,

$$p_0 = \frac{\pi p_1^+ + (1 - \pi)p_1^-}{1 + r} \tag{18}$$

with the risk-neutral probability π determined by the same formula as for calls, as shown in Equation 17.

Let us construct a simple example. Let S_0 be £40 and the risk-free rate be 5%. The up and down factors are u = 1.20 and d = 0.75. Thus, the next two possible prices of the asset are $S_1^+ = £40(1.20) = £48$ and $S_1^- = £40(0.75) = £30$. Consider a call and a put that have exercise prices of £38. Then the next two possible values of the call and put are

$$c_1^+ = \text{Max}(0,£48 - £38) = £10$$

$$c_1^- = \text{Max}(0,£30 - £38) = £0$$

$$p_1^+ = \text{Max}(0,£38 - £48) = £0$$

$$p_1^- = \text{Max}(0,£38 - £30) = £8$$

Next we compute the risk-neutral probability,

$$\pi = \frac{1 + 0.05 - 0.75}{1.20 - 0.75} = 0.667$$

The values of the call and put are

$$c_0 = \frac{0.667(£10) + (1 - 0.667)£0}{1.05} = £6.35$$

and

$$p_0 = \frac{0.667(£0) + (1 - 0.667)£8}{1.05} = £2.54$$

The binomial model, as we see it here, is extremely simple. In reality, of course, there are more than two possible next-period prices for the underlying. As it turns out, we can extend the number of periods and subdivide an option's life into an increasing number of smaller time periods. In that case, we can obtain a more accurate and realistic model for option pricing, one that is widely used in practice. Given our objective in this reading of understanding the basic ideas behind derivative pricing, the one-period model is sufficient for the time being.

---

24 A long position in h units of the underlying would be hedged with one long put. The formula for h is the same as the one given here for calls, with call prices in the numerator instead of put prices.

EXAMPLE 8

Binomial Valuation of Options

1 Which of the following terms directly represents the volatility of the underlying in the binomial model?

  A The standard deviation of the underlying

  B The difference between the up and down factors

  C The ratio of the underlying value to the exercise price.

2 Which of the following is *not* a factor in pricing a call option in the binomial model?

  A The risk-free rate

  B The exercise price

  C The probability that the underlying will go up

3 Which of the following *best* describes the binomial option pricing formula?

  A The expected payoff is discounted at the risk-free rate plus a risk premium.

  B The spot price is compounded at the risk-free rate minus the volatility premium.

  C The expected payoff based on risk-neutral probabilities is discounted at the risk-free rate.

Solution to 1:

B is correct. The up and down factors express how high and how low the underlying can go. Standard deviation does not appear directly in the binomial model, although it is implicit. The ratio of the underlying value to the exercise price expresses the moneyness of the option.

Solution to 2:

C is correct. The actual probabilities of the up and down moves are irrelevant to pricing options. The risk-free and exercise price are, of course, highly relevant.

Solution to 3:

C is correct. Risk-neutral probabilities are used, and discounting is at the risk-free rate. There is no risk premium incorporated into option pricing because of the use of arbitrage.

We have now seen how to obtain the price of a European option. Let us now consider what happens if the options are American, meaning they have the right to be exercised early.

4.3 American Option Pricing

First, we will use upper case letters for American call and put prices: C_0 and P_0. Second, we know that American options possess every characteristic of European options and one additional trait: They can be exercised at any time prior to expiration.

Early exercise cannot be required, so the right to exercise early cannot have negative value. Thus, American options cannot sell for less than European options. Thus, we can state the following:

$$C_0 \geq c_0$$
$$P_0 \geq p_0 \tag{19}$$

Given the price of the underlying at S_0, the early-exercise feature means that we can exercise the option at any time. So, we can claim the value Max($0,S_0 - X$) for calls and Max($0,X - S_0$) for puts. These values establish new minimum prices for American calls and puts,

$$C_0 = \text{Max}(0,S_0 - X)$$
$$P_0 = \text{Max}(0,X - S_0) \tag{20}$$

For call options, we previously learned that a European call has a minimum value given by Equation 10, which is restated here:

$$c_0 \geq \text{Max}\left[0,S_0 - X/(1+r)^T\right]$$

Comparing Max($0,S_0 - X$) (the minimum for American calls) with Max[$0,S_0 - X/(1 + r)^T$] (the minimum for European calls) reveals that the latter is either the same or higher. There are some circumstances in which both minima are zero, some in which the American minimum is zero and the European minimum is positive, and some in which both are positive, in which case $S_0 - X/(1 + r)^T$ is unquestionably more than $S_0 - X$. Given that an American call price cannot be less than a European call price, we have to reestablish the American call minimum as Max[$0,S_0 - X/(1 + r)^T$].

For put options, we previously learned that a European put has a minimum value given by Equation 11, which is restated here:

$$p_0 \geq \text{Max}\left[0,X/(1+r)^T - S_0\right]$$

Comparing Max($0,X - S_0$) (the minimum for American puts) with Max[$0,X/(1 + r)^T - S_0$] (the minimum for European puts) reveals that the former is never less. In some circumstances, they are both zero. In some, $X - S_0$ is positive and $X/(1 + r)^T - S_0$ is negative, and in some cases both are positive but $X - S_0$ is unquestionably more than $X/(1 + r)^T - S_0$. Thus, the American put minimum value is the exercise value, which is Max($0,X - S_0$).

So, now we have new minimum prices for American calls and puts:

$$C_0 \geq \text{Max}\left[0,S_0 - X/(1+r)^T\right]$$
$$P_0 \geq \text{Max}(0,X - S_0) \tag{21}$$

Thus, in the market these options will trade for at least these values.

Let us return to the previous examples for the minimum values. The exercise price is €60, the risk-free rate is 4%, and the expiration is $T = 0.75$. Consider the two cases below:

Underlying: S_0 = €70

- The minimum European call price was previously calculated as €11.74. The exercise value of the American call is Max(0,€70 – €60) = €10. The American call has to sell for at least as much as the European call, so the minimum price of the American call is €11.74.
- The minimum European put price was €0.00. This is also the exercise value of the American put [Max(0,€60 – €70) = €0.00], so the minimum price of the American put is still €0.00

Underlying: S_0 = €50

- The minimum European call price was previously calculated as €0.00. The exercise value of the American call is Max(0,€50 – €60) = €0.00, so €0.00 is still the minimum price of the American call.
- The minimum European put price was previously calculated as €8.26. The exercise value of the American put is Max(0,€60 – €50) = €10. So, €10 is the minimum price of the American put.

The call result leads us to a somewhat surprising conclusion. With the exception of what happens at expiration when American and European calls are effectively the same and both worth the exercise value, an American call is always worth more in the market than exercised. That means that an American call will never be exercised early. This result is probably not intuitive.

Consider a deep in-the-money call. One might think that if the holder expected the underlying to not increase any further, exercise might be justified. Yet, we said the call would sell for more in the market than its exercise value. What is the rationale? If the investor thinks the underlying will not go up any further and thus expects no further gains from the option, why would she prefer the underlying? Would the investor be happier holding the underlying, which she believes is not expected to increase? Moreover, she would tie up more funds exercising to acquire the underlying than if she just held on to the option or, better yet, sold it to another investor.

So far, however, we have left out a possible factor that can affect early exercise. Suppose the underlying is a stock and pays dividends. When a stock goes ex-dividend, its price instantaneously falls. Although we will omit the details, an investor holding a call option may find it worthwhile to exercise the call just before the stock goes ex-dividend. The capture of the dividend, thereby avoiding the ex-dividend drop in the price of the underlying, can make early exercise worthwhile. If the underlying is a bond, coupon interest can also motivate early exercise. But if there are significant carrying costs, the motivation for early exercise is weakened. Storage costs lend a preference for owning the option over owning the underlying.

Because the minimum value of an American put exceeds the minimum value of the European put, there is a much stronger motivation for early exercise. Suppose you owned an American put on a stock that is completely bankrupt, with a zero stock price and no possibility of recovery. You can either wait until expiration and capture its exercise value of $\text{Max}(0,X - S_T) = \text{Max}(0,X - 0) = \text{Max}(0,X) = X$, or you can capture that value by exercising now. Obviously now is better. As it turns out, however, the underlying does not need to go all the way to zero. There is a critical point at which a put is so deep in-the-money that early exercise is justified. This rationale works differently for a call. A deep in-the-money put has a limit to its ultimate value. It can get no deeper than when the underlying goes to zero. For a call, there is no limit to its moneyness because the underlying has no upper limit to its price.

Although dividends and coupon interest encourage early exercise for calls, they discourage early exercise for puts. The loss from the decline in the price of the underlying that is avoided by exercising a call just before the decline works to the benefit of a put holder. Therefore, if a put holder were considering exercising early, he would be better off waiting until right after the dividend or interest were paid. Carrying costs on the underlying, which discourage exercise for calls, encourage exercise for puts.

At this point, we cannot determine the critical prices at which American options are best exercised early. We require more knowledge and experience with option pricing models, which is covered in more advanced material.

EXAMPLE 9

American Option Pricing

1 With respect to American calls, which of the following statements is *most* accurate?

A American calls should be exercised early if the underlying has reached its expected maximum price.

B American calls should be exercised early if the underlying has a lower expected return than the risk-free rate.

C American calls should be exercised early only if there is a dividend or other cash payment on the underlying.

2 The effect of dividends on a stock on early exercise of a put is to:

A make early exercise less likely.

B have no effect on early exercise.

C make early exercise more likely.

Solution to 1:

C is correct. Cash payments on the underlying are the only reason to exercise American calls early. Interest rates, the expected return on the underlying, and any notion of a maximum price is irrelevant. But note that a dividend does not mean that early exercise should automatically be conducted. A dividend is only a necessary condition to justify early exercise for calls.

Solution to 2:

A is correct. Dividends drive down the stock price when the dividend is paid. Thus, all else being equal, a stock paying dividends has a built-in force that drives down the stock price. This characteristic discourages early exercise, because stock price declines are beneficial to holders of puts.

SUMMARY

This reading on derivative pricing provides a foundation for understanding how derivatives are valued and traded. Key points include the following:

- The price of the underlying asset is equal to the expected future price discounted at the risk-free rate, plus a risk premium, plus the present value of any benefits, minus the present value of any costs associated with holding the asset.
- An arbitrage opportunity occurs when two identical assets or combinations of assets sell at different prices, leading to the possibility of buying the cheaper asset and selling the more expensive asset to produce a risk-free return without investing any capital.
- In well-functioning markets, arbitrage opportunities are quickly exploited, and the resulting increased buying of underpriced assets and increased selling of overpriced assets returns prices to equivalence.

- Derivatives are priced by creating a risk-free combination of the underlying and a derivative, leading to a unique derivative price that eliminates any possibility of arbitrage.
- Derivative pricing through arbitrage precludes any need for determining risk premiums or the risk aversion of the party trading the option and is referred to as risk-neutral pricing.
- The value of a forward contract at expiration is the value of the asset minus the forward price.
- The value of a forward contract prior to expiration is the value of the asset minus the present value of the forward price.
- The forward price, established when the contract is initiated, is the price agreed to by the two parties that produces a zero value at the start.
- Costs incurred and benefits received by holding the underlying affect the forward price by raising and lowering it, respectively.
- Futures prices can differ from forward prices because of the effect of interest rates on the interim cash flows from the daily settlement.
- Swaps can be priced as an implicit series of off-market forward contracts, whereby each contract is priced the same, resulting in some contracts being positively valued and some negatively valued but with their combined value equaling zero.
- At expiration, a European call or put is worth its exercise value, which for calls is the greater of zero or the underlying price minus the exercise price and for puts is the greater of zero and the exercise price minus the underlying price.
- European calls and puts are affected by the value of the underlying, the exercise price, the risk-free rate, the time to expiration, the volatility of the underlying, and any costs incurred or benefits received while holding the underlying.
- Option values experience time value decay, which is the loss in value due to the passage of time and the approach of expiration, plus the moneyness and the volatility.
- The minimum value of a European call is the maximum of zero and the underlying price minus the present value of the exercise price.
- The minimum value of a European put is the maximum of zero and the present value of the exercise price minus the price of the underlying.
- European put and call prices are related through put–call parity, which specifies that the put price plus the price of the underlying equals the call price plus the present value of the exercise price.
- European put and call prices are related through put–call–forward parity, which shows that the put price plus the value of a risk-free bond with face value equal to the forward price equals the call price plus the value of a risk-free bond with face value equal to the exercise price.
- The values of European options can be obtained using the binomial model, which specifies two possible prices of the asset one period later and enables the construction of a risk-free hedge consisting of the option and the underlying.
- American call prices can differ from European call prices only if there are cash flows on the underlying, such as dividends or interest; these cash flows are the only reason for early exercise of a call.
- American put prices can differ from European put prices, because the right to exercise early always has value for a put, which is because of a lower limit on the value of the underlying.

PRACTICE PROBLEMS

1 For a risk-averse investor, the price of a risky asset, assuming no additional costs and benefits of holding the asset, is:

A unrelated to the risk-free rate.

B directly related to its level of risk.

C inversely related to its level of risk.

2 An arbitrage opportunity is *least likely* to be exploited when:

A one position is illiquid.

B the price differential between assets is large.

C the investor can execute a transaction in large volumes.

3 An arbitrageur will *most likely* execute a trade when:

A transaction costs are low.

B costs of short-selling are high.

C prices are consistent with the law of one price.

4 An arbitrage transaction generates a net inflow of funds:

A throughout the holding period.

B at the end of the holding period.

C at the start of the holding period.

5 Which of the following combinations replicates a long derivative position?

A A short derivative and a long asset

B A long asset and a short risk-free bond

C A short derivative and a short risk-free bond

6 Most derivatives are priced by:

A assuming that the market offers arbitrage opportunities.

B discounting the expected payoff of the derivative at the risk-free rate.

C applying a risk premium to the expected payoff of the derivative and its risk.

7 The price of a forward contract:

A is the amount paid at initiation.

B is the amount paid at expiration.

C fluctuates over the term of the contract.

8 Assume an asset pays no dividends or interest, and also assume that the asset does not yield any non-financial benefits or incur any carrying cost. At initiation, the price of a forward contract on that asset is:

A lower than the value of the contract.

B equal to the value of the contract.

C greater than the value of the contract.

9 With respect to a forward contract, as market conditions change:

A only the price fluctuates.

B only the value fluctuates.

C both the price and the value fluctuate.

10 The value of a forward contract at expiration is:

A positive to the long party if the spot price is higher than the forward price.

B negative to the short party if the forward price is higher than the spot price.

C positive to the short party if the spot price is higher than the forward price.

11 At the initiation of a forward contract on an asset that neither receives benefits nor incurs carrying costs during the term of the contract, the forward price is equal to the:

A spot price.

B future value of the spot price.

C present value of the spot price.

12 Stocks BWQ and ZER are each currently priced at $100 per share. Over the next year, stock BWQ is expected to generate significant benefits whereas stock ZER is not expected to generate any benefits. There are no carrying costs associated with holding either stock over the next year. Compared with ZER, the one-year forward price of BWQ is *most likely*:

A lower.

B the same.

C higher.

13 If the net cost of carry of an asset is positive, then the price of a forward contract on that asset is *most likely*:

A lower than if the net cost of carry was zero.

B the same as if the net cost of carry was zero.

C higher than if the net cost of carry was zero.

14 If the present value of storage costs exceeds the present value of its convenience yield, then the commodity's forward price is *most likely*:

A less than the spot price compounded at the risk-free rate.

B the same as the spot price compounded at the risk-free rate.

C higher than the spot price compounded at the risk-free rate.

15 Which of the following factors *most likely* explains why the spot price of a commodity in short supply can be greater than its forward price?

A Opportunity cost

B Lack of dividends

C Convenience yield

16 When interest rates are constant, futures prices are *most likely*:

A less than forward prices.

B equal to forward prices.

C greater than forward prices.

17 In contrast to a forward contract, a futures contract:

A trades over-the-counter.

B is initiated at a zero value.

C is marked-to-market daily.

18 To the holder of a long position, it is more desirable to own a forward contract than a futures contract when interest rates and futures prices are:

A negatively correlated.

B uncorrelated.

C positively correlated.

19 The value of a swap typically:

A is non-zero at initiation.
B is obtained through replication.
C does not fluctuate over the life of the contract.

20 The price of a swap typically:
A is zero at initiation.
B fluctuates over the life of the contract.
C is obtained through a process of replication.

21 The value of a swap is equal to the present value of the:
A fixed payments from the swap.
B net cash flow payments from the swap.
C underlying at the end of the contract.

22 If no cash is initially exchanged, a swap is comparable to a series of forward contracts when:
A the swap payments are variable.
B the combined value of all the forward contracts is zero.
C all the forward contracts have the same agreed-on price.

23 For a swap in which a series of fixed payments is exchanged for a series of floating payments, the parties to the transaction:
A designate the value of the underlying at contract initiation.
B value the underlying solely on the basis of its market value at the end of the swap.
C value the underlying sequentially at the time of each payment to determine the floating payment.

24 A European call option and a European put option are written on the same underlying, and both options have the same expiration date and exercise price. At expiration, it is possible that both options will have:
A negative values.
B the same value.
C positive values.

25 At expiration, a European put option will be valuable if the exercise price is:
A less than the underlying price.
B equal to the underlying price.
C greater than the underlying price.

26 The value of a European call option at expiration is the greater of zero or the:
A value of the underlying.
B value of the underlying minus the exercise price.
C exercise price minus the value of the underlying.

27 For a European call option with two months until expiration, if the spot price is below the exercise price, the call option will *most likely* have:
A zero time value.
B positive time value.
C positive exercise value.

28 When the price of the underlying is below the exercise price, a put option is:
A in-the-money.
B at-the-money.

C out-of-the-money.

29 If the risk-free rate increases, the value of an in-the-money European put option will *most likely*:

A decrease.

B remain the same.

C increase.

30 The value of a European call option is inversely related to the:

A exercise price.

B time to expiration.

C volatility of the underlying.

31 The table below shows three European call options on the same underlying:

	Time to Expiration	Exercise Price
Option 1	3 months	$100
Option 2	6 months	$100
Option 3	6 months	$105

The option with the highest value is *most likely*:

A Option 1.

B Option 2.

C Option 3.

32 The value of a European put option can be either directly or inversely related to the:

A exercise price.

B time to expiration.

C volatility of the underlying.

33 Prior to expiration, the lowest value of a European put option is the greater of zero or the:

A exercise price minus the value of the underlying.

B present value of the exercise price minus the value of the underlying.

C value of the underlying minus the present value of the exercise price.

34 A European put option on a dividend-paying stock is *most likely* to increase if there is an increase in:

A carrying costs.

B the risk-free rate.

C dividend payments.

35 Based on put-call parity, a trader who combines a long asset, a long put, and a short call will create a synthetic:

A long bond.

B fiduciary call.

C protective put.

36 Which of the following transactions is the equivalent of a synthetic long call position?

A Long asset, long put, short call

B Long asset, long put, short bond

C Short asset, long call, long bond

37 Which of the following is *least likely* to be required by the binomial option pricing model?

A Spot price

B Two possible prices one period later

C Actual probabilities of the up and down moves

38 To determine the price of an option today, the binomial model requires:

A selling one put and buying one offsetting call.

B buying one unit of the underlying and selling one matching call.

C using the risk-free rate to determine the required number of units of the underlying.

39 Assume a call option's strike price is initially equal to the price of its underlying asset. Based on the binomial model, if the volatility of the underlying decreases, the lower of the two potential payoff values of the hedge portfolio:

A decreases.

B remains the same.

C increases.

40 Based on the binomial model, an increase in the actual probability of an upward move in the underlying will result in the option price:

A decreasing.

B remaining the same.

C increasing.

41 If a call option is priced higher than the binomial model predicts, investors can earn a return in excess of the risk-free rate by:

A investing at the risk-free rate, selling a call, and selling the underlying.

B borrowing at the risk-free rate, buying a call, and buying the underlying.

C borrowing at the risk-free rate, selling a call, and buying the underlying.

42 An at-the-money American call option on a stock that pays no dividends has three months remaining until expiration. The market value of the option will *most likely* be:

A less than its exercise value.

B equal to its exercise value.

C greater than its exercise value.

43 At expiration, American call options are worth:

A less than European call options.

B the same as European call options.

C more than European call options.

44 Which of the following circumstances will *most likely* affect the value of an American call option relative to a European call option?

A Dividends are declared

B Expiration date occurs

C The risk-free rate changes

45 Combining a protective put with a forward contract generates equivalent outcomes at expiration to those of a:

A fiduciary call.

B long call combined with a short asset.

C forward contract combined with a risk-free bond.

46 Holding an asset and buying a put on that asset is equivalent to:

A initiating a fiduciary call.

B buying a risk-free zero-coupon bond and selling a call option.

C selling a risk-free zero-coupon bond and buying a call option.

47 If an underlying asset's price is less than a related option's strike price at expiration, a protective put position on that asset versus a fiduciary call position has a value that is:

A lower.

B the same.

C higher.

48 Based on put–call parity, which of the following combinations results in a synthetic long asset position?

A A long call, a short put, and a long bond

B A short call, a long put, and a short bond

C A long call, a short asset, and a long bond

49 For a holder of a European option, put–call–forward parity is based on the assumption that:

A no arbitrage is possible within the spot, forward, and option markets.

B the value of a European put at expiration is the greater of zero or the underlying value minus the exercise price.

C the value of a European call at expiration is the greater of zero or the exercise price minus the value of the underlying.

50 Under put–call–forward parity, which of the following transactions is risk free?

A Short call, long put, long forward contract, long risk-free bond

B Long call, short put, long forward contract, short risk-free bond

C Long call, long put, short forward contract, short risk-free bond

SOLUTIONS

1 C is correct. An asset's current price, S_0, is determined by discounting the expected future price of the asset by r (the risk free rate) plus λ (the risk premium) over the period from 0 to T, as illustrated in the following equation:

$$S_0 = \frac{E(S_T)}{(1 + r + \lambda)^T}$$

Thus, an asset's current price inversely relates to its level of risk via the related risk premium, λ.

A is incorrect because an asset's current price in spot markets is calculated using the risk-free rate plus a risk premium.

B is incorrect because an asset's current price in spot markets is inversely related, not directly related, to its level of risk.

2 A is correct. An illiquid position is a limit to arbitrage because it may be difficult to realize gains of an illiquid offsetting position. A significant opportunity arises from a sufficiently large price differential or a small price differential that can be employed on a very large scale.

3 A is correct. Some arbitrage opportunities represent such small price discrepancies that they are only worth exploiting if the transaction costs are low. An arbitrage opportunity may require short-selling assets at costs that eliminate any profit potential. If the law of one price holds, there is no arbitrage opportunity.

4 C is correct. Arbitrage is a type of transaction undertaken when two assets or portfolios produce identical results but sell for different prices. A trader buys the asset or portfolio with the lower price and sells the asset or portfolio with the higher price, generating a net inflow of funds at the start of the holding period. Because the two assets or portfolios produce identical results, a long position in one and short position in the other means that at the end of the holding period, the payoffs offset. Therefore, there is no money gained or lost at the end of the holding period, so there is no risk.

5 B is correct. A long asset and a short risk-free asset (meaning to borrow at the risk-free rate) can be combined to produce a long derivative position.

A is incorrect because a short derivative and a long asset combine to produce a position equivalent to a long risk-free bond, not a long derivative.

C is incorrect because a short derivative and a short risk-free bond combine to produce a position equivalent to a short asset, not a long derivative.

6 B is correct. Virtually all derivative pricing models discount the expected payoff of the derivative at the risk-free rate.

A is incorrect because derivatives are priced by assuming that the market is free of arbitrage opportunities via the principle of no arbitrage, not by assuming that the market offers them.

C is incorrect because the application of a risk premium to the expected payoff of the derivative and its risk is not appropriate in the pricing of derivatives. An investor's risk premium is not relevant to pricing a derivative.

7 B is correct. The forward price is agreed upon at the start of the contract and is the fixed price at which the underlying will be purchased (or sold) at expiration. Payment is made at expiration. The value of the forward contract may change over time, but the forward price does not change.

8 C is correct. The price of a forward contract is a contractually fixed price, established at initiation, at which the underlying will be purchased (or sold) at expiration. The value of a forward contract at initiation is zero; therefore, the forward price is greater than the value of the forward contract at initiation.

9 B is correct. The value of the forward contract, unlike its price, will adjust as market conditions change. The forward price is fixed at initiation.

10 A is correct. When a forward contract expires, if the spot price is higher than the forward price, the long party profits from paying the lower forward price for the underlying. Therefore, the forward contract has a positive value to the long party and a negative value to the short party. However, if the forward price is higher than the spot price, the short party profits from receiving the higher forward price (the contract value is positive to the short party and negative to the long party).

11 B is correct. At initiation, the forward price is the future value of the spot price (spot price compounded at the risk-free rate over the life of the contract). If the forward price were set to the spot price or the present value of the spot price, it would be possible for one side to earn an arbitrage profit by selling the asset and investing the proceeds until contract expiration.

12 A is correct. The forward price of each stock is found by compounding the spot price by the risk-free rate for the period and then subtracting the future value of any benefits and adding the future value of any costs. In the absence of any benefits or costs, the one-year forward prices of BWQ and ZER should be equal. After subtracting the benefits related to BWQ, the one-year forward price of BWQ is lower than the one-year forward price of ZER.

13 A is correct. An asset's forward price is increased by the future value of any costs and decreased by the future value of any benefits: $F_0(T) = S_0(1 + r)^T - (\gamma - \theta)(1 + r)^T$. If the net cost of carry (benefits less costs) is positive, the forward price is lower than if the net cost of carry was zero.

14 C is correct. When a commodity's storage costs exceed its convenience yield benefits, the net cost of carry (benefits less costs) is negative. Subtracting this negative amount from the spot price compounded at the risk-free rate results in an addition to the compounded spot price. The result is a commodity forward price which is higher than the spot price compounded. The commodity's forward price is less than the spot price compounded when the convenience yield benefits exceed the storage costs and the commodity's forward price is the same as the spot price compounded when the costs equal the benefits.

15 C is correct. The convenience yield is a benefit of holding the asset and generally exists when a commodity is in short supply. The future value of the convenience yield is subtracted from the compounded spot price and reduces the commodity's forward price relative to it spot price. The opportunity cost is the risk-free rate. In the absence of carry costs, the forward price is the spot price compounded at the risk-free rate and will exceed the spot price. Dividends are benefits that reduce the forward price but the lack of dividends has no effect on the spot price relative to the forward price of a commodity in short supply.

16 B is correct. When interest rates are constant, forwards and futures will likely have the same prices. The price differential will vary with the volatility of interest rates. In addition, if futures prices and interest rates are uncorrelated, forward and futures prices will be the same. If futures prices are positively correlated with interest rates, futures contracts are more desirable to holders of long positions than are forwards. This is because rising prices lead to future profits that are reinvested in periods of rising interest rates, and falling prices lead to losses that occur in periods of falling interest rates. If futures prices are

negatively correlated with interest rates, futures contracts are less desirable to holders of long positions than are forwards. The more desirable contract will tend to have the higher price.

17 C is correct. Futures contracts are marked-to-market on a daily basis. The accumulated gains and losses from the previous day's trading session are deducted from the accounts of those holding losing positions and transferred to the accounts of those holding winning positions. Futures contracts trade on an exchange, forward contracts are over-the-counter transactions. Typically both forward and futures contracts are initiated at a zero value.

18 A is correct. If futures prices and interest rates are negatively correlated, forwards are more desirable to holders of long positions than are futures. This is because rising prices lead to futures profits that are reinvested in periods of falling interest rates. It is better to receive all of the cash at expiration under such conditions. If futures prices and interest rates are uncorrelated, forward and futures prices will be the same. If futures prices are positively correlated with interest rates, futures contracts are more desirable to holders of long positions than are forwards.

19 B is correct. Valuation of the swap during its life appeals to replication and the principle of arbitrage. Valuation consists of reproducing the remaining payments on the swap with other transactions. The value of that replication strategy is the value of the swap. The swap price is typically set such that the swap contract has a value of zero at initiation. The value of a swap contract will change during the life of the contract as the value of the underlying changes in value.

20 C is correct. Replication is the key to pricing a swap. The swap price is determined at initiation by replication. The value (not the price) of the swap is typically zero at initiation and the fixed swap price is typically determined such that the value of the swap will be zero at initiation.

21 B is correct. The principal of replication articulates that the valuation of a swap is the present value of all the net cash flow payments from the swap, not simply the present value of the fixed payments of the swap or the present value of the underlying at the end of the contract.

22 B is correct. When two parties engage in a series of forward contracts and initially agree on a price of $FS_0(T)$, some of the forward contracts have positive values and some have negative values, but their combined value equals zero.

A is incorrect because for a swap, all payments are fixed and equal, not variable.

C is incorrect because forward prices are determined by the spot price and the net cost of carry, meaning that forward contracts expiring at different times will have different prices, not the same price.

23 C is correct. On each payment date, the swap owner receives a payment based on the value of the underlying at the time of each respective payment.

A is incorrect because in a swap involving a series of fixed payments exchanged for a series of floating payments, each floating payment reflects the value of the underlying at the time of payment, not a designated value at contract initiation.

B is incorrect because in a swap involving a series of fixed payments exchanged for a series of floating payments, each floating payment is based on the value of the underlying at the time of each respective payment, not on the market value at the end of the swap.

24 B is correct. If the underlying has a value equal to the exercise price at expiration, both options will have zero value since they both have the same exercise price. For example, if the exercise price is $25 and at expiration the underlying price is \$25, both the call option and the put option will have a value of zero. The value of an option cannot fall below zero. The holder of an option is not obligated to exercise the option; therefore, the options each have a minimum value of zero. If the call has a positive value, the put, by definition, must have a zero value and vice versa. Both cannot have a positive value.

25 C is correct. A European put option will be valuable at expiration if the exercise price is greater than the underlying price. The holder can put (deliver) the underlying and receive the exercise price which is higher than the spot price. A European put option would be worthless if the exercise price was equal to or less than the underlying price.

26 B is correct. The value of a European call option at expiration is the greater of zero or the value of the underlying minus the exercise price.

27 B is correct. A European call option with two months until expiration will typically have positive time value, where time value reflects the value of the uncertainty that arises from the volatility in the underlying. The call option has a zero exercise value if the spot price is below the exercise price. The exercise value of a European call option is $\text{Max}(0,S_t - X)$, where S_t is the current spot price at time t and X is the exercise price.

28 A is correct. When the price of the underlying is below the exercise price for a put, the option is said to be in-the-money. If the price of the underlying is the same as the exercise price, the put is at-the-money and if it is above the exercise price, the put is out-of-the-money.

29 A is correct. An in-the-money European put option decreases in value with an increase in the risk-free rate. A higher risk-free rate reduces the present value of any proceeds received on exercise.

30 A is correct. The value of a European call option is inversely related to the exercise price. A lower exercise price means there are more potential outcomes at which the call expires in-the-money. The option value will be greater the lower the exercise price. For a higher exercise price, the opposite is true. Both the time to expiration and the volatility of the underlying are directly (positively) related to the value of a European call option.

31 B is correct. The value of a European call option is inversely related to the exercise price and directly related to the time to expiration. Option 1 and Option 2 have the same exercise price; however, Option 2 has a longer time to expiration. Consequently, Option 2 would likely have a higher value than Option 1. Option 2 and Option 3 have the same time to expiration; however, Option 2 has a lower exercise price. Thus, Option 2 would likely have a higher value than Option 3.

32 B is correct. The value of a European put option can be either directly or indirectly related to time to expiration. The direct effect is more common, but the inverse effect can prevail the longer the time to expiration, the higher the risk-free rate, and the deeper in-the-money is the put. The value of a European put option is directly related to the exercise price and the volatility of the underlying.

33 B is correct. Prior to expiration, the lowest value of a European put is the greater of zero or the present value of the exercise price minus the value of the underlying.

34 C is correct. Payments, such as dividends, reduce the value of the underlying which increases the value of a European put option. Carrying costs reduce the value of a European put option. An increase in the risk-free interest rate may decrease the value of a European put option.

35 A is correct. A long bond can be synthetically created by combining a long asset, a long put, and a short call. A fiduciary call is created by combining a long call with a risk free bond. A protective put is created by combining a long asset with a long put.

36 B is correct. According to put–call parity, a synthetic call can be constructed by combining a long asset, long put, and short bond positions.

37 C is correct. The actual probabilities of the up and down moves in the underlying do not appear in the binomial option pricing model, only the pseudo or "risk-neutral" probabilities. Both the spot price of the underlying and two possible prices one period later are required by the binomial option pricing model.

38 C is correct. Pricing an option relies on the facts that a perfectly hedged investment earns the risk-free rate and that, based on the binomial option pricing model, the size of the two possible changes in the option price (meaning the potential step up or step down in the option value) after one period are equivalent.

39 B is correct. When the volatility of the underlying decreases, the value of the option also decreases, meaning that the upper payoff value of the hedge portfolio combining them declines. However, the lower payoff value remains at zero.

40 B is correct. The binomial model does not consider the actual probabilities of upward and downward movements in determining the option value. Thus, a change in this probability has no effect on the calculated option price.

41 C is correct. If an option is trading above the value predicted by the binomial model, investors can engage in arbitrage by selling a call, buying shares of the underlying, and funding the transaction by borrowing at the risk-free rate. This will earn a return in excess of the risk-free rate.

42 C is correct. Prior to expiration, an American call option will typically have a value in the market that is greater than its exercise value. Although the American option is at-the-money and therefore has an exercise value of zero, the time value of the call option would likely lead to the option having a positive market value.

43 B is correct. At expiration, the values of American and European call options are effectively the same; both are worth the greater of zero and the exercise value.

44 A is correct. When a dividend is declared, an American call option will have a higher value than a European call option because an American call option holder can exercise early to capture the value of the dividend. At expiration, both types of call options are worth the greater of zero and the exercise value. A change in the risk-free rate does not affect the relative values of American and European call options.

45 A is correct. Put–call forward parity demonstrates that the outcome of a protective put with a forward contract (long put, long risk-free bond, long forward contract) equals the outcome of a fiduciary call (long call, long risk-free bond). The outcome of a protective put with a forward contract is also equal to the outcome of a protective put with asset (long put, long asset).

46 A is correct. Under put–call parity, initiating a fiduciary call (buying a call option on an asset that expires at time T together with a risk-free zero-coupon bond that also expires at time T) is equivalent to holding the same asset and initiating a protective put on it (buying a put option with an exercise price of X that can be used to sell the asset for X at time T).

47 B is correct. On the one hand, buying a call option on an asset and a risk-free bond with the same maturity is known as a fiduciary call. If the fiduciary call expires in the money (meaning that the value of the call, $S_T - X$, is greater than the risk-free bond's price at expiration, X), then the total value of the fiduciary call is $(S_T - X) + X$, or S_T. On the other hand, holding an underlying asset, S_T, and buying a put on that asset is known as a protective put. If the put expires out of the money, meaning that the value of the asset, S_T, is greater than the put's value at expiration, 0, then the total value of the protective put is $S_T - 0$, or S_T. A protective put and a fiduciary call produce the same result.

48 A is correct. One can synthetically create a long asset position by buying a call, shorting a put, and buying a bond.

B is incorrect because combining a short call and a short bond with the right to sell (not buy) another asset via a long put could not result in a new synthetic long asset position.

C is incorrect because combining a long call, a short asset, and a long bond creates a long put, not a synthetic long asset.

49 A is correct. Put–call–forward parity is based on the assumption that no arbitrage is possible within the spot, forward, and option markets.

B is incorrect because the value of a European put at expiration is the greater of either zero or the exercise price minus the value of the underlying, not the greater of zero or the underlying value minus the exercise price. In addition, put–call–forward parity is related to the equality of a fiduciary call and a synthetic protective put or to a protective put and a synthetic fiduciary call, not specifically to the value of a put at expiration.

C is incorrect because the value of a European call at expiration is the greater of either zero or the underlying value minus the exercise price, not the greater of zero or the exercise price minus the value of the underlying. In addition, put–call–forward parity is related to the equality of a fiduciary call and a synthetic protective put or to a protective put and a synthetic fiduciary call, not specifically to the value of a call at expiration.

50 A is correct. Purchasing a long forward contract and a risk-free bond creates a synthetic asset. Combining a long synthetic asset, a long put, and a short call is risk free because its payoffs produce a known cash flow of the value of the exercise price.

Glossary

A priori probability A probability based on logical analysis rather than on observation or personal judgment.

Abnormal return The amount by which a security's actual return differs from its expected return, given the security's risk and the market's return.

Absolute advantage A country's ability to produce a good or service at a lower absolute cost than its trading partner.

Absolute dispersion The amount of variability present without comparison to any reference point or benchmark.

Absolute frequency The number of observations in a given interval (for grouped data).

Accelerated book build An offering of securities by an investment bank acting as principal that is accomplished in only one or two days.

Accelerated methods Depreciation methods that allocate a relatively large proportion of the cost of an asset to the early years of the asset's useful life.

Accounting costs Monetary value of economic resources used in performing an activity. These can be explicit, out-of-pocket, current payments, or an allocation of historical payments (depreciation) for resources. They do not include implicit opportunity costs.

Accounting profit Income as reported on the income statement, in accordance with prevailing accounting standards, before the provisions for income tax expense. Also called *income before taxes* or *pretax income*.

Accounts payable Amounts that a business owes to its vendors for goods and services that were purchased from them but which have not yet been paid.

Accounts receivable turnover Ratio of sales on credit to the average balance in accounts receivable.

Accrued expenses Liabilities related to expenses that have been incurred but not yet paid as of the end of an accounting period—an example of an accrued expense is rent that has been incurred but not yet paid, resulting in a liability "rent payable." Also called *accrued liabilities*.

Accrued interest Interest earned but not yet paid.

Acid-test ratio A stringent measure of liquidity that indicates a company's ability to satisfy current liabilities with its most liquid assets, calculated as (cash + short-term marketable investments + receivables) divided by current liabilities.

Acquisition method A method of accounting for a business combination where the acquirer is required to measure each identifiable asset and liability at fair value. This method was the result of a joint project of the IASB and FASB aiming at convergence in standards for the accounting of business combinations.

Action lag Delay from policy decisions to implementation.

Active investment An approach to investing in which the investor seeks to outperform a given benchmark.

Active return The return on a portfolio minus the return on the portfolio's benchmark.

Active strategy In reference to short-term cash management, an investment strategy characterized by monitoring and attempting to capitalize on market conditions to optimize the risk and return relationship of short-term investments.

Activity ratios Ratios that measure how efficiently a company performs day-to-day tasks, such as the collection of receivables and management of inventory. Also called *asset utilization ratios* or *operating efficiency ratios*.

Add-on rates Bank certificates of deposit, repos, and indexes such as Libor and Euribor are quoted on an add-on rate basis (bond equivalent yield basis).

Addition rule for probabilities A principle stating that the probability that *A* or *B* occurs (both occur) equals the probability that *A* occurs, plus the probability that *B* occurs, minus the probability that both *A* and *B* occur.

Agency bonds See *quasi-government bond*.

Agency RMBS In the United States, securities backed by residential mortgage loans and guaranteed by a federal agency or guaranteed by either of the two GSEs (Fannie Mae and Freddie Mac).

Aggregate demand The quantity of goods and services that households, businesses, government, and foreign customers want to buy at any given level of prices.

Aggregate demand curve Inverse relationship between the price level and real output.

Aggregate income The value of all the payments earned by the suppliers of factors used in the production of goods and services.

Aggregate output The value of all the goods and services produced in a specified period of time.

Aggregate supply The quantity of goods and services producers are willing to supply at any given level of price.

Aggregate supply curve The level of domestic output that companies will produce at each price level.

Aging schedule A breakdown of accounts into categories of days outstanding.

All-or-nothing (AON) orders An order that includes the instruction to trade only if the trade fills the entire quantity (size) specified.

Allocationally efficient A characteristic of a market, a financial system, or an economy that promotes the allocation of resources to their highest value uses.

Alternative data Non-traditional data types generated by the use of electronic devices, social media, satellite and sensor networks, and company exhaust.

Alternative investment markets Market for investments other than traditional securities investments (i.e., traditional common and preferred shares and traditional fixed income instruments). The term usually encompasses direct and indirect investment in real estate (including timberland and farmland) and commodities (including precious metals); hedge funds, private equity, and other investments requiring specialized due diligence.

Alternative trading systems Trading venues that function like exchanges but that do not exercise regulatory authority over their subscribers except with respect to the conduct of the subscribers' trading in their trading systems. Also called *electronic communications networks* or *multilateral trading facilities*.

American depository receipt A US dollar-denominated security that trades like a common share on US exchanges.

American depository share The underlying shares on which American depository receipts are based. They trade in the issuing company's domestic market.

American-style Type of option contract that can be exercised at any time up to the option's expiration date.

Amortisation The process of allocating the cost of intangible long-term assets having a finite useful life to accounting periods; the allocation of the amount of a bond premium or discount to the periods remaining until bond maturity.

Amortised cost The historical cost (initially recognised cost) of an asset, adjusted for amortisation and impairment.

Amortizing bond Bond with a payment schedule that calls for periodic payments of interest and repayments of principal.

Amortizing loan Loan with a payment schedule that calls for periodic payments of interest and repayments of principal.

Annual percentage rate The cost of borrowing expressed as a yearly rate.

Annuity A finite set of level sequential cash flows.

Annuity due An annuity having a first cash flow that is paid immediately.

Anticipation stock Excess inventory that is held in anticipation of increased demand, often because of seasonal patterns of demand.

Antidilutive With reference to a transaction or a security, one that would increase earnings per share (EPS) or result in EPS higher than the company's basic EPS—antidilutive securities are not included in the calculation of diluted EPS.

Arbitrage 1) The simultaneous purchase of an undervalued asset or portfolio and sale of an overvalued but equivalent asset or portfolio, in order to obtain a riskless profit on the price differential. Taking advantage of a market inefficiency in a risk-free manner. 2) The condition in a financial market in which equivalent assets or combinations of assets sell for two different prices, creating an opportunity to profit at no risk with no commitment of money. In a well-functioning financial market, few arbitrage opportunities are possible. 3) A risk-free operation that earns an expected positive net profit but requires no net investment of money.

Arbitrage-free pricing The overall process of pricing derivatives by arbitrage and risk neutrality. Also called the *principle of no arbitrage.*

Arbitrageurs Traders who engage in arbitrage. See *arbitrage.*

Arithmetic mean The sum of the observations divided by the number of observations.

Arms index A flow of funds indicator applied to a broad stock market index to measure the relative extent to which money is moving into or out of rising and declining stocks.

Artificial intelligence Computer systems that exhibit cognitive and decision-making ability comparable (or superior) to that of humans.

Asian call option A European-style option with a value at maturity equal to the difference between the stock price at maturity and the average stock price during the life of the option, or $0, whichever is greater.

Ask The price at which a dealer or trader is willing to sell an asset, typically qualified by a maximum quantity (ask size). See *offer.*

Ask size The maximum quantity of an asset that pertains to a specific ask price from a trader. For example, if the ask for a share issue is $30 for a size of 1,000 shares, the trader is offering to sell at $30 up to 1,000 shares.

Asset allocation The process of determining how investment funds should be distributed among asset classes.

Asset-backed securities A type of bond issued by a legal entity called a *special purpose entity* (SPE) on a collection of assets that the SPE owns. Also, securities backed by receivables and loans other than mortgages.

Asset-based loan A loan that is secured with company assets.

Asset-based valuation models Valuation based on estimates of the market value of a company's assets.

Asset beta The unlevered beta; reflects the business risk of the assets; the asset's systematic risk.

Asset class A group of assets that have similar characteristics, attributes, and risk/return relationships.

Asset swap Converts the periodic fixed coupon of a specific bond to a Libor plus or minus a spread.

Asset utilization ratios Ratios that measure how efficiently a company performs day-to-day tasks, such as the collection of receivables and management of inventory.

Assets Resources controlled by an enterprise as a result of past events and from which future economic benefits to the enterprise are expected to flow.

Assignment of accounts receivable The use of accounts receivable as collateral for a loan.

At the money An option in which the underlying's price equals the exercise price.

Auction A type of bond issuing mechanism often used for sovereign bonds that involves bidding.

Autarkic price The price of a good or service in an autarkic economy.

Autarky A state in which a country does not trade with other countries.

Automated Clearing House (ACH) An electronic payment network available to businesses, individuals, and financial institutions in the United States, US Territories, and Canada.

Automatic stabilizer A countercyclical factor that automatically comes into play as an economy slows and unemployment rises.

Available-for-sale Under US GAAP, debt securities not classified as either held-to-maturity or held-for-trading securities. The investor is willing to sell but not actively planning to sell. In general, available-for-sale debt securities are reported at fair value on the balance sheet, with unrealized gains included as a component of other comprehensive income.

Average accounting rate of return (ARR) Over the life of a project, the AAR can be defined as the average net income divided by the average book value.

Average fixed cost Total fixed cost divided by quantity produced.

Average life See *weighted average life.*

Average product Measures the productivity of inputs on average and is calculated by dividing total product by the total number of units for a given input that is used to generate that output.

Average revenue Total revenue divided by quantity sold.

Average total cost Total cost divided by quantity produced.

Average variable cost Total variable cost divided by quantity produced.

Back simulation Another term for the historical method of estimating VaR. This term is somewhat misleading in that the method involves not a *simulation* of the past but rather what *actually happened* in the past, sometimes adjusted to reflect the fact that a different portfolio may have existed in the past than is planned for the future.

Back-testing With reference to portfolio strategies, the application of a strategy's portfolio selection rules to historical data to assess what would have been the strategy's historical performance.

Backup lines of credit A type of credit enhancement provided by a bank to an issuer of commercial paper to ensure that the issuer will have access to sufficient liquidity to repay maturing commercial paper if issuing new paper is not a viable option.

Balance of payments A double-entry bookkeeping system that summarizes a country's economic transactions with the rest of the world for a particular period of time, typically a calendar quarter or year.

Balance of trade deficit When the domestic economy is spending more on foreign goods and services than foreign economies are spending on domestic goods and services.

Balance sheet The financial statement that presents an entity's current financial position by disclosing resources the entity controls (its assets) and the claims on those resources (its liabilities and equity claims), as of a particular point in time (the date of the balance sheet). Also called *statement of financial position* or *statement of financial condition*.

Balance sheet ratios Financial ratios involving balance sheet items only.

Balanced With respect to a government budget, one in which spending and revenues (taxes) are equal.

Balloon payment Large payment required at maturity to retire a bond's outstanding principal amount.

Bar chart A price chart with four bits of data for each time interval—the high, low, opening, and closing prices. A vertical line connects the high and low. A cross-hatch left indicates the opening price and a cross-hatch right indicates the close.

Barter economy An economy where economic agents as house-holds, corporations, and governments "pay" for goods and services with another good or service.

Base rates The reference rate on which a bank bases lending rates to all other customers.

Basic EPS Net earnings available to common shareholders (i.e., net income minus preferred dividends) divided by the weighted average number of common shares outstanding.

Basis point Used in stating yield spreads, one basis point equals one-hundredth of a percentage point, or 0.01%.

Basket of listed depository receipts An exchange-traded fund (ETF) that represents a portfolio of depository receipts.

Bearer bonds Bonds for which ownership is not recorded; only the clearing system knows who the bond owner is.

Behavioral finance A field of finance that examines the psychological variables that affect and often distort the investment decision making of investors, analysts, and portfolio managers.

Behind the market Said of prices specified in orders that are worse than the best current price; e.g., for a limit buy order, a limit price below the best bid.

Benchmark A comparison portfolio; a point of reference or comparison.

Benchmark issue The latest sovereign bond issue for a given maturity. It serves as a benchmark against which to compare bonds that have the same features but that are issued by another type of issuer.

Benchmark rate Typically the yield-to-maturity on a government bond having the same, or close to the same, time-to-maturity.

Benchmark spread The yield spread over a specific benchmark, usually measured in basis points.

Bernoulli random variable A random variable having the outcomes 0 and 1.

Bernoulli trial An experiment that can produce one of two outcomes.

Best bid The highest bid in the market.

Best effort offering An offering of a security using an investment bank in which the investment bank, as agent for the issuer, promises to use its best efforts to sell the offering but does not guarantee that a specific amount will be sold.

Best-in-class An ESG implementation approach that seeks to identify the most favorable companies in an industry based on ESG considerations.

Best offer The lowest offer (ask price) in the market.

Beta A measure of the sensitivity of a given investment or portfolio to movements in the overall market.

Bid The price at which a dealer or trader is willing to buy an asset, typically qualified by a maximum quantity.

Bid–ask spread The difference between the prices at which dealers will buy from a customer (bid) and sell to a customer (offer or ask). It is often used as an indicator of liquidity.

Bid–offer spread The difference between the prices at which dealers will buy from a customer (bid) and sell to a customer (offer or ask). It is often used as an indicator of liquidity.

Bid size The maximum quantity of an asset that pertains to a specific bid price from a trader.

Big Data The vast amount of data being generated by industry, governments, individuals, and electronic devices that arises from both traditional and non-traditional data sources.

Bilateral loan A loan from a single lender to a single borrower.

Binomial model A model for pricing options in which the underlying price can move to only one of two possible new prices.

Binomial random variable The number of successes in n Bernoulli trials for which the probability of success is constant for all trials and the trials are independent.

Binomial tree The graphical representation of a model of asset price dynamics in which, at each period, the asset moves up with probability p or down with probability $(1 - p)$.

Bitcoin A cryptocurrency using blockchain technology that was created in 2009.

Block brokers A broker (agent) that provides brokerage services for large-size trades.

Blockchain A type of digital ledger in which information is recorded sequentially and then linked together and secured using cryptographic methods.

Blue chip Widely held large market capitalization companies that are considered financially sound and are leaders in their respective industry or local stock market.

Bollinger Bands A price-based technical analysis indicator consisting of a moving average plus a higher line representing the moving average plus a set number of standard deviations from average price (for the same number of periods as used to calculate the moving average) and a lower line that is a moving average minus the same number of standard deviations.

Bond Contractual agreement between the issuer and the bondholders.

Bond equivalent yield A calculation of yield that is annualized using the ratio of 365 to the number of days to maturity. Bond equivalent yield allows for the restatement and comparison of securities with different compounding periods.

Bond indenture The governing legal credit agreement, typically incorporated by reference in the prospectus. Also called *trust deed*.

Bond market vigilantes Bond market participants who might reduce their demand for long-term bonds, thus pushing up their yields.

Bond yield plus risk premium approach An estimate of the cost of common equity that is produced by summing the before-tax cost of debt and a risk premium that captures the additional yield on a company's stock relative to its bonds. The additional yield is often estimated using historical spreads between bond yields and stock yields.

Bonus issue of shares A type of dividend in which a company distributes additional shares of its common stock to shareholders instead of cash.

Book building Investment bankers' process of compiling a "book" or list of indications of interest to buy part of an offering.

Book value The net amount shown for an asset or liability on the balance sheet; book value may also refer to the company's excess of total assets over total liabilities. Also called *carrying value*.

Boom An expansionary phase characterized by economic growth "testing the limits" of the economy.

Bottom-up analysis An investment selection approach that focuses on company-specific circumstances rather than emphasizing economic cycles or industry analysis.

Break point In the context of the weighted average cost of capital (WACC), a break point is the amount of capital at which the cost of one or more of the sources of capital changes, leading to a change in the WACC.

Breakeven point The number of units produced and sold at which the company's net income is zero (Revenues = Total cost); in the case of perfect competition, the quantity at which price, average revenue, and marginal revenue equal average total cost.

Bridge financing Interim financing that provides funds until permanent financing can be arranged.

Broad money Encompasses narrow money plus the entire range of liquid assets that can be used to make purchases.

Broker 1) An agent who executes orders to buy or sell securities on behalf of a client in exchange for a commission. 2) See *futures commission merchants*.

Broker–dealer A financial intermediary (often a company) that may function as a principal (dealer) or as an agent (broker) depending on the type of trade.

Brokered market A market in which brokers arrange trades among their clients.

Budget surplus/deficit The difference between government revenue and expenditure for a stated fixed period of time.

Bullet bond Bond in which the principal repayment is made entirely at maturity.

Business risk The risk associated with operating earnings. Operating earnings are uncertain because total revenues and many of the expenditures contributed to produce those revenues are uncertain.

Buy-side firm An investment management company or other investor that uses the services of brokers or dealers (i.e., the client of the sell side firms).

Buyback A transaction in which a company buys back its own shares. Unlike stock dividends and stock splits, share repurchases use corporate cash.

Call An option that gives the holder the right to buy an underlying asset from another party at a fixed price over a specific period of time.

Call market A market in which trades occur only at a particular time and place (i.e., when the market is called).

Call money rate The interest rate that buyers pay for their margin loan.

Call option An option that gives the holder the right to buy an underlying asset from another party at a fixed price over a specific period of time.

Call protection The time during which the issuer of the bond is not allowed to exercise the call option.

Callable bond A bond containing an embedded call option that gives the issuer the right to buy the bond back from the investor at specified prices on pre-determined dates.

Candlestick chart A price chart with four bits of data for each time interval. A candle indicates the opening and closing price for the interval. The body of the candle is shaded if the opening price was higher than the closing price, and the body is clear if the opening price was lower than the closing price. Vertical lines known as wicks or shadows extend from the top and bottom of the candle to indicate the high and the low prices for the interval.

Cannibalization Cannibalization occurs when an investment takes customers and sales away from another part of the company.

Capacity The ability of the borrower to make its debt payments on time.

Capital account A component of the balance of payments account that measures transfers of capital.

Capital allocation line (CAL) A graph line that describes the combinations of expected return and standard deviation of return available to an investor from combining the optimal portfolio of risky assets with the risk-free asset.

Capital asset pricing model (CAPM) An equation describing the expected return on any asset (or portfolio) as a linear function of its beta relative to the market portfolio.

Capital budgeting The process that companies use for decision making on capital projects—those projects with a life of one year or more.

Capital consumption allowance A measure of the wear and tear (depreciation) of the capital stock that occurs in the production of goods and services.

Capital deepening investment Increases the stock of capital relative to labor.

Capital expenditure Expenditure on physical capital (fixed assets).

Capital lease See *finance lease*.

Capital market expectations An investor's expectations concerning the risk and return prospects of asset classes.

Capital market line (CML) The line with an intercept point equal to the risk-free rate that is tangent to the efficient frontier of risky assets; represents the efficient frontier when a risk-free asset is available for investment.

Capital market securities Securities with maturities at issuance longer than one year.

Capital markets Financial markets that trade securities of longer duration, such as bonds and equities.

Capital rationing A capital rationing environment assumes that the company has a fixed amount of funds to invest.

Capital restrictions Controls placed on foreigners' ability to own domestic assets and/or domestic residents' ability to own foreign assets.

Capital stock The accumulated amount of buildings, machinery, and equipment used to produce goods and services.

Capital structure The mix of debt and equity that a company uses to finance its business; a company's specific mixture of long-term financing.

Captive finance subsidiary A wholly-owned subsidiary of a company that is established to provide financing of the sales of the parent company.

Carry The net of the costs and benefits of holding, storing, or "carrying" an asset.

Carrying amount The amount at which an asset or liability is valued according to accounting principles.

Carrying value The net amount shown for an asset or liability on the balance sheet; book value may also refer to the company's excess of total assets over total liabilities. For a bond, the purchase price plus (or minus) the amortized amount of the discount (or premium).

Cartel Participants in collusive agreements that are made openly and formally.

Cash collateral account Form of external credit enhancement whereby the issuer immediately borrows the credit-enhancement amount and then invests that amount, usually in highly rated short-term commercial paper.

Cash conversion cycle A financial metric that measures the length of time required for a company to convert cash invested in its operations to cash received as a result of its operations; equal to days of inventory on hand + days of sales outstanding – number of days of payables. Also called *net operating cycle.*

Cash flow additivity principle The principle that dollar amounts indexed at the same point in time are additive.

Cash flow from operating activities The net amount of cash provided from operating activities.

Cash flow from operations The net amount of cash provided from operating activities.

Cash flow yield The internal rate of return on a series of cash flows.

Cash market securities Money market securities settled on a "same day" or "cash settlement" basis.

Cash markets See *spot markets.*

Cash prices See *spot prices.*

Cash-settled forwards See *non-deliverable forwards.*

CBOE Volatility Index A measure of near-term market volatility as conveyed by S&P 500 stock index option prices.

Central bank funds market The market in which deposit-taking banks that have an excess reserve with their national central bank can loan money to banks that need funds for maturities ranging from overnight to one year. Called the Federal or Fed funds market in the United States.

Central bank funds rates Interest rates at which central bank funds are bought (borrowed) and sold (lent) for maturities ranging from overnight to one year. Called Federal or Fed funds rates in the United States.

Central banks The dominant bank in a country, usually with official or semi-official governmental status.

Certificate of deposit An instrument that represents a specified amount of funds on deposit with a bank for a specified maturity and interest rate. CDs are issued in various denominations and can be negotiable or non-negotiable.

Change in polarity principle A tenet of technical analysis that once a support level is breached, it becomes a resistance level. The same holds true for resistance levels; once breached, they become support levels.

Change of control put A covenant giving bondholders the right to require the issuer to buy back their debt, often at par or at some small premium to par value, in the event that the borrower is acquired.

Character The quality of a debt issuer's management.

Classified balance sheet A balance sheet organized so as to group together the various assets and liabilities into subcategories (e.g., current and noncurrent).

Clawback A requirement that the general partner return any funds distributed as incentive fees until the limited partners have received back their initial investment and a percentage of the total profit.

Clearing The process by which the exchange verifies the execution of a transaction and records the participants' identities.

Clearing instructions Instructions that indicate how to arrange the final settlement ("clearing") of a trade.

Clearinghouse An entity associated with a futures market that acts as middleman between the contracting parties and guarantees to each party the performance of the other.

Closed economy An economy that does not trade with other countries; an *autarkic economy.*

Closed-end fund A mutual fund in which no new investment money is accepted. New investors invest by buying existing shares, and investors in the fund liquidate by selling their shares to other investors.

Code of ethics An established guide that communicates an organization's values and overall expectations regarding member behavior. A code of ethics serves as a general guide for how community members should act.

Coefficient of variation (CV) The ratio of a set of observations' standard deviation to the observations' mean value.

Coincident economic indicators Turning points that are usually close to those of the overall economy; they are believed to have value for identifying the economy's present state.

Collateral manager Buys and sells debt obligations for and from the CDO's portfolio of assets (i.e., the collateral) to generate sufficient cash flows to meet the obligations to the CDO bondholders.

Collateral trust bonds Bonds secured by securities such as common shares, other bonds, or other financial assets.

Collateralized bond obligations A structured asset-backed security that is collateralized by a pool of bonds.

Collateralized debt obligation Generic term used to describe a security backed by a diversified pool of one or more debt obligations.

Collateralized loan obligations A structured asset-backed security that is collateralized by a pool of loans.

Collateralized mortgage obligation A security created through the securitization of a pool of mortgage-related products (mortgage pass-through securities or pools of loans).

Collaterals Assets or financial guarantees underlying a debt obligation that are above and beyond the issuer's promise to pay.

Combination A listing in which the order of the listed items does not matter.

Commercial paper A short-term, negotiable, unsecured promissory note that represents a debt obligation of the issuer.

Committed capital The amount that the limited partners have agreed to provide to the private equity fund.

Committed lines of credit A bank commitment to extend credit up to a pre-specified amount; the commitment is considered a short-term liability and is usually in effect for 364 days (one day short of a full year).

Commodity swap A swap in which the underlying is a commodity such as oil, gold, or an agricultural product.

Common market Level of economic integration that incorporates all aspects of the customs union and extends it by allowing free movement of factors of production among members.

Common shares A type of security that represent an ownership interest in a company.

Common-size analysis The restatement of financial statement items using a common denominator or reference item that allows one to identify trends and major differences; an example is an income statement in which all items are expressed as a percent of revenue.

Common stock See *common shares.*

Company analysis Analysis of an individual company.

Comparable company A company that has similar business risk; usually in the same industry and preferably with a single line of business.

Comparative advantage A country's ability to produce a good or service at a lower relative cost, or opportunity cost, than its trading partner.

Competitive strategy A company's plans for responding to the threats and opportunities presented by the external environment.

Complements Goods that tend to be used together; technically, two goods whose cross-price elasticity of demand is negative.

Complete markets Informally, markets in which the variety of distinct securities traded is so broad that any desired payoff in a future state-of-the-world is achievable.

Component cost of capital The rate of return required by suppliers of capital for an individual source of a company's funding, such as debt or equity.

Compounding The process of accumulating interest on interest.

Comprehensive income The change in equity of a business enterprise during a period from nonowner sources; includes all changes in equity during a period except those resulting from investments by owners and distributions to owners; comprehensive income equals net income plus other comprehensive income.

Conditional expected value The expected value of a stated event given that another event has occurred.

Conditional probability The probability of an event given (conditioned on) another event.

Conditional variances The variance of one variable, given the outcome of another.

Consistent With reference to estimators, describes an estimator for which the probability of estimates close to the value of the population parameter increases as sample size increases.

Constant-yield price trajectory A graph that illustrates the change in the price of a fixed-income bond over time assuming no change in yield-to-maturity. The trajectory shows the "pull to par" effect on the price of a bond trading at a premium or a discount to par value.

Constituent securities With respect to an index, the individual securities within an index.

Consumer surplus The difference between the value that a consumer places on units purchased and the amount of money that was required to pay for them.

Contingency provision Clause in a legal document that allows for some action if a specific event or circumstance occurs.

Contingent claims Derivatives in which the payoffs occur if a specific event occurs; generally referred to as options.

Contingent convertible bonds Bonds that automatically convert into equity if a specific event or circumstance occurs, such as the issuer's equity capital falling below the minimum requirement set by the regulators. Also called *CoCos*.

Continuation patterns A type of pattern used in technical analysis to predict the resumption of a market trend that was in place prior to the formation of a pattern.

Continuous random variable A random variable for which the range of possible outcomes is the real line (all real numbers between $-\infty$ and $+\infty$ or some subset of the real line).

Continuous time Time thought of as advancing in extremely small increments.

Continuous trading market A market in which trades can be arranged and executed any time the market is open.

Continuously compounded return The natural logarithm of 1 plus the holding period return, or equivalently, the natural logarithm of the ending price over the beginning price.

Contra account An account that offsets another account.

Contract rate See *mortgage rate.*

Contraction The period of a business cycle after the peak and before the trough; often called a *recession* or, if exceptionally severe, called a *depression*.

Contraction risk The risk that when interest rates decline, the security will have a shorter maturity than was anticipated at the time of purchase because borrowers refinance at the new, lower interest rates.

Contractionary Tending to cause the real economy to contract.

Contractionary fiscal policy A fiscal policy that has the objective to make the real economy contract.

Contracts for differences See *non-deliverable forwards.*

Contribution margin The amount available for fixed costs and profit after paying variable costs; revenue minus variable costs.

Controlling shareholders A particular shareholder or block of shareholders holding a percentage of shares that gives them significant voting power.

Convenience yield A non-monetary advantage of holding an asset.

Conventional bond See *plain vanilla bond.*

Conventional cash flow A conventional cash flow pattern is one with an initial outflow followed by a series of inflows.

Convergence The tendency for differences in output per capita across countries to diminish over time; in technical analysis, a term that describes the case when an indicator moves in the same manner as the security being analyzed.

Conversion price For a convertible bond, the price per share at which the bond can be converted into shares.

Conversion ratio For a convertible bond, the number of common shares that each bond can be converted into.

Conversion value For a convertible bond, the current share price multiplied by the conversion ratio.

Convertible bond Bond that gives the bondholder the right to exchange the bond for a specified number of common shares in the issuing company.

Convertible preference shares A type of equity security that entitles shareholders to convert their shares into a specified number of common shares.

Convexity adjustment For a bond, one half of the annual or approximate convexity statistic multiplied by the change in the yield-to-maturity squared.

Core inflation The inflation rate calculated based on a price index of goods and services except food and energy.

Corporate governance The system of internal controls and procedures by which individual companies are managed.

Correlation A number between −1 and +1 that measures the comovement (linear association) between two random variables.

Correlation coefficient A number between −1 and +1 that measures the consistency or tendency for two investments to act in a similar way. It is used to determine the effect on portfolio risk when two assets are combined.

Cost averaging The periodic investment of a fixed amount of money.

Cost of capital The rate of return that suppliers of capital require as compensation for their contribution of capital.

Cost of carry See *carry*.

Cost of debt The cost of debt financing to a company, such as when it issues a bond or takes out a bank loan.

Cost of preferred stock The cost to a company of issuing preferred stock; the dividend yield that a company must commit to pay preferred stockholders.

Cost-push Type of inflation in which rising costs, usually wages, compel businesses to raise prices generally.

Cost structure The mix of a company's variable costs and fixed costs.

Counterparty risk The risk that the other party to a contract will fail to honor the terms of the contract.

Coupon rate The interest rate promised in a contract; this is the rate used to calculate the periodic interest payments.

Cournot assumption Assumption in which each firm determines its profit-maximizing production level assuming that the other firms' output will not change.

Covariance A measure of the co-movement (linear association) between two random variables.

Covariance matrix A matrix or square array whose entries are covariances; also known as a variance–covariance matrix.

Covenants The terms and conditions of lending agreements that the issuer must comply with; they specify the actions that an issuer is obligated to perform (affirmative covenant) or prohibited from performing (negative covenant).

Covered bond Debt obligation secured by a segregated pool of assets called the cover pool. The issuer must maintain the value of the cover pool. In the event of default, bondholders have recourse against both the issuer and the cover pool.

Credit analysis The evaluation of credit risk; the evaluation of the creditworthiness of a borrower or counterparty.

Credit curve A curve showing the relationship between time to maturity and yield spread for an issuer with comparable bonds of various maturities outstanding, usually upward sloping.

Credit default swap (CDS) A type of credit derivative in which one party, the credit protection buyer who is seeking credit protection against a third party, makes a series of regularly scheduled payments to the other party, the credit protection seller. The seller makes no payments until a credit event occurs.

Credit derivatives A contract in which one party has the right to claim a payment from another party in the event that a specific credit event occurs over the life of the contract.

Credit enhancements Provisions that may be used to reduce the credit risk of a bond issue.

Credit-linked coupon bond Bond for which the coupon changes when the bond's credit rating changes.

Credit-linked note (CLN) Fixed-income security in which the holder of the security has the right to withhold payment of the full amount due at maturity if a credit event occurs.

Credit migration risk The risk that a bond issuer's creditworthiness deteriorates, or migrates lower, leading investors to believe the risk of default is higher. Also called *downgrade risk*.

Credit risk The risk of loss caused by a counterparty's or debtor's failure to make a promised payment. Also called *default risk*.

Credit scoring model A statistical model used to classify borrowers according to creditworthiness.

Credit spread option An option on the yield spread on a bond.

Credit tranching A structure used to redistribute the credit risk associated with the collateral; a set of bond classes created to allow investors a choice in the amount of credit risk that they prefer to bear.

Credit-worthiness The perceived ability of the borrower to pay what is owed on the borrowing in a timely manner; it represents the ability of a company to withstand adverse impacts on its cash flows.

Cross-default provisions Provisions whereby events of default such as non-payment of interest on one bond trigger default on all outstanding debt; implies the same default probability for all issues.

Cross-price elasticity of demand The percentage change in quantity demanded for a given percentage change in the price of another good; the responsiveness of the demand for Product A that is associated with the change in price of Product B.

Cross-sectional analysis Analysis that involves comparisons across individuals in a group over a given time period or at a given point in time.

Cross-sectional data Observations over individual units at a point in time, as opposed to time-series data.

Crossing networks Trading systems that match buyers and sellers who are willing to trade at prices obtained from other markets.

Crowding out The thesis that government borrowing may divert private sector investment from taking place.

Cryptocurrency An electronic medium of exchange that lacks physical form.

Cryptography An algorithmic process to encrypt data, making the data unusable if received by unauthorized parties.

Cumulative distribution function A function giving the probability that a random variable is less than or equal to a specified value.

Cumulative preference shares Preference shares for which any dividends that are not paid accrue and must be paid in full before dividends on common shares can be paid.

Cumulative relative frequency For data grouped into intervals, the fraction of total observations that are less than the value of the upper limit of a stated interval.

Cumulative voting A voting process whereby each shareholder can accumulate and vote all his or her shares for a single candidate in an election, as opposed to having to allocate their voting rights evenly among all candidates.

Currencies Monies issued by national monetary authorities.

Currency option bonds Bonds that give the bondholder the right to choose the currency in which he or she wants to receive interest payments and principal repayments.

Currency swap A swap in which each party makes interest payments to the other in different currencies.

Current account A component of the balance of payments account that measures the flow of goods and services.

Current assets Assets that are expected to be consumed or converted into cash in the near future, typically one year or less. *Also called liquid assets.*

Current cost With reference to assets, the amount of cash or cash equivalents that would have to be paid to buy the same or an equivalent asset today; with reference to liabilities, the undiscounted amount of cash or cash equivalents that would be required to settle the obligation today.

Current government spending With respect to government expenditures, spending on goods and services that are provided on a regular, recurring basis including health, education, and defense.

Current liabilities Short-term obligations, such as accounts payable, wages payable, or accrued liabilities, that are expected to be settled in the near future, typically one year or less.

Current ratio A liquidity ratio calculated as current assets divided by current liabilities.

Current yield The sum of the coupon payments received over the year divided by the flat price; also called the *income* or *interest yield* or *running yield.*

Curve duration The sensitivity of the bond price (or the market value of a financial asset or liability) with respect to a benchmark yield curve.

Customs union Extends the free trade area (FTA) by not only allowing free movement of goods and services among members, but also creating a common trade policy against nonmembers.

CVaR Conditional VaR, a tail loss measure. The weighted average of all loss outcomes in the statistical distribution that exceed the VaR loss.

Cyclical See *cyclical companies.*

Cyclical companies Companies with sales and profits that regularly expand and contract with the business cycle or state of economy.

Daily settlement See *mark to market* and *marking to market.*

Dark pools Alternative trading systems that do not display the orders that their clients send to them.

Data mining The practice of determining a model by extensive searching through a dataset for statistically significant patterns. Also called *data snooping.*

Data science An interdisciplinary field that brings computer science, statistics, and other disciplines together to analyze and produce insights from Big Data.

Data snooping See *data mining.*

Day order An order that is good for the day on which it is submitted. If it has not been filled by the close of business, the order expires unfilled.

Day's sales outstanding Estimate of the average number of days it takes to collect on credit accounts.

Days in receivables Estimate of the average number of days it takes to collect on credit accounts.

Days of inventory on hand An activity ratio equal to the number of days in the period divided by inventory turnover over the period.

Dealers A financial intermediary that acts as a principal in trades.

Dealing securities Securities held by banks or other financial intermediaries for trading purposes.

Death cross A technical analysis term that describes a situation where a short-term moving average crosses from above a longer-term moving average to below it; this movement is considered bearish.

Debentures Type of bond that can be secured or unsecured.

Debt incurrence test A financial covenant made in conjunction with existing debt that restricts a company's ability to incur additional debt at the same seniority based on one or more financial tests or conditions.

Debt-rating approach A method for estimating a company's before-tax cost of debt based upon the yield on comparably rated bonds for maturities that closely match that of the company's existing debt.

Debt-to-assets ratio A solvency ratio calculated as total debt divided by total assets.

Debt-to-capital ratio A solvency ratio calculated as total debt divided by total debt plus total shareholders' equity.

Debt-to-equity ratio A solvency ratio calculated as total debt divided by total shareholders' equity.

Declaration date The day that the corporation issues a statement declaring a specific dividend.

Decreasing returns to scale When a production process leads to increases in output that are proportionately smaller than the increase in inputs.

Deductible temporary differences Temporary differences that result in a reduction of or deduction from taxable income in a future period when the balance sheet item is recovered or settled.

Deep learning Machine learning using neural networks with many hidden layers.

Deep learning nets Machine learning using neural networks with many hidden layers.

Default probability The probability that a borrower defaults or fails to meet its obligation to make full and timely payments of principal and interest, according to the terms of the debt security. Also called *default risk.*

Default risk The probability that a borrower defaults or fails to meet its obligation to make full and timely payments of principal and interest, according to the terms of the debt security. Also called *default probability.*

Default risk premium An extra return that compensates investors for the possibility that the borrower will fail to make a promised payment at the contracted time and in the contracted amount.

Defensive companies Companies with sales and profits that have little sensitivity to the business cycle or state of the economy.

Defensive interval ratio A liquidity ratio that estimates the number of days that an entity could meet cash needs from liquid assets; calculated as (cash + short-term marketable investments + receivables) divided by daily cash expenditures.

Deferred coupon bond Bond that pays no coupons for its first few years but then pays a higher coupon than it otherwise normally would for the remainder of its life. Also called *split coupon bond.*

Deferred income A liability account for money that has been collected for goods or services that have not yet been delivered; payment received in advance of providing a good or service.

Deferred revenue A liability account for money that has been collected for goods or services that have not yet been delivered; payment received in advance of providing a good or service.

Deferred tax assets A balance sheet asset that arises when an excess amount is paid for income taxes relative to accounting profit. The taxable income is higher than accounting profit and income tax payable exceeds tax expense. The company expects to recover the difference during the course of future operations when tax expense exceeds income tax payable.

Deferred tax liabilities A balance sheet liability that arises when a deficit amount is paid for income taxes relative to accounting profit. The taxable income is less than the accounting profit and income tax payable is less than tax expense. The company expects to eliminate the liability over the course of future operations when income tax payable exceeds tax expense.

Defined benefit pension plans Plans in which the company promises to pay a certain annual amount (defined benefit) to the employee after retirement. The company bears the investment risk of the plan assets.

Defined contribution pension plans Individual accounts to which an employee and typically the employer makes contributions during their working years and expect to draw on the accumulated funds at retirement. The employee bears the investment and inflation risk of the plan assets.

Deflation Negative inflation.

Degree of confidence The probability that a confidence interval includes the unknown population parameter.

Degree of financial leverage (DFL) The ratio of the percentage change in net income to the percentage change in operating income; the sensitivity of the cash flows available to owners when operating income changes.

Degree of operating leverage (DOL) The ratio of the percentage change in operating income to the percentage change in units sold; the sensitivity of operating income to changes in units sold.

Degree of total leverage The ratio of the percentage change in net income to the percentage change in units sold; the sensitivity of the cash flows to owners to changes in the number of units produced and sold.

Degrees of freedom (df) The number of independent observations used.

Delta The sensitivity of the derivative price to a small change in the value of the underlying asset.

Demand curve Graph of the inverse demand function. A graph showing the demand relation, either the highest quantity willingly purchased at each price or the highest price willingly paid for each quantity.

Demand function A relationship that expresses the quantity demanded of a good or service as a function of own-price and possibly other variables.

Demand-pull Type of inflation in which increasing demand raises prices generally, which then are reflected in a business's costs as workers demand wage hikes to catch up with the rising cost of living.

Demand shock A typically unexpected disturbance to demand, such as an unexpected interruption in trade or transportation.

Dependent With reference to events, the property that the probability of one event occurring depends on (is related to) the occurrence of another event.

Depository bank A bank that raises funds from depositors and other investors and lends it to borrowers.

Depository institutions Commercial banks, savings and loan banks, credit unions, and similar institutions that raise funds from depositors and other investors and lend it to borrowers.

Depository receipt A security that trades like an ordinary share on a local exchange and represents an economic interest in a foreign company.

Depreciation The process of systematically allocating the cost of long-lived (tangible) assets to the periods during which the assets are expected to provide economic benefits.

Depression See *contraction.*

Derivative pricing rule A pricing rule used by crossing networks in which a price is taken (derived) from the price that is current in the asset's primary market.

Derivatives A financial instrument whose value depends on the value of some underlying asset or factor (e.g., a stock price, an interest rate, or exchange rate).

Descriptive statistics The study of how data can be summarized effectively.

Development capital Minority equity investments in more mature companies that are seeking capital to expand or restructure operations, enter new markets, or finance major acquisitions.

Diffuse prior The assumption of equal prior probabilities.

Diffusion index Reflects the proportion of the index's components that are moving in a pattern consistent with the overall index.

Diluted EPS The EPS that would result if all dilutive securities were converted into common shares.

Diluted shares The number of shares that would be outstanding if all potentially dilutive claims on common shares (e.g., convertible debt, convertible preferred stock, and employee stock options) were exercised.

Diminishing balance method An accelerated depreciation method, i.e., one that allocates a relatively large proportion of the cost of an asset to the early years of the asset's useful life.

Diminishing marginal productivity Describes a state in which each additional unit of input produces less output than previously.

Direct debit program An arrangement whereby a customer authorizes a debit to a demand account; typically used by companies to collect routine payments for services.

Direct financing leases Under US GAAP, a type of finance lease, from a lessor perspective, where the present value of the lease payments (lease receivable) equals the carrying value of the leased asset. No selling profit is recognized at lease inception. The revenues earned by the lessor are financing in nature.

Direct format With reference to the cash flow statement, a format for the presentation of the statement in which cash flow from operating activities is shown as operating cash receipts less operating cash disbursements. Also called *direct method.*

Direct method See *direct format.*

Direct taxes Taxes levied directly on income, wealth, and corporate profits.

Direct write-off method An approach to recognizing credit losses on customer receivables in which the company waits until such time as a customer has defaulted and only then recognizes the loss.

Disbursement float The amount of time between check issuance and a check's clearing back against the company's account.

Discount To reduce the value of a future payment in allowance for how far away it is in time; to calculate the present value of some future amount. Also, the amount by which an instrument is priced below its face (par) value.

Discount interest A procedure for determining the interest on a loan or bond in which the interest is deducted from the face value in advance.

Discount margin See *required margin.*

Discount rates In general, the interest rate used to calculate a present value. In the money market, however, discount rate is a specific type of quoted rate.

Discounted cash flow models Valuation models that estimate the intrinsic value of a security as the present value of the future benefits expected to be received from the security.

Discounted payback period the number of years it takes for the cumulative discounted cash flows from a project to equal the original investment.

Discouraged worker A person who has stopped looking for a job or has given up seeking employment.

Discrete random variable A random variable that can take on at most a countable number of possible values.

Discriminatory pricing rule A pricing rule used in continuous markets in which the limit price of the order or quote that first arrived determines the trade price.

Diseconomies of scale Increase in cost per unit resulting from increased production.

Dispersion The variability around the central tendency.

Display size The size of an order displayed to public view.

Distressed investing Investing in securities of companies in financial difficulty. Private equity funds that specialize in distressed investing typically buy the debt of mature companies in financial difficulty.

Distributed ledger A type of database that may be shared among entities in a network.

Distributed ledger technology Technology based on a distributed ledger.

Divergence In technical analysis, a term that describes the case when an indicator moves differently from the security being analyzed.

Diversification ratio The ratio of the standard deviation of an equally weighted portfolio to the standard deviation of a randomly selected security.

Dividend A distribution paid to shareholders based on the number of shares owned.

Dividend discount model (DDM) A present value model that estimates the intrinsic value of an equity share based on the present value of its expected future dividends.

Dividend discount model based approach An approach for estimating a country's equity risk premium. The market rate of return is estimated as the sum of the dividend yield and the growth rate in dividends for a market index. Subtracting the risk-free rate of return from the estimated market return produces an estimate for the equity risk premium.

Dividend payout ratio The ratio of cash dividends paid to earnings for a period.

Divisor A number (denominator) used to determine the value of a price return index. It is initially chosen at the inception of an index and subsequently adjusted by the index provider, as necessary, to avoid changes in the index value that are unrelated to changes in the prices of its constituent securities.

Domestic content provisions Stipulate that some percentage of the value added or components used in production should be of domestic origin.

Double bottoms In technical analysis, a reversal pattern that is formed when the price reaches a low, rebounds, and then sells off back to the first low level; used to predict a change from a downtrend to an uptrend.

Double coincidence of wants A prerequisite to barter trades, in particular that both economic agents in the transaction want what the other is selling.

Double declining balance depreciation An accelerated depreciation method that involves depreciating the asset at double the straight-line rate. This rate is multiplied by the book value of the asset at the beginning of the period (a declining balance) to calculate depreciation expense.

Double top In technical analysis, a reversal pattern that is formed when an uptrend reverses twice at roughly the same high price level; used to predict a change from an uptrend to a downtrend.

Down transition probability The probability that an asset's value moves down in a model of asset price dynamics.

Downgrade risk The risk that a bond issuer's creditworthiness deteriorates, or migrates lower, leading investors to believe the risk of default is higher. Also called *credit migration risk.*

Drag on liquidity When receipts lag, creating pressure from the decreased available funds.

Drawdown A percentage peak-to-trough reduction in net asset value.

Dual-currency bonds Bonds that make coupon payments in one currency and pay the par value at maturity in another currency.

DuPont analysis An approach to decomposing return on investment, e.g., return on equity, as the product of other financial ratios.

Duration A measure of the approximate sensitivity of a security to a change in interest rates (i.e., a measure of interest rate risk).

Duration gap A bond's Macaulay duration minus the investment horizon.

Dutch Book theorem A result in probability theory stating that inconsistent probabilities create profit opportunities.

Early repayment option See *prepayment option.*

Earnings per share The amount of income earned during a period per share of common stock.

Earnings surprise The portion of a company's earnings that is unanticipated by investors and, according to the efficient market hypothesis, merits a price adjustment.

Economic costs All the remuneration needed to keep a productive resource in its current employment or to acquire the resource for productive use; the sum of total accounting costs and implicit opportunity costs.

Economic indicator A variable that provides information on the state of the overall economy.

Economic loss The amount by which accounting profit is less than normal profit.

Economic order quantity–reorder point (EOQ–ROP) An approach to managing inventory based on expected demand and the predictability of demand; the ordering point for new inventory is determined based on the costs of ordering and carrying inventory, such that the total cost associated with inventory is minimized.

Economic profit Equal to accounting profit less the implicit opportunity costs not included in total accounting costs; the difference between total revenue (TR) and total cost (TC). Also called *abnormal profit* or *supernormal profit*.
Economic stabilization Reduction of the magnitude of economic fluctuations.
Economic union Incorporates all aspects of a common market and in addition requires common economic institutions and coordination of economic policies among members.
Economies of scale Reduction in cost per unit resulting from increased production.
Effective annual rate The amount by which a unit of currency will grow in a year with interest on interest included.
Effective convexity A *curve convexity* statistic that measures the secondary effect of a change in a benchmark yield curve on a bond's price.
Effective duration The sensitivity of a bond's price to a change in a benchmark yield curve.
Effective interest rate The borrowing rate or market rate that a company incurs at the time of issuance of a bond.
Efficient market A market in which asset prices reflect new information quickly and rationally.
Elastic Said of a good or service when the magnitude of elasticity is greater than one.
Elasticity The percentage change in one variable for a percentage change in another variable; a general measure of how sensitive one variable is to a change in the value of another variable.
Elasticity of demand A measure of the sensitivity of quantity demanded to a change in a product's own price: $\%\Delta Q^D/\%\Delta P$.
Elasticity of supply A measure of the sensitivity of quantity supplied to a change in price: $\%\Delta Q^S/\%\Delta P$.
Electronic communications networks See *alternative trading systems*.
Electronic funds transfer (EFT) The use of computer networks to conduct financial transactions electronically.
Elliott wave theory A technical analysis theory that claims that the market follows regular, repeated waves or cycles.
Embedded option Contingency provisions that provide the issuer or the bondholders the right, but not the obligation, to take action. These options are not part of the security and cannot be traded separately.
Empirical probability The probability of an event estimated as a relative frequency of occurrence.
Employed The number of people with a job.
Engagement/active ownership An ESG investment style that uses shareholder power to influence corporate behavior through direct corporate engagement (i.e., communicating with senior management and/or boards of companies), filing or co-filing shareholder proposals, and proxy voting that is directed by ESG guidelines.
Enterprise risk management An overall assessment of a company's risk position. A centralized approach to risk management sometimes called firmwide risk management.
Enterprise value A measure of a company's total market value from which the value of cash and short-term investments have been subtracted.
Equal weighting An index weighting method in which an equal weight is assigned to each constituent security at inception.
Equipment trust certificates Bonds secured by specific types of equipment or physical assets.
Equity Assets less liabilities; the residual interest in the assets after subtracting the liabilities.
Equity risk premium The expected return on equities minus the risk-free rate; the premium that investors demand for investing in equities.
Equity swap A swap transaction in which at least one cash flow is tied to the return to an equity portfolio position, often an equity index.
ESG An acronym that encompasses environmental, social and governance.
ESG integration The integration of qualitative and quantitative environmental, social, and governance factors into traditional security and industry analysis; also known as *ESG incorporation*.
ESG investing The consideration of environmental, social, and governance factors in the investment process.
Estimate The particular value calculated from sample observations using an estimator.
Estimation With reference to statistical inference, the subdivision dealing with estimating the value of a population parameter.
Estimator An estimation formula; the formula used to compute the sample mean and other sample statistics are examples of estimators.
Ethical principles Beliefs regarding what is good, acceptable, or obligatory behavior and what is bad, unacceptable, or forbidden behavior.
Ethics The study of moral principles or of making good choices. Ethics encompasses a set of moral principles and rules of conduct that provide guidance for our behavior.
Eurobonds Type of bond issued internationally, outside the jurisdiction of the country in whose currency the bond is denominated.
European option An option that can only be exercised on its expiration date.
European-style Said of an option contract that can only be exercised on the option's expiration date.
Event Any outcome or specified set of outcomes of a random variable.
Ex-dividend date The first date that a share trades without (i.e., "ex") the dividend.
Excess kurtosis Degree of kurtosis (fatness of tails) in excess of the kurtosis of the normal distribution.
Exchanges Places where traders can meet to arrange their trades.
Exclusionary screening An ESG implementation approach that excludes certain sectors or companies that deviate from an investor's accepted standards. Also called *negative screening* or *norms-based screening*.
Execution instructions Instructions that indicate how to fill an order.
Exercise The process of using an option to buy or sell the underlying.
Exercise price The fixed price at which an option holder can buy or sell the underlying. Also called *strike price*, *striking price*, or *strike*.
Exercise value The value obtained if an option is exercised based on current conditions. Also known as *intrinsic value*.
Exhaustive Covering or containing all possible outcomes.
Expansion The period of a business cycle after its lowest point and before its highest point.
Expansionary Tending to cause the real economy to grow.
Expansionary fiscal policy Fiscal policy aimed at achieving real economic growth.

Expected inflation The level of inflation that economic agents expect in the future.

Expected loss Default probability times Loss severity given default.

Expected value The probability-weighted average of the possible outcomes of a random variable.

Expenses Outflows of economic resources or increases in liabilities that result in decreases in equity (other than decreases because of distributions to owners); reductions in net assets associated with the creation of revenues.

Experience curve A curve that shows the direct cost per unit of good or service produced or delivered as a typically declining function of cumulative output.

Export subsidy Paid by the government to the firm when it exports a unit of a good that is being subsidized.

Exports Goods and services that an economy sells to other countries.

Extension risk The risk that when interest rates rise, fewer prepayments will occur because homeowners are reluctant to give up the benefits of a contractual interest rate that now looks low. As a result, the security becomes longer in maturity than anticipated at the time of purchase.

Externality An effect of a market transaction that is borne by parties other than those who transacted.

Extra dividend A dividend paid by a company that does not pay dividends on a regular schedule, or a dividend that supplements regular cash dividends with an extra payment.

Extreme value theory A branch of statistics that focuses primarily on extreme outcomes.

Face value The amount of cash payable by a company to the bondholders when the bonds mature; the promised payment at maturity separate from any coupon payment.

Factor A common or underlying element with which several variables are correlated.

Fair value The amount at which an asset could be exchanged, or a liability settled, between knowledgeable, willing parties in an arm's-length transaction; the price that would be received to sell an asset or paid to transfer a liability in an orderly transaction between market participants.

Fed funds rate The US interbank lending rate on overnight borrowings of reserves.

Federal funds rate The US interbank lending rate on overnight borrowings of reserves.

Fiat money Money that is not convertible into any other commodity.

Fibonacci sequence A sequence of numbers starting with 0 and 1, and then each subsequent number in the sequence is the sum of the two preceding numbers. In Elliott Wave Theory, it is believed that market waves follow patterns that are the ratios of the numbers in the Fibonacci sequence.

Fiduciary call A combination of a European call and a risk-free bond that matures on the option expiration day and has a face value equal to the exercise price of the call.

FIFO method The first in, first out, method of accounting for inventory, which matches sales against the costs of items of inventory in the order in which they were placed in inventory.

Fill or kill See *immediate or cancel order*.

Finance lease From the lessee perspective, under US GAAP, a type of lease which is more akin to the purchase of an asset by the lessee. From the lessor perspective, under IFRS, a lease which "transfers substantially all the risks and rewards incidental to ownership of an underlying asset."

Financial account A component of the balance of payments account that records investment flows.

Financial flexibility The ability to react and adapt to financial adversity and opportunities.

Financial leverage The extent to which a company can effect, through the use of debt, a proportional change in the return on common equity that is greater than a given proportional change in operating income; also, short for the financial leverage ratio.

Financial leverage ratio A measure of financial leverage calculated as average total assets divided by average total equity.

Financial risk The risk that environmental, social, or governance risk factors will result in significant costs or other losses to a company and its shareholders; the risk arising from a company's obligation to meet required payments under its financing agreements.

Financing activities Activities related to obtaining or repaying capital to be used in the business (e.g., equity and long-term debt).

Fintech Technological innovation in the design and delivery of financial services and products in the financial industry.

Firm commitment offering See *underwritten offering*.

First-degree price discrimination Where a monopolist is able to charge each customer the highest price the customer is willing to pay.

First lien debt Debt secured by a pledge of certain assets that could include buildings, but may also include property and equipment, licenses, patents, brands, etc.

First mortgage debt Debt secured by a pledge of a specific property.

Fiscal multiplier The ratio of a change in national income to a change in government spending.

Fiscal policy The use of taxes and government spending to affect the level of aggregate expenditures.

Fisher effect The thesis that the real rate of interest in an economy is stable over time so that changes in nominal interest rates are the result of changes in expected inflation.

Fisher index The geometric mean of the Laspeyres index.

Fixed charge coverage A solvency ratio measuring the number of times interest and lease payments are covered by operating income, calculated as (EBIT + lease payments) divided by (interest payments + lease payments).

Fixed costs Costs that remain at the same level regardless of a company's level of production and sales.

Fixed-for-floating interest rate swap An interest rate swap in which one party pays a fixed rate and the other pays a floating rate, with both sets of payments in the same currency. Also called *plain vanilla swap* or *vanilla swap*.

Fixed rate perpetual preferred stock Nonconvertible, noncallable preferred stock that has a fixed dividend rate and no maturity date.

Flags A technical analysis continuation pattern formed by parallel trendlines, typically over a short period.

Flat price The full price of a bond minus the accrued interest; also called the *quoted* or *clean* price.

Float In the context of customer receipts, the amount of money that is in transit between payments made by customers and the funds that are usable by the company.

Float-adjusted market-capitalization weighting An index weighting method in which the weight assigned to each constituent security is determined by adjusting its market capitalization for its market float.

Float factor An estimate of the average number of days it takes deposited checks to clear; average daily float divided by average daily deposit.

Floaters See *floating-rate notes.*

Floating-rate notes A note on which interest payments are not fixed, but instead vary from period to period depending on the current level of a reference interest rate.

Flotation cost Fees charged to companies by investment bankers and other costs associated with raising new capital.

Foreclosure Allows the lender to take possession of a mortgaged property if the borrower defaults and then sell it to recover funds.

Foreign currency reserves Holding by the central bank of non-domestic currency deposits and non-domestic bonds.

Foreign direct investment Direct investment by a firm in one country (the source country) in productive assets in a foreign country (the host country).

Foreign exchange gains (or losses) Gains (or losses) that occur when the exchange rate changes between the investor's currency and the currency that foreign securities are denominated in.

Foreign portfolio investment Shorter-term investment by individuals, firms, and institutional investors (e.g., pension funds) in foreign financial instruments such as foreign stocks and foreign government bonds.

Forward commitments Class of derivatives that provides the ability to lock in a price to transact in the future at a previously agreed-upon price.

Forward contract An agreement between two parties in which one party, the buyer, agrees to buy from the other party, the seller, an underlying asset at a later date for a price established at the start of the contract.

Forward curve A series of forward rates, each having the same timeframe.

Forward market For future delivery, beyond the usual settlement time period in the cash market.

Forward price The fixed price or rate at which the transaction scheduled to occur at the expiration of a forward contract will take place. This price is agreed on at the initiation date of the contract.

Forward rate The interest rate on a bond or money market instrument traded in a forward market. A forward rate can be interpreted as an incremental, or marginal, return for extending the time-to-maturity for an additional time period.

Forward rate agreements A forward contract calling for one party to make a fixed interest payment and the other to make an interest payment at a rate to be determined at the contract expiration.

Fractile A value at or below which a stated fraction of the data lies.

Fractional reserve banking Banking in which reserves constitute a fraction of deposits.

Free cash flow The actual cash that would be available to the company's investors after making all investments necessary to maintain the company as an ongoing enterprise (also referred to as free cash flow to the firm); the internally generated funds that can be distributed to the company's investors (e.g., shareholders and bondholders) without impairing the value of the company.

Free cash flow to equity (FCFE) The cash flow available to a company's common shareholders after all operating expenses, interest, and principal payments have been made, and necessary investments in working and fixed capital have been made.

Free-cash-flow-to-equity models Valuation models based on discounting expected future free cash flow to equity.

Free cash flow to the firm (FCFF) The cash flow available to the company's suppliers of capital after all operating expenses have been paid and necessary investments in working capital and fixed capital have been made.

Free float The number of shares that are readily and freely tradable in the secondary market.

Free trade When there are no government restrictions on a country's ability to trade.

Free trade areas One of the most prevalent forms of regional integration, in which all barriers to the flow of goods and services among members have been eliminated.

Frequency distribution A tabular display of data summarized into a relatively small number of intervals.

Frequency polygon A graph of a frequency distribution obtained by drawing straight lines joining successive points representing the class frequencies.

Full integration An ESG investment style that focuses on the explicit inclusion of ESG factors into the traditional financial analysis of individual stocks for the purpose of valuation (e.g., as inputs into cash flow forecasts and/or cost-of-capital estimates).

Full price The price of a security with accrued interest; also called the *invoice* or *dirty* price.

Fundamental analysis The examination of publicly available information and the formulation of forecasts to estimate the intrinsic value of assets.

Fundamental value The underlying or true value of an asset based on an analysis of its qualitative and quantitative characteristics. Also called *intrinsic value.*

Fundamental weighting An index weighting method in which the weight assigned to each constituent security is based on its underlying company's size. It attempts to address the disadvantages of market-capitalization weighting by using measures that are independent of the constituent security's price.

Funds of hedge funds Funds that hold a portfolio of hedge funds, more commonly shortened to *funds of funds.*

Future value (FV) The amount to which a payment or series of payments will grow by a stated future date.

Futures contract A variation of a forward contract that has essentially the same basic definition but with some additional features, such as a clearinghouse guarantee against credit losses, a daily settlement of gains and losses, and an organized electronic or floor trading facility.

Futures price The agreed-upon price of a futures contract.

FX swap The combination of a spot and a forward FX transaction.

G-spread The yield spread in basis points over an actual or interpolated government bond.

Gains Asset inflows not directly related to the ordinary activities of the business.

Game theory The set of tools decision makers use to incorporate responses by rival decision makers into their strategies.

Gamma A numerical measure of how sensitive an option's delta (the sensitivity of the derivative's price) is to a change in the value of the underlying.

GDP deflator A gauge of prices and inflation that measures the aggregate changes in prices across the overall economy.

General partner The partner that runs the business and ultimately bears unlimited liability for the business's debts and obligations.

Geometric mean A measure of central tendency computed by taking the *n*th root of the product of *n* non-negative values.

Giffen goods Goods that are consumed more as the price of the good rises because it is a very inferior good whose income effect overwhelms its substitution effect when price changes.

Gilts Bonds issued by the UK government.

Giro system An electronic payment system used widely in Europe and Japan.

Global depository receipt A depository receipt that is issued outside of the company's home country and outside of the United States.

Global minimum-variance portfolio The portfolio on the minimum-variance frontier with the smallest variance of return.

Global registered share A common share that is traded on different stock exchanges around the world in different currencies.

Gold standard With respect to a currency, if a currency is on the gold standard a given amount can be converted into a prespecified amount of gold.

Golden cross A technical analysis term that describes a situation where a short-term moving average crosses from below a longer-term moving average to above it; this movement is considered bullish.

Good-on-close An execution instruction specifying that an order can only be filled at the close of trading. Also called *market on close.*

Good-on-open An execution instruction specifying that an order can only be filled at the opening of trading.

Good-till-cancelled order An order specifying that it is valid until the entity placing the order has cancelled it (or, commonly, until some specified amount of time such as 60 days has elapsed, whichever comes sooner).

Goodwill An intangible asset that represents the excess of the purchase price of an acquired company over the value of the net assets acquired.

Government equivalent yield A yield that restates a yield-to-maturity based on 30/360 day-count to one based on actual/actual.

Green bonds A bond used in green finance whereby the proceeds are earmarked towards environmental-related products.

Green finance A type of finance that addresses environmental concerns while achieving economic growth.

Grey market The forward market for bonds about to be issued. Also called "when issued" market.

Gross domestic product The market value of all final goods and services produced within the economy in a given period of time (output definition) or, equivalently, the aggregate income earned by all households, all companies, and the government within the economy in a given period of time (income definition).

Gross margin Sales minus the cost of sales (i.e., the cost of goods sold for a manufacturing company).

Gross profit Sales minus the cost of sales (i.e., the cost of goods sold for a manufacturing company).

Gross profit margin The ratio of gross profit to revenues.

Grouping by function With reference to the presentation of expenses in an income statement, the grouping together of expenses serving the same function, e.g. all items that are costs of goods sold.

Grouping by nature With reference to the presentation of expenses in an income statement, the grouping together of expenses by similar nature, e.g., all depreciation expenses.

Growth cyclical A term sometimes used to describe companies that are growing rapidly on a long-term basis but that still experience above-average fluctuation in their revenues and profits over the course of a business cycle.

Growth investors With reference to equity investors, investors who seek to invest in high-earnings-growth companies.

Guarantee certificate A type of structured financial instrument that provides investors capital protection. It combines a zero-coupon bond and a call option on some underlying asset.

Haircut See *repo margin.*

Harmonic mean A type of weighted mean computed by averaging the reciprocals of the observations, then taking the reciprocal of that average.

Head and shoulders pattern In technical analysis, a reversal pattern that is formed in three parts: a left shoulder, head, and right shoulder; used to predict a change from an uptrend to a downtrend.

Headline inflation The inflation rate calculated based on the price index that includes all goods and services in an economy.

Hedge funds Private investment vehicles that typically use leverage, derivatives, and long and short investment strategies.

Hedge portfolio A hypothetical combination of the derivative and its underlying that eliminates risk.

Held-to-maturity Debt (fixed-income) securities that a company intends to hold to maturity; these are presented at their original cost, updated for any amortisation of discounts or premiums.

Herding Clustered trading that may or may not be based on information.

Hidden order An order that is exposed not to the public but only to the brokers or exchanges that receive it.

High-frequency trading A form of algorithmic trading that makes use of vast quantities of data to execute trades on ultra-high-speed networks in fractions of a second.

High-water mark The highest value, net of fees, that a fund has reached in history. It reflects the highest cumulative return used to calculate an incentive fee.

Histogram A bar chart of data that have been grouped into a frequency distribution.

Historical cost In reference to assets, the amount paid to purchase an asset, including any costs of acquisition and/or preparation; with reference to liabilities, the amount of proceeds received in exchange in issuing the liability.

Historical equity risk premium approach An estimate of a country's equity risk premium that is based upon the historical averages of the risk-free rate and the rate of return on the market portfolio.

Historical simulation Another term for the historical method of estimating VaR. This term is somewhat misleading in that the method involves not a *simulation* of the past but rather what *actually happened* in the past, sometimes adjusted to reflect the fact that a different portfolio may have existed in the past than is planned for the future.

Holder-of-record date The date that a shareholder listed on the corporation's books will be deemed to have ownership of the shares for purposes of receiving an upcoming dividend.

Holding period return The return that an investor earns during a specified holding period; a synonym for total return.

Homogeneity of expectations The assumption that all investors have the same economic expectations and thus have the same expectations of prices, cash flows, and other investment characteristics.

Horizon yield The internal rate of return between the total return (the sum of reinvested coupon payments and the sale price or redemption amount) and the purchase price of the bond.

Horizontal analysis Common-size analysis that involves comparing a specific financial statement with that statement in prior or future time periods; also, cross-sectional analysis of one company with another.

Horizontal demand schedule Implies that at a given price, the response in the quantity demanded is infinite.

Hostile takeover An attempt by one entity to acquire a company without the consent of the company's management.

Household A person or a group of people living in the same residence, taken as a basic unit in economic analysis.

Human capital The accumulated knowledge and skill that workers acquire from education, training, or life experience and the corresponding present value of future earnings to be generated by said skilled individual.

Hurdle rate The rate of return that must be met for a project to be accepted.

Hypothesis With reference to statistical inference, a statement about one or more populations.

Hypothesis testing With reference to statistical inference, the subdivision dealing with the testing of hypotheses about one or more populations.

I-spread The yield spread of a specific bond over the standard swap rate in that currency of the same tenor.

Iceberg order An order in which the display size is less than the order's full size.

If-converted method A method for accounting for the effect of convertible securities on earnings per share (EPS) that specifies what EPS would have been if the convertible securities had been converted at the beginning of the period, taking account of the effects of conversion on net income and the weighted average number of shares outstanding.

Immediate or cancel order An order that is valid only upon receipt by the broker or exchange. If such an order cannot be filled in part or in whole upon receipt, it cancels immediately. Also called *fill or kill*.

Impact lag The lag associated with the result of actions affecting the economy with delay.

Implicit price deflator for GDP A gauge of prices and inflation that measures the aggregate changes in prices across the overall economy.

Implied forward rates Calculated from spot rates, an implied forward rate is a break-even reinvestment rate that links the return on an investment in a shorter-term zero-coupon bond to the return on an investment in a longer-term zero-coupon bond.

Implied volatility The volatility that option traders use to price an option, implied by the price of the option and a particular option-pricing model.

Import license Specifies the quantity of a good that can be imported into a country.

Imports Goods and services that a domestic economy (i.e., house-holds, firms, and government) purchases from other countries.

In the money Options that, if exercised, would result in the value received being worth more than the payment required to exercise.

Incentive fee Fees paid to the general partner from the limited partner(s) based on realized net profits.

Income Increases in economic benefits in the form of inflows or enhancements of assets, or decreases of liabilities that result in an increase in equity (other than increases resulting from contributions by owners).

Income elasticity of demand A measure of the responsiveness of demand to changes in income, defined as the percentage change in quantity demanded divided by the percentage change in income.

Income tax paid The actual amount paid for income taxes in the period; not a provision, but the actual cash outflow.

Income tax payable The income tax owed by the company on the basis of taxable income.

Income trust A type of equity ownership vehicle established as a trust issuing ownership shares known as units.

Increasing marginal returns When the marginal product of a resource increases as additional units of that input are employed.

Increasing returns to scale When a production process leads to increases in output that are proportionately larger than the increase in inputs.

Incremental cash flow The cash flow that is realized because of a decision; the changes or increments to cash flows resulting from a decision or action.

Indenture Legal contract that describes the form of a bond, the obligations of the issuer, and the rights of the bondholders. Also called the *trust deed*.

Independent With reference to events, the property that the occurrence of one event does not affect the probability of another event occurring.

Independent projects Independent projects are projects whose cash flows are independent of each other.

Independently and identically distributed (IID) With respect to random variables, the property of random variables that are independent of each other but follow the identical probability distribution.

Index-linked bond Bond for which coupon payments and/or principal repayment are linked to a specified index.

Index of Leading Economic Indicators A composite of economic variables used by analysts to predict future economic conditions.

Indexing An investment strategy in which an investor constructs a portfolio to mirror the performance of a specified index.

Indifference curve A curve representing all the combinations of two goods or attributes such that the consumer is entirely indifferent among them.

Indirect format With reference to cash flow statements, a format for the presentation of the statement which, in the operating cash flow section, begins with net income then shows additions and subtractions to arrive at operating cash flow. Also called *indirect method*.

Indirect method See *indirect format*.

Indirect taxes Taxes such as taxes on spending, as opposed to direct taxes.

Industry A group of companies offering similar products and/or services.

Industry analysis The analysis of a specific branch of manufacturing, service, or trade.

Inelastic Said of a good or service when the magnitude of elasticity is less than one. Insensitive to price changes.

Inferior goods A good whose consumption decreases as income increases.

Inflation The percentage increase in the general price level from one period to the next; a sustained rise in the overall level of prices in an economy.

Inflation-linked bond Type of index-linked bond that offers investors protection against inflation by linking the bond's coupon payments and/or the principal repayment to an index of consumer prices. Also called *linkers*.

Inflation premium An extra return that compensates investors for expected inflation.

Inflation rate The percentage change in a price index—that is, the speed of overall price level movements.

Inflation Reports A type of economic publication put out by many central banks.

Inflation uncertainty The degree to which economic agents view future rates of inflation as difficult to forecast.

Information cascade The transmission of information from those participants who act first and whose decisions influence the decisions of others.

Information-motivated traders Traders that trade to profit from information that they believe allows them to predict future prices.

Informationally efficient market A market in which asset prices reflect new information quickly and rationally.

Initial coin offering An unregulated process whereby companies raise capital by selling crypto tokens to investors in exchange for fiat money or another agreed-upon cryptocurrency.

Initial margin The amount that must be deposited in a clearinghouse account when entering into a futures contract.

Initial margin requirement The margin requirement on the first day of a transaction as well as on any day in which additional margin funds must be deposited.

Initial public offering (IPO) The first issuance of common shares to the public by a formerly private corporation.

Input productivity The amount of output produced by workers in a given period of time—for example, output per hour worked; measures the efficiency of labor.

Intangible assets Assets lacking physical substance, such as patents and trademarks.

Interbank market The market of loans and deposits between banks for maturities ranging from overnight to one year.

Interbank money market The market of loans and deposits between banks for maturities ranging from overnight to one year.

Interest Payment for lending funds.

Interest coverage A solvency ratio calculated as EBIT divided by interest payments.

Interest-only mortgage A loan in which no scheduled principal repayment is specified for a certain number of years.

Interest rate A rate of return that reflects the relationship between differently dated cash flows; a discount rate.

Interest rate swap A swap in which the underlying is an interest rate. Can be viewed as a currency swap in which both currencies are the same and can be created as a combination of currency swaps.

Intergenerational data mining A form of data mining that applies information developed by previous researchers using a dataset to guide current research using the same or a related dataset.

Intermarket analysis A field within technical analysis that combines analysis of major categories of securities—namely, equities, bonds, currencies, and commodities—to identify market trends and possible inflections in a trend.

Internal rate of return (IRR) The discount rate that makes net present value equal 0; the discount rate that makes the present value of an investment's costs (outflows) equal to the present value of the investment's benefits (inflows).

Internet of Things A network arrangement of structures and devices whereby the objects on the network are able to interact and share information.

Interpolated spread The yield spread of a specific bond over the standard swap rate in that currency of the same tenor.

Interquartile range The difference between the third and first quartiles of a dataset.

Interval With reference to grouped data, a set of values within which an observation falls.

Interval scale A measurement scale that not only ranks data but also gives assurance that the differences between scale values are equal.

Intrinsic value See *exercise value*.

Inventory blanket lien The use of inventory as collateral for a loan. Though the lender has claim to some or all of the company's inventory, the company may still sell or use the inventory in the ordinary course of business.

Inventory investment Net change in business inventory.

Inventory turnover An activity ratio calculated as cost of goods sold divided by average inventory.

Inverse demand function A restatement of the demand function in which price is stated as a function of quantity.

Inverse floater A type of leveraged structured financial instrument. The cash flows are adjusted periodically and move in the opposite direction of changes in the reference rate.

Investing activities Activities associated with the acquisition and disposal of property, plant, and equipment; intangible assets; other long-term assets; and both long-term and short-term investments in the equity and debt (bonds and loans) issued by other companies.

Investment banks Financial intermediaries that provide advice to their mostly corporate clients and help them arrange transactions such as initial and seasoned securities offerings.

Investment opportunity schedule A graphical depiction of a company's investment opportunities ordered from highest to lowest expected return. A company's optimal capital budget is found where the investment opportunity schedule intersects with the company's marginal cost of capital.

Investment policy statement (IPS) A written planning document that describes a client's investment objectives and risk tolerance over a relevant time horizon, along with constraints that apply to the client's portfolio.

Investment property Property used to earn rental income or capital appreciation (or both).

January effect Calendar anomaly that stock market returns in January are significantly higher compared to the rest of the months of the year, with most of the abnormal returns reported during the first five trading days in January. Also called *turn-of-the-year effect*.

Joint probability The probability of the joint occurrence of stated events.

Joint probability function A function giving the probability of joint occurrences of values of stated random variables.
Just-in-time (JIT) method Method of managing inventory that minimizes in-process inventory stocks.
Key rate duration A method of measuring the interest rate sensitivities of a fixed-income instrument or portfolio to shifts in key points along the yield curve.
Keynesians Economists who believe that fiscal policy can have powerful effects on aggregate demand, output, and employment when there is substantial spare capacity in an economy.
Kondratieff wave A 54-year long economic cycle postulated by Nikolai Kondratieff.
Kurtosis The statistical measure that indicates the combined weight of the tails of a distribution relative to the rest of the distribution.
Labor force The portion of the working age population (over the age of 16) that is employed or is available for work but not working (unemployed).
Labor productivity The quantity of goods and services (real GDP) that a worker can produce in one hour of work.
Laddering strategy A form of active strategy which entails scheduling maturities on a systematic basis within the investment portfolio such that investments are spread out equally over the term of the ladder.
Lagging economic indicators Turning points that take place later than those of the overall economy; they are believed to have value in identifying the economy's past condition.
Laspeyres index A price index created by holding the composition of the consumption basket constant.
Law of demand The principle that as the price of a good rises, buyers will choose to buy less of it, and as its price falls, they will buy more.
Law of diminishing marginal returns The observation that a variable factor's marginal product must eventually fall as more of it is added to a fixed amount of the other factors.
Law of diminishing returns The smallest output that a firm can produce such that its long run average costs are minimized.
Law of one price The condition in a financial market in which two equivalent financial instruments or combinations of financial instruments can sell for only one price. Equivalent to the principle that no arbitrage opportunities are possible.
Lead underwriter The lead investment bank in a syndicate of investment banks and broker–dealers involved in a securities underwriting.
Leading economic indicators Turning points that usually precede those of the overall economy; they are believed to have value for predicting the economy's future state, usually near-term.
Legal tender Something that must be accepted when offered in exchange for goods and services.
Lender of last resort An entity willing to lend money when no other entity is ready to do so.
Leptokurtic Describes a distribution that has fatter tails than a normal distribution.
Lessee The party obtaining the use of an asset through a lease.
Lessor The owner of an asset that grants the right to use the asset to another party.
Letter of credit Form of external credit enhancement whereby a financial institution provides the issuer with a credit line to reimburse any cash flow shortfalls from the assets backing the issue.
Level of significance The probability of a Type I error in testing a hypothesis.
Leverage In the context of corporate finance, leverage refers to the use of fixed costs within a company's cost structure. Fixed costs that are operating costs (such as depreciation or rent) create operating leverage. Fixed costs that are financial costs (such as interest expense) create financial leverage.
Leveraged buyout A transaction whereby the target company's management team converts the target to a privately held company by using heavy borrowing to finance the purchase of the target company's outstanding shares.
Liabilities Present obligations of an enterprise arising from past events, the settlement of which is expected to result in an outflow of resources embodying economic benefits; creditors' claims on the resources of a company.
Life-cycle stage The stage of the life cycle: embryonic, growth, shakeout, mature, declining.
LIFO layer liquidation With respect to the application of the LIFO inventory method, the liquidation of old, relatively low-priced inventory; happens when the volume of sales rises above the volume of recent purchases so that some sales are made from relatively old, low-priced inventory. Also called *LIFO liquidation.*
LIFO method The last in, first out, method of accounting for inventory, which matches sales against the costs of items of inventory in the reverse order the items were placed in inventory (i.e., inventory produced or acquired last are assumed to be sold first).
LIFO reserve The difference between the reported LIFO inventory carrying amount and the inventory amount that would have been reported if the FIFO method had been used (in other words, the FIFO inventory value less the LIFO inventory value).
Likelihood The probability of an observation, given a particular set of conditions.
Limit down A limit move in the futures market in which the price at which a transaction would be made is at or below the lower limit.
Limit order Instructions to a broker or exchange to obtain the best price immediately available when filling an order, but in no event accept a price higher than a specified (limit) price when buying or accept a price lower than a specified (limit) price when selling.
Limit order book The book or list of limit orders to buy and sell that pertains to a security.
Limit up A limit move in the futures market in which the price at which a transaction would be made is at or above the upper limit.
Limitations on liens Meant to put limits on how much secured debt an issuer can have.
Limited partners Partners with limited liability. Limited partnerships in hedge and private equity funds are typically restricted to investors who are expected to understand and to be able to assume the risks associated with the investments.
Line chart In technical analysis, a plot of price data, typically closing prices, with a line connecting the points.
Linear interpolation The estimation of an unknown value on the basis of two known values that bracket it, using a straight line between the two known values.
Linear scale A scale in which equal distances correspond to equal absolute amounts. Also called *arithmetic scale.*
Linker See *inflation-linked bond.*

Liquid market Said of a market in which traders can buy or sell with low total transaction costs when they want to trade.
Liquidation To sell the assets of a company, division, or subsidiary piecemeal, typically because of bankruptcy; the form of bankruptcy that allows for the orderly satisfaction of creditors' claims after which the company ceases to exist.
Liquidity The ability to purchase or sell an asset quickly and easily at a price close to fair market value. The ability to meet short-term obligations using assets that are the most readily converted into cash.
Liquidity premium An extra return that compensates investors for the risk of loss relative to an investment's fair value if the investment needs to be converted to cash quickly.
Liquidity ratios Financial ratios measuring the company's ability to meet its short-term obligations.
Liquidity risk The risk that a financial instrument cannot be purchased or sold without a significant concession in price due to the size of the market.
Liquidity trap A condition in which the demand for money becomes infinitely elastic (horizontal demand curve) so that injections of money into the economy will not lower interest rates or affect real activity.
Load fund A mutual fund in which, in addition to the annual fee, a percentage fee is charged to invest in the fund and/or for redemptions from the fund.
Loan-to-value ratio The ratio of a property's purchase price to the amount of its mortgage.
Lockbox system A payment system in which customer payments are mailed to a post office box and the banking institution retrieves and deposits these payments several times a day, enabling the company to have use of the fund sooner than in a centralized system in which customer payments are sent to the company.
Locked limit A condition in the futures markets in which a transaction cannot take place because the price would be beyond the limits.
Lockup period The minimum holding period before investors are allowed to make withdrawals or redeem shares from a fund.
Logarithmic scale A scale in which equal distances represent equal proportional changes in the underlying quantity.
London interbank offered rate (Libor) Collective name for multiple rates at which a select set of banks believe they could borrow unsecured funds from other banks in the London interbank market for different currencies and different borrowing periods ranging from overnight to one year.
Long The buyer of a derivative contract. Also refers to the position of owning a derivative.
Long-lived assets Assets that are expected to provide economic benefits over a future period of time, typically greater than one year. Also called *long-term assets.*
Long position A position in an asset or contract in which one owns the asset or has an exercisable right under the contract.
Long-run average total cost The curve describing average total cost when no costs are considered fixed.
Longitudinal data Observations on characteristic(s) of the same observational unit through time.
Look-ahead bias A bias caused by using information that was unavailable on the test date.
Loss aversion The tendency of people to dislike losses more than they like comparable gains.
Loss severity Portion of a bond's value (including unpaid interest) an investor loses in the event of default.
Losses Asset outflows not directly related to the ordinary activities of the business.
Lower bound The lowest possible value of an option.
M^2 A measure of what a portfolio would have returned if it had taken on the same total risk as the market index.
M^2 alpha Difference between the risk-adjusted performance of the portfolio and the performance of the benchmark.
Macaulay duration The approximate amount of time a bond would have to be held for the market discount rate at purchase to be realized if there is a single change in interest rate. It indicates the point in time when the coupon reinvestment and price effects of a change in yield-to- maturity offset each other.
Machine learning Computer based techniques that seek to extract knowledge from large amounts of data by "learning" from known examples and then generating structure or predictions. ML algorithms aim to "find the pattern, apply the pattern."
Macroeconomics The branch of economics that deals with aggregate economic quantities, such as national output and national income.
Maintenance covenants Covenants in bank loan agreements that require the borrower to satisfy certain financial ratio tests while the loan is outstanding.
Maintenance margin The minimum amount that is required by a futures clearinghouse to maintain a margin account and to protect against default. Participants whose margin balances drop below the required maintenance margin must replenish their accounts.
Maintenance margin requirement The margin requirement on any day other than the first day of a transaction.
Management buy-ins Leveraged buyout in which the current management team is being replaced and the acquiring team will be involved in managing the company.
Management buyout A leveraged buyout event in which a group of investors consisting primarily of the company's existing management purchase at least controlling interest in its outstanding shares. At the extreme, they may purchase all shares and take the company private.
Management fee A fee based on assets under management or committed capital, as applicable, also called a *base fee.*
Manufacturing resource planning (MRP) The incorporation of production planning into inventory management. A MRP analysis provides both a materials acquisition schedule and a production schedule.
Margin The amount of money that a trader deposits in a margin account. The term is derived from the stock market practice in which an investor borrows a portion of the money required to purchase a certain amount of stock. In futures markets, there is no borrowing so the margin is more of a down payment or performance bond.
Margin bond A cash deposit required by the clearinghouse from the participants to a contract to provide a credit guarantee. Also called a *performance bond.*
Margin call A request for the short to deposit additional funds to bring their balance up to the initial margin.
Margin loan Money borrowed from a broker to purchase securities.
Marginal cost The cost of producing an additional unit of a good.
Marginal probability The probability of an event *not* conditioned on another event.

Marginal product Measures the productivity of each unit of input and is calculated by taking the difference in total product from adding another unit of input (assuming other resource quantities are held constant).

Marginal propensity to consume The proportion of an additional unit of disposable income that is consumed or spent; the change in consumption for a small change in income.

Marginal propensity to save The proportion of an additional unit of disposable income that is saved (not spent).

Marginal revenue The change in total revenue divided by the change in quantity sold; simply, the additional revenue from selling one more unit.

Marginal value curve A curve describing the highest price consumers are willing to pay for each additional unit of a good.

Mark to market The revaluation of a financial asset or liability to its current market value or fair value.

Market anomaly Change in the price or return of a security that cannot directly be linked to current relevant information known in the market or to the release of new information into the market.

Market bid–ask spread The difference between the best bid and the best offer.

Market-capitalization weighting An index weighting method in which the weight assigned to each constituent security is determined by dividing its market capitalization by the total market capitalization (sum of the market capitalization) of all securities in the index. Also called *value weighting.*

Market discount rate The rate of return required by investors given the risk of the investment in a bond; also called the *required yield* or the *required rate of return.*

Market float The number of shares that are available to the investing public.

Market liquidity risk The risk that the price at which investors can actually transact—buying or selling—may differ from the price indicated in the market.

Market model A regression equation that specifies a linear relationship between the return on a security (or portfolio) and the return on a broad market index.

Market multiple models Valuation models based on share price multiples or enterprise value multiples.

Market-on-close An execution instruction specifying that an order can only be filled at the close of trading.

Market order Instructions to a broker or exchange to obtain the best price immediately available when filling an order.

Market-oriented investors With reference to equity investors, investors whose investment disciplines cannot be clearly categorized as value or growth.

Market rate of interest The rate demanded by purchasers of bonds, given the risks associated with future cash payment obligations of the particular bond issue.

Market risk The risk that arises from movements in interest rates, stock prices, exchange rates, and commodity prices.

Market value The price at which an asset or security can currently be bought or sold in an open market.

Marketable limit order A buy limit order in which the limit price is placed above the best offer, or a sell limit order in which the limit price is placed below the best bid. Such orders generally will partially or completely fill right away.

Markowitz efficient frontier The graph of the set of portfolios offering the maximum expected return for their level of risk (standard deviation of return).

Matching principle The accounting principle that expenses should be recognized in the same period in which the associated revenue is recognized.

Matching strategy An active investment strategy that includes intentional matching of the timing of cash outflows with investment maturities.

Matrix pricing Process of estimating the market discount rate and price of a bond based on the quoted or flat prices of more frequently traded comparable bonds.

Maturity premium An extra return that compensates investors for the increased sensitivity of the market value of debt to a change in market interest rates as maturity is extended.

Maturity structure A factor explaining the differences in yields on similar bonds; also called *term structure.*

Mean absolute deviation With reference to a sample, the mean of the absolute values of deviations from the sample mean.

Mean–variance analysis An approach to portfolio analysis using expected means, variances, and covariances of asset returns.

Measure of central tendency A quantitative measure that specifies where data are centered.

Measure of value A standard for measuring value; a function of money.

Measurement scales A scheme of measuring differences. The four types of measurement scales are nominal, ordinal, interval, and ratio.

Measures of location A quantitative measure that describes the location or distribution of data; includes not only measures of central tendency but also other measures such as percentiles.

Median The value of the middle item of a set of items that has been sorted into ascending or descending order; the 50th percentile.

Medium of exchange Any asset that can be used to purchase goods and services or to repay debts; a function of money.

Medium-term note A corporate bond offered continuously to investors by an agent of the issuer, designed to fill the funding gap between commercial paper and long-term bonds.

Menu costs A cost of inflation in which businesses constantly have to incur the costs of changing the advertised prices of their goods and services.

Mesokurtic Describes a distribution with kurtosis identical to that of the normal distribution.

Mezzanine financing Debt or preferred shares with a relationship to common equity resulting from a feature such as attached warrants or conversion options. Mezzanine financing is subordinate to both senior and high-yield debt but is senior to equity. It is referred to as "mezzanine" because of its location on the balance sheet.

Microeconomics The branch of economics that deals with markets and decision making of individual economic units, including consumers and businesses.

Minimum efficient scale The smallest output that a firm can produce such that its long-run average total cost is minimized.

Minimum-variance portfolio The portfolio with the minimum variance for each given level of expected return.

Minority shareholders A particular shareholder or block of shareholders holding a small proportion of a company's outstanding shares, resulting in a limited ability to exercise control in voting activities.

Minsky moment Named for Hyman Minksy: A point in a business cycle when, after individuals become overextended in borrowing to finance speculative investments, people start realizing that something is likely to go wrong and a panic ensues leading to asset sell-offs.

Mismatching strategy An active investment strategy whereby the timing of cash outflows is not matched with investment maturities.

Modal interval With reference to grouped data, the most frequently occurring interval.

Mode The most frequently occurring value in a set of observations.

Modern portfolio theory (MPT) The analysis of rational portfolio choices based on the efficient use of risk.

Modified duration A measure of the percentage price change of a bond given a change in its yield-to-maturity.

Momentum oscillators A graphical representation of market sentiment that is constructed from price data and calculated so that it oscillates either between a high and a low or around some number.

Monetarists Economists who believe that the rate of growth of the money supply is the primary determinant of the rate of inflation.

Monetary policy Actions taken by a nation's central bank to affect aggregate output and prices through changes in bank reserves, reserve requirements, or its target interest rate.

Monetary transmission mechanism The process whereby a central bank's interest rate gets transmitted through the economy and ultimately affects the rate of increase of prices.

Monetary union An economic union in which the members adopt a common currency.

Money A generally accepted medium of exchange and unit of account.

Money convexity For a bond, the annual or approximate convexity multiplied by the full price.

Money creation The process by which changes in bank reserves translate into changes in the money supply.

Money duration A measure of the price change in units of the currency in which the bond is denominated given a change in its yield-to-maturity.

Money market The market for short-term debt instruments (one-year maturity or less).

Money market securities Fixed-income securities with maturities at issuance of one year or less.

Money market yield A yield on a basis comparable to the quoted yield on an interest-bearing money market instrument that pays interest on a 360-day basis; the annualized holding period yield, assuming a 360-day year.

Money multiplier Describes how a change in reserves is expected to affect the money supply; in its simplest form, 1 divided by the reserve requirement.

Money neutrality The thesis that an increase in the money supply leads in the long-run to an increase in the price level, while leaving real variables like output and employment unaffected.

Money-weighted return The internal rate of return on a portfolio, taking account of all cash flows.

Moneyness The relationship between the price of the underlying and an option's exercise price.

Monopolistic competition Highly competitive form of imperfect competition; the competitive characteristic is a notably large number of firms, while the monopoly aspect is the result of product differentiation.

Monopoly In pure monopoly markets, there are no substitutes for the given product or service. There is a single seller, which exercises considerable power over pricing and output decisions.

Monte Carlo simulation An approach to estimating a probability distribution of outcomes to examine what might happen if particular risks are faced. This method is widely used in the sciences as well as in business to study a variety of problems.

Moral principles Beliefs regarding what is good, acceptable, or obligatory behavior and what is bad, unacceptable, or forbidden behavior.

Mortgage-backed securities Debt obligations that represent claims to the cash flows from pools of mortgage loans, most commonly on residential property.

Mortgage loan A loan secured by the collateral of some specified real estate property that obliges the borrower to make a predetermined series of payments to the lender.

Mortgage pass-through security A security created when one or more holders of mortgages form a pool of mortgages and sell shares or participation certificates in the pool.

Mortgage rate The interest rate on a mortgage loan; also called *contract rate* or *note rate*.

Moving average The average of the closing price of a security over a specified number of periods. With each new period, the average is recalculated.

Moving-average convergence/divergence oscillator (MACD) A momentum oscillator that is constructed based on the difference between short-term and long-term moving averages of a security's price.

Multi-factor model A model that explains a variable in terms of the values of a set of factors.

Multi-market indexes Comprised of indexes from different countries, designed to represent multiple security markets.

Multi-step format With respect to the format of the income statement, a format that presents a subtotal for gross profit (revenue minus cost of goods sold).

Multilateral trading facilities See *alternative trading systems*.

Multinational corporation A company operating in more than one country or having subsidiary firms in more than one country.

Multiplication rule for probabilities The rule that the joint probability of events *A* and *B* equals the probability of *A* given *B* times the probability of *B*.

Multiplier models Valuation models based on share price multiples or enterprise value multiples.

Multivariate distribution A probability distribution that specifies the probabilities for a group of related random variables.

Multivariate normal distribution A probability distribution for a group of random variables that is completely defined by the means and variances of the variables plus all the correlations between pairs of the variables.

Municipal bonds A type of non-sovereign bond issued by a state or local government in the United States. It very often (but not always) offers income tax exemptions.

Munis A type of non-sovereign bond issued by a state or local government in the United States. It very often (but not always) offers income tax exemptions.

Mutual fund A comingled investment pool in which investors in the fund each have a pro-rata claim on the income and value of the fund.

Mutually exclusive projects Mutually exclusive projects compete directly with each other. For example, if Projects A and B are mutually exclusive, you can choose A or B, but you cannot choose both.

***n* Factorial** For a positive integer n, the product of the first n positive integers; 0 factorial equals 1 by definition. n factorial is written as $n!$.

Narrow money The notes and coins in circulation in an economy, plus other very highly liquid deposits.

Nash equilibrium When two or more participants in a non-coop-erative game have no incentive to deviate from their respective equilibrium strategies given their opponent's strategies.

National income The income received by all factors of production used in the generation of final output. National income equals gross domestic product (or, in some countries, gross national product) minus the capital consumption allowance and a statistical discrepancy.

Natural language processing Computer programs developed to analyze and interpret human language.

Natural rate of unemployment Effective unemployment rate, below which pressure emerges in labor markets.

Negative screening An ESG investment style that focuses on the exclusion of certain sectors, companies, or practices in a fund or portfolio on the basis of specific ESG criteria.

Neo-Keynesians A group of dynamic general equilibrium models that assume slow-to-adjust prices and wages.

Net book value The remaining (undepreciated) balance of an asset's purchase cost. For liabilities, the face value of a bond minus any unamortized discount, or plus any unamortized premium.

Net exports The difference between the value of a country's exports and the value of its imports (i.e., value of exports minus imports).

Net income The difference between revenue and expenses; what remains after subtracting all expenses (including depreciation, interest, and taxes) from revenue.

Net operating cycle An estimate of the average time that elapses between paying suppliers for materials and collecting cash from the subsequent sale of goods produced.

Net present value (NPV) The present value of an investment's cash inflows (benefits) minus the present value of its cash outflows (costs).

Net profit margin An indicator of profitability, calculated as net income divided by revenue; indicates how much of each dollar of revenues is left after all costs and expenses. Also called *profit margin* or *return on sales.*

Net realisable value Estimated selling price in the ordinary course of business less the estimated costs necessary to make the sale.

Net revenue Revenue after adjustments (e.g., for estimated returns or for amounts unlikely to be collected).

Net tax rate The tax rate net of transfer payments.

Neural networks Computer programs based on how our own brains learn and process information.

Neutral rate of interest The rate of interest that neither spurs on nor slows down the underlying economy.

New classical macroeconomics An approach to macroeconomics that seeks the macroeconomic conclusions of individuals maximizing utility on the basis of rational expectations and companies maximizing profits.

New Keynesians A group of dynamic general equilibrium models that assume slow-to-adjust prices and wages.

No-load fund A mutual fund in which there is no fee for investing in the fund or for redeeming fund shares, although there is an annual fee based on a percentage of the fund's net asset value.

Node Each value on a binomial tree from which successive moves or outcomes branch.

Nominal GDP The value of goods and services measured at current prices.

Nominal rate A rate of interest based on the security's face value.

Nominal risk-free interest rate The sum of the real risk-free interest rate and the inflation premium.

Nominal scale A measurement scale that categorizes data but does not rank them.

Non-accelerating inflation rate of unemployment Effective unemployment rate, below which pressure emerges in labor markets.

Non-agency RMBS In the United States, securities issued by private entities that are not guaranteed by a federal agency or a GSE.

Non-cumulative preference shares Preference shares for which dividends that are not paid in the current or subsequent periods are forfeited permanently (instead of being accrued and paid at a later date).

Non-current assets Assets that are expected to benefit the company over an extended period of time (usually more than one year).

Non-current liabilities Obligations that broadly represent a probable sacrifice of economic benefits in periods generally greater than one year in the future.

Non-cyclical A company whose performance is largely independent of the business cycle.

Non-deliverable forwards Cash-settled forward contracts, used predominately with respect to foreign exchange forwards. Also called *contracts for differences.*

Non-financial risks Risks that arise from sources other than changes in the external financial markets, such as changes in accounting rules, legal environment, or tax rates.

Non-participating preference shares Preference shares that do not entitle shareholders to share in the profits of the company. Instead, shareholders are only entitled to receive a fixed dividend payment and the par value of the shares in the event of liquidation.

Non-recourse loan Loan in which the lender does not have a shortfall claim against the borrower, so the lender can look only to the property to recover the outstanding mortgage balance.

Non-renewable resources Finite resources that are depleted once they are consumed, such as oil and coal.

Non-sovereign bonds A bond issued by a government below the national level, such as a province, region, state, or city.

Non-sovereign government bonds A bond issued by a government below the national level, such as a province, region, state, or city.

Nonconventional cash flow In a nonconventional cash flow pattern, the initial outflow is not followed by inflows only, but the cash flows can flip from positive (inflows) to negative (outflows) again (or even change signs several times).

Nonparametric test A test that is not concerned with a parameter, or that makes minimal assumptions about the population from which a sample comes.

Nonsystematic risk Unique risk that is local or limited to a particular asset or industry that need not affect assets outside of that asset class.

Normal distribution A continuous, symmetric probability distribution that is completely described by its mean and its variance.

Normal goods Goods that are consumed in greater quantities as income increases.

Normal profit The level of accounting profit needed to just cover the implicit opportunity costs ignored in accounting costs.

Notching Ratings adjustment methodology where specific issues from the same borrower may be assigned different credit ratings.

Note rate See *mortgage rate.*

Notice period The length of time (typically 30–90 days) in advance that investors may be required to notify a fund of their intent to redeem some or all of their investment.

Notional principal An imputed principal amount.

Number of days of inventory An activity ratio equal to the number of days in a period divided by the inventory ratio for the period; an indication of the number of days a company ties up funds in inventory.

Number of days of payables An activity ratio equal to the number of days in a period divided by the payables turnover ratio for the period; an estimate of the average number of days it takes a company to pay its suppliers.

Number of days of receivables Estimate of the average number of days it takes to collect on credit accounts.

Objective probabilities Probabilities that generally do not vary from person to person; includes a priori and objective probabilities.

Off-the-run Seasoned government bonds are off-the-run securities; they are not the most recently issued or the most actively traded.

Offer The price at which a dealer or trader is willing to sell an asset, typically qualified by a maximum quantity (ask size).

Official interest rate An interest rate that a central bank sets and announces publicly; normally the rate at which it is willing to lend money to the commercial banks. Also called *official policy rate* or *policy rate.*

Official policy rate An interest rate that a central bank sets and announces publicly; normally the rate at which it is willing to lend money to the commercial banks.

Oligopoly Market structure with a relatively small number of firms supplying the market.

On-the-run The most recently issued and most actively traded sovereign securities.

One-sided hypothesis test A test in which the null hypothesis is rejected only if the evidence indicates that the population parameter is greater than (smaller than) θ_0. The alternative hypothesis also has one side.

One-tailed hypothesis test A test in which the null hypothesis is rejected only if the evidence indicates that the population parameter is greater than (smaller than) θ_0. The alternative hypothesis also has one side.

Open economy An economy that trades with other countries.

Open-end fund A mutual fund that accepts new investment money and issues additional shares at a value equal to the net asset value of the fund at the time of investment.

Open interest The number of outstanding contracts in a clearinghouse at any given time. The open interest figure changes daily as some parties open up new positions, while other parties offset their old positions.

Open market operations The purchase or sale of bonds by the national central bank to implement monetary policy. The bonds traded are usually sovereign bonds issued by the national government.

Operating activities Activities that are part of the day-to-day business functioning of an entity, such as selling inventory and providing services.

Operating breakeven The number of units produced and sold at which the company's operating profit is zero (revenues = operating costs).

Operating cash flow The net amount of cash provided from operating activities.

Operating cycle A measure of the time needed to convert raw materials into cash from a sale; it consists of the number of days of inventory and the number of days of receivables.

Operating efficiency ratios Ratios that measure how efficiently a company performs day-to-day tasks, such as the collection of receivables and management of inventory.

Operating lease An agreement allowing a lessee to use some asset for a period of time; essentially a rental.

Operating leverage The use of fixed costs in operations.

Operating profit A company's profits on its usual business activities before deducting taxes. Also called *operating income.*

Operating profit margin A profitability ratio calculated as operating income (i.e., income before interest and taxes) divided by revenue. Also called *operating margin.*

Operating risk The risk attributed to the operating cost structure, in particular the use of fixed costs in operations; the risk arising from the mix of fixed and variable costs; the risk that a company's operations may be severely affected by environmental, social, and governance risk factors.

Operational independence A bank's ability to execute monetary policy and set interest rates in the way it thought would best meet the inflation target.

Operational risk The risk that arises from inadequate or failed people, systems, and internal policies, procedures, and processes, as well as from external events that are beyond the control of the organization but that affect its operations.

Operationally efficient Said of a market, a financial system, or an economy that has relatively low transaction costs.

Opportunity cost The value that investors forgo by choosing a particular course of action; the value of something in its best alternative use.

Option A financial instrument that gives one party the right, but not the obligation, to buy or sell an underlying asset from or to another party at a fixed price over a specific period of time. Also referred to as *contingent claim* or *option contract.*

Option-adjusted price The value of the embedded option plus the flat price of the bond.

Option-adjusted spread OAS = Z-spread – Option value (in basis points per year).

Option-adjusted yield The required market discount rate whereby the price is adjusted for the value of the embedded option.

Option contract See *option.*

Option premium The amount of money a buyer pays and seller receives to engage in an option transaction.

Order A specification of what instrument to trade, how much to trade, and whether to buy or sell.

Order-driven markets A market (generally an auction market) that uses rules to arrange trades based on the orders that traders submit; in their pure form, such markets do not make use of dealers.

Order precedence hierarchy With respect to the execution of orders to trade, a set of rules that determines which orders execute before other orders.

Ordinal scale A measurement scale that sorts data into categories that are ordered (ranked) with respect to some characteristic.

Ordinary annuity An annuity with a first cash flow that is paid one period from the present.

Ordinary shares Equity shares that are subordinate to all other types of equity (e.g., preferred equity). Also called *common stock* or *common shares*.

Organized exchange A securities marketplace where buyers and seller can meet to arrange their trades.

Other comprehensive income Items of comprehensive income that are not reported on the income statement; comprehensive income minus net income.

Out-of-sample test A test of a strategy or model using a sample outside the time period on which the strategy or model was developed.

Out of the money Options that, if exercised, would require the payment of more money than the value received and therefore would not be currently exercised.

Outcome A possible value of a random variable.

Over-the-counter (OTC) markets A decentralized market where buy and sell orders initiated from various locations are matched through a communications network.

Overbought A market condition in which market sentiment is thought to be unsustainably bullish.

Overcollateralization Form of internal credit enhancement that refers to the process of posting more collateral than needed to obtain or secure financing.

Overfitting An undesirable result from fitting a model so closely to a dataset that it does not perform well on new data.

Overlay/portfolio tilt An ESG investment style that focuses on the use of certain investment strategies or products to change specific aggregate ESG characteristics of a fund or investment portfolio to a desired level (e.g., tilting an investment portfolio toward a desired carbon footprint).

Oversold A market condition in which market sentiment is thought to be unsustainably bearish.

Own price The price of a good or service itself (as opposed to the price of something else).

Own-price elasticity of demand The percentage change in quantity demanded for a percentage change in good's own price, holding all other things constant.

Owners' equity The excess of assets over liabilities; the residual interest of shareholders in the assets of an entity after deducting the entity's liabilities. Also called *shareholders' equity* or *shareholders' funds*.

Paasche index An index formula using the current composition of a basket of products.

Paired comparisons test A statistical test for differences based on paired observations drawn from samples that are dependent on each other.

Paired observations Observations that are dependent on each other.

Pairs arbitrage trade A trade in two closely related stocks involving the short sale of one and the purchase of the other.

Panel data Observations through time on a single characteristic of multiple observational units.

Par curve A sequence of yields-to-maturity such that each bond is priced at par value. The bonds are assumed to have the same currency, credit risk, liquidity, tax status, and annual yields stated for the same periodicity.

Par value The amount of principal on a bond.

Parallel shift A parallel yield curve shift implies that all rates change by the same amount in the same direction.

Parameter A descriptive measure computed from or used to describe a population of data, conventionally represented by Greek letters.

Parametric test Any test (or procedure) concerned with parameters or whose validity depends on assumptions concerning the population generating the sample.

Pari passu On an equal footing.

Partial duration See *key rate duration.*

Participating preference shares Preference shares that entitle shareholders to receive the standard preferred dividend plus the opportunity to receive an additional dividend if the company's profits exceed a pre-specified level.

Pass-through rate The coupon rate of a mortgage pass-through security.

Passive investment A buy and hold approach in which an investor does not make portfolio changes based on short-term expectations of changing market or security performance.

Passive strategy In reference to short-term cash management, it is an investment strategy characterized by simple decision rules for making daily investments.

Payable date The day that the company actually mails out (or electronically transfers) a dividend payment.

Payback period the number of years required to recover the original investment in a project. The payback is based on cash flows.

Payment date The day that the company actually mails out (or electronically transfers) a dividend payment.

Payments system The system for the transfer of money.

Peak The highest point of a business cycle.

Peer group A group of companies engaged in similar business activities whose economics and valuation are influenced by closely related factors.

Pennants A technical analysis continuation pattern formed by trendlines that converge to form a triangle, typically over a short period.

Per capita real GDP Real GDP divided by the size of the population, often used as a measure of the average standard of living in a country.

Per unit contribution margin The amount that each unit sold contributes to covering fixed costs—that is, the difference between the price per unit and the variable cost per unit.

Percentiles Quantiles that divide a distribution into 100 equal parts.

Perfect competition A market structure in which the individual firm has virtually no impact on market price, because it is assumed to be a very small seller among a very large number of firms selling essentially identical products.

Perfectly elastic When the quantity demanded or supplied of a given good is infinitely sensitive to a change in the value of a specified variable (e.g., price).

Perfectly inelastic When the quantity demanded or supplied of a given good is completely insensitive to a change in the value of a specified variable (e.g., price).

Performance bond See *margin bond.*

Performance evaluation The measurement and assessment of the outcomes of investment management decisions.

Performance fee Fees paid to the general partner from the limited partner(s) based on realized net profits.

Period costs Costs (e.g., executives' salaries) that cannot be directly matched with the timing of revenues and which are thus expensed immediately.

Periodicity The assumed number of periods in the year, typically matches the frequency of coupon payments.

Permanent differences Differences between tax and financial reporting of revenue (expenses) that will not be reversed at some future date. These result in a difference between the company's effective tax rate and statutory tax rate and do not result in a deferred tax item.

Permissioned networks Networks that are fully open only to select participants on a DLT network.

Permissionless networks Networks that are fully open to any user on a DLT network.

Permutation An ordered listing.

Perpetual bonds Bonds with no stated maturity date.

Perpetuity A perpetual annuity, or a set of never-ending level sequential cash flows, with the first cash flow occurring one period from now. A bond that does not mature.

Personal consumption expenditures All domestic personal consumption; the basis for a price index for such consumption called the PCE price index.

Personal disposable income Equal to personal income less personal taxes.

Personal income A broad measure of household income that includes all income received by households, whether earned or unearned; measures the ability of consumers to make purchases.

Plain vanilla bond Bond that makes periodic, fixed coupon payments during the bond's life and a lump-sum payment of principal at maturity. Also called *conventional bond.*

Platykurtic Describes a distribution that has relatively less weight in the tails than the normal distribution.

Point and figure chart A technical analysis chart that is constructed with columns of X's alternating with columns of O's such that the horizontal axis represents only the number of changes in price without reference to time or volume.

Point estimate A single numerical estimate of an unknown quantity, such as a population parameter.

Point of sale (POS) Systems that capture transaction data at the physical location in which the sale is made.

Policy rate An interest rate that a central bank sets and announces publicly; normally the rate at which it is willing to lend money to the commercial banks.

Population All members of a specified group.

Population mean The arithmetic mean value of a population; the arithmetic mean of all the observations or values in the population.

Population standard deviation A measure of dispersion relating to a population in the same unit of measurement as the observations, calculated as the positive square root of the population variance.

Population variance A measure of dispersion relating to a population, calculated as the mean of the squared deviations around the population mean.

Portfolio company In private equity, the company in which the private equity fund is investing.

Portfolio demand for money The demand to hold speculative money balances based on the potential opportunities or risks that are inherent in other financial instruments.

Portfolio planning The process of creating a plan for building a portfolio that is expected to satisfy a client's investment objectives.

Position The quantity of an asset that an entity owns or owes.

Positive screening An ESG investment style that focuses on the inclusion of certain sectors, companies, or practices in a fund or portfolio on the basis of specific minimum ESG criteria.

Posterior probability An updated probability that reflects or comes after new information.

Potential GDP The level of real GDP that can be produced at full employment; measures the productive capacity of the economy.

Power of a test The probability of correctly rejecting the null—that is, rejecting the null hypothesis when it is false.

Precautionary money balances Money held to provide a buffer against unforeseen events that might require money.

Precautionary stocks A level of inventory beyond anticipated needs that provides a cushion in the event that it takes longer to replenish inventory than expected or in the case of greater than expected demand.

Preference shares A type of equity interest which ranks above common shares with respect to the payment of dividends and the distribution of the company's net assets upon liquidation. They have characteristics of both debt and equity securities. Also called *preferred stock.*

Preferred stock See *preference shares.*

Premium In the case of bonds, premium refers to the amount by which a bond is priced above its face (par) value. In the case of an option, the amount paid for the option contract.

Prepaid expense A normal operating expense that has been paid in advance of when it is due.

Prepayment option Contractual provision that entitles the borrower to prepay all or part of the outstanding mortgage principal prior to the scheduled due date when the principal must be repaid. Also called *early repayment option.*

Prepayment penalty mortgages Mortgages that stipulate a monetary penalty if a borrower prepays within a certain time period after the mortgage is originated.

Prepayment risk The uncertainty that the timing of the actual cash flows will be different from the scheduled cash flows as set forth in the loan agreement due to the borrowers' ability to alter payments, usually to take advantage of interest rate movements.

Present value (PV) The present discounted value of future cash flows: For assets, the present discounted value of the future net cash inflows that the asset is expected to generate; for liabilities, the present discounted value of the future net cash outflows that are expected to be required to settle the liabilities.

Present value models Valuation models that estimate the intrinsic value of a security as the present value of the future benefits expected to be received from the security. Also called *discounted cash flow models.*

Pretax margin A profitability ratio calculated as earnings before taxes divided by revenue.

Price elasticity of demand Measures the percentage change in the quantity demanded, given a percentage change in the price of a given product.

Price index Represents the average prices of a basket of goods and services.

Price limits Limits imposed by a futures exchange on the price change that can occur from one day to the next.

Price multiple A ratio that compares the share price with some sort of monetary flow or value to allow evaluation of the relative worth of a company's stock.

Price priority The principle that the highest priced buy orders and the lowest priced sell orders execute first.

Price relative A ratio of an ending price over a beginning price; it is equal to 1 plus the holding period return on the asset.

Price return Measures *only* the price appreciation or percentage change in price of the securities in an index or portfolio.

Price return index An index that reflects *only* the price appreciation or percentage change in price of the constituent securities. Also called *price index*.

Price stability In economics, refers to an inflation rate that is low on average and not subject to wide fluctuation.

Price takers Producers that must accept whatever price the market dictates.

Price to book value A valuation ratio calculated as price per share divided by book value per share.

Price to cash flow A valuation ratio calculated as price per share divided by cash flow per share.

Price to earnings ratio (P/E ratio or P/E) The ratio of share price to earnings per share.

Price to sales A valuation ratio calculated as price per share divided by sales per share.

Price value of a basis point A version of money duration, it is an estimate of the change in the full price of a bond given a 1 basis point change in the yield-to-maturity.

Price weighting An index weighting method in which the weight assigned to each constituent security is determined by dividing its price by the sum of all the prices of the constituent securities.

Priced risk Risk for which investors demand compensation for bearing (e.g. equity risk, company-specific factors, macroeconomic factors).

Primary bond markets Markets in which issuers first sell bonds to investors to raise capital.

Primary capital markets (primary markets) The market where securities are first sold and the issuers receive the proceeds.

Primary dealers Financial institutions that are authorized to deal in new issues of sovereign bonds and that serve primarily as trading counterparties of the office responsible for issuing sovereign bonds.

Primary market The market where securities are first sold and the issuers receive the proceeds.

Prime brokers Brokers that provide services that commonly include custody, administration, lending, short borrowing, and trading.

Principal The amount of funds originally invested in a project or instrument; the face value to be paid at maturity.

Principal–agent relationship A relationship in which a principal hires an agent to perform a particular task or service; also known as an *agency relationship*.

Principal amount Amount that an issuer agrees to repay the debt holders on the maturity date.

Principal business activity The business activity from which a company derives a majority of its revenues and/or earnings.

Principal value Amount that an issuer agrees to repay the debt holders on the maturity date.

Principle of no arbitrage See *arbitrage-free pricing*.

Prior probabilities Probabilities reflecting beliefs prior to the arrival of new information.

Priority of claims Priority of payment, with the most senior or highest ranking debt having the first claim on the cash flows and assets of the issuer.

Private equity fund A hedge fund that seeks to buy, optimize, and ultimately sell portfolio companies to generate profits. See *venture capital fund*.

Private equity securities Securities that are not listed on public exchanges and have no active secondary market. They are issued primarily to institutional investors via non-public offerings, such as private placements.

Private investment in public equity (PIPE) An investment in the equity of a publicly traded firm that is made at a discount to the market value of the firm's shares.

Private placement Typically, a non-underwritten, unregistered offering of securities that are sold only to an investor or a small group of investors. It can be accomplished directly between the issuer and the investor(s) or through an investment bank.

Probability A number between 0 and 1 describing the chance that a stated event will occur.

Probability density function A function with non-negative values such that probability can be described by areas under the curve graphing the function.

Probability distribution A distribution that specifies the probabilities of a random variable's possible outcomes.

Probability function A function that specifies the probability that the random variable takes on a specific value.

Producer price index Reflects the price changes experienced by domestic producers in a country.

Production function Provides the quantitative link between the levels of output that the economy can produce and the inputs used in the production process.

Productivity The amount of output produced by workers in a given period of time—for example, output per hour worked; measures the efficiency of labor.

Profession An occupational group that has specific education, expert knowledge, and a framework of practice and behavior that underpins community trust, respect, and recognition.

Profit The return that owners of a company receive for the use of their capital and the assumption of financial risk when making their investments.

Profit and loss (P&L) statement A financial statement that provides information about a company's profitability over a stated period of time. Also called the *income statement*.

Profit margin An indicator of profitability, calculated as net income divided by revenue; indicates how much of each dollar of revenues is left after all costs and expenses.

Profitability index (PI) For a simple project, the PI is the present value of a project's future cash flows divided by the initial investment.

Profitability ratios Ratios that measure a company's ability to generate profitable sales from its resources (assets).

Project sequencing To defer the decision to invest in a future project until the outcome of some or all of a current project is known. Projects are sequenced through time, so that investing in a project creates the option to invest in future projects.

Promissory note A written promise to pay a certain amount of money on demand.

Property, plant, and equipment Tangible assets that are expected to be used for more than one period in either the production or supply of goods or services, or for administrative purposes.

Prospectus The document that describes the terms of a new bond issue and helps investors perform their analysis on the issue.

Protective put An option strategy in which a long position in an asset is combined with a long position in a put.

Proxy contest Corporate takeover mechanism in which shareholders are persuaded to vote for a group seeking a controlling position on a company's board of directors.

Proxy voting A process that enables shareholders who are unable to attend a meeting to authorize another individual to vote on their behalf.

Pseudo-random numbers Numbers produced by random number generators.

Public offer See *public offering.*

Public offering An offering of securities in which any member of the public may buy the securities. Also called *public offer.*

Pull on liquidity When disbursements are paid too quickly or trade credit availability is limited, requiring companies to expend funds before they receive funds from sales that could cover the liability.

Pure discount bonds See *zero-coupon bonds.*

Pure-play method A method for estimating the beta for a company or project; it requires using a comparable company's beta and adjusting it for financial leverage differences.

Put An option that gives the holder the right to sell an underlying asset to another party at a fixed price over a specific period of time.

Put–call–forward parity The relationship among puts, calls, and forward contracts.

Put–call parity An equation expressing the equivalence (parity) of a portfolio of a call and a bond with a portfolio of a put and the underlying, which leads to the relationship between put and call prices.

Put/call ratio A technical analysis indicator that evaluates market sentiment based upon the volume of put options traded divided by the volume of call options traded for a particular financial instrument.

Put option An option that gives the holder the right to sell an underlying asset to another party at a fixed price over a specific period of time.

Putable bonds Bonds that give the bondholder the right to sell the bond back to the issuer at a predetermined price on specified dates.

Quantile A value at or below which a stated fraction of the data lies. Also called *fractile.*

Quantitative easing An expansionary monetary policy based on aggressive open market purchase operations.

Quantity equation of exchange An expression that over a given period, the amount of money used to purchase all goods and services in an economy, $M \times V$, is equal to monetary value of this output, $P \times Y$.

Quantity theory of money Asserts that total spending (in money terms) is proportional to the quantity of money.

Quartiles Quantiles that divide a distribution into four equal parts.

Quasi-fixed cost A cost that stays the same over a range of production but can change to another constant level when production moves outside of that range.

Quasi-government bonds A bond issued by an entity that is either owned or sponsored by a national government. Also called *agency bond.*

Quick assets Assets that can be most readily converted to cash (e.g., cash, short-term marketable investments, receivables).

Quick ratio A stringent measure of liquidity that indicates a company's ability to satisfy current liabilities with its most liquid assets, calculated as (cash + short-term marketable investments + receivables) divided by current liabilities.

Quintiles Quantiles that divide a distribution into five equal parts.

Quota rents Profits that foreign producers can earn by raising the price of their goods higher than they would without a quota.

Quotas Government policies that restrict the quantity of a good that can be imported into a country, generally for a specified period of time.

Quote-driven market A market in which dealers acting as principals facilitate trading.

Quoted interest rate A quoted interest rate that does not account for compounding within the year. Also called *stated annual interest rate.*

Quoted margin The specified yield spread over the reference rate, used to compensate an investor for the difference in the credit risk of the issuer and that implied by the reference rate.

Random number An observation drawn from a uniform distribution.

Random number generator An algorithm that produces uniformly distributed random numbers between 0 and 1.

Random variable A quantity whose future outcomes are uncertain.

Range The difference between the maximum and minimum values in a dataset.

Ratio scales A measurement scale that has all the characteristics of interval measurement scales as well as a true zero point as the origin.

Real GDP The value of goods and services produced, measured at base year prices.

Real income Income adjusted for the effect of inflation on the purchasing power of money. Also known as the *purchasing power of income.* If income remains constant and a good's price falls, real income is said to rise, even though the number of monetary units (e.g., dollars) remains unchanged.

Real interest rate Nominal interest rate minus the expected rate of inflation.

Real risk-free interest rate The single-period interest rate for a completely risk-free security if no inflation were expected.

Realizable (settlement) value With reference to assets, the amount of cash or cash equivalents that could currently be obtained by selling the asset in an orderly disposal; with reference to liabilities, the undiscounted amount of cash or cash equivalents expected to be paid to satisfy the liabilities in the normal course of business.

Rebalancing Adjusting the weights of the constituent securities in an index.

Rebalancing policy The set of rules that guide the process of restoring a portfolio's asset class weights to those specified in the strategic asset allocation.

Recession A period during which real GDP decreases (i.e., negative growth) for at least two successive quarters, or a period of significant decline in total output, income, employment, and sales usually lasting from six months to a year.

Recognition lag The lag in government response to an economic problem resulting from the delay in confirming a change in the state of the economy.

Recourse loan Loan in which the lender has a claim against the borrower for any shortfall between the outstanding mortgage balance and the proceeds received from the sale of the property.

Redemption yield See *yield to maturity.*

Redemptions Withdrawals of funds by investors, as allowed by the notice period and other terms in the partnership agreement.

Refinancing rate A type of central bank policy rate.

Registered bonds Bonds for which ownership is recorded by either name or serial number.

Relative/best-in-class screening An ESG investment style that focuses on sectors, companies, or projects selected for ESG performance relative to industry peers.

Relative dispersion The amount of dispersion relative to a reference value or benchmark.

Relative frequency With reference to an interval of grouped data, the number of observations in the interval divided by the total number of observations in the sample.

Relative price The price of a specific good or service in comparison with those of other goods and services.

Relative strength analysis A comparison of the performance of one asset with the performance of another asset or a benchmark based on changes in the ratio of the securities' respective prices over time.

Relative strength index A technical analysis momentum oscillator that compares a security's gains with its losses over a set period.

Renewable resources Resources that can be replenished, such as a forest.

Rent Payment for the use of property.

Reorganization Agreements made by a company in bankruptcy under which a company's capital structure is altered and/or alternative arrangements are made for debt repayment; US Chapter 11 bankruptcy. The company emerges from bankruptcy as a going concern.

Replication The creation of an asset or portfolio from another asset, portfolio, and/or derivative.

Repo A form of collateralized loan involving the sale of a security with a simultaneous agreement by the seller to buy the same security back from the purchaser at an agreed-on price and future date. The party who sells the security at the inception of the repurchase agreement and buys it back at maturity is borrowing money from the other party, and the security sold and subsequently repurchased represents the collateral.

Repo margin The difference between the market value of the security used as collateral and the value of the loan. Also called *haircut.*

Repo rate The interest rate on a repurchase agreement.

Repurchase agreement A form of collateralized loan involving the sale of a security with a simultaneous agreement by the seller to buy the same security back from the purchaser at an agreed-on price and future date. The party who sells the security at the inception of the repurchase agreement and buys it back at maturity is borrowing money from the other party, and the security sold and subsequently repurchased represents the collateral.

Repurchase date The date when the party who sold the security at the inception of a repurchase agreement buys the security back from the cash lending counterparty.

Repurchase price The price at which the party who sold the security at the inception of the repurchase agreement buys the security back from the cash lending counterparty.

Required margin The yield spread over, or under, the reference rate such that an FRN is priced at par value on a rate reset date.

Required rate of return See *market discount rate.*

Required yield See *market discount rate.*

Required yield spread The difference between the yield-to-maturity on a new bond and the benchmark rate; additional compensation required by investors for the difference in risk and tax status of a bond relative to a government bond. Sometimes called the *spread over the benchmark.*

Reserve accounts Form of internal credit enhancement that relies on creating accounts and depositing in these accounts cash that can be used to absorb losses. Also called *reserve funds.*

Reserve funds See *reserve accounts.*

Reserve requirement The requirement for banks to hold reserves in proportion to the size of deposits.

Resistance In technical analysis, a price range in which selling activity is sufficient to stop the rise in the price of a security.

Responsible investing The practice of identifying companies that can efficiently manage their financial, environmental, and human capital resources to generate attractive long-term profitability; often synonymous with *sustainable investing.*

Restricted payments A bond covenant meant to protect creditors by limiting how much cash can be paid out to shareholders over time.

Retracement In technical analysis, a reversal in the movement of a security's price such that it is counter to the prevailing longerterm price trend.

Return-generating model A model that can provide an estimate of the expected return of a security given certain parameters and estimates of the values of the independent variables in the model.

Return on assets (ROA) A profitability ratio calculated as net income divided by average total assets; indicates a company's net profit generated per dollar invested in total assets.

Return on equity (ROE) A profitability ratio calculated as net income divided by average shareholders' equity.

Return on sales An indicator of profitability, calculated as net income divided by revenue; indicates how much of each dollar of revenues is left after all costs and expenses. Also referred to as *net profit margin.*

Return on total capital A profitability ratio calculated as EBIT divided by the sum of short- and long-term debt and equity.

Revaluation model Under IFRS, the process of valuing long-lived assets at fair value, rather than at cost less accumulated depreciation. Any resulting profit or loss is either reported on the income statement and/or through equity under revaluation surplus.

Revenue The amount charged for the delivery of goods or services in the ordinary activities of a business over a stated period; the inflows of economic resources to a company over a stated period.

Reversal patterns A type of pattern used in technical analysis to predict the end of a trend and a change in direction of the security's price.

Reverse repo A repurchase agreement viewed from the perspective of the cash lending counterparty.

Reverse repurchase agreement A repurchase agreement viewed from the perspective of the cash lending counterparty.

Reverse stock split A reduction in the number of shares outstanding with a corresponding increase in share price, but no change to the company's underlying fundamentals.

Revolving credit agreements The strongest form of short-term bank borrowing facilities; they are in effect for multiple years (e.g., 3–5 years) and may have optional medium-term loan features.

Rho The sensitivity of the option price to the risk-free rate.

Ricardian equivalence An economic theory that implies that it makes no difference whether a government finances a deficit by increasing taxes or issuing debt.

Risk Exposure to uncertainty. The chance of a loss or adverse outcome as a result of an action, inaction, or external event.

Risk averse The assumption that an investor will choose the least risky alternative.

Risk aversion The degree of an investor's inability and unwillingness to take risk.

Risk budgeting The establishment of objectives for individuals, groups, or divisions of an organization that takes into account the allocation of an acceptable level of risk.

Risk exposure The state of being exposed or vulnerable to a risk. The extent to which an organization is sensitive to underlying risks.

Risk factor/risk premium investing An ESG investment style that focuses on the inclusion of ESG information in the analysis of systematic risks as, for example, in smart beta and factor investment strategies (similar to size, value, momentum, and growth strategies).

Risk governance The top-down process and guidance that directs risk management activities to align with and support the overall enterprise.

Risk management The process of identifying the level of risk an organization wants, measuring the level of risk the organization currently has, taking actions that bring the actual level of risk to the desired level of risk, and monitoring the new actual level of risk so that it continues to be aligned with the desired level of risk.

Risk management framework The infrastructure, process, and analytics needed to support effective risk management in an organization.

Risk-neutral pricing Sometimes said of derivatives pricing, uses the fact that arbitrage opportunities guarantee that a risk-free portfolio consisting of the underlying and the derivative must earn the risk-free rate.

Risk-neutral probabilities Weights that are used to compute a binomial option price. They are the probabilities that would apply if a risk-neutral investor valued an option.

Risk premium An extra return expected by investors for bearing some specified risk.

Risk shifting Actions to change the distribution of risk outcomes.

Risk tolerance The amount of risk an investor is willing and able to bear to achieve an investment goal.

Risk transfer Actions to pass on a risk to another party, often, but not always, in the form of an insurance policy.

Robo-adviser A machine-based analytical tool or service that provides technology-driven investment solutions through online platforms.

Robust The quality of being relatively unaffected by a violation of assumptions.

Rule of 72 The principle that the approximate number of years necessary for an investment to double is 72 divided by the stated interest rate.

Running yield See *current yield*.

Safety-first rules Rules for portfolio selection that focus on the risk that portfolio value will fall below some minimum acceptable level over some time horizon.

Safety stock A level of inventory beyond anticipated needs that provides a cushion in the event that it takes longer to replenish inventory than expected or in the case of greater than expected demand.

Sales Generally, a synonym for revenue; "sales" is generally understood to refer to the sale of goods, whereas "revenue" is understood to include the sale of goods or services.

Sales risk Uncertainty with respect to the quantity of goods and services that a company is able to sell and the price it is able to achieve; the risk related to the uncertainty of revenues.

Sales-type leases Under US GAAP, a type of finance lease, from a lessor perspective, where the present value of the lease payments (lease receivable) exceeds the carrying value of the leased asset. The revenues earned by the lessor both a selling profit at inception and financing (interest) revenues.

Sample A subset of a population.

Sample excess kurtosis A sample measure of the degree of a distribution's kurtosis in excess of the normal distribution's kurtosis.

Sample kurtosis A sample measure of the degree of a distribution's peakedness.

Sample mean The sum of the sample observations, divided by the sample size.

Sample selection bias Bias introduced by systematically excluding some members of the population according to a particular attribute—for example, the bias introduced when data availability leads to certain observations being excluded from the analysis.

Sample skewness A sample measure of degree of asymmetry of a distribution.

Sample standard deviation The positive square root of the sample variance.

Sample statistic A quantity computed from or used to describe a sample.

Sample variance A sample measure of the degree of dispersion of a distribution, calculated by dividing the sum of the squared deviations from the sample mean by the sample size minus 1.

Sampling The process of obtaining a sample.

Sampling distribution The distribution of all distinct possible values that a statistic can assume when computed from samples of the same size randomly drawn from the same population.

Sampling error The difference between the observed value of a statistic and the quantity it is intended to estimate.

Sampling plan The set of rules used to select a sample.

Say on pay A process whereby shareholders may vote on executive remuneration (compensation) matters.

Say's law Named for French economist J.B. Say: All that is produced will be sold because supply creates its own demand.

Scatter plot A two-dimensional plot of pairs of observations on two data series.

Scenario analysis Analysis that shows the changes in key financial quantities that result from given (economic) events, such as the loss of customers, the loss of a supply source, or a catastrophic event; a risk management technique involving examination of the performance of a portfolio under specified situations. Closely related to stress testing.

Screening The application of a set of criteria to reduce a set of potential investments to a smaller set having certain desired characteristics.

Seasoned offering An offering in which an issuer sells additional units of a previously issued security.

Second-degree price discrimination When the monopolist charges different per-unit prices using the quantity purchased as an indicator of how highly the customer values the product.

Second lien A secured interest in the pledged assets that ranks below first lien debt in both collateral protection and priority of payment.

Secondary bond markets Markets in which existing bonds are traded among investors.

Secondary market The market where securities are traded among investors.

Secondary precedence rules Rules that determine how to rank orders placed at the same time.

Sector A group of related industries.

Sector indexes Indexes that represent and track different economic sectors—such as consumer goods, energy, finance, health care, and technology—on either a national, regional, or global basis.

Secured bonds Bonds secured by assets or financial guarantees pledged to ensure debt repayment in case of default.

Secured debt Debt in which the debtholder has a direct claim—a pledge from the issuer—on certain assets and their associated cash flows.

Securitization A process that involves moving assets into a special legal entity, which then uses the assets as guarantees to secure a bond issue.

Securitized assets Assets that are typically used to create asset-backed bonds; for example, when a bank securitizes a pool of loans, the loans are said to be securitized.

Security characteristic line A plot of the excess return of a security on the excess return of the market.

Security market index A portfolio of securities representing a given security market, market segment, or asset class.

Security market line (SML) The graph of the capital asset pricing model.

Security selection The process of selecting individual securities; typically, security selection has the objective of generating superior risk-adjusted returns relative to a portfolio's benchmark.

Self-investment limits With respect to investment limitations applying to pension plans, restrictions on the percentage of assets that can be invested in securities issued by the pension plan sponsor.

Sell-side firm A broker/dealer that sells securities and provides independent investment research and recommendations to their clients (i.e., buy-side firms).

Semi-strong-form efficient market A market in which security prices reflect all publicly known and available information.

Semiannual bond basis yield An annual rate having a periodicity of two; also known as a *semiannual bond equivalent yield*.

Semiannual bond equivalent yield See *semiannual bond basis yield*.

Semideviation The positive square root of semivariance (sometimes called *semistandard deviation*).

Semilogarithmic Describes a scale constructed so that equal intervals on the vertical scale represent equal rates of change, and equal intervals on the horizontal scale represent equal amounts of change.

Semivariance The average squared deviation below the mean.

Seniority ranking Priority of payment of various debt obligations.

Sensitivity analysis Analysis that shows the range of possible outcomes as specific assumptions are changed.

Separately managed account (SMA) An investment portfolio managed exclusively for the benefit of an individual or institution.

Serial maturity structure Structure for a bond issue in which the maturity dates are spread out during the bond's life; a stated number of bonds mature and are paid off each year before final maturity.

Settlement The process that occurs after a trade is completed, the securities are passed to the buyer, and payment is received by the seller.

Settlement date Date when the buyer makes cash payment and the seller delivers the security.

Settlement price The official price, designated by the clearinghouse, from which daily gains and losses will be determined and marked to market.

Share repurchase A transaction in which a company buys back its own shares. Unlike stock dividends and stock splits, share repurchases use corporate cash.

Shareholder activism Strategies used by shareholders to attempt to compel a company to act in a desired manner.

Shareholder engagement The process whereby companies engage with their shareholders.

Shareholders' equity Assets less liabilities; the residual interest in the assets after subtracting the liabilities.

Sharpe ratio The average return in excess of the risk-free rate divided by the standard deviation of return; a measure of the average excess return earned per unit of standard deviation of return.

Shelf registration Type of public offering that allows the issuer to file a single, all-encompassing offering circular that covers a series of bond issues.

Short The seller of an asset or derivative contract. Also refers to the position of being short an asset or derivative contract.

Short position A position in an asset or contract in which one has sold an asset one does not own, or in which a right under a contract can be exercised against oneself.

Short-run average total cost The curve describing average total cost when some costs are considered fixed.

Short selling A transaction in which borrowed securities are sold with the intention to repurchase them at a lower price at a later date and return them to the lender.

Shortfall risk The risk that portfolio value will fall below some minimum acceptable level over some time horizon.

Shutdown point The point at which average revenue is equal to the firm's average variable cost.

Simple interest The interest earned each period on the original investment; interest calculated on the principal only.

Simple random sample A subset of a larger population created in such a way that each element of the population has an equal probability of being selected to the subset.

Simple random sampling The procedure of drawing a sample to satisfy the definition of a simple random sample.

Simple yield The sum of the coupon payments plus the straight-line amortized share of the gain or loss, divided by the flat price.

Simulation Computer-generated sensitivity or scenario analysis that is based on probability models for the factors that drive outcomes.
Simulation trial A complete pass through the steps of a simulation.
Single-step format With respect to the format of the income statement, a format that does not subtotal for gross profit (revenue minus cost of goods sold).
Sinking fund arrangement Provision that reduces the credit risk of a bond issue by requiring the issuer to retire a portion of the bond's principal outstanding each year.
Situational influences External factors, such as environmental or cultural elements, that shape our behavior.
Skewed Not symmetrical.
Skewness A quantitative measure of skew (lack of symmetry); a synonym of skew.
Small country A country that is a price taker in the world market for a product and cannot influence the world market price.
Smart beta Involves the use of simple, transparent, rules-based strategies as a basis for investment decisions.
Smart contract A computer program that is designed to self-execute on the basis of pre-specified terms and conditions agreed to by parties to a contract.
Socially responsible investing An investment approach that excludes investments in companies or industries that deviate from an organization's beliefs and sometimes includes investments with favorable environmental or social profiles.
Solvency With respect to financial statement analysis, the ability of a company to fulfill its long-term obligations.
Solvency ratios Ratios that measure a company's ability to meet its long-term obligations.
Solvency risk The risk that an organization does not survive or succeed because it runs out of cash, even though it might otherwise be solvent.
Sovereign A bond issued by a national government.
Sovereign bond A bond issued by a national government.
Sovereign yield spread An estimate of the country spread (country equity premium) for a developing nation that is based on a comparison of bonds yields in country being analyzed and a developed country. The sovereign yield spread is the difference between a government bond yield in the country being analyzed, denominated in the currency of the developed country, and the Treasury bond yield on a similar maturity bond in the developed country.
Spearman rank correlation coefficient A measure of correlation applied to ranked data.
Special dividend A dividend paid by a company that does not pay dividends on a regular schedule, or a dividend that supplements regular cash dividends with an extra payment.
Special purpose entity A non-operating entity created to carry out a specified purpose, such as leasing assets or securitizing receivables; can be a corporation, partnership, trust, limited liability, or partnership formed to facilitate a specific type of business activity. Also called *special purpose vehicle* or *variable interest entity*.
Special purpose vehicle See *special purpose entity*.
Specific identification method An inventory accounting method that identifies which specific inventory items were sold and which remained in inventory to be carried over to later periods.
Speculative demand for money The demand to hold speculative money balances based on the potential opportunities or risks that are inherent in other financial instruments. Also called *portfolio demand for money*.
Speculative money balances Monies held in anticipation that other assets will decline in value.
Split coupon bond See *deferred coupon bond*.
Sponsored A type of depository receipt in which the foreign company whose shares are held by the depository has a direct involvement in the issuance of the receipts.
Spot curve A sequence of yields-to-maturity on zero-coupon bonds. Sometimes called *zero* or *strip curve* because coupon payments are "stripped" off of the bonds.
Spot markets Markets in which assets are traded for immediate delivery.
Spot prices The price of an asset for immediately delivery.
Spot rates A sequence of market discount rates that correspond to the cash flow dates; yields-to-maturity on zero-coupon bonds maturing at the date of each cash flow.
Spread In general, the difference in yield between different fixed income securities. Often used to refer to the difference between the yield-to-maturity and the benchmark.
Spread over the benchmark See *required yield spread*.
Spread risk Bond price risk arising from changes in the yield spread on credit-risky bonds; reflects changes in the market's assessment and/or pricing of credit migration (or downgrade) risk and market liquidity risk.
Spurious correlation A correlation that misleadingly points toward associations between variables.
Stackelberg model A prominent model of strategic decision making in which firms are assumed to make their decisions sequentially.
Stagflation When a high inflation rate is combined with a high level of unemployment and a slowdown of the economy.
Staggered boards Election process whereby directors are typically divided into multiple classes that are elected separately in consecutive years—that is, one class every year.
Stakeholder management The identification, prioritization, and understanding of the interests of stakeholder groups, and managing the company's relationships with these groups.
Stakeholders Individuals or groups of individuals who may be affected either directly or indirectly by a decision and thus have an interest, or stake, in the decision.
Standard deviation The positive square root of the variance; a measure of dispersion in the same units as the original data.
Standard normal distribution The normal density with mean (μ) equal to 0 and standard deviation (σ) equal to 1.
Standardizing A transformation that involves subtracting the mean and dividing the result by the standard deviation.
Standards of conduct Behaviors required by a group; established benchmarks that clarify or enhance a group's code of ethics.
Standing limit orders A limit order at a price below market and which therefore is waiting to trade.
Stated annual interest rate A quoted interest rate that does not account for compounding within the year. Also called *quoted interest rate*.
Statement of changes in equity (statement of owners' equity) A financial statement that reconciles the beginning-of-period and end-of-period balance sheet values of shareholders' equity; provides information about all factors affecting shareholders' equity. Also called *statement of owners' equity*.

Statement of financial condition The financial statement that presents an entity's current financial position by disclosing resources the entity controls (its assets) and the claims on those resources (its liabilities and equity claims), as of a particular point in time (the date of the balance sheet).

Statement of financial position The financial statement that presents an entity's current financial position by disclosing resources the entity controls (its assets) and the claims on those resources (its liabilities and equity claims), as of a particular point in time (the date of the balance sheet).

Statement of operations A financial statement that provides information about a company's profitability over a stated period of time.

Statistic A quantity computed from or used to describe a sample of data.

Statistical inference Making forecasts, estimates, or judgments about a larger group from a smaller group actually observed; using a sample statistic to infer the value of an unknown population parameter.

Statistically significant A result indicating that the null hypothesis can be rejected; with reference to an estimated regression coefficient, frequently understood to mean a result indicating that the corresponding population regression coefficient is different from 0.

Statutory voting A common method of voting where each share represents one vote.

Step-up coupon bond Bond for which the coupon, which may be fixed or floating, increases by specified margins at specified dates.

Stock dividend A type of dividend in which a company distributes additional shares of its common stock to shareholders instead of cash.

Stock-out losses Profits lost from not having sufficient inventory on hand to satisfy demand.

Stock split An increase in the number of shares outstanding with a consequent decrease in share price, but no change to the company's underlying fundamentals.

Stop-loss order See *stop order.*

Stop order An order in which a trader has specified a stop price condition. Also called *stop-loss order.*

Store of value The quality of tending to preserve value.

Store of wealth Goods that depend on the fact that they do not perish physically over time, and on the belief that others would always value the good.

Straight-line method A depreciation method that allocates evenly the cost of a long-lived asset less its estimated residual value over the estimated useful life of the asset.

Straight voting A shareholder voting process in which shareholders receive one vote for each share owned.

Strategic analysis Analysis of the competitive environment with an emphasis on the implications of the environment for corporate strategy.

Strategic asset allocation The set of exposures to IPS-permissible asset classes that is expected to achieve the client's long-term objectives given the client's investment constraints.

Strategic groups Groups sharing distinct business models or catering to specific market segments in an industry.

Street convention Yield measure that neglects weekends and holidays; the internal rate of return on cash flows assuming payments are made on the scheduled dates, even when the scheduled date falls on a weekend or holiday.

Stress testing A specific type of scenario analysis that estimates losses in rare and extremely unfavorable combinations of events or scenarios.

Strong-form efficient market A market in which security prices reflect all public and private information.

Structural (or cyclically adjusted) budget deficit The deficit that would exist if the economy was at full employment (or full potential output).

Structural subordination Arises in a holding company structure when the debt of operating subsidiaries is serviced by the cash flow and assets of the subsidiaries before funds can be passed to the holding company to service debt at the parent level.

Structured financial instruments Financial instruments that share the common attribute of repackaging risks. Structured financial instruments include asset-backed securities, collateralized debt obligations, and other structured financial instruments such as capital protected, yield enhancement, participation and leveraged instruments.

Subjective probability A probability drawing on personal or subjective judgment.

Subordinated debt A class of unsecured debt that ranks below a firm's senior unsecured obligations.

Subordination Form of internal credit enhancement that relies on creating more than one bond tranche and ordering the claim priorities for ownership or interest in an asset between the tranches. The ordering of the claim priorities is called a senior/subordinated structure, where the tranches of highest seniority are called senior followed by subordinated or junior tranches. Also called *credit tranching.*

Substitutes Said of two goods or services such that if the price of one increases the demand for the other tends to increase, holding all other things equal (e.g., butter and margarine).

Sunk cost A cost that has already been incurred.

Supervised learning A machine learning approach that makes use of labeled training data.

Supply shock A typically unexpected disturbance to supply.

Support In technical analysis, a price range in which buying activity is sufficient to stop the decline in the price of a security.

Support tranche A class or tranche in a CMO that protects the PAC tranche from prepayment risk.

Supranational bonds A bond issued by a supranational agency such as the World Bank.

Surety bond Form of external credit enhancement whereby a rated and regulated insurance company guarantees to reimburse bondholders for any losses incurred up to a maximum amount if the issuer defaults.

Survey approach An estimate of the equity risk premium that is based upon estimates provided by a panel of finance experts.

Survivorship bias The bias resulting from a test design that fails to account for companies that have gone bankrupt, merged, or are otherwise no longer reported in a database.

Sustainable growth rate The rate of dividend (and earnings) growth that can be sustained over time for a given level of return on equity, keeping the capital structure constant and without issuing additional common stock.

Sustainable investing The practice of identifying companies that can efficiently manage their financial, environmental, and human capital resources to generate attractive long-term profitability; often synonymous with *responsible investing.*

Sustainable rate of economic growth The rate of increase in the economy's productive capacity or potential GDP.

Swap contract An agreement between two parties to exchange a series of future cash flows.

Syndicated loans Loans from a group of lenders to a single borrower.

Syndicated offering A bond issue that is underwritten by a group of investment banks.

Systematic risk Risk that affects the entire market or economy; it cannot be avoided and is inherent in the overall market. Systematic risk is also known as non-diversifiable or market risk.

Systematic sampling A procedure of selecting every *k*th member until reaching a sample of the desired size. The sample that results from this procedure should be approximately random.

***t*-Test** A hypothesis test using a statistic (*t*-statistic) that follows a *t*-distribution.

Tactical asset allocation The decision to deliberately deviate from the strategic asset allocation in an attempt to add value based on forecasts of the near-term relative performance of asset classes.

Target balance A minimum level of cash to be held available—estimated in advance and adjusted for known funds transfers, seasonality, or other factors.

Target capital structure A company's chosen proportions of debt and equity.

Target independent A bank's ability to determine the definition of inflation that they target, the rate of inflation that they target, and the horizon over which the target is to be achieved.

Target semideviation The positive square root of target semivariance.

Target semivariance The average squared deviation below a target value.

Tariffs Taxes that a government levies on imported goods.

Tax base The amount at which an asset or liability is valued for tax purposes.

Tax expense An aggregate of an entity's income tax payable (or recoverable in the case of a tax benefit) and any changes in deferred tax assets and liabilities. It is essentially the income tax payable or recoverable if these had been determined based on accounting profit rather than taxable income.

Tax loss carry forward A taxable loss in the current period that may be used to reduce future taxable income.

Taxable income The portion of an entity's income that is subject to income taxes under the tax laws of its jurisdiction.

Taxable temporary differences Temporary differences that result in a taxable amount in a future period when determining the taxable profit as the balance sheet item is recovered or settled.

Technical analysis A form of security analysis that uses price and volume data, which is often displayed graphically, in decision making.

Technology The process a company uses to transform inputs into outputs.

Tender offer Corporate takeover mechanism which involves shareholders selling their interests directly to the group seeking to gain control.

Tenor The time-to-maturity for a bond or derivative contract. Also called *term to maturity*.

Term maturity structure Structure for a bond issue in which the bond's notional principal is paid off in a lump sum at maturity.

Term structure See *maturity structure*.

Term structure of credit spreads The relationship between the spreads over the "risk-free" (or benchmark) rates and times-to-maturity.

Term structure of yield volatility The relationship between the volatility of bond yields-to-maturity and times-to-maturity.

Terminal stock value The expected value of a share at the end of the investment horizon—in effect, the expected selling price. Also called *terminal value*.

Terminal value The expected value of a share at the end of the investment horizon—in effect, the expected selling price.

Terms of trade The ratio of the price of exports to the price of imports, representing those prices by export and import price indexes, respectively.

Text analytics The use of computer programs to analyze and derive meaning from typically large, unstructured text- or voice-based datasets.

Thematic investment An ESG investing style that focuses on investing in themes or assets specifically relating to ESG factors, such as clean energy, green technology, or sustainable agriculture.

Third-degree price discrimination When the monopolist segregates customers into groups based on demographic or other characteristics and offers different pricing to each group.

Time-period bias The possibility that when we use a time-series sample, our statistical conclusion may be sensitive to the starting and ending dates of the sample.

Time-series data Observations of a variable over time.

Time tranching The creation of classes or tranches in an ABS/MBS that possess different (expected) maturities.

Time value The difference between the market price of the option and its intrinsic value.

Time value decay Said of an option when, at expiration, no time value remains and the option is worth only its exercise value.

Time value of money The principles governing equivalence relationships between cash flows with different dates.

Time-weighted rate of return The compound rate of growth of one unit of currency invested in a portfolio during a stated measurement period; a measure of investment performance that is not sensitive to the timing and amount of withdrawals or additions to the portfolio.

Tokenization The process of representing ownership rights to physical assets on a blockchain or distributed ledger.

Top-down analysis An investment selection approach that begins with consideration of macroeconomic conditions and then evaluates markets and industries based upon such conditions.

Total comprehensive income The change in equity during a period resulting from transaction and other events, other than those changes resulting from transactions with owners in their capacity as owners.

Total cost The summation of all costs, for which costs are classified as fixed or variable.

Total factor productivity A scale factor that reflects the portion of growth that is not accounted for by explicit factor inputs (e.g. capital and labor).

Total fixed cost The summation of all expenses that do not change as the level of production varies.

Total invested capital The sum of market value of common equity, book value of preferred equity, and face value of debt.

Total probability rule A rule explaining the unconditional probability of an event in terms of probabilities of the event conditional on mutually exclusive and exhaustive scenarios.

Total probability rule for expected value A rule explaining the expected value of a random variable in terms of expected values of the random variable conditional on mutually exclusive and exhaustive scenarios.

Total return Measures the price appreciation, or percentage change in price of the securities in an index or portfolio, plus any income received over the period.

Total return index An index that reflects the price appreciation or percentage change in price of the constituent securities plus any income received since inception.

Total return swap A swap in which one party agrees to pay the total return on a security. Often used as a credit derivative, in which the underlying is a bond.

Total variable cost The summation of all variable expenses.

Tracking error The standard deviation of the differences between a portfolio's returns and its benchmark's returns; a synonym of active risk.

Tracking risk The standard deviation of the differences between a portfolio's returns and its benchmarks returns. Also called *tracking error*.

Trade creation When regional integration results in the replacement of higher cost domestic production by lower cost imports from other members.

Trade credit A spontaneous form of credit in which a purchaser of the goods or service is financing its purchase by delaying the date on which payment is made.

Trade diversion When regional integration results in lower-cost imports from non-member countries being replaced with higher-cost imports from members.

Trade payables Amounts that a business owes to its vendors for goods and services that were purchased from them but which have not yet been paid.

Trade protection Government policies that impose restrictions on trade, such as tariffs and quotas.

Trade surplus (deficit) When the value of exports is greater (less) than the value of imports.

Trading securities Under US GAAP, a category of debt securities held by a company with the intent to trade them. Also called *held-for-trading securities*.

Traditional investment markets Markets for traditional investments, which include all publicly traded debts and equities and shares in pooled investment vehicles that hold publicly traded debts and/or equities.

Transactions money balances Money balances that are held to finance transactions.

Transactions motive In the context of inventory management, the need for inventory as part of the routine production–sales cycle.

Transfer payments Welfare payments made through the social security system that exist to provide a basic minimum level of income for low-income households.

Transparency Said of something (e.g., a market) in which information is fully disclosed to the public and/or regulators.

Treasury Inflation-Protected Securities A bond issued by the United States Treasury Department that is designed to protect the investor from inflation by adjusting the principal of the bond for changes in inflation.

Treasury stock method A method for accounting for the effect of options (and warrants) on earnings per share (EPS) that specifies what EPS would have been if the options and warrants had been exercised and the company had used the proceeds to repurchase common stock.

Tree diagram A diagram with branches emanating from nodes representing either mutually exclusive chance events or mutually exclusive decisions.

Trend A long-term pattern of movement in a particular direction.

Treynor ratio A measure of risk-adjusted performance that relates a portfolio's excess returns to the portfolio's beta.

Triangle patterns In technical analysis, a continuation chart pattern that forms as the range between high and low prices narrows, visually forming a triangle.

Trimmed mean A mean computed after excluding a stated small percentage of the lowest and highest observations.

TRIN A flow of funds indicator applied to a broad stock market index to measure the relative extent to which money is moving into or out of rising and declining stocks.

Triple bottoms In technical analysis, a reversal pattern that is formed when the price forms three troughs at roughly the same price level; used to predict a change from a downtrend to an uptrend.

Triple tops In technical analysis, a reversal pattern that is formed when the price forms three peaks at roughly the same price level; used to predict a change from an uptrend to a downtrend.

Trough The lowest point of a business cycle.

True yield The internal rate of return on cash flows using the actual calendar including weekends and bank holidays.

Trust deed The governing legal credit agreement, typically incorporated by reference in the prospectus. Also called *bond indenture*.

Trust receipt arrangement The use of inventory as collateral for a loan. The inventory is segregated and held in trust, and the proceeds of any sale must be remitted to the lender immediately.

Turn-of-the-year effect Calendar anomaly that stock market returns in January are significantly higher compared to the rest of the months of the year, with most of the abnormal returns reported during the first five trading days in January.

Two-fund separation theorem The theory that all investors regardless of taste, risk preferences, and initial wealth will hold a combination of two portfolios or funds: a risk-free asset and an optimal portfolio of risky assets.

Two-sided hypothesis test A test in which the null hypothesis is rejected in favor of the alternative hypothesis if the evidence indicates that the population parameter is either smaller or larger than a hypothesized value.

Two-tailed hypothesis test A test in which the null hypothesis is rejected in favor of the alternative hypothesis if the evidence indicates that the population parameter is either smaller or larger than a hypothesized value.

Two-week repo rate The interest rate on a two-week repurchase agreement; may be used as a policy rate by a central bank.

Type I error The error of rejecting a true null hypothesis.

Type II error The error of not rejecting a false null hypothesis.

Unanticipated (unexpected) inflation The component of inflation that is a surprise.

Unconditional probability The probability of an event *not* conditioned on another event.

Underemployed A person who has a job but has the qualifications to work a significantly higher-paying job.

Underlying An asset that trades in a market in which buyers and sellers meet, decide on a price, and the seller then delivers the asset to the buyer and receives payment. The underlying is the asset or other derivative on which a particular derivative is based. The market for the underlying is also referred to as the *spot market*.

Underwriter A firm, usually an investment bank, that takes the risk of buying the newly issued securities from the issuer, and then reselling them to investors or to dealers, thus guaranteeing the sale of the securities at the offering price negotiated with the issuer.

Underwritten offering A type of securities issue mechanism in which the investment bank guarantees the sale of the securities at an offering price that is negotiated with the issuer. Also known as *firm commitment offering*.

Unearned revenue A liability account for money that has been collected for goods or services that have not yet been delivered; payment received in advance of providing a good or service. Also called *deferred revenue* or *deferred income*.

Unemployed People who are actively seeking employment but are currently without a job.

Unemployment rate The ratio of unemployed to the labor force.

Unexpected inflation The component of inflation that is a surprise.

Unit elastic An elasticity with a magnitude of negative one. Also called *unitary elastic*.

Unit labor cost The average labor cost to produce one unit of output.

Unit normal distribution The normal density with mean (μ) equal to 0 and standard deviation (σ) equal to 1.

Units-of-production method A depreciation method that allocates the cost of a long-lived asset based on actual usage during the period.

Univariate distribution A distribution that specifies the probabilities for a single random variable.

Universal owners Long-term investors, such as pension funds, that have significant assets invested in globally diversified portfolios.

Unlimited funds An unlimited funds environment assumes that the company can raise the funds it wants for all profitable projects simply by paying the required rate of return.

Unsecured debt Debt which gives the debtholder only a general claim on an issuer's assets and cash flow.

Unsponsored A type of depository receipt in which the foreign company whose shares are held by the depository has no involvement in the issuance of the receipts.

Unsupervised learning A machine learning approach that does not make use of labeled training data.

Up transition probability The probability that an asset's value moves up.

Validity instructions Instructions which indicate when the order may be filled.

Valuation allowance A reserve created against deferred tax assets, based on the likelihood of realizing the deferred tax assets in future accounting periods.

Valuation ratios Ratios that measure the quantity of an asset or flow (e.g., earnings) in relation to the price associated with a specified claim (e.g., a share or ownership of the enterprise).

Value at risk (VaR) A money measure of the minimum value of losses expected during a specified time period at a given level of probability.

Value investors With reference to equity investors, investors who are focused on paying a relatively low share price in relation to earnings or assets per share.

VaR See *value at risk*.

Variable costs Costs that fluctuate with the level of production and sales.

Variance The expected value (the probability-weighted average) of squared deviations from a random variable's expected value.

Variation margin Additional margin that must be deposited in an amount sufficient to bring the balance up to the initial margin requirement.

Veblen goods Goods that increase in desirability with increasing price.

Vega A measure of the sensitivity of an option's price to changes in the underlying's volatility.

Venture capital Investments that provide "seed" or startup capital, early-stage financing, or later-stage financing (including mezzanine-stage financing) to companies that are in early development stages and require additional capital for expansion or preparation for an initial public offering.

Venture capital fund A hedge fund that seeks to buy, optimize, and ultimately sell portfolio companies to generate profits. See *private equity fund*.

Vertical analysis Common-size analysis using only one reporting period or one base financial statement; for example, an income statement in which all items are stated as percentages of sales.

Vertical demand schedule Implies that some fixed quantity is demanded, regardless of price.

Volatility As used in option pricing, the standard deviation of the continuously compounded returns on the underlying asset.

Voluntarily unemployed A person voluntarily outside the labor force, such as a jobless worker refusing an available vacancy.

Voluntary export restraint A trade barrier under which the exporting country agrees to limit its exports of the good to its trading partners to a specific number of units.

Vote by proxy A mechanism that allows a designated party—such as another shareholder, a shareholder representative, or management—to vote on the shareholder's behalf.

Warehouse receipt arrangement The use of inventory as collateral for a loan; similar to a trust receipt arrangement except there is a third party (i.e., a warehouse company) that supervises the inventory.

Warrant Attached option that gives its holder the right to buy the underlying stock of the issuing company at a fixed exercise price until the expiration date.

Weak-form efficient market hypothesis The belief that security prices fully reflect all past market data, which refers to all historical price and volume trading information.

Wealth effect An increase (decrease) in household wealth increases (decreases) consumer spending out of a given level of current income.

Weighted average cost method An inventory accounting method that averages the total cost of available inventory items over the total units available for sale.

Weighted average cost of capital A weighted average of the aftertax required rates of return on a company's common stock, preferred stock, and long-term debt, where the weights are the fraction of each source of financing in the company's target capital structure.

Weighted average coupon rate Weighting the mortgage rate of each mortgage loan in the pool by the percentage of the mortgage outstanding relative to the outstanding amount of all the mortgages in the pool.

Weighted average life A measure that gives investors an indication of how long they can expect to hold the MBS before it is paid off; the convention-based average time to receipt of all principal repayments. Also called *average life.*

Weighted average maturity Weighting the remaining number of months to maturity for each mortgage loan in the pool by the amount of the outstanding mortgage balance.

Weighted mean An average in which each observation is weighted by an index of its relative importance.

Wholesale price index Reflects the price changes experienced by domestic producers in a country.

Winsorized mean A mean computed after assigning a stated percent of the lowest values equal to one specified low value, and a stated percent of the highest values equal to one specified high value.

Working capital The difference between current assets and current liabilities.

Working capital management The management of a company's short-term assets (such as inventory) and short-term liabilities (such as money owed to suppliers).

World price The price prevailing in the world market.

Yield The actual return on a debt security if it is held to maturity.

Yield duration The sensitivity of the bond price with respect to the bond's own yield-to-maturity.

Yield to maturity Annual return that an investor earns on a bond if the investor purchases the bond today and holds it until maturity. It is the discount rate that equates the present value of the bond's expected cash flows until maturity with the bond's price. Also called *yield-to-redemption* or *redemption yield.*

Yield to redemption See *yield to maturity.*

Yield-to-worst The lowest of the sequence of yields-to-call and the yield-to-maturity.

Zero-coupon bonds Bonds that do not pay interest during the bond's life. It is issued at a discount to par value and redeemed at par. Also called *pure discount bonds.*

Zero volatility spread (Z-spread) Calculates a constant yield spread over a government (or interest rate swap) spot curve.